P9-APO-125

INTERNATIONAL RETAILING

Brenda Sternquist

Michigan State University

INTERNATIONAL RETAILING

Brenda Sternquist

Michigan State University

Fairchild Publications

New York

DEDICATION

To my parents, Harriet and Orland Sternquist;
my brothers Sheridan and his wife Phyllis, John and his wife Nancy,
and Alan; and my son, Gavin Witter.

Cover Design: Eva Ruutopold
Figure Illustrations: Dolores Bego

Library of Congress Catalog Card Number: 97-061477

ISBN: 1-56367-103-4

GST R 133004424

Printed in the United States of America

PREFACE

With the trend toward economic unification, the development of regional trading blocks, and the economic growth of developing countries, interest in international business has never been greater. Courses on international business, international marketing, and now international retailing are proliferating. The current trend in retailing and merchandising programs across the United States is to add content in international retailing, yet there are almost no books available on the domestic distribution systems in other countries. Since there are, by contrast, so many books on retailing in the United States, is it any wonder that manufacturers from other countries have been so successful in entering the U.S. market? I have written *International Retailing* to fill the gap for teaching materials for a course on international retailing and to supplement more general courses on retailing.

International Retailing is based on over 13 years of original research conducted in foreign countries and on information about international retailing obtained from stockbrokers' retail analyst reports from around the world. Comparisons are made to the United States throughout, but I have tried to avoid an ethnocentric bias. The text concentrates on how economic unification measures have affected the distribution of consumer goods throughout the world and suggests how they will affect it in the future. I profile the retail industry in a variety of foreign countries, as well as particular foreign companies. I have conducted research in each country included except those in eastern Europe. Two of my colleagues have done research in central and eastern Europe, and I have relied on them for accuracy in the countries where I have not worked.

This book is organized into five parts. Part I introduces the international retail environment and lays the groundwork for understanding the retail environment in specific countries around the world; it provides a theoretical context for what follows. Chapter 1 deals with internationalization of retailing as a phenomenon. Chapter 2 focuses on the relationship between international culture and human behavior. Chapter 3 discusses the retail environment in developing countries and how it changes as a country develops economically. Licensing, franchising, and strategic alliances are the focus of Chapter 4, as much international activity for retailers begins as licensing arrangements or as joint ventures. The final chapter in Part I (Chapter 5) is about retailing in multinational markets, the phenomenon of several countries entering into trade agreements, such as the North American Free Trade Agreement (NAFTA).

Parts II, III, and IV focus on retailing in particular areas of the world. Part II covers North America, with a look at retailing in the United States (Chapter 6) and in Mexico and Canada (Chapter 7). Part III covers retailing in Europe. The chapters in this unit are divided into the geographical and cultural bands of northern Europe (Chapter 8), middle Europe (Chapter 9), southern Europe (Chapter 10), and eastern Europe (Chapter 11). Not every country considered a part of Europe is included. This is because some countries do not have distinguishing retail characteristics or major retailers who have expanded internationally. The selection of countries for inclusion was based on whether an overview of that country could be used to generalize about other countries. For instance, the concentration of retailing in German department stores is unmatched, with two retail companies controlling 90% of the department store industry. This characteristic enables me to explain how such a concentration affects market mix variables, such as price. If the reader encounters a similar situation in another country, he or she should be able to compare it with the German retail environment.

Part IV is devoted to retailing in Asia, where I have conducted most of my research. I know Tokyo and Hong Kong better than I know Chicago or Detroit. Chapter 12 looks at retailing in Japan, the first foreign retail market I studied, beginning in 1984. When I went to do my first series of interviews there, I felt unable to ask an intelligent question. Although I had read everything I could find, it did not prepare me for understanding just how much Japanese culture influences how the Japanese sell goods. To explain the difference to students, I usually start by stretching my arms out as wide as I can. Then I tell them that one hand is the United States, the other is Japan; retailing in every other country falls somewhere in the middle. Knowing about retailing in the United States and Japan will enable students to analyze retailing anywhere else in the world. Chapter 13 is about the overseas Chinese markets of Hong Kong and Taiwan. The final chapter in Part IV (Chapter 14) is about retailing in the People's Republic of China (PRC), or mainland China. This is a particularly exciting time to be studying China because it is undergoing a major change from a planned to a free market economy.

Part V contains a single chapter (Chapter 15) that rounds out the text by returning to theoretical issues. This chapter focuses on a theory to explain the internationalization of retailers and offers a prognosis for future international trends.

Each chapter in *International Retailing* begins with a list of learning objectives and concludes with a summary, a list of key terms, a series of discussion questions, and a list of endnotes. Maps are included in order to position the featured country in its geographical context.

Following each of the five parts there are substantial analyses of particular retail companies, 19 in all. These company focuses are a major feature of this text. The rich information provided about each company helps readers see how retailers within a particular country operate. All but two of these sections were written as a research assignment by senior level and graduate students in undergraduate and graduate courses that I teach on international retailing. The two focuses on Russian retailers were written by colleagues at Michigan State University. Finding information on many of these foreign companies is very difficult, for often there is very little available, and much of that is in a foreign language. I have selected the most outstanding papers. After much scrutiny and editing they appear in this book along with their authors' names. A series of discussion questions has the effect of making each focus a case study and highlights issues introduced in preceding chapters. Each time I read a company focus, I acquire a little more information to help me in my research on international retailing. The focuses supply me with a vocabulary of important retailers from around the world. I hope they will do so for the reader as well.

The text concludes with a bibliography of works cited and an index. Technical terms used in the text and boldfaced at their first occurrence are boldfaced in the index for easy identification. This enables the index to function as a glossary, as the number of the page on which the term is defined also appears in boldface.

An instructor's guide, prepared by Linda S. Niehm and Vanessa Prier Wickliffe, doctoral students at Michigan State University, accompanies the text. In addition to such features as test questions, the guide includes video suggestions. In particular, it suggests where instructors can incorporate into their syllabus specific films produced by the Merchandising Management team at Michigan State University. These films can be purchased individually and obtained from Fairchild Publications by calling customer service at 1-800-932-4724.

ACKNOWLEDGMENTS

This book is the result of collaboration with many people. I am grateful to the following reviewers selected by the publisher who provided so many good and useful suggestions at various stages in the development of this book: Holly Bastow-Shoop, North Dakota State University; Marianne Bickle, Colorado State University; Kitty Dickerson, University of Missouri; Carl L. Dyer, University of Tennessee; Fay Gibson, University of North Carolina-Greensboro; Jan M. Hathcote, University of Georgia; Richard Hise, Texas A & M University; Cynthia Jasper, University of Wisconsin-Madison; Rita Kean, University of Nebraska; Sherri Lotz, University of Arizona; Martha Moran, University of Massachusetts-Amherst; Soyeon Shim, University of Arizona; Bart Weitz, University of Florida at Gainesville; and Sarah Wise, University of South Carolina.

Three European colleagues who reviewed the chapters on Europe deserve my thanks for their thoughtful suggestions: Luca Pellegrini (Italy), Andrea Tordjman (France), and especially Leigh Sparks (U.K.). Leigh provided me with many documents which I had not seen. His insight and suggestions helped greatly.

The Merchandising Management team at Michigan State University also deserves my greatest appreciation: Judy Osbun for her support and creative ideas, Linda Good and Patricia Huddleston for their cheerleading and for their contribution of two company focuses on eastern Europe, and Dawn Pysarchik for her insight into retailing in India and Korea.

I also want to thank the students in my undergraduate and graduate international retailing courses and in my graduate course on Japanese distribution for contributing the company focuses that are a part of this book. In particular, I want to single out undergraduate Lori Garijo, who authored or coauthored three cases and who also worked with me on the international franchising chapter, where she developed the summary table of international retail franchisers. She was probably most helpful when she read a chapter and said, "Dr. S., you have to give these kids a story to convey the point or they are just not going to get it." I thank Lori for her special perspective from the trenches.

Conducting international retailing research is expensive. Funding sources that have made this process possible include: College of Human Ecology Travel Grants, Michigan State University Research Initiation Grants, Michigan State University Foreign Travel Fund, Michigan State University Agriculture Experiment Station, United States Department of Agriculture Challenge

Grants, Isetan Department Store (Japan), Marui Department Store (Japan), Hoso Bunko Foundation (Japan), and Japan Telecommunications Advancement Foundation (Japan).

As much as money, it is the people you know that helps foster international research. I would like to thank Gunner Sletmo, whose brainstorm it was to have an International Retailing Symposium in Montreal, Canada; Tomoyoshi Ogawa, my Japanese research colleague for 10 years and the person responsible for nearly everything I know about Japanese retailing; Shanghai University International College of Business, especially Professors Zhou Xi Qiao and Ying Chengmin, who arranged interviews and translators for my four research trips to Shanghai; Ms. Hu at the Chinese Academy of Social Sciences in Beijing, who has been my research colleague and has tracked down artists for direct purchase possibilities; Barry Davies of Manchester Polytechnic, who helped arrange U.K. interviews in 1993 and who, with his wife, Christine, extended the hospitality of their home to me and my son; and Robert Moran, President of Sears-Mexico, who made interview appointments for me with the most important retail executives in Mexico. I thank the hundreds of retail executives, government officials, and retail analysts who have granted me interviews.

Last but not least, I want to acknowledge my son, Gavin Witter. With humor, curiosity, and encouragement, he has been my research assistant in Asia and Europe and knows more about international retailing than is healthy for a kid his age.

BRIEF CONTENTS

Part IV

RETAILING IN ASIA

Part V

REGIONALIZATION AND INTERNATIONALIZATION OF RETAILING

CONTENTS

Part I Overview

The chapters in Part I of this book provide an introduction to the international retailing environment, laying the groundwork for understanding the retail environment in specific countries around the world. Chapter 1 begins with an overview of issues related to the internationalization of retailing and a discussion of how international retailing differs from international marketing. Retailing is geographically tied. Although manufacturers have the option of producing their product in one location and then exporting that product, to be a retailer, one must operate within a given country. The retail function is the direct-to-consumer link; thus, retailers must have a physical presence in the market. This presence may differ for various types of retailers. For instance, a mail-order company's presence may be a catalog and distribution facilities, rather than a retail store. Both approaches, however, constitute a physical presence. In Chapter 1, I discuss why a retailer might internationalize, and I tie the reasons into several theories that help to explain the internationalization decision. At the end of Part I, Company Focus I.1 presents the case of Marks & Spencer plc. This British company has expanded in many international markets, but its success at home has not always been duplicated in foreign markets. The Marks & Spencer story demonstrates that internationalization is not a natural extension for a world-class retailer but, rather, cause for examining and altering strategies.

Factors of production (land, labor, capital, and entrepreneurship) influence a country's comparative advantage, and these factors can also be used to understand a retailer's comparative advantage. Dunning's theory of the eclectic firm, presented in Chapter 1, focuses on three types of advantages a company might use to decide whether it should internationalize, and the attractiveness of various expansion alternatives. The macro-marketing environment is an environment that the retailer cannot control. Retailers monitor and evaluate this environment and use this information when they make company decisions. The final theoretical concept introduced in Chapter 1 is that of global versus multinational strategies. This concept relates to the type of management control and standardization a retailer will use in international expansion.

Chapter 2 focuses on international culture and human behavior. This chapter highlights the ways in which people from different societies are taught to understand space, possessions, friendships, agreements, and time. Each person becomes acculturated to his or her particular culture through aspects of everyday society: material elements, social institutions, human interaction, aesthetics, and language. In this chapter, I discuss findings from Hofstede's study of culture. Hofstede identified four major dimensions of difference that can be used to generalize about groups of countries. Throughout this chapter, I adapt Hofstede's ideas to convey retailing concepts.

In Chapter 3, I look at retailing in developing countries. Certain characteristics are typical of retailing in less developed countries. Consumers bargain for prices, there is little use of formal credit, product choice is limited, and retailers compete by virtue of having a scarce product rather than through strategic or price considerations. As a country develops, the market changes from a seller's market to a buyer's market. Power changes from the suppliers (sellers) to the consumers (buyers). The last part of this chapter looks at Samiee's theory of economic development and retail change. I will use this framework later to discuss changes in the People's Republic of China as it moves from a planned to a free market economy.

Chapter 4 provides a discussion of licensing, franchising, and strategic alliances. This chapter begins with a theoretical explanation of franchising and then looks at different types of international franchisers. Retailers have a particularly difficult decision in determining whether to franchise or not. Franchising means that one is sharing one's company secrets with others. Those outside the company can easily exploit these advantages. Franchising can be helpful in achieving rapid expansion, but the long-term effects on a company's proprietary knowledge can be harmful. The final part of this chapter includes a discussion of international strategic alliances. Buying alliances have been particularly popular and successful for international retailers. European retailers have been very successful participating in buying alliances. Other types of strategic alliances go further than just buying associations. Strategic alliances are a powerful means for international expansion, but they have their own problems. Company Focus I.2 on Isetan and Barneys joint venture, presented at the end of Part I, is a good example of the negative aspects of this type of agreement.

The world is becoming segregated not by countries, but by trading groups. Chapter 5, the concluding chapter in Part I, focuses on multinational markets. In addition to discussing the advantages and disadvantages of multinational markets, I also provide a discussion of five levels of multinational markets. There is a hierarchical development of markets, based on the control countries give to the market integration. Countries relinquish control of their markets as they move up the hierarchy. Trade groups such as the European Union (EU) and North American Free Trade Agreement (NAFTA) are becoming more important than countries.

The chapters in Part I provide a theoretical framework for understanding the country-specific chapters that follow. By reading Chapter 3, on retailing in developing countries, you will understand informal markets in a country such as Mexico. By understanding the hierarchy behind formal multinational markets described in Chapter 5, you will better understand Europe's problem with monetary unification. Knowledge of both theories and country-specific characteristics is necessary to predict future international retail developments.

TOYS "R" US
Exit
Entrance

1

Internationalization of Retailing

After reading this chapter, you will understand:

- Concepts that make international retailing different from international marketing.
- Entry strategies available to international retailers, and how these strategies affect a retailer's market exposure and long-term potential for internationalization.
- Why retailers engage in international expansion.
- How the four factors of production help to explain the theory of comparative advantage and how they help apply Dunning's theory of the eclectic firm to retail internationalization.
- Why the macro-marketing environments affect a retailer's decision to enter foreign markets.
- How to classify a retailer's international expansion as global or multinational and use this classification to predict a retailer's international expansion.

THIS CHAPTER PRESENTS concepts and theories necessary for understanding international retailing. I begin by exploring the ways in which international retailing differs from international marketing. Next, I outline reasons why companies decide to pursue internationalization and analyze the types of firms that expand into foreign markets. At the end of the chapter, I present a decision-making framework that can be used to analyze a company's decision to internationalize.

GEOGRAPHY OF RETAILING

The focus of this book is international retail markets. My intent is to discuss concepts and theories that will help you to understand differences in global retail markets and the process of retail internationalization. Retailing is geographically tied. To conduct a retailing business in a foreign market, a company must have a physical presence there. Although manufacturers can produce a product at home and then export it throughout the world, retailers must be physically present wherever they are doing business. Each country in the world has different rules and regulations for retailing. To operate in such disparate environments requires both knowledge and experience. If a manufacturer wants to sell a product in the European Union (EU), for example, that manufacturer needs only to make sure that the product meets ISO 9000 regulations—product standards set by the International Organization for Standardization—which apply to every country in the EU. The regulations of EU countries are thus harmonized into one standard. However, a retailer wishing to operate in the EU needs to meet a different set of regulatory requirements for each country being considered.

Often when we think of geography, we think in terms of physical geography; that is, where things are. When I went to school, geography was synonymous with learning the capitals of all of the states and countries. Nevertheless, real geographers know that geography includes the study of both cultural geography and economic geography. In the United States and other countries, different regions reflect **cultural geography,** how people live their lives in different regions of the country or world. The Deep South has a pattern of life that is very different from life in New England. Americans who live on the East Coast are very different from those who live on the West Coast.

Economic geography relates to the distribution of industrialization or wealth. The designation "Group of Seven" (G7) is used when referring to the seven most developed countries in the world. This designation applies to the United States, Japan, Germany, France, the United Kingdom, Italy, and Canada. These countries are not found next to each other, yet their level of economic development makes consumption practices similar.

Economic geography affects retailing both within individual countries and throughout the world. Consumers who are geographically adjacent may be vastly different economically. Consider the example of Malaysia and Singapore. Retailing in Singapore is sophisticated and diverse. Retailing in adjacent Malaysia is primitive. Cultural and economic borders determine rates of retail growth.

Retailing activity is tied to economic activity. In Chapter 3, I will discuss how retailing changes with economic activity. Retailers become larger and more integrated. Consumers, not suppliers, gain market power. Retailing advancement depends on infrastructures such as transportation, communication, and packaging. These infrastructures become more modern with economic development.

Companies that produce products can become international, effortlessly. Most manufacturers begin their international operations when a foreign consumer approaches them, wanting to buy their product. At this point, it is not the marketer that is international, it is the customer.

The major issue for international marketing is one of standardization versus adaptation. Some products are global products, meaning they can be sold in foreign markets with virtually no adaptation. This is what is meant by **standardization.** Most products, however, need some changes in the product or promotion strategy to fit new markets. This is what is meant by **adaptation.** In retailing, the product is the retail business. Even if the retailer operates using a standard format throughout the world, the company is being placed in the middle of a culturally different surrounding. This explains why a global offering such as Kentucky Fried Chicken was viewed as a posh restaurant when it was first introduced in China. Although the retail offering was not altered, the product and pricing positioned it as an exclusive offer in this market.

Manufacturers who become involved in foreign markets have several alternatives for getting their products to users. They may choose the least involvement, exporting their product to a foreign country through a distributor. Because they have a distributor in the foreign country, they may incur few of the financial risks or headaches involved in international sales. Retailers do not have this option. They sell products to the ultimate user; this means they need to be located where the ultimate user is geographically. Retailers must have a physical presence in the markets where they want sales. Mail-order retailers have a presence in the market, not as a store, but through a medium, such as a catalog. It is as difficult to obtain mailing lists for catalogs as it is to set retail store location strategy. The catalog is their physical presence in the market. Mail-order retailers also must have a behind-stage presence, such as a distribution center.

A retailer's required physical presence in the market also presents unique problems unlike those encountered by international marketers. In particular, the element of culture is a more important variable for retailers than for manufacturers.

Retailers fall far behind manufacturers in internationalization efforts. Of the top 100 retail companies in the world, only 56 operate outside their home markets. Only five of those retailers generate more than 50% of their sales in foreign markets. IKEA, the Scandinavian home furnishings specialty store that has moved into 18 countries, generated the largest proportion of revenues—89%—from global operations.[1]

Wal-Mart Stores, Inc., the giant discount department store chain, dominates the list of 100 largest retail companies (See Chapter 1 Appendix, p. 44). If Wal-Mart were a nation, its revenue would be equal to the 34th largest economy, just behind that of Greece. However, even Wal-Mart's exposure to international markets is small. The company generates only 2.9% of its sales from international operations in four countries. Three of these countries are the North American Free Trade Agreement (NAFTA) partners: the United States, Canada, and Mexico. Wal-Mart's only other international operations are in Hong Kong and mainland China. (Wal-Mart's Chinese sales are not included in these figures because these stores opened in 1996.) Company Focus I.3, presented at the end of Part I, outlines Wal-Mart's international involvement.

ENTRY STRATEGY

When a manufacturer is interested in expanding internationally, certain choices will determine its level of involvement and financial commitment (Figure 1.1). The lowest level of involvement is to **export,** shipping a product to a foreign country. When a manufacturer exports merchandise, it incurs a limited level of risk, but it also has limited exposure to the market. This means that the manufacturer does not learn how to conduct business in that market; someone else, generally a distributor, is handling the details. A second level of exposure for a manufacturer is to **license** the product or company name. When a company licenses its name, it allows another company to produce a product under that company name. With licensing, a manufacturer places itself at risk of losing control of product quality and distribution in the foreign country. The financial risk with licensing, as with exporting, is small. Licensing, like exporting, does not give the company exposure to the foreign market, and no significant learning takes place. The third level of involvement for a manufacturer is to enter a **joint venture** with a company in the destination country. Joint ventures exist when two companies join together to form a new business entity. This type of international involvement offers the company knowledge of the new market. The last level of involvement is to open a **wholly owned subsidiary,** the manufacturer's own company, in the foreign market. In effect, the manufacturer sets up a facility in the foreign country, produces the product, and sells the product there. This offers the greatest exposure to the foreign market, and it also provides the greatest opportunity to learn about the new market.

Retailers have different international expansion choices. The lowest level of involvement for a retailer is through a licensing or franchising arrangement. **Licensing** arrangements for retailers, like those for manufacturers, allow a foreign company to use the licensing company's name. For example, Carrefour SA, the French hypermarket chain, licenses its name in Taiwan. Retailers sacrifice control in this type of arrangement, and it is unusual in retailing. Generally, retail companies use **franchising.** Through the franchise arrangement, the franchiser gives imitators the right to use the

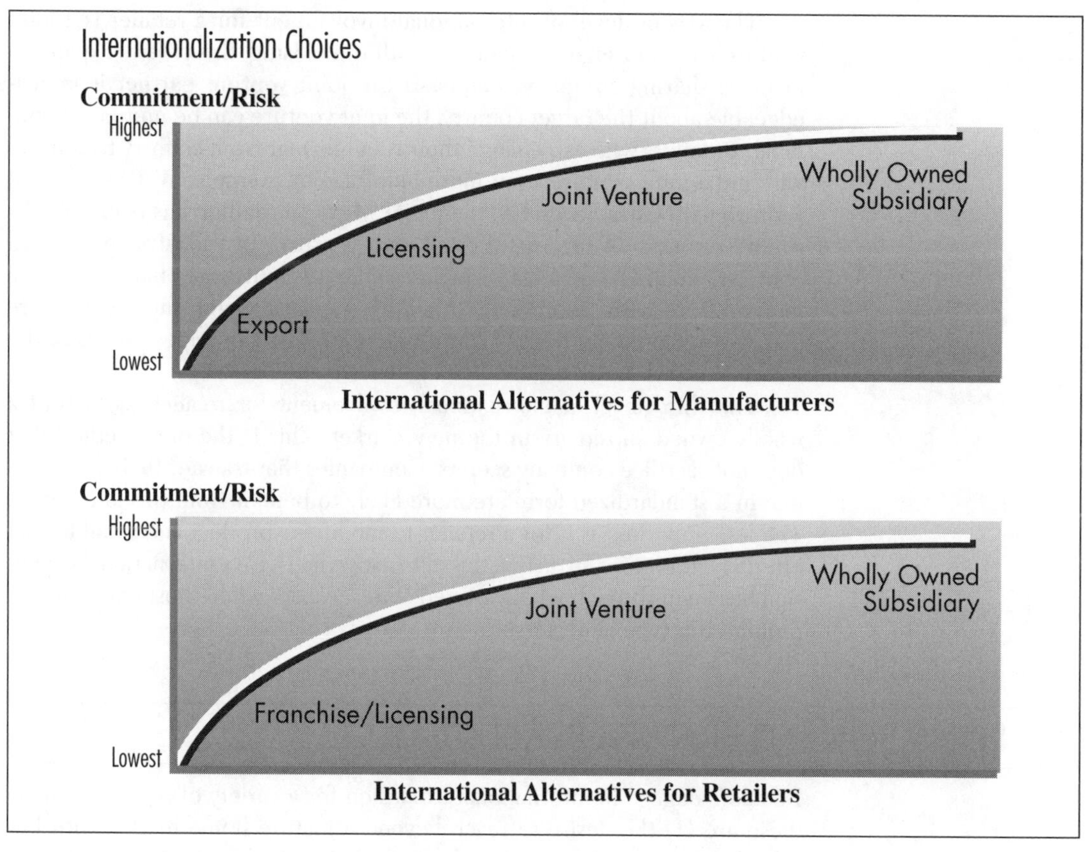

Figure 1.1 For manufacturers, the export alternative carries the least amount of risk when internationalizing. For retailers, who must have a presence in the market in order to internationalize, the least risky option is to franchise or license; the downside to this strategy, however, is that they lose control of their concept.

retailer's name; the retailer, in turn, gives the franchisee the training needed to run the business. Every franchise agreement is different, but each gives some elements of distinctive retail format to the franchisee. If a retailer has a distinctive retail format and it provides this format to franchisees, the retailer is selling its trade secrets. Franchising may thus be good for short-term profitability, but it makes it difficult for the retailer to enter the market later as a wholly owned subsidiary. This is an important consideration, because although franchisees are very popular and have been successful in foreign markets, their presence can block future expansion opportunities. Fast-food businesses in the United States have successfully entered international markets using franchisees. McDonald's Corp., for one, expands internationally using franchisees exclusively. Other retailers, such as Benetton and The Body Shop, have used a combination of licensing, franchising, and wholly owned subsidiaries for their international expansion.

The second level of international involvement for a retailer is a joint venture with a foreign company. As with franchising, this type of expansion involves sharing company secrets. If the joint venture partner is knowledgeable about the target country, the joint venture can be mutually beneficial. Retailers who can change their retail format from country to country will find a joint venture even more helpful. For example, Wal-Mart's joint venture with Cifra SA de CV, the major Mexican retailer, has been called a superb example of successful retail joint ventures by industry analysts. In contrast, when Isetan, a major Japanese department store chain, entered a joint venture with Barneys, a New York specialty chain, the results were disastrous. Company Focus I.2 at the end of Part I provides details of the Isetan-Barneys affair.

The third level of international involvement for retailers is to start a wholly owned subsidiary in the new market. This is the only method that does not sacrifice company secrets. Companies that transfer their retail format in a standardized form are more likely to benefit from this alternative. The less important it is for a retailer to modify its product and retail format offerings, the more attractive this alternative is. IKEA's international expansion has been through wholly owned stores, except where host governments prohibit this type of ownership.

REASONS FOR INTERNATIONALIZING

Retailers engage in international expansion for a variety of reasons. Among these are (1) the desire to reach beyond a mature home market with low growth potential, (2) a need to diversify their investment, (3) a situation in which expansion at home is blocked by legislation, (4) the possession of a unique market format, (5) intense competition at home, (6) an economic downturn at home, or (7) the desire to secure first-mover advantages.

United States retailers have been slow to internationalize because they have a big home market. Until U.S. national retail chains saturated their home market, there was little motivation for them to expand elsewhere. Other countries, such as the Netherlands, are so small that retailers who want to grow are forced into international markets.

MATURE HOME MARKET—LOW GROWTH POTENTIAL

Retail formats, like new products, go through four stages: introduction, growth, maturity, and decline. Retail formats that have reached the maturity stage do not continue to show growth in sales. However, retail formats that are not considered innovative or exciting in the home market may be viewed as new and interesting in a foreign market. For instance, warehouse clubs peaked in popularity in the United States in the late 1980s, but these formats are now entering Asian and South American markets with great pizzazz. Toys "R" Us, Inc. began expanding into Asia and Europe because it had already opened stores in most of the U.S. locations that seemed appropriate for its format.

Often retailers view the expansion into a foreign market, using their existing retail format, as less risky than staying at home and adapting to a new retail format. Large-scale retailers are most likely to expand to less developed countries. Kmart Corporation's expansion to Prague, in the Czech Republic, is one example. Wal-Mart's expansion into Mexico and China also seems to fit this model.

NEED TO DIVERSIFY INVESTMENT

The old adage, "don't put all your eggs in one basket," is true in business investment. During the 1970s, Delhaize, a family-owned Belgian food retailer, decided it did not want to have all of its investment in Europe. The company concluded that having some investments in the United States would be a prudent move, and it acquired the Food Lion supermarket chain. However, Delhaize did not take over day-to-day operation and management of Food Lion. Purchasing this business was not a part of a retail format diversification strategy. It was part of a financial portfolio diversification strategy.

Some countries are more attractive to retailers than others. The United States is an attractive investment area because of its stable political climate and the low level of government involvement in business operations. However, it is also one of the most over-stored countries, making competition great. **Over-stored** means that a country has too much retail space per consumer. The United States may have as much as 30% too much retail space. As a result, domestic cannibalization—obtaining sales in one store, at the expense of another store—is continuing at a rapid rate.

EXPANSION AT HOME BLOCKED BY LEGISLATION

Many countries have strict rules that limit retail expansion, restrict a retailer's ability to terminate employees, and regulate hours of operation. Japan is often cited for its restrictive legislation. However, most European countries have laws that are just as restrictive as Japan's. Governments put most of these laws into effect to protect small businesses and employees.

A Japanese law called the *Daiten Ho* (Large-Scale Retail Store Law) once regulated the opening of stores of more than 1,000 square meters. When a new, large store was proposed, small shops in the area determined whether they wanted the new business as a neighbor. As might be expected, these small businesses were usually not eager to have a large-scale competitor in their midst. As a result, it often took up to 10 years to open a new store. In response to intense pressure from the United States, Japan finally reduced the restrictiveness of this law. New measures introduced in 1990 and 1997 have been put into place to reduce the time needed to get new store approval. New applications are supposed to take less than 18 months. Belgium has a similar set of laws called the Padlock Laws and France has the *Loi Royer*.

POSSESSION OF A UNIQUE MARKET FORMAT

It is difficult for a retail store to protect new ideas. Retail innovations cannot be patented or copyrighted. Once a new retail format is introduced, competitors begin to imitate it. One of the best ways for retailers with a unique retail format to exploit the benefits of this format is to expand aggressively into foreign markets, knowing that if they do not expand themselves, imitators will replicate their unique format and enjoy the benefits of innovation.

The Body Shop is a good example of this strategy. The Body Shop retails bath supplies with a unique assortment of scents and all-natural ingredients. The company makes a point of finding product ingredients that are indigenous to a local area, and uses these products in its worldwide store offerings. Sales in the United States have been in decline. In 1997, the company decided to hire its first vice president of marketing and conduct market research to identify its customer base. The Body Shop has operated without any formal marketing officer for 17 years.[2]

Benetton is unique, not so much because of its retail format, which is similar to that of many other retailers, but because of the company's controversial promotional messages. The company image is very strong, sometimes so strong as to be detrimental to the sale of merchandise. Benetton also has a unique method of dyeing merchandise after the products have been manufactured. This gives the company more flexibility to change color offerings based on consumer reaction.

INTENSE COMPETITION AT HOME

Some markets are more competitive than others. Retailers in highly competitive markets such as Japan or the United States may thus decide to enter other markets with greater growth potential and less competition. The wave of Japanese department stores that has moved into Hong Kong is a good example of this strategy. The first movers were not the most competitive retailers seeking to become global retailers, but instead those retailers who had stagnant or declining market share in Japan. United States retailers that have moved into Mexico provide another example. In the United States, Kmart has been losing its battle with Wal-Mart for supremacy in the discount retailing arena. Rather than continuing to cannibalize its stores in the United States, Kmart decided to expand internationally in areas where it would not face direct competition from Wal-Mart. However, Kmart's expansion into the Czech Republic and Slovakia, Singapore, and Mexico has not been successful, and the company has withdrawn.

ECONOMIC DOWNTURN AT HOME

Recessions hit retailers early and hard. During periods of poor economic growth in the home market, international expansion may appear very desirable. In the early 1990s, Japan's retail sales declined for 44 straight months before finally posting an increase in the third quarter of 1995. The People's Republic of China, by contrast, has had double-digit retail sales increases for more than five years in this period.

Retailers have the additional advantage of being able to open new stores with little lead time. If the economic climate at home is less than optimal, they can quickly move into another location. After the Berlin Wall fell in 1989, West German retailers sent mobile stores to East German cities. Often, these mobile stores consisted of nothing more than semitrailer trucks filled with merchandise. The trucks would be driven to the center of an East German town or city and, presto, the West German retailer would be open for business. The smaller the retailer, the quicker such moves based on economic conditions can be made.

United States retailers such as Wal-Mart and Kmart expanded into Mexico just before the 1994 peso devaluation, which devastated the Mexican economy. Wal-Mart anticipated aggressive expansion in Mexico, but this expansion has been delayed until the host country's economy rebounds.

FIRST-MOVER ADVANTAGES

Every city has a limited number of ideal retail sites. One of the oldest adages used to explain retail success is "location, location, location." The problem of finding a good location is greater for large-scale stores such as department stores and mass merchandisers than it is for specialty stores. In Hong Kong, there are three major shopping areas: the Golden Mile in Kowloon, Pacific Place in Central, and Causeway Bay. If a department store does not locate in one of these major shopping areas, its future is in trouble. The Japanese retailer Seibu only entered the Hong Kong market when a location in the new development of Pacific Place became available. Before Pacific Place was built, there were few sites suitable for Seibu's pioneer Hong Kong store. In 1997, however, Seibu transferred management of the store to a Hong Kong retailer, Dixon Concepts.

Location is very important to retailer success, therefore the importance of being first in the market, when the premier sites are still available, is extremely important. Manufacturers have a far broader range of locational alternatives than retailers. Because manufacturers do not need direct access to consumers, they can build their factories on the periphery of cities, or in rural areas where land is less expensive. Good location is so important to retailers that it can be the deciding factor in a company's decision to expand internationally.

TYPES OF RETAIL FIRMS THAT EXPAND INTO INTERNATIONAL MARKETS

All types of retailers contemplate international expansion. The strong, the weak, the unique, and the standard all aspire to expand. Where a retailer will go can be predicted based on its categorization as one of these four general types.

THE STRONG

Strong companies seek international markets when worldwide distribution is their goal. Although McDonald's is the strongest competitor in the fast-food business, the company realized that if it did not take its retail format into international markets, imitators would replicate it, denying the company future international growth. Innovators of a new idea have the best chance of maintaining a dominant market share if they continue to expand. (Figure 1.2).

Strong companies have their choice of where to expand. They also have a choice of whether to expand in their initial retail format or in a modification of that format. IKEA is an example of a strong company. In each market it has entered, the company has become a market-share leader.

THE WEAK

Weak companies are often forced into international expansion when they cannot maintain a market share in the home market. Their internationalization is an attempt to find a market with less cutthroat competition. Kmart's entry into the Czech and Slovak market in 1992 exemplifies this strategy. No strong foreign competition existed in Prague, where domestic department stores were being privatized after having been state-owned for years. This market appeared to offer an ideal situation for a company unsure of retaining its competitive edge in the domestic U.S. market. However, as noted earlier, this move was not successful. Several years later, Kmart sold its Czech and Slovak stores to the UK-owned food retailer, Tesco plc. Kmart had also entered the Canadian and Mexican markets only to withdraw in 1997. The company is attempting to consolidate its strength in the United States with its core business, as a discount retailer.

THE UNIQUE

Unique companies have a variety of expansion alternatives. Most often, unique companies expand using an exact replication of their standard format. Although they can expand to both less developed and more developed countries, they may choose to focus on more developed countries, in which a distinctive global

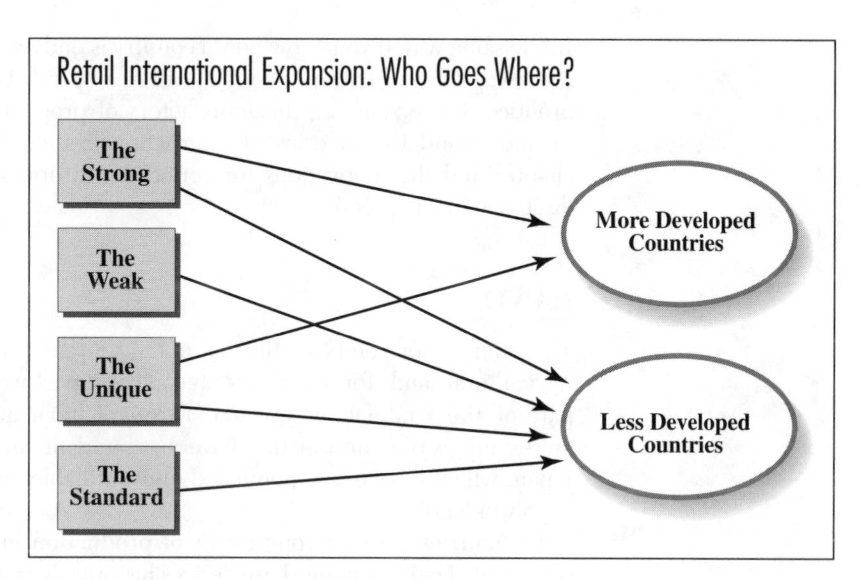

Figure 1.2
The profile of a retail company can be used to predict where the retailer will go. Strong and unique companies may expand to either more developed countries or less developed countries. The weak and standard companies will tend to expand to less developed countries, where their retail offering will face less competition.

consumer is found. A set of consumers exists from the so-called "Triad"—United States, Japan, and Europe—that is barely indistinguishable in its consumption characteristics. Unique retailers are suppliers to this global consumer. These retailers generally use a specialty store format; they are lifestyle retailers.

THE STANDARD

Standard companies expand to international markets to capitalize on their large-scale format. These retailers focus on a type of vocational technical training, which trains sales employees to provide high levels of service. Locating in areas where land and labor are inexpensive best serves these stores. They need to identify countries where consumers' disposable income is increasing. Generally the movement of a standard company is from a more developed country to a less developed country. The French hypermarkets' entry into Spain is an example of this type of movement.

FACTORS OF PRODUCTION

Theories of international trade focus on explaining trade flows. The basic determinants of what a country will make are called factors of production. There are four factors of production: land, labor, capital, and entrepreneurship. In effect, these factors are for countries what personal assets are to people. One person may be very intelligent, another very athletic. These assets determine what types of things the person will be good at doing.

In the same way, if you know how a country is endowed with respect to land, labor, capital, and entrepreneurship, you can predict what it will efficiently produce. Understanding the four factors of production will also help you to understand the theories of internationalization discussed later in this chapter and the motivations for countries to form multinational markets, discussed in Chapter 5.

LAND

The land factor refers to the natural resources used to produce things. Agricultural land, forests, rivers, and oil reserves would all be considered part of the land factor. Canada, Russia, China, and the United States are examples of countries that have an abundant supply of land resources. Japan, which has heavily populated and untillable areas, illustrates a weak supply of land.

Countries with a strong factor of production in land tend to be self-sufficient. Their economic base derives historically from agriculture. Without a strong agricultural base, a country is forced to engage in international trade to obtain the resources needed for production. Countries with land as a strong factor of production can adopt isolationist views; those without land cannot.

Countries with a weak land factor will try to protect land from development. Germany is a good example of a country that has enacted restrictive retail development laws to retain its green spaces. Large-scale stores are restricted to urban areas. This limits the introduction of certain retail formats, such as warehouse clubs, that require a vast expanse of land.

LABOR

Labor as a factor of production does not refer to the skilled labor force, but rather to unskilled and semiskilled workers. Countries with a low minimum wage are considered strong in this factor. Less developed countries generally have a stronger supply of labor because their minimum wage is low. However, they sometimes camouflage the true labor rate because of high social welfare costs associated with doing business in their country. In Mexico, for instance, the minimum wage is about $0.70 per hour. However, government-mandated worker benefits nearly triple the actual wage.

Countries with a strong labor factor will attract labor-intensive industries such as apparel manufacturing. The production of apparel moves from one geographical region to another as the costs of labor increase with economic development.

Countries can attract some retailers such as large department stores by offering lower-cost labor. In Hong Kong, department stores imported workers from mainland China because they could pay them lower wages. Service industries flourish where there is a large disparity between the rich and the poor. The rich need to be able to afford to hire; the poor are needed as the service providers. Fast-food retailers have typically hired teenagers to work in their operations. A few years ago companies like McDonald's and Burger King had difficulty finding teenage employees in wealthy East Coast communities. Teenagers in these communities viewed their time as more valuable than the wage paid by the fast-food retailers. The companies solved the problem by recruiting workers who were retired and wanted only a supplementary income.

CAPITAL

Capital refers to money, machinery, and infrastructure. Countries with these resources are considered strong in this factor. The United States and Germany are examples of countries that have a strong factor for capital. Because both are considered safe countries in which to invest, they have more resources to lend to entrepreneurs. The capital resource is generally stronger in more developed countries.

United States and Germany are considered "safe" because they have stable political systems and currencies that do not fluctuate wildly. For many years, Brazil was known as a country with an unstable economic environment. Inflation was so high that prices had to be changed daily in stores. Investors did not see the Brazilian economy as a stable place to put their capital. In 1994, Brazil introduced a new system, called the *plano real,* that created a new, more stable currency and ended hyperinflation. Before the introduction of the plan, inflation in Brazil was running at 60% annually. Later in 1994, it was 5%.[3]

ENTREPRENEURSHIP

Entrepreneurship refers to creative management and ideas; that is, how people solve problems and look for opportunities. Entrepreneurship as a factor of production does not simply refer to small business management as we often use the term. Small business management is a part of this factor, but not the whole factor. One of major exports of the United States is management, reflecting the country's strong factor in this area. Germany is another country with strong abilities in entrepreneurship. Particularly in retail innovations, France has also shown strong entrepreneurship. The French were the first to develop hypermarkets, a retail format that they have transferred successfully to other countries.

Industries are often described as being labor intensive or capital intensive. The apparel industry is an example of a labor-intensive industry. The basic unit of production is the sewing machine. Increasing output means adding more workers. Labor-intensive industries generally have diseconomies of scale. With **economies of scale,** as an organization gets bigger, it produces things more efficiently, reducing costs. With **diseconomies of scale** the opposite occurs. As the organization gets bigger, it produces things less efficiently, increasing costs. Have you ever worked on a group project with many people? You may have found that the effort to get everyone together and working as a team was more time-consuming than just doing the work yourself or with a smaller group. Often, we assume that having more people working on something will reduce the effort of everyone, but this rarely happens. Whether you have a group of four or fourteen people, it is not uncommon for three or four people to do 90% of the work.

The chemical industry is capital intensive, meaning that machines, not people determine output. Capital-intensive industries generally have economies of scale. The more they produce, the lower the per unit cost.

Industries are not 100% labor intensive or 100% capital intensive. Nevertheless, it helps to have some idea about how an industry is classified. The important point is that labor-intensive industries will naturally gravitate to those countries that have a strong labor factor of production (i.e., a low minimum wage). Capital-intensive industries will gravitate to those countries that have a strong capital factor of production (i.e., money, high technology machinery, and the infrastructure needed to support it).

These factors will help you to understand the theory of comparative advantage which is presented next. This theory is the building block for other theories discussed in this book.

THEORY OF COMPARATIVE ADVANTAGE

International trade theory is based on the idea of comparative advantage. Understanding this idea is important in determining which countries will initiate and welcome contact with the world. Some countries choose to remain isolated from other countries. For many years, China, one of the greatest civilizations in the world, rejected trade with other countries. Japan kept its doors closed until forced, literally at gunpoint, to accept trade with outsiders. Today, North Korea has little interaction with the rest of the world.

The ideas of absolute and relative advantage help to explain how and when we expect international trade to develop. Suppose you know a surgeon who also loves to do woodworking. If he spent his day doing surgery, he could make $4,000 a day. If he concentrated on making cabinets, he could make $1,000 a day. Even if both of those figures are greater than what other surgeons or other woodworkers could make, it is still in his best interests to focus on what will give him the greatest economic return—surgery—and have someone else do the cabinetmaking. The fact that this person can make more than others in either category means he has an absolute advantage.

In international trade, a country that can produce things more efficiently than its trading partners has an **absolute advantage.** In the example provided in Table 1.1, Country X can be seen to produce both cotton textiles and wine more efficiently than Country Y. It has the absolute advantage over Country Y. For the most efficient trade, the country with the absolute advantage should produce what it is more difficult for its trading partner to produce. This situation is called **relative advantage.** In this example,

TABLE 1.1

Comparison of Country X and Country Y Production of Textiles and Wine

	Production Per Day	
	Cotton Textiles	**Wine**
Country X	5,000 yds (in millions)	4,000 bottles (in thousands)
Country Y	3,000 yds (in millions)	1,000 bottles (in thousands)

Country X should produce wine and Country Y should produce cotton. The idea of relative advantage applies when a country produces what it can make the most money selling, and trades with other countries for other goods. In effect, the country is focusing its production efforts on what will give it the greatest overall gains.

Let's expand on the preceding example. Suppose Country Y is considering trade alternatives with Country Z. Both countries can produce footwear and cotton textiles. If Country Y devotes all of its resources to producing footwear, it can produce 6 million pairs of shoes a year. If it devotes all of its resources to producing cotton textiles, it can produce 10 million yards of cotton textiles. If Country Z concentrates its resources in the same way, it can produce 3 million pairs of shoes or 8 million yards of cotton textiles. In this situation, Country Y has the absolute advantage. It can produce both shoes and cotton textiles more efficiently than Country Z. However, it can still be in Country Y's best interests to focus its production efforts on the commodity that is harder for Country Z to produce—in this case, shoes.

Relative advantage depends on one's strengths and the strengths of one's trading partners. Some countries do everything well. Maybe they have large amounts of each factor of production and can choose to produce whatever they want. Even here, there is good reason for countries to specialize, producing the products that are more difficult for other countries to produce and then trading for other products. This idea is referred to as the specialization of labor.

The theory of comparative advantage explains how countries choose what they will produce. We can relate this theory to the ideas about factors of production discussed earlier. As we saw, factors of production are the elements of land, labor, capital, and entrepreneurship that each country possesses in different degrees. Each type of industry has different requirements for production efficiency. As previously mentioned, apparel manufacturing requires labor as a factor of production; as a result, the apparel manufacturing industry has moved, over the years, to countries that have low-cost labor. Once, the United States had a healthy apparel manufacturing industry. However, as wages increased in the United States, other low-wage countries became more attractive locations for apparel production. First, apparel production moved to Japan. Then, as wages increased in Japan, apparel production moved to Korea.

As wages increased in Korea, apparel production moved to the People's Republic of China. Each geographical move is prompted by the need to find low-cost labor, the basic factor of production for apparel.

Of course, government officials do not one day suddenly suggest, "Well, it's time to switch from apparel manufacturing, which is labor intensive, to computer software production, which is entrepreneurship intensive." Instead, a natural trend becomes apparent in the country's trade relations. When an industry begins to gather trade deficits, analysts know the industry is no longer competitive. Countries facing this situation have two options: either they allow the natural flow of trade to continue, or they attempt to build trade barriers to reduce the natural trade flows.

BARRIERS TO TRADE

Countries restrict natural trade flows by putting tariffs on imported goods. A **tariff** is a tax placed on imported goods. This tax is added to the cost of these goods and makes them more expensive. When a country puts tariffs on imported merchandise, it makes the people who buy that merchandise pay higher prices. Essentially, these people pay to support the domestic industry.

There are three types of tariffs: specific, ad valorem, and combination. A **specific tariff** is a certain dollar amount added to each product. For instance, if shoes have a $2 specific tariff, $2 is added to the cost of each imported pair of shoes. Specific tariffs encourage importers to ship more expensive merchandise. A $2 tariff is 20% of a $10 pair of shoes, but only 10% of a $20 pair of shoes. An **ad valorem tariff** is a percent of the value of the imported goods. A 10% ad valorem tariff on a $10 pair of shoes would be $1. A 10% ad valorem tariff on a $30 pair of shoes would be $3. A **combination tariff** is a combination of a specific and an ad valorem tariff. You might have a combination tariff of $2 plus 10% ad valorem tariff. For a $40 pair of shoes that would be $2 + $40(.10) = $6.

Quotas are a numerical restriction on the amount of merchandise that can enter a country. Countries allocate quotas to other countries as part of negotiated trade agreements. For instance, the United States might tell Equador that it can ship 500,000 pairs of shoes to this country. After that level is reached, any additional shoes shipped to the United States must be held in storage until the next quota period. Quotas increase the price of products because they restrict supply. The smaller the supply, the higher the price.

Both tariffs and quotas are regressive. By this we mean they hurt lower-income people proportionately more than higher-income people. Particularly with products such as apparel, low-income people buy more low-cost import products. For many years, the U.S. government protected the apparel industry because that industry employed many people. Only in the past 10 years has the government phased out its protection program. Similarly, France and Japan have a long history of restricting agricultural imports. They do this to protect their farmers from competition that might put them out of business.

Governments also use currency exchange to reduce imports. **Currency exchange** is the value of a country's currency. Each day in the *Wall Street Journal,* you can find a chart that tells what the currencies from around the world are worth (Figure 1.3). Traders from around the world buy and sell currencies every day. However, countries also maintain an official currency exchange for the exchange of goods and services between countries. Governments can keep this official currency rate artificially low to discourage imports. If the dollar exchange rate is low, consumers will need more dollars to purchase foreign merchandise. Let me give you an example. When I first started going to Japan in 1985, $1 U.S. purchased nearly 200 yen. Today, the dollar purchases only 100 yen. A can of vending machine coffee costs about 240 yen. In 1985, it cost me just a little over a dollar for a can of coffee. Now the can would cost $2.40. The same is true when products are exported from Japan to the United States. If the dollar is low, it costs more dollars to buy Japanese products. This makes them seem expensive relative to other domestic products.

Governments always want to show a favorable balance of trade. A **favorable balance of trade** means that one exports more than one imports. As we just saw, by keeping the official value of the dollar low, the United States can discourage imports by making those imports more expensive. Keep in mind that the value of the dollar is different for each currency in the world. You can use the accompanying chart from the *Wall Street Journal* (Figure 1.3) to determine the value of the U.S. dollar in comparison to other world currencies. Currency exchange is a relative economic indicator, though. The number of dollars needed to buy yen has no bearing on the number of dollars needed to buy British pounds.

DUNNING'S THEORY OF THE ECLECTIC FIRM

In discussing the process by which retail companies move into international markets, it is useful to have a framework to help explain who will internationalize. Dunning[4] developed a theory that attempts to explain why companies would consider expanding into a foreign country. In contrast to the four factors of production, which are relevant to countries, Dunning's theory focuses on three components a *company* must have to spur its international expansion. Dunning's three components are (1) ownership advantages, (2) internalization advantages, and (3) location advantages. He believes that the more of these advantages a company has, the more likely it is that the company will internationalize.

OWNERSHIP ADVANTAGES

Ownership advantages are unique elements that belong to the company. These advantages can be either **asset based** or **transaction based.** Asset-based ownership advantages are possessions of the company, such as a well-

CURRENCY TRADING

EXCHANGE RATES

Monday, August 4, 1997

The New York foreign exchange selling rates below apply to trading among banks in amounts of $1 million and more, as quoted at 4 p.m. Eastern time by Dow Jones and other sources. Retail transactions provide fewer units of foreign currency per dollar.

Country	U.S. $ equiv. Mon	U.S. $ equiv. Fri	Currency per U.S. $ Mon	Currency per U.S. $ Fri
Argentina (Peso)	1.0014	1.0014	.9986	.9986
Australia (Dollar)	.7403	.7396	1.3508	1.3521
Austria (Schilling)	.07614	.07631	13.133	13.104
Bahrain (Dinar)	2.6525	2.6525	.3770	.3770
Belgium (Franc)	.02597	.02598	38.500	38.490
Brazil (Real)	.9237	.9234	1.0826	1.0830
Britain (Pound)	1.6300	1.6305	.6135	.6133
1-month forward	1.6281	1.6286	.6142	.6140
3-months forward	1.6241	1.6245	.6157	.6156
6-months forward	1.6178	1.6187	.6181	.6178
Canada (Dollar)	.7252	.7240	1.3790	1.3812
1-month forward	.7265	.7254	1.3765	1.3786
3-months forward	.7289	.7277	1.3720	1.3741
6-months forward	.7320	.7308	1.3662	1.3683
Chile (Peso)	.002402	.002398	416.30	416.95
China (Renminbi)	.1202	.1202	8.3205	8.3203
Colombia (Peso)	.0008981	.0008986	1113.43	1112.90
Czech. Rep. (Koruna)	....	....	....	....
Commercial rate	.02863	.02897	34.928	34.513
Denmark (Krone)	.1405	.1409	7.1150	7.0950
Ecuador (Sucre)	....	....	....	....
Floating rate	.0002475	.0002475	4040.00	4040.00
Finland (Markka)	.1795	.1801	5.5695	5.5525
France (Franc)	.1588	.1592	6.2985	6.2820
1-month forward	.1591	.1595	6.2855	6.2699
3-months forward	.1597	.1601	6.2629	6.2464
6-months forward	.1605	.1610	6.2287	6.2114
Germany (Mark)	.5358	.5368	1.8662	1.8630
1-month forward	.5371	.5379	1.8620	1.8591
3-months forward	.5391	.5400	1.8548	1.8517
6-months forward	.5424	.5433	1.8438	1.8407
Greece (Drachma)	.003435	.003447	291.13	290.10
Hong Kong (Dollar)	.1292	.1292	7.7425	7.7425
Hungary (Forint)	.005025	.005094	198.99	196.31
India (Rupee)	.02797	.02794	35.755	35.793
Indonesia (Rupiah)	.0003839	.0003821	2605.00	2617.00
Ireland (Punt)	1.4426	1.4480	.6932	.6906
Israel (Shekel)	.2825	.2823	3.5400	3.5424
Italy (Lira)	.0005470	.0005495	1828.00	1820.00
Japan (Yen)	.008445	.008446	118.42	118.40
1-month forward	.008482	.008483	117.89	117.89
3-months forward	.008555	.008556	116.89	116.88
6-months forward	.008672	.008670	115.32	115.34
Jordan (Dinar)	1.4094	1.4075	.7095	.7105
Kuwait (Dinar)	3.2776	3.2808	.3051	.3048
Lebanon (Pound)	.0006505	.0006504	1537.25	1537.50
Malaysia (Ringgit)	.3797	.3790	2.6335	2.6385
Malta (Lira)	2.4969	2.5063	.4005	.3990
Mexico (Peso)	....	....	....	....
Floating rate	.1280	.1276	7.8100	7.8350
Netherland (Guilder)	.4758	.4767	2.1016	2.0978
New Zealand (Dollar)	.6421	.6433	1.5574	1.5545
Norway (Krone)	.1298	.1297	7.7038	7.7108
Pakistan (Rupee)	.02496	.02496	40.070	40.070
Peru (new Sol)	.3794	.3791	2.6358	2.6377
Philippines (Peso)	.03390	.03436	29.500	29.100
Poland (Zloty)	.2882	.2881	3.4700	3.4715
Portugal (Escudo)	.005296	.005310	188.82	188.31
Russia (Ruble) (a)	.0001724	.0001724	5800.50	5800.00
Saudi Arabia (Riyal)	.2666	.2666	3.7506	3.7505
Singapore (Dollar)	.6817	.6781	1.4670	1.4748
Slovak Rep. (Koruna)	.02858	.02872	34.992	34.817
South Africa (Rand)	.2148	.2158	4.6545	4.6330
South Korea (Won)	.001125	.001125	889.00	889.25
Spain (Peseta)	.006346	.006364	157.59	157.14
Sweden (Krona)	.1240	.1246	8.0614	8.0237
Switzerland (Franc)	.6555	.6550	1.5255	1.5267
1-month forward	.6580	.6573	1.5197	1.5213
3-months forward	.6625	.6619	1.5095	1.5108
6-months forward	.6694	.6689	1.4939	1.4951
Taiwan (Dollar)	.03490	.03478	28.654	28.752
Thailand (Baht)	.03160	.03110	31.650	32.150
Turkey (Lira)	.00000619	.00000625	161610.00	159935.00
United Arab (Dirham)	.2723	.2723	3.6720	3.6720
Uruguay (New Peso)	....	....	....	....
Financial	.1044	.1058	9.5800	9.4550
Venezuela (Bolivar)	.002021	.002015	494.88	496.37
SDR	1.3490	1.3549	.7413	.7381
ECU	1.0575	1.0611	....	....

Special Drawing Rights (SDR) are based on exchange rates for the U.S., German, British, French, and Japanese currencies. Source: International Monetary Fund.

European Currency Unit (ECU) is based on a basket of community currencies.

a-fixing, Moscow Interbank Currency Exchange.

The Wall Street Journal daily foreign exchange data for 1996 and 1997 may be purchased through the Readers' Reference Service (413) 592-3600.

Figure 1.3
The exchange rates between the U.S. dollar and selected foreign currencies are published daily in financial newspapers. This table shows the currency exchange rates as published in the August 5, 1997, *Wall Street Journal*.

known brand name, patents, or copyrights. Transaction-based advantages encompass how a company does things. It could be the knowledge that is a part of a sophisticated logistics system, a method for producing private label products, a sophisticated merchandising information system, or a just-in-time inventory system. You might think of both types of assets as the company's secrets. The more important these secrets are, the more important it is to protect them. As previously noted, retail secrets are difficult to protect from imitation. Most new ideas are visible to competitors who will attempt to imitate them to enhance their own position. Retail secrets cannot be protected through patents or copyrights. This makes the guarding of secrets even more difficult.

Transaction-based advantages are generally connected with tacit learning. **Tacit learning** means that you learn to do something by doing it, as in playing the piano. You cannot play the piano without some degree of hands-on experience. In retailing, a customer service program such as Nordstrom's would be difficult to transfer to another company without a great deal of tacit learning. The British call tacit knowledge "learning by doing." The American term, "on-the-job training," says the same thing. A retail company could directly purchase an asset-based advantage; however, the company's employees would have to be trained for it to gain a transaction-based advantage.

INTERNALIZATION ADVANTAGES

In simple terms, **internalization advantages** have to do with a company's ability to keep its own secrets. **Internalization** means a company's knowledge base is not shared with others. I usually refer to this as keeping a company's secrets. The Coca-Cola Co. could have made a lot of money by selling the recipe for its soft drink. However, the company realized the importance of internalizing this information. If Coca-Cola decided to sell its secrets, we would say they were externalizing the secret. Entering a franchising arrangement is a way in which many retailers share their secrets. This is dangerous for retailers who have important information that helps them to remain distinctive. Many retailers enter franchising arrangements with companies in a foreign country. They accept the short-term return (i.e., franchising fees) because they do not think they will ever be interested in entering the foreign country as a wholly owned subsidiary. However, if these retailers later decide they do want to enter the market, they have already supplied franchisees—and potential competitors—with their most important pieces of information: information about how the company remains competitive.

LOCATIONAL ADVANTAGES

Locational advantages relate to how suitable the host country is with respect to the firm's strategies. Pellegrini[5] identified three issues relevant to international retailing: cultural proximity, market size, and competitors' moves.

CULTURAL PROXIMITY Cultural proximity refers to how similar patterns of life are in two countries. The more similar the cultures, the greater the chance that retail expansion will be successful. Sharing of a language often influences our judgment about cultural proximity, but a common language is not nearly as important to cultural similarity as we might believe. The United States and Belgium, for instance, share a pattern of life more similar than the United States and Great Britain. Many people mistakenly believe that language is the best indicator of similarities. People in Great Britain and the United States speak English, but the meanings of many words are often quite different, leading to an incorrect asummption of similarity (Box 1.1).

Canadian retailers have not been successful in the United States, but U.S. retailers are successful in Canada. Canadian retailers are inclined to view the U.S. market as equivalent to Canada, just bigger (a concept called psychic distance paradox[6]). **Psychic distance paradox** occurs when we deal with two cultures that seem to be very similar; it is not likely to occur when we readily acknowledge that cultures are very different. The U.S. retailers

BOX 1.1 CROSSING BORDERS

You Say You Speak English?

The English speak English, North Americans speak English, but can we communicate? It is difficult unless you understand that in England:

Newspapers are sold at *book stalls*.

The *ground floor* is the main floor, while the first floor is what we call the second, and so on up the building.

An apartment house is a *block of flats*.

You will be putting your clothes not in a closet, but in a *cupboard*.

A closet usually refers to the W.C. or *water closet*, which is the toilet.

When one of your British friends says she is going to *"spend a penny,"* she is going to the ladies' room.

A *bathing dress* or *bathing costume* is what the British call a bathing suit, and for those who want to go shopping, it is essential to know that a *tunic* is a blouse; a *stud* is a collar button, nothing more; and garters are *suspenders*.

Suspenders are *braces*.

If you want to buy a sweater, you should ask for a *jumper* or a *jersey* as the recognizable item will be marked in British clothing stores.

A *ladder* is not used for climbing but refers to a run in a stocking.

If you *called up* someone, it means to your British friend that you have drafted the person—probably for military service. To *ring someone up* is to telephone them.

You put your packages in the *boot* of your car not the trunk.

When you *table* something, you mean you want to discuss it, not postpone it as in the U.S.

Queer, when used by a British person, means only feeling funny.

Any reference by you to an M.D. will probably not bring a doctor. The term means *mental deficient* in Britain.

When the desk clerk asks what time you want to be *knocked up* in the morning, he is only referring to your wake-up call.

A *billion* means a million million (1,000,000,000,000) and not a thousand million as in the U.S.

Source: Cateora, P. R. (1996). *International Marketing*. 9th ed. Chicago: Irwin, p. 139.

moving into Canada were national chains. They approached the Canadian market as a foreign market, not as an extension of domestic operations.

Cultural proximity is more important for mass retailers and becomes less significant when retail ideas involve narrowly defined consumer markets that are similar in various countries.

MARKET SIZE Market saturation in the home country is an impetus for foreign direct investment by retailers. Ample space for expansion must be available, particularly if the firm needs to reach a certain size to exploit economies of scale. Germany restricts expansion to protect the environment. I interviewed one German retail executive who estimated that there were fewer than five locations available in Germany that were suitable for a department store expansion. The lack of available areas for expansion forces retailers to seek international locations.

Legal restrictions governing growth in the home country can be considered a motive for companies to move to foreign locations. Many countries, such as Japan, Belgium, France, and Italy, severely restrict the opening of large stores. The purpose of these restrictions is to protect smaller stores.

COMPETITORS' MOVES A first-mover advantage may be lost if competitors enter a foreign market. Competitors may secure prime retail locations and block out other firms. An innovator entering a new market is nearly always more successful than the imitators that follow. Competitors' moves are more important to retailers than to manufacturers because retailers are geographically based businesses.

Watching the U.S. mass merchandisers Wal-Mart and Kmart internationalize into Canada and Mexico has been similar to observing a championship chess match. One player's moves require the opponent's countermoves. In this game, the winner was Wal-Mart; Kmart is withdrawing from the Canadian market.

MACRO-MARKETING DECISION-MAKING FRAMEWORK

A retail company does not have control over every element that affects its business. The environmental elements the company cannot control are called the **macro-environment.** The macro-environment consists of five subenvironments: economic, competitive, technological, social, and governmental. To gain a competitive edge, a company should monitor these environments and use the information to change the elements of the environment that are controllable, the **micro-environment.** The micro-environment consists of price, product, promotion, distribution, and management. The macro-environment is different for each country that a company may consider entering. It is very important that multinational companies monitor this environment carefully.

The economic environment is a very important consideration for retailers. Some countries do not allow foreign firms of any kind to operate within them. China did not open its doors to foreign joint ventures until 1992. **Foreign joint ventures** are partnerships between a foreign company and a local company. India and North Korea still do not allow foreign joint ventures, much less foreign ownership. To enter China, Yaohan, a mass merchandiser originating in Japan but currently with corporate headquarters in Shanghai, had to enter an agreement with a Chinese retailer. Yaohan chose Number One Department Store, the largest retailer in Shanghai. Wal-Mart entered a joint venture with Cifra, the largest retailer in Mexico. In 1997, Wal-Mart purchased 12% of Cifra's outstanding shares. This gives Wal-Mart a majority of the voting stock. Cifra has 381 stores in Mexico, including 21 Wal-Mart Supercenters and 28 Sam's Clubs.[7] Company Focus I.3 highlights the internationalization of Wal-Mart.

ECONOMIC ENVIRONMENT

The biggest consideration for a company entering a foreign market is the basis of the economic system. In a centrally planned economy, there will be little opportunity for foreign retailers to enter the market. Under this system, the government determines what merchandise will be produced and where it will be distributed. North Korea is one of the few remaining centrally planned systems. Countries such as the People's Republic of China (PRC) actually have a mixed system. The PRC is today privatizing stores that were once government owned and allowing free market retailers to sell merchandise carried by the government stores. Russia and most parts of the former Soviet Union are undergoing similar transformations. There is a wide continuum of economic systems between socialist and capitalist countries. Most European countries and Mexico are more socialistic than the United States. In these countries, businesses must provide a high level of social welfare programs including unemployment compensation, health care, and child care. The United States and Hong Kong are capitalistic. They give companies a freer hand in conducting business within their borders.

The economic environment includes the current economic health of the area. Inflation, unemployment rates, disposable income, and savings rates have an influence on retail health and viability. Retail sales are a barometer for economic change. Consumers can postpone expenditures for nonessential purchases. Thus, when sales for nonessentials increase, it is an indicator of overall economic health.

The economic environment is important in helping a retailer assess whether a country is an attractive destination. But even if a country is identified as an attractive destination because of economic factors, it may still be a difficult area to enter. Japan is a good example of a country that, before the economic bubble burst, was viewed as a very attractive destination for foreign retailers. However, the competitive environment in Japan is very intense, and most of the best locations are taken. In short, the economic environment said "go," but the competitive environment said "no."

COMPETITIVE ENVIRONMENT

There are four major types of competitive environments: monopoly, oligopoly, monopolistic competition, and perfect competition. The competitive environment is classified in terms of number of producers and number of consumers. Each competitive situation has a set of subcharacteristics related to price. The categorization is based on the number of suppliers, numbers of buyers, and whether the product is homogeneous or differentiated (Figure 1.4).

MONOPOLY The first type of competitive environment is a **monopoly.** This is a situation in which there is one supplier and many buyers. Monopolies exist in the United States when an individual or company is awarded a

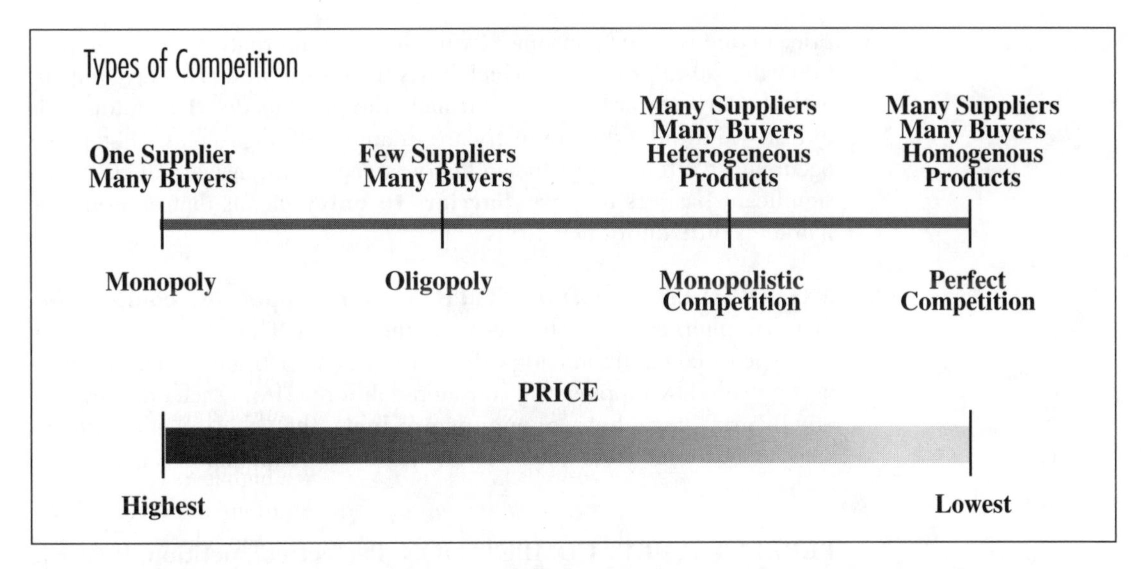

Figure 1.4 Competition is defined by the number of suppliers and the number of buyers operating in the market. Price will be highest when there is only one producer, because there is no competition to challenge the producer on price. Monopolistic competition and pure competition have many suppliers and many buyers. The difference between these two types of competition is the product. If consumers view the products of all the suppliers as the same, it is pure competition. This type of competition will result in the lowest price possible.

patent or copyright, or when the government deems that a particular service is vital to the country. Monopolies that provide an essential service are utility companies and transportation providers, such as Amtrak, the U.S. national rail service. The United States used to have more service providers that were considered essential, such as the long distance telephone companies. We now know that, even for essential service providers, competition gives consumers lower prices and greater choice.

Overall, competition reduces the price consumers pay. Monopolies will tend to charge the highest possible price because there is no competition. Some monopolies do not charge high prices, but these are usually distinguished by their lack of service. Before market reforms in mainland China and in Russia, the state owned all the stores. The prices were set very low, particularly for necessities. However, selection and service were terrible.

OLIGOPOLY Oligopolies are the next type of competition. In this market situation, a few companies control the market. Generally, an industry is considered an oligopoly if it has a 4/50 concentration. This means that the top four companies provide 50% of the market. Oligopolies avoid competing on price, instead choosing to compete on service. There is a simple explanation for this. Because there are only a few competitors, comparing various offerings is very easy for consumers. If the price of one is lower, consumers will select that alternative. Price competition will lead to price wars, which hurts the entire industry. The company with the largest market share is usually the price leader. The automobile industry and the airline industry are examples of oligopolies. Oligopolies occur most often where the industry is capital intensive and there are significant barriers to entry. **Barriers to entry** means that entering the market is difficult for new firms.

MONOPOLISTIC COMPETITION In **monopolistic competition,** many suppliers and many buyers are in the market. The difference between this type of competition and perfect or pure competition is that the products provided by suppliers are considered different from each other by buyers. By providing a **heterogeneous product**—that is, one that consumers view as different from their competitors'—the companies can charge a higher price.

PERFECT (PURE) COMPETITION Perfect competition, similar to monopolistic competition, has many suppliers and buyers; however, consumers do not view the products as being different. Agricultural products are a good example of this type of competitive environment. When we go into a grocery store, we generally do not specify that we want to buy Farmer Brown's milk. Milk is just milk; the product is homogeneous. In perfect competition, price will be a perfect interplay of supply and demand. The lowest price will be found in this competitive environment.

The differences between monopolistic and perfect competition most often confuse people. Consider the purchase of bananas. Usually when we go to a grocery store to buy bananas, we just find an attractive bunch and purchase it. However, one consumer might notice a little sticker on a bunch that says "Chiquita Bananas." The well-known advertising jingle runs through that person's mind. "I'm Chiquita Banana and I would like to say. . ." If this consumer buys the Chiquita Bananas, he or she has moved from a situation of perfect competition to one of monopolistic competition. By considering Chiquita Bananas superior, or at least more desirable, the consumer may be willing to pay a higher price. The product—bananas—is no longer perceived as homogeneous but as heterogeneous.

TECHNOLOGICAL ENVIRONMENT

The technological environment consists of equipment and infrastructures that make retailing more efficient and profitable. The PRC has a problem with power failures. This does not bode well for industries that depend on refrigeration units or computer usage. In 1989, I visited one of the first government-owned supermarkets in Shanghai. When supermarkets first opened, they sold primarily staple packaged merchandise, not refrigerated or frozen food. Shortly after this pioneering supermarket opened in Shanghai, it put in a large chest freezer for frozen meat. I asked the store owner about this, knowing that most Chinese did not have freezer space in their homes. The manager said the frozen meat was considered a novelty. People bought the frozen meat, took it home, thawed it out, and cooked it. The supermarket also had computers at the checkout lanes, with scanning capability. However, the scanning devices were not hooked up. The computers were used like old-fashioned cash registers, and as a place to store the money. Although these checkout clerks used the computers to add up the bill, sales clerks in department stores generally still use an abacus. We often see the latest technology appearing in developing countries as foreign retailers enter and bring their innovations.

Sometimes governments help promote technological adaptations. For instance, several years ago, France introduced a computer telephone system called Minitel. Most homes in France had this system, and people used it as an electronic phone book and as a system for making reservations. The benefit is that French consumers soon became acquainted with and began using the computer system as part of their daily activities.

One of the most important technological advances required for modern retailing systems is an up-to-date packaging system. As a country begins to develop economically, retailers begin to use more self-service. Packaging protects products from consumers unaccustomed to self-service. At later stages of economic development, packaging plays a role in making the product more attractive and less perishable.

SOCIAL ENVIRONMENT

The social environment for retailing is very important. In some cultures, shopping is a woman's major activity. A homemaker spends her day selecting ingredients for the evening meal. As she goes about her shopping, she exchanges news and information with the shop owners and other shoppers. The marketplace thus serves a variety of important functions; it is not simply a place to obtain products.

There was a time when women in the United States loved to shop. Shopping was considered a pleasurable way to spend leisure time. I know few professional women who still feel this way. Today's working women and mothers look for places where they can get in and out quickly and conveniently. Women want to reduce the time they spend shopping so they can maximize their time with family and friends. Retailers are now struggling to come up with ideas that will make shopping fun again.

Even teenagers, once called "mall rats," are turning up their noses at mall environments. Malls are becoming "uncool." Tower Records, for one, has adopted a strategy of avoiding mall locations, focusing instead on freestanding locations in shopping neighborhoods. Tower is anticipating that its target market, teenagers and young adults, are looking for a less sanitized shopping environment than the typical mall.

GOVERNMENTAL ENVIRONMENT

The last type of macro-environment is the governmental and legal system. "Red-Tape Traumas" (Box 1.2) illustrates how governmental regulations affect business in the "Big Three" countries: the United States, Japan, and Germany.

A legal system applies only within a specific country. No country has the authority to dictate to another country what is legal and what is illegal. No supreme judicial body solves the legal problems of the world. Although the World Court considers grievances of its member countries, the court has no authority or ability to intervene.

There are four major types of legal systems: code law, common law, Islamic law, and Marxist law. Most countries allowing foreign ownership of retailing are either code-law or common-law countries. Countries with Islamic-law and Marxist-law systems discourage exposure to outside influences.

Code-law countries require that every action fit within a preexisting law. France and Italy are examples of code-law countries, in which registration determines ownership. Tradition, past practices, and legal precedence influences a **common-law** country's decisions. Common law changes as society changes. Countries that were once under the British legal system are likely to be common-law countries. The United States, Great Britain, Canada, and Australia are common-law countries. In a code-law country, a man and woman would need to be formally married to be protected by joint property rights. The marriage certificate is their registration of the relationship. In common-law countries, if a man and woman live together for a period, functioning as husband and wife but never formally marrying, they can be considered married. If they separate, both people can sue for ownership of property. This is where we get the term "common-law wife." Common law is also the basis for palimony suits.

Have you ever heard the saying, "possession is nine-tenths of the law?" This phrase also has its basis in common law. Suppose my neighbor put up a fence between our two properties. If the fence were two feet over onto my property but I did not say anything about it for several years, I could lose my ownership rights to that land. My neighbor could make the claim that I knowingly allowed him to claim those two extra feet of property. Prior use establishes ownership under common law.

In a code-law country, patents and copyrights are determined by registration. In a common-law country, patents and copyrights are determined by the party that can prove it had the idea first.

Islamic law is based on interpretation of the Koran. This type of legal system is found in Pakistan, Iran, and other Islamic countries. Islamic law prescribes a total pattern of life for its followers. It includes issues such as property rights, economic decision-making, and types of economic freedoms.[8] Charging interest is illegal under Islamic law. As you might expect, this makes business capitalization very difficult. Islamic banks have

BOX 1.2

Red-Tape Traumas

By Bob Davis, Peter Gumbel, and David P. Hamilton.

You think the government's on your back? Just look at Big Government through the eyes of discount retailers in the world's Big Three economies.

In Recklinghausen, in Germany's industrial Ruhr, Allkauf SB-Warenhaus GmbH has struggled to build a store for 15 years. The discounter owns the land, but that doesn't matter much. Local authorities can — and do — bar new stores if they believe existing ones will suffer. Even at best, it takes about five years to get authorization. And if a community opposes a store, Allkauf Chairman Eugen Viehof says, "there's no use even trying."

In the city of Saga on Japan's southernmost island of Kyushu, Mr Max Corp. has spent three years persuading more than 20 farmers to sell their land and petition the government to rezone it for commercial use. Next come at least 18 months of haggling with local merchants, who legally can demand concessions when new stores open nearby. Mr Max expects to open its new outlet by early 1997, but to placate opposition will almost certainly have to shrink the store's planned size at least 20% and pay inflated membership fees to a local trade association.

In Abilene, Kan., Duckwall-Alco Stores Inc. can act quickly. It sneaks into small Midwestern towns and quietly takes options on property. Only then is the local mayor contacted. "I say, 'We're a discounter and want to move into your town,'" says John Hedeen, Alco's vice president for real estate. "There's silence on the line. They think, 'My God, this will ruin the town.'" But if the property is already zoned commercial the town can do little. (Eventually, most towns wind up welcoming the stores and the new jobs.)

The American Advantage

Most businesses around the world complain about red tape, often with good reason. But a comparison of regulatory burdens in the U.S., Japan and Germany shows that wile many American businesses have valid complaints, they generally have it much easier than their foreign counterparts. "If you look at the details of the system, few people in the U.S. would substitute the Japanese or German economies for their own," says Edward Hudgins, director of regulatory studies for the libertarian Cato Institute in Washington.

Each nation's regulations reflect and reinforce its brand of capitalism—predatory in the U.S., paternal in Germany and protected in Japan—and its social values. It's easier to open a business in the U.S. than in Germany because Germans value social consensus above risk-taking, but it's harder to hire people because Americans worry more about discrimination lawsuits. It's easier to import children's clothes in the U.S. than Japan because Japanese bureaucrats defend a jumble of import restrictions, but it's harder to open bank branches across the U.S. because Americans strongly defend state prerogatives.

Although global competitions makes many industries around the world resemble their rivals, business conditions on their home turfs vary strikingly. Government rules in the Big Three economies affect managers, workers and customers of discount chains, for example, very differently, with Germany's many regulations pushing prices of most goods much higher than in the U.S. and even Japan.

A Hovering Presence

Retailing has yet to become a global business like the auto industry, even though the three retailers sell generally similar merchandise. One big influence on each of these chains isn't a government agency at all but the world's largest retailer: Wal-Mart Stores Inc. Alco's strategy is run-and-hide, opening stores—typically with 18,000 square feet—in towns with fewer than 5,000 people. It figures Wal-Mart won't bother with such small markets, and it feels safe so long as no Wal-Mart is within about 30 miles.

In Germany and Japan, where retail consolidation lags behind that in the U.S., Allkauf and Mr Max dream of becoming the next Wal-Mart. Allkauf wants

Continued

Red-Tape
continued

to emulate Wal-Mart's electronic scanners and computerized inventory controls to cut costs. Its stores usually have at least 50,000 square feet. Mr Max wants to copy Wal-Mart's mega-size, opening 100,000-square-foot stores in a format it calls "Hyper Mall Merx"—a U.S.-style shopping center anchored by a Mr Max and a supermarket and including a dozen small retailers.

Of the three discount chains, Moenchengladbach-based Allkauf is by far the largest, with sales of $2.55 billion in its latest fiscal year and 9,000 employees. Fukuoka-based Mr Max's sales totaled $588.3 million; it has 518 permanent employees and more than 500 part-timers. Alco, of Abilene, rang up sales of $242.1 million and has 3,500 employees. Allkauf, which is closely held, doesn't report net income; Mr Max earned $11.7 million and Alco $4.1 million in their latest years.

In a store's day-to-day operations, the hand of government is nearly invisible in the U.S. Alco stores open every day except Thanksgiving, Christmas and Easter and stay open as late as they choose, though 8 p.m. is usually late enough for customers on the prairie. Each season, the stores feature a sale in the center aisle—of Halloween candy, of Christmas ornaments, of lawn furnishings in spring.

Germany, though, has a welter of rules, some dating to the Kaiser's era, limiting store hours and competition. That gives store clerks regular hours and helps Allkauf's smaller rivals but inconveniences customers. Allkauf stores can be open only 68½ hours a week and must close at 6:30 p.m. on weekdays and at 2 p.m. on Saturdays. Sunday shopping is forbidden. At Allkauf's Moenchengladbach store, the crush of shoppers is unbearable on Friday evenings and Saturday mornings; the rest of the week, the store is fairly quiet.

Meanwhile, under a Hitler-era "rebate law," German stores can hold full-scale "sales" only twice a year, usually in January and late July. Even then, they can't discount food. The rules are enforced by regulatory cops from the industry-run Central Institute for the Combating of Unfair Competition, which fielded 20,000 complaints about violations in 1994. There's talk in parliament of easing the restrictions, but so far nothing has changed. "Every structure must have rules ensuring order so as not to hurt the rights of others," says Reiner Muenker, the institute's deputy director.

Forced 'Holidays'

At first glance, Japan seems a shoppers' paradise by comparison. Mr Max usually can stay open until 8 p.m. But to placate smaller retailers, Japanese law requires it to take 24 days of "holiday" a year, closing its stores twice a month for no other reason.

And Mr Max faces restrictions that would appall a U.S. retailer. It can't give discount coupons, for fear of violating laws designed to protect consumers from "confusion." Moreover, the government's antitrust watchdog, the Fair Trade Commission, forbids it to discount such copyrighted products as compact disks, books and magazines. (Mr Max offers a 10% break on CD purchases anyway but doesn't advertise it so as not to draw fire.)

Mr Max faces one of its toughest government burdens when importing goods, which it needs to do to keep prices low. Motioning toward the kitchenware in a store near corporate headquarters in Fukuoka, Yoshiaki Hirano, Mr Max's 37-year-old president, sounds as frustrated as U.S. trade negotiators describing Japan's barriers.

Japanese customs officials once decreed that each carton of Thai-made plastic food containers must be tested six times, once for each of three different-size containers and their lids. So Mr Max decided to buy from a domestic wholesaler and now charges about $3.45 a container. "If we could have imported, we could sell for maybe one-third or one-fourth what the Japanese consumer pays now," Mr. Hirano says.

Another time, Japan's health authorities held up a shipment of American-made baby-size T-shirts because they contained too much Formalin, a chemical the ministry claims causes skin disease. Mr Max eventually gave up on that issue, too. "We're just asking them, 'If it's good enough for a U.S. child, why can't we sell it here?' " says Toshio Yamamoto, Mr Max's merchandising manager.

Other rules rankle, too. Japanese fire codes were designed for cramped, multi-story buildings. So, Mr Max must install fire shutters that lower automatically to contain a fire, even though fires wouldn't spread vertically in its big single-story stores. The codes also require an exit at the end of each aisle. Mr Max builds the doors but then, despite the local inspectors, put shelves and products in front of them. In all, Mr Max calculates that the requirements add 30% to construction costs.

In the U.S., Alco wrestles with liability laws. Alco won't sell exercise equipment or child car-seats unless the supplier carries as much as $5 million in liability insurance. And the retailer won't buy property unless the owner certifies that any environmental mess has been cleaned up. That's necessary, Alco executives say, because under U.S. law retailers can be sued for problems arising from the goods they sell or the property they buy even if they didn't create the problems.

Alco also faces tough anti-discrimination laws — and U.S. commitments to a multiethnic society that are lacking in Germany and Japan. Alco gives store managers a list of questions they can't ask job applicants: Don't ask a woman if she wants to be called Miss, Mrs. or Ms., don't talk about "mother tongue," and don't ask where an applicant was born. Such questions, Alco worries, could be used in a lawsuit by someone rejected for a job.

In the U.S., of course, an employer would be especially leery about asking a job applicant about religious preferences, even if the question might seem appropriate. But in Germany, employers don't have a problem: A person's religion is listed on work papers because, by law, German churches get a slice of income-tax revenue, and the tax authorities need to know which denomination should receive the money.

Minimum Wages

Even more critical for Alco are minimum-wage levels. Its clerks and cashiers make the federal minimum of $4.25 an hour. Department supervisors earn $6 an hour. None get health insurance. Yet in rural Kansas, where four-bedroom houses sell for $50,000 and jobs are scarce, Alco often has five applicants for every opening. The stores frequently hire mothers who work part time while their children are in school. Alco worries that the government will raise the minimum wage by 25 cents an hour, which, the company calculates, would have reduced last year's $6.7 million pretax earnings by $912,000—about 15%.

Alco's mix of cheap wages, cheap land and cookie-cutter buildings helps it keep prices low by international standards. A gallon of Alco paint, for instance, costs about $12; Allkauf's and Mr Max's equivalents cost about $60. A 25-inch Magnavox color television set goes for $399 at Alco, compared with the $570 Allkauf charges for a 25-inch Condor and the $468 Mr Max charges for a 25-inch Sharp. Alco isn't always the cheapest, though. The Japanese chain sells Ma Montre brand jeans for $14.88, Alco sells Rustler jeans for $14.99, and Allkauf sells Red Baron jeans for $36.

Germany's regulatory system is designed to keep peace between labor and management even if consumers pay more. Through its collective-bargaining system, clerks at Allkauf and throughout German retailing earn the equivalent of $16 an hour and get six weeks of vacation. Forget about firing them. Unions have a major say in setting severance pay. When Allkauf closed a Hanover store, it ended up paying just over $20,000 to each of its 100 employees there. When Alco closes a Midwest store, by contrast, it pays no severance. Alco helps workers fill out unemployment-compensation forms, gives them a letter of thanks and asks whether they are willing to move to another location.

The Japanese minimum wage isn't a problem for Mr Max, which pays part-time employees about $6.60 an hour, some 10% above the local minimum wage. After adjusting for Japan's steep cost of living, which is almost twice that of the U.S., the part-timers earn less than Alco wages. Mr. Max's career (or "lifetime") employees, all university graduates, start at about $32,000 a year, roughly as much as a veteran Alco store manager. Japanese workers benefit from a national social-security system that provides health care and a small pension, although they must make income-based contributions; career employees get more generous company-sponsored health and pension plans, plus a chance at rapid advancement.

No rules prevent Mr Max from laying off career workers, but Mr. Hirano says he wouldn't do so for fear of damaging the

Continued

Red-Tape
continued

company's reputation among college seniors. In addition, the Labor Ministry scrutinizes all firings for cause and weighs in when its investigators think that a company acted unjustly. The ministry is known for leaning quietly on employers to prevent layoffs.

While the German regulatory system is virtually immovable, Japan is slowly loosening its rules. For years, Japan's Large-Scale Retail Store law made opening new stores nightmarish. Now, Mr Max owes its growth to 1990 changes that facilitated expansion. Local retailers can't stop big stores from opening, though they can still insist on restrictions.

Mr Max usually has to scale back the size of planned stores to win their approval, somtimes as much as 70%. Once, in Saga, merchants even made it promise *not* to close one of its older consumer-electronics stores in a nearby shopping center. They feared for their own businesses if it pulled out.

Now Mr Max can co-opt some opposition by opening mall-size retailing centers. "We're in a position to ask [local retailers] to join us," says Mr. Hirano, who once worked as a New York investment banker. With greater leverage, Mr Max can open stores faster. It started building its latest Hyper Mall Merx only two years after buying the property—slow by U.S. standards but fast compared with the nearly eight years Mr Max needed to get approval in the town of Kasuga, near Fukuoka.

For Allkauf, German unification was a breakthrough that allowed it to expand in ways impossible in West Germany. Federal authorities were so eager to provide goods for people to buy that they waived most store-opening rules in East Germany. And East Germans were so starved of goods that, for several years, they bought like crazy, often on credit. Allkauf's revenues grew 25% during those years.

Neither Japan nor Germany, though, is likely to match one advantage of the U.S. regulatory system: A company can start over. In 1989, crushed by debt and too much competition from Wal-Mart and Kmart Corp., Alco filed for bankruptcy protection. All three nations have bankruptcy laws, but they are used more extensively in the U.S., where business failure isn't considered a moral disgrace.

Over the next two years, Alco negotiated to repay its unsecured creditors, settling for nine cents on the dollar, and devised a new retail strategy. By 1991, it was out of bankruptcy proceedings. Three years later, it raised $13 million in a public stock offering. Hardly any company likes government rules, but in this case they gave Alco a second chance.

Source: The Wall Street Journal, (1997). December 14.

developed a solution. Instead of providing interest-bearing loans, a bank will purchase company stock, then sell it back to the company later for a greater amount. The difference between the purchase and resale price equals the additional charge paid as interest in non-Islamic countries.

Marxist law is based on a code-law system. The basic premise of Marxist law is that of socialist ownership. North Korea still uses Marxist law. The state owns all the factories, retail stores, and educational institutions. Mainland China is now operating under a mixed system, privatizing most of what the state owned. In 1992, China changed its system to allow foreign retail joint ventures; however, no laws were written to cover these ventures. At a recent meeting with officials who write the joint venture laws in China, I was asked why so few U.S. companies were interested in entering China. I replied that the lack of established rules for the joint ventures was certain to hamper U.S.

retailers' interests. The first foreign retailers to begin moving into China were Japanese. These retailers entered China before rules were written, and some retailers have since learned that operating under Marxist law can be fraught with uncertainty. After building the biggest retail store in China, Yaohan, the first Japanese retailer to enter a retailing joint venture in China, found out that the government expected it to build a housing project for residents of the area who had been displaced by the store. From a Marxist viewpoint this expectation makes a great deal of sense; but not so to the capitalist retailers.

GOVERNMENT INFLUENCES ON OWNERSHIP Governments have a major impact on retailing in areas other than the legal system. As we saw in Box 1.2, each country has laws that regulate where new stores can be opened, what hours they can be open, and what kinds of products they can sell. Recall that in Japan, the *Daiten Ho* (Large-Scale Retail Store Law) once made the approval process for new stores very difficult. Obtaining permission to open new stores sometimes took 10 years or more. Japan has since altered this law to make the process less time-consuming. Now the maximum time for application review is 12 months.

Governments can also force retailers operating within their country to relinquish ownership. There are four types of governmental interference with ownership: confiscation, expropriation, domestication, and nationalization.

With **confiscation,** the government simply takes over a company, making no payment to the owners. Generally, a country confiscates property only during times of political strife. After property is confiscated, a government may sell the assets and then close the business. The result of confiscation is that the government gains the company assets.

Expropriation occurs when the government takes over a company but compensates the owners in some nominal way. For instance, a government that gives business owners $1 for each $100 in property value is using expropriation. The key point is that the owner does not have a choice in selling the property. By giving some token payment, however, the government can justify its actions more readily. In the 1950s, the communist government took over private property in China. Several large foreign retailers, such as Wing On and Sincere of Hong Kong, lost their retail stores in Shanghai. As with confiscation, the government may dispose of the assets and then close the business. Again, the result is that the government gains the company assets.

Domestication refers to the situation in which a government forces a company to transfer ownership in the company to **nationals** (the people who live in the country). Domestication often occurs when strong nationalistic sentiments arise over foreign ownership of a country's property. Suppose Mexico were to pass a foreign ownership law, restricting the percentage of ownership allowed by foreigners. If a company wanted to continue to operate in Mexico, it would need to sell part of its company to people in Mexico. When Sears first entered the Mexican market, the company set the stage for becoming an important addition to the Mexican business environment. Sears used a process called **predetermined domestication.** That is, the company undertook domestication as part of a long-term market strategy. Predetermined domestication includes four dimensions: (1) Selling equity in the company at a fair market price; (2) Including nationals in middle- and upper-management positions, not just in low-level positions; (3) Purchasing merchandise from the host country; and (4) Including host country suppliers in the company's global operations. If domestication occurs gradually, it can be beneficial to the company. Selling equity to locals expands the company's financing base. Using locals as managers is less expensive and also adds to the company's cultural awareness: Purchasing merchandise locally lowers costs. By undertaking predetermined domestication, a company is ensuring itself against government-forced domestication.

Nationalization occurs when the government takes over the ownership of a business and operates it as a government institution. Generally, nationalization occurs throughout an industry, not just on a company-by-company basis. Governments nationalize industries under the guise of protecting the national welfare of the country. The Canadian government nationalized the railroads in Canada to bring all ownership under one domain. In the 1950s, as mentioned, the Chinese government nationalized all industry, bringing all property and business ownership under the domain of the People's Republic of China.

The international macro-marketing environment includes economic, competitive, technological, social, and government environments. A retailer must understand these environments before it can determine where to go—and how to internationalize. Salmon and Tjordman[9] developed a theory of internationalization based on centralized versus decentralized decision-making. The centralized expansion method is called a global strategy. The decentralized method is called a multinational strategy.

GLOBAL VERSUS MULTINATIONAL STRATEGIES

Have you been to a McDonald's in a foreign country? McDonald's looks the same in Hong Kong as it does in Chicago. The same basic ingredients are there: Big Macs and french fries. In Germany, the restaurant looks the same but you will encounter beer on the menu. In Japan, things are a bit different—McDonald's sports some odd-looking blue drinks, but the familiar Big Mac and fries are still there. The same experience holds true if you walk into a Laura Ashley store or a Body Shop throughout the world. Such retailers use a **global strategy;** that is, they replicate their standard format throughout the world. Other retailers change their products and strategy to adapt to other parts of the world; they use a **multinational strategy.**

GLOBAL STRATEGIES

IKEA, Benetton, and McDonald's are among those classified as using a global strategy. These retailers assume that their customers are similar throughout the world. This does not mean they assume that mass markets are the same throughout the world, rather, that wherever they decide to move there will be a target consumer who identifies with their retail offering.

Global companies have several characteristics. They are generally **vertically integrated.** Vertical integration occurs when a company expands to a different level in the production hierarchy. If a company expands in the direction of raw materials, it is called **backward vertical integration.** If it expands in the direction of the consumer, it is called **forward vertical integration.** Let's look at some examples using an actual company, Levi Strauss & Co. Levi Strauss produces jeans. If the company were to acquire a textile plant, it would be moving toward the raw materials; an instance of backward vertical integration. Levi Strauss has begun to open its own retail stores; the company is thus moving closer to the consumer (forward vertical integration).

Global retailers sell only their private label products or products for which the manufacturers carry product risk. **Private label** products are products made to the retailer's specifications and not sold at other retail stores. Benetton uses a network of subcontractors to produce its product. These subcontractors use the same know-how, technology, and standards to provide a uniform product for Benetton. This dependence on a private label line means these retailers require a longer lead time before production is completed. A **lead time** is the period between when the design for a product is completed and when production is finished. Retailers of private label lines thus concentrate on products with a long life cycle, avoiding fashion-sensitive merchandise that is more risky.

Foot Locker sells national brands but negotiates for exclusive features such as colors or detailing for its stores. Tower Records operates in an industry where unsold merchandise can be returned. Bookstores also have this type of industry-wide returns system

Logistics plays an important part in the retail strategy of global companies. **Logistics** refers to the system of moving merchandise from producer to consumer. Warehouses, transportation systems, and computer information networks are part of the logistics system. Global retailers supply stores around the world from several centralized warehouses, which they fully automate and integrate. Because global retailers faithfully replicate their format in new markets they enter, they can expand at a rapid rate. This rapid expansion is also necessary to ensure adequate store coverage to support the centralized warehouse.

Global companies use centralized management to achieve this type of standardized retail operation. **Centralized management** means that policies related to the product line, merchandising, service, advertising, and prices are determined at the corporate level. Most companies do not use a 100% global strategy. Toys "R" Us, Inc., is a good example of a company that generally uses a global strategy but does not carry 100% private label merchandise. Toys "R" Us adjusts its product offerings and prices according to the location it is entering.

Global companies are generally specialty retailers with a narrow and distinct product line. Returning to Dunning's theory, these companies specialize in ownership advantages, both asset-based and transaction-based. The asset-based advantages are the company reputation and private label line. The transaction-based advantages are superior logistics, centralized management, and the ability to expand into new markets quickly.

MULTINATIONAL STRATEGY

Retailers using a multinational strategy adapt their retail offerings as they enter foreign markets. They consider their retail subsidiaries as a portfolio of businesses that they must manage and adapt to each market they enter. French hypermarkets and food supermarkets, overall, are good examples of the multinational strategy. The selling of food is quite culturally bound. Therefore, it is unlikely a store selling food could be successful without adaptation. Multinational retailers focus on securing locational advantages. They seek markets that are geographically adjacent, culturally similar, with low levels of competition. Multinational retailers have decentralized management to allow them to be more sensitive to cultural nuances. Carrefour and Promodès, French hypermarkets, are examples of such retailers. Multinational retailers often use mixed management teams made up of native and expatriate executives.

These retailers have a more difficult time expanding because they are not just replicating a standard format but instead inventing a new offering. They also do not benefit from economies of scale, as do global retailers. Multinational retailers are successful because of their acquired experience, but unlike global retailers, the international expansion of their network does not reduce their costs of retailing, supplying, and advertising. Carrefour's international expansion, summarized below, shows a pattern of success and learning.

Photo 1.1
This Toys "R" Us store is on reclaimed land in Hong Kong Harbor. The location is excellent, just adjacent to the Starr Ferry, one of the two major transportation links from central Hong Kong to Tsim Sha Shui. *Courtesy of the author.*

Photo 1.2
This Toys "R" Us store is located in Saudi Arabia. Toys "R" Us is a global retailer; the format is recognizable wherever the stores are located. *Courtesy of Amal Aswailem.*

Photo 1.3
This picture was taken at a Toys "R" Us store in Japan during "doll" season, when young girls are given dolls elaborately dressed in traditional kimonos, and when hotels and restaurants feature displays of dolls. *Courtesy of AP/Wide World Photos.*

- 1969: Belgium (out in 1978)
- 1969: United Kingdom (out in 1983)
- 1972: Italy (out in 1984)
- 1973: Spain (43 stores in 1993)
- 1974: Brazil (29 stores in 1993)
- 1976: Austria (out in 1979)
- 1977: Germany (out in 1979)
- 1982: Argentina (7 stores in 1993)
- 1988: United States (out in 1994)
- 1989: Taiwan (7 stores in 1993)
- 1990: Portugal (2 stores in 1993)
- 1993: Italy (5 stores today)
- 1993: Malaysia (1 store in 1994)
- 1993: Turkey (1 stores in 1993)

Carrefour has exited countries in which it was not successful (Belgium, the United Kingdom, Italy, Austria, Germany, the United States). All are developed countries with a high degree of competition. The countries in which Carrefour has been the most successful are Spain and Brazil. Carrefour made a second entry into Italy in 1993, after gaining a great deal of knowledge from its other international experiences. This time, the format was successful.

Multinational retailers usually concentrate their expansion in a limited number of countries, attempting to gain market share. The movement of French hypermarkets into Spain illustrates this approach. French hypermarkets moved into Spain in the mid to late 1970s. They now have the dominant market share there. Japanese department stores moved into Hong Kong in the same way, dominating the department store market share within just a few years.

Multinational retailers are most successful in businesses where bulk, weight, or perishability of the merchandise inhibits international procurement. Large retailers, department stores, and mass merchandisers who face extreme competition in the home market may engage in this expansion strategy to find markets where competition is less severe. Retailers may also use this format for expansion if their expansion in the home market is blocked because of government restrictions against large-scale retailers. Such laws make expansion in Japan, Belgium, France, and Germany difficult. As a result, large-scale retailers in these markets may seek international expansion as their most desirable growth avenue.

Global Companies

- Centralized management
- Standard format
- Rapid expansion
- Private label or industries in which manufacturers hold product risk

Multinational Companies

- Decentralized management
- Adapts
- Stages expansion
- National brands and private label

Major features of global and multinational companies are summarized above. Dunning's ownership advantages and internalization advantages are very important to global companies. Their ownership advantages include a distinctive retail format and often a private label product. They use centralized management to maintain these advantages. Locational advantages are more important to multinational companies. Because they adapt to culture, they must know the target culture and be able to translate that knowledge into products. Multinational companies therefore obtain much greater knowledge because they are adapting to each change.

SUMMARY

This chapter provides the conceptual overview for understanding international retailing. The study of international retailing and retail internationalization is very different from the study of international marketing and market internationalization. Retailing is geographically based. Laws regulating international trade do not affect international retailing, as the retailers can source in each domestic market. Instead, retailers need to be aware of intra-country business laws and regulations.

Retailers must assess their company's strengths and the relative attractiveness of continued domestic growth or international growth. They must determine whether it is important to keep company knowledge to themselves and use it for their continued international expansion.

Figure 1.5
Deciding how to internationalize takes into consideration ownership advantages and the need to internalize company information. Deciding where to go takes into consideration locational advantages.

Retailers use the macro-environment—economic, competitive, technological, social, and governmental—to make decisions about their retail offering. This decision is twofold: First, should they enter the foreign market? And, if they decide to enter the market, should they use a standard retail format (global), or should they adapt their retail offering (multinational)? The issues are who should go, where to go, and how to go. Such issues are also related to the decision to rely on centrally versus decentrally managed operations.

This decision framework is summarized in Figure 1.5. Factors of production—land, labor, capital, and entrepreneurship—influence a country's level of economic development and the choice of country when internationalizing. The macro-environment influences a country's locational advantage. A company's ownership advantages will influence whether it will internalize its secrets. This decision will, in turn, influence whether the company uses a standard format or a format that is individualized for each country.

KEY TERMS

absolute advantage
ad valorem tariff
adaptation
asset based
backward vertical integration
barriers to entry
centralized management
code law
combination tariff
common law
confiscation
cultural geography
currency exchange
diseconomies of scale
domestication
economic geography
economies of scale
export
expropriation
favorable balance of trade
foreign joint venture
forward vertical integration
franchising
global strategy
heterogeneous product
internationalization advantage
internationalization
Islamic law
joint venture
lead time
license
licensing
locational advantages
logistics
macro-environment
Marxist law
micro-environment
monopolistic competition
monopoly
multinational strategy
nationalization
nationals
oligopoly
over-stored
ownership advantages
perfect competition
predetermined domestication
private label
psychic distance paradox
quota
relative advantage
specific tariff
standardization
tacit learning
tariff
transaction based
vertically integrated
wholly owned subsidiary

DISCUSSION QUESTIONS

1. Consider the macro-marketing environment (economic, competitive, technological, social, and governmental/legal). How would each of these environments affect a manufacturer distributing to the country versus a retailer operating in a country?
2. Retailers and manufacturers have different international expansion options. Use Dunning's theory of the eclectic firm to explain the risks and benefits of franchising.
3. Some theories discuss retail internationalization in terms of push and pull factors. Push factors nudge retailers out of their home markets. Pull factors attract retailers into new markets. Although I have not used these terms, can you explain how each of the following reasons for internationalization could be considered push or pull factors? These reasons are (a) mature home market—low growth potential, (b) need to diversify investment, (c) expansion at home blocked by legislation, (d) possession of a unique market format, (e) intense competition at home, (e) economic downturn at home, and (g) first-mover advantages.
4. What is the relationship between Dunning's theory of the eclectic firm and Salmon and Tordjman's theory of internationalization through global versus multinational retailers?

ENDNOTES

1. Coopers & Lybrand. (1995). *Global Powers of Retailing.* Chain Store Age Special Report.
2. Parker-Pope, T. (1996). "Body Shop Considers a Makeover for Its Image to End U.S. Losses." *Wall Street Journal,* November 12, p. B4.
3. Coopers & Lybrand. (1996). *Global Retailing: Assignment Latin America.*
4. Dunning, J. H., and M. McQueen. (1982). "The Eclectic Theory of the Multinational Enterprise and the International Hotel Industry." In A. M. Rugman, ed., *New Theories of the Multinational Enterprise.* Beckenham, Kent: Croom Helm, pp. 79–106.
5. Pelligrini, L. (1991). "The Internationalization of Retailing and 1992 Europe." *Journal of Marketing Channels,* Vol. 1, No. 2, pp. 3–27.
6. Evans, W., H. Lane, and S. Grady. (1992). *Border Crossings: Doing Business in the US.* Scarborough, Ontario, Canada: Prentice-Hall.
7. "Wal-Mart Kicks Off $1.2B Offer for Cifra." (1997). *Women's Wear Daily,* July 28, p. 20.
8. Cateora, P. R. (1996). *International Marketing.* 9th ed. Chicago: Irwin.
9. Salmon, W., and A. Tordjman. (1990). "The Internationalization of Retailing." *International Journal of Retailing,* Vol. 4, No. 2, pp. 3–16.

CHAPTER 1 APPENDIX

The Top 100 Global Retailers

Sales Rank	Company	Trading Names	Format Types
1	Wal-Mart Stores, Inc.[b]	Wal-Mart, Sam's Clubs, Bud's Warehouse Outlets, Food-4-Less, Hypermart*USA, Value Clubs, Superama, Bodega Aurrera, Aurrera, Vips, Suburbia	Discount Stores Warehouse Clubs, Supercenters
2	Metro Holding AG[b]	Metro, Makro, Huma, Meister, Primus & BLV, Winner's Point, (see Kaufhof Group and Asko Deutsche Kaufhaus AG)	Shopping Centers, Supermarkets, Specialty Stores, Department Stores
3	Kmart Corporation[b]	Kmart, Borders, Builders Square	Discount Stores, Specialty Stores, DIY
4	Sears, Roebuck and Co.[a,b]	Sears	Department Stores
5	Tenglemann Warenhandelsgesellschaft	Tenglemann, Plus, Kaiser's, Obi, Ledi, Grosso-Markt, Magnet, Gubi, Rude Reste Rampe, Wissol, Tenga, Basis, Lauf & Kauf, (see Great Atlantic & Pacific Tea, Inc.)	Shopping Centers, Supermarkets, Drug Stores, Specialty Stores
6	The Daiei, Inc.	Daiei, Topos, D-Mart, Bundle Exotic Town, Holiday Mart, Kuo's Wholesale Membership Club, Lawson	Supermarkets, Department Stores, Convenience Stores, Specialty Stores
7	Ito-Yokado Co., Ltd.	7-Eleven, Ito-Yokado, Marudai, Maruki Tobishima, Mary Ann, York-Benimaru, York Mart, Steps, Daikuma, Oshman's, Robinson's, York (see Southland)	Superstores, Specialty Stores, Supermarkets, Discount Stores, Department Stores
8	Aldi	ALDI	Supermarkets
9	Carrefour SA	Brepa, Carcoop, Carrefour, Euromarche, GML, Presicarre, Pryca, Sofidis, Sogara, Sogramo, Superest, Erteco, Carfuel, Carma, Vacances, Providange, Al Gran Sole, Ed L'Epicier, Ed le Maraócher, Europa Discount, Picard Surgelés	Hypermarkets, Discount Stores, Convenience Stores, Specialty Stores
10	Kroger Company	Kroger, Dillion Food Stores, King Soopers, Fry's Food Stores, City Market, Gerbes Supermarkets, Sav-Mor, Kwik Shop, Quik Stop Markets, Time Saver Stores, Tom Thumb Food Stores, Turkey Hill Minit Markets, Loaf 'N Jug, Mini-Mart	Supermarkets, Convenience Stores
11	Dayton Hudson Corporation	Target, Mervyn's, Dayton's, Hudson's, Marshall Field's	Discount Stores, Department Stores
12	J.C. Penney Company, Inc.	JCPenney	Department Stores, Mail Order, Drug Stores

Countries with Retail Operations	Country of Origin/ Global Locations*	Percent International Revenues	1994 Sales (US$ Millions)
4	United States US, CN, MX, HK	2.9%	82,494
15	Switzerland/Germany GC, IT, NL, PL, UK, AS, CN, CR, HK, FR, US, GR, BG, DK, SZ	24.0%	52,000
6	United States US, CN, CR, SV MX, SG	3.5%	34,025
3	United States US, CN, MX	1.2%	33,099
10	Germany FR, IT, NL, UK, AS, PL, CR, HK, US, GR	50.0%	32,400
1	Japan JP	0.0%	29,545
6	Japan JP, US, CN, TW, HK, AL	23.9%	28,175
10	Germany BG, DK, FR, IT, NL, UK, AS, PL, US, GR	NA	24,900
14	France PT, SP, TW, TK, MX, CN, SK, TD, UK, AR, BR, FR, IT, MY	37.1%	24,577
1	United States US	0.0%	22,959
1	United States US	0.0%	21,311
2	United States US, CL	0.0%	21,082

Continued

*See page 59 for country key.

CHAPTER 1 APPENDIX

The Top 100 Global Retailers

Sales Rank	Company	Trading Names	Format Types
13	Jusco Co., Ltd.	Jusco, Mini Stop, Wellmart, Cox, Blue Grass, Nustep, JUS-Photo, The Body Shop, Talbots, Megamart, Maxvalu	Supermarkets, Discount Stores, Mail-Order
14	American Stores Company	Lucky Stores, Jewel Osco, Super Saver, Acme Markets, Jewel Food Stores, Osco Drug, Sav-on, RxAmerica	Supermarkets, Drug Stores
15	J Sainsbury plc	J Sainsbury; SavaCentre, Homebase, Shaw's	Supermarkets, Hypermarkets, DIY
16	Promodès SA[b]	Continent, Champion, Dia, Shopi, 8 a Huit, Codec, Promocash, Prodirest, Superscore, Score, Continente, Mini-Markets	Hypermarkets, Supermarkets, Cash & Carry, Convenience Stores
17	Auchan[b]	Auchan, Alcamco	Hypermarkets
18	Price/Costco, Inc.	Price Costco	Warehouse Clubs
19	Koninklijke Ahold, NV[c]	Albert Heijn, Gall & Gall, Etos, Jamin, De Tuinen, Ter Huume, Pingo Doce, Tops, Mana, Finast, BI-LO, Giant, Edwards, Red Food	Supermarkets, Specialty Stores
20	Safeway	Safeway	Supermarkets
21	Tesco plc	Tesco, Catteau, Global, Wm. Low	Supermarkets
22	Karstadt Group[c]	Karstadt, Hertie, Runners Point, Wehmeyer, Schrmann, Shaulandt, WOM, Neckermann Versand, Baby-Walz, Saalfrank, Kastner & Ohler, Optic point, Hertie Wir Kinder	Department Stores, Mail-Order, Specialty Stores
23	Otto Versand GmbH	Otto, Post-Shop, Apart, Trend, Otto-Extra, Garten, Otto Wohnen, Geschenke-Boutique, Heimwerker, Grattan, Bon Prix, Heine, Alba Moda, Sport-Scheck, Schwab, 3 Suisses, Eddie Bauer, Margarèta, Spiegel, New Hampton, Blanche Porte, VPC Promotion, Bequet, Venta, Beyela, Arcadia Internacional, Postalmarket, Euronova, 3 Pagon, Look Again	Mail-Order
24	Nichii Co., Ltd.	Nichii, Vivre, Saty, Dac City	Supermarkets, Department Stores
25	Kaufhof Group	Kaufhof, Kaufhof Mode & Sport, Horten, Kaufhalle, Media Markt, Saturn, Reno, Vobis, Mac Fash, Jagquues' Whin-Depot, Versandaus, Wenz, Oppermann, Hawesko, Hanscalisches Wein-und Sehl-Kontor	Department Stores, Mail-Order, Specialty Stores

Countries with Retail Operations	Country of Origin/ Global Locations*	Percent International Revenues	1994 Sales (US$ Millions)
5	Japan JP, US, NL, HK, CN	10.0%	19,586
1	United States US	0.0%	18,355
2	United Kingdom UK, US	12.3%	17,398
7	France FR, SP, GR, IT, PT, GC, US	39.4%	17,072
4	France FR, IT, SP, US	12.0%	16,750
5	United States US, CN, UK, MX, SK	16.4%	16,481
4	Netherlands NL, US, CR, PT	48.3%	15,931
2	United States US, CN	21.7%	15,627
3	United Kingdom UK, FR, HK	2.9%	15,474
6	Germany GR, FR, BG, NL, AS, SZ	6.8%	14,912
15	Germany AS, BG, CN, GR, FR, UK, HK, NL, IT, JP, PL, PT, SP, SZ, US	49.0%	14,800
1	Japan JP	0.0%	14,545
11	Germany GR, NL, AS, FR, BG, SZ, IT, SP, PL, HK, LX	8.5%	13,620

Continued

*See page 59 for country key.

CHAPTER 1 APPENDIX

The Top 100 Global Retailers

Sales Rank	Company	Trading Names	Format Types
26	SHV Holdings	Makro	Supermarkets
27	Selyu Ltd.	Family Mart	Supermarkets, Convenience Stores
28	Casino Guichard-Perrachon	Casino, Smart and Final, Gèant, Rallye Super	Hypermarkets, Supermarkets, Convenience Stores
29	Pinault Printemps-Redoute	La Redoute, Printemps, Prisunic, Conforama, Fnac, Cyrillus, Daxon, Edmèe de Roubaix, La Maison de Valèrie, Vert Baudet, Redoute-Femme, Prènatal, Anne Weyburn, Taillisime, Somewhere, Secrets de Beautè, Jardin de Florimon, Vestro, Empire	Mail-Order, Department Stores, Supermarkets Specialty Stores
30	Home Depot, Inc.	Home Depot	DIY
31	May Department Stores Company	Lord & Taylor, Foley's, Robinsons-May, Hecht's, Filene's, Kaufmann's, Famous-Barr, Meier & Frank, Payless ShoeSource	Department Stores, Specialty Stores
32	Albertson's Inc.	Albertson's	Supermarkets
33	Asko Deutsche Kaufhaus AG[b]	ASKO, real, Praktiker, Möbel Unger, Adler, extra, C&C, tip Discount Handels, Meierei C. Bolle, Deutsche SB-Kauf, Joh. Contzen, Saarländische Fleischwaren-Verkaufsgesellschaft, MASSA	Hypermarkets Supermarkets, DIY Specialty Stores
34	Coles Myer Ltd.[b]	Bi-Lo, Coles Supermarkets, Grace Bros, Myer, Myer Direct, Fosseys, Kmart, Target, Katies, Officeworks, Liquorland, World 4 Kids, Liquorland Vintage Cellars	Supermarkets, Department Stores, Discount Stores, Specialty Stores
35	Takashimaya Co., Ltd.	Takashimaya	Department Stores, Mail-Order, Specialty Stores
36	Groupe Delhaize "Le Lion"	AD, Club Foods, AB, Delvita, tom & Co., Caddy Home, Delhaize, Dail Budget, Di, P.G., (see Food Lion)	Supermarkets, Drugstores, Discount Stores, Specialty Stores
37	Lidl & Schwarz Stiftung & Co., KG	Lidl, Kaufland, A&O, Ruef & Co. KG	Shopping Centers, Supermarkets, Discount Stores, Cash & Carry
38	Melville Corporation	CVS, Marshalls, Wilsons, Bobs, Chess King, Accessory Lady, Meldisco, Footaction, Thom McAn, Kay-Bee, Linens 'n Things, This End Up, Prints Plus	Drug Stores, Specialty Stores

Countries with Retail Operations	Country of Origin/ Global Locations*	Percent International Revenues	1994 Sales (US$ Millions)
14	Netherlands NL, US, UK, GR, FR, SP, SZ, BG, PT, HK, BZ, AG, TW, TD	85.3%	13,556
2	Japan JP, HK	0.0%	13,009
3	France FR, US, MX	8.9%	12,929
17	France FR, SP, PT, SZ, GR, BG, AS, UK, GC, IT, CY, TW, TD, LX, NL, HK, JP	20.5%	12,765
2	United States US, CN	NA	12,477
1	United States US	0.0%	12,223
1	United States US	0.0%	11,895
4	Germany GR, AS, LX, SZ	1.5%	11,667
2	Australia AL, NZ	1.5%	11,648
1	Japan JP	0.0%	11,618
5	Belgium BL, GC, CR, US, FR	76.2%	11,393
9	Germany FR, IT, BG, AS, UK, SP, PT, NL, GR	N/A	11,300
1	United States US	0.0%	11,286

Continued

*See page 59 for country key.

CHAPTER 1 APPENDIX

The Top 100 Global Retailers

Sales Rank	Company	Trading Names	Format Types
39	Winn-Dixie Stores, Inc.[b]	Winn-Dixie, Marketplace, Buddies, The City Meat Markets	Supermarkets
40	Marks & Spencer plc	Marks & Spencer, Brooks Brothers, Kings Supermarkets	Department Stores, Specialty Stores, Supermarkets
41	Great Atlantic & Pacific Tea Co. Inc.	A&P, Waldbaum's, Food Emporium, Super Fresh, Farmer Jack, Kohl's, Dominion, Miracle Food Mart	Supermarkets
42	Mitsukoshi Ltd.	Mitsukoshi	Department Stores, Mail Order
43	Jardine Matheson Holdings[d]	Wellcome, Franklins, Woolworths, Simago, 7-Eleven, Mannings, Guardian, Big Fresh, Cold Storage	Supermarkets, Convenience Stores, Drug Stores, Specialty Stores
44	George Weston Ltd.	Loblaws, The Real Canadian Superstore, The Real Canadian Wholesale, Save-Easy, The Real Atlantic Superstore, SuperValu, National, Zehrs Food Plus, Zehrs Markets, The Supercentre, Atlantic Grocer, Dominion, OK! Economy, The Real Superstore, That Stanley!, National Market	Supermarkets
45	Walgreen Co.	Walgreen, Healthcare Plus	Drugstores, Mail-Order
46	Quelle Schickedanz AG & CO[b]	Quelle, Apollo-Optik, Mobel-Hess, Quelle, Peter Hahn, Elegance, Top Shop, Fashion Shop, Chic Sportiv, Modern Classic, Lady's Collection, Mobel-Katalog, Garten Quelle, Schopflin, Quelle Technorama	Specialty Stores, Department Stores, Mail-Order
47	Argyll Group plc	Safeway, Presto	Supermarkets, Discount Stores
48	Toys "R" Us, Inc.	Toys "R" Us, Kids "R" Us	Specialty Stores
49	Publix Super Markets, Inc.	Publix	Supermarkets
50	Uny Co. Ltd.	Sagami, U-Store, Circle K	Department Stores, Specialty Stores, Convenience Stores
51	Woolworths Limited[b]	Big W, Woolworths Variety, Rockmans, Dick Smith, Safeway, Purity, Roelf Vos, Mac's Liquor, Food For Less, Woolworths, Crazy Prices	Supermarkets, Department Stores, Specialty Stores

Countries with Retail Operations	Country of Origin/ Global Locations*	Percent International Revenues	1994 Sales (US$ Millions)
2	United States US, BS	1.2%	11,082
10	United Kingdom UK, FR, IR, BG, SP, NL, HK, CN, US, JP	12.0%	10,427
2	United States US, CN	1.2%	10,332
7	Japan JP, HK, US, UK, GR, SP, IT	10.0%	9,954
10	Hong Kong HK, CN, JP, SG, TW, TD, AL, NZ, SP, UK	63.0%	9,569
2	Canada CN, US	20.6%	9,516
1	United States US	0.0%	9,235
6	Germany GR, FR, NL, BG, AS, SZ	12.0%	9,036
1	United Kingdom UK	0.0%	8,907
21	United States US, AL, AS, BG, CN, DK, FR, GR, HK, JP, LX, MY, NL, PT, SG, SP, SW, SZ, TW, UE, UK	24.0%	8,746
1	United States US	0.0%	8,665
2	Japan JP, HK	10.0%	8,524
2	Australia AL, NZ	0.3%	8,400

Continued

*See page 59 for country key.

CHAPTER 1 APPENDIX

The Top 100 Global Retailers

Sales Rank	Company	Trading Names	Format Types
52	Federated Department Stores	Jordan Marsh, Bloomingdale's, The Bon Marche, Burdines, Lazarus, Rich's, Goldsmith's, Stern's, Macy's, Bullock's, Aeropostale, Charter Club, MCO	Department Stores, Mail-Order
53	Woolworth Corporation	Foot Locker, After Thoughts, Carimar, Accessory Lady, Rubin, Reflexions, Kinney, Lady Foot Locker, Kids Mart, Champs Sports, Northern Reflections, Little Folks, Athletic X-Press, Williams the Shoemen, Weekend Edition, The San Francisco Music Box Company, Kids Foot Locker, Mathers, Randy River, Moderna, Der Schuh, Footquarters, Vic Jenens, Karuba, Northern Gateway, Going to the Game!, Canary Island, Northern Elements, Silk & Satin, The Best of Times, Gallery One, World, Foot Locker, Northern Traditions, Lady Plus, Colorado, Ashbrooks, Woolworth, The Bargin! Shop, The Rx Place, Rx Place Drug mart, Farmas	Specialty Stores, Department Stores
54	Cora	Cora, Record, Match-Nord, Match-Est, Truffaut	Hypermarkets, Supermarkets, Specialty Stores
55	ASDA	ASDA, Dales	Superstores, Discount Stores Supermarkets
56	Coop Switzerland	Co-op	Department Stores, Hypermarkets, Supermarkets, Grocery Stores
57	Food Lion, Inc.	Food Lion	Supermarkets
58	SPAR Handels-Aktiengesellschaft	Spar, Eurospar, Interspar, Bauspar, Netto, Kodi	Supermarkets, Superstores, Specialty Stores, Hypermarkets, Discount Stores, DIY
59	Docks de France SA	Mommouth, Atac, Suma, Sebeco, Lil' Champ, Eco Serve	Hypermarkets, Supermarkets, DIY Convenience Stores
60	Daimaru	Daimaru	Department Stores, Supermarkets
61	Kingfisher plc	B&O, Comet, Superdrug, FW Woolworh, Darty	Department Stores, Drug Stores, Specialty Stores

Countries with Retail Operations	Country of Origin/ Global Locations*	Percent International Revenues	1994 Sales (US$ Millions)
1	United States US	0.0%	8,316
13	United States US, CN, MX, GR, UK, BG, LX, NL, FR, SP, IT, AL, HK	34.4%	8,293
1	France FR	0.0%	8,138
1	United Kingdom UK	0.0%	8,097
1	Switzerland SZ	0.0%	8,005
1	United States US	0.0%	7,933
1	Germany GR	0.0%	7,870
3	France FR, SP, US	11.9%	7,859
1	Japan JP	0.0%	7,647
2	United Kingdom UK, FR	15.5%	7,579

Continued

*See page 59 for country key.

CHAPTER 1 APPENDIX

The Top 100 Global Retailers

Sales Rank	Company	Trading Names	Format Types
62	Limited, Inc.	Express, Lerner New York, Lane Bryant, The Limited, Henri Bendel, Victoria's Secret, Cacique, Structure, Abercrombie & Fitch Co., Bath & Body Works, Penhaligon's, The Limited Too	Specialty Stores, Mail-Order
63	El Corte Ingles	El Corte Ingles, Hipercor	Department Stores, Hypermarkets
64	Army & Airforce Exchange Service[c]	PX, BX	Grocery Stores, Specialty Stores
65	Montgomery Ward Holding Corp.	Montgomery Ward, The Apparel Store, Auto Express, Electronic Avenue, Gold 'N Gems, Home Ideas, Lechmere, Montgomery Ward Direct L.P.	Department Stores, Mail-Order
66	GIB Group	Sarma, Inno, Maxi GB, Rob, Unic, Nopri, Brico, Obi, Homebase, Aki, Scotty's, Handy Andy, Pearle Vision Center, Christiaensen, Disport, Super GB, Bigg's, Auto 5, Fnac, Club	Supermarkets, DIY, Specialty Stores, Hypermarkets, Department Stores, Grocery Stores
67	Southland	7-Eleven, High's Dairy Stores, Quik Mart, Super-7	Convenience Stores
68	Co op AG	Coop, Wandmaker, Plaza, SKY, PRO, Depot	Shopping Centers, DIY, Department Stores, Superstores, Specialty Stores, Supermarkets
69	Seibu Department Stores Group	Seibu	Department Stores
70	R.H. Macy & Co., Inc.	Macy's, Bullock's, Aeropostale, Charter Club, MCO	Department Stores, Specialty Stores
71	Lowe's Companies, Inc.	Lowe's	DIY
72	Meijer	Meijer	Superstores
73	The Boots Company plc	Boots, The Chemists, Boots Opticians, Childrens World, Do It All, Halfords, A.G. Stanley, Sephora	Drugstores, Specialty Stores
74	Vendex International NV[c]	Vroom & Dreesmann, Kreymborg, Hunkemöeller, Kien, Claudia Straeter, Perry Sport, Siebel, Stoutenbeek Wooncentrum, Lederland, Dixons, EDah, Konmar, Basicmarkt, Dagmerkt, Torro, Pet's Place, Edi, Eda, Battard, America Today, Schaap + Citroen, Royal Gold, Van Reeuwijk, LuigiLucardi, Kijkshop/Best Sellers, Klick, Mondileder-Stoutenbeek, Electro-Jacobs, Guco, Heijmans, Rovato, Valkenberg	Department Stores, Specialty Stores Supermarkets

Countries with Retail Operations	Country of Origin/ Global Locations*	Percent International Revenues	1994 Sales (US$ Millions)
2	United States US, UK	0.0%	7,321
3	Spain SP, PT, US	NA	7,104
27	United States NA	39.0%	7,053
1	United States US	0.0%	7,038
8	Belgium BG, PL, UK, FR, SP, PT, US, LX	24.8%	6,955
2	United States US, CN	17.3%	6,760
1	Germany GR	0.0%	6,726
2	Japan JP, HK	NA	6,462
1	United States US	0.0%	6,163
1	United States US	0.0%	6,111
1	United States US	0.0%	6,000
1	United Kingdom UK	0.0%	5,965
8	Netherlands NL, BG, LX, GR, FR, SP, AS, SZ	23.5%	5,720

*See page 59 for country key.

Continued

CHAPTER 1 APPENDIX

The Top 100 Global Retailers

Sales Rank	Company	Trading Names	Format Types
75	Circuit City Stores, Inc.	Circuit City	Specialty Stores
76	C & A Breninkmeyer (German operations)	C&A	Specialty Stores
77	Dillard Department Stores	Dillards	Department Stores
78	Isetan Co., Ltd.	Isetan	Department Stores
79	Galeries Lafayette	Galeries Lafayette, Nouvelles Galeries, Monoprix, Super M, Inno, Uniprix, BHV	Department Stores, Mail-Order
80	Marui Co., Ltd.	Marui, in The Room	Department Stores
81	Best Buy Co., Inc.	Best Buy	Specialty Stores
82	H-E-B Grocery	H.E. Butt Food Stores, H.E. Butt Super Food/Drug Stores, Pantry Food Stores, Marketplace	Supermarkets
83	Vons Companies Inc.	Vons, Pavilions, EXPO	Supermarkets
84	Matsuzakaya Co., Ltd.	Matsuzakaya	Department Stores
85	Tandy Corporation[b]	Radio Shack, Computer City, Incredible Universe, McDuff Electronics and Appliance Supercenters, VideoConcepts, The Edge in Electronics	Specialty Stores
86	Isosceles plc	Gateway Foodmarkets, Somerfield, Food Giant, Solo	Supermarkets
87	Tokyu Department Store Co., Ltd.	Tokyu	Department Stores
88	The Great Universal Stores plc[b]	GUS Catalogue Order Ltd., Family Hampers Ltd, G.U.S. Merchandise Corporation Ltd, White Arrow Express Ltd, Kay and Co. Ltd, Universal Versand GmbH, Halens Postorder, Vedia SA, Burberrys, The Scotch House Ltd, G.U.S. Canada, Lewis Stores Ltd, John England, Kit, Choice, Family Album, Fashion Extra, Great Universal, Personal Selection, Marshall Ward, John Meyers, John Noble, Trafford, My Shop, Royal Welsh Warehouses, Wehkamp B.V.	Mail-Order, Specialty Stores
89	Comptoirs Modernes	Stoc, Carrefour, Comod, Merca Plus, Marché Plus	Supermarkets, Hypermarkets

Countries with Retail Operations	Country of Origin/ Global Locations*	Percent International Revenues	1994 Sales (US$ Millions)
1	United States US	0.0%	5,583
1	Germany GR	0.0%	5,550
1	United States US	0.0%	5,546
3	Japan JP, HK, SP	NA	5,409
2	France FR, SG	NA	5,315
1	Japan JP	0.0%	5,194
1	United States US	0.0%	5,080
1	United States US	0.0%	5,000
1	United States US	0.0%	4,997
1	Japan JP	0.0%	4,981
4	United States US, CN, SW, DK	0.0%	4,944
1	United Kingdom UK	0.0%	4,841
1	Japan JP	0.0%	4,765
7	United Kingdom UK, AS, SW, SZ, US, SA, CN	24.4%	4,740
2	France FR, SP	0.9%	4,643

Continued

*See page 59 for country key.

CHAPTER 1 APPENDIX

The Top 100 Global Retailers

Sales Rank	Company	Trading Names	Format Types
90	AVA AG	Marktkauf, Kaufmarkt, Suba, Heico, Dixi, Basar, Krane, Sinus	Department Stores, Supermarkets, DIY, Specialty Stores
91	Cifra SA de CV	Bodega Aurrera, Superama, Gran Bazar, Wal-Mart Supercenter, Suburbia, Almacenes Aurrera, Sam's Club	Department Stores, Warehouse Stores, Supermarkets, Hypermarkets, Specialty Stores
92	IKEA	IKEA	Specialty Stores
93	Eckerd Corporation	Eckerd	Drug Stores
94	Rite Aid Corporation	Rite Aid	Drug Stores
95	Nagasakiya Co., Ltd.	Home Center, Nagasakiya, Sunkus	Superstores, Convenience Stores, Specialty Stores
96	Kwik Save	Kwik Save	Supermarkets
97	Office Depot Inc.	Office Depot, The Office Place	Specialty Stores
98	Hudson's Bay Company	The Bay, Zellers	Department Stores, Discount Stores, Specialty Stores
99	Pathmark Holdings, Inc.	Pathmark	Supermarkets, Drug Stores
100	Izumiya Co., Ltd.	Izumiya	Discount Stores

Source: Coopers & Lybrand. (1995). *Global Powers of Retailing. Chain Store Age Special Report,* p. 7.

DIY = do-it-yourself

*See country key.

[a] Store counts include franchised units.

[b] C&L estimate—percent of revenue generated globally.

[c] Parent company's operations are diversified—percent of revenue generated globally has been calculated based upon total consolidated revenues.

[d] Retail operations in Asian regions other than Hong Kong have been included in domestic revenues.

Countries with Retail Operations	Country of Origin/ Global Locations*	Percent International Revenues	1994 Sales (US$ Millions)
1	Germany GR	0.0%	4,622
1	Mexico MX	0.0%	4,619
18	Sweden SW, GR, SZ, NL, UK, BG, US, AS, FR, CN, DK, NW, CR, HG, PL, SV, AL, IT	88.9%	4,590
1	United States US	0.0%	4,549
1	United States US	0.0%	4,534
1	Japan JP	0.0%	4,350
1	United Kingdom UK	0.0%	4,289
2	United States US, CN	NA	4,266
1	Canada CN	0.0%	4,266
1	United States US	0.0%	4,182
1	Japan JP	0.0%	4,070

Abbrev.	Country	Abbrev.	Country	Abbrev.	Country	Abbrev.	Country
AR	Argentina	CY	Cyprus	LX	Luxembourg	SK	South Korea
AL	Australia	DK	Denmark	MY	Malaysia	SP	Spain
AS	Austria	FR	France	MX	Mexico	SW	Sweden
BS	Bahamas	GR	Germany	NL	Netherlands	SZ	Switzerland
BG	Belgium	GC	Greece	NZ	New Zealand	TD	Thailand
BZ	Brazil	HK	Hong Kong	NW	Norway	TK	Turkey
CN	Canada	HG	Hungary	PL	Poland	TW	Taiwan
CR	Czech Republic	IR	Ireland	PT	Portugal	UE	United Arab Emirates
CL	Chile	IS	Israel	SG	Singapore	UK	United Kingdom
CH	China	IT	Italy	SV	Slovakia	US	United States
		JP	Japan	SA	South Africa		

118
119
120

2

International Culture and Human Behavior

After reading this chapter, you will understand:

- **Why culture affects international retailing.**
- **How high context and low context cultures differ in their use/understanding of space, material possessions, friendship patterns, agreements across cultures, and time.**
- **The methods by which societies teach their members to belong to their own cultural group.**
- **How Hofstede's cultural dimensions model helps to categorize groups of nations on four major dimensions. These theoretical dimensions of difference can be used to strategically position international retailers' offerings.**

THE FOCUS OF international retailing is on the marketing link that directly touches consumers. It is impossible to understand the retail system within a country without understanding the culture of that country. Culture influences what people purchase and how those items are used. Artifacts that may look the same in different countries may serve very different purposes. For instance, on my first trip to Japan, I was touring a department store in

Tokyo. We were in the housewares division and I saw a big display of what looked to me like trays Americans would use to serve breakfast in bed. The quantity of "breakfast-in-bed" trays was very large. This led me to comment to my Japanese host, "The Japanese must be very romantic, with such an emphasis on serving breakfast in bed." My Japanese host looked a little puzzled, but then explained that what I had called "breakfast trays" were, in fact, short-legged tables that sit over the sunken heating element in a Japanese home. Japanese families sit around this table with their feet down in a sunken floor unit outfitted with an electrical heating device. The table has a quilt over it to preserve the heat and keep everyone warm. It was not quite the use I had envisioned.

This chapter explores the ways in which culture alters our view of the world. Retailing is greatly affected by culture. In fact, most retail failures in international markets can be attributed to cultural factors.

DEFINING CULTURE

"Primary socialization" is the term social theorists use to describe the process by which people in a society learn symbols and their meanings within that society. We use this process to classify the world around us.[1] Culture provides the kind of shared understanding among people in a society that allows them to predict and coordinate social activity. Although

Photo 2.1
The Japanese *kotatsu* is a low dining table. Family members sit on the floor while dining or drinking tea. When I first saw one in a department store I thought it was a breakfast-in-bed tray.

we "learn" culture, it is not homogeneous throughout society. Differences in gender, ethnicity, region, social class, and religion all influence the way in which an individual is socialized to his or her culture.

We view culture through learned behavior. The functions of what a social group does are very much the same; food, housing, and emotional ties to others are basic requirements for all individuals. However, the ways that societies meet these requirements may differ significantly.

Some countries are considered **multicultural,** meaning that they have several or many cultures within their borders. India, China, the United States, Canada, and South Africa are examples of multicultural countries. Other countries such as those in Scandinavia (Denmark, Norway, and Sweden) are generally considered to comprise one cultural group. This is, of course, a generalization. In the rural Swedish community of South Dakota where I grew up, one of the favorite topics of jokes and conversations was the differences between Swedes and Norwegians. The Latin American countries of Venezuela, Columbia, and Ecuador are also considered to be one cultural group.[2]

One of the simplest ways to explain group differences is through the designation high context and low context cultures. Being able to categorize countries on this dimension will help you to make many retail generalizations.

HIGH CONTEXT AND LOW CONTEXT CULTURES

Edward Hall, a noted sociologist, was the first to identify these two theoretical dimensions of culture. Hall made the distinction between cultures where meaning of individual behavior depends on the situation (termed **high context**) and those where meaning is based on the words, not the situation (termed **low context**). Without exchanging words, people in high context cultures can communicate quite effectively. Nonverbal exchanges occur in low context cultures too; however, the meaning is generally unintentional. Words convey most of the important meanings.

Nonverbal messages have important and intended meanings in high context cultures. To read these nonverbal messages requires a similarity of background. High context cultures teach children this communication in the family from an early age. Other social institutions such as school, religious organizations, and work continue this process, known as acculturation. If a country has one religion, one language, and a highly coordinated educational system, this type of acculturation process is more likely.

Saudi Arabia and Japan are two of the countries rated high context. Southern European countries, Chile and Mexico, and most of industrialized Asia, except China and India are also high context countries. Figure 2.1 presents a distribution of selected countries on the high versus low context continuum.

In low context cultures, intentions and feelings are expressed verbally. Situations do not change the meaning of words and behavior. What you say is

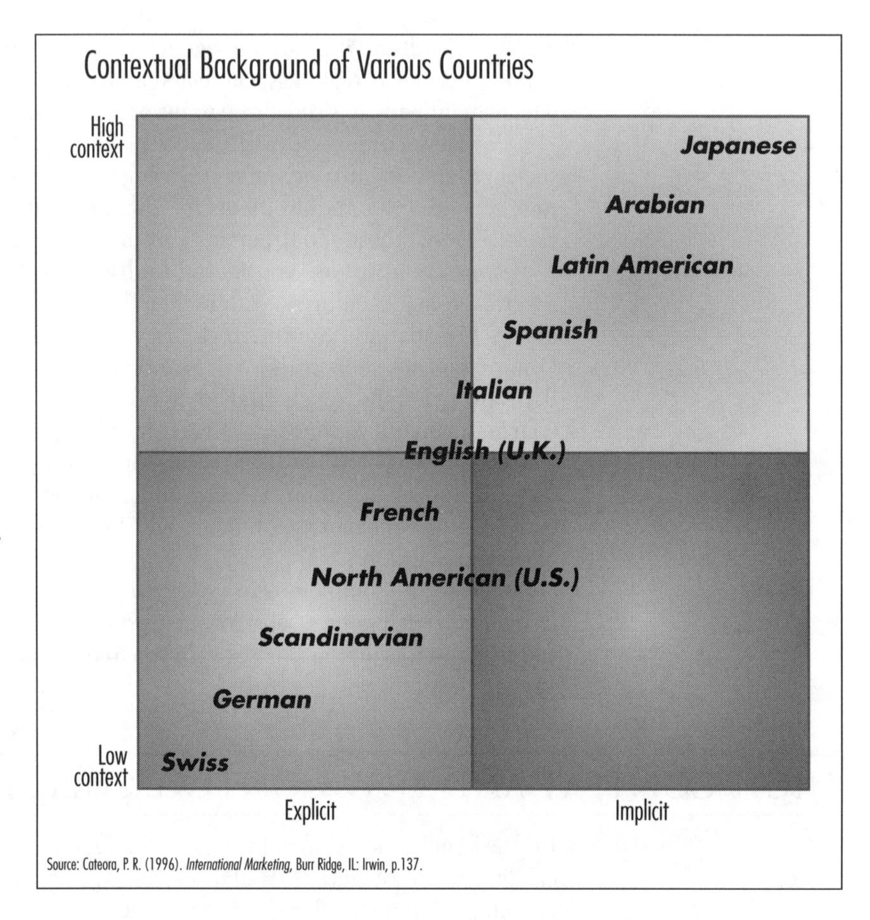

Figure 2.1
In high context countries, such as Japan and Saudi Arabia, the cultural context is as important as what is actually said; the speaker and the listener use a common understanding of the context. Low context countries, such as Germany and Switzerland, communicate information explicitly, with words.

what you mean. This type of communication system occurs most often in countries that are multicultural and where people have different value systems. The United States, Switzerland, Germany, the Scandinavian countries, India, China, Australia, and New Zealand are countries with low context cultures.

The difference between high context and low context cultures is illustrated through what Hall called the "silent languages." These languages include: space, material possessions, friendship patterns, agreements across cultures, and time. (In the following discussion, AE stands for American–Northern European cultures.)

SPACE

Space refers to the distance between two people having a conversation. Perceptions of appropriate space are one of the most common differences between cultures. For example, Middle-Eastern men stand very close to each other when they have a conversation. This closeness would make most Americans feel uncomfortable. A visitor to shops in Middle-Eastern countries will notice that they are very crowded. Merchandise is crammed into every area, and people can hardly move without bumping into each other. A Middle-Eastern shop is a busy, crowded place; a place that would give Americans claustrophobia.

AE cultures like an organized uncluttered look for stores. Research has shown that consumers in these cultures psychologically associate merchandise that is crammed into a store with sales. Similarly, if stores lay out sale merchandise too neatly, people are distrustful.

AE cultures like private spaces. The most prestigious offices are those that are large, spacious, and private. It is preferable to have a secretary or two who screen entrants. In contrast, in Japan, a high context culture, a person who has a private office, away from the action, is considered no longer important to the company. That person has been "put out to pasture." An important Japanese executive has his desk in the center of a large office that includes his whole department. Assistants have desks around the room. Everyone is within shouting distance. An interoffice memo is unheard of in a Japanese office system. If you want to tell someone something, you shout at him, or get up and go over to talk with him.

MATERIAL POSSESSIONS

Material culture is a term that describes the learned social meaning of possessions. Retailing influences the diffusion of material culture. Countries often limit the opening of foreign retailers because they are uncomfortable with the distribution of that culture's material objects.

Designer brand names express social status. Before the economic bubble burst in Japan, consumption of designer brands was very high. Although this trend has slowed, conspicuous consumption is still

Photo 2.2
Restaurants in Saudi Arabia have two entrances; women, children, and families eat on one side, single men on the other side. The wall to the left of the male customer in this photo separates the two sides. The Muslim religion calls for this type of separation. *Courtesy of Amal Aswailem.*

evident among the Japanese. **Conspicuous consumption** means that people purchase possessions to express their wealth and status.

McCracken[3] has observed that new objects have only recently taken on great value to consumers worldwide. In Europe, it was once the **patina,** or appearance of age, that made objects desirable. Silver and furniture passed down through generations held greater value than products bought new. Old wealth was seen as more desirable than new wealth. We would expect such high context cultures to place greater value on objects with family history; the family history is the object's context.

When a high context culture's material culture is threaten by a low culture's crassness, concerns about the social order become evident. Youth in developing countries who drink Coke, and wear Nike shoes and Levi jeans pose a threat to the older cultural norms. This new material culture is visible for all to see, and difficult for the older generation to ignore. The increased visibility of changing consumption patterns may be one reason that foreign retailers are often barred from doing business in countries with less developed or planned economies.

FRIENDSHIP PATTERNS

The way that people relate to one another illustrates cultural patterns. Friendships and even marriages in the United States tend to be temporary, rather than permanent. In addition, Americans often develop immediate friendships with people. Within hours of making a new friend, Americans may reveal intimate information—the type of information that other cultures would take decades to reveal, if it were revealed at all. For this reason, people from other cultures sometimes view Americans as friendly but shallow.

Such informality is also found in the way retail salespersons address customers in the United States. Salesclerks and waitresses are quick to adopt a person's first name or refer to the person with familiar terms such as "dear" or "honey." Salespeople believe they are being helpful by giving customers advice.

Interpersonal communications in other cultures may be very different from the informal American norm. For example, in Japan, only very close personal friends use a person's first name. Females and younger Japanese are more likely to use friends' first names than males or the older generation. In fact, male Japanese friends who are in their forties commonly refer even to their close friends by their last names. Even the patterns and methods of giving gifts differ across cultures (Box 2.1).

AGREEMENTS ACROSS CULTURES

Low context cultures rely on contracts that list the specifics of an agreement. They expect partners to keep the specific terms of the contract. Americans have a phrase for this, "adhering to the letter of the law." High

BOX 2.1

It's Not the Gift that Counts, but How You Present It

Giving a gift in another country requires careful attention to culturally appropriate behavior. Here are a few suggestions:

Japan:

- Do not open a gift in front of a Japanese counterpart unless asked and do not expect the Japanese person to open your gift.
- Avoid ribbons and bows as part of gift wrapping. Bows as we know them are considered unattractive and ribbon colors can have different meanings.
- Do not offer a gift depicting a fox or badger. The fox is the symbol of fertility; the badger, cunning.

Europe:

- Avoid red roses and white flowers, even numbers, and the number 13. Do not wrap flowers in paper.
- Do not risk the impression of bribery by spending too much on a gift.

Arab Countries:

- Do not give a gift when you first meet someone. It may be interpreted as a bribe.
- Do not present the gift when alone with the recipient unless you know the person well. Gifts should be given in front of others in less personal relationships.

Latin America:

- Do not give a gift until after a somewhat personal relationship has developed unless it is given to express appreciation for hospitality.
- Gifts should be given during social encounters, not in the course of business.
- Avoid the colors black and purple; both are associated with the Catholic Lenten season.

China:

- Never make an issue of a gift presentation—publicly or privately.
- Gifts should be presented privately, with the exception of collective ceremonial gifts at banquets.

Source: Cateora, P. R. (1996). *International Marketing*. Chicago: Irwin, p. 109.

context cultures rely more on general agreement with the basic intent of the partners.

Doing business in Japan can be very frustrating for foreigners who do not understand this concept. They may spend long periods negotiating the specific details of a contract only to have their Japanese partners ignore the contract once it has been signed. In Chapter 12, I discuss some specific cultural terms related to this behavior.

The Japanese use time to their advantage in contract signing. They know that Americans are impatient to get things done. Thus, the Japanese will often delay meetings until they gain favorable concessions.

TIME

In Germany, grocery stores generally close at 7:00 P.M. In 1996, Germany voted down a law that would have allowed retail stores to remain open later at night, giving working couples additional time to shop. It was felt that expanding opening hours would unfairly restrict the time that the salesclerks could spend with their families. Later that year, Germany passed a law that allowed stores to stay open one hour later.

Hall has identified two types of time systems, which he calls monochronic and polychronic time. Monochronic time is based on the northern European model, in which one thing is scheduled at a time. Polychronic time is based on the Mediterranean model, which entails involvement in several things at once. The two systems are logically and empirically very distinct, and difficult to mix.[4] Polychronic time focuses on people and completion of transactions rather than adherence to preset schedules. Appointments are not considered important and are broken frequently. For polychronic people, time is less tangible; they generally do not think of time as wasted or saved.

The polychronic environment in the markets, stores, and souks of Mediterranean and Arab countries can be very frustrating for northern Europeans or Americans. The shopping atmosphere seems chaotic. Customers all compete for the attention of one clerk who is trying to wait on everyone at once. There is no apparent order, no line or number to suggest who has been waiting the longest.[5]

The same patterns can be seen at the office of an important government official in a Mediterranean country. The private office has a large reception area. Small groups of people wait here and are visited by the minister or his aides. They conduct most of the actual business outside the formal office in the semipublic setting. The official will move from group to group conferring with each in turn. For those whose problems are more difficult to solve, the minister will return again and again until a solution has been found. The minister, like the clerk in the store, is waiting on several groups at once, the essence of polychronic time.

Hall makes the point that we can relate polychronic time to feminine lives. Think of the way a mother takes care of her family. She does not rigidly set a certain amount of time for each family member; instead, she spends a few minutes supervising one child then moves to another child while folding the clothes and making dinner. Polychronic cultures put the emphasis on human relationships, not on schedules. Although a society may be more oriented to polychronic time or monochronic time, it may also successfully combine the two. Japan is a society that is polychronic time-oriented when dealing with other Japanese, but monochronic time-oriented when dealing with outsiders. The Japanese ability to combine the best of both orientations can be seen in their success in international markets.

Monochronic time is not better than polychronic time. It is just a different way of viewing the world. Societies that rely on monochronic time feel that time is theirs to be managed and controlled. Time does not have such a designation for societies that are polychronic time-oriented.

The next part of this chapter focuses on the building blocks of culture. Societies build culture through product use, people's interactions with each other, art, and language. Retailing affects and is affected by each of these.

Photo 2.3
Most food in Saudi Arabia is purchased in outdoor markets like this one. Saudi women are reluctant to visit an outdoor market alone; male members of the household are the major shoppers at this type of market. *Courtesy of Amal Aswailem.*

DIMENSIONS OF CULTURE

Societies may be very different from one another. However, the basic tools a society needs to make its members a part of it are quite similar. We call these tools cultural universals. Cultural universals include material elements, social institutions, humans and their universe, aesthetics, and language.

MATERIAL ELEMENTS

Material elements are dependent on a country's infrastructure. The basic economic and technological systems available in a country affect the products that can be sold. Technological advancements are also a leading cause of cultural change.

Economics is the manner in which a society uses its capabilities and benefits from these capabilities. This includes the production of goods and services, their distribution and consumption, means of exchange, and the income derived from the creation of utilities. Material culture affects the amount demanded, the quality of products demanded, and the functions of the products.[6]

Less developed countries may not have the idea of preventive maintenance. Owning an expensive automobile that requires dealer servicing may not be an option for a person living in such a country. Owning a car that can be worked on by oneself is probably a better option.

When Russia and China used strict government planning systems, few luxury consumer goods were available to the average person. The government only supported purchases of goods that would help industrial production, not goods that would enrich consumers' lives. Under a planned economy, retailing is viewed with a disdainful eye. It is seen as a negative influence that corrupts people by creating desires for non-necessities. The value put on what others think about a person's purchase is the basis for the next section.

SOCIAL INSTITUTIONS

Reference groups are an important part of consumers' socialization process. **Reference groups** provide values and attitudes that influence and shape purchasing behavior. The family is an important reference group when children are young. Adolescents are more likely to respond to the influence of peers.

The concept of family differs throughout the world. In the United States, a family may be several unrelated single people living together. Asians are likely to consider a married couple's parents and grandparents part of their intimate family.

Three other groups of people have an impact on consumers' decisions: change agents, opinion leaders, and gatekeepers. **Change agents** influence consumption decisions, but they are outside the person's reference group. Change agents are people with great visibility, such as politicians and actors. When a change agent uses a product, there may be a mad rush of others imitating this behavior.

Opinion leaders are people within a consumer's reference group who influence purchases. Opinion leaders are taste setters at a local level. Their influence is greater than change agents.

Gatekeepers are individuals who have the authority to decide what consumers will purchase. Parents are gatekeepers for younger children. They control the money and can decide what is a reasonable purchase. Retail buyers are gatekeepers. They select the merchandise a retail store will offer. If they do not select the products for the store, the consumer will not have that product as a purchase alternative.

In the movie "101 Dalmatians," the female villain wanted to use the puppies to make a spotted coat. After the movie became a hit, fake fur Dalmatian coats were seen everywhere. The character in the movie was a change agent. The first people to wear spotted coats were opinion leaders. The retail buyers who either selected or failed to select the spotted coats six months before the film came out were gatekeepers.

In the next section, we will consider how people are influenced by nonhuman cultural dimensions. These groups of cultural influences include religion, belief systems, superstitions, and other related world views.

HUMANS AND THE UNIVERSE

Feng Shui is an important element in Chinese culture. It is the belief that constructed environments like buildings and roads must be positioned in harmony with the spirits. The Chinese will call in a *Feng Shui* expert before they begin construction on a new building. In fact, the Regent Hotel in Hong Kong altered its construction plans to improve its connections with the spirits. The Chinese also believe that man should live in harmony with and not attempt to control nature. In Chinese culture, much of what occurs is viewed as fate. If products do not perform as they should, Chinese consumers often believe it is their fault for selecting inferior products rather than the fault of the manufacturer.

Retailers need to consider such culturally linked beliefs when internationalizing. For instance, McDonald's Corp. has had to alter its standard fast-food menu to do business in India. The reason? Most Indians are Hindu, a religious group that considers cows sacred.

Ethnocentrism is the tendency to consider one's own culture as superior to others. Many Americans are surprised to find that their culture is not the envy of the world. A colleague from Great Britain told me his students often remark, "Americans are so stupid." His reply was, "If they are so stupid, why are they so rich?" A Swedish colleague told me she could never live in the United States. She said, "The U.S. is such a hard society. You do not take care of your poor and elderly." Most international marketing mistakes are made because people do not put aside their **self-reference criterion,** the unconscious reference to one's own cultural values.

AESTHETICS

A culture's aesthetic values affect what people buy. Standards of beauty, appreciation, and meaning as well as various methods of artistic expression affect consumers' purchases. Objects of art also differ from society to society. As an example, I often visit museums on Sunday when in Japan. Tokyo has many wonderful art galleries. In the Ginza area, during one visit, I noticed a sign for an art museum. I made a special trip to Ginza, paid my admission fee, and entered the gallery. The entire museum was devoted to calligraphy scrolls. The museum contained wall after wall of Japanese writing, which I could not read or really appreciate. I sat on a bench for a while so my departure would not be so rapid as to be embarrassing.

Until about 75 years ago, the Chinese bound girls' feet, beginning in infancy. Small feet were considered a source of beauty. The foot-binding process is not pretty. The toes are broken and bent under the foot. Walking becomes very difficult. Tiny bound feet gained an erotic dimension. Catching a glimpse of the space between the toes had much the same arousal factor as a glimpse of breast cleavage for today's men.

LANGUAGE

A Japanese colleague once asked me, "What is the meaning of 'Speak Lark'?" I looked at her with a puzzled expression. She pointed to a huge billboard with a picture of a blond woman enjoying a Lark brand of cigarette. The billboard's text was "Speak Lark." I told her that it did not have a real meaning. Differences in language have caused many mistakes in international marketing. Literal translations of company names and advertising themes rarely work. It is more important to translate to an equivalent idea.

Japanese has three different writing systems, hiragana, katakana, and kanji. The kanji is based on a pictorial representation of the object. The word for one tree looks like a single tree. The word for a forest is a combination of three symbols for a tree. This is quite a simple example for a very complex writing system. Although I have attended two years of Japanese classes and had a private tutor for one year, the amount of Japanese I can speak, much less read, is minuscule.

Japanese advertising often features English words that have little meaning to the message being presented. The English words are included because they look attractive, or convey a Western flavor or attitude. This may seem bizarre until you consider that American advertising often includes Japanese symbols just for decoration. When Americans see Japanese letters, they see an illustration—a symbol of another culture—not a word that has meaning.

HOFSTEDE'S CULTURAL DIMENSIONS MODEL

The distinction between high context and low context culture provides a means for broadly classifying cultural groups. The building blocks of culture, in turn, determine an individual's pattern of daily life. Another useful model for describing cultural groups is Hofstede's dimensions of difference. These four major dimensions can also be generalized to retail situations.

Geert Hofstede,[7] a researcher from the Netherlands, has developed one of the most frequently used theories of cultural differences. He developed a paradigm to study the impact of national culture on individual behavior. What makes his work so unique is that he developed the model after examining the values and beliefs of 116,000 IBM employees in 40 countries throughout the world. Later he expanded this study to 10 other countries. Hofstede developed a typology consisting of four national, cultural dimensions through which society can be classified. These four dimensions are **individualism, uncertainty avoidance, power distance,** and **masculinity/femininity.** This typology is often used in international management. However, there are important, distinct implications for international retailing.

INDIVIDUALISM

This dimension encompasses the dichotomy between individualism and collectivism. Table 2.1 summarizes the essential elements of this dimension. The foundation of this dimension is I (individualism) versus we (collectivism). Hofstede did not make the transfer from these cultural dimensions to retailing. However, we might predict certain things about societies that are at the extremes of these two dimensions.

We would expect small businesses and entrepreneurism to flourish in individualistic societies. Greater product variety and consumption with the purpose of differentiating the purchaser from others are also predictable.

TABLE 2.1

Hofstede's Dimension of Individualism

Collectivist	Individualist	Applications to Retailing and Consumer Behavior
In society, people are born into extended families or clans who protect them in exchange for loyalty.	In society, everybody is supposed to take care of himself or herself and his or her immediate family.	Government support for small businesses versus no government involvement.
"We" consciousness holds sway.	"I" consciousness holds sway.	Government control of retail sector and state ownership of stores versus individual entrepreneurs.
Identity is based in the social system.	Identity is based in the individual.	Status comes from employment with large, old companies versus status is given to the entrepreneur and self-owner.
The emphasis is on belonging to organizations; membership is the ideal.	The emphasis is on individual initiative and achievement; leadership is the ideal.	Teamwork and group achievement versus individual initiative and leadership.
Private life is invaded by organizations and clans to which one belongs; opinions are predetermined.	Everybody has a right to a private life and opinion.	Company has the right to know about employee's life versus separation of work and private life.
Value standards differ for in-groups and out-groups (particularism).	Value standards should apply to all (universalism).	Group member gives purchase rights versus all consumers have the right to purchase any products they chose.

Source: Adapted with the author's permission from Hofstede, G. (1992). "Motivation, Leadership, and Organization: Do American Theories Apply Abroad?" In H. Lane and J. DiStefano, eds., *International Management Behavior,* 2nd Edition. Boston: PWS-Kent, pp. 98–122. Reprinted from *Organizational Dynamics*, Summer 1980.

In collectivist societies, we could predict that consumers would use products to convey the status of group membership. Brand names are likely to be dominant in collectivist cultures.

UNCERTAINTY AVOIDANCE

The dimension of uncertainty avoidance focuses on a society's willingness to take risks. Societies in which people avoid risks are viewed by Hofstede as high in uncertainty avoidance. Societies in which people believe in taking risks are low in uncertainty avoidance. The major dimensions of uncertainty avoidance are summarized in Table 2.2

The Japanese place great importance on gift giving and carefully choose the type of store where they purchase a gift. The prestige of the store reduces

TABLE 2.2

Hofstede's Dimension of Uncertainty Avoidance

Low Uncertainty Avoidance	High Uncertainty Avoidance	Applications to Retailing and Consumer Behavior
Ease and lower stress are are experienced.	Higher anxiety and stress are experienced.	Shopping is an enjoyable, family experience versus stressful and to be minimized.
Time is free.	Time is money.	Full service versus self-service as ideal.
Aggressive behavior is frowned upon.	Aggressive behavior of self and others is accepted.	Low-key sales approach versus hard sell.
More acceptance of dissent is entailed.	A strong need for consensus is involved.	Products purchased to show individualism versus products that maintain affiliation to the group.
Deviation is not considered threatening; greater tolerance is shown.	Deviant persons and ideas are dangerous; intolerance holds sway.	Deviance is demonstrated through visible products such as clothes versus through thoughts and secret acts.
More positive feelings toward younger people are seen.	Younger people are suspect.	Youth as important target group versus youth as troublemakers to be monitored.
If rules cannot be kept, we should change them.	If rules cannot be kept, we are sinners and should repent.	Common law applied to commercial activities versus prescribed application of law.
Belief is placed in generalists and common sense.	Belief is placed in experts and their knowledge.	Innovations come from the common person versus innovations come from from powerful and wealthy people.

Source: Adapted with the author's permission from Hofstede, G. (1992). "Motivation, Leadership, and Organization: Do American Theories Apply Abroad?" In H. Lane and J. DiStefano, eds., *International Management Behavior,* 2nd Edition. Boston: PWS-Kent, pp. 98–122. Reprinted from *Organizational Dynamics,* Summer 1980. All rights reserved, Geert Hofstede.

TABLE 2.3

Hofstede's Dimension of Power Distance

Small Power Distance	Large Power Distance	Applications to Retailing and Consumer Behavior
Inequality in society should be minimized.	There should be an order of inequality in this world in which everybody has a rightful place; high and low are protected by this source.	Purchases avoid the illusion of wealth and power versus conspicuous consumption and flaunting of wealth.
Hierarchy means an inequality of roles, established for convenience.	Hierarchy means existential inequality.	Salespeople are empowered to handle customer problems versus only upper managers can address problems.
Superiors are accessible.	Superiors are inaccessible.	Success of small retailers who interact with customers versus large companies in which chief executive officers are distant from consumers.
All should have equal rights.	Power holders are entitled to privileges.	Everyone waits in the same line to be serviced versus the powerful go to the front of the line.
People at various power levels feel less threatened and are more prepared to trust people.	Other people are a potential threat to one's power and can rarely be trusted.	General supervision, flexible work time versus highly rigid work schedules.

Source: Adapted with the author's permission from Hofstede, G. (1992). "Motivation, Leadership, and Organization: Do American Theories Apply Abroad?" In H. Lane and J. DiStefano, eds., *International Management Behavior,* 2nd Edition. Boston: PWS-Kent, pp. 98–122. Reprinted from *Organizational Dynamics,* Summer 1980.

the risk of purchasing the gift. In Japan, a society high in uncertainty avoidance, large retailers with a long history provide the lowest levels of risk associated with a purchase. A purchase from a small retailer carries greater risk.

POWER DISTANCE

This dimension refers to how well a society tolerates inequality. Small power distance societies believe that they should reduce inequality. Large power distance societies believe there should be an ordered inequality in the world. In this view, everyone has a rightful place, high and low, and the order protects this rightful place. The major elements of the power distance concept are presented in Table 2.3.

Malaysia, Guatemala, Panama, and the Philippines have the largest power distance; Denmark, Norway, and Sweden the smallest. In large power distance societies, power holders are entitled to privileges. Those in power are expected to look and act powerful.

MASCULINITY/FEMININITY

This dimension looks at how distinctly roles in society are defined. The contrast is between masculine and feminine orientations. This dimension does not relate to which of the sexes has power within the society. Rather, is used to describe how people live their lives and what is important to them. Societies with a masculine orientation focus on assertiveness, domination, and high performance. In this orientation, money and things are important; big and fast are considered beautiful; independence is the ideal. Societies with a feminine orientation believe that there should be equality between the sexes. Quality of life is important, and interdependence is the ideal. Small and slow are considered beautiful. People in masculine societies "live to work." People in feminine societies "work to live." The major elements of these dimensions are outlined in Table 2.4.

TABLE 2.4

Hofstede's Dimension of Masculinity/Femininity

Feminine	Masculine	Applications to Retailing and Consumer Behavior
Men needn't be assertive, but can also assume nurturing roles.	Men should be assertive. Women should be nurturing.	Sex-neutral products versus sex-specific products.
Sex roles in society are more fluid.	Sex roles in society are clearly differentiated.	Same as above.
There should be equality between the sexes.	Men should dominate in society.	Men and women as bosses and entrepreneurs versus men as captains of industry.
Quality of life is important.	Performance is what counts.	Environmentally friendly companies versus high profit at all cost companies.
You work in order to live.	You live in order to work.	Retailers close during evenings and weekends versus importance of 24-hour shopping.
People and environment are are important.	Money and things are important.	Green products versus large market share products.
Interdependence is the ideal.	Independence is the ideal.	Cooperatives versus corporate retailers.
Service provides the motivation.	Ambition provides the drive.	Long-term sustainable customer service versus high growth, short-lived products.
One sympathizes with the unfortunate.	One admires the successful achiever.	Corporate sponsorship of community events versus separation of corporate and community goals.
Small and slow are beautiful.	Big and fast are beautiful.	Unique and independent businesses versus large corporations.

Source: Adapted with the author's permission from Hofstede, G. (1992). "Motivation, Leadership, and Organization: Do American Theories Apply Abroad?" In H. Lane and J. DiStefano, eds., *International Management Behavior,* 2nd Edition. Boston: PWS-Kent, pp. 98–122. Reprinted from *Organizational Dynamics,* Summer 1980.

COMBINING DIMENSIONS

A more complete profile of the dimensions of difference between nations becomes evident when two dimensions are viewed together. Figure 2.2 combines the individualism with power distance rating on a grid. It groups similar countries together in a shaded area. Most Asian and Central and South American countries cluster together in a group that embodies large power distance and low individualism. The United States falls within a group that displays small power distance and high individualism. Australia, Great Britain, the Netherlands, Canada, and New Zealand are part of the U.S. group.

Masculinity/femininity and uncertainty avoidance are profiled together in Figure 2.3. The United States falls within a group in the weak uncertainty avoidance and high masculine orientation quadrant. Ireland, Great Britain, India, the Philippines, New Zealand, South Africa, Canada, and Australia are other countries in this group. We could predict that individuals in this group believe taking risks is important for success. They judge success by performance, power, money, and things. They live to work.

The Scandinavian countries cluster together in the weak uncertainty avoidance and high feminine orientation quadrant. We could predict that individuals in this group believe in taking risks, as well. However, they judge success in terms of quality of life. People and the environment are important. They work to live, rather than letting work consume their lives.

In the next section, some of these cultural elements are put together into a model to help describe the cross-cultural process.

MODEL OF CROSS-CULTURAL BEHAVIOR

Retail success can change consumer behavior. The introduction of McDonald's set the stage for a variety of fast-food formats in the United States. This cultural change has also occurred in many of the countries McDonald's entered following its success in its home market. McDonald's did not originate the fast-food idea. However, the company's aggressive franchising efforts made it a worldwide symbol of Americana.

A model for analyzing cross-cultural buying behavior is presented in Figure 2.4 p. 80. This model could be used to analyze the spread of new retail formats throughout a large country, where different regions represent different cultural groups. It is used more frequently to study how new products or retail formats are adopted from country to country.

We can use the example of McDonald's introduction into Japan to explore the model. Let's begin at the top. The *change agent,* in this instance, is the first McDonald's franchise operator, Den Fujita, a Japanese entrepreneur. Fujita started an import business at the age of 25, importing golf clubs and Florsheim shoes. He switched to women's accessories shortly after, correctly deciding that women were more likely to purchase imported designer

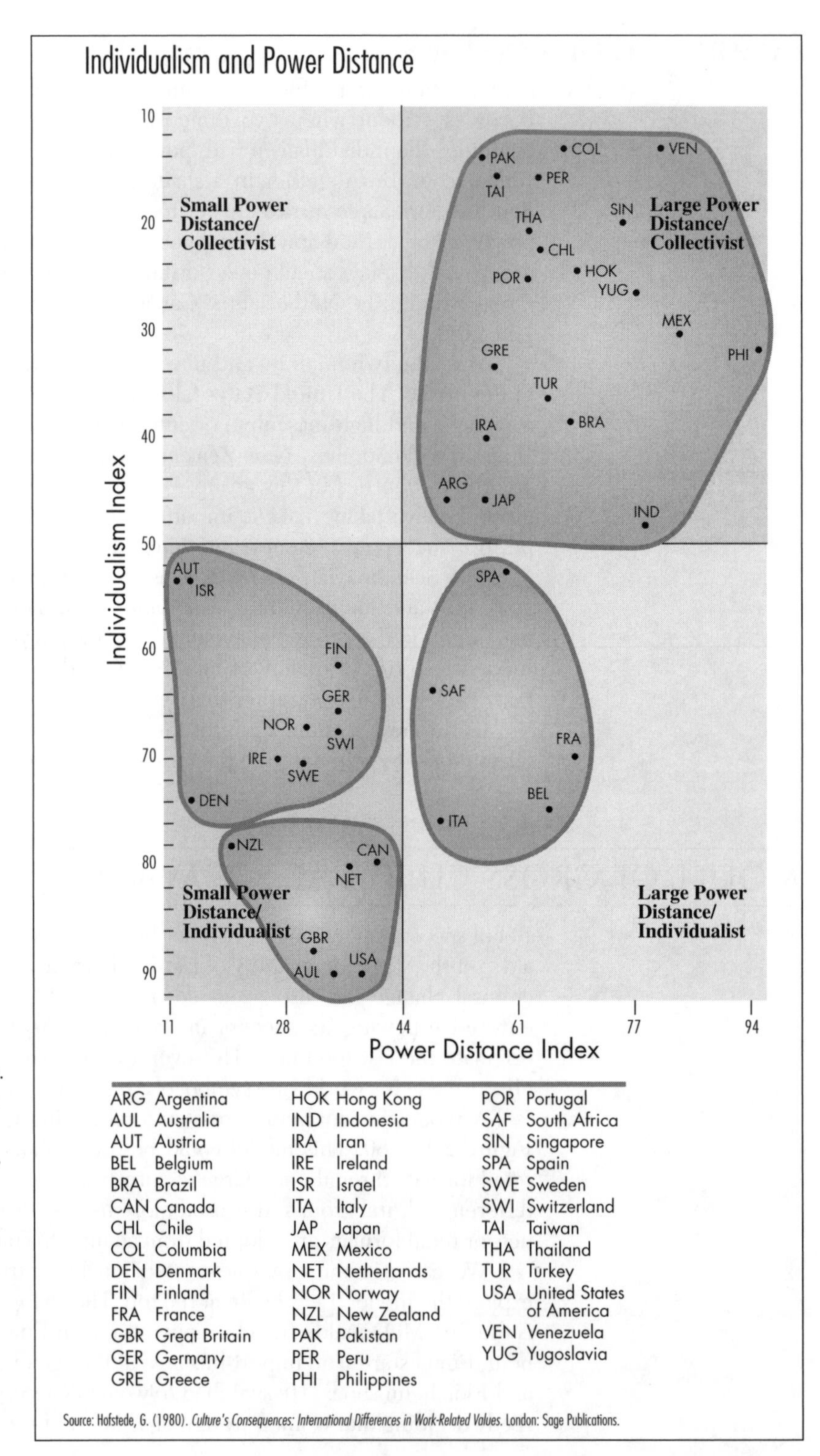

Figure 2.2
Hofstede's four dimensions of difference help us to understand people from various cultures. This figure indexes the power distance and the individualism dimensions. The United States, Great Britain, New Zealand, the Netherlands, Canada, and Australia fall in the small power distance/individualist quadrant. *Small power distance* refers to the belief that people are equal. *Individualist* refers to the importance of individual rather than group, or collectivist, efforts.

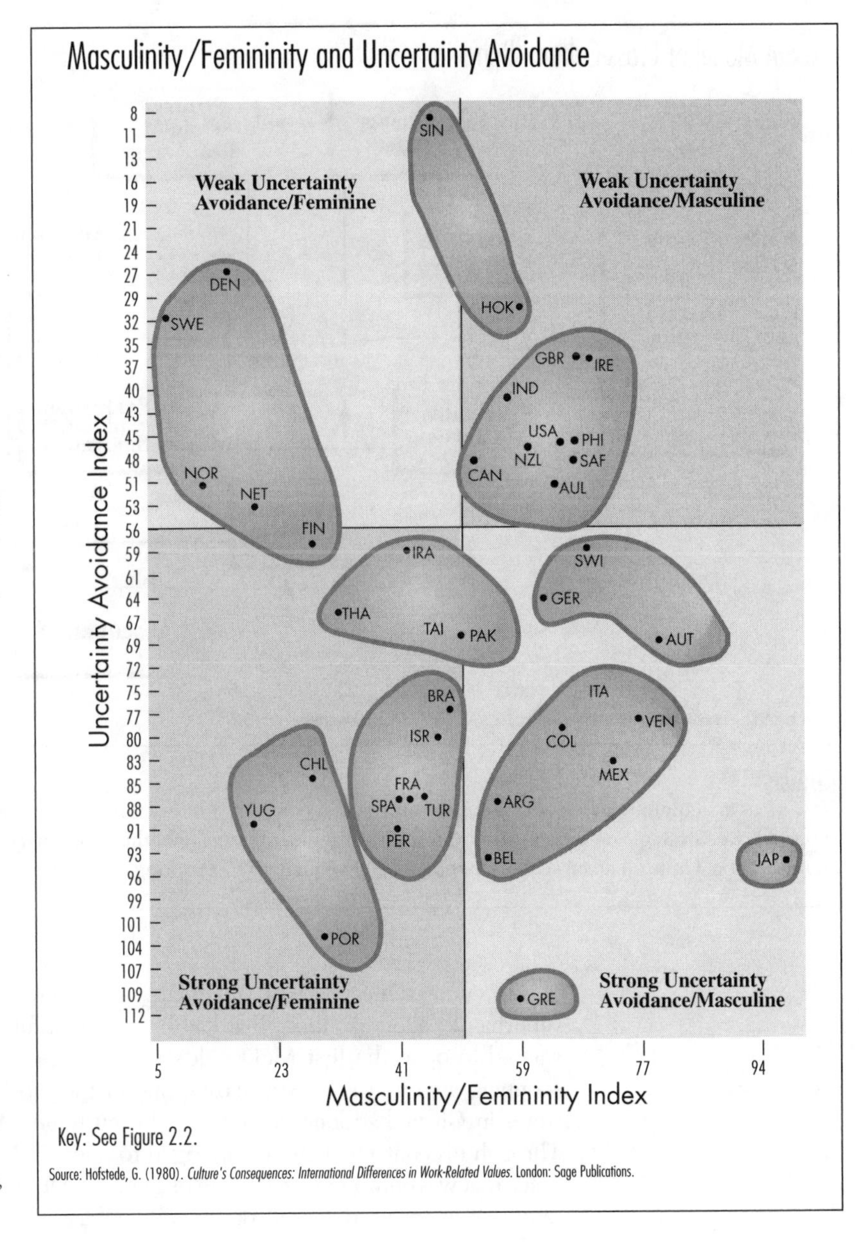

Figure 2.3
This figure indexes the uncertainty avoidance and masculinity dimensions of Hofstede's four dimensions of difference. Uncertainty avoidance refers to how people view risk: those who are high on uncertainty avoidance do not take risks; those who are low on uncertainty avoidance view risk taking as a part of life and believe you must gamble to gain. Masculinity/femininity refers to how well-defined male and female roles are in society. Societies that are high on the masculinity dimension have a "live to work" attitude, valuing things that are big, fast, and beautiful. Societies that are high on femininity have a "work to live" attitude: they value relationships, and men and women share in child-rearing. Countries that are low on uncertainty avoidance and high on the femininity dimension are Denmark, Sweden, Norway, the Netherlands, and Finland.

products. Fujita found out through his trading company representative in Chicago that McDonald's was interested in internationalizing. Typically, McDonald's only approved single franchises to individuals. Fujita, however, convinced the company, first, that it should approve the opening of several restaurants throughout Japan and, second, that he should be given a free hand in running the restaurants.

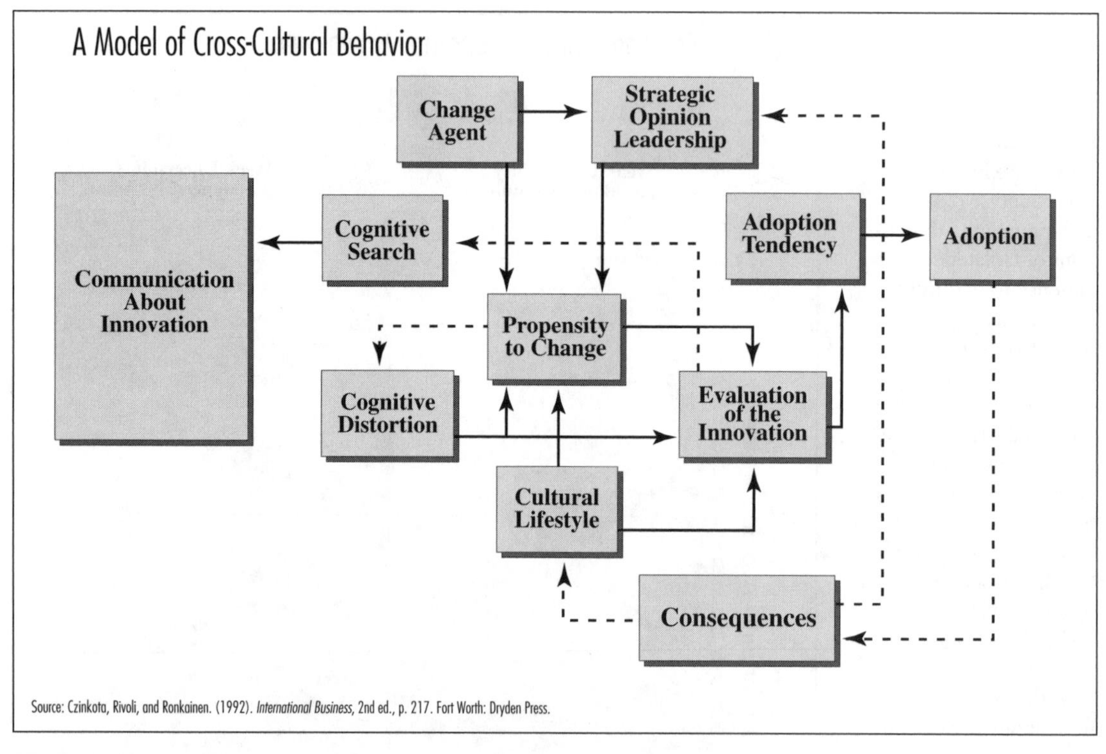

Figure 2.4
New ideas are communicated across cultures through a complex process, which could be diagrammed as shown above. Strategic opinion leaders and change agents influence whether average consumers will adopt an innovation. Cultural norms can influence the consequences of adopting an innovation.

He ignored the advice of McDonald's analysts who recommended finding a suburban location like those that had been successful in the United States. He wanted to open the first McDonald's in Ginza, the most famous and busiest shopping area in Tokyo. Mitsukoshi, one of the most prestigious department stores in Ginza, had long been one of his customers for women's accessories. Through his contacts there, he arranged to open a McDonald's restaurant in a space that was only one-fifth the size of a normal McDonald's. The space was the same space he used to sell designer handbags. Fujita designed a compact kitchen and substituted stand-up customer counters instead of seats. There was one catch. The department store did not want construction at the location to inconvenience its regular shoppers. Mitsukoshi is closed on Mondays. Fujita thus had from 6:00 P.M. Sunday to 9:00 A.M. Tuesday to construct his tiny restaurant. That is 39 hours to assemble a store that normally takes three months.

Fujita accepted the terms. He rented a warehouse on the outskirts of Tokyo where his construction crews practiced assembling a McDonald's unit in the allocated 39 hours. They went through trial runs, assembling the store and tearing it down until they got the time down. Fujita telexed Chicago that the grand opening would be July 20, 1971. The grand man of McDonald's, Ray Kroc, and other McDonald's officials arrived in Tokyo on Saturday, July 17, to attend the opening. They asked to see the store. Fujita took them to the Mitsukoshi window where the store would be and said, "Here's where it goes." McDonald's officials could not believe Fujita's story. They were frantic about the scheduled grand opening.

The construction crew performed their well-rehearsed movements, however, and when the officials showed up for the grand opening, the restaurant was ready. Three days after the first unit opened, Fujita opened another in Shinjuku, one of the busiest commuter train terminals in Tokyo. A day later, a third unit was opened. All were successful. After 18 months, Fujita had 19 McDonald's restaurants throughout Japan.[8]

In the model, *strategic opinion leadership* refers to the actions by which a change agent appeals to influencers within a cultural group. Convinced that Japan's youth would be the ones most likely to accept the fast-food concept, Fujita aimed his advertising at children and young families. This group of Japanese were those with the greatest *propensity to change.* Fujita said, "The eating habits of older Japanese are very conservative, but we could teach the children that the hamburger was something good." Fujita went so far as to make advertising claims that hamburgers would improve the health of Japanese children, making them grow bigger and stronger. Much to the chagrin of McDonald's officials, he even claimed that hamburgers would lighten Japanese skin.

Fujita made marketing modifications to succeed in Japan. He clarified that McDonald's Japan was run by Japanese not by Americans. This reduced the *cognitive distortion* and increased the *evaluation of the innovation.* He advertised on television, making sure the spots had a Japanese flavor (*communication about innovation*). This communication was intended to stimulate consumers' *cognitive search,* seeking to find out more about the fast-food concept. He changed the pronunciation of the McDonald's name to Makudonaldo because the name was difficult for Japanese to pronounce. For the same reason, Ronald McDonald became Donald McDonald. This improved the *adoption tendency* and, ultimately, the Japanese consumer's *adoption* of McDonald's restaurants. As the popularity of McDonald's restaurants increased, the *consequences* of adoption became clearer. Youthful consumers who might have purchased a traditional Japanese boxed lunch were now opting for fast foods. Just like families in the United States, Japanese families' *cultural lifestyles* have changed. Fast-food outlets are expanding throughout the country. Each year, fewer families sit down to a traditional family meal for breakfast, lunch, or dinner.

Not all internationalization of retail innovations alters culture. Most of international retailing goes unnoticed by consumers within a country. Few people know, or care that a retail concept is of foreign origin. Each year, many retailers expand internationally, only to retreat shortly afterwards. Retail innovations have a life cycle, like a product life cycle, that can be used to predict success.

SUMMARY

Culture influences retailing in many ways, but retailing can also influence culture. Over time, the products we purchase and how we purchase them influences culture. Culture is a learned pattern of life. We are socialized into our culture as children and continue to learn about it until we die. In this chapter, I have presented some theoretical concepts that can help you generalize about and predict behavior of people from other cultures.

Understanding whether groups have a polychronic or monochronic time–orientation helps us to be patient if we are monochronic time–oriented, or tolerant of rushing if we are polychronic time–oriented. Knowing that a group of people are high context communicators helps us understand that we probably will not understand all of what is being communicated unless we are a part of that culture. Low context cultures can communicate quite adequately with each other because they put everything into words. However, low context cultures will never have the depth of silent communication present in high context interactions.

Hofstede's cultural dimensions provide another mechanism for generalizing about cultural groups. Some of his dimensions, such as individualism versus collectivism, can be related to monochronic time and polychronic time, and high context versus low context. Countries that are classified as being individualist are also monochronic time–oriented and low context.

In this chapter, we have seen how retailing can affect cultural change. Retailing both affects and is affected by economic change. In the next chapter, we will consider the evolution of retailing with increased economic development.

KEY TERMS

change agents
conspicuous consumption
ethnocentrism
femininity
gatekeepers
high context
individualism
low context
masculinity
multicultural
opinion leaders
patina
power distance
reference groups
self-reference criterion
uncertainty avoidance

DISCUSSION QUESTIONS

1. It is often said that culture is learned behavior. Give three examples of learned behaviors that affect international retailing.
2. Provide three examples of high context cultures and three examples of low context cultures. How would you expect these cultures to feel about Hall's silent languages of (a) space, (b) material possessions, (c) friendship patterns, (d) agreements across cultures, and (e) time.
3. Societies teach their members to belong to their cultural group through material elements, social institutions, belief systems, aesthetics, and language. What people and institutions have provided you with your cultural perspective in these areas?
4. Use Hofstede's cultural dimensions model to make some strategic decisions about a specific retail activity. Suppose you are interested in opening a toy store in Japan. Japan is considered low on individualism, high on power distance, high on masculinity, and low on risk tolerance. How would your decisions reflect these dimensions?
5. No doubt you have heard people say, "English is the international language of business. If you want to do business with me, you'd better speak my language." What is the term for this view and what are the repercussions for international retailers?

ENDNOTES

1. Terpstra, V., and K. David. (1985). *The Cultural Environment of International Business.* Cincinnati, OH: South-Western.
2. Johansson, J. (1997). *Global Marketing: Foreign Entry, Local Marketing and Global Management.* Chicago, IL: Irwin.
3. McCracken, G. (1988). *Culture and Consumption.* Bloomington: Indiana University Press.
4. Hall, E. (1983). *The Dance of Life.* New York: Anchor Books-Doubleday.
5. Hall. (1983).
6. Cateora, P. R. (1996). *International Marketing.* 9th ed. Chicago: Irwin.
7. Hofstede, G. (1980). *Culture's Consequences: International Differences in Work-Related Values.* Beverly Hills, CA: Sage Publications.
8. Love, J. (1995). *McDonald's: Behind the Arches.* New York: Bantam.

3

Retailing in Developing Countries

After reading this chapter, you will understand:

- Characteristics of traditional retailers and how economic development affects these characteristics.
- How the role of retail buyer as gatekeeper of products is an important market transition by which retailers become assemblers of goods.
- Characteristics of buyer's and seller's markets and how these characteristics affect power within the distribution system.
- Why prices need to be fixed for modern retail systems to function.
- How female employment is related to self-service retailing.

DEFINING DEVELOPING COUNTRIES

Economists generally classify a country's level of development by its **gross domestic product** (GDP); that is, the total value of goods and services produced during the year by people in that country. The World Bank compiles an index that lists countries according to their rank, from least developed to most developed. The index number is clean and simple and handy to use. This index, shown in Chapter 3 Appendix, p. 113, includes per capita gross national product (GNP), measured in U.S. dollars, and a rating of each country's purchasing power parity (PPP), expressed as a percentage of an individual's purchasing power in the United States. This table provides the basis for the brief tables introducing the discussions of individual countries in the chapters that follow.

As a student of retailing, you might consult these figures and have little idea about the way people actually live in these countries. I find that more tangible elements help me to understand how people live their lives. Table 3.1 provides several concrete measures of everyday living. This table gives number of rooms per dwelling and number of persons per room. Nevertheless, what I find really interesting is the percent of households that have what we might consider everyday necessities. These necessities are piped water, flush toilets, and electrical lighting. The table includes only a representative sampling of countries, but this is enough to give you an idea of how different countries compare.

To me, toilets provide a good indicator of everyday living standards. The toilets at the Beijing airport are awful. During my first trip to Beijing, I noticed there was never any toilet paper in the bathroom. Then I took a trip to Beijing when China was lobbying to hold the Olympics. What a change; not only was there toilet paper in the bathroom, but a valet was handing out the nicely folded squares of toilet paper as people went into the stalls. Unfortunately, this was a lobbying effort; the next time I went to Beijing, the airport toilets again lacked toilet paper.

Use of toilet paper is, of course, a culturally prescribed behavior. Only one out of five high-income consumers in India uses toilet paper. An Indian native, educated at the London Business School, is quoted as saying, "I'd be willing to bet that no minister in the entire Indian cabinet uses toilet paper."[1] The *Wall Street Journal* article in Box 3.1 contains some interesting comparisons of the difficulties in marketing Western products to consumers in India and China.

STAGES OF DEVELOPMENT

There are measures of economic development other than the availability of toilets and toilet paper. Rostow, for instance, classified countries according to production and consumption capability.[2]

BOX 3.1

Marketing Gurus Say: In India, Think Cheap, Lose the Cold Cereal

By Miriam Jordan

Bombay, India—How do you pitch spaghetti in a country where people eat with a bare hand? Or disposable lighters to consumers so frugal, they refill them?

Such are the marketing riddles that confound Western multinational companies in India. Furnishing answers is the business of marketing guru K. M. S. Ahluwalia.

When Avon Products Inc. came calling, Titoo—as Mr. Ahluwalia is nicknamed—advised the cosmetics giant not to go ringing doorbells in India, where only bric-a-brac salesmen sell door-to-door. Since founding India's largest market-research firm, ORG-MARG, Titoo has served as a guide to multinationals like Coca-Cola Co., Gillette Co., and Unilever PLC that are wooing India's seemingly Western-oriented consumers.

"Repeat after me," he says in an interview, reciting his mantra for Western clients: "India is different, India is different, India is different."

This reality check is in order. Many Western companies see vast riches in this market of 950 million consumers. Most of India's people are poor, but the middle class is estimated to equal in number the entire U.S. population, though it isn't nearly as well off. Free-market reforms launched five years ago have given more Indians a taste of prosperity. They now have a wider choice of products and greater exposure to Western lifestyles: MTV and "Baywatch" are beamed into many living rooms via satellite television.

But Western consumer marvels are colliding with a force that belies appearances and can't be swept aside as quickly as India's formerly socialist economy: its 4,000-year-old culture.

"I'd be willing to bet that no minister in the entire Indian cabinet uses toilet paper," declares Titoo, a 50-year-old London Business School graduate and former advertising man, who counts himself among those in favor of traditional Indian cleansing. Though he hasn't surveyed the politicians, he has polled consumers, and found that only one out of five high-income earners use toilet paper.

The outlook isn't any better for antiperspirants in this sweltering country, as Gillette discovered. Indians typically bathe twice a day—it's a mammoth market for soap—but deodorant penetration is just 2% among urban dwellers.

India's outward modernity can be deceptive. "Indians are capable of living in several centuries at once," says Daraius Ardeshir, managing director of Nestle India Ltd., the local unit of the Swiss food company. "When I visit my father's house, I still kiss his feet," he says.

Indians who study in the U.S. and Britain often return home to arranged marriages. Even many people who have chosen their own spouses opt to move in with their extended families. Such traditional family bonds inhibit Western marketers' access: Yuppies, deferring to their elders, don't make household-purchasing decisions.

The response to consumer products launched in India over the past three years has disappointed many multinational companies hoping for quick success. When Titoo's team recently surveyed marketing managers in India, only 27% of food-company marketers said their expectations had been met; among those selling consumer items, the figure was 33%.

A sweeping new Gallup poll of consumer attitudes confirms what tough customers Indians can be. In India, where urban temperatures top 110 degrees in the summer, just 1% of households have an air conditioner, Gallup found—and only 1% plan to buy one within the next two years.

Marketing problems include nightmarish distribution hassles and a diverse population with dozens of regional groups—each with its own language. A more fundamental challenge is to strike the right cultural chord.

Lesson one: Indians are champion recyclers. Even as they

Continued

In India, Think Cheap
continued

prosper, they remain frugal. For many middle-class smokers, for example, it would be inconceivable to throw away a disposable cigarette lighter when it can be refilled cheaply.

A similar challenge frustrates sanitary napkin marketers. "You'd think that in a country with a huge population, you'd make a fortune selling sanitary napkins," says P. H. Lele, executive vice president of Johnson & Johnson Ltd., a unit of the U.S. personal-care-products giant.

Not yet. Indian women recycle old cotton saris or sheets instead. Fewer than 2% of all Indian women and just 23% of adult urban women use sanitary napkins.

India's men are a hard sell, too. India is the world's largest market for razor blades—but not for disposable shavers. Less than 1% of blades bought in cities are attached to a plastic handle. People can't stand to toss them away. Still, Gillette believes the market will come around. "India has the size as well as the fuzz," says Pradeep Pant, managing director of Indian Shaving Products Ltd., a Gillette-controlled joint venture.

Cultural psychologist Sudhir Kakar says frugality has deep historical roots in India. Mohandas K. Gandhi, who led India's fight for independence from Britain, tapped this value when he urged countrymen to spin their own cloth for clothing instead of buying British imports.

And Indians have never had a social-security system to fall back on. Though median household income is only $480, the private savings rate is an impressive 24%. "Unconsciously," says Dr. Kakar, the psychologist, "even the richest man fears sinking into the sea of poverty that surrounds him."

This mindset drives Indian consumers—wealthy or not—to spend a little money at a time, even though that may not be the cheapest way to buy a product. And so marketers don't recommend selling family-sized packages of detergents, shampoos or tea leaves.

To trim costs, Indians often ignore manufacturers' instructions. If a drink mix calls for a heaping teaspoon, they'll plop in a level teaspoon. "Culturally, we are underdosers," says Rama Bijapurkar, a McKinsey & Co. consultant. "We underconsume to be economical."

But frugality isn't the main cultural hurdle for multinationals. Of all areas, food is the most treacherous, since many Indians believe food shapes personality, mood and the mind.

Tang orange drink may have succeeded in outer space, but it burned on entry in India, where people believe that citrus and milk are bad for the stomach—and sour your mood—when consumed at the same time. Kraft Foods International, a unit of Philip Morris Cos., positioned Tang as a drink for breakfast, when tea with milk is customary. Kraft, which also marketed Maxwell House coffee in India, quit the country in the early 1990s. In China, Tang's futuristic image has made it such a hit that Kraft has just opened a $20 million plant outside the city of Tianjin.

Kellogg Co. is getting a cold shoulder from Indians, who prefer hot food for breakfast because they feel it infuses them with energy. Consumers indulged their curiosity when Kellogg's Corn Flakes arrived two years ago. Recently, though, sales have plummeted, people close to the company say, as Indians returned to their breakfast of flat bread with eggs or cooked vegetables. Indians are willing to try new foods, marketers have concluded, but usually return to traditional fare.

To be sure, the popularity of Western restaurants such as Kentucky Fried Chicken and Pizza Hut demonstrates Indians' appetite for new cuisines. But that change hasn't entered the home. At least not when a Western food, such as cold cereal, is pitched as a replacement for a main meal. "As long as it's a food for casual eating, you have a good chance of succeeding," says Sunil Alagh, managing director of Indian biscuit maker Britannia Industries Ltd. "When you try to get into the main meal, that's where you flop."

Nestle SA has learned that the snack is where it's at for Western food companies. In 1983, Nestle launched its Maggi brand of instant noodles. Unlike competitor Unilever, which tried to convert Indians to eating pasta meals, Nestle has recently found success by pitching Maggi noodles as a snack between meals. Its advertisements showed children playfully shoving the noodles into their mouths. Most Indians eat with their fingers.

Nestle is setting an example for other food companies in India by working the margins of the market, localizing its products and appeasing price-conscious housewives, who typically control half of the family budget. Between 1991 and 1995, Nestle India more than doubled its sales to 10 billion rupees ($280 million) and increased net profit 50% to 532 million rupees.

In the process, the company adapted to the Indian reality "rather than saying, 'This is good for you, eat it,' " says Mr. Ardeshir, the managing director. "If you want to be big in India, you have to get in with local foods."

Nestle has created an Indian instant coffee, Sunrise, which is blended with chicory to give a strong and familiar flavor. Sunrise outsells the world-famous Nescafe in India. The company also markets mixes for traditional desserts, as well as a mint that's flavored with betel nut, a popular mild stimulant. It has commissioned local pickle maker Chordia Foods Ltd. to manufacture Indian chutneys under the Nestle name.

But the right product needs the right price, even among Nestle's elite target market of India's 20 million wealthiest households. More than half of 119 Nestle products sold in India cost less than 25 rupees (70 cents). Sales of Maggi noodles have tripled since January 1994, when the price was cut to about 14 cents from 19 cents a package. "It took us 10 years to realize we can have a mass market," says Mr. Ardeshir, who concedes that Nestle stumbled after entering India in 1962.

Despite the dramatic economic changes in India in the past five years, the most successful consumer-product multinationals are those that have been in India for decades—though success is relative. After 35 years in India, Johnson & Johnson's turnover of $50 million is roughly equal to its sales in Malaysia, home to just 19 million people.

While newer entrants must sit tight through years of losses, at least one marketing executive is prospering: Titoo. His company's turnover has surged 56% a year on average since 1991, as multinationals troop into his office. This year he will sell a stake in his firm to a Dutch publishing and information company, one of several suitors. "I'm getting rich," he says, "but I'm losing my hair."

Source: *The Wall Street Journal,* October 11, 1996.

TABLE 3.1

Living Standards in Selected Countries

Country	Rooms per Dwelling	Persons per Room	Percent of Households: Piped Water	Flush Toilets	Electric Lighting
Brazil	4.6	1.1	55	76	69
Chile	2.9	1.6	70	59	88
Costa Rica	4.1	1.4	88	60	73
El Salvador	1.7	3.5	35	28	39
Ethiopia	2.0	2.6	83	NA	62
Guatemala	2.4	2.7	30	18	40
Hong Kong	3.1	0.5	98	80	93
Indonesia	3.3	1.2	12	15	30
Japan	4.6	0.7	93	46	98
Peru	2.4	2.3	49	43	48
Saudi Arabia	3.1	1.9	46	26	61
Singapore	2.1	2.3	48	42	37
Sri Lanka	2.2	2.5	18	10	15
United States	5.3	0.5	99	99	99

Source: Cateora, P. R. (1996). *International Marketing.* 9th ed. Chicago: Irwin, p. 247. NA = not available.

Rostow became well known for presenting a model that classifies countries by five stages of development: (1) the traditional society, (2) the preconditions for takeoff, (3) the takeoff, (4) the drive to maturity, and (5) the age of high mass consumption. Countries in the first three stages are considered underdeveloped. Those above stage 3 are considered developed. A country's stage of development in this model can be tied to specific retailing strategies, as the following discussion illustrates.

STAGE 1: THE TRADITIONAL SOCIETY

Countries in this stage lack the capability of significantly increasing their level of productivity. There is a marked absence of systematic application of the methods of modern science and technology. Literacy levels are low.

RETAIL APPLICATION

Countries such as Rwanda, Mozambique, Ethiopia, Tanzania, and Burundi could fit under this classification. Vendors, moving from village to village with a bag of assorted merchandise, dominate retailing in these countries. Stores in permanent locations also have very scrambled merchandise. **Scrambled merchandise** means that they sell an unrelated grouping of merchandise. A vendor might have clothes, food, magazines, and soft drinks as part of the merchandise assortment.

STAGE 2: THE PRECONDITIONS FOR TAKE-OFF

This second stage includes those societies that are in the process of transition to the take-off stage. During this period, the advances of modern science are beginning to be applied in agriculture and production. The development of transportation, communications, power, education, health, and other public undertakings are begun in a small but important way.

RETAIL APPLICATION

Countries such as Mali and Nigeria probably fit this classification. Retailers are mainly situated in permanent structures, although their merchandise is still very scrambled. If retail businesses are not government-owned, they are single-family, single-unit operations.

STAGE 3: THE TAKE-OFF

At this stage, countries achieve a growth pattern that becomes a normal condition. People and social overhead have been developed to sustain steady development. Agricultural and industrial modernizations lead to rapid expansion in these areas.

RETAIL APPLICATION

Countries such as China, Vietnam, and Zimbabwe fit this description. Foreign retailers are eager to enter the market. Supermarkets and superettes are emerging. Superettes are small-scale supermarkets, a self-service format that is introduced into developing countries before full-scale supermarket development. Commercial activities include the development of modern retail formats in shopping centers.

STAGE 4: THE DRIVE TO MATURITY

After take-off, countries maintain sustained progress and their economies seek to extend modern technology to all fronts of economic activity. The economy takes on international involvement. In this stage, an economy shows that it has the technological and entrepreneurial skills to produce anything, but not everything, it chooses to produce.

RETAIL APPLICATION

Countries in this stage include the so-called "Four Tigers"—Hong Kong, Korea, Singapore, and Taiwan. Supermarkets and other forms of modern retailing are well-established, although they may coexist with traditional wet markets. **Wet markets,** like farmers' markets, are places where producers come to sell their merchandise. They are usually outdoors and do not have

Photo 3.1
One of the most basic forms of retailing is an itinerant trader selling merchandise out of a bag. This Liberian merchant travels from village to village selling his wares.
Courtesy of the United Nations/B. Wolff.

refrigeration facilities. Shopping centers may have been overbuilt during the take-off phase and are currently experiencing decline.

STAGE 5: THE AGE OF HIGH MASS CONSUMPTION

The age of high mass consumption leads to shifts in a country's leading economic sectors toward durable consumer goods and services. Real income per capita rises to the point where a very large number of people have significant amounts of discretionary income.[3]

RETAIL APPLICATION

This stage would include most countries listed under high-income economies in Chapter 3 Appendix, p. 113. Their retail offerings are very specialized. Logistics is an important part of improving distribution efficiencies. Retailers are integrated both vertically and horizontally. Recall that in Chapter 2, I explained that vertical integration occurs when a company moves into another level of the distribution channel (e.g., Levi Strauss, a manufacturer, opening retail stores). Horizontal integration occurs when a company expands at the same channel level (e.g., one retailer purchases another retailer).

Although these indicators of development are important, conditions are less predictable now than they were in the past. In the past 20 years, several countries have experienced an explosion in economic development. The trend began with the "Four Tigers"—Hong Kong, Korea, Singapore, and Taiwan. The speed of their economic growth has been amazing. In these countries and other highly developed countries, traditional retail systems coexist with modern forms of retailing. Knowing how such traditional retail systems operate is important and is the basis for understanding the impact of modern retail systems. Traditional retail systems share a set of characteristics that are tied to their level of economic development. With greater prosperity, the retail systems change form. Less developed markets are controlled by sellers; more developed markets are controlled by buyers.

TRADITIONAL RETAIL SYSTEMS

Traditional retail systems are made up of small and independent stores. Shopkeepers in these systems generally know their customers. Shopping is a daily activity, time-consuming but pleasant, that is usually carried out by women. In such a system, the female head of household would likely spend some time chatting with each of the shopkeepers whom she encounters each day. Daily shopping in this environment is thus a social and cultural exchange, as well as an economic activity.

I once worked with a graduate student from Ecuador. He came from an affluent family in Quito and he was married to a very talented interior

Photo 3.2
These small shops in Damascus, Syria, are located in permanent store locations, overflowing into the street. The shops are barely large enough for one customer; the owner parks himself outside. *Courtesy of the United Nations.*

designer who was just finishing her undergraduate degree at Michigan State University. After graduation, they would return to Ecuador. He explained that when they returned to Ecuador, his wife would not work because although they had a live-in cook, it would take his wife, as female head of the household, most of the day to do the shopping for the family meal.

In most countries with traditional retail systems, the female head of household does the shopping. Nonetheless, this has not been the case in Saudi Arabia, where cultural restrictions have traditionally prohibited women from driving and have discouraged them from going out of the house. A Saudi woman would typically make up the shopping list, but a male member of the household would do the actual shopping.[4] Increasingly, however, Saudi women are shopping at the modern supermarkets that are opening.

There is a relationship between women seeking employment outside the home and the emergence of modern self-service supermarkets. It is not clear, however, which comes first. Are self-service supermarkets introduced because women are entering the professional work force and have less time to do the family shopping? Or does it follow that when self-service supermarkets enter the retail system, the time women need to spend shopping is reduced and therefore they have time to seek employment outside the home? Probably neither scenario is totally correct. The two situations are complementary to each other.

When I was growing up on a farm in South Dakota, traditional grocery stores were located just one mile from our home in one direction and one-quarter mile in the other. Each of these grocery stores relied on business from a five-mile radius of farm families. Before I had graduated from the eighth grade, both of the grocery stores had closed.

Students are often tempted to think that these types of traditional retailers disappeared from American society after the early 1950s. In fact, ethnic areas in large cities such as New York and Los Angeles still have a traditional retail sector. Most European and Asian cities also have traditional retail sectors, coexisting with modern supermarkets.

Traditional retail systems, as we will see next, are characterized by fragmented markets, long channels, atomistic competition, limited product variety, flexible prices with bargaining, and informal credit.

FRAGMENTED MARKETS

In **fragmented markets,** the decision-making unit is the individual shop. Each shop operates independently of others. There are no chains of stores. Stores have little power within the distribution system. As a country becomes more developed, the role of coordinated chains becomes more prevalent. Stores join together to obtain economies of scale in purchasing and possibly promotion. With greater economic development, markets become more integrated.

LONG CHANNELS

A **channel** is the path products take from producer to retailer. The length of a channel is related to the economic development within a country. In very traditional retail settings the channel is quite long, often encompassing several different stages of distribution.

Let's look at a specific example. Although Japan is a highly developed country, it has retained a large traditional retail sector that operates alongside the modern retail sector. A Japanese homemaker will generally visit several small mom-and-pop stores daily or every other day to select food. Japanese homes are small, making storage a problem. In addition, the Japanese like very fresh fish and food products; shopping on a daily basis ensures the freshest fish and produce available. Because the mom-and-pop stores in Japan are also very small, making storage a problem, they rely on frequent deliveries. Large stores in urban areas might buy direct from the manufacturer or from a first-level (primary) wholesaler. Small stores in urban areas generally buy from a second-level (secondary) wholesaler. Mom-and-pop stores in less urban areas of Japan may purchase from a third-level (tertiary) wholesaler. In the case of fish, which is very perishable, the product may pass through even more wholesalers than less perishable merchandise.

An important activity for wholesalers is to break bulk cartons and distribute a smaller amount of a product to retailers. A wholesaler may order a case containing 100 dozen eggs. These are then divided among perhaps 20 retailers, with each receiving five dozen eggs to sell each day. In a traditional retail system, where stores are small, retailers purchase a small amount at a time, making the role of wholesalers very important. *The smaller the order placed, the longer the channel.*

Product characteristics also influence channel length. *The more perishable the product, the longer the channel.* When I tell this to students in my class, they do not think it makes sense. It would seem that a shorter channel would get perishable products to customers faster. Nevertheless, longer channels are really a speed track. Perhaps you have seen a depiction of the method old-fashioned firefighters used to put out fires. Each firefighter did not carry his bucket to the fire and pour it on. Instead, one person filled the buckets, which were then passed from person to person in a "bucket brigade." Product distribution is like that bucket brigade. If you have watched people building a wall of sand bags to keep a river within its banks, you have seen that same type of bucket brigade. This time, the buckets were sand bags being passed from one link to the next. Passing the bucket or the sand bag to the next person in line is like passing the product to another intermediary.

The distribution of fresh fish is one of the longest channels in food sales. Fish must be very fresh. Daily, if not twice a day, delivery is required to maintain quality. If a product is not perishable, a larger amount can be purchased at one time and stored.

ATOMISTIC COMPETITION

Traditional retail systems feature geographical competition and, eventually, geographical concentration and customer draw. Because each individual unit does not have much competitive pull, the retailers benefit by creating a central place to attract customers. A central place means that consumers will be drawn to the location because of the greater variety offered there. Additional competitors are advantageous because they add to the attraction of the location as a central place. This concept is the basis for **central place theory.**[5]

In Chapter 7, which discusses Mexico, I talk about informal markets. These markets focus their offerings to create a draw for customers. Dozens of vendors locate in the same area creating an additional draw for customers. According to central place theory, the maximum distance customers will travel for convenience goods is much smaller than the distance they will travel for specialized goods.[6] Figure 3.1 represents this graphically.[7] If you are going to purchase a carton of milk, and that is your only purchase, you will go to the closest convenience store. You will purchase the milk and leave. If you are shopping for a pair of shoes, you will travel to an area that has a wide selection of shoes. You will probably pass by individual stores that sell shoes on your way to the geographically concentrated shoe-selling area. This might be a mall, or a central business district. When you are at the location, you will visit all the shoe stores that could possibly have shoes in your price and quality range. As Figure 3.1 illustrates, shopping for specialized goods has a different shopping pattern than shopping for convenience goods. This is represented by the wider demand cones (greater distance you are willing to travel) and the

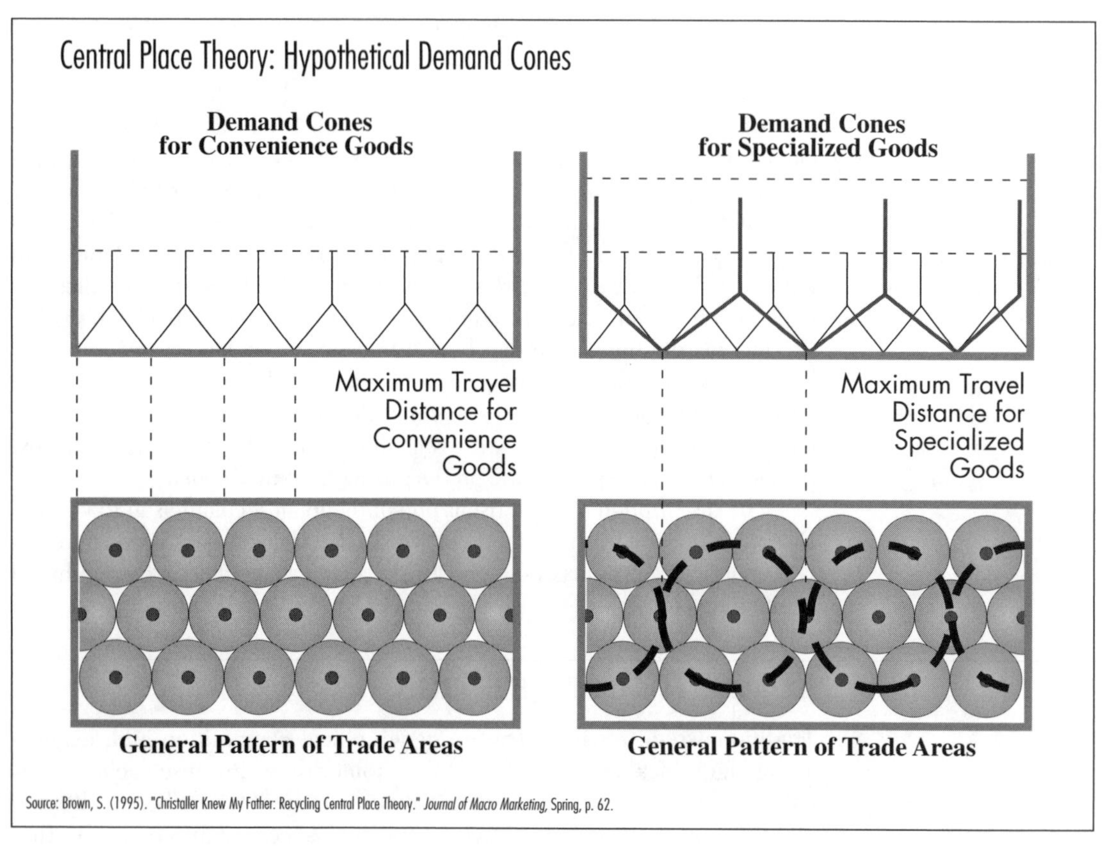

Figure 3.1
Convenience goods are goods that you purchase frequently. You shop at the most convenient location for the product; you do not travel much distance to make the purchase. Specialized goods benefit from a central place where people can comparison shop. The maximum travel distance for specialized goods is much greater than for convenience goods. In this illustration the demand cone, or shopping area, is twice as large for specialized goods than for convenience goods.

circular flow in the general pattern of trade area (visiting each shoe store that might have shoes you are interested in purchasing).

Beach vendors understand central place theory. Rather than spreading themselves out throughout a beach area, they concentrate their sales in one area. Several vendors selling hot dogs, together with others selling ice cream, become a beach fast-food outlet. Instead of being competition for each other, each vendor is an attraction, a contribution to the central place. Suppose you are on the beach. Suddenly you have the desire for a cold drink. You look up and see a vendor one block from you with a sign that says Coca-Cola. You also know that three blocks away, a cluster of vendors sell all types of food and cold drinks. If you know that a Coca-Cola is what you want, you would go to the

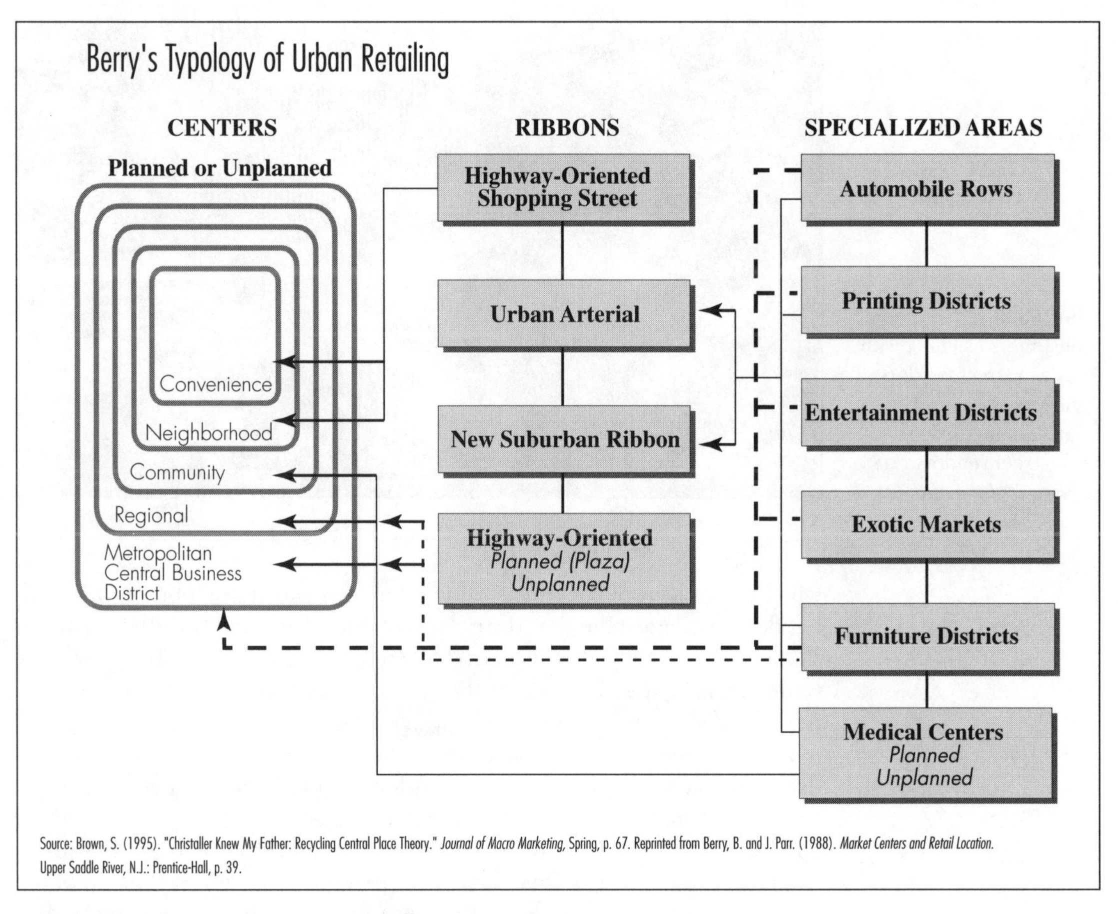

Source: Brown, S. (1995). "Christaller Knew My Father: Recycling Central Place Theory." *Journal of Macro Marketing*, Spring, p. 67. Reprinted from Berry, B. and J. Parr. (1988). *Market Centers and Retail Location.* Upper Saddle River, N.J.: Prentice-Hall, p. 39.

Figure 3.2
According to Berry, specialized shopping areas are connected to shopping centers by ribbons of shopping. Convenience and neighborhood centers are connected by traditional shopping highway-oriented streets. Community, regional, and metropolitan central business districts are linked to specialized areas by urban arterial, new suburban ribbon, and highway-oriented roads.

closest vendor, buy your drink, and leave. The Coca-Cola is a convenience good in this instance; you know you are going to buy this product so you go to the closest market offering. Now consider what you would do if you are not quite sure what you want to drink. You might be interested in iced tea, or bottled water instead of a Coca-Cola. In this case, you would be inclined to travel the greater distance and visit several vendors to decide what you want to drink.

A three-category typology of urban retailing can be used to extend the central place concept[8] (Figure 3.2). The typology focuses on *centers* and *specialized areas.* Centers are the central business district, or other planned or unplanned shopping centers. Specialized areas are groupings of retailers

Photo 3.3
Consumers haggling with Mexican street vendors. Nearly every church courtyard in Mexico contains street vendors.
Courtesy of the author.

who have gathered. These clustering retailers create automobile rows, printing districts, entertainment districts, exotic markets, and furniture districts. *Ribbons* are linear shopping areas that stretch along the major transportation routes, joining the centers and the specialized areas. Such ribbons include traditional shopping streets and highway-oriented shopping areas.

I have seen some evidence that these three categories may exist in informal markets. In Mexico City, informal markets are a part of every cathedral square. The cathedral and the market in a square could be considered the center in Berry's typology. On side streets from the square, ribbons of informal vendors line the narrow linear street. At the end of the street, an opening is found; it is the home of a specialized group of retailers such as handbag merchants. These retailers gather together to create a draw for consumers. The stores are independently operated, but they recognize that by gathering, they gain the advantages of a central place.

LIMITED PRODUCT VARIETY

In Mexico, I visited many small shops. Nearly every store would have the same selection. Even in the informal shopping sectors in Cancún, where there are lots of tourist dollars, the stores selling belts would all display nearly identical belts. The stores selling lace dresses would have virtually the same dresses. The vendors of chessboards would have the same three or four chess sets. The same scenario holds true in traditional markets throughout the world. Why would these small retailers sell the same merchandise? Are they not aware that they could increase their sales by selling a unique product?

The answer to these questions is found in the limited number of suppliers who will do business with these retailers. Because they are so small, the retailers need to find suppliers who will give them a constant source of products. The few suppliers, for their part, feel little motivation to provide good service to their small retailers, and the selection they offer is limited. As Mexico or another country becomes more developed, however, we would expect to see more suppliers. This competition would force all of the suppliers to provide service to their retailers and to provide a wider product choice.

As this process continued, manufacturers might begin to differentiate themselves from other manufacturers by developing brand names. When a manufacturer develops a brand name, it is giving consumers a guarantee about the product. It guarantees that the product will meet certain standards whenever it is purchased. For canned vegetables, the guarantee may be one of food safety and product quality. In clothing, the guarantee may be expectations related to fit and product durability. A manufacturer that develops a brand name can charge a premium for the product to offset the price of enforcing its product guarantee.

Manufacturers can promote their products in two ways. They can promote to the retailer, convincing the retailer than they have the best product selection for the price; this is done with trade promotion. An alternative is to promote the product to the consumer by establishing a brand name. The expense of reaching a consumer audience is much greater, but it gives the manufacturer greater protection from competition.

In many developing countries, foreign brands carry the highest prestige. In the People's Republic of China, however, foreign companies were not allowed to advertise or sell their products for more than 30 years. During China's planned economy, local manufacturers could not use brand names and could not even promote their own products. The central

Photo 3.4
Wooden kitchen utensils for sale in Souk El Hammadeya in Damascus, Syria. *Courtesy of the United Nations.*

government would tell the manufacturers what to produce and which large government wholesaler to ship it to. Even with this attempt to depersonalize production, however, consumers began to recognize that products from some manufacturers were superior to others. Consumers would line up to buy bicycles from Number One Bicycle Manufacturer because this manufacturing facility gained a word-of-mouth reputation as being superior to other bicycle manufacturers.

FLEXIBLE PRICES AND BARGAINING

It takes time to shop in a less developed country. Small shops generally do not have prices marked, and even when the price is marked, it is negotiable. In small shops, the price an item is sold for is at the owner's discretion. For non-food items, the initial asking price is much greater than what the retailer will actually accept. A shopper will ask the owner the price of an item. The owner quotes a price. The shopper may then offer half of what the owner is asking, and the bargaining begins from there. There is an unwritten rule about bargaining in good faith. Bargaining without the intent to buy is a bit like being labeled a "tease." If the shopper begins negotiations with a vendor and is given a good price, the shopper should be prepared to make a purchase. Shops with flexible prices do not accept merchandise returns.

The shopkeeper might settle on a lower price for the first sale of the day, or the final sale of the day, to bring good luck. When retailers change their format from being independents to being chains, they generally move away from flexible pricing. One reason is that store managers cannot be trusted to make the same decision an owner or operator would make.

Department stores are often the first fixed-price merchants to appear as a country develops economically. With so many salespeople in a department store, the pricing decisions need to be centrally made and communicated through fixed prices.

INFORMAL CREDIT

Small retailers frequently extend credit to their customers. This informal credit is used to stimulate sales and to develop a long-term partnership between the retailer and the consumer. Consumers may buy from a particular retailer because they can receive credit rather than because the retailer has the most attractive products and pricing.

The introduction of formal credit is an important step as a country becomes more economically developed. Formal credit can be taken by a consumer from one location to another. Some companies gain their market presence through attractive credit policies. Sears, Roebuck and Co. uses this strategy. Its lenient credit requirements enable young families or people with few credit alternatives to buy their first appliances from Sears. Credit is an important aspect in consumer freedom. It allows consumers to buy good quality products, perhaps not at the lowest possible price, but at a price they can afford over a specified period. In Mexico, a company called Eurika has also used this type of easy credit policy. In Eurika's case, a unique sales promotional program was also developed. Relatives in the United States can purchase electrical appliances for relatives or friends in Mexico. The use of formal credit allows consumers to make more rational purchase decisions for large-ticket items. In other words, they can select the lowest-priced/best-quality product rather than a product sold by a retailer who will finance the purchase.

Several of the macro-environmental factors described in Chapter 1 affect retailing in less developed countries. In such countries, it is likely that the government uses regulation to control distribution channels. Price controls are quite prevalent, products are subsidized, and rationing contributes to the black market. Consumers use forward buying when inflation is expected to cause prices to increase. In less developed countries, it is likely that the government owns distribution or cooperatives. Greece is an example of a country in which the government has controlled distribution of consumer products.

In less developed countries, retailers depend on suppliers to extend supplier credit. This ultimately causes retailers to become dependent on suppliers. Just as consumers become tied to retailers through the credit they owe, retailers become tied to the suppliers they owe. Among the Overseas Chinese (a term used to refer to Chinese people living in Taiwan. Singapore, Malaysia, the United States, and other countries), the Chinese business group extends credit to the persons who are a part of their group. This family funding replaces the venture capital available in other markets.

RETAIL EVOLUTION

SELLER'S MARKET TO BUYER'S MARKET

A **seller's market** exists when consumers want to buy more products than sellers can provide. Sellers have the power in this type of market, and consumers must settle for what is available. At Michigan State University, tickets to hockey games have sold out every season for more than 11 years. More people want to buy hockey tickets than the current supply provides. Those people who hold hockey tickets are subscribers who have bought tickets for years. In this instance, the ticket holders can sell their tickets for more than face value, a practice known as scalping.

Scalping occurs in retailing, also. In seller's markets, the sellers hold products that are in great demand. They can charge higher prices for these products. Seller's markets for most products exist in developing countries.

A **buyer's market** exists when sellers have more products available than consumers want. Here, sellers compete to gain sales, and buyers have the market strength. This system occurs in most developed countries. The competition for consumers' dollars reduces prices, benefiting consumers.

Instead of scalping, a buyer's market is characterized by discounting. Suppliers reduce their price to gain consumers' purchases. If the Michigan State hockey team did not do well for years, ticket holders might begin to sell their season tickets. In fact, this has happened with Michigan State University football tickets. At most home games, $20 tickets can be purchased at the door for $5. Football tickets have become a buyer's market.

The relationship between buyers and sellers is altered depending on whether the situation is a buyer's or a seller's market. Excellent research exploring this phenomenon is available. Kale developed several research propositions that highlight the differences between buyer's and seller's markets. **Propositions,** which are generalizations about how events are related, are the basis for theory. **Theory** is our best explanation for how a series of events are related. Good theory is just a summary of reality before we have identified what is real. Kale's research focused on manufacturer and supplier relationships, but with some altering of terms, his findings have great relevance to understanding the roles of retailers (buyers) and their suppliers (sellers). His generalizations also make a meaningful contribution to understanding the relationship between consumers (buyers) and retailers (sellers).

Kale presents his theory of relationships in three stages: initiation, implementation, and review (Table 3.2). I will discuss each of these stages separately to clarify how they relate to buyer's and seller's markets.

INITIATION This is the introductory stage of a buyer-seller relationship. In a buyer's market, the retailer will evaluate suppliers in an objective manner. Does this supplier have the quality of merchandise the retailer wants to sell in the store? Can this supplier provide good delivery and service? Does this supplier sell the same products to competitors? In a seller's market, the retailer does not have many choices of suppliers. Suppliers have the power. In a seller's market, the initiation process will be informal and the decision of whom to sell to will be based on subjective and personal criteria.

IMPLEMENTATION This is the performance part of the relationship. In a buyer's market, a supplier's performance will determine market power. If a supplier is providing a product that sells successfully and this product is consistently made available to the retailer, the supplier will have power. In a seller's market, there are few alternatives for the retailer, so performance of the supplier is not what conveys power. Power comes by virtue of the lack of alternative suppliers. Even if a supplier is not performing adequately, the retailer will continue to deal with the supplier because there are no alternatives. Because performance will not affect power, the supplier is inclined to provide poorer and poorer service.

TABLE 3.2

Differences in the Supplier-Retailer Relationship in a Buyer's versus a Seller's Market

Relationship Stage	Buyer's Market	Seller's Market
Initiation	▪ Formal, well-thought-out ▪ Supplier chooses retailer based on objective criteria	▪ Relatively less well-thought-out ▪ Supplier chooses retailer, based on relatively subjective and personal criteria ▪ Supplier has many choices of retailers, whereas retailer's choices are few
Implementation	Channel Power ▪ Supplier's role performance determines retailer's dependence and supplier's power	Channel Power ▪ The lack of alternative channel participation opportunities determines retailer's dependence and supplier's power
	Supplier's Power and Influence Strategies (to alter retailer's decision-making) ▪ Powerful supplier → unpressurized influence strategies ▪ Less powerful supplier → relatively pressurized influence strategies	Supplier's Power and Influence Strategies (to alter retailer's decision-making) ▪ Powerful supplier → relatively pressurized influence strategies ▪ Less powerful supplier → unpressurized influence strategies
Review	Retailer's Dependence and Attributed Supplier ▪ Negatively correlated to supplier ▪ Supplier attributes credit to retailer ▪ If losing, supplier blames self, retailer, or the situation; the supplier-retailer dependence varies accordingly ▪ Retailer is concerned more about equity in a channel relationship	Retailer's Dependence and Attributed Supplier ▪ Positively correlated to supplier ▪ Supplier attributes credit to self ▪ If losing, supplier and retailer blame one another; resulting in channel conflict ▪ Retailer grudgingly maintains the channel relationship; motivational investment is reduced; searches for another supplier, which is very time-consuming and may not materialize

Source: Kale, S. H. (1989). "Impact of Market Characteristics on Producer-Distributor Relationships." In Pellegrini, L., and S. K. Reddy, eds., *Retail and Marketing Channel,* New York: Routledge, pp. 100–114.

In a buyer's market, more powerful suppliers use unpressurized influence strategies, while less powerful suppliers use pressurized influence strategies. The more dependent the retailer is on the supplier, the less the retailer will acknowledge this dependence. In a seller's market, powerful suppliers use pressurized influence strategies and the less powerful use unpressurized influence strategies. The more dependent the retailer is on the supplier, the more power the retailer attributes to the supplier.

REVIEW PROCESS In a buyer's market, if the relationship is successful the supplier will credit the retailer. Suppliers are concerned with equity in a buyer-supplier relationship. This sets the stage for relationship marketing. In a seller's market, if a supplier is doing well, it credits itself. If the dyad is not doing well, they blame each other, creating channel conflict. In a seller's market, the retailer grudgingly continues the relationship, constantly looking for a new supplier. This search is time-consuming and detracts from current performance.

The role of retailers changes with economic development. In less developed countries, retailers sell whatever they can get. This situation is one of opportunistic sourcing. As retailers acquire more choices of suppliers, they take on a new role: retailers become merchandise assemblers.

THE IMPORTANCE OF RETAILER AS ASSEMBLER OF GOODS

I believe that the role of retailer as assembler of goods is an important mark of retail maturity as a country moves from a less developed to a more developed status. In less developed countries, retailers sell what they have access to. They do not search the market to find products that fit the needs of their clientele. As a country develops and competition increases, retailers need to differentiate themselves, focusing on products their customers really want and need. At this stage, retailers take on a different role. Rather than serving as warehouses of what is available, they become interpreters of their customer's tastes: gatekeepers to the desired products. They search the market looking for merchandise that distinguishes them, as retailers. The assumption of the role of gatekeeper is important. Before this transition occurs, consumers wander from one retailer to another. When the gatekeeper role emerges, retailers become the assemblers of goods for consumers. This eases the burden of shopping for consumers as retailers strive to offer consumers the best products for their money.

THEORY OF ECONOMIC DEVELOPMENT AND RETAIL CHANGE

Samiee[8] provides a summary of research propositions that can serve as the foundation for a theory of economic development and retail change. Although these propositions are an excellent contribution to international retailing research, I think several are incorrect or in need of modification. Table 3.3 provides examples of instances in which Saimee's explanation of the relationship does not seem accurate.

Siamee organizes the propositions under seven categories: environment, consumer characteristics, channel characteristics, retail and wholesaling practices, channel communication, market research, and channel performance.

TABLE 3.3

Analysis of Samiee's (1993) Research Propositions: Economic Development and Retail Change

Channel/Retailing Element	Proposition	Sternquist's Observations
Environment	The level of economic development significantly influences the structure of the distribution channels in less developed countries such that:	
	▮ Channels are longer and less efficient	▮ Longer yes, but this has nothing to do with efficiency
	▮ Channels are a major source of employment	▮ Not necessarily
	▮ Major segments of the population are self-sufficient (e.g., food and apparel)	▮ Not necessarily
	▮ There is a sellers' market in many product categories	▮ Yes, most sectors are seller's markets
	Government regulations and controls influence the distribution channels through:	
	▮ Frequent or ongoing price controls, subsidized products, and rationing leading to the presence of black markets	▮ Yes
	▮ Consumers practice forward-buying in hyper-inflationary environments	▮ Yes
	▮ Government-supported or -owned distributors and cooperatives	▮ Yes
	Buyers and sellers in the channel know each other well and channel operations are influenced by high-context cultures that impact various aspects of business communications and negotiations	Yes, high-context relationships are evident in the social dimensions of shopping
Consumer Characteristics	Consumer characteristics in less developed countries lead to retailers' need for smaller but more frequent purchases from their suppliers, which, in turn, may lead to product and package modification by manufacturers; typically, the following are expected:	
	▮ Smaller packages of products	▮ Yes
	▮ Smaller cases containing a larger variety of products	▮ Yes
	▮ Product modifications to ensure longer shelf-life	▮ Yes
	▮ Package modifications to ensure safe delivery	▮ Yes
	▮ Retailers offer credit to their regular clientele on an informal basis	▮ Yes

Continued

TABLE 3.3

Analysis of Samiee's (1993) Research Propositions: Economic Development and Retail Change

Channel/Retailing Element	Proposition	Sternquist's Observations
	▮ Shopping is a more important form of social interaction as compared with developed nations	▮ Yes
Channel Characteristics	Channel structures are fragmented and the networks are uncoordinated. The channel is further characterized by:	▮ Yes
	▮ Relatively small institutions	▮ Yes
	▮ Channel members are generalists and their functions become more specialized (i.e., separated) with economic development	▮ Yes, scrambled merchandise
	▮ Retail establishments vary in form and functions performed and may cater to a different class of customers as compared with developed nations	▮ Yes
	▮ Limited financial and managerial resources	▮ Yes
	▮ Adoption and popularity of self-service retailing are dependent on the availability of packaged goods and on a shortage of labor	▮ No, packaging follows the self-service industry; shortage of labor is not related to self-service, the origins of self-service are not related to cost reduction but instead to consumer exposure to products and prestige of the retail innovation; self-service stores first locate in wealthiest sections of the city
	▮ Limited presence of vertical marketing systems	▮ Yes
Retail and Wholesaling Practice	As compared with developed nations, less developed countries' retailing practices are characterized by:	
	▮ Limited working capital of channel members, particularly retailers	▮ Yes, capital if available comes from family members
	▮ Intermediaries typically obtain financing for purchases with no or low interest or carrying charges from suppliers	▮ Yes
	▮ Dominance of family-owned and -operated firms	▮ Yes
	▮ Sporadic or routine importing by various channel members	▮ Yes
	▮ Limited vendor loyalty	▮ Yes, this is elaborated and supported by Kale (see earlier discussion in this chapter)
	▮ More emphasis on carrying and dispensing bulk or staple products	▮ Yes

TABLE 3.3

Analysis of Samiee's (1993) Research Propositions: Economic Development and Retail Change

Channel/Retailing Element	Proposition	Sternquist's Observations
Channel Communication	Channel communication is characterized by the limited availability and use of print media and various forms of intra-channel promotion	■ No, informal means of communication are available; extensive print and radio communication are found in all but the most undeveloped countries
	Numerous brokers and agents are instrumental in the communications process as they expedite transactions, such that:	
	■ They assist in providing total market coverage	■ No
	■ They are specialized by customer or channel member, region, or product	■ No
Market Research	The following patterns are generally expected:	
	■ Little use of formal market information is made by less developed countries' channel members; use of market research increases with greater economic development and the size of the channel member; in less developed countries, retailers typically do not have market research departments and seldom use outside suppliers	■ No, the difference is probably related to size, not economic development
	■ Informal and underground distribution channels play major roles in LDCs and this activity is not reflected in official statistics	■ Yes, and this informal activity can be highly effective
Channel Performance	Retail performance is lower than in the developed markets and is characterized by:	
	■ Flexible, but generally low, channel markups	■ No; it is different for product groups but markups are higher with less competition and become lower with greater competition
	■ The practice of one-price policy increases with increased foreign participation in the distribution sector	■ No; fixed price comes with larger stores, or chain operations; it is not related to foreign retailers' market participation
	■ Prices, terms of sales, and payment arrangements are negotiable; low net profit margins	■ No

Samiee, S. (1993). "Retailing and Channel Considerations in Developing Countries: A Review and Research Propositions." *Journal of Business Research,* Vol. 27, pp. 103–130. Reprinted with permission from Elsevier Science Inc.

ENVIRONMENT

Channels in less developed countries are longer; however, channel length does not mean that the channel is inefficient. Long channels could mean that retailers are holding smaller inventory, or that they are selling very perishable products. The concept of channel length indicting inefficiency is simply inaccurate. For years, a popular argument held that Japan's distribution system is inefficient, because the Japanese have longer channels. But if one controls for the perishability of the product, there is no difference between channel length in the United States and Japan.

Governments do play a much greater role in less developed countries. Price controls, rules excluding foreign ownership, and state-owned distributors are some problems in this environment. Most developing countries have some laws that limit foreign ownership of retail activities.

CONSUMER CHARACTERISTICS

I think the propositions outlined by Saimee are accurate. Retailers need packaging to protect merchandise through the transportation and selling phase. In less developed countries, packaging is protective, not provocative. Shopping is an enjoyable activity, an important level of social interaction.

CHANNEL CHARACTERISTICS

Earlier, I used the term scrambled merchandise. Samiee uses the term retail generalists. We are observing the same phenomena. Retailers in less developed countries do not narrowly define their product offerings. They carry whatever products they think they can sell. Over the past two years, my colleagues who conduct research in Russia noticed that the kiosks in Moscow had begun to

Photo 3.5
These small shops in Mexico carry very mixed merchandise. The store at center right is closed; the sliding corrugated door pulls down and locks for security. When all of these shops are similarly closed, it is nearly impossible to tell that this is a shopping street. There is no window shopping in this neighborhood. *Courtesy of the author.*

define and focus their product lines. Previously, a kiosk might have sold razors, magazines, shirts, and gum. Now it might be focusing only on magazines.

Saimee makes a statement in this section regarding self-service retailing. He says that self-service retailing is dependent on the availability of packaged goods and on a shortage of labor. I believe he has the relationships reversed, and this is a serious error. Self-service enters less developed countries in a predictable pattern. The first self-service stores are supermarkets or superettes. Developers put these self-service stores in the wealthiest sections of the city. Prices in these first supermarkets are very high. They gain a successful niche with wealthy local residents and expatriates (foreigners) living in the area. Customers pay the high prices because the supermarket is considered a prestigious place to buy food and because it carries some imported products. The packaging industry to support this initial supermarket offering is developed by the supermarket itself. Supermarkets have their own shrink wrap and disposable trays. It is only later that an independent packaging industry emerges to provide service to the supermarkets. Also, self-service does not emerge to save labor costs. It originates to give consumers more control over their exposure to products, handling and examining the product.

RETAIL AND WHOLESALING PRACTICE

Samiee's propositions in this section parallel my findings. In less developed countries, the businesses are small and family owned. Working capital, if it is available at all, comes from other family members. Commercial credit is not available to these businesses.

There is limited vendor loyalty. Kale's work reinforces the point that in seller's markets the buyer is constantly looking for a better provider. How well a supplier performs its role does not define the retailer-supplier relationship; instead, the relationship continues because there are few alternatives.

CHANNEL COMMUNICATIONS

Channel communication in less developed countries can be very good, but it is informal communication. Word-of-mouth advertising is an important element in less developed country channel communications.

Except in the least developed countries, there are communication media. Print media actually flourish in less developed countries. China in the 1930s had many newspapers, radio stations, and television stations.

MARKET RESEARCH

Samiee considers the absence of formal market research a phenomenon of less developed countries. I do not agree. Few retailers in the United States conduct formal market research. Those that do are very large retailers. If the

Photo 3.6
Fresh fruit is displayed at this stall in a Lebanese market. Such markets do not have refrigeration. *Courtesy of the United Nations.*

size variable is removed, there is probably no difference between the use of market research in less developed and more developed countries. For example, most research conducted in Japan is grassroots research. Manufacturers hire employees to sell merchandise in retail stores. By having their employees, not the retailers, talk with customers, the manufacturers get direct feedback about their product lines.

CHANNEL PERFORMANCE

Samiee indicates that markups and net profit margins are lower in a less developed country and increase with greater development. I think the relationship is more complex than this. This proposition is also not compatible with one of Samiee's previous propositions stating that less developed countries are typically seller's markets. In seller's markets, there is little competition, and without competition, price is higher. Profit margins are also probably different for various types of merchandise. In food retailing, the lowest profit margins are found in the most developed countries. It may be that profit margins in certain types of merchandise have a curvilinear relationship. At lower levels of development, profit margins are the lowest, then they increase with market development, and finally fall again when competition becomes intense.

Samiee also offers a proposition to the effect that use of a one-price policy increases with greater foreign participation. I do not think a one-price policy has anything to do with foreign participation. It depends, instead, on store size and whether a store is operated by non-owners or family members. When larger stores, such as department stores, enter a market area, fixed pricing is adopted. These large stores can be foreign or local; the effect will be the same. Historical development of retailing in Japan, China, and Mexico supports this idea. The change agent that moves a society toward fixed pricing rather than bargaining is the size of the retailer and the need to give agency power to the salesperson to continue flexible pricing. **Agency power** means you give someone else the authority to act in your behalf. In a large store with many salespersons, an owner who did not adopt fixed pricing would have to entrust each employee with agency power to negotiate the sales price.

SUMMARY

Traditional retail systems have a number of characteristics. They are fragmented, with retailers operating as single units. This gives them limited negotiating power with suppliers. Markets in less developed countries are typically supplier's markets. This means there is a greater demand for products than there is a supply. Suppliers can dictate terms to buyers and have little motivation to provide good service.

Channels are long. Long channels correspond to small purchases. Consumers purchase a little each time they shop. Retailers carry small inventories. Each level of the channel depends on the next level to warehouse products.

Product variety is limited in less developed markets. There are few brand names and little competition other than price competition. Prices are flexible with informal bargaining and informal credit. This informal credit applies both to consumers and to interim channel credit.

KEY TERMS

agency power
buyer's market
central place theory
channel
fragmented markets
gross domestic product
propositions
scrambled merchandise
seller's market
theory
wet market

DISCUSSION QUESTIONS

1. How does female labor participation affect retailing? How do modern forms of retailing facilitate female labor participation?
2. Why do prices need to become fixed in a modern retail format?
3. Discuss the role of retail buyer as gatekeeper. How does this change the importance of retailing to the marketing system?
4. What is a fragmented retail system? Why would a retailer remain in a fragmented system when an integrated system would offer economies of scale?
5. How do the roles of retailer and supplier change when one is dealing with a seller's market versus a buyer's market?

ENDNOTES

1. Jordon, M. (1996). "Marketing Gurus Say: In India, Think Cheap, Lose the Cold Cereal." *Wall Street Journal,* October 11, p. A9.
2. Rostow, W. W. (1960). *The Stages of Economic Growth.* London: Cambridge University Press.
3. Cateora, P. R. (1996). *International Marketing.* 9th ed. Chicago: Irwin, p. 316.
4. Alawi, H. (1986). "Saudi Arabia: Making Sense of Self-Service." *International Marketing Review,* Spring, pp. 21–38.
5. Christaller, W. (1963). *Central Places in Southern Germany.* (C. Baskin, trans.). Englewood Cliffs, N.J.: Prentice-Hall.
6. Brown, S. (1995). "Christaller Knew My Father: Recycling Central Place Theory." *Journal of Macro Marketing,* Spring, pp. 60–73.
7. Berry, B. (1967). *Geography of Market Centres and Retail Distribution.* Englewood Cliffs, N.J.: Prentice-Hall.
8. Berry, B. (1963). *Commercial Structure and Commercial Blight; Retail Patterns and Processes in the City of Chicago.* Research Paper No. 85. Chicago: University of Chicago, Department of Geography.
9. Samiee, S. (1993). "Retailing and Channel Considerations in Developing Countries: A Review and Research Propositions," *Journal of Business Research,* Vol. 27, pp. 103–130.

CHAPTER 3 APPENDIX

Basic Economic Indicators of the World's Nations

	Population (millions) mid-1995	Surface area (thousands of sq. km)	GNP per capita[a] dollars 1995	GNP per capita[a] avg. ann. growth % 1985–95	PPP estimates of GNP per capita[b] US=100 1987	PPP estimates of GNP per capita[b] US=100 1995	Poverty % of people living on less than $1 a day (PPP) 1981–95	Life expectancy at birth (years) 1995	Adult illiteracy % 1995
Low-income economies	**3,179.9 t**	**40,606 t**	**430 w**	**3.8 w**				**63 w**	**34 w**
excluding China & India	**1,050.3 t**	**27,758 t**	**290 w**	**−1.4 w**				**56 w**	**46 w**
1 †Mozambique	16.2	802	80	3.6	2.5	3.0	—	47	60
2 Ethiopia	56.4	1,097	100	−0.3	2.0	1.7	33.8	49	65
3 Tanzania[c]	29.6	945	120	1.0	2.6	2.4	16.4	51	32
4 Burundi	6.3	28	160	−1.3	3.2	2.3	—	49	65
5 Malawi	9.8	118	170	−0.7	3.1	2.8	—	43	44
6 Chad	6.4	1,284	180	0.6	2.5	2.6	—	48	52
7 Rwanda	6.4	26	180	−5.4	3.8	2.0	45.7	46	40
8 Sierra Leone	4.2	72	180	−3.6	3.2	2.2	—	40	—
9 Nepal	21.5	141	200	2.4	4.0	4.3	53.1	55	73
10 Niger	9.0	1,267	220	—	3.6	2.8	61.5	47	86
11 Burkina Faso	10.4	274	230	−0.2	3.3	2.9	—	49	81
12 Madagascar	13.7	587	230	−2.2	3.1	2.4	72.3	52	—
13 Bangladesh	119.8	144	240	−2.1	4.8	5.1	—	58	62
14 Uganda	19.2	236	240	−2.7	4.7	5.5	50.0	42	38
15 Vietnam	73.5	332	240	—	—	—	—	68	6
16 Guinea-Bissau	1.1	36	250	−2.0	2.8	2.9	87.0	38	45
17 Haiti	7.2	28	250	−5.2	5.8	3.4	—	57	55
18 Mali	9.8	1,240	250	0.8	2.3	2.0	—	50	69
19 Nigeria	111.3	924	260	1.2	4.4	4.5	28.9	53	43
20 Yemen, Rep.	15.3	528	260	—	—	—	—	53	—
21 Cambodia	10.0	181	270	—	—	—	—	53	35
22 Kenya	26.7	580	280	0.1	5.7	5.1	50.2	58	22
23 Mongolia	2.5	1,567	310	−3.8	10.6	7.2	—	65	—
24 Togo	4.1	57	310	−2.7	5.5	4.2	—	56	48
25 Gambia, The	1.1	11	320	—	4.5	3.5	—	46	61
26 Central African Republic	3.3	623	340	−2.4	5.0	4.0	—	48	40
27 India	929.4	3,288	340	3.2[e]	4.4	5.2	52.5	62	48
28 Lao PDR	4.9	237	350	2.7	—	—	—	52	43
29 Benin	5.5	113	370	−0.3	6.9	6.5	—	50	63
30 Nicaragua	4.4	130	380	−5.4	11.8	7.4	43.8	68	34
31 Ghana	17.1	239	390	1.4	7.4	7.4	—	59	—
32 Zambia	9.0	753	400	−0.8	4.2	3.5	84.6	46	22
33 Angola	10.8	1,247	410	−6.1	8.9	4.9	—	47	—
34 Georgia[d]	5.4	70	440	−17.0	28.1	5.5	—	73	—

Continued

CHAPTER 3 APPENDIX

Basic Economic Indicators of the World's Nations

	Population (millions) mid-1995	Surface area (thousands of sq. km)	GNP per capita[a] dollars 1995	GNP per capita[a] avg. ann. growth % 1985–95	PPP estimates of GNP per capita[b] US=100 1987	PPP estimates of GNP per capita[b] US=100 1995	Poverty % of people living on less than $1 a day (PPP) 1981–95	Life expectancy at birth (years) 1995	Adult illiteracy % 1995
Low-income economies	**3,179.9t**	**40,606t**	**430w**	**3.8w**				**63w**	**34w**
excluding China & India	**1,050.3t**	**27,758t**	**290w**	**−1.4w**				**56w**	**46w**
35 Pakistan	129.9	796	460	1.2	8.4	8.3	11.6	60	62
36 Mauritania	2.3	1,026	460	0.5	6.0	5.7	31.4	51	—
37 Azerbaijan[d]	7.5	87	480	−16.3	21.8	5.4	—	70	—
38 Zimbabwe	11.0	391	540	−0.6	8.6	7.5	41.0	57	15
39 Guinea	6.6	246	550	1.4	—	—	26.3	44	—
40 Honduras	5.9	112	600	0.1	7.9	7.0	46.5	67	27
41 Senegal	8.5	197	600	—	7.3	6.6	54.0	50	67
42 China	1,200.2	9,561	620	8.3	6.3	10.8	29.4	69	19
43 Cameroon	13.3	475	650	−6.6	15.1	7.8	—	57	37
44 Côte d'Ivoire	14.0	322	660	—	8.2	5.9	17.7	55	60
45 Albania	3.3	29	670	—	—	—	—	73	—
46 Congo	2.6	342	680	−3.2	11.5	7.6	—	51	25
47 Kyrgyz Republic[d]	4.5	199	700	−6.9	13.6	6.7	18.9	68	—
48 Sri Lanka	18.1	66	700	2.6	10.6	12.1	4.0	72	10
49 Armenia[d]	3.8	30	730	−15.1	25.4	8.4	—	71	—
Middle-income economies	**1,590.9t**	**60,838t**	**2,390w**	**−0.7w**				**68w**	**18w**
Lower-middle-income	**1,152.6t**	**40,323t**	**1,670w**	**−1.3w**				**67w**	**—**
50 Lesotho	2.0	30	770	1.2	6.1	6.6	50.4	61	29
51 Egypt, Arab Rep.	57.8	1,001	790	1.1	14.3	14.2	7.6	63	49
52 Bolivia	7.4	1,099	800	1.8	9.1	9.4	7.1	60	17
53 Macedonia, FYR	2.1	26	860	—	—	—	—	73	—
54 Moldova[d]	4.3	34	920	—	—	—	6.8	69	—
55 Uzbekistan[d]	22.8	447	970	23.9	12.6	8.8	—	70	—
56 Indonesia	193.3	1,905	980	6.0	9.8	14.1	14.5	64	16
57 Philippines	68.6	300	1,050	1.5	10.3	10.6	27.5	66	5
58 Morocco	26.6	447	1,110	0.9	13.2	12.4	1.1	65	56
59 Syrian Arab Republic	14.1	185	1,120	0.9	18.5	19.7	—	68	—
60 Papua New Guinea	4.3	463	1,160	2.3	8.5	9.0	—	57	28
61 Bulgaria	8.4	111	1,330	22.6	23.4	16.6	2.6	71	—
62 Kazakstan[d]	16.6	2,717	1,330	28.6	24.2	11.2	—	69	—
63 Guatemala	10.6	109	1,340	0.3	13.2	12.4	53.3	66	44
64 Ecuador	11.5	284	1,390	0.8	15.8	15.6	30.4	69	10
65 Dominican Republic	7.8	49	1,460	2.1	13.7	14.3	19.9	71	18
66 Romania	22.7	238	1,480	23.8	22.2	16.2	17.7	70	—

CHAPTER 3 APPENDIX

Basic Economic Indicators of the World's Nations

	Population (millions) mid-1995	Surface area (thousands of sq. km)	GNP per capita[a] dollars 1995	GNP per capita[a] avg. ann. growth % 1985–95	PPP estimates of GNP per capita[b] US=100 1987	PPP estimates of GNP per capita[b] US=100 1995	Poverty % of people living on less than $1 a day (PPP) 1981–95	Life expectancy at birth (years) 1995	Adult illiteracy % 1995
Middle-income economies	**1,590.9t**	**60,838t**	**2,390w**	**−0.7w**				**68w**	**18w**
Lower-middle-income	**1,152.6t**	**40,323t**	**1,670w**	**−1.3w**				**67w**	—
67 Jamaica	2.5	11	1,510	3.6	11.3	13.1	4.7	74	15
68 Jordan	4.2	89	1,510	−4.5	23.8	15.1	2.5	70	13
69 Algeria	28.0	2,382	1,600	−2.4	26.5	19.6	1.6	70	38
70 El Salvador	5.6	21	1,610	2.8	8.2	9.7	—	67	29
71 Ukraine[d]	51.6	604	1,630	−9.2	20.7	8.9	—	69	—
72 Paraguay	4.8	407	1,690	1.2	13.3	13.5	—	68	8
73 Tunisia	9.0	164	1,820	1.9	18.3	18.5	3.9	69	33
74 Lithuania[d]	3.7	65	1,900	−11.7	25.2	15.3	2.1	69	—
75 Colombia	36.8	1,139	1,910	2.6	20.7	22.7	7.4	70	9
76 Namibia	1.5	824	2,000	2.9	15.8	15.4	—	59	—
77 Belarus[d]	10.3	208	2,070	−5.2	26.3	15.6	—	70	—
78 Russian Federation[d]	148.2	17,075	2,240	−5.1	30.9	16.6	1.1	65	—
79 Latvia[d]	2.5	65	2,270	−6.6	24.5	12.5	—	69	—
80 Peru	23.8	1,285	2,310	−1.6	17.9	14.0	49.4	66	11
81 Costa Rica	3.4	51	2,610	2.8	19.8	21.7	18.9	77	5
82 Lebanon	4.0	10	2,660	—	—	—	—	68	8
83 Thailand	58.2	513	2,740	8.4	16.2	28.0	0.1	69	6
84 Panama	2.6	76	2,750	−0.4	26.1	22.2	25.6	73	9
85 Turkey	61.1	779	2,780	2.2	20.4	20.7	—	67	18
86 Poland	38.6	313	2,790	1.2	21.5	20.0	6.8	70	—
87 Estonia[d]	1.5	45	2,860	−4.3	25.5	15.6	6.0	70	—
88 Slovak Republic	5.4	49	2,950	−2.8	17.6	13.4	12.8	72	—
89 Botswana	1.5	582	3,020	6.1	15.3	20.7	34.7	68	30
90 Venezuela	21.7	912	3,020	0.5	33.0	29.3	11.8	71	9
Upper-middle-income	**438.3t**	**20,514t**	**4,260w**	**0.2w**				**69w**	**14w**
91 South Africa	41.5	1,221	3,160	−1.1	22.4	18.6	23.7	64	18
92 Croatia	4.8	57	3,250	—	—	—	—	74	—
93 Mexico	91.8	1,958	3,320	0.1	27.8	23.7	14.9	72	10
94 Mauritius	1.1	2	3,380	5.4	39.0	49.0	—	71	17
95 Gabon	1.1	268	3,490	−8.2	—	—	—	55	37
96 Brazil	159.2	8,512	3,640	−0.8	24.2	20.0	28.7	67	17
97 Trinidad and Tobago	1.3	5	3,770	−1.7	38.1	31.9	—	72	2
98 Czech Republic	10.3	79	3,870	−1.8	44.9	36.2	3.1	73	—
99 Malaysia	20.1	330	3,890	5.7	22.9	33.4	5.6	71	17

Continued

CHAPTER 3 APPENDIX

Basic Economic Indicators of the World's Nations

	Population (millions) mid-1995	Surface area (thousands of sq. km)	GNP per capita[a] dollars 1995	GNP per capita[a] avg. ann. growth % 1985–95	PPP estimates of GNP per capita[b] US=100 1987	PPP estimates of GNP per capita[b] US=100 1995	Poverty % of people living on less than $1 a day (PPP) 1981–95	Life expectancy at birth (years) 1995	Adult illiteracy % 1995
Upper-middle-income	**438.8t**	**20,514t**	**4,260w**	**0.2w**				**69w**	**14w**
100 Hungary	10.2	93	4,120	−1.0	28.9	23.8	0.7	70	—
101 Chile	14.2	757	4,160	6.1	24.6	35.3	15.0	72	5
102 Oman	2.2	212	4,820	0.3	33.2	30.2	—	70	—
103 Uruguay	3.2	177	5,170	3.1	23.6	24.6	—	73	3
104 Saudi Arabia	19.0	2,150	7,040	−1.9	43.0	—	—	70	37
105 Argentina	34.7	2,767	8,030	1.8	31.6	30.8	—	73	4
106 Slovenia	2.0	20	8,200	—	—	—	—	74	—
107 Greece	10.5	132	8,210	1.3	44.2	43.4	—	78	—
Low- & middle-income	**4,770.8t**	**101,444t**	**1,090w**	**0.4w**				**65w**	**30w**
Sub-Saharan Africa	**583.3t**	**24,271t**	**490w**	**−1.1w**				**52w**	**43w**
East Asia and Pacific	**1,706.4t**	**16,249t**	**800w**	**7.2w**				**68w**	**17w**
South Asia	**1,243.0t**	**5,133t**	**350w**	**2.9w**				**61w**	**51w**
Europe and Central Asia	**487.6t**	**24,355t**	**2,220w**	**−3.5w**				**68w**	**—**
Middle East and N. Africa	**272.4t**	**11,021t**	**1,780w**	**−0.3w**				**66w**	**39w**
Latin America and Caribbean	**477.9t**	**20,414t**	**3,320w**	**0.3w**				**69w**	**13w**
High-income economies	**902.2t**	**32,039t**	**24,930w**	**1.9w**				**77w**	**—**
108 Korea, Rep.	44.9	99	9,700	7.7	27.3	42.4	—	72	f
109 Portugal	9.9	92	9,740	3.6	41.6	47.0	—	75	—
110 Spain	39.2	505	13,580	2.6	50.5	53.8	—	77	—
111 New Zealand	3.6	271	14,340	0.8	63.3	60.6	—	76	f
112 Ireland	3.6	70	14,710	5.2	44.2	58.1	—	77	f
113 †Israel	5.5	21	15,920	2.5	56.3	61.1	—	77	—
114 †Kuwait	1.7	18	17,390	1.1	86.3	88.2	—	76	21
115 †United Arab Emirates	2.5	84	17,400	−2.8	84.4	61.1	—	75	21
116 United Kingdom	58.5	245	18,700	1.4	72.0	71.4	—	77	f
117 Australia	18.1	7,713	18,720	1.4	70.1	70.2	—	77	f
118 Italy	57.2	301	19,020	1.8	72.5	73.7	—	78	f
119 Canada	29.6	9,976	19,380	0.4	84.6	78.3	—	78	f
120 Finland	5.1	338	20,580	−0.2	72.9	65.8	—	76	f
121 †Hong Kong	6.2	1	22,990[e]	4.8	70.7	85.1	—	79	8
122 Sweden	8.8	450	23,750	−0.1	77.7	68.7	—	79	f

CHAPTER 3 APPENDIX

Basic Economic Indicators of the World's Nations

	Population (millions) mid-1995	Surface area (thousands of sq. km)	GNP per capita[a] dollars 1995	GNP per capita[a] avg. ann. growth % 1985–95	PPP estimates of GNP per capita[b] US=100 1987	PPP estimates of GNP per capita[b] US=100 1995	Poverty % of people living on less than $1 a day (PPP) 1981–95	Life expectancy at birth (years) 1995	Adult illiteracy % 1995
High-income economies	**902.2t**	**32,039t**	**24,930w**	**1.9w**				**77w**	—
123 Netherlands	15.5	37	24,000	1.9	70.5	73.9	—	78	*f*
124 Belgium	10.1	31	24,710	2.2	76.3	80.3	—	77	*f*
125 France	58.1	552	24,990	1.5	77.6	78.0	—	78	*f*
126 †Singapore	3.0	1	26,730	6.2	56.1	84.4	—	76	9
127 Austria	8.1	84	26,890	1.9	75.0	78.8	—	77	*f*
128 United States	263.1	9,364	26,980	1.3	100.0	100.0	—	77	*f*
129 Germany	81.9	357	27,510	—	—	74.4	—	76	*f*
130 Denmark	5.2	43	29,890	1.5	78.7	78.7	—	75	*f*
131 Norway	4.4	324	31,250	1.7	78.6	81.3	—	78	*f*
132 Japan	125.2	378	39,640	2.9	75.3	82.0	—	80	*f*
133 Switzerland	7.0	41	40,630	0.2	105.4	95.9	—	78	*f*
World	**5,673.0t**	**133,483t**	**4,880w**	**0.8w**				**67w**	—

†Economics classified by the United Nations or otherwise regarded by their authorities as developing. [a] Atlas method. [b] Purchasing power parity (PPP) as a percentage of purchasing power in the United States. [c] In all tables, GDP and GNP cover mainland Tanzania. [d] Estimates for economies of the former Soviet Union are preliminary; their classification will be kept under review. [e] Data refer to GDP. [f] According to UNESCO, illiteracy is less than 5 percent. t. = total w. = weighted average.

Source: World Bank. (1997). *World Development Report*. 1997. New York: Oxford University Press, pp. 214–215.

ELEVEn
が安く買える!
Shop America
カタログ
ショッピング
ショップ-アメリカ
会員
募集
ペンタの空

4

Licensing, Franchising, and Strategic Alliances

After reading this chapter, you will understand:

- Why retailers license or franchise their businesses.
- The theoretical basis for franchising and international franchising.
- The role of strategic international alliances for retailers and the criteria for selecting partners.
- How retailers can develop partnership alternatives that help them to sustain important competitive advantages.

AS WE SAW IN CHAPTER 1, retailers expanding internationally do not have all the options available to manufacturing companies. Manufacturers can produce at home and then simply sell their products overseas. International retailers must have a presence in the market. The levels of international involvement for retailers are licensing, franchising, joint venture, and wholly owned subsidiary. Of these, licensing offers the least control; a wholly owned subsidiary offers the most. On a continuum it would look something like this:

Licensing . . . . Franchising . . . . Joint Venture . . . . Wholly Owned Subsidiary

Least Control ⟷ *Most Control*

In this chapter, I first explore the reasons why retailers would choose to license or franchise their businesses. Next, I present a theory of franchising that differentiates among four types of franchisors. A discussion of strategic alliances follows, in which two types of strategic alliances are contrasted. The chapter concludes with a discussion of the ways in which companies can use strategic alliances to their greatest benefit when expanding into international markets.

LICENSING

Licensing refers to the offering of a company's know-how or other intangible assets to another company for a fee, royalty, or other type of payment. The licensee obtains the use of the licensor's proprietary knowledge. The licensor receives financial gain and the opportunity to have greater visibility for its retail concept. The drawback is that the licensee partner may eventually become a competitor, gaining market momentum with the specific knowledge gained from the licensor.

A retail company that allows a foreign retailer to use its company name has probably entered into a licensing arrangement. Promodès, a French hypermarket retailer, has a licensing contract with a retailer in Taiwan. Promodès does not have any influence over the licensee's operations. Instead it offers the licensee the chance to buy its merchandise, including Promodès private label products. The licensee can also hire Promodès executives as consultants, but the Taiwanese interests must pay for this service.

There are great risks in licensing. The most important risk is that the company is giving up one of its most important assets, its company name. If the licensee runs the company in a sloppy manner, it reflects on the licensor. Furthermore, licensing agreements may offer little protection to the licensor. Table 4.1 provides an overview of important considerations that should be included in a licensing agreement. Generally a licensor receives 5% of sales royalty. However, this can vary. Walt Disney World Co. receives 7% of royalties from its Japanese licensee. When it decided to open a theme park in Europe, Disney had learned from its licensee arrangement in Japan. This time the company chose a joint venture arrangement that would give it more control.

Manufacturers are more likely than retailers to use licensing. A manufacturer may license a retailer or manufacturer in a foreign country to produce products under its name. The products are generally meant to be sold in that foreign country. The products produced under the licensing arrangement may be the same quality as those produced in the manufacturer's other factories, or they may not.

Retailing is a way of doing business, a learning-by-doing type of education. Large-scale retailers are more likely to license than to franchise. Specialty stores, are more likely to offer a franchise arrangement. The designations used in Chapter 1—multinational versus global retailers—are helpful here. International expansion using a multinational format means the retailer uses decentralized management and adjusts the store to cultural differences. This

TABLE 4-1

Elements of a Licensing Contract

Technology Package

- Definition/description of the licensed industrial property (patents, trademarks, know-how)
- Know-how to be supplied and its method of transfer
- Supply of raw materials, equipment, and intermediate goods

Use Conditions

- Field of use of licensed technology
- Territorial rights for manufacture and sale
- Sublicensing rights
- Safeguarding trade secrets
- Responsibility for defense/infringement action on patents and trademarks
- Exclusion of competitive products
- Exclusion of competitive technology
- Maintenance of product standards
- Performance requirements
- Rights of licensee to new products and technology
- Reporting requirements
- Auditing/inspection rights of licensor
- Reporting requirements of licensee

Compensation

- Currency of payment
- Responsibilities for payment of local taxes
- Disclosure fee
- Running royalties
- Minimum royalties
- Lump-sum royalties
- Technical assistance fees
- Sales to and/or purchases from licensee
- Fees for additional new products
- Grantback of product improvements by licensee
- Other compensation

Other Provisions

- Contract law to be followed
- Duration and renewal of contract
- Cancellation/termination provisions
- Procedures for the settlement of disputes
- Responsibility for government approval of the license agreement

Source: Adapted from Johansson, J. K. (1997). *Global Marketing.* New York: Times Mirror Books, p. 196.

Photo 4.1
The GUM department store in Moscow, Russia, leases space to other retailers, such as Galleries Lafayette shown here. This GUM location, close to Red Square and the Kremlin, is very desirable.
Courtesy of WWD.

format is more compatible with licensing than with franchising. International expansion using a global format means the retailer uses centralized management, a standard retail offering throughout the world, and often private label merchandise. This format is more characteristic of franchising.

FRANCHISING

Franchising is a type of licensing arrangement that provides the seller with greater control over the retail format. A **franchise** is the right to operate a business under a company's name. The **franchisor** is selling the right to a proven way of doing business. The **franchisee** is buying this right. McDonald's Corp. is a worldwide franchisor. It sells the right to use the McDonald's name and method of operation. If you decided to open a McDonald's restaurant, you would be a franchisee. In the most tightly controlled franchise operations, a company provides a complete retail operation. The companies with the most successful international franchise operations are those that have developed a strong franchise network in their home market before internationalizing.

Franchisees may receive a total system for conducting business, including how to recruit and train employees. The local franchisee raises the necessary capital and manages the franchise, paying an initial fee and a royalty percentage on total sales to the franchisor. Table 4.2 provides examples of several major international franchisors and summarizes their requirements for opening one of their franchises.

Under U.S. law, the basic elements of a franchise include:

- A contract (but it need not be in writing to be covered by the U.S. statutes).
- A system.
- A branding, i.e., trademark, service mark, trade name, etc.
- A granting of rights.
- Payment of money.

Franchising has grown rapidly. In 1971, approximately 150 U.S. companies were involved in international franchising. The number increased to 354 by 1986.[1] The International Franchise Association surveyed its members in 1992, finding that one-half of the franchisors without foreign units planned to expand internationally, and 93% of those with international operations intended to increase the size of those operations.[2]

There are two general types of franchises, direct and master. A **direct franchise** is given to each individual store owner. Each application is considered separately. One individual might obtain multiple franchises, but each is applied for individually. The advantage of this type of franchise is that it is more likely to consist of owner-operators. These owner-operators will care for the store differently than hired managers.

The second type of franchise, a **master franchise,** is given to an individual who is then given the right to develop a particular state, country, or region. The holder of a master franchise is generally given the right to sublease franchise agreements throughout the region. A master franchise holder becomes an intermediary between the corporate franchisor and the individual franchisees. This type of franchise is the newest form of retail expansion. Athlete's Foot Group, Inc. has used this method to expand internationally, awarding a master franchise for each country.

General Nutrition Companies, Inc. (GNC) is a provider of vitamins and nutritional supplements in the United States. It operates 3,047 retail stores in all 50 states, Puerto Rico, and 18 foreign countries. Of these, 1,873 are company-owned and 1,174 are franchised. Recently, GNC gave its Israeli-market master franchise to an Israeli citizen who had operated one of the company's most successful U.S. franchise locations in the 1990s before returning to Israel. By the year 2003, GNC estimates that 15 stores will be opened in Israel.

TABLE 4.2

Summary of Franchise Requirements of Selected International Retail Franchisors

Name and Address of Business	Product or Service Offering	International Locations
The Athlete's Foot 1950 Vaughn Rd. Kennesaw, GA 30144 (800) 524-6444	Athletic footwear	Located in over 20 countries, including France, Canada, and Australia
Baskin-Robbins 31 Baskin Robbins Pl. Glendale, CA 91201 (800) 331-0031	Food: ice cream and yogurt	Located in 44 countries, including India
Candleman Corp. 1021 Industrial Park Rd. P.O. Box 731 Brainerd, MN 56401 (800) 328-3453	Candles and candle accessories	Located in Canada and the United States
Dunkin' Donuts 14 Pacella Park Dr. Randolph, MA 02368 (800) 777-9983	Food: donuts, coffee, muffins, and bagels	Located in over 20 countries including China and Israel
Golf USA Inc. 3705 W. Memorial Rd., Ste. 801 Oklahoma City, OK 73120 (800) 488-1107	Golf apparel and equipment	Located in five countries including Canada
The Mad Science Group 5460 Royalmount, Ste. 204 Mount Royal, QUE H4P 1H7 Canada (514) 344-6691	Children's science programs and products	Located in Canada and the United States
Mail Boxes Etc. 6060 Cornerstone Ct. West San Diego, CA 92121-3795 (800) 456-0414	Mail services, packaging, and shipping	Located in over 50 countries, including Spain, Israel, and Thailand
Mango P.O. Box 280 08184 Palau de Plegamans Barcelona, Spain (34-3) 864-44 44	Fashionable women's apparel	Located in various countries, including Spain, France, Greece, and Portugal
MotoPhoto Inc. 4444 Lake Center Dr. Dayton, OH 45426 (800) 733-6686	Photo processing, camera accessories, and portrait studios	Located in Canada, Scandinavia, and the United States

Franchising Fee	Capital Requirements	Training and Support Available
$25,000	$175,000–$325,000	**Yes:** two-week training program and ongoing support provided
$15,000	$60,000–$89,000	**Yes:** not specified
$25,000	Approximately $200,000	**Yes:** start-up assistance and support provided
$40,000	$200,000 liquid; $400,000 minimum net worth	**Yes:** not specified
$30,000–$40,000	$156,400–$312,500	**Yes:** one-week classroom and one-week on-site training; support also provided
$23,500	None	**Yes:** not specified
$24,950	$97,430–$145,650 (total investment)	**Yes:** two-week training course, one-week in-store training; and ongoing support provided
$35,000	Not specified	**Yes:** support provided
$35,000	$100,000 cash investment; $176,000 total investment	**Yes:** not specified

Continued

TABLE 4.2

Summary of Franchise Requirements of Selected International Retail Franchisors

Name and Address of Business	Product or Service Offering	International Locations
Pearle Vision, Inc. 2534 Royal Ln. Dallas, TX 75229 (972) 277-5000	Optical retail outlet	Located in six countries, including Canada, and the U.S. Virgin Islands
Software City 26 W. Forest Ave. Englewood, NJ 07631 (201) 569-8900	Computers and computer-related products	Located in four countries including: United States, Guam, Saudi Arabia, and Canada
Subway 325 Bic Drive Milford, CT 06460 (203) 877-4281	Food: submarine sandwiches and salads	Located in 55 countries, including Brazil, Australia, and Peru
Taco Bell Corp. (Pepsico Inc.) 1790 Von Karman Irvine, CA 92714 (714) 863-4500	Food: Mexican fast food	Located in 5 countries
USA Baby 857 N. Larch Ave. Elmhurst, IL 60126 (800) 323-4108	Infant and children's furniture	Located in Canada and the United States

References for franchise chart: *The Franchise Handbook* (Summer 1997), published by Enterprise Magazines, Inc., Wisconsin.

The Athlete's Foot: *The Franchise Handbook,* p. 207. Also used: http://www.theathletesfoot.com/France.htm; also: http://www.theathletesfoot.com/Canada.htm; also: http://www.theathletesfoot.com/Australa.htm; also. http://www.betheboss.com.

Baskin-Robbins: *The Franchise Handbook,* p. 123. Also used: http://www3elibrary.com and http://www.franchise-update.com/india.htm.

Candleman Corp: *The Franchise Handbook,* p. 153. Also used: http://www.franchise1.com/comp/candle.html.

Dunkin' Donuts: *The Franchise Handbook,* p. 115. Also used: http://www.franchise1.com/comp/dunkin1.html; also: http://www.seattle-pi.com/pi/getaways/010997/chi09.html.

Golf USA: *The Franchise Handbook,* p. 208.

The Mad Science Group: *The Franchise Handbook,* p. 82.

Franchising Fee	Capital Requirements	Training and Support Available
$30,000	$134,000–$2,472,750; $110,000 cash investment	**Yes:** not specified
$15,000	$50,000–$200,000	**Yes:** intensive training program and support is available
$10,000	$64,170–$149,950	**Yes:** two-week training and follow-up support provided
$35,000	$200,000 net worth; $125,000 liquid assets	**Yes:** not specified
$7,500–$16,500	$200,000–$250,000	**Yes:** not specified

Mail Boxes Etc.: *The Franchise Handbook,* p. 74. Also used: http://www.mbe.com

Mango: http://www.entremkt.com; also: http://www.mango.es/e/fue.htm

MotoPhoto: *The Franchise Handbook,* p. 185. Also used: http://www.franchise-update.com/motopho.htm

Pearle Vision: *The Franchise Handbook,* p. 182. Also used: http://www.elibrary.com

Software City: *The Franchise Handbook,* p. 88.

Subway: *The Franchise Handbook,* p. 150. Also used: http://www.franchise@subway.com/franchise/international/location.htm

Taco Bell Corp.: *The Franchise Handbook,* p. 129.

USA Baby: *The Franchise Handbook.* p. 84.

Source: Compiled by the author.

THEORY OF FRANCHISING

There are three perspectives that can explain why a firm would decide to franchise: (1) to extend limited resources, (2) to improve administrative efficiency, and (3) to provide risk management. The first perspective suggests that firms franchise to extend their scarce corporate resources. Because the franchisee puts up an initial fee and much of the initial capital investment, franchisors can expand their markets without having to generate capital themselves. This may be particularly relevant to fast-food franchises, for whom many units are needed to achieve brand name recognition and market share.

The administrative efficiency perspective derives from **agency theory,** which predicts that individuals who own their own stores will be more likely to perform at a high level than would hired managers. Owners of franchised units earn salary in relation to performance and are less likely to need monitoring. Hired managers can be monitored, but at a great cost to the company. For instance, when Taco Bell Corp. uses hired managers, the company relies on a variety of incentives to enhance the managers' performance. It pays higher-than-industry-average salaries and gives managers more decision-making and unit-performance bonuses.

The final perspective for explaining the decision to franchise is risk management. This view suggests that franchisors will reduce risk by using corporate ownership only in areas that are more reliable and will franchise in locations that may have higher risk. Higher risk may be due to geographical distance and cultural differences.[3] This idea is supported by the practice of franchisors who repurchase franchise units that yield higher sales.[4]

Experience and size are important factors that help determine whether a company will pursue international franchising.[5] Both experience and size can help reduce the percieved risk of international operations. The primary reasons companies give for not expanding internationally are sufficient opportunities at home and lack of international knowledge and competencies.[6]

As we will see in the next section, a successful international franchising strategy depends on maximizing both managerial abilities and risk management. The theory presented next organizes international franchisors into four groups.

THEORY OF INTERNATIONAL FRANCHISING

Fladmoe-Lindquist, in an article on international franchising,[7] identifies a typology for understanding international franchise types. The typology utilizes resource-based theory. According to this theory, know-how-based resources or routines for operating provide competitive advantage to firms. In addition, some companies are simply better than others at generating ideas and new ways to do things. Resource-based theory emphasizes the importance of not just possessing resources, but of continual organization learning. Growth of a firm involves combining existing resources and capabilities with the ability to develop new resources and capabilities. Effective learning requires that the franchisor acquire and process information, thus creating knowledge. This is the basis for new franchise strategies for international franchisors as they learn about the international competitive environment.

Table 4.3 is a summary of Fladmoe-Lindquist's typology. She identifies four types of international franchisors: constrained franchisors, integrating franchisors, conventional franchisors, and worldwide franchisors. An important point made by Fladmoe-Lindquist is that learning and capabilities are not constant over time. The ability of companies to learn and integrate knowledge is stronger at some points in time than at others. This helps to explain why franchisors expand at some times, retreat at others, and sit idle for periods of time.

Constrained franchisors have limited international management capabilities and little capacity for learning. A company in this category is not likely to pursue significant international franchise development. Such "locally international" franchisors will limit their international expansion to the country closest to them, geographically or culturally. Many American companies have extended their franchise operations to Canada but have little interest in going elsewhere. Bruegger's Bagels is an example of a constrained franchisor. Bruegger's opened its first bagel shop in 1983 but did not begin franchising until 1991. The company's international growth interest is limited to Canada.[8]

Integrating franchisors have limited international franchising capabilities but considerable capacity for learning from experience and integrating experiences into operations. These firms are more likely to initiate international expansion early in their life cycle. The British franchisor Tie Rack Plc fits this typology. Tie Rack expanded within Great

TABLE 4.3

International Franchising Capabilities and Capacity for Development

Capacity for Developing International Capabilities	Existing International Franchising Capabilities	
	Low	**High**
High	*Integrating franchisors* ▮ Pursue cautious growth ▮ Use multiple forms of franchising ▮ Proactive evaluation	*Worldwide franchisors* ▮ Focus on global markets ▮ Use multiple forms of franchising ▮ Both proactive and reactive
Low	*Constrained franchisors* ▮ Locally international ▮ Limited involvement in international markets ▮ Reactive evaluation	*Conventional franchisors* ▮ Focus on several foreign markets ▮ Use fewer forms of franchising ▮ Often reactive with some proactive efforts

Fladmoe-Lindquist, K. (1996). "International Franchising: Capabilities and Development." *Journal of Business Venturing*, Vol. 11, p. 428. Reprinted wtih permission from Elsevier Science Inc.

Britain before considering international expansion. The company enters each market using an approach that reflects an awareness of different national tastes, regulations, and franchise partners. The French market was entered using a master license with a joint venture partner. In Norway, a direct license for a single shop with an independent franchisee was used instead. Tie Rack entered the U.S. market with a wholly owned subsidiary of the franchisor.[9]

Conventional franchisors have some of the capabilities needed for international expansion but do not have a great ability to develop what is needed to succeed in a broader global setting. If they expand internationally, retailers in this group typically find themselves in a less-than-ideal location. They are likely to enter a market and then withdraw. These franchisors are also apt to expand into international franchising through foreign solicitations by prospective franchisees. A businessperson from South Africa who approaches Gap Inc., a retailer of casual clothing, about opening a Gap franchise in Cape Town, is an example of a foreign solicitation by a prospective franchisee. Gap has not selected South Africa as a strategic area where it should expand its offerings. It is simply responding to an offer from an outside businessperson.

This is similar to what happens to manufacturing firms. Many manufacturing firms begin their international involvement responding to unsolicited orders from foreign countries: an order is placed by a company in a foreign country, the manufacturer responds by exporting the product to them. It is a first step in internationalization, but it is an opportunistic, not a strategic decision. The British franchisor, Fastframe, fits this profile. The firm had been successful in Britain, but was not really ready for international expansion. An American convinced Fastframe to expand to California. Although the firm has been moderately successful, management admits they made many mistakes in the initial effort. This includes poor research regarding project viability, poor site selection, and short-sighted contract provisions that constrained the franchisor.[10]

Worldwide franchisors are generally larger franchisors with a greater amount of experience and greater capabilities in both administrative efficiency and host country risk management. These franchisors operate in many countries. They use a variety of ownership and franchise agreement configurations. They have operated internationally for a long period of time, gathering additional knowledge in a variety of markets. McDonald's would fit into this group. These companies make mistakes during their early international expansion efforts, but they integrate these experiences into their international franchising routines and capabilities and go on to hold successful worldwide positions.

A retailer may start as one type of franchise developer and shift to another typology. A traditional method of movement is for a constrained franchisor to become a conventional franchisor. In this scenario, a domestic or "locally international" franchisor moves to a broader international position without having internalized or integrated any new knowledge into the franchise operations. The company is able to follow this path because it has

Photo 4.2
A mother and child are leaving a 7-Eleven store in Japan. These convenience stores offer non-product services, such as fax facilities and payment centers for purchasing from catalogs or paying utility bills. *Courtesy of AP/ Wide World Photos.*

been relatively successful at home and in neighboring markets. It believes it is time to attempt a more extensive international position. However, this can be a risky move. Success in home and neighboring markets combined with a lower level of "international awareness" can result in expansion to foreign markets before the company develops an understanding of host country risk. Actually, success is a very poor teacher, because when you succeed, you rarely go back and examine why you succeeded. Greater learning comes from failure, or at least problems that need to be attended to. Midas, a U.S. automobile parts retailer, entered the British market using home-based corporate employees. The employees were sent on temporary rather than permanent assignments. They missed an important opportunity to develop their international capabilities with a permanent, locally based organization. This is an example of a company moving from constrained to conventional franchisor. Most of Midas's British franchise units failed.

Companies may also move from constrained to integrating franchisors. This move occurs primarily among domestic franchisors who increase their set of capabilities before attempting to broaden their international operations. This is a proactive pattern of internationalization. Tie Rack's expansion into France, Scandinavia, and the United States reflects this type of analytical capabilities development.[11] Tie Rack used each international step to broaden its knowledge and capabilities before entering another geographical area.

A franchisor that maintains the learning capacity developed as an integrating franchisor may develop into a worldwide franchisor. The path generally begins with a retailer moving from a constrained to an integrating and then to a worldwide franchisor. Subway's ability to stay entrepreneurial[12] and Midas's successful expansion to other countries after its initial failure in Great Britain are good examples of this route.[13]

Some companies make the change from conventional franchisor to worldwide franchisor. This change requires that the company put great energy into finding new ideas and products for foreign markets. This type of franchisor usually finds itself operating in several international markets as a series of reactive responses to foreign franchisees. This happened to International Dairy Queen Inc. during the early days of its international expansion. The company found itself in less obscure markets because potential franchisees solicited it. Dairy Queen was smart enough to recognize that additional skills and capabilities were needed to continue successful operations.

The last type of movement occurs among franchisors with high capabilities from the start. These companies move from integrating franchisors to worldwide franchisors. They begin operations already in a learning mode and continue to integrate new information while gaining resources and capabilities along the way. If the capacity for learning and integration does not diminish, such firms are likely to expand worldwide more quickly than any other type of franchisor. As Fladmoe-Lindquist's international franchisor typology emphasizes, a company's capabilities (ownership advantages) and willingness and readiness to learn from previous actions will determine its ability to take advantage of international franchising opportunities.

REGULATION OF FRANCHISING

Most countries do not have laws that deal specifically with franchising. Although the United States—the leader in franchise development—does have specific franchising laws, in Europe, only France and Spain have such laws. Franchising thrives in Japan, yet there is no specific law that relates to this business activity.

Central and South America, including Mexico, have experienced a great increase in franchise development. There are more than 800 members in Latin American franchise associations. In 1994, Mexico introduced a set of disclosure requirements that are similar to the franchise laws in the United States and France. Brazil enacted its own franchising law about the same time as Mexico. Both Mexico's and Brazil's laws include a stipulation that the franchisee has 10 days to review the information and make a decision regarding the franchise purchase. Spain's law requires that franchisors register their companies with a government registry and deliver key investment information to prospective franchisees at least 20 days before the franchisee signs the purchase contract or pays any money. Russia has a franchise law that relies less on the delivery of investment information and more on registration and requirements of the franchise relationship.

Running a successful international franchising empire requires careful and continuous quality control. McDonald's restaurants are an example of a tightly run and successful franchising system. McDonald's franchise system is considered one of the most successful in the world. McDonald's has a reputation for solid franchisor-franchisee relationships. Its franchise system is built on the idea that McDonald's Corp. should only make money from its franchisees' food sales. McDonald's headquarters does not sell equipment, food, or packaging to its franchisees. All equipment and supplies are purchased from company-approved, third-party suppliers. When this philosophy was originated, it was quite unique. Until that time, franchise operations made much of their money by selling equipment.

When a franchisee in Paris failed to keep its restaurant clean, McDonald's terminated the relationship. The franchisee took McDonald's to court but lost and received a scolding from the French judge for letting a great organization like McDonald's down.

Recently, franchisors have begun teaming business concepts together. The idea of dual branding or co-branding is changing the look of franchising by combining two or more concepts under one roof. Ideally, co-branding creates synergy between concepts. Baskin-Robbins and Dunkin' Donuts offer this type of synergy. Traffic is highest for Dunkin' Donuts in the morning and highest for Baskin-Robbins in the afternoon.

Franchising allows retailers to expand very rapidly because they are relying on the capital invested by franchisees. This system works particularly well for specialty stores. The Body Shop is one of the best known and most successful international franchising operations. If the company had used internal funds for expansion, it would probably still have shops only in small towns in Great Britain. Benetton began as a franchisor but now only supplies merchandise to the affiliated but independent Benetton stores.

As previously noted, the major problem with franchising is that the founding company relinquishes its company secrets to the franchisee. The company gains quick growth and immediate returns but loses control of its company secrets and the information that has made it unique. Strategic alliances, which will be discussed next, are another method for joint expansion activities.

STRATEGIC INTERNATIONAL ALLIANCES

Strategic alliances are business relationships established by two or more companies who cooperate out of mutual need and to share risk in achieving a common objective. This means that the companies involved determine that:

- Common objectives exist.
- One partner's weakness is offset by the other's strength.
- Reaching the objectives alone is too costly, takes too much time, or will be too risky.
- Together their respective strengths make possible what otherwise would be unattainable.

To be considered a strategic alliance, three characteristics need to be present. The alliances must be horizontal, collaborative, and mutually beneficial to all parties. Companies form strategic alliances to fill the gaps in skills. Good alliances operate like good marriages; poor alliances, in turn, are very similar to bad marriages.

To be characterized as **horizontal,** partners in the alliance must be at the same channel level. A retailer-to-retailer alliance would be horizontal. A retailer-to-manufacturer alliance would be vertical. Strategic alliances would only include the retailer-to-retailer agreements.

An alliance based on mutually defined objectives is **collaborative.** Strategic alliances are not dictated from a stronger channel member to a weaker member.

In a **mutually beneficial** arrangement, as one would expect, benefits occur for all of the participants. In the period from the 1950s through the 1970s, many international retail alliances were formed. However, most of these alliances were formed to limit political risk or meet legal requirements in a specific country. For instance, until 1988, a foreign company could not invest in Mexico without a Mexican partner, who had to own 51% of the enterprise. These business alliances generally were not strategic, that is, formed to be collaborative, horizontal, and mutually beneficial. Rather, they were *legislated* joint ventures.

Today, the purpose of strategic international alliances is to be competitive in global markets by meeting or exceeding new standards for products and technology use. Most successful strategic international alliances are between partners of equal strength in their home markets. The strategic international alliance between Wal-Mart and Cifra, the Mexican retailer, is a good example

Photo 4.3
Wal-Mart has opened supercenters in Mexico City. The company's alliance with the Mexican retailer Cifra is considered one of the most successful retail alliances in the world. *Courtesy of the author.*

of this new breed of business cooperation. Cifra has long held the position of the dominant retailer in Mexico. It has a variety of retail formats, a long history in Mexico, and strong partnerships with local suppliers. In turn, Wal-Mart brought to the alliance with Cifra one of the most sophisticated logistics and purchasing systems in the world. Company Focus I.3, which provides an overview of Wal-Mart's international activities, is included at the end of Part I. Wal-Mart has had mixed success in its international strategic alliances.

There are three major reasons why a retailer would form a strategic alliance:

1. To create new retail companies in another country with a local retailer as partner.
2. To enhance purchasing power.
3. To facilitate exchange of knowledge or know-how.

These reasons are not mutually exclusive. In the Wal-Mart-Cifra alliance, all three of these reasons were a motivation for the parties involved.

ALLIANCE TYPES

Not all alliances fit the description of being strategic alliance; they are just retail alliances, generally formed to enhance purchasing power and develop private label products. Some of these retail alliances would meet some but not all the strategic alliance criteria. There are two types of retail alliances. **Equity alliances** include a cross shareholding between members; that is, members own shares of the other members' stocks. **Nonequity alliances** involve collaboration in business activities that can be mutually beneficial,

Photo 4.4
Even before the peso devaluation, which increased the price of imported merchandise by 30% to 40%, most of the merchandise sold in Wal-Mart's Mexico stores was of domestic origin. This lessened the impact of the peso devaluation. *Courtesy of the author.*

TABLE 4.4

European Retail Alliances (as of January 1995)

Alliance Name (date of formation)	Alliance Center	Members	Domicile	Turnover (ecu billions) (1993)	Number Of Outlets (1993)
Associated Marketing Services (AMS) (1989)	Switzerland	Ahold	Netherlands	12.46	2,132
		Allkauf	Germany	3.31	292
		Argyll	UK	7.19	841
		Casino	France	9.48	3,311
		Hakon	Norway	1.84[a]	416[a]
		ICA	Sweden	5.55	2,840[a]
		Kesko	Finland	3.83	2,007[a]
		Mercadonna	Spain	1.14	160
		Rinascente	Italy	3.13	740
		Superquin	Ireland	0.13[b]	21
		Jer. Martins	Portugal	0.59	169
		Edeka[c]	Germany	15.30	11,618
			TOTAL	**63.95**	**24,547**
Deuro Buying (1990)	Switzerland	Carrefour	France	18.57	647
		Makro	Netherlands	4.44	171
		Metro	Switzerland	29.6	1,434
		NAF[d]	Netherlands	28.8[a]	12,088[a]
			TOTAL	**81.41**	**14,340**
European Marketing Distribution (EMD) (1989)	Switzerland	Markant	Germany	33.78	24,276
		Markant	Netherlands	1.49	2,218[a]
		ZEV	Austria	2.98	2,407[a]
		Euromadi	Spain	5.43	6,801[a]
		Selex	Italy	2.13	1,100[a]
		Uniarme	Portugal	0.69	68[a]
		Nisa	UK	12.80	3,040[a]
		Musgrave	Ireland	1.14	387[a]
		Supervib	Denmark	2.45	666[a]
			TOTAL	**62.89**	**40,963**
Eurogroup (1988)	Germany	GIB	Belgium	7.70	1,768
		Vendex	Netherlands	4.78	705
		Rewe Zentr.	Germany	23.25	8,479
		Co-op Schw.	Switzerland	5.61	1,729
			TOTAL	**41.34**	**12,681**
Buying Internat Group Spar (BIGS) (1990)	Netherlands	Spar	Austria	2.15	N/A
		Unidis	Belgium	0.41[a]	N/A
		Bernag Ovag	Switzerland	0.10[a]	N/A
		Dagrofa	Denmark	0.86[a]	N/A
		Spar	UK	1.64[a]	N/A

TABLE 4.4

European Retail Alliances (as of January 1995)

Alliance Name (date of formation)	Alliance Center	Members	Domicile	Turnover (ecu billions) (1993)	Number Of Outlets (1993)
		Hellaspar	Greece	0.17[a]	N/A
		Despar	Italy	2.23[a]	N/A
		BWG/Spar	Ireland	2.38[a]	N/A
		Unil	Norway	0.09[a]	N/A
		Unigro	Netherlands	2.04[a]	N/A
		Dagab	Sweden	1.63[a]	N/A
		Tukospar	Finland	1.78[a]	N/A
			TOTAL	**15.48**	
Inter Coop/NAF Internat (1971)	Denmark	CCU	Bulgaria	1.83	13,000
		FDB	Denmark	3.54	1,276
		BVK	Germany	3.41	1,120
		SOK	Finland	3.02	1,138
		Tradeka	Finland	0.80	726
		FNCC	France	N/A	N/A
		CWS	UK	8.66	4,600
		AFEOSZ	Hungary	0.93	12,739
		Coop Union	Iceland	0.42	177
		Coop Italia	Italy	4.91	1,245
		JCCU	Japan	20.98	2,450
		NKL	Norway	2.23	1,291
		KF	Sweden	5.65	1,812
		Coop Union	Slovakia	0.49	6,636
			TOTAL	**56.87**	**48,210**
SEDD (1994)	Not known	Sainsbury	UK	13.21	419
		Esselunga	Italy	1.49[a]	75[a]
		Delhaize	Belgium	8.06[a]	1,377[a]
		Docks de France	France	4.84[a]	1,451[a]
			TOTAL	**27.60**	**3,322**
Total of All Alliances				**349.54**[e]	**144,063**[f]

ecu = European Currency Units

[a]1992.

[b]Estimate.

[c]Edeka joined AMS in January 1995. Edeka owns 1,650 shops itself and supplies 9,950 independent retailers.

[d]NAF is an alliance itself.

[e]NAF is excluded from Deuro to prevent double counting.

[f]Excludes BIGS.

Source: Adapted from data provided by the Institute of Grocery Distribution. In Robinson, T., and C. M. Clarke-Hill. (1995). "International Alliances in European Retailing." In P. McGoldnick and G. Davies, eds., *International Retailing Trends and Strategies.* London: Pitman Publishing, pp. 136–137. (1994)

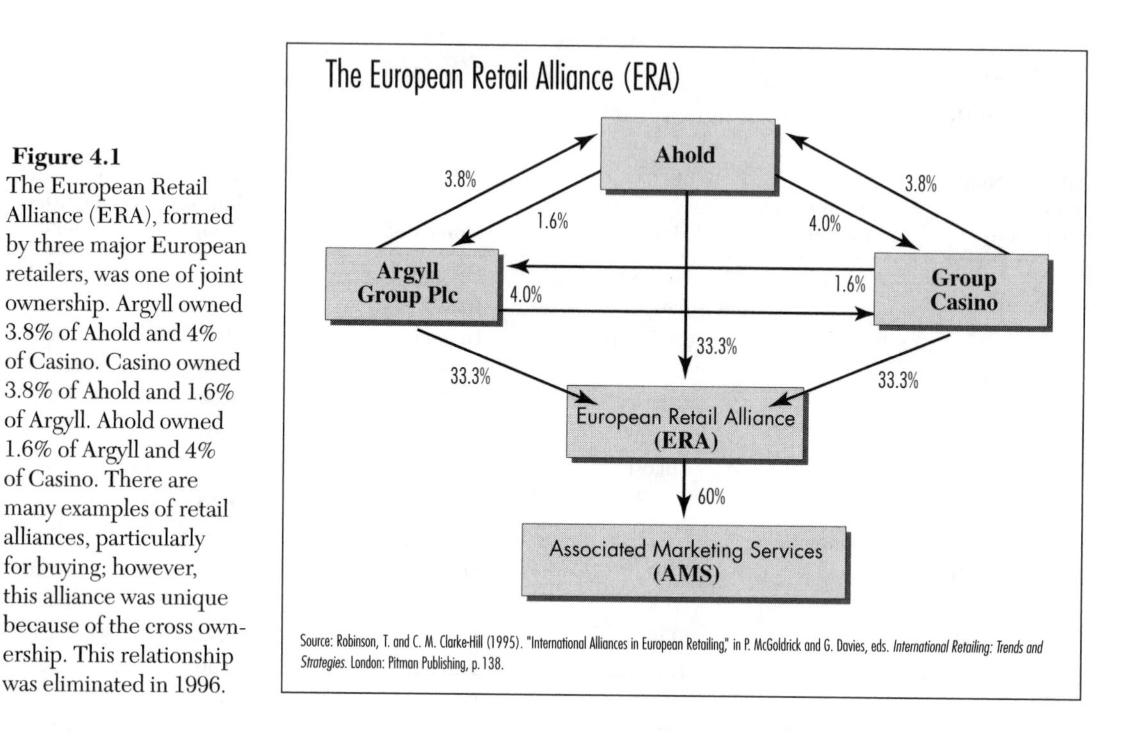

Figure 4.1
The European Retail Alliance (ERA), formed by three major European retailers, was one of joint ownership. Argyll owned 3.8% of Ahold and 4% of Casino. Casino owned 3.8% of Ahold and 1.6% of Argyll. Ahold owned 1.6% of Argyll and 4% of Casino. There are many examples of retail alliances, particularly for buying; however, this alliance was unique because of the cross ownership. This relationship was eliminated in 1996.

such as cooperative buying groups, branding, expertise exchange, and product marketing.[14] Nonequity groups generally have a central office to administer the work of the alliance. They often refer to these offices as alliances with central secretariats. Such alliances are more fluid than the equity alliances, with members entering and leaving. A list of the major European retail alliances is presented in Table 4.4. Since these alliances are quite fluid, this list will be immediately out of date.

Retailers may belong to several strategic alliances. In Europe, until 1996 three companies—Koninklijke Ahold NV, Argyll Group plc, and Casino Guichard-Perrachon—made up the cross shareholding alliance called the European Retail Alliance (ERA). This was an equity alliance: Ahold owned 4% of Casino and 1.6% of Argyll; Argyll owned 4% of Casino and 3.8% of Ahold; Casino owned 3.8% of Ahold and 1.6% of Argyll. Each of the three companies owned one-third of ERA, which in turn owned 60% of Associated Marketing Services (AMS). Figure 4.1 illustrates this relationship visually. AMS includes a broader retail membership. The three core ERA retailers gained from the additional purchasing power of the bigger group. In 1996, the ERA relationship was dissolved; however, AMS still exists.

Retail alliances also occur in Japan; however, a major retailer who becomes the anchor for the group generally dominates these alliances.

There are five major Japanese department store buying groups: Daimaru, ADO (All Nippon Department Store Development Organization), Hi-Land Group, Mitsukoshi, and JMA (Japan Department Stores Management Group). Many buying groups also exist in the Japanese food industry.

JOINT VENTURES

Joint ventures are formed when two or more retailers come together to create a new enterprise. The joint venture may be considered a strategic alliance if it has the three characteristics of a strategic alliance. Earlier, I mentioned that many of the international retail alliances of the 1950s through the 1970s were formed to meet host government regulations related to local ownership. In such cases, the joint venture would not be considered a strategic alliance because there is no evidence that it meets the requirement of being collaborative and mutually beneficial. The joint ventures created by governments that require a certain level of local ownership might be compared to a shotgun wedding. The two parties are legally joined, but they are not necessarily happy about the situation. In contrast, a strategic alliance is like a marriage based on love and respect. Each partner gains from the joining (mutually beneficial), they share a similar objective (a wonderful life together), and the partnership is between two equals (horizontal).

SUMMARY

Licensing, franchising, and strategic alliances involve sharing company secrets. The problems for retailers involved in these types of arrangements can be significant. Of these methods of cooperation, strategic alliances provide retailers with the greatest potential to gain market presence over the long run.

Companies originally used joint ventures in foreign markets because they were mandated by the host country. Today, many countries will not allow wholly owned foreign retailers to operate within their borders. Countries do this to protect their local investment interests. Some of the most successful international expansion involves strategic alliances. Strategic alliances are characterized by being horizontal, collaborative, and mutually beneficial to all parties. When used in good faith, the strengths gained in a strategic alliance are great. When the partners do not operate as faithful partners, the outcome is trouble. At the end of Part I, Company Focus I.2 describes the strategic alliance and joint venture between Isetan and Barneys. Isetan is a major Japanese department store; Barneys, one of the most prestigious men's and women's specialty stores in New York. In their joint venture, things went terribly wrong. Read the company focus and ask yourself whether this could have been prevented.

KEY TERMS

agency theory
collaborative
direct franchise
equity alliance
franchise
franchisee
franchisor
horizontal
joint ventures
master franchise
mutually beneficial
nonequity alliance
strategic alliances

DISCUSSION QUESTIONS

1. What are the advantages and disadvantages of licensing and franchising for the companies described below?
   a. Photoark is a company that has just developed a unique method of developing film at home. Consumers purchase the film and chemicals from a Photoark store, then take them home to shoot and develop. To keep the photo quality high, it is very important that while the chemicals are held in the store, they be maintained at a constant temperature and that inventory be no more than five days old. Photoark wants to expand internationally. The company knows that its technology will be copied by other retailers in a few years, and its wants to gain market presence rapidly.
   b. Treetops is a book retailer that focuses on selling innovative books. Its selection is vast; in whatever market it enters it is the largest store in the area. Treetops could be considered a category killer. Its most important business asset is an excellent logistics system, which the company uses in moving merchandise from one store to another to take advantage of regional preferences in books.
2. Why would the Walt Disney World Co. choose to use a licensing arrangement in Japan but a joint venture in France? Knowing what you know about Disney, what mode of international expansion would you suggest?
3. Conventional franchisors often expand because of a solicitation from a businessperson in a foreign country. What is wrong with responding to these invitations to franchise?
4. Identify areas in which strategic international alliances would be a superior expansion route. What factors make the decision different for retailers as compared to manufacturers?
5. How can you determine if a joint venture is a strategic alliance? Are all strategic alliances joint ventures? Are all joint ventures strategic alliances? Explain your answer.

ENDNOTES

1. U.S. Department of Commerce, 1988.
2. International Franchising Association (IFA). (1992). *Franchising in the Economy: 1989–1992.* Washington, D.C.: IFA Educational Foundation.
3. Fladmoe-Lindquist, K. (1996). "International Franchising: Capabilities and Development." *Journal of Business Venturing,* Vol. 11, pp. 419–438.
4. Martin, R. E. (1988). "Franchising and Risk Management." *American Economic Review,* Vol. 78, No. 5, pp. 954–968.
5. Huszagh, S. M., F. W. Huszagh, and F. McIntyre. (1992). "International Franchising in the Context of Competitive Strategy and the Theory of the Firm." *International Marketing Review,* Vol. 9, No. 5, pp. 5–18.
6. Aydin, N., and M. Kacker. (1990). "International Outlook of U.S. Based Franchisers." *International Marketing Review,* Vol. 7, No. 2, pp. 43–53.
7. Fladmoe-Lindquist. (1996).
8. *Entrepreneur.* (1996). "Seventeenth Annual Franchise 500." January, pp. 211–311.
9. Delnevo, R. (1990). "Tie Rack, plc. Case Study." In M. Abell, ed., *The International Franchise Option.* London: Waterlow Publishers, pp. 339–347.
10. Fladmoe-Lindquist. (1996).
11. Delnevo (1990).
12. Entrepreneur (1996).
13. Shook, C. and R. Shook. (1993). *Franchising: The Business Strategy that Changed the World.* Englewood Cliffs, N.J.: Prentice-Hall.
14. Robinson, T. M., and C. M. Clarke-Hill. (1994). "Competitive Advantage Through Strategic Retail Alliances: A European Perspective," presented at Recent Advances in Retailing and Service Science Conference, University of Alberta, Canada, May 1994.
15. Robinson, T., and C. M. Clarke-Hill. (1995). "International Alliances in European Retailing." In P. McGoldrick and G. Davies, eds., *International Retailing Trends and Strategies.* London: Pitman Publishing, pp. 133–150.

1
EURO

5

Retailing in Multinational Markets

After reading this chapter, you will understand:

- Some of the benefits and drawbacks of multinational cooperation.
- How factors of production influence the success of multinational groups and whether multinational cooperative agreements will be beneficial to consumers.
- The hierarchical structure of multinational markets.
- The antecedents to further levels of multinational cooperation.
- The effect different levels of cooperation have on domestic retailers and international retailers.

ALONG WITH THE VIEW of the world as a market comes the idea of multinational markets that link countries for trade. The United States, Canada, and Mexico have joined to form the North American Free Trade Association. Fifteen European countries now form the European Union (EU). The EU has grown out of a 1952 agreement between six original members. It has been expanded four times, in 1973, 1981, 1986, and 1995. It is estimated that by the year 2000, the EU will be twice as large as it currently is, a result of new members joining the current group of countries. Later in this chapter, I will identify which countries are a part of the EU and which countries are being considered for the fifth enlargement. Latin American countries have formed a multitude of trade associations, some with more success than others. Asian countries have tremendous potential for creating multinational markets, and have joined together in a series of cooperative agreements. African countries have been the least successful in forging successful multinational arrangements. This can be explained by the instability of countries in that region.

Multinational agreements are most successful when member nations have dissimilar production capabilities. Production capabilities are directly related to a country's factors of production, discussed in Chapter 1. Multinational agreements between countries having different strengths offer the greatest long-term gains. A low-wage country that joins a country with strong capital and entrepreneurship creates a self-sufficient market relationship.

Multinational cooperation offers some benefits and some drawbacks to member nations. Multinational markets also display a pattern of development ranging from the least formal to the most formal. The least formal level of agreement is a regional cooperative group. The next level is a free trade area; internal barriers to trade are eliminated at this level. The third level is a full customs union, in which internal barriers are eliminated and common external barriers are established with external trading partners. The fourth level is a common market. A common market agreement eliminates internal barriers to trade, establishes common external barriers, and adds the free flow of capital and labor. The highest multinational level is a political union. A political union includes the removal of internal barriers of trade, establishes common external barriers to trade, allows for the free flow of capital and labor, and adds the establishment of a unifying economic logic. I will discuss each of these levels of agreement in more detail later in the chapter, but first let's talk about the benefits and drawbacks of multinational integration.

BENEFITS OF MULTINATIONAL MARKETS

The four major benefits of multinational markets can be summarized as follows: (1) large mass markets are attractive to mass merchandisers, (2) improved channels of distribution provide a benefit to all types of retailers operating outside a local community, (3) increased trade with member nations can be an advantage to the participating members but a disadvantage to those outside the trade block, and (4) consumers benefit from lower costs if the multinational market includes countries with diverse factors of production.

LARGE MASS MARKET

When countries remove barriers to the free flow of merchandise between borders, they increase the potential customer base. Rules and regulations that impeded the flow of merchandise are removed, increasing the sales area.

Large mass markets are a benefit to retailers because they can take advantage of economies of scale in purchasing merchandise. The United States has had one of the largest mass markets in the world. This has encouraged the growth of national chains. Because of this large mass market, the most important retail innovations have occurred in the United States. Greater volume sets the stage for technological innovations and the profitable use of private label sourcing. There is a flip side to this benefit, though. Because U.S. retailers have had such a large mass market, they have not expanded internationally. Unlike European or Japanese retailers, who needed to expand because of national saturation, U.S. retailers are latecomers to internationalization. American retailers have grown into national chains, expanding throughout the large U.S. mass market.

Large mass markets are more important to particular types of retailers. Mass merchandisers and discount operations benefit most from multinational markets. It is probably not a surprise that the early U.S. international retailers were mass merchandisers such as Sears and discounters such as Wal-Mart and Kmart. A second advantage of multinational markets derives from the ease of moving from one country to another. The ease of movement relates to products, people, and promotions.

IMPROVED CHANNELS OF DISTRIBUTION, ADVERTISING, AND TRANSPORTATION

If you traveled through Europe before 1992, you experienced customs officials at the boundary of each country. At these checkpoints, you were required to show your passport and answer questions about your travel purpose. Now, when you move from France to Germany, for example, you may not realize that you have entered another country. The experience is similar to going from Michigan to Indiana. The only indication that you have entered another state is a sign, "Welcome to Indiana." The same situation occurs for merchandise moving from one EU country to another. Before 1992, transportation trucks were required to stop at customs, complete documentation forms, pay a tariff, and answer questions about the merchandise destination. All of this adds to the costs of distribution. Likewise, removing these requirements reduces the cost of distribution.

Less regulation and supervision of cargo reduce transportation costs in multinational markets. Standard regulations related to freight cargo containers reduce the need to repack containers to meet national regulations.

Retailers can also economize advertising through a mass market. Although countries are still free to decide advertising standards, the regulations are straightforward. In Germany, using comparative advertising is not legal. Retailers in Germany are allowed to advertise sales only twice a year.

Improved access to consumers and the attraction of a larger mass market lead to greater trade flows within the multinational market.

INCREASED TRADE WITH MEMBER NATIONS

The greatest benefits of multinational markets occur when member nations have complementary, not competitive, resources and factors of production. Mexico, for instance, has a lower labor cost than either the United States or Canada. Under the North American Free Trade Agreement (NAFTA), tariffs among these countries were reduced. This would encourage production of more labor- intensive products south of the border. Opponents of NAFTA maintain that having a country with a low labor cost as a part of the multinational market is disastrous, leading to the loss of jobs. However, this is exactly what an agreement such as NAFTA should do. Mexico, with an abundant supply of labor and low minimum wage, should produce labor-intensive products, leaving the United States and Canada with higher paying jobs based in technology. When the EU added Spain to its multinational market, the same concern was expressed. Many Europeans believed that jobs would be lost elsewhere in Europe. When a country's factors of production are viewed as complementary resources rather than competitors, the arrangement is much more likely to be successful.

Agricultural products are often the most contested area of trade because each country views the maintenance of an agricultural industry as important to its national well-being, and agriculture production is often duplicated among member countries. Continental Europe banned British beef exports when mad cow disease erupted in Britain. This ban was probably related more to market protection than to health interests. Earlier, Britain had banned French poultry exports, supposedly to protect British citizens from a poultry virus. In separate cases, France has banned Italian wine and the Irish have banned all poultry and eggs from other member countries. The reasons given were always related to health; however, the evidence points to market protection rather than health issues. The European Commission is a regulatory group that settles the European common market trade disputes. In each of these instances, the Commission charged the countries with violations of EU regulations.

Generally, countries that form a multinational market are located in close geographical proximity; however, this is not always the case. One of the newest multinational trade agreements is the Asian Pacific Economic Cooperation (APEC). A summary of economic data for the 18 APEC members is included in Table 5.1; Figure 5.1 shows the geographical location of member countries.

CONSUMER BENEFITS OF LOWER INTERNAL TARIFF BARRIERS

Tariffs are taxes on imported products. Reducing tariffs makes these products less expensive. This affects consumption, allowing consumers to purchase more of these and other goods, as well as increasing the standard of living. When consumers purchase products produced within their multinational trading group, the cost to consumers should be lower.

The more diverse the production capabilities of these member countries, the greater the cost savings for consumers. As we saw earlier, adding Mexico to NAFTA provided a low-wage producer to this multinational market. This created initial panic from special interest groups representing U.S. labor. Presidential candidate Ross Perot commented at the time that NAFTA had created a great big sucking sound—the sound of U.S. jobs going south. In fact, this has not happened. Low-wage jobs lost to Mexico have been replaced with new jobs in other sectors of the economy.

DRAWBACKS OF MULTINATIONAL MARKETS

At this point in the discussion, you may believe that there are only minor drawbacks to multinational markets. Of course, that is not true. Although the benefits outweigh the drawbacks, there are some winners and losers among countries engaging in multinational cooperation. For one thing, the more similar the production capabilities of the member countries, the less the economic gain. Competition also increases within the multinational block. This can be advantageous for consumers, who will likely benefit from lower prices. However, it will probably cause a consolidation of market players. Weak firms will go out of business and marginal firms will consolidate.

Another drawback is that the market, at first appearance, seems like a single market. This can lead retailers to misunderstand the need to be adaptive to cultural differences. Furthermore, inflation can be a problem if there is insufficient competition within the market to keep prices low. Finally, the increased layer of government involvement can contribute to inflation as well as to an overall problem with excessive red tape. Let's look at each of these, in turn.

INCREASED COMPETITION

After tariffs are eliminated, competition becomes much more intense. To understand why, consider the following examples of different schools' athletic teams. Suppose you went to a small high school of only 40 students. Your school needs 11 members to make a soccer team. As one of the 40 students, you have a very good chance of making the team. Now suppose your school is consolidated with another high school of 300 students. The chance that you will make the soccer team as one of 340 competing students is much less. However, the greater pool of potential players probably ensures that your school will have a much more competitive team.

In a multinational market, this increased competition will mean lower costs to consumers and a natural consolidation of companies. Companies that are capital-intensive will benefit from consolidation; companies that are labor-intensive may experience little change.

TABLE 5.1

1993 Major Economic Data for 18 APEC Members[a]

Country	Population (millions)	Land Area (1,000 sq. km)	GDP[b] ($ billions)	Per Capita GDP[b] ($)	GDP Growth Rate (%)	Exports ($ billions)	Imports ($ billions)
1. Australia	17.7	7,680	285	16,100	3.0	42.5	45.6
2. Brunei	0.268	5.77	4.02	15,500	3.6	2.37	2.6
3. Canada	28.8	9,980	545	19,000	2.4	141	138
4. Chile	13.8	756	43.7	3,160	6.0	9.55	11
5. China	1,210	9,600	545	452	13.4	91.6	104
6. Hong Kong	5.92	1.07	115	19,400	5.5	135	139
7. Indonesia	189	1,920	143	755	6.5	36.8	28.3
8. Japan	125	378	4,220	33,700	0.2	363	241
9. Malaysia	19.2	330	57.6	3,100	8.5	47.1	45.6
10. Mexico	91.2	1,960	361	4,010	1.0	47.2	63.9
11. New Zealand	3.46	271	44.6	12,900	4.6	10.4	9.65
12. Papua New Guinea	4.06	462	3.85	950	1.7	2.21	1.65
13. Philippines	65.7	299	54.1	824	1.7	11.3	18
14. Singapore	2.87	0.64	55.1	19,200	9.9	74.1	85.4
15. South Korea	44.1	99	331	7,510	5.5	83.5	84.3
16. Taiwan	20.9	36	216	10,400	5.9	85	771
17. Thailand	58.6	514	110	1,910	7.9	37.1	46.1
18. United States	258	9,370	6,290	24,400	3.0	465	603

[a]Refer to Figure 5.1 for the location of member countries.
[b]GDP and per capita GDP—1991 for Brunei; 1992 for Thailand and Malaysia; GNP for Papua New Guinea; GDP growth rate—0 real; GNP growth rate for Papua New Guinea.
Source: *The Nikkei Weekly*, November 13, 1995, p. 21.

LOOKS LIKE A SINGLE MARKET, BUT IT'S NOT

Careless assessment of the remaining cultural complexity of multinational markets poses the next disadvantage. It is tempting to view multinational markets as one mass market, but that is a dangerous assumption.

Are the United States and Mexico really any more similar after NAFTA than they were before? Probably not. Evidence even points toward the opposite effect. Similarly, there are signs that individual country identities are even more important after Europe's unification than they were before. When the European countries became joined at the hip economically, they cried out for a national identity in other ways. For instance, France has since

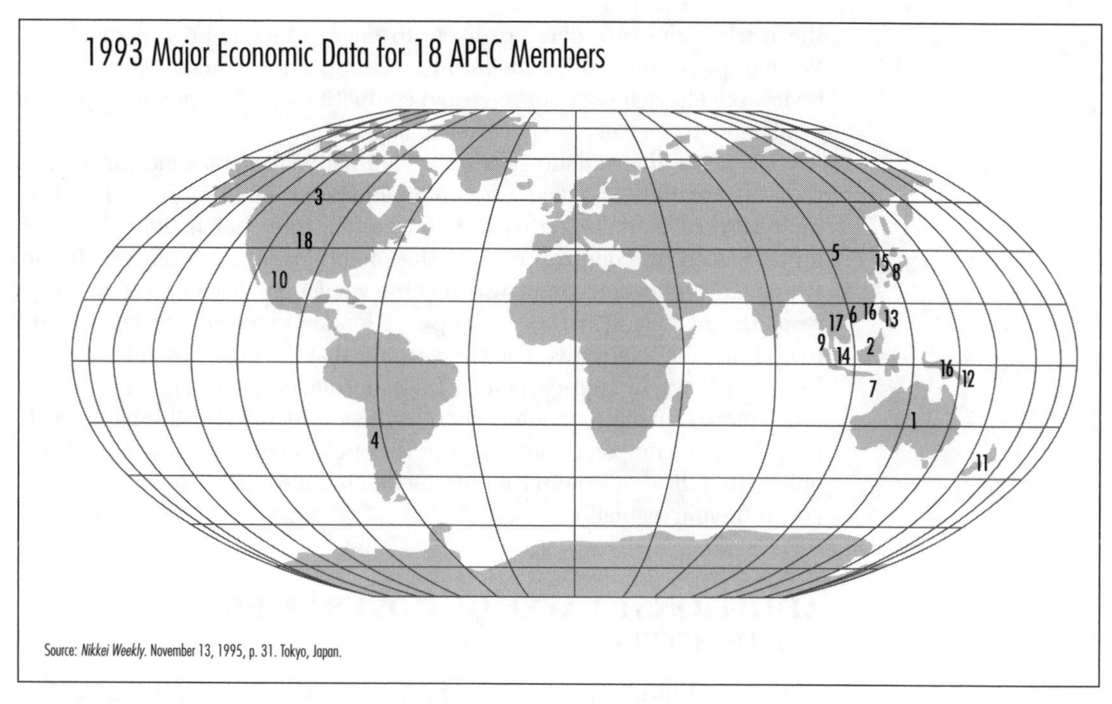

Figure 5.1
The APEC member nations represent a vast assortment of natural resources and people.

passed a very restrictive law requiring that when a French word exists for a product being described in advertising or another form of communication, the French word must be used.

Even without the consideration of national pride and preservation of a national identity, there exists the problem of considering a heterogeneous group of people as homogeneous. If you have moved from one part of the United States to another part, you have probably experienced different cultures. The lifestyle of Los Angelinos is very different from that of New Yorkers, or even Michiganders. Treating an entire country or multinational market as one large mass market is generally a mistake.

INFLATION

Competition within a multinational market increases, as we have seen, but competition from countries outside the market decreases. Decreased competitive pressures, in turn, lead to increased prices for consumers.

Why would inflation be a problem in a multinational market? The answer depends on the partners taking part in the integration. If integration leads to oligopoly, the competitive structure in which a few companies control the market, the providers are likely to engage in non-price competition. Without price competition, built-in (structural) price increases occur. If you review the characteristics of price and competition in an oligopoly, discussed in Chapter 1, you can predict what will happen.

We know that inflation within a multinational market increases when trade with countries outside the multinational membership is reduced. In multinational markets, tariffs decrease among member nations; however, tariffs placed on countries outside the membership may increase. Before European unification, there was much speculation that unification would result in a so-called **Fortress Europe**—a market that would be less friendly to non-member countries. The concern was that if companies did not establish a presence in Europe before 1992, entrance to the market would be much more difficult thereafter. There is some evidence that this has come to pass. Foreign companies entering the European market need to comply not only with individual country requirements, but also with a separate level of governmental regulation.

ADDITIONAL LAYER OF GOVERNMENT COMPLEXITY

Government involvement with business is rarely viewed as productive. In a multinational market, there is an additional level of governmental considerations. Let's look at Europe. The European Commission is the executive body of the EU. It is headquartered in Brussels. There are 17 commissioners: two representatives from each of the larger member countries and one from each smaller member. Each of the commissioners oversees three directorates, which oversee different segments of industry, such as agriculture and transportation. Retail trade falls under Directorate 23, called the Committee for Commerce and Distribution. This committee also oversees enterprise policy, commerce, tourism, and social economy. Some industry segments are well-organized and present an effective lobby to protect industry interests. The retailing industry has not done this.

The **ISO 9000** regulations, developed by the International Organization for Standardization, were designed to set minimum standards for European products. The 1992 regulations for the common market require that member states set minimum common standards, called downward harmonization. The minimum standards are those required for sale throughout the EU. **Downward harmonization** means that countries cannot prohibit the sale of products that do not meet their previous regulations.[1]

Complaints of noncompliance with the ISO regulations have erupted throughout Europe. For instance, Germany requires that beer contain no preservatives. This is a violation of the downward harmonization principle. Countries within the EU can handle this lack of similarity by requiring labeling of—but not by banning—the product that does not meet another country's home standard.

In Europe, few of these product regulations directly affect retailers. However, each country continues to make and enforce its own rules about hours of operation, the building of large-scale retail stores, the doing of part-time and overtime work, and Sunday trading practices. A summary of commercial legislation regarding hours of operation in the EU countries is included in Table 5.2.

You now have a better idea about some of the benefits and drawbacks involved with multinational markets. Multinational markets develop in a hierarchy from the least integrated to the most integrated. At each level, an additional element of integration is added. These elements deal with (1) internal trade barriers, (2) external trade barriers, (3) free flow of capital and labor, and (4) unifying political and economic systems, as we will see next.

TABLE 5.2

Commercial Legislation in EU Regarding Retail Hours of Operation

Country	Weekdays	Sundays
Germany	Tues.–Fri.: 6 AM to 8 PM	Closed
Austria (to be voted)	Mon.–Fri.: 7:30 AM to 7:30 PM Sat.: 7:30 AM to 5 PM; total 66 hours	Closed
Belgium	Mon.–Sat.: 5 AM to 8 PM To 9 PM Fri., and before bank holidays	15 openings per year; more in tourist towns
Netherlands	Mon.–Fri.: 12 hours between 8 AM and 9 PM Sat.: 10 hours maximum; total: 70 hours	Closed, except tourist towns
UK	No restrictions	Over 280 square meters (3,014 square feet): six hours between 10 AM and 6 PM
Spain	Supermarkets: 8 AM to 2 PM and 4 PM to 9 PM; Hypermarkets: 10 AM to 10 PM; total 72 hours	By region: at least eight per year
Portugal	Mon.–Sat.: 6 AM to 12 midnight	6 AM to 12 midnight; large stores: 8 AM to 1 PM
Italy	Mon.–Sat.: 9 AM to 8 PM; total: 66 hours Closed a half day a week (by region)	Closed, except tourist towns
Greece	Mon.: 8 AM to 8:30 PM Tues.–Fri.: 8 AM to 9 PM Sat.: 8 AM to 8 PM	Closed, except tourist towns
Poland	Mon.–Fri.: 7:30 AM to 9 PM Sat.: 8:30 AM to 5 PM	8:30 AM to 3 PM

Source: *Retail News Letter*, December 1996, No. 441, p. 2.

LEVELS OF MULTINATIONAL COOPERATION

REGIONAL COOPERATIVE GROUP

The lowest level of integration is a **regional cooperative group.** This is an agreement between countries to jointly participate and to develop certain industries or infrastructures beneficial to the economies of member countries. With this level of involvement, there is no elimination or lowering of internal tariffs or any other agreements regarding trade with other countries. This level of agreement generally leads to a higher level of participation in multinational markets.

FREE TRADE AREA

The **free trade area** level of involvement is the first to have any direct effect on retailing. If countries establish a free trade area, they eliminate or reduce internal barriers between member nations. They establish no common external barriers and there is no free flow of capital and labor. NAFTA is an example of this type of agreement. Canada, Mexico, and the United States have agreed to reduce tariffs among themselves, eventually having no tariffs. This type of agreement is an important step toward becoming a multinational market, but it is inherently unstable, because external trade relationships are not similar.

Since the member countries have separate agreements with external trading partners, there is a weak link in this type of trade agreement. For example, if the United States charges 16% tariffs on merchandise coming from France, and Canada charges 13% tariffs on the same French merchandise, these products will flow through Canada to their destination in the United States. This is illustrated graphically in Figure 5.2. Until the United States and Canada establish similar external agreements with trading partners, there will always be a weak link. In the case of NAFTA, the three countries have reduced this problem by passing domestic content laws. Domestic content laws require that a certain proportion of a product must be produced in the trade group to qualify for trade under NAFTA terms.

As we will see in the next section, a full customs union is a more stable level of multinational agreement than a free trade area because it gets rid of the weak link, that is, the different external trade agreements. If NAFTA is successful, it is likely that the three countries will move to a higher level of involvement.

Retailers in a free trade area may move to other countries within the member nations to take advantage of lower costs for land and labor. If a company depends on a high degree of service, it may benefit from relocating to the lower-wage, developing country. Companies with mature retail formats may find that the less developed country in the group offers locational

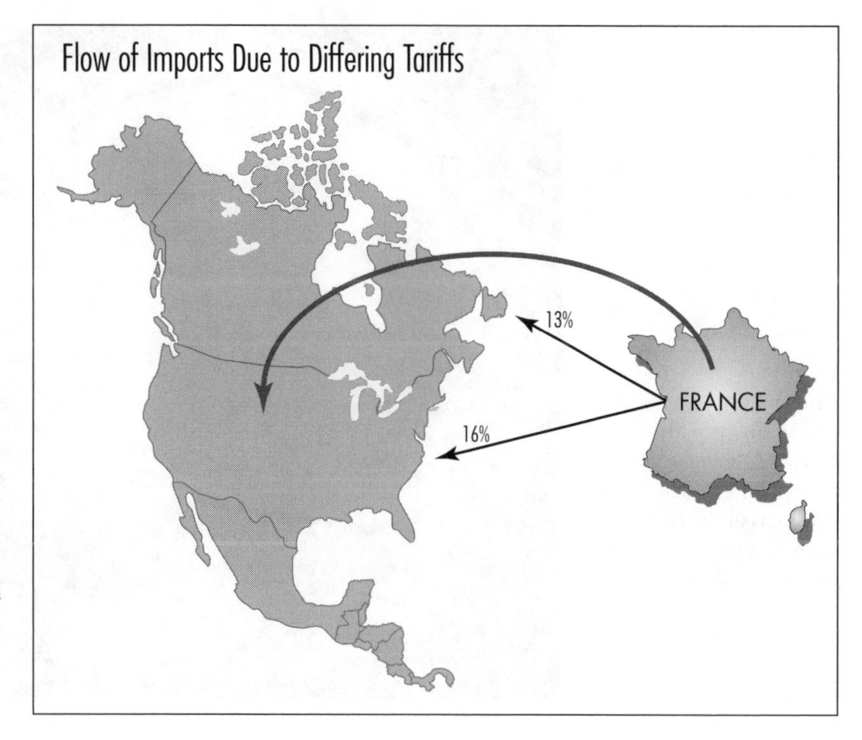

Figure 5.2
If countries remove internal barriers to trade but do not establish common external barriers, goods will flow through the country with the lowest tariffs. In this hypothetical example, the merchandise from France would flow through Canada into the United States.

advantages. Consumers in less developed countries may view a retail format as more innovative than consumers who live in more developed countries.

FULL CUSTOMS UNION

A **full customs union** eliminates or reduces internal trade barriers; in addition, it establishes the same external barriers to trade. There is no free flow of capital or labor. This level of multinational trade is stable because the external barriers have been harmonized. Retailers benefit from this level of involvement because they have similar sources and costs of supply.

Most countries moving from a free trade area to a common market pass through this stage. The EU was a customs union before becoming a common market. Customs unions exist between France and Monaco, Italy and San Marino, and Switzerland and Liechtenstein.[2]

COMMON MARKET

Common markets eliminate the internal barriers, establish the same external barriers, and allow the free flow of capital and labor. The EU is an exam-

Photo 5.1
Dutch Finance Minister Garret Zalm presents the winning design for the coins of the EURO currency, the currency to be used by the European countries that formed the European Union (EU). *Courtesy of AFP Photo/Marcel Antonisse.*

ple of this type of agreement. Retailers operating in a common market benefit from the lower cost of products, which are the result of the elimination of internal barriers. They also have the advantage of similar external barriers, making a stable and equalized trading situation. Labor-intensive retailers such as department stores benefit because they can recruit employees from lower-wage countries to work in the domestic market. Banking institutions benefit because they can extend financing to less developed countries. Consumers benefit from this level of cooperation due to the increased competition. However, if the EU is a good indicator, the laws governing retail trade remain the domain of domestic concerns.

There are three common markets in Latin America: the Andean Common Market (Ancom), the Central American Common Market (CACM), and the Southern Cone Common Market (Mercosur). Table 5.3 shows which European countries belong to the EU, as well as listing similar multinational market groups in Latin America. Mercosur, composed of four members of the Latin American Integration Association (LAIA), includes the Latin American powerhouse countries, Argentina, Brazil, Paraguay, and Uruguay. It is Latin America's largest common market with a population of 185 million people. A bilateral agreement with the United States was negotiated with Mercosur under the American Initiative Enterprise. The CACM

TABLE 5.3

Multinational Market Groups in Europe and Latin America

Association	Members
European Union (EU)	
From 1952 (original ECSC membership):	Belgium, Germany (former East Germany joined in 1991), France, Italy, Luxembourg, The Netherlands
From 1973 (first enlargement):	Denmark, Republic of Ireland, United Kingdom
From 1981 (second enlargement):	Greece
From 1986 (third enlargement):	Portugal, Spain
From 1995 (fourth enlargement):	Austria, Finland, Sweden
Countries being considered for the fifth enlargement:	Bulgaria, Cyprus, Czech Republic, Estonia, Hungary, Latvia, Lithuania, Malta, Poland, Romania, Slovakia, Slovenia
Andean Common Market (Ancom)	Bolivia, Columbia, Ecuador, Peru, Venezuela, Panama (Associate)
Central American Common Market (CACM)	Guatemala, El Salvador, Costa Rica, Nicaragua, Honduras
Caribbean Community and Common Market (CARICOM)	Antigua and Barbuda, Barbados, Belize, Dominica, Grenada, Guyana, Jamaica, Montserrat, St. Kitts-Nevis Anguilla, St. Lucia, St. Vincent, Trinidad-Tobago
Latin American Integration Association (LAIA)	Argentina, Bolivia, Brazil, Chile, Colombia, Ecuador, Mexico, Paraguay, Peru, Uruguay, Venezuela
Southern Cone Common Market (Mercosur)	Argentina, Brazil, Paraguay, Uruguay

Sources: http://eubasics@allmansland.com (1997); Cateora, P. R. (1996). *International Marketing.* 9th ed. Chicago: Irwin, p. 285; *International Trade Statistics Yearbook 1.* (1990). New York: United Nations; and *International Marketing Data and Statistics.* (1994). 18th ed. London: Euromonitor Publications.

union was the first to take the concept of a common market a step further. This union has implemented **sectoral development,** a process by which the union's governing body allocates production responsibility for certain manufactured products to particular countries. In this way, countries within the union do not duplicate production and the group is guaranteed the total CACM market for a product. CACM includes Guatemala, El Salvador, Costa Rica, Nicaragua, and Honduras. Earlier, I mentioned that multinational markets are most successful if they have different strengths in factors of production. This group of five countries has very similar factor endowments. Using the concept of sectoral development allows them to concentrate production and suppliers in a particular area. The total population for the group is around 25 million people.

Sectoral development can have negative effects on retailers. Transportation costs would increase for all products not allocated to the home country. Retailers would not be able to develop their own private sources to produce products unless the production capability for those products had been allocated to their country. Also, prices would likely increase for consumers because competition would be reduced.

POLITICAL UNION

The highest level of multinational cooperation is a **political union.** It has all the elements of a common market—a lowering or elimination of internal barriers of trade, the establishment of common external barriers of trade, and the free flow of capital and labor—plus a unifying economic logic. The United States is a type of political union. There are no tariffs between states. States do not enter into individual agreements with external trading partners; rather, the United States government negotiates these agreements as a unified block. People can move from one state to another to take jobs. The United States is unified under the economic ideology of capitalism.

The British Commonwealth is an example of a voluntary political union. The Council for Mutual Economic Assistance (COMECON) is an example of involuntary unification. COMECON was a centrally controlled group of countries organized by then-Soviet leader Joseph Stalin as a way to rebuild the eastern European countries after World War II. Since 1989, however, the eastern European countries have begun declaring their independence from the former USSR. Today, the future of COMECON is uncertain. Its leaders do not have the strength to keep the cooperative agreement together.

The eastern European countries that formed COMECON were lulled into a false sense of security during the years of Soviet domination. For years, they supplied Russia with goods and services produced through the government-dictated system. When the Soviet federation disbanded, the eastern European countries were left with antiquated industries that were not competitive with world markets. These countries are now struggling to bridge their postcommunist relationships and evolve into a world of competitive producers. The Commonwealth of Independent States (CIS) is a new configuration in eastern Europe. It includes 11 republics that were once part of the USSR.

Although a political union is the highest form of multinational cooperation, there are several major problems with this type of agreement. The economic logic of the member countries may be similar, but not their economic levels. In addition, language barriers and cultural barriers exist among members. There is also a tendency to consider these markets as difficult to penetrate. A summary of the stages of multinational cooperation is presented in Figure 5.3.

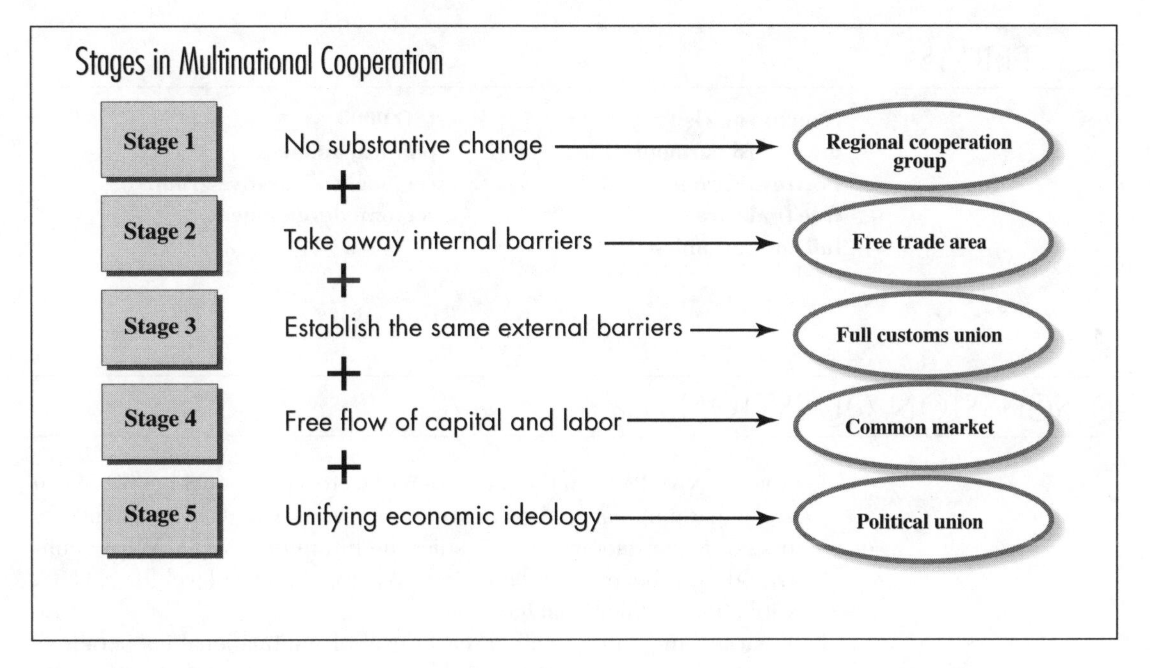

Figure 5.3
Regional cooperation group is the first level of multinational cooperation. At each step, an additional type of unification is added. The highest level is a political union. At this level, there are no internal barriers to trade, the countries have the same external barriers, capital and labor flow freely, and there is a unifying economic ideology.

SUMMARY

The countries of the world are pairing off into economic units as never before. This multinational cooperation will only accelerate in the 21st century. Countries that do not belong to a strong, diverse trade group will be left behind. The history of multinational cooperation is not long. In fact, the longest lasting political union is COMECON, the involuntary union of communist and socialist countries. However, analysis of this union can help us to understand free market multinational cooperation.

The world will be watching the EU over the coming years. This association of countries represents the highest level of a true multinational market group available for study. If the EU's success continues, we can anticipate that the NAFTA group will increase its membership and move to a higher level of integration, such as a full customs union or common market.

KEY TERMS

common market
downward harmonization
Fortress Europe
free trade area
full customs union
ISO 9000
political union
regional cooperative group
sectoral development

DISCUSSION QUESTIONS

1. Analyze NAFTA from the standpoint of factors of production. Since you know that multinational groups are more successful if there is a diverse base of factor endowments, predict the future of NAFTA. What countries do you believe will be added? What is the ideal level for NAFTA within the multinational hierarchy?
2. What are the antecedents of each level of multinational cooperation? Are these steps essential or could a group jump from a free trade area to a political union?
3. How does access to a multinational market affect domestic retailers? What about international retailers from within the block? Or international retailers from outside the block?
4. Europe has used a system of downward harmonization for product standards. What would be the effect of changing this system?

ENDNOTES

1. Wolfe, A. (1991). "Single European Market: National or Euro-Brands." *International Journal of Advertising*, pp. 49–58.
2. Cateora, P. R. (1996). *International Marketing*. 9th ed. Chicago: Irwin.

COMPANY FOCUS I.1

MARKS & SPENCER

Sarah Marie De Nardi-Cole

Marks & Spencer plc—or *Marks & Sparks,* as natives of the United Kingdom so lovingly refer to it—celebrated its centennial in 1984. From the beginning, it has been attracting the attention of customers and retailers alike. The purpose of this case study is to explore one specific area in which the company has been extremely successful and has proved itself a pioneer in the rubric of British retailing: internationalization.

Description of the Company

Target Market

Marks & Spencer's ideal customer is someone who is looking for good quality, classic-style clothing. If you are in the market for corduroy flares, Marks & Spencer is not the store for you. Marks & Spencer has said that its core customer is a 25- to 55-year-old average British person, male or female, the epitome of middle England.[1] The typical Marks & Spencer customer is middle to upper class, as well as a little older.

Product

All of the merchandise offered at Marks & Spencer is sold under the store's private label, *St. Michael.* Most of the products are manufactured in the United Kingdom with one known exception: hosiery. An agreement between Marks & Spencer and Sara Lee Corp., better known in the United States as Hanes and L'Eggs, stipulates that hosiery items manufactured by Sara Lee and labeled *Sara Lee for St. Michael* are sold through the various Marks & Spencer outlets.[2]

Marks & Spencer's products fall into two categories: food and general merchandise. General merchandise includes men's, women's, and children's fashions, and encompasses all areas of clothing such as slacks, suits for both sexes, handbags, footwear, sweaters, dresses, socks, ties, lingerie (for both sexes), as well as goods for the home (towels, soaps, etc.), toys for children, books, and a newer line of cosmetics.

In the area of food, there is also a wide product range. All of the products in the food areas are also sold under the St. Michael name. Marks & Spencer offers more prepared products than it's competitors and averages 15 to 20 varieties of product categories.[3] The company's stores carry a variety of perishables by way of fruits and vegetables. In fact, Marks & Spencer claims to have at least a dozen different ways to purchase broccoli,[4] and about 120 ways to buy chicken breasts.[5]

All tastes can be found at Marks & Spencer, including (but not limited to) Indian, American, Thai, Chinese, Italian, French, and of course English, Scottish, and Irish.[6] Marks & Spencer's groceries also offer an interesting range of beverages: bottled waters, beer, wines, and, of course, a wide selection of teas and biscuits.

Finally, in addition to the edible and potable goods offered at Marks and Spencer, the company also offers financial services. One of the financial products offered to its customers is the Marks & Spencer credit card, which provides credit to shoppers. It is, however, the only credit source used at the company. If customers do not pay with a Marks & Spencer card, they must pay with cash. With the credit card, customers can receive a credit limit of 20 times what they deposit. Customers then earn interest on the balance when their deposits are greater than their purchases.[7] Other financial products include personal loans, personal equity plans, unit trusts, and life insurance.

Price

Typically, Marks & Spencer's pricing strategy was to fix a price limit for all the merchandise sold in its stores so that working-class customers could afford it. The company then searched for products that could result in profit while selling at the price fixed for its working-class patrons.[8]

Today, Marks & Spencer still believes in a sort of one-price range strategy internationally. It accomplishes this by maintaining close relationships with its suppliers. This relationship helps Marks & Spencer get good prices on merchandise through economies of scale. Marks & Spencer stipulates all manufacturing details to its suppliers, from the number of stitches in a buttonhole to length of a hemline. In this way, Marks & Spencer can be assured the quality it desires while, at the same time, having the power to negotiate on price.

Coats Viyella plc. is a large clothing manufacturer based out of Manchester. This company sells around $400 million of apparel goods annually to Marks & Spencer.[9] Smaller manufacturers would not be able to handle any other accounts besides Marks & Spencer. This is where Marks & Spencer derives some of its bargaining power.

What does this mean to consumers? It means simply that at Marks & Spencer customers will not be required to pay a high price for something of mediocre quality. With respect to prices on food items, Marks & Spencer has the same sort of relationship with its manufacturers, which, in return, means moderately priced items. The general price range in the grocery section is roughly between U.S. $1.50 and U.S. $4.50 (£1 to £3) for anything from side vegetable dishes to ready-made meals.[10]

Place

Marks & Spencer stores have two formats. The first format consists of clothing and housewares, with the basement of the store usually being dedicated to grocery items. The second format is nothing but grocery items. Marks & Spencer stores were, in the beginning, all centrally located in the *high street* area of bigger cities (*high street* meaning Main Street in British English). Some changes have come about in this area due to competition, however, and Marks & Spencer can now also be found located on the outskirts of town. In fact, in one instance, due to the lack of space in Great Britain, Marks & Spencer set up an agreement with one of its competitors, Tesco, to share a parking lot (or *car park* in British vernacular) but have competing facilities.

As for size, the chain average is 35,000 to 40,000 square feet, (3,252 to 3,716 square meters) but size varies depending on location. Marks & Spencer has a minimum net space requirement of 100,000 square feet (9,290 square meters) for stores found at the outskirts of towns.[11]

Promotion

Marks & Spencer tends to frown on advertising and, in fact, tends to avoid it.[12] Some exceptions are made, but most often Marks & Spencer depends on word-of-mouth. The Marks & Spencer name is well-known throughout the world and the company relies on this fact for its advertising needs. An all-out advertising campaign is only undertaken when there is a new product or a new retail format. For instance, the new Marks & Spencer store in Paris required some advertising to compensate for low name recognition.[13] Marks & Spencer also depends on its pleasant store layout, its quality for price strategy, and its large selection to sell its goods.

History

It all began when Michael Marks met a wholesaler merchant in Leeds who offered to lend him £5. Marks asked if he could use this sum to buy purchases from the warehouse.[14] This marked the beginning of Marks' peddling.

The peddling soon led to bigger and better things. Marks opened a stall in the Leeds market. From the start, an interesting strategy to attract customers as well as to facilitate communications was put in motion. Marks took all of the items he offered that were sold for a penny, and put them in one area of his stall. Above this section he placed a sign saying, "Don't ask the price, it's a penny."[15] His penny-pricing concept was so successful that Marks decided to carry, from then on, only items costing a penny. By 1901, Marks had acquired 11 shops, 24 stalls, and a new partner, Tom Spencer, who had been a cashier at the warehouse where Marks was lent the £5 to begin his business.[16] Marks & Spencer boasted shops in other cities besides Leeds, including Manchester, Birmingham, Newcastle, and finally London.[17]

By the time Simon Marks (Michael Marks' son) assumed full control of the company, it had 10 stores in market halls, with a total of 145 branch stores in all. The majority of these stores were located in London. The philosophy of providing value for money was still religiously followed at Marks & Spencer, even though the price offered was no longer a penny. For instance, management at Marks & Spencer established a price limit of 5 shillings per item in 1927.

Marks & Spencer was able to put a price limit on its items because of another business principle it deemed invaluable—efficient distribution methods. In 1926, Simon Marks introduced the now famous St. Michael label, named after the company's founder, Michael Marks. Management gradually replaced other brands with its own until 1949, when all Marks & Spencer stores were selling only the private label. This was an important move by the company and is one of the main reasons Marks & Spencer is so successful today. Although neither of the partners at that time wanted to get into their own production, they realized the advantages of buying in bulk and the influence they enjoyed over the manufacturers when so doing.

Marks & Spencer continued to follow the principles that it had developed, which included:

encouraging suppliers to maintain high quality standards in production and working environment, offering customers a selective range of high quality merchandise, simplified operating procedures, and supporting British industry and buying abroad only when new ideas, technology, quality and value were not available in the U.K.[18] (page 38).

These principles are what helped the company to expand. In fact, Marks & Spencer had its first taste of international expansion as early as 1940.

Marks & Spencer Today

Today, few people in the world have not heard of Marks & Spencer, especially in the retailing realm, where the company is considered Britain's leading retailer. Marks & Spencer has had such an impact in the United Kingdom that it has been said that the nation's evolution is shown through the changes and progress at Marks & Spencer.[19] As for success, evidence of this would be that by 1994 the company had captured 18% of the U.K. market. At that time, 33% of British women were wearing Marks & Spencer undergarments. Market share in some areas was up to 40%. Men's suits had captured 20% market share.[20] Profits in 1994 grossed £851 million ($1.39 billion) on sales of £6.5 billion ($10.6 billion). This made Marks & Spencer Britain's most profitable retailer. Marks & Spencer stores today are present throughout England and Ireland, with 55 stores in London alone.[21] The United Kingdom is not the only site, however, for successful Marks & Spencer outlets, which are now located around the globe. These outlets come in various forms. To comply with foreign government restrictions, Marks & Spencer now has franchises, subsidiaries, and wholly owned stores under names other than Marks & Spencer, such as Brooks Brothers and Kings Supermarkets.

As of 1996, there were 645 locations of Marks & Spencer worldwide, with 373 stores in the United Kingdom, Europe, Hong Kong, and Canada. The countries in which Marks & Spencer owns outlets (with the number of outlets and their locations) are as follows:[22]

- *Belgium:* 3 stores in Brussels, Antwerp, Liege.
- *Canada:* 48 stores in Barrie, Ontario; Bramlea, Ontario; Burlington, Ontario; Calgary, Alberta; Coquitlan, British Columbia; Dieppe, New Brunswick; Edmonton, Alberta; Etobicoke, Ontario; Halifax, Nova Scotia; Hamilton, Ontario (2); Kelowna, British Columbia; Kingston, Ontario; Kitchener, Ontario; London, Ontario; Mississauga, Ontario; Montreal, Quebec.
- *France:* 17 stores in Belle Epine, Boulevard Haussmann, La Defence Quatre Temps, Lille, Lyon, Marseille, Nantes, Nice, Parly (2), Reims, Rosny (2), Rouen, Rue de Rivoli, Strasbourg, Toulouse, Velizy (2), Villiers en Biere.
- *Germany:* 1 store in Cologne.
- *Hong Kong:* 7 stores in Causeway Bay, Central, Harbour City, Queen's Road, Central Queensway, Shatin, Taikoo Shing.
- *Ireland:* 2 stores in Cork, Dublin.
- *Spain:* 5 stores in Barcelona, Madrid, Serrano, Seville, Valencia.
- *The Netherlands:* 2 stores in Amsterdam, The Hague.

As for franchises, in 1996 Marks & Spencer had operations (followed by the number and their locations) in the following countries:[23]

- *Austria:* 3 stores in Vienna.
- *The Bahamas:* 5 stores in Nassau, Freeport, Cayman Islands.
- *Bermuda:* 1 store in Hamilton.
- *Canary Islands:* 4 stores in Gran Canaria, Tenerife.
- *Cyprus:* 8 stores in Limassol, Larnaca, Paphos, Paralimini, Nicosia.
- *The Czech Republic:* 1 store in Prague.
- *Finland:* 5 stores in Helsinki.
- *Gibraltar:* 1 store in Gibraltar.
- *Greece:* 9 stores in Athens, Crete, Kavala, Thessaloniki, Larissa.
- *Hungary:* 2 stores in Budapest.
- *Indonesia:* 6 stores in Jakarta.
- *Israel:* 7 stores in Tel Aviv, Jerusalem, Haifa, Kfar Saba, Ashdod, Rechorot.
- *Jersey:* 2 stores in St. Helier, St. Brelades.
- *Malaysia:* 2 stores in Kuala Lumpur.
- *Malta:* 2 stores in Valletta, Sliena.
- *The Philippines:* 2 stores in Valletta, Manila.
- *Portugal:* 6 stores in Lisbon, Oporto.
- *Singapore:* 7 stores in Singapore.
- *Thailand:* 6 stores in Bangkok.
- *Turkey:* 1 store in Istanbul.

Finally, stores owned by Marks & Spencer, but not under the name of Marks & Spencer, include Brooks

Brothers, Inc. located in the District of Columbia and in the following U.S. states:[24] Alabama, California, Connecticut, Florida, Georgia, Illinois, Kentucky, Louisiana, Maryland, Massachusetts, Michigan, Minnesota, Missouri, New Jersey, New York, North Carolina, Ohio, Oklahoma, Pennsylvania, Tennessee, Texas, Virginia, and Washington. The Kings Supermarkets are all located in New Jersey.

Having clarified that Marks & Spencer is, indeed, an international retailer, we can move on to look at how they became international.

Evolution of an International Retailer

Luca Pellegrini, in his article "Alternatives for Growth and Internationalization in Retailing," talks about the different modes of internationalization for retailers.[25] He maintains that most retailers follow the same pattern. In the appendix to that article, Pellegrini gives examples of different retailers and describes how they became international. One of these companies is Marks & Spencer. Pellegrini illustrates its international growth in steps:

Step 1—Original market.
Step 2—Adjacent market.
Step 3—Other national market.
Step 4—Other similar countries for Marks & Spencer; this would be France, Belgium, Spain, and the Netherlands.
Step 5—Other similar countries.
Step 6—Other foreign countries.
Steps 1 through 6 were all carried out with the original store type.
Step 7—Other similar countries: D'Allairds, Peoples (CDN)—retail men's and women's wear.
Step 8—Brooks Brothers (USA)—department stores.
Step 9—Kings Supermarket (USA)—supermarkets.
Steps 7 through 9 involved similar store types.

As we can see, Marks & Spencer did not stray far from its original format. The way in which Pellegrini portrays Marks & Spencer's internationalization is valid. However, he neglects to mention the very first step the company took in internationalizing. This first step was taken, as mentioned previously, as early as the 1940s.

Marks & Spencer's first attempt at internationalization was exporting.[26] This is an interesting concept for a retailer because, in most cases, exporting is a strategy used by manufacturers when internationalizing. Exporting is seen as a way to "test the waters," so to speak. For a retailer to do so is unusual. This factor supports the concept that Marks & Spencer is a "manufacturer without factories." Because of its close and controlling relationship with suppliers, Marks & Spencer was able to export its unique private label brand—St. Michael—to foreign countries.

There is not much in print about Marks & Spencer exportations; Briggs simply notes that by 1955, the Marks & Spencer Export Corporation was exporting goods worth £703,000 ($1,146,000) overseas.[27] Its exporting continues today. In Marks & Spencer's 1996 online annual report, export store sales are reported as having increased by 11.7% and total shipments from the United Kingdom to subsidiaries and franchises by 12.3%.[28]

After first exporting in the 1940s, Marks & Spencer went overseas. Contrary to what might be expected, however, the company went overseas somewhat by force. This was due in part to its own saturation of the British market, as well as to economic and political factors. The political pressure that Marks & Spencer felt was perhaps the determining factor. At that time, some members of the Labour Party were threatening that leading retailers might be candidates for a future nationalization program.[29] These two factors combined with the perceived cultural proximity of Canada were enough to make the management of Marks & Spencer believe that going there was a sensible decision. It would be safe to assume, as well, that the market south of the Canadian border was also deemed as very attractive.

In 1973, Marks & Spencer bought three Canadian chains—People's Department Stores, Inc. (budget-priced stores), D'Allaird's (clothing for older women), and Walker's clothing stores—which were made into stores similar to the Marks & Spencer stores in Britain.[30] The company's entry into Canada received much negative press, and for a valid reason. It had made a mistake on entering into the new market. Marks & Spencer had assumed that Canada was so culturally similar to Britain that no modifications to its retail format were needed. The company's strategy was simply to transport the formula that had been working so well in Britain to Canada.[31] When they realized their mistake, management at Marks & Spencer went about correcting it. Eventually, they began to use merchandise made mostly in Canada, and the food department was expanded. In addition to changing the marketing mix, Marks & Spencer eventually closed some of the inner city outlets and opened others in suburban areas.[32] However, the company was slow to change its habits, and this resulted in an operating loss of 9.7 million Canadian dollars (US $7 million) for 1988.[33] The Canadian venture was difficult for Marks & Spencer. The company lost money for the first decade of its existence.[34] The stores operating under the D'Allaird's name have since been closed in order to help management concentrate on improving performance in other Canadian operations.[35]

Although its first overseas experience was not a pleasant one, Marks & Spencer was not deterred. The company next decided to enter a European market. Perhaps this was because this market was physically closer to Great Britain. In addition, even though the languages are different, European cultures are similar in many aspects. Marks & Spencer decided to venture into France, opening its first outlet in Paris in 1975. The location was prime, on the Boulevard Haussman, which is in an area of Paris renowned for its boutiques. French consumer habits were studied and a marketing mix was planned. The products offered would differ from those sold in the United Kingdom in an attempt to shape the offering to the market. Clothes were made to have a somewhat snugger fit, and French wines were added to the grocery area.[36] The company soon noticed, however, that the French items were staying on the shelves and the British imports were quickly disappearing. This convinced Marks & Spencer executives to change their marketing mix, and the store has known great success since. This positive experience abroad served as a catalyst not only for the company to open stores in different provinces in France (by 1990, there were eight stores in France), but also for it to expand to Belgium. Belgians also got to know Marks & Spencer in 1975. The first store opened in Brussels, and it was followed seven years later by another store in Antwerp.[37]

Realizing that its operations in Europe were well underway, and that business in Canada was slowly improving, resulting in profit, Marks & Spencer decided to enter the U.S. market. Incidentally, Marks & Spencer found it appropriate to go into its second North American market the same way it entered the first: by acquisition. In April of 1988, Marks & Spencer purchased Brooks Brothers, and in August of the same year, Kings Supermarkets. Brooks Brothers and Marks & Spencer actually had quite a lot in common. Both sold only private label goods, both worked closely with their manufacturers, and both had been around since the latter 1800s and early 1900s. Both also had a very well-developed, loyal customer base.

Although the pair had much in common, this acquisition received a great deal of bad press. This is principally because Marks & Spencer paid $750 million—an enormous sum—to acquire Brooks Brothers. In fact, this figure amounted to 30 times the chain's estimated net profits for 1987 (the year before the acquisition).[38]

Management at Marks & Spencer did not let the bad press discourage them and went ahead with the deal. The agreement had its sweet side. Not only did Marks & Spencer get the U.S. chain consisting of 47 stores, but it also got a 21-store joint venture with Daido Worsted Mills in Japan. In addition, a special agreement stipulated that the previous owners of Brooks Brothers, the Canadian Campeau organization, could not compete against Brooks Brothers in the United States or in Japan for five years. At the time of the acquisition, Brooks Brothers also had three factories in Long Island City and North Carolina, it's own charge card, and a direct marketing catalogue.[39]

After the takeover, the Brooks Brothers' product line changed slightly. The first change was an expansion of the sportswear selection and additions to the women's line.[40] In addition to widening the product base, and in an effort to attract a younger clientele, Marks & Spencer cut prices and opened stores in outlet shopping centers.[41] Besides acquiring a new customer base, Marks & Spencer also acquired new products for its European stores. The company has been known to take a Brooks Brothers classic like the $259 blazer, examine it, and duplicate it to sell through its outlets in Europe.[42]

The Kings Supermarkets have also witnessed a few changes. This chain, which had been family owned and profitable since 1936, was well-known for quality and innovation. Because of the strong national brand loyalty in the United States, Marks & Spencer decided that having a mixture of national brands in addition to its own St. Michael brand would provide a better merchandise mix in stores.

After entering the American market, further expansion in Europe seemed like the best bet. Building on its past successes in France and Belgium, Marks & Spencer opened its doors in Madrid, Spain, in 1990. As in Paris, the location chosen was in an ideal area, situated in the well-known shopping district of Calle Serrano. Before opening this store, however, Marks & Spencer had tested the market by venturing into a franchise agreement with Galerias Preciados (Marks &

Spencer already had departments within the existing Galerias stores). Then the company moved to open its own store.

This expansion marked not only the company's first attempt to enter a Spanish-speaking country, but also its first joint venture. The joint venture was between Marks & Spencer and Cortefiel, one of Spain's most successful retailers.[43] An explanation for the decision to enter the joint venture could be the somewhat unstable political environment in Spain at that time. The country had just emerged from an oppressive dictatorship period under Franco not too long before the Marks & Spencer opening.

Finally, after Europe and North America, Marks & Spencer turned to another area of industrialized nations, the Far East. As the company had already acquired Brooks Brothers outlets in Japan, expanding into Hong Kong seemed like the next logical step. In the early 1990s, Marks & Spencer opened three outlets in Hong Kong. The merchandise for these outlets was sourced from Great Britain, and in 1994, Marks & Spencer concentrated on building an adequate distribution center to enable it to supply merchandise in a more timely and cost-effective manner.[44]

After opening outlets in the Far East, Marks & Spencer decided to return to an area of the world in which it had previously known success, Europe. In January 1996, Marks & Spencer announced that it would be opening its first outlet in Germany,[45] Europe's largest and wealthiest nation, with a large population not to mention a clothing market that is double the size of the United Kingdom's. The site chosen for the first store was Cologne.

Future Projections

Marks & Spencer can truly be called an international retailer. What does the future have in store for the company? Clearly, more expansion, both domestic and international. One may think that the United Kingdom is saturated and that there is no place else for Marks & Spencer to go but abroad. Nevertheless, if there is one thing to be learned from the Marks & Spencer story, it is that improvements can always be made. There is still growth potential for this quasi-national British landmark. It plans on opening new stores, as well as extending the ones that already exist.[46] It is also considering TV shopping as an option for future U.K. growth.[47]

Even though Far East sales were down in 1995, probably due to the costs of opening the company's seventh outlet in Hong Kong during that year (it has since opened its eighth), this region of the world has also been judged a potential area for business. These outlets are boutique/specialty stores not full-scale department stores. Some stores have been been repositioned to sell only underwear and hosiery. Marks & Spencer opened a store in South Korea in 1997. Marks & Spencer decided against opening a store in Japan due to excessive property costs but has established a resident office in Shanghai, China, that could amount to a future opening—most likely resulting in a joint venture because of the strict political barriers to foreign retailers.[48] Europe is also a target for future growth. Marks & Spencer plans to open additional stores in Germany. Continued business will also be pursued in Spain. As for other cities in Europe, the company has plans for Paris. Comparable in size to London, but with only 7 stores compared to London's 55, Paris is seen as one city in Europe where new outlets are conceivable. Finally, a little closer to home, the company plans on further growth in the Republic of Ireland.

Conclusions

It is possible to extrapolate Marks & Spencer's recipe for success in analyzing the company's future projections. The key ingredients would be innovation, determination, and, surely, perspiration. We can see that the company's growth is cyclical. It did not give up on internationalizing when the Canadian venture did not go as planned. Instead, management learned from its mistakes and used this knowledge to grow elsewhere. In addition, it would appear all too easy for a company to become overzealous as the result of success in one region and consequently want to make this new market its home. This is not what Marks & Spencer did. The company went back to the Asian market after its European success, and then back to the European market after its Asian success while constantly improving its current operations and opening franchises in all regions of the world. Finally, if there is one keystone in Marks & Spencer's success, it is efficient distribution through close relations with suppliers. Marks & Spencer started on this creed when Michael Marks first started peddling. The fact that it has kept this tradition for well over a century is remarkable and commendable, not to mention undoubtedly, traditionally British.

DISCUSSION QUESTIONS

1. Marks & Spencer has a close relationship with its suppliers. Describe the advantages and disadvantages of such a relationship for both sides.
2. Marks & Spencer's private label, St. Michael, has been in existence for over 50 years, yet in the United States, a strategy of mixing national brands and private labels was used. What is the attraction to the development of a private label for retailers?
3. Examine the list of areas in which franchises and wholly owned stores were pursued. What conclusions can be drawn?
4. What is meant by economy of scale? Give examples of how Marks & Spencer takes advantage of this. Are there any examples of economy of scale to be found in the study?
5. Marks & Spencer has been called a manufacturer without factories because of the tight relationship it has with manufacturers. Upon acquiring Brooks Brothers, Marks & Spencer also acquired factories that were producing merchandise for Brooks Brothers. The company sold these factories and has stated that it is not ready to get into production for itself. Discuss why large retailers such as Marks & Spencer may be hesitant to expand vertically.
6. Certain changes had to be made to Marks & Spencer's merchandise mix in Canada. More items produced in Canada were included. In France, the French items were left on the shelves and the British imports flew out of the store. Discuss the cultural differences that may explain the predicaments.
7. Marks & Spencer offers financial services as well as general merchandise to its customers. Its credit card program varies greatly from those used by department stores in the United States in that customers make a deposit (e.g., $5) and receive credit for four times their deposit ($20). When customers' deposits exceed their expenses, interest is earned on the difference (e.g., deposit $5, credit equals $20 [four times deposit equals credit]). If purchases equal $15, the remaining balance of $5 can collect interest. Could this be the next step for U.S. retailers? Why or why not?
8. Acquisition was used in both Canada and the United States, two countries that are perceived as culturally similar but geographically much larger than the United Kingdom and at quite a distance from the company's headquarters. Wholly owned subsidiaries were used in France and Belgium with a joint venture in Spain. Marks & Spencer's sights are now set on China. Studying past strategies used, what predictions could be made, if any, regarding the company's entrance into China's market?
9. Marks & Spencer uses a single brand, and has similar outlet requirements for all of its stores, but it does shape it's merchandise somewhat to local markets. Would Marks & Spencer be considered a global or a multinational retailer and why?
10. Discuss Marks & Spencer's steps to international growth as discussed by Luca Pellegrini. What would a logical Step 10 be?

ENDNOTES

1. "British Institutions: Marks & Spencer Store of Value." (1993). *The Economist,* Vol. 327, June 26, p. 63.
2. Wahl, M. (1993). "Pushing Yankee Products in Lord Rayner's Court." *Brandweek,* Vol. 24, July 12, p. 26.
3. Schurer, M. (1995). "Marks & Spencer." *Supermarket Business,* Vol. 50, February, p. 108.
4. Schurer (1995).
5. Marcom, J. Jr. (1991). "Blue Blazers and Guacamole." *Forbes,* Vol. 148, November 25, pp. 64–68.
6. Salmans, S. (1980). "Mixed Fortunes at M&S." *Management Today,* November, pp. 66–73.
7. Tse, K. K. (1985). *Marks & Spencer: Anatomy of Britain's Most Efficiently Managed Company.* Great Britain: Pergamon Press.

8. Tse (1985).
9. Marcom (1991).
10. Schurer (1995).
11. Smith New Court Securities, PLC. (1995). *Marks & Spencer Company Report,* May 25.
12. Salmans (1980).
13. Salmans (1980).
14. Sieff, I. (1970). *Memoirs.* London: C. Tinling & Co. Ltd.
15. Tse (1985).
16. Briggs, A. (1992). "St. Michael Marks and Spencer PLC." In A. Hast, ed., *International Directory of Company Histories,* Vol. 5. Detroit: St. James Press, pp. 124–126.
17. Briggs (1992).
18. Whitehead, M. (1994). "Marks & Spencer—Britain's Leading Retailer: Quality and Value Worldwide." *Management Decisions,* Vol. 32, pp. 38–41.
19. *The Economist* (June 26, 1993).
20. Bower, J. and J. Matthews. (1994). "Marks & Spencer: Sir Richard Greenbury's Quiet Revolution." *Harvard Business School Publishing,* pp. 1–29.
21. "Annual Report Marks & Spencer Worldwide." (Online). (1996). Available: www.marks-and-spencer.co.uk/annual/global.html.
22. "Annual Report Marks & Spencer Worldwide." (1996).
23. "Annual Report Marks & Spencer Worldwide." (1996).
24. "Brooks Brothers Clothing." (Online). (1996). Available: www.marks-and-spencer.com/worldwide/brooks.html.
25. Pelligrini, L. (1994). "Alternatives for Growth and Internationalization." *The International Review of Retail, Distribution and Consumer Research,* Vol. 4, No. 2, pp. 121–148.
26. Briggs (1992).
27. Briggs (1992).
28. "Annual Report Marks & Spencer Worldwide." (1996).
29. Whitehead (1994).
30. Weiner, S. (1989). "Low Marks, Few Sparks." *Forbes,* Vol. 144, September 18, pp. 146–147.
31. Maremont, M. (1988). "Marks & Spencer Pays a Premium For Pinstripes, *Business Week,* April 18, p. 67.
32. Salmans (1980).
33. Weiner (1989).
34. Maremont (1988).
35. "Annual Report Marks & Spencer Worldwide." (1996).
36. Salmans (1980).
37. Whitehead, M. (1991). "International Franchising —Marks & Spencer: A Case Study." *International Journal of Retail and Distribution Management,* Vol. 19, pp. 10–12.
38. Maremont (1988).
39. Whitehead (1991).
40. Bhargava, S. W. (1993). "What's Next, Grunge Bathrobes?" *Business Week,* June 21, pp. 64–68.
41. Moshavi, S. (1994). "Calling All Mall Rats." *Forbes,* Vol. 153, April 25, p. 123.
42. Marcom (1991).
43. Whitehead (1994).
44. Bower and Matthews (1994).
45. "Annual Report Marks & Spencer Worldwide." (1996).
46. Gilbert Eliott & Company. (1996). *Marks & Spencer Annual Report,* March 22.
47. Smith New Court Securities, PLC (1995).
48. Smith New Court Securities, PLC (1995).

COMPANY FOCUS I.2

ISETAN AND BARNEYS JOINT VENTURE

Lori Garijo

Isetan Department Stores

History

Many leading Japanese department stores began as kimono shops, and Isetan Company, Ltd. is no exception. Founded in 1886 by Tanji Kosuge, Isetan was then known as the Iseya Tanji Drapery. This store was located in the Kanda District of Tokyo.[1] Kosuge chose this location because it was heavily populated and near a busy intersection, which guaranteed steady customer traffic. The location was also close to many geisha districts, and the geisha became primary customers. Kosuge's business quickly expanded, and he began to display his merchandising skills using new and innovative (for the time) ideas. Kosuge would send salesmen out to visit customers with samples of the store's original products, and he experimented with keeping the store open at night. Seasonal sales were also introduced, and soon, Kosuge was buying out other kimono stores.[2]

Although the store was prospering, other retailers were attempting to alter their stores to a department store format. In 1907, Kosuge changed the name of his store to Isetan, a combination of the first two syllables of Iseya with the first syllable of Tanji.[3] It is not clear if Kosuge was planning to change Isetan's format, but at the time of his death in 1916, Isetan was still a kimono shop.

Isetan was taken over by Kosuge's son-in-law Gihei Takahashi, who had been working for the store since 1908. Takahashi took his wife's family name of Kosuge, and when his father-in-law died, he also took the first name of Tanji.[4]

Under Kosuge II, Isetan began the transformation to a department store format. Kosuge II created the Isetan Partnership in 1917 to run the store and to give Isetan a more businesslike stature. Unfortunately, the Great Kanto Earthquake of 1923 occurred during the transformation planned by Kosuge II. Although the earthquake was a devastating occurrence, the event actually pushed Isetan into the department store format.[5] When Isetan reopened in 1924, it expanded its merchandise offerings with household goods, toys, children's clothing, cosmetics, and stationery. The earthquake changed many things, including the street configuration of Kanda. Kanda was no longer a busy, profitable area.[6]

In 1930, Isetan became a limited company, renamed Isetan Company Ltd., and moved its store to the city of Shinjuku. Shinjuku was the perfect location for the department store. Considered a city subcenter of Tokyo, Shinjuku attracted large numbers of middle-class families. This location allowed Isetan to prosper.[7] During World War II, Isetan's growth was slowed, but the store continued to operate. After the war, retailers experienced a change in consumer tastes. Consumers had become influenced by the Western-style clothing they had been exposed to during the Allied occupation. Isetan noticed this change and used it as an opportunity to become a fashion leader. Kosuge II also used this time to introduce modern merchandising techniques. Kosuge began "dividing up customers very specifically on the basis of age, sex, taste, and spending power."[8]

In 1960, Kosuge II gave control of Isetan to his son Toshio, who also took the name Tanji. Under Kosuge III, Isetan cemented its reputation for innovation. Kosuge III realized that car ownership was growing and Isetan became the first Japanese department store to have a parking garage. In 1963, the store added a Pierre Balmain salon to introduce designer brands. Another important innovation during this time period was the development of a sizing system for women's clothing. This system has been utilized by all Japanese department stores. In 1968, Isetan opened an annex that was entirely devoted to menswear. By opening this annex, Kosuge felt that Isetan's male consumers could be targeted more effectively. The Isetan Research Institute Company Ltd. was established in 1967. The Institute's purpose was to collect and analyze information about fashion and consumer trends. By the end of the 1960s, Isetan was the leading fashion merchandiser in Japan.[9]

Expansion
Isetan began its international expansion with the opening of a store in Singapore in 1972. The subsidiary Isetan (Singapore) Ltd. was created to control Isetan's interests in Singapore.[10] Isetan is Singapore's oldest Japanese retailer and is currently located in the well-known Shaw House, a large retailing complex that also houses five movie theaters and 10 restaurants. Isetan occupies five floors of the complex and targets affluent consumers. This is evident by the merchandise that Isetan offers: designer labels Escada, Valentino, and Ungaro; household goods from Wedgewood and Royal Copenhagen; and many other gift and souvenir items.[11,12]

Isetan (Singapore) suffered net losses in 1994 and 1995. The company restructured itself and discontinued operations that had proven unprofitable, such as its In-Kids outlets. Isetan also reduced its excess inventory (through warehouse sales), controlled operating expenses, and reduced agency lines such as Donna Karan.[13,14] The agency lines required a large inventory investment. After the restructuring, Isetan (Singapore) realized a net profit of $1.99 million for the fiscal year ending March 31, 1996.[15] It is surprising that Isetan was able to realize a profit after the losses that were incurred by the parent company due to the Isetan-Barneys' joint venture.

In 1973, Isetan again entered the international market with the opening of a store in Hong Kong. A second branch store was opened in 1987. The Hong Kong stores mainly targeted Japanese tourists. Unfortunately, the Hong Kong expansion was not profitable for Isetan, and the last of the two stores closed in 1996.[16,17]

In the 1980s, Isetan expanded into other areas. Several subsidiaries were created, and they illustrate the new diversification of the company. The subsidiaries include: J. F. Corporation, Isetan's supplier of original brands; Queens Isetan Co., Ltd., which runs a chain of supermarkets and gourmet food stores; and the Isetan Finance Company, Ltd., which oversees the non-banking financial operations for the company.[18] Most of these subsidiaries were created under Kuniyasu Kosuge, who was given control of the company by his father, Kosuge III, in 1984.

The company continued to grow under Kuniyasu's control, and more stores were opened in Vienna, London, and Thailand.[19] Kuniyasu financed Isetan's expansion by issuing warrants. Warrants are options to purchase stock at a fixed price in the future. Unfortunately, a large number of warrants were exercised and it became clear that 33% of Isetan's stock was controlled by outsiders.[20] The real estate developer, Shuwa Corp., held the largest amount of "outsider" stock at 22.9%. Beause Shuwa Corp. was facing its own cash shortage, it considered selling its Isetan shares. Ito-Yokado, a Japanese mass merchandise store chain, was approached by Shuwa to buy the shares.[21] In May of 1993, Mitsubishi Bank (of whom Isetan is a partial member) stepped in and forced Kuniyasu to resign. Kuniyasu Kosuge remains at Isetan, but only as a figurehead. Mitsubishi Bank did not buy the shares from Shuwa, but the bank placed two of its executives on Isetan's board of directors to oversee a restructuring of the company.[22,23]

Kazuma Koshiba, a former executive in Isetan's marketing department, was hired as the new president of Isetan. Koshiba sold several of the extravagant, unprofitable subsidiaries and concentrated on increasing Isetan's net profit. Cost-cutting measures were implemented. For example, in newly opened stores, Isetan began to employ part-time workers instead of full-time workers.[24] While Koshiba continues to rid Isetan of many of its unprofitable ventures, the fate of Isetan stores in China is unclear. The Chinese locations, which opened in 1993, are not yet profitable. It is unlikely, however, that Isetan will pull out of China due to the tremendous potential of that market.

Koshiba is still in the process of fixing Isetan's problems. Isetan is currently embroiled in a legal battle concerning a joint venture with Barneys New York. This joint venture agreement was made while Isetan was under the leadership of Kuniyasu Kosuge and was inherited by Koshiba.

Isetan-Barneys Joint Venture

Barneys Inc. is the parent company of Barneys New York, a well-known clothing retailer based in the same city. Barneys was founded by Barney Pressman in 1923, and was known for its discounted men's suits.[25] In the 1970s, the price and quality of Barneys merchandise was elevated by Pressman's son, Fred. In the 1980s, Fred Pressman's sons, Gene and Bob, turned Barneys into a trendy upscale store. High fashion designer labels became more frequent, and Barneys' first women's department was opened. In the late 1980s, a 70,000 square foot (6,500 square meters) women's store was added to the 17th Street flagship store.[26] It was also during this time period that Gene and Bob Pressman began looking for a partner to help them expand.

Isetan was enjoying the economic prosperity of Japan in the 1980s. New stores were opened in other

Asian countries, and Isetan had diversified into other retailing formats, such as sports clubs and restaurants.[27] Kuniyasu Kosuge (then president of Isetan) was introduced to the Pressmans through representatives of Goldman, Sachs & Company.[28] A joint venture between Isetan and Barneys was discussed. Both companies could benefit from a joint venture. Barneys could gain expansion financing, and Isetan could gain a prestigeous store name to use in specialty store expansion in Japan.

The Agreement

In 1989, a joint venture agreement between Isetan and Barneys was signed. Isetan agreed to finance the establishment of an unspecified number of Barneys stores across the United States and Asia. In exchange for the financing, Isetan would obtain exclusive licensing rights to the Barneys name in Asia. Isetan would also receive training in Barneys merchandising techniques.[29,30]

Isetan gave the Pressmans $12 million to finance the smaller stores and later agreed to give them $236 million to build three large stores in New York, Chicago, and Beverly Hills.[31,32] Isetan was given half-ownership of the new stores, and was entitled to receive monthly rent payments from these stores. The rent payments were to be based on the sales volume and property value of each store location.[33–35]

This joint venture appeared beneficial for both partners. Barneys Japan opened on November 3, 1990 in Shinjuku, and Barneys shops within Isetan department stores followed later.[36] Plans were being made to move Barneys' flagship store from 17th Street to a new upscale address on Madison Avenue. Barneys and Isetan were also collaborating on the development and manufacturing of a private label line to be sold in Japan and the United States.[37] Although the joint venture seemed to function smoothly, it would soon become apparent that the venture was not as perfect as observers believed.

Signs of Trouble

The first sign that the joint venture was beginning to unravel came in the Fall of 1991. Isetan was in another partnership with the Metropolitan Life Insurance Company. The goal of this particular partnership was the development of office space on the floors above the Barneys store (which was under construction) on Madison Avenue. Without warning, Met Life backed out of the deal.[38,39] The cause of the Met Life pullout is not clear. What is known is that Isetan and the Pressmans were relying on the cost projections for building a store in the first nine floors of the existing building on Madison Avenue; these projections were given by Met Life. The Pressmans have a reputation for extravagant spending. Perhaps Met Life suspected the Pressmans were incapable of staying within those projections. Concerned that its investment in the Barneys store was in jeopardy, Isetan bought out Met Life's interest in the upper floors for $120 million.[40]

The second troubling sign occurred in late 1992. Barneys needed more money to continue the construction of the new flagship store, as well as the stores in Chicago and Beverly Hills. This occurrence was particularly disturbing because the Madison Avenue store was scheduled to open in 1992. There were also problems with the Beverly Hills store, which caused the construction budget for that store to double.[41] Isetan had originally agreed upon a commitment of $236 million to finance the construction of the three big stores. Although Isetan felt uneasy about loaning more money to the Pressmans, it continued to do so. To reassure Isetan, the Pressmans agreed to personally guarantee the $168 million in loans.[42]

The third disturbing sign began with rumors that Barneys was frequently late in paying its debts. Soon, it was obvious that the allegations were more than rumors. Suppliers began complaining about extremely late payments from Barneys. It was later found that Barneys paid on average 42 days late compared with the industry average of 15 days.[43] As the complaints continued to grow, the Pressmans found that the opening of the Beverly Hills store was threatened by suppliers who were holding back shipments to the store. The Pressmans responded by blaming the late payments on "managerial distraction, bungling, and a new voicemail system."[44] The Pressmans also published an incomplete set of financial figures in an attempt to show that Barneys was financially sound.

In what was probably the most disturbing sign of trouble to Isetan, after March 1995, Barneys stopped paying interest on its short-term loans to the company, and did not pay the January 1996 rent that was owed to Isetan.[45,46]

Bankruptcy

On January 11, 1996, Barneys filed for Chapter 11 bankruptcy protection. In addition, Barneys filed a lawsuit against Isetan for $50 million. The $50 million was the amount of rent collected by Isetan from Barneys for 1995–1996. Barneys claimed that it was forced to file for bankruptcy due to Isetan's discontinuation of financial backing. The intention of filing Chapter 11 was to force Isetan to adhere to the original agreement.[47]

On January 25, 1996, Isetan filed a countersuit against Barneys, and petitioned a bankruptcy judge to order Barneys to pay $3 million in back rent on the New York, Chicago, and Beverly Hills stores. Isetan argued that it was the only post-petition creditor that Barneys was refusing to pay.[48] The petition was considered on January 31, 1996.[49]

On February 8, 1996, Isetan, which had earlier objected to Barneys seeking of debtor-in-possession financing, withdrew its objection and agreed to a $3.25 million settlement from Barneys by which Isetan would receive payments on the $3.25 million from Barneys through April 19, 1996.[50] Extending the settlement of February 8, Barneys agreed to continue payments to Isetan through June 27.

Isetan returned to court, this time seeking the return of the $168 million in loans that it had made to Barneys. Isetan claimed that the loans were personally guaranteed by the Pressmans.

In response, Barneys added Kenneth Klee to its legal team. Klee, a top bankruptcy lawyer, is one of the authors of the U.S. Bankruptcy Code.[51]

Controversy

The ongoing legal battle between Isetan and Barneys has been complicated by contradictions. These contradictions have led to speculation that perhaps the Pressmans are guilty of fraud. Here are a few of the contradictions that have led to the speculations.

In regard to Barneys claim that it was forced to seek Chapter 11 protection, Barneys cited that it was fearful that Isetan would terminate its leases, and that fear was a determining factor in its decision.[52] This claim can be contrasted with a statement made by Irving Rosenthal, Barneys chief financial officer, on January 16, 1996. Rosenthal stated that Barneys had less than $1 million in cash on hand.[53] It is possible that the real reason for Barneys' bankruptcy petition was its almost total lack of operating cash.

Barneys claimed that suppliers were often paid late due to "managerial distractions" and a new voice-mail system. This claim can be contrasted with a partial list of Barneys' major unsecured creditors:[54]

Hugo Boss Fashions . . . . *owed $3.7 million*
Donna Karan Menswear . . . . *owed $2.1 million*
Giorgio Armani Menswear . . . . *owed $252,255*
Hermès . . . . *owed $66,144*

Isetan claimed that loans made to Barneys were personally guaranteed by the Pressmans. In contrast, the Pressmans claimed that all of the money, including the personal guarantees, were to be converted into Barneys stock, not to exceed 49%.[55] Considering Barneys' grim financial status, this arrangement would be beneficial only to Barneys. Once the loans were converted into stock, Barneys' rent payments on the three big stores (approximately $2 million per month) would cease. In 1997, Dixon Concepts of Hong Kong was in the processs of acquiring Barneys.

Conclusion

Although this dispute will eventually be resolved by the courts, the repercussions from this battle will be felt for years to come. The damage done to the trust between partnerships of foreign powers has already taken place. International retailers are awaiting the decision from this case, and regardless of the outcome, the decision will likely affect the future of foreign joint ventures.

DISCUSSION QUESTIONS

1. Is the Isetan-Barneys relationship a strategic alliance?
2. What are Isetan's motivations for international expansion? How would you assess their international expansion strategy thus far?
3. Using Dunning's theory (see Chapter 1), assess Isetan's decision to expand initially in Hong Kong, Singapore, and China.

ENDNOTES

1. Lloyd-Owen, J. (1992). "Isetan Company Limited." In A. Hast, ed., *International Directory of Company Histories,* Vol. 5. Detroit: St. James Press, pp. 85–87.
2. Lloyd-Owen (1992).
3. Lloyd-Owen (1992).
4. Lloyd-Owen (1992).
5. Lloyd-Owen (1992).
6. Lloyd-Owen (1992).
7. Lloyd-Owen (1992).
8. Lloyd-Owen (1992).
9. Lloyd-Owen (1992).
10. "Singapore's Isetan/Pft-2: Revenue Up 9.4%." (1996). *Wall Street Journal,* June 21.
11. "Shaw House." (1996). Singapore Shopping Centers [http: //www.iipl.com.sg]
12. "Isetan Makes $2 Million Profit After Two Years of Losses." (1996). *Asian Retailing* [http: // www.montar.com/grocery/news/singaport/isetan.html].
13. *Wall Street Journal* (June 21, 1996).
14. *Asian Retailing* (1996).
15. *Wall Street Journal* (June 21, 1996).
16. Lloyd-Owen (1992).
17. *Retail News Letter.* (1996). February, No. 432.
18. Lloyd-Owen (1992).
19. Lloyd-Owen (1992).
20. Spaeth, A. (1996). "Burned in the U.S.A.—Japan's Isetan Drops a Bundle on a Misguided Spending Spree with its Flashy New York Partner." *Time International,* February 5.
21. Akamatsu, T. (1993). "Shuwa and Ito-Yokado Haggle with Mitsubishi Bank over Isetan Shares." *Tokyo Business Today,* November, p. 62.
22. Spaeth (1996).
23. Akamatsu (1993).
24. "Japanese Retailing: The Recovery Department." (1995). The Economist, December 2, pp. 64, 69.
25. Spaeth (1996).
26. Strom, S. (1996). "A Match Not Made in Heaven: Another U.S.-Japan Deal Falls Through." *New York Times,* January 12, D-3.
27. Spaeth (1996).
28. Strom, S., and J. Steinhauer. (1996). "Barneys May Be Bankrupt, but its Founding Family is Unbowed." *New York Times,* January 21, sec. 3, p. 1.
29. Strom and Steinhauer (1996).
30. Spaeth (1996).
31. Steinhauer, J. (1996). "New Tactic for Barneys: Bankruptcy Brawl for Two Companies." *New York Times,* January 14, sec. 1, p. 19.
32. Strom and Steinhauer (1996).
33. Steinhauer (1996).
34. Strom and Steinhauer (1996).
35. Spaeth (1996).
36. "Pressmans in Joint Venture to Open Barneys Units in Japan." (1989). *Daily News Record,* March 21, p. 3.
37. *Daily News Record* (1989).
38. Strom (1996).
39. Strom and Steinhauer (1996).
40. Strom and Steinahuer (1996).
41. Strom and Steinhauer (1996).
42. Strom and Steinahuer (1996).
43. Strom and Steinhauer (1996).
44. Strom (1996).
45. WuDunn, S. (1996). "Japan Retailer Riles $168 Million Suit Against Barneys." *New York Times,* January 13, p. 37.
46. "Pressman Brothers Sued for Barneys Debt; Isetan to Recover Unpaid Loans." (1996). *Comtex Scientific Corporation,* January 12.
47. Strom (1996).
48. Lee, D. (1996). "Briefly; Retailing." *Los Angeles Times,* January 25, D-2.
49. Bernstein, J. (1996). "Short Cuts/Another Record for Blue Chips—Just Barely." *Newsday,* February 10, A23.
50. Pyle, A. (1996). "Briefly; Retailing." *Los Angeles Times,* April 25, D-2.
51. "Barneys to Add Klee to its Legal Team." (1996). *Wall Street Journal,* July 11.
52. Lee (1996).
53. "Barneys Says it has Less than $1 Million Cash." (1996). *New York Times,* January 17, D-4.
54. WuDunn (1996).
55. Strom and Steinhauer (1996).

COMPANY FOCUS I.3

WAL-MART

Barbara Frazier

Wal-Mart is the world's largest retailer. In 1996, the company operated 1,995 Wal-Mart stores, 433 Sam's Club Warehouse Stores, and 239 Supercenters in the United States. Internationally, it was operating 134 stores in Canada, 41 units in Mexico, 5 in Brazil, 4 in Argentina, 2 in China, and 1 in Indonesia in 1996.[1]

Wal-Mart Stores, Inc. consists of the Wal-Mart division, a national discount retailer offering family apparel, health and beauty aids, household needs, electronics, toys, fabric and crafts, lawn and garden, jewelry, and shoes. In addition, some Wal-Mart stores offer a pharmacy, automotive services, garden centers, restaurants, vision centers and 1-hour photo labs. This division operates on an everyday low price strategy predicated on aggressive cost control.

Sam's Club is a members-only warehouse club offering name-brand merchandise at warehouse prices for office use, resale to customers, and for personal use. The strategy of this division is to compensate for narrow profit margins through high volume. Sam's Club limits its merchandise mix to 3,500 items, including food products, janitorial products, auto supplies, small building equipment and hardware, snack items, office supplies, computers and equipment, electronics, small appliances, apparel, jewelry, and home furnishings.

Wal-Mart Supercenters are full-line grocery departments combined with Wal-Mart's general merchandise stores. Grocery areas include bakery, delicatessen, frozen foods, meat, produce, and dairy departments. Bud's Warehouse Outlets is a working warehouse outlet offering bulk displays of manufacturers' closeouts.[2]

Wal-Mart International Division includes joint ventures and wholly owned Wal-Mart stores, Supercenters, and Sam's Clubs in Mexico, Canada, Brazil, Argentina, mainland China, and Indonesia.[3]

History

Wal-Mart has grown to its giant status in a short 35 years. Founder Sam Walton learned basic retailing skills as a Ben Franklin franchisee. After becoming disenchanted with Ben Franklin's restrictive merchandising and sourcing policies, and the loss of his original lease, Walton purchased Harrison's Variety Store in Bentonville, Arkansas in May 1950. He renamed the store Walton's 5 & 10, and used unorthodox sales techniques, cost-reduction practices, and an emphasis on low prices and high quality to build a chain of discount department stores in the United States. By 1970, Walton had a total of 32 outlets, and had incorporated under the Wal-Mart, Inc. name. Sales increased from $31 million in 1970 to $33 billion in 1990, while the number of units increased to 1,531 in the same period. In 1991, Wal-Mart overtook Sears as the leading U.S. retailer. The first Sam's Clubs warehouses were opened in the mid-1980s.[4] The company acquired the 107-store Pace Membership Warehouses, Inc. in 1994, strengthening its position in the membership warehouse club sector.[5]

Wal-Mart continued to expand its domestic network, opening 57 new stores in the first 9 months of 1996. Eighty-seven existing Wal-Mart stores were converted to Supercenters in the same period. International expansion included the addition of 1 Supercenter in Argentina, 4 Wal-Mart stores in Canada, 2 units in China, and 13 Mexican units.[6]

The company's tremendous growth has yielded some impressive facts. Its 1996 annual report boasts that 60 million customers visit its stores each week. An average of $360 is spent annually for every man, woman, and child in America. The firm employs 675,000 associates, and yields $307 per square foot ($28.52 per square meter) annually. Based on revenues, Wal-Mart is the twelfth largest company in the world.[7]

Competitive Advantages

Wal-Mart has built its success on a deceptively simple strategy: offer low prices and a clean, friendly shopping environment; control costs; and streamline logistical and distribution strategies. Sam Walton's early experience in squeezing the lowest prices from his suppliers, and being equally miserly with the company's expenses, earned Wal-Mart a reputation for offering greater value than its competitors on name-brand merchandise.

Lower prices were welcomed by dollar-conscious U.S. consumers pinched by the economic swings of the 1970s, 1980s, and 1990s. Newer physical plants allowed Wal-Mart to present a cleaner, more comfortable place to shop than its nearest competitor, Kmart. The retailer's roots in rural America, and Sam Walton's obsession with customer service, had built a culture of friendliness and hospitality, which also gave it an advantage over Kmart and Sears.[8]

The firm's founder endowed the firm with a cost-cutting conscience, which extends from the corporate office to front-line associates. Expense reduction has been enhanced by the sheer size of the organization and by exacting standards of efficiency imposed by company executives at every level. A state-of-the-art distribution system was integral to cost-cutting efforts, reducing costly receiving errors and speeding bulk merchandise from supplier to consumer.[9]

Sam Walton chose the location for his first store, not by careful market analysis, but based on where his wife wanted to raise their family. His early expansion strategy to serve small, rural communities has been the foundation of the company's growth. In the United States, Wal-Mart has targeted underserved rural communities of less than 30,000 that had been ignored by the competition. The company's expansion sites radiate out from its distribution centers, which allowed it to control distribution costs.[10] More recently, Supercenter expansion has followed a more volume-oriented approach, targeting areas with populations averaging 61,000. Recent supercenter expansions are clustered within twelve contiguous states in the midsection of the United States. The average income for Wal-Mart's markets is around $25,000, compared to Kmart's $31,000.[11]

Wal-Mart is welcomed by most communities because of its contribution to the local tax base. When the company purchases property for a new store, it leaves extra space next to its building for possible future expansion, which prevents developers from erecting adjacent shopping centers. It also prohibits small stores and restaurants from building in its parking lots.[12]

Wal-Mart has built an efficient logistics and distribution system and sophisticated communication and inventory replenishment systems as a result of its U.S. experience in supplying stores in remote rural locations. Its exacting standards of efficiency and decision to locate distribution centers strategically, so they are no more than one day's drive from its stores, have led to distribution costs of 1.3% of sales, compared to 3% to 5% for its competitors.[13]

Wal-Mart sources its merchandise from 28 countries. Many of its sources are small firms, which may rely on Wal-Mart for a major portion of their orders. The company has developed a reputation for hard bargaining tactics with its suppliers, with price and timely delivery the main issues. Wal-Mart works closely with its manufacturers to develop new products and improve quality. To do business with Wal-Mart, even small companies may be required to invest in computer-based electronic data interchange (EDI) systems to receive orders and send invoices.

Wal-Mart has realized much of its cost advantages through the development of a quick response inventory replenishment system.[14] Suppliers are given access to Wal-Mart's sales for their own product lines, enabling them to improve sales forecasts and inventory control.[15] A 1996 pilot project between Wal-Mart and Warner-Lambert was designed to allow joint development of sales forecasts that incorporated information about all factors, including everything from planned store layout changes to meteorological data.[16]

Supporting Wal-Mart's pricing, inventory, and expense control and distribution strategy is the company's commitment to customer service. Its small-town Southern roots built a people-oriented culture that has endured as it has grown. The company's legendary "10-foot rule" reminds associates to pleasantly acknowledge any customer who is within 10 feet.[17]

Community involvement has played a major part in Wal-Mart's overall strategy.[18] In 1996, the company gave more than $81 million dollars to hospitals and nonprofit agencies. It also underwrites college scholarships and provides industrial development grants to towns and cities to help them bolster their economic bases. The company supports the Support American Manufacturing program, which shows smaller manufacturing companies how to improve their operations. Wal-Mart also supports programs to educate the public about recycling and other environmental issues. Three Environmental Demonstration Stores have been built in Kansas, Oklahoma, and California to serve as "test tubes" for environmentally friendly building materials and experimental methods for conserving energy and water.[19,20]

Wal-Mart counts its ability to motivate its workforce as a key strategic tool.[21] The company concentrates on staffing key positions with individuals who subscribe to the Wal-Mart philosophy. Flexibility is achieved by avoiding unnecessary management layers. Innovative ideas are encouraged by providing a high degree of autonomy to its associates and by fostering a climate of respect for employee ideas and opinions.[22] The company takes special care to preserve this culture through a computerized training program that not only keeps employees informed about their jobs and store operations, but also reinforces the basic tenets of the "Wal-Mart way."[23]

International Expansion

Wal-Mart began its international expansion in Mexico in 1991 as a joint venture with the Mexican retailer, Cifra. What began as a small warehouse club concept in Mexico City called Club Aurrera has grown into the six-country international division with stores in Canada, Mexico, Argentina, Brazil, Indonesia, and China. Wal-Mart also operates stores in Puerto Rico.

Sales for the international division were $3.7 billion for 1996, with an operating loss of $16 million.[24] Investment of millions of dollars into these new markets has brought criticism from skeptics. Shareholders have been vocal in their concern over the company's shift in the balance of store openings away from the United States to other countries.[25] As of the end of fiscal 1996, only the company's operations in Canada and Mexico were profitable.[26] Analysts expect, however, that the international division could represent 10% of the company's total revenues by the year 2000, and continue to grow at a pace faster than the revenue growth for the traditional discount store division.[27]

Wal-Mart's shift toward expansion outside the United States was the result of a saturated domestic market in which the company already serves the most desirable areas with its 2,000-plus units. Rather than follow the product diversification strategies of its nearest competitors, Kmart and Sears, Wal-Mart has pursued a geographical strategy through which it could apply its proprietary know-how in distribution, supplier negotiation, and merchandising to consumers outside the United States. Each country in which Wal-Mart has located has a burgeoning economy and an emerging middle class, and is under-stored in comparison to its citizens' growing purchasing power. As in the post-World War II environment in the United States, Wal-Mart is offering products for young families on a budget in Mexico, South America, China, and Indonesia.[28]

To be considered as an expansion target, a country must have suppliers that are able to provide a major portion of the merchandise assortment. Labor costs in the foreign markets that Wal-Mart has entered are favorable. The company is willing to work with countries to help them build the transportation infrastructure necessary to support future expansion in their countries.[29] The political climate has been generally favorable in developing countries, which leads to less risk when entering foreign markets.[30]

For Wal-Mart, ownership advantages that have led the company toward a global expansion strategy are its size, sophisticated distribution system, and its reputation. As the world's largest retailer, the company has a reputation as a formidable power when bargaining with its suppliers. Its immense size and profitable position domestically have allowed the international division to invest aggressively in expansion and be patient in realizing returns on those investments. Wal-Mart's "one store at a time" expansion strategy involves opening several stores in a new market, but postponing aggressive expansion until those stores are solid performers.[31]

When Wal-Mart enters a less-developed country, its executives share the company's expertise in building a distribution infrastructure with the country's government officials, encouraging the host nation to build the distribution capabilities necessary for Wal-Mart's expansion. State of the art inventory replenishment systems perfected in the United States have also given Wal-Mart an advantage when entering foreign markets.[32]

To win international customers, Wal-Mart uses its well-tested merchandising strategy of offering value, price, and friendly customer service to consumers. Consumers in emerging nations have rarely encountered retailers like Wal-Mart, with its clean, efficient, and broadly merchandised stores.[33] Store openings in new countries are colossal affairs, with thousands of price-conscious consumers flocking to clear shelves of milk, paper products, and electronics. When entering a new country, Wal-Mart plans its merchandise assortment to reflect the native population, and sources a large share of items from local suppliers. In Brazil, China, and Indonesia, about 80% of the merchandise carried in Wal-Mart's stores is locally sourced. Wal-Mart works closely with local suppliers to help them develop new products and improve quality. The company promotes national programs in each country that encourage consumers to buy local products, much like the "Buy American" program used in the United States.[34] A review of Wal-Mart's activities in international markets follows.

Mexico

Mexico City is the home of the world's largest Wal-Mart. Wal-Mart entered the Mexican market in 1991 with a 50/50 partnership with Cifra, Mexico's largest retailing group. Cifra achieved success by targeting different income groups with a saturation approach. The partnership with Wal-Mart matches Cifra's market knowledge and buying power with Wal-Mart's expertise in logistics and distribution.[35] The devaluation of the peso in 1994 and economic crisis in 1995, coupled with an erratic and inconsistent regulatory environment, have taken some of the wind out of the sails of the Wal-Mart–Cifra joint venture recently. Despite less than ideal conditions, however, the Wal-Mart–Cifra partnership enjoys the majority share of the discount retailing market in Mexico and is a profit-making venture. In 1997, Wal-Mart made a public offer to buy a controlling interest in Cifra. Cifra would continue to operate the 381 stores in Mexico. This figure includes 21 Wal-Mart Supercenters and 28 Sam's Clubs.[36] These stores are targeted toward a young, emerging middle-class market. Grand openings in Mexican markets feature singing mariachis and in-line skating employees. Stores offer a full line of groceries, tortilla shops, and a binational array of merchandise categories that mirror U.S. assortments.[37]

Although Wal-Mart has been cautious about expansion in this market due to economic hard times, the company planned to open eight new Supercenters in Mexico in 1997, estimated at $200 million in new investment in the country.

Canada

Wal-Mart entered the Canadian market through the acquisition of 122 Woolco stores in 1993. Headquartered in Toronto, Ontario, Wal-Mart Canada, Inc. is a wholly owned subsidiary of Wal-Mart Stores. The company operates 136 Wal-Marts across Canada and employs more than 22,000 associates. Since its launch, it has captured more than 40% market share in the discount sector and ranked first among Canada's six top discount and major department stores in terms of offering value and service.[38] Zellers and Kmart are principal competitors in Canada and have been devoting most of their resources to the price war with Wal-Mart.[39] The company planned to open two new stores in 1997, one in Ontario and one in Quebec. Wal-Mart recently appointed a former Zeller's executive as its vice-president and general merchandise manager.[40]

Brazil

Wal-Mart entered the Brazilian market in a joint venture with Los Americanas in November 1995.[41] The first store opening in São Paulo brought 200,000 shoppers. Wal-Mart competes with Carrefour (France) and Makro (Netherlands) in this market. Unlike other markets that Wal-Mart has entered, it enjoys no price advantage in Brazil. Its competitors, which enjoy long-standing relationships with local vendors, are comparable to Wal-Mart in appearance and operation. Wal-Mart has a clear competitive advantage in its customer service strategies, which its competitors do not cultivate.[42] The company has tapped into an abundance of highly skilled Brazilian workers, who are eager to assume the decision-making power given to Wal-Mart associates.[43] At the end of 1996, Wal-Mart had two Wal-Mart Stores and three Sam's Club Warehouse Stores in Brazil, employing over 2,400 associates.

Argentina

Argentina is the first market that Wal-Mart has entered as a wholly owned venture. As of December 1996, the company operated three Supercenters and three Sam's Clubs and planned to open four additional Supercenters and one to two Sam's Clubs in 1997. The biggest problem for Wal-Mart is absorbing the incredible sales volume generated by its Argentinian units. Sales estimates for the average supercenter is around $180 million, about three times the average for a U.S. unit. On a typical Saturday, staple stocks of milk and paper products completely disappear. Company management has worked to overcome these problems by planning new units with larger back rooms, and encouraging category management by vendors.[44] Over 1,700 employees staff stores in Argentina.

Competition is fierce in this market. The country's dominant retailer is France's Carrefour, which has 14 stores and 20 years' experience in the Argentine market. Analysts believe that this will be the toughest fight for Wal-Mart in foreign markets.[45,46]

People's Republic of China

In a joint venture agreement, Wal-Mart opened an 180,000 square foot (16,700 square meter) supercenter and a 115,000 square foot (10,700 square meter) Sam's Club in Shenzen, China in August 1996. Breaking with its traditional store formats, Wal-Mart built its three-story Supercenter in a four-tower, 30-story apartment building in China's active free enterprise zone. About 1,500 associates work in Wal-Mart's Chinese stores. Chinese consumers are less mobile than those in the United States, so the stores were sited within walking distance of 300,000 people. Customer response has been enthusiastic. High-ticket items are moving well in Shenzen, which enjoys the highest average income levels in China. The stores cater to local tastes by stocking dried fish, preserved plums, soy bean milk, and even three-snake rice wine.[47–49] Adjusting the apparel mix has been more difficult, although denim and other casual apparel have been well received.[50]

In 1994, Wal-Mart entered the Hong Kong market in a joint venture agreement with a business partner from Thailand.[51] It used a mini-warehouse club format, which consumers summarily rejected. Hong Kong customers, who value convenience, quality, service, and store atmosphere over price and bulk purchases, were not interested in the products available at the store, which was closed in 1995.[52] Wal-Mart has used the lessons learned in the Hong Kong venture to prepare for its entry into the world's largest consumer market. Analysts predict that the company could be as prevalent in China as it is in the United States by 2003. Competitors in Shenzen include France's Carrefour, which opened a 36,000 square foot (3,300 square meter) supercenter with lower prices than Wal-Mart; and Japanese retailers Yoahan and Jusco.[53] In addition to announcing plans to open one or more additional stores in the Shenzen zone, Wal-Mart has been investigating other Chinese markets in southern coastal areas as well as in northern and central China.[54]

Indonesia

Wal-Mart opened its second Supercenter in Jakarta in January 1997 in a licensing agreement with Lippo Group, Indonesia's most powerful conglomerate. The licensing agreement is a close working arrangement, with Wal-Mart paid on a fee-for-services basis. The Supercenter is a four floor, 180,000 square foot (16,700 square meter) anchor in the new Megamal in an affluent section of the city. The store offers a deli, bakery, floral departments, housewares, home decor, electronics, and appliances, and employs more than 800 associates. The company plans to develop private label apparel programs with local manufacturers and is investigating the possibility of leasing arrangements with food operators such as Pizza Hut.[55]

Wal-Mart's major competitor in Indonesia is Mega M, the supercenter format of the country's largest retail chain, Matahari.[56] Matahari prepared for the invasion of Wal-Mart for a year and a half, sending teams around the world to gather information about the American invader. Mega M and Wal-Mart compete head on for price dominance as neighbors in the Supermal, where Wal-Mart's first store is located.[57]

The consumer profile for Jakarta indicates that 60% of the city's population are middle- to upper-income, giving them high purchasing power. Consumer research studies indicate that shopping patterns in Indonesia have been shifting to a brand, quality, and image orientation. Indonesian consumers tend to rate the image of imported products higher than that of domestic goods. While Marks & Spencer and J. C. Penney offer only imported goods in their Indonesian stores, Wal-Mart has entered the market with an orientation to local products.[58]

Wal-Mart has had to bend its ethics policies to accommodate Indonesian business traditions. In the United States, Wal-Mart maintains strict rules prohibiting employees from accepting so much as a soft drink from a supplier, but Indonesian business partners have been insulted by a refusal, so Wal-Mart has adapted its standards to fit the culture. Indonesian employees are learning to give input to their supervisors on how to run the stores, a practice foreign to Indonesian culture.[59]

Future plans in Indonesia include development of private label apparel programs with local manufacturers. Wal-Mart is considering several more Supercenters in Jakarta, but does not plan to expand outside of the city in the foreseeable future.[60]

Future Growth

Wal-Mart, Inc. has managed to surpass all competitors who have dared to face the firm. In addition to its domination of its home market, it has become the market leader in both Mexico and Canada. CEO Bobby Martin, of the international division, states that the division's strategy is to become the dominant retailer in every market that the company serves.

Industry analysts and company insiders alike agree that Wal-Mart's success has come by way of its ability to learn by doing. Expertise in distribution, communication, and cost control gained in the home market laid the foundation for its expansion into Mexico and Canada. The company has used lessons learned in Mexico and Puerto Rico to drive its expansion into South America. It applied the lessons learned in the failure of the Hong Kong store to its strategy in China.

Wal-Mart has also played the role of teacher in the markets it has entered. It has transferred knowledge about American retail distribution, promotion, and pricing tactics to its competitors in foreign market, which Wal-Mart officials find encouraging. According to Martin, the rapid adoption of Wal-Mart strategies by competitors helps to place the power in the hands of the consumer, which benefits Wal-Mart.[61]

Wal-Mart's expansion plans include opening new Wal-Mart Stores, Supercenters, and Sam's Clubs in the United States, as well as adding new distribution centers. International expansion includes new stores in each of its foreign markets.[62] According to analysts, Chile, Columbia, and Venezuela are also being considered. Although the company has been researching the Korean market,[63] no definite entry plans have been announced.

Wal-Mart is poised to take full advantage of the globalization of retailing. Armed with the best retail logistical and operational know-how on the planet, some analysts forecast that revenues for the International division will equal that of its domestic operation by the year 2005. The company is in the process of setting a new standard of retailing worldwide. Wal-Mart executives acknowledge that the road ahead will not be easy. Start-up costs are enormous, and the company is taking the long view in expectations about return on investment.[64] The same concepts that guided its founder appear to be at work as the company moves into the 21st century: offer low prices with a dose of friendly service and the relentless pursuit of efficiency.[65] As Sam Walton said, "There's absolutely no limit to what plain, ordinary working people can accomplish if they're given the opportunity and the encouragement and the incentive to do their best."[66]

DISCUSSION QUESTIONS

1. In Part I, I discussed the fact that large-scale retailers are most likely to expand initially into countries that are geographically and culturally similar to the home market. Both Wal-Mart and Kmart expanded into Canada and Mexico. Wal-Mart has been more successful than Kmart. What elements of their strategy can explain this success?
2. Wal-Mart's most recent expansion has been to Asia. Asia is neither geographically nor culturally similar to the home market. What are some of the problems with expanding into this area?
3. Wal-Mart's joint venture with Cifra in Mexico is very successful. Wal-Mart's joint venture with a Thai company in Hong Kong was not successful. What differences between these two types of joint ventures could help explain the success of one and the failure of the other?

ENDNOTES

1. *Wal-Mart, Inc. Annual Report.* (1996).
2. *Wal-Mart Company Report.* (1996).
3. *Wal-Mart 10-Q Report.* (1996).
4. Vance, S., and R. Scott, (1994). *Wal-Mart: A History of Sam Walton's Retail Phenomenon.* New York: Maxwell Macmillan International, pp. 7–9.
5. *Wal-Mart Company Report.* (1996).
6. *Wal-Mart 10-Q Report.* (1996).
7. *Wal-Mart Annual Report.* (1996).
8. Vance and Scott (1994), p. 100.
9. Vance and Scott (1994), p. 92.
10. Vance and Scott (1994), p. 84.
11. Speer, T. (1994). "Where Will Wal-Mart Strike Next?" *American Demographic,* August 1, p. 11.
12. "Wal-Mart Stores, Inc." (1992). *Crain's Chicago Business,* Vol. 15, No. 36, September 2.
13. Vance and Scott (1994), p. 92.
14. Macht, J. (1995). "Are You Ready For Electronic Partnering?" *INC. Magazine,* Vol. 17, November 1, p. 43.
15. "Wal-Mart Stores, Inc." (1992).
16. "Sharing IS Secrets." (1996). *Computerworld,* Vol. 30, No. 39, pp. 1, 131.
17. *Wal-Mart Annual Report.* (1996).
18. Vance and Scott (1994).
19. Troy, M. (1997). "Wal-Mart Bows to New Boise Concept Store." *Discount Store News,* Vol. 36, No. 4, pp. 1, 54.
20. Wal-Mart Stores Home Page. (1997). www.wal-mart.com.
21. *Wal-Mart Annual Report.* (1996).
22. Vance and Scott (1994), pp. 100-104.
23. *Wal-Mart Annual Report.* (1996).
24. *Wal-Mart Annual Report.* (1996).

25. "Wal-Mart Vaults the Great Wall of China." (1997). *Discount Store News,* Vol. 36, No. 2, p. 23.
26. Hisey, P. (1996). "Wal-Mart's Martin in Brazil: We're Here for the Long Run." *Discount Store News,* Vol. 35, No. 22, November 18, pp. 1, 14.
27. Hisey (1996).
28. Johnson, J. (1996). "The World According to Martin." *Discount Merchandiser,* Vol. 36, No. 9, pp. 35–37.
29. Johnson (1996).
30. Hisey (1996).
31. Hisey (1996).
32. Johnson (1996).
33. Johnson (1996).
34. Johnson (1996).
35. Millman, J. (1991). "The Merchant of Mexico." *Forbes,* Vol. 148, No. 3, pp. 80–81.
36. "Wal-Mart Kicks Off $1.2B offer for CIFRA." (1997). *Women's Wear Daily,* July 28.
37. Washington-Valdez, D. (1995). "Wal-Mart Now in Mexico's Largest Border City." *Gannett News Service,* October 20.
38. "Wal-Mart Canada Announces Phase One of 1997 Expansion." (1997). Press Release, *Canada Newswire,* January 28.
39. "Chain Store Age Global Powers of Retailing Supplement." (1996) *Chain Store Age,* December, p. 16B.
40. "Chain Store Age Global Powers of Retailing Supplement." (1996).
41. Hisey (1996).
42. "Wal-Mart Makes Robust Strides in Brazil." (1997). *Discount Store News,* Vol. 36, No. 2, p. 27.
43. Kohler, K. (1996). "Brazil: With Stability Comes Opportunity." *Chain Store Age,* Section 2: Global Retailing: Assignment Latin America Supplement, pp. 9–10.
44. "Wal-Mart International Reshapes the World Retailing Order."(1997). *Discount Store News,* Vol. 36, No. 2, p. 21.
45. Shepard, L. (1996). "Business Week International Editions: International Business: South America: Wal-Mart Undercuts the Price Cutters." *Business Week International,* February 26, p. 19.
46. "Wal-Mart International Reshapes the World Retailing Order." (1997).
47. Halverson, R. (1996). "Wal-Mart Pulls out of Joint Venture, But Not Out of China." *Discount Store News,* Vol. 35, No. 3, p. 4.
48. Halverson (1996).
49. "China Attracts Western Retailers Willing to Learn Its Ways; Asia: Megastore Operators Are Looking Beyond the Risks and Courting the Nation's Growing Middle Class." (1997). *Los Angeles Times Wire,* February 16, Business: p. 15.
50. "Wal-Mart International Reshapes the World Retailing Order." (1997).
51. Coleman, C. (1995). "Wal-Mart Seeks Entry into Korean Market." *Korea Times,* June 6.
52. Herndon, N. (1995). "Hong Kong Shoppers Cool to Wal-Mart's Value Club." *Marketing News,* Vol. 29, No. 24, p. 1.
53. Halverson (1996).
54. Halverson (1996).
55. Mammarella, J. (1996). "Price War Rages as Wal-Mart Opens Second Store in Indonesia." *Discount Store News,* Vol. 35, No. 1, January 6, pp. 1, 90.
56. "Wal-Mart Redefines Retail in Indonesia." (1997). *Discount Store News,* Vol. 36, No. 2, p. 22.
57. Mammarella (1996).
58. "Foreign Retailers Eye the Growing Middle-Upper Income Group." (1996). *Indonesian Commercial Newsletter,* Vol. 23, No. 210, p. 34.
59. "Wal-Mart Learns, When In Jakarta, . . ." (1997). *Discount Store News,* Vol. 36, No. 2, January 20, p. 12.
60. Mammarella (1996).
61. Hisey (1996).
62. *Wal-Mart Annual Report.* (1996).
63. Coleman (1995).
64. Hisey (1996).
65. Pellet, J. (1995). "Wal-Mart: Yesterday and Today." *Discount Merchandiser,* Vol. 35, No. 9, pp. 66–67.
66. *Wal-Mart Annual Report.* (1996).

Part II Retailing in North America

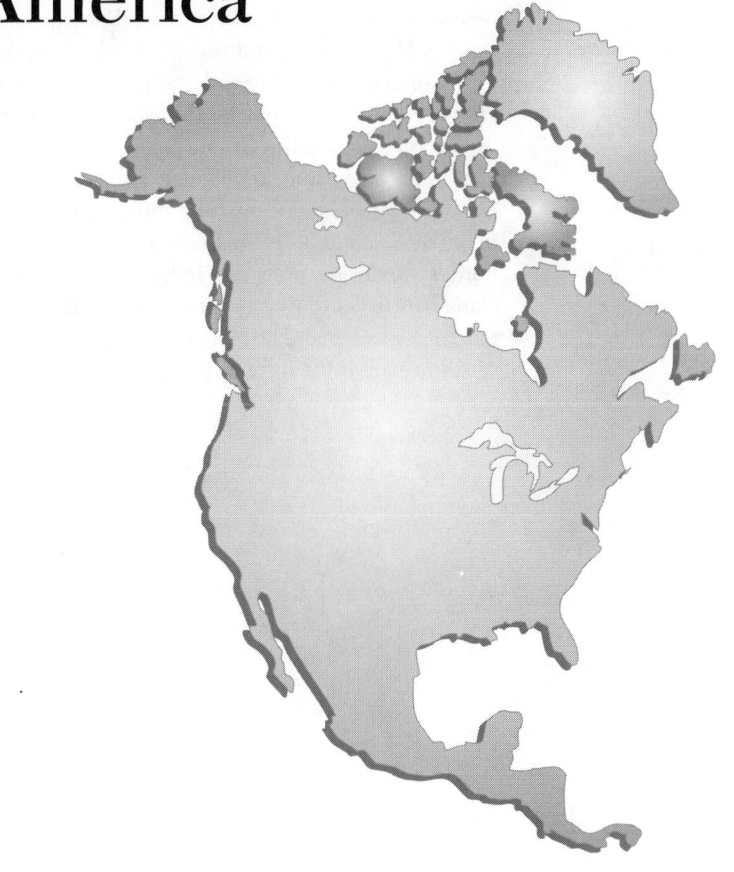

Part II of this text concerns retailing in North America. The three countries discussed in this section—the United States, Mexico, and Canada—have quite different retail environments. In the chapter on the United States, I do not discuss types of retailers, but instead describe several characteristics that differentiate the U.S. retail market from many other markets. It is not my intent to say that no other country has these characteristics. The United Kingdom has been more aggressive in developing private label products than the United States. Hong Kong's retail industry has developed under less governmental regulation than exists in the United States. Nevertheless, these characteristics will provide a set of benchmarks that you can use intellectually to summarize and compare the retailing environment of countries throughout the world.

Mexico is a developing country with a mixed retail system. Modern retailers exist side by side with informal street markets. These informal street markets are very profitable in Mexico. They have low overhead as there is no building rent and employees are generally family members. In recent years, such markets have become sophisticated, emulating some aspects of product layout used in modern supermarkets.

Canada, like the United States, experienced a recession during the 1990s. However, its economy has not experienced the kind of recent economic expansion found in the United States. As a result, retailing has suffered greatly. U.S. retailers, using knowledge gained from expansion within the United States, have been successfully moving into Canadian locations. Most of the major U.S. national chains now have representation in Canada. Such cross-border expansion does not seem to work both ways. Ninety percent of the Canadian firms that attempt expansion into the United States fail. The U.S. market looks big and attractive to Canadian retailing. What is more difficult to see, however, is the intense market competitiveness in the United States.

Anchorage
Seattle
Chicago
New York
UNITED STATES
Los Angeles
Atlanta
Dallas
Houston
Miami

6

Retailing in the United States

After reading this chapter, you will understand:

- How the role of retailing changes when retailers become assemblers of merchandise.
- Why buyers are considered profit centers in the United States and how this designation makes U.S. retailing different from retailing in other parts of the world.
- The importance of retailers providing definitive retail options for consumers.
- The role of distribution in a free market system and how the concepts of sorting, spatial closure, and temporal closure are organized in a formal logistics system.

THE U.S. RETAIL SYSTEM possesses several characteristics that set it apart from many other retail systems in the world. In this chapter, I will discuss these characteristics and contrast them to the retailing environment in other countries. Preceding this discussion, a short overview outlines the evolution of retailing in the United States, tying the changing retail environment to key events in the nation's history. The chapter concludes with a segment focusing on a theory of distribution in a free market system. Three problems affecting distribution in this type of system are explored, and retailing responses to these problems are described.

COUNTRY BACKGROUND

Industrial growth began in the United States in the early 1800s and continued until the Civil War. In the years before that war, businesses were still small. Production capacity of industry was limited because hand labor was the unit of production. Most business served a small local market.

The Civil War changed American life dramatically. Machines replaced hand labor. More important, a new nationwide network of railroads allowed businesses to distribute goods throughout a broader area. Inventors developed new products, and businesses made the products in large quantities. Investors and bankers provided large amounts of capital. The country had a vast array of natural resources. Big businesses grew and helped complementary businesses prosper.

This industrial growth affected American life. The new business activity centered in the cities, bringing people from rural areas to urban centers in large numbers. Between 1870 and 1916, the country's population exploded. More than 25 million immigrants entered the United States. Immigration and natural population growth more than doubled the U.S. population, from 40 million to 100 million inhabitants. This population boom helped the country by providing a large market for products and by providing workers for the factories.

In the late 1800s, the railroad system bridged the continent. Train service increased from 9,000 miles in 1850 to 200,000 miles in 1900. Within the cities, train service helped to bring consumers to the city centers. Huge department stores emerged in growing cities. Marshall Field of Chicago, R. H. Macy of New York, and John Wanamaker's of Philadelphia led the inner city department store growth. Montgomery Ward and Richard Sears began mail-order companies to serve people who lived far from stores.

Mass production of the automobile in the early 20th century brought another significant change. With personal transportation, families began to populate the suburbs. Retailing followed this population shift by inventing the suburban shopping mall. Today, few countries in the world have a higher use of individual automobiles. The U.S. retail environment is focused more than ever on the importance of location as a retail growth factor. Table 6.1 presents selected demographic and economic data for the United States.

THE DIVERSE RETAIL ENVIRONMENT

The retail industry in the United States is very diverse. Nearly every geographical area has a variety of retail formats that have value and meaning for consumers. Value and meaning for consumers is an important idea. Take, for instance, discount stores. Most American consumers believe that they can purchase merchandise at a lower price through discount outlets. They believe that this merchandise is identical to the full-price merchandise in

TABLE 6.1

United States: Selected Demographic and Economic Data

	Population (millions) mid-1995	Area (thousands of sq. km)	GNP per capita: Dollars 1995	GNP per capita: Avg. ann. growth (%) 1985–95	PPP estimates of GNP per capita U.S. = 100: 1987	PPP estimates of GNP per capita U.S. = 100: 1995	Life expectancy at birth (years) 1995	Adult illiteracy (%) 1995
High-income economies	102.24	32,039t	24,930w	1.9w			77w	
United States	263.1	9,364	26,980	1.3	100.0	100.0	77	a

Source: World Bank (1997). a = less than 5%. t = total. PPP = purchasing power parity. w = weighted average.

department stores. In this instance, the discount store has meaning and value to consumers.

When discount stores first enter a country, consumers are understandably wary about buying merchandise from these retailers, believing that only inferior products could possibly be sold in such a store. As consumers become more comfortable and experienced with buying from discount stores, their attitudes change from disbelief that anyone would buy merchandise from a discount store to disbelief that anyone would buy certain types of merchandise anywhere other than at a discount store. Think about the last time you bought an electrical appliance. If you are a U.S. consumer, you probably bought this product from a discount store such as Best Buy. You probably only compared prices at one or two stores, because these retailers guarantee their prices as being the lowest available. This means if you find the same product for a lower price someplace else, they will refund the difference. In this way, these stores eliminate price as a risk factor.

You probably would not buy some products at a discount store. Nevertheless, you have a clear-cut idea of what products you would purchase there. You might not consider buying clothes at a mass merchandiser, but you are likely to buy household supplies there. A department store may seem like the only appropriate place to buy a wedding gift, but if you were buying the same product for yourself you might buy it at a discount store.

Self-service is another important characteristic of distinctive types of retail formats. In more developed countries, self-service is considered part of a low cost, discount strategy. In less developed countries, the introduction of self-service has nothing to do with a discount image, it reflects consumers'

Photo 6.1
Sears, Roebuck and Company advertised itself as the cheapest supply house on earth. This 1897 Sears catalog features a 68-cent revolver. The catalog provided an important retail link to rural Americans.

freedom to hold and examine products without relying on salespersons. When self-service is first introduced to a less developed country, packaging is needed to protect the products from consumers. In developed countries, packaging is used to entice consumers to hold products.

I was talking to a class of business students at Shanghai University-International Business School in the 1990s. Self-service food stores were just being introduced to the People's Republic of China (PRC). I asked the

Photo 6.2
Warehouse stores feature products sold out of open boxes on warehouse pallets. Products are often packaged together or sold in commercial-size containers. Many shoppers, like the one in this picture, are overwhelmed by the volume. *Courtesy of SN.*

group how they felt about these stores. A young woman volunteered, "When I go into a self-service store, I feel free as a bird. Free to hold merchandise and select those things that are right for me as a consumer." I was very surprised that self-service was such an emotional experience for this young woman. A few months later, I happened to be talking with my mother. Somehow we began to talk about the introduction of self-service stores into the United States. To my surprise, my mother's first experience in a self-service store in the late 1950s was very similar to that of the young Chinese student. She used some of the same words, saying that she had felt free to compare products and really evaluate them.

Thirty years separate these two phenomena. During most of that time, China was closed to outside influences—a period corresponding to the cultural revolution and central government ownership of all businesses. Self-service stores were not introduced into Communist China until economic reforms were introduced. A planned economy does not endeavor to make shopping more efficient or enjoyable.

The retail industry in the United States uses a variety of formats that have meaning and value to consumers. But this alone does not fully explain the dynamic environment of U.S. retailing. After studying retailing in other countries, I began to identify several characteristics that set U.S. retailing apart from retailing in other countries. It is important to consider these characteristics before exploring retailing in other parts of the world. In Chapter 2, I talked about the self-reference criterion. This is the assumption that every other part of the world does or should do things as we do. It is also important to keep this assumption in mind as you compare U.S. retailing to retailing elsewhere in the world. You will find that retailing in the United States is quite different from retailing in other parts of the world, but different is not necessarily better.

WHAT SETS THE U.S. RETAIL INDUSTRY APART FROM THAT OF OTHER COUNTRIES?

There are many characteristics that differentiate retailing in the United States from retailing in other countries. However, the following features stand out in my mind as being uniquely definitive of the U.S. system.

LITTLE GOVERNMENT REGULATION

The United States has the most lenient government attitude toward the regulation of retailing of any country in the world. The governments of Japan and most countries in Europe regulate the hours that a store can be open. Opening new large-scale retail stores is very difficult in Belgium, France, Italy, Spain, and Japan. Terminating unneeded employees is very difficult in Europe. None of these areas are regulated by government in the United States.

In Italy, every store operator has to attend a school to learn how to run his or her particular type of business. In the United States there are no education or knowledge requirements for store owners. The Italian government determines where retail stores will be located. For instance, if you wanted to open a toy store, you would have to wait until a toy store location became available. In the United States, as long as an area is zoned for commercial development, most types of retail stores can be opened. The exception to this is liquor stores, which require a special license.

Retail researchers from Europe and Japan generally hold one big misconception about retailing in the United States. They believe that the Robinson-Patman Act plays a major role in U.S. pricing. It does not. In fact, most retailers and manufacturers have never heard of this act, and it has little influence on their business. The Robinson-Patman Act is an effort to specify illegal price discrimination. According to the act, illegal price discrimination exists when different prices are charged for goods of "like grade and quality . . . where the effect of such discrimination may be substantially to lessen competition or tend to create a monopoly in any line of commerce, or to insure, destroy, or prevent competition with any person who knowingly receives the benefit of such discrimination or with customers of either of them."[1] Price discrimination is permissible when (1) there is a cost-savings (economies of scale) in the size of order, (2) the goods are subject to deterioration, obsolescence, or seasonal changes, and (3) there is no injury to competition. The general rule of thumb is that if a volume discount is offered to all customers who can order in the bulk specified, there is no price discrimination.

RETAILERS ARE ASSEMBLERS OF LINES OF GOODS

Each retail store or chain of stores has individuals whose major responsibility is to select merchandise for the store. These retail buyers serve an important function. Based on their view of their store's customers, they filter thousands of merchandise offerings, selecting merchandise that they view as the best value for the price in styles that will appeal to their customers. In other words, the buyers assemble products from which their consumers choose.

In many countries, manufacturers determine merchandise offerings in the retail stores. The manufacturers provide the merchandise, provide their own salespersons, and accept the return of unsold merchandise. The manufacturers take the product risk, and likewise claim the largest share of the profit margin.

RETAIL BUYERS ARE CONSIDERED PROFIT CENTERS

This characteristic is one of the most important. The role of buyer as profit center is more important for non-food retailers than for food retailers. Retail buyers have a very important role in U.S. stores. U.S. companies evaluate buyers on their performance, sales, maintained markup, and turnover on a year-to-date basis. They reward buyers who have outstanding figures; they terminate those who fail to perform. In most companies, the buying role is totally separated from the selling role. Buyers may visit the departments they buy for, but their visits are to obtain information, not to sell merchandise. The degree of separation, buying from selling, is unique to U.S. stores. Retailers in some other countries have professional buyers, but they generally do not have the autonomy of buyers in the United States.

U.S. buyers make decisions in the same way as an individual consumer. In most cases, they individually select merchandise. They examine the items in a vendor's line and make a "yes" or "no" decision about each item. Buyers in China and Japan select a vendor but do not individually select each item. Furthermore, buyers in many countries must consult other executives or managers before making a purchase decision. This team decision-making is more similar to industrial buying in the United States.

In the United States, centralized buying is a common practice. Buyers in this case make selections for stores located throughout the country. What is lost in not customizing the product line for various geographic locations is replaced by economies of scale that make possible an increase in volume and discount pricing.

Photo 6.3
A vendor shows a retail buyer the product line at the 1997 July Gifts & Accessories Mart™ in Chicago. In the United States, retail buyers select items individually, like a consumer. Each individual product will receive a "yes" or "no" evaluation. Retail buyers play a very important role as gatekeepers of consumer choice. *Courtesy of Peggy VaGenius.*

Some companies use a system of buyers and allocators. The buyers select the merchandise for a wide variety of stores and the allocators determine the actual number of units that each store receives. These figures are based on past sales figures. Retailers may transfer merchandise that is not selling at one store to another store location. However, this process is expensive.

Some stores, such as Nordstrom, do not use centralized buying. Buyers live in the geographical areas where the company has stores, and they buy merchandise in those areas. Most national department stores chains formerly had local buyers and centralized buyers, but attempts to consolidate expenses have pushed stores to eliminate the two levels of buying.

J. C. Penney Company, Inc. has the management of each store determine the merchandise the store will sell. Corporate buyers in Dallas originally select the merchandise that managers will view and select for their stores. The managers then view the merchandise through closed circuit television and place orders. They send the orders to the corporate headquarters, and the buyers place the company's orders with the vendors.

IMPORTANCE OF NATIONAL CHAINS

Few other countries have the extensive network of national retail chains that characterizes the United States. These national chains include mass merchandisers, convenience stores, warehouse clubs, supermarkets, and specialty stores. Although department stores are less likely to have a national presence, they have a strong regional presence. Dayton Hudson Corporation, for example, has stores throughout the Midwest. These national chains are the result of the large U.S. mass market.

Malls prefer national chains because their chance of failure is less than that of smaller chains or independents. Malls do not like to have empty spaces. The purchasing power of national chains allows them to have great power in the distribution channel. Many national chains, such as Gap and The Limited, sell their own private label exclusively. This removes them from competition with the national brand name discounters. However, finding the same stores in every major mall creates a degree of shopping boredom among consumers. United States malls use department stores as mall anchors. In France and Germany, a hypermarket (mixed food and non-food) retailer is likely to be the anchor. Toys "R" Us, profiled in Company Focus II.1, established stores across the United States before expanding internationally. The sales volume for this company gives it negotiating strength.

SOPHISTICATED LOGISTICS

In retailing, logistics is the act of moving merchandise from a manufacturer to a store. Merchandise might go from the manufacturer to a distribution center and then to a store, or directly from a manufacturer to the retail store. Sometimes the merchandise goes from a manufacturer to a wholesaler and then to a retailer. When I owned a retail store, we would frequently buy jeans from a cash-and-carry wholesaler. We would buy 10 pairs of jeans and when those sold, we would and go and buy 10 more pairs.

The discount mass merchandisers were the first to introduce technologically sophisticated logistics systems. Retailer-operated distribution centers emerged wherever national chains had enough stores to justify their existence. These sophisticated distribution centers made the chains more autonomous by ensuring that they had the merchandise available when their stores needed it. The Limited, for instance, has a distribution center that is completely computerized. Humans do not handle merchandise. Computers **pick** (select) the merchandise, based on orders from the individual stores. The merchandise comes from the manufacturer on hangers. The computer system selects the merchandise, hangs it in a box, and affixes a mailing label for the ordering stores.

Kmart's distribution system uses **cross docking** whenever possible. Merchandise comes by truck from the manufacturers. The trucks back into the warehouse and mini-loaders transport merchandise to the distribution trucks heading for the store. This eliminates unloading the merchandise and having it sit on the floor.

Nearly all the national and regional chains have computerized retail inventory systems (RIS) to provide instantaneous information about inventory. Before these systems were introduced, retailers knew what merchandise they received but not how much merchandise they had sold until they did an actual physical count at the end of the year. Even small retailers can now know how much inventory they have at any instant.

STRONG MANUFACTURERS—NATIONAL BRAND NAMES

Discount retailers cannot develop without strong national brand names. The United States has well-known national brands in most merchandising categories. In some countries, the manufacturers are very small, and they never establish national or international recognition. Discount retailers receive recognition when consumers can determine that they are buying the same product for less in a discount store. Japan's discount industry has faltered because although the industry introduced low-cost stores, these stores did not have wide access to national brand names. If consumers cannot compare a discount store's products with products sold in traditional retailers, they will not perceive the discount offering as having value.

The food retailing industry is manufacturer dominated. Manufacturers spend large amounts of money on new product introduction and advertising.

Levi Strauss has worldwide brand recognition. The company has been opening retail stores throughout the world. This forward vertical integration will allow it to gain maximum exposure for the Levi's name. Company Focus II.2 at the end of Part II discusses Levi Strauss's international expansion.

STRONG PRIVATE LABELS

Private labels began in the United States as a low-cost alternative to nationally known brand names. Supermarket chains introduced the first generic brands to cut their costs and offer lower prices to consumers. Store brands rapidly followed. Supermarket chains in the United States positioned the cost of store brands between that of the generic and the national brand names. In the United Kingdom, store brand foods are positioned at the higher price points, intending to compete with the best-known national brands in quality and value for price.

The strategy of 100% private label has paid off for Gap. The company has 1,430 Gap and Gap Kids stores in six countries. For the last decade, profit gains have averaged 28% per year. A decade ago, Gap had 10 designers; in 1997, they had 80 designers. Gap's designers put a 1,000-item line together four times a year. They spent 10 weeks preparing for the Fall 1997 preview. Each Gap designer is paired with a product specialist who evaluates costs, finds fabric sources, and reports on what is selling well and what is not.[2]

The line between designer and retailer used to be distinctly drawn. Fashion designers created apparel; retailers sold it. But retailers now realize that to break out of the "cycle of sameness," they need a distinct product. Federated, which owns stores such as Bloomingdale's and Macy's, assembled a design team of more than 400. Private labels and brands account for 15% of Federated sales in 1997. This is up from less than 5% in 1994. Limited, Inc., Casual Corner, and Ann Taylor Stores, Inc. are doing the same thing. Even Sears and J. C. Penney are putting together top-rate in-house design teams. The six-year old Arizona line is the most successful private label brand J. C. Penney has ever had. The label accounts for 5% of the company's total retail sales. The Canyon River Blues line at Sears has grown to a $200 million enterprise. Sears expects its private brand business to double to $4 billion between the years 1997 and 2000.[3]

Department stores introduced private labels to provide a hedge for themselves against brand name discounting. High status retailers found that they could gain great margins on merchandise that carried their store's name. Mass merchandisers entered the private label program to give them expanded merchandise choices and increase their profit margins. Specialty stores such as Gap and The Limited established their market presence by selling only private label products. Consumers identified with being a Limited customer, or a Gap customer.

RETAILERS CAN TERMINATE EMPLOYEES

The right to terminate employees may seem like a little thing, but retailing is very labor-intensive. Labor is one of a retailer's most important expenses. In the United States, retailers can hire and fire employees based on their sales needs. This is not so in most European countries. In Italy, retailers will close their doors for a month in the summer to allow employees to take a vacation. It is not that the retailers are so socially concerned. Rather, they are required by law to do this, as they cannot hire part-time employees while the vacationing employees are away.

Photo 6.4
Gap stores in Paris sell 100% private label merchandise, like Gap stores in the United States. Many retail stores are investing large amounts of money on design teams to create unique product offerings. *Courtesy of WWD.*

RETAILERS HIRE COLLEGE GRADUATES

Most U.S. retailers hire management trainees with college degrees. Retail buyers and managers in major U.S. retail companies are among the most educated in the world. They are also given much responsibility early in their careers. After graduating from a university and completing a training program, a new employee is put into an assistant buyer or assistant manager position. After three to five years, if the person does well, she or he could expect to be a buyer or a department manager. In Japan, by contrast, new workers might work on the sales floor for 10 years before being promoted to management. Even then, horizontal moves within the organization would be more common than vertical (upward) moves.

German retailers hire high school graduates and offer an educational program as part of their company advancement plan. The educational program is not like the six- to eight-week training program offered by U.S. retailers; it is a multiyear program. French retailers work with universities to provide extensive internship programs. Students study a subject at the university; then they are put into an employment situation that applies the concepts.

PERMANENT MERCHANDISE MARKETS

Throughout the United States, there are large markets where retailers can go to buy merchandise. These markets allow small retailers to have the same access as large retailers to hundreds of manufacturers. The permanent

Figure 6.1
Permanent merchandise markets are found throughout the United States, one of the few countries in the world with this extensive system. Retail buyers visit these markets to select merchandise for their stores. Having many manufacturers together in one location makes finding new suppliers much easier.

merchandise markets provide an affordable way for retailers to find unique merchandise. Most other countries do not have such permanent merchandise markets. Instead, retailers buy from manufacturers with whom they have long-term relationships.

Permanent merchandise markets also give retailers information about market trends. Markets have special promotions, called a market week. During this time, additional vendors come to the market to display their products and show retailers market trends. Permanent markets enable smaller retailers to have access to many suppliers. Without a central market, small business owners must spend additional time and money visiting suppliers. A map of permanent markets is included in Figure 6.1.

SHORT CHANNELS

Retailers in the United States generally buy directly from the manufacturer. This is the shortest channel possible. The prevalence of large national chains also reduces the number of steps in the channel. However, short channels have more to do with the type of merchandise purchased than they have to do with efficiencies.

As stated before, permanent merchandise markets make it possible for small retailers to purchase directly from manufacturers. However, a manufacturer may require that a retailer place a minimum order of a dozen items of each product or a minimum order of $5,000. In this case, the retailer can go to a wholesaler and buy smaller amounts of the merchandise for a slightly higher price. Wholesalers play an important role in breaking down bulk quantities and shipping in smaller lots.

Compared with food consumers in other developed countries such as Europe and Japan, U.S. consumers purchase less perishable merchandise. In many parts of Europe and in Japan, the family cook will stop on a daily basis to purchase fresh produce to use in cooking. As we might expect, channel lengths are longer in these countries.

Greater volume ——→ Shorter channel
More perishable ——→ Longer channels

PRODUCTION IS BASED ON ORDERS

This characteristic relates only to non-food merchandise. Manufacturers produce a product line, have samples made, show these samples to retail buyers, and then collect orders. They produce only those products for which sufficient orders are received. Those products with insufficient orders are canceled. Generally, a manufacturer produces only a limited supply of extra products. Thus, if merchandise gets into the store and sells very well, there is usually no chance to reorder. The more basic the merchandise, the more likely it is that manufacturers will produce more than orders and retailers will have access to reorders.

If merchandise does not sell, the retailer continues to lower the price until someone finally buys it. Large dominant retailers may pressure their suppliers for markdown money to share profit loss due to slow-selling merchandise, but this is a recent trend. In general, retail stores carry the product risk in the United States.

Some categories of merchandise, such as cosmetics and books, are sold under the consignment system in U.S. stores. In these cases, manufacturers carry the product risk for this merchandise. They also decide when they will take markdowns.

HEALTHY INDEPENDENT RETAILERS

The United States has the healthiest small retailer sector of any country in the world. Government subsidies or entitlements do not protect small retailers. Therefore, they have to be competitive, based on their own strengths, flexibility, and uniqueness. Small retailers in the United States have a high failure rate, but the result is a very healthy segment of successful independent retailers.

Independent retailers provide the variety that makes retailing interesting. These independent retailers are located outside the mall area. Some major retailers such as Tower Records, are beginning to avoid mall locations, believing that teenagers are tired of the artificiality of the mall.

In the next section, I will look at the functions of retailing in a free market system. The theory presented does not relate just to the United States, it applies to any system operating under the market mechanism. The primary focus of a free market system is to match demand with supply. Later in Parts III and IV, I will discuss retailing in planned economies. The functions there are quite different.

THEORY OF DISTRIBUTION IN A FREE MARKET SYSTEM

A free market means that producers are free to produce as much of and whatever they wish. Consumers are free to purchase as much of and whatever they wish. Matching the needs of suppliers and consumers requires some problem-solving and planning. Three basic problems need to be resolved in the distribution of consumer products in a free market system.[3] They are:

1. The need to match specialized production with specific demand (sorting).
2. The need to resolve spatial discrepancy, transporting the products from the place of production to the place of consumption (spatial closure).
3. The need to equalize supply with demand over different time periods (temporal closure).

SORTING

Matching production with demand is an issue in free markets, but not in planned markets. In a planned market, the government tells each manufacturing facility what it should produce and how much it should produce. The government then tells the manufacturers where the merchandise should be shipped. If consumers want to purchase the merchandise, they are limited to the choices that are available from the government manufacturers. In a planned economy, there is no incentive for factories to produce things that consumers actually want, their only customer is the government. In a free market, if consumers do not like one factory's products, they can choose products from another factory. If a manufacturer does not produce what consumers want, the products will not sell and eventually the manufacturer will go out of business.

Production is often geographically concentrated. Much of the home furniture industry is in North Carolina. Office furniture is produced primarily in Michigan. However, all U.S. consumers can buy furniture for their homes and offices throughout the United States. Furthermore, large-scale manufacturers tend to produce a certain type of product for a period, and then change to produce a different type of product. This is called a production run. Just because a factory produces a particular type of table during January, however, does not mean consumers will want to purchase those tables in January, or at any other particular time during the year. Demand is scattered in time and geography.

Wroe Alderson developed the theoretical concept of **sorting.** According to Alderson, sorting includes (1) standardization, (2) accumulation, (3) allocation, and (4) assortment.

STANDARDIZATION The process of **standardization** involves collecting uniform products from different suppliers. When you look into an egg carton, you expect the eggs to all be the same size. Eggs are graded as large, extra large, and so on. The eggs come from many farmers, but the egg processing plant washes the eggs and puts them together into standard groups.

ACCUMULATION **Accumulation** is the process of matching supply and demand. It consists of assembling standard products into large quantities. Accumulation is usually carried out in a location geographically closer to consumers than standardization. A mass merchandiser's distribution center would be an example of this function. Merchandise from a variety of suppliers comes into the warehouse. The warehouse manager, however, determines what is an efficient ordering volume for the merchandise.

ALLOCATION **Allocation** refers to the process by which the stores determine what supply they need to satisfy customer demand. Earlier in this chapter, I mentioned that some specialty stores have employees called allocators. A central buyer selects the stores' merchandise, but the allocator determines the number of items that will be sent to each store.

ASSORTMENT With an **assortment,** a retailer achieves a customized selection of merchandise to satisfy a specific target customer. A department store offers a product assortment that appeals to its specific clientele. The store must arrange an overall merchandise assortment, including men's and women's clothing, appliances, and housewares[4].

Sorting resolves the product-discrepancy problem created by specialization of production. A difference between a developing and a highly industrialized economy is the degree to which the distribution infrastructure can do sophisticated sorting. Sorting efficiency is essential for an advanced economy.

An example can help to illustrate the four processes involved in sorting. After a major hurricane struck Florida, a group of logistics experts were sent to the area to set up a relief distribution center. The efforts of the distribution center focused on solving the sorting problem; that is, how to match supply with demand. First, the logistics team needed to establish some standards for medical equipment and food supplies. Rubber gloves of the sterilized type were needed. Blood supplies had to be put into groups: A positive, AB, and so on. Baby food needed to be assembled according to different nutritional needs. Next, the team needed to determine what the supply of these products would be. Area hospitals and emergency centers were contacted to accumulate a large amount of the needed equipment and supplies. Once the supply was determined, the team designated relief groups that would be sent to different shelters. For instance, one shelter would house people who needed medical help. Another shelter would be for families with young children. The team's allocation and assort-

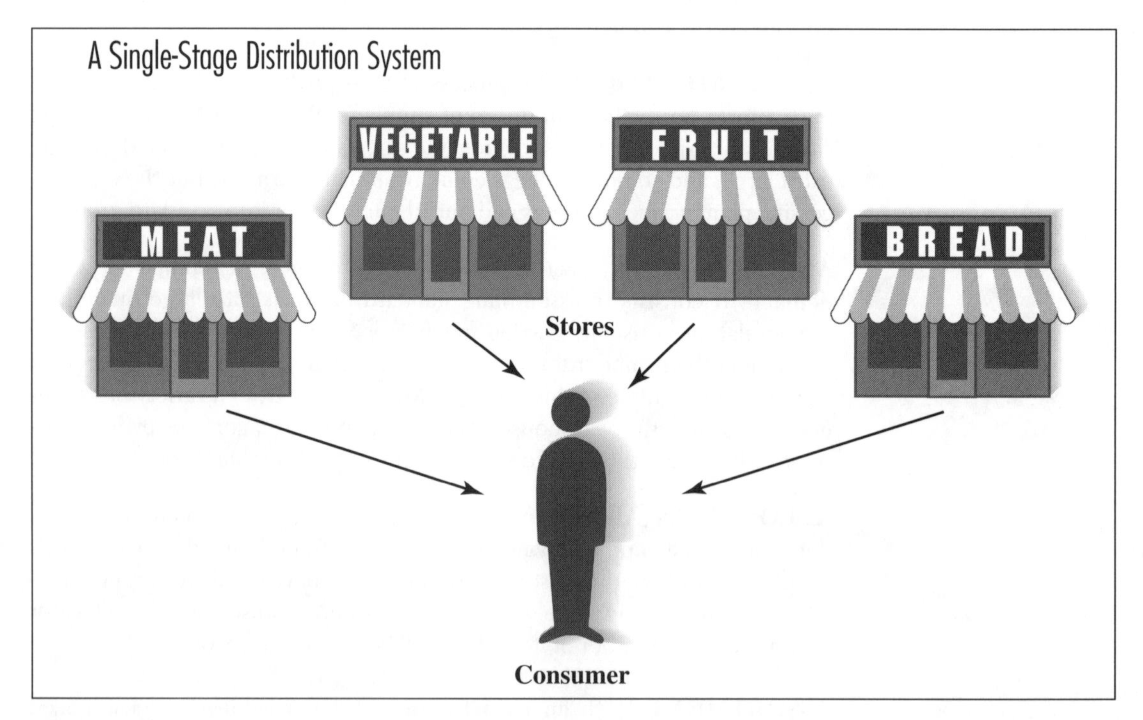

Figure 6.2
In a single-stage distribution system, consumers must visit each store to purchase products. It takes a long time to do shopping with this system.

ment efforts included determining the needs of each center so that diapers and baby food, for instance, would not be sent to centers without young children.

SPATIAL CLOSURE

Spatial closure relates to the transportation of products to consumers via a direct market, a central market, or a multistage system. Without the central market, purchasers must make individual trips to each of the potential suppliers (Figure 6.2). A multistage distribution system adds a degree of complexity. However, it is also the characteristic of more advanced economies (Figure 6.3). In this system, the retail buyers act as specialists, assembling the best possible set of merchandise for consumers. This idea is referred to as the **principle of minimum transactions.**[5] The introduction of buyers serves to reduce total transactions and is the basic justification for using a multistage distribution structure. In many developing countries, it takes women all day to do the food shopping. Rather than visit a supermarket where many choices are provided

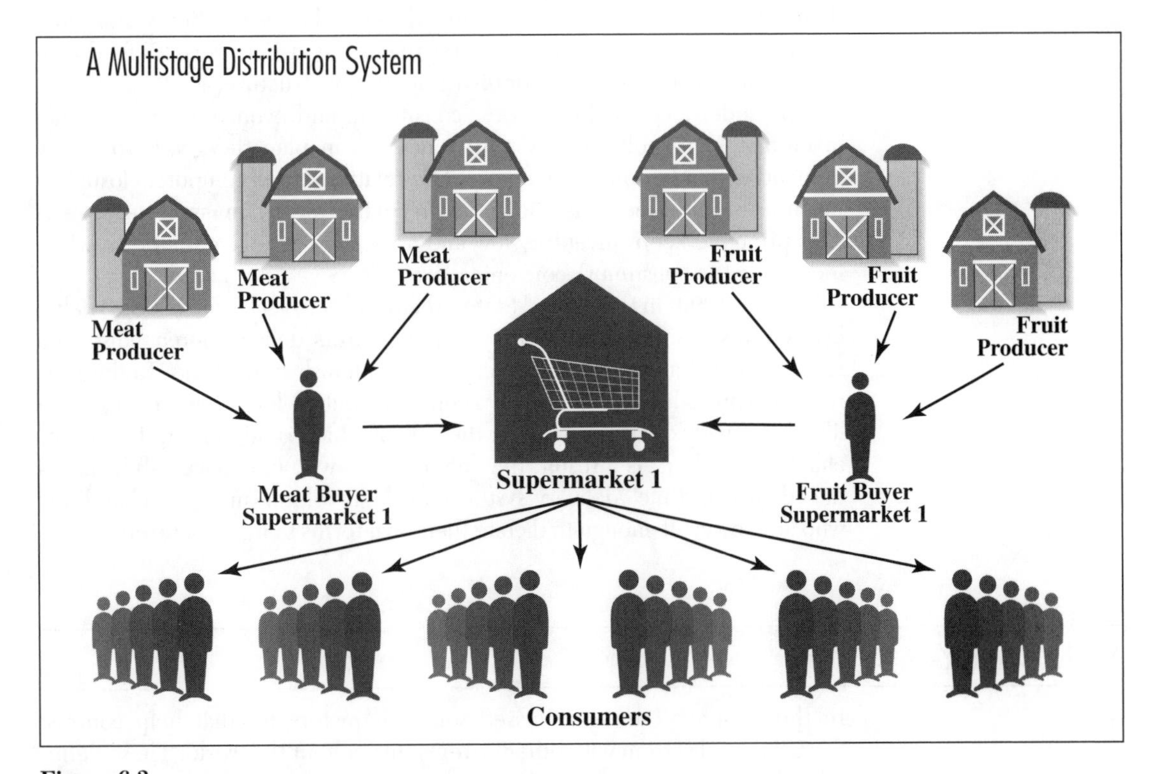

Figure 6.3
In a multistage distribution system, specialized retail buyers visit many suppliers and select a wide variety of products for sale. Buyers for the supermarket take over the function of going from one supplier to another. This system greatly streamlines shopping.

under one roof, a woman will make a trip to the meat shop, the bread shop, the vegetable shop, and so on. Shopping in these countries is time-consuming and inefficient, involving numerous separate transactions. When supermarkets are introduced to developing countries, suddenly it is possible to purchase all the ingredients for a meal in one transaction rather than five or more.

Middlemen might be added for a variety of reasons other than just for efficiency. Bucklin[6] called these intermediaries service outputs. They include (1) lot size, or the ability to procure small quantities; (2) waiting time, or the length of time it takes following purchases to obtain the actual goods; (3) market decentralization, or the proximity of goods to the buyer; and (4) product variety, or combinations of goods that most closely match demand. These factors help to explain the Japanese distribution system, discussed in Chapter 12.

TEMPORAL CLOSURE

Temporal closure refers to the fact that there is a difference between the time when manufacturers produce products and the time when consumers demand products. Products must flow through the distribution system in a timely manner. I have heard estimates that 10 to 20% of Russia's food production spoils because of a poor distribution infrastructure.

In underdeveloped countries, consumers and even retailers stockpile inventory. In a multistage system, retailers can plan the goods to satisfy demand with a minimum inventory. The relationship of temporal closure to inventory requirements is known as the **principle of massed reserves.**[7] This principle keeps inventory low and associated storage costs down while increasing the consumer's convenience.

In the 1990s in the United States, the trend is to seek "just in time" delivery systems. Using such a system, manufacturers deliver merchandise to a retail store just as it becomes necessary to replenish store stocks. In this way, retailers can reduce their costs by keeping inventory low. However, a system like this usually creates a backlog, the cost of which is put off on the weaker channel member. As a result, the only retailers who have successfully introduced "just in time" delivery systems are high-volume mass-merchandisers who are powerful enough to dictate their own terms to manufacturers.

SUMMARY

In this chapter, I have discussed some characteristics that help contrast the U.S. retail system with other systems throughout the world. These definitive features include: little government regulation; retailers assembling merchandise lines instead of manufacturers; retail buyers serving as profit centers; powerful national chains; technologically sophisticated logistics systems; strong national brand names; strong private labels; easy termination of employees; college-educated management trainees; permanent merchandise marts; short channels; production based on orders; and healthy independent retailers. Of course, retail systems in other countries have some of these same characteristics. As I talk about these countries in the following chapters, I will try to point out these similarities.

Chapter 7 focuses on Mexico and Canada, our North American Free Trade Agreement (NAFTA) neighbors. Although U.S. retailers have moved into Canada and Mexico, the results have been mixed. U.S. retailers are quite successful in Canada; however, when Canadian retailers have tried to enter the United States, they have not been successful. Several major U.S. retailers have entered Mexico, and then pulled out. A major contributor to this initial failure was the devaluation of the peso, which occurred at nearly the same time that U.S. retailers entered that market.

KEY TERMS

accumulation
allocation
assortment
cross docking
pick
principle of massed reserves
principle of minimum transactions
sorting
spatial closure
standardization
temporal closure

DISCUSSION QUESTIONS

1. When retail buyers are considered profit centers, they are rewarded for taking procurement risk. However, pay for retail buyers in such countries as Japan is based primarily on seniority. Characterize how you view the buying process to be different, based on risk-taking or security compensation.
2. An important characteristic of retailers in the United States is their role as assemblers of lines of merchandise. Explain this concept using the central market concept presented in Figures 6.2 and 6.3. Can you use this central market concept to explain why being an independent retailer is somewhat easier in the United States than in countries without permanent markets?
3. Bucklin discussed service outputs such as lot size, waiting time, market decentralization, and product variety. Would wholesalers add or detract from the degree of product variety found in a country? Explain.

ENDNOTES

1. Bowersox, D., and M. B. Cooper. (1992). *Strategic Marketing: Channel Management.* New York: McGraw-Hill, p. 157.
2. Berner, R. (1997). "How Gap's Own Design Shop Keeps Its Imitators Hustling." *Wall Street Journal,* March 13, p. B1.
3. Berner, R. (1997). "Now the Hot Designers on Seventh Avenue Work for Macy's, Sears." *Wall Street Journal,* March 13, p. B1.
4. Bowersox and Cooper (1992).
5. Bowersox and Cooper (1992).
6. Hall, M. (1951). *Distributive Trading.* London: Hutchinson's University Library.
7. Bucklin, L. (1966). *A Theory of Distribution Structure.* Berkeley, Calif.: IBER Special Publications.
8. Hall (1951), p. 80.

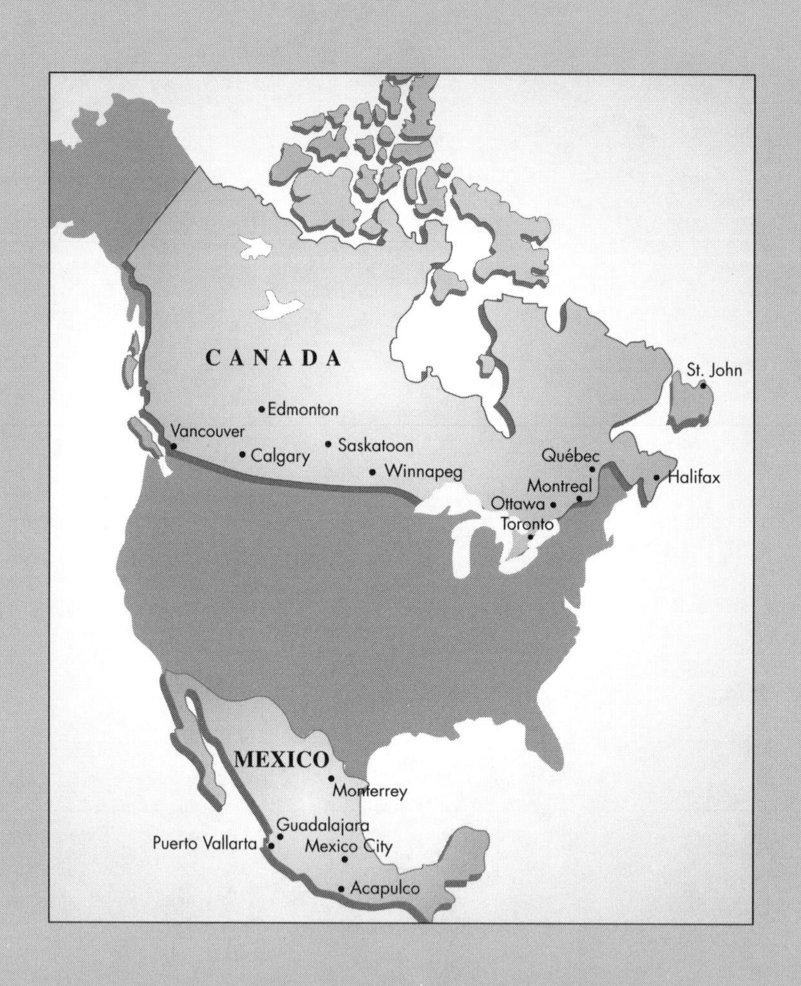
CANADA
Edmonton
Vancouver
Calgary
Saskatoon
Winnapeg
St. John
Québec
Montreal
Halifax
Ottawa
Toronto
MEXICO
Monterrey
Guadalajara
Puerto Vallarta
Mexico City
Acapulco

7

Retailing in Mexico and Canada

After reading this chapter, you will understand:

- Why U.S. retailers are expanding at a rapid rate in both Mexico and Canada.
- How currency devaluation has affected foreign retailers in Mexico, and what strategic decisions these retailers need to adopt to remain competitive.
- Why Mexico's informal retailing sector affects modern retail formats.
- How informal retailing sectors create a sense of place, drawing customers to their location.
- How foreign chains are creating intense competition for Canadian retailers.

MEXICO AND CANADA, the United States' North American Free Trade Agreement (NAFTA) partners represent very different retailing environments. In Mexico, modern superstores operate in juxtaposition to street vendors and informal merchant markets. Canada, in contrast, offers a retailing environment similar in many ways to that of the United States. Both markets, however, offer many opportunities to foreign retailers seeking to expand their international operations.

Most observers expected that NAFTA would affect the manufacturing industries of member nations more than other sectors of their economies. As a surprise to most, retailing has been affected significantly by NAFTA. Since the early 1990s, foreign-based volume retailers have been entering the Mexican and Canadian markets in even greater numbers. Several Mexican retailers, in turn, have entered joint ventures and strategic alliances with foreign-based volume retailers to gain operational expertise and capital. Most of the U.S. movement of retailers into Canada has been acquisition based. The Canadian market is just emerging from the recession. Canadian retailers have been muscled out by financially strong U.S. retailers.

MEXICO

COUNTRY BACKGROUND

Mexicans have a strong sense of nationalism. Their country's history of revolution has contributed to this sense of unity. Mexicans exalt their pre-conquest native civilization, downplaying the role of the Spaniards in their cultural history.

Highly advanced civilizations developed in central Mexico before the arrival of the Spaniards in 1519. A 300-year colonial period followed. During this time, the native population declined from 28 million in 1520 to little more than 1 million by the end of the 18th century. The Spanish rulers excluded from government not only native Indians, but also those persons of pure Spanish descent born in the New World.

By the early 19th century, the unrepresented groups were resentful and a rebellion began with the battle cry, "Death to the Spaniards." In 1821, Mexico declared independence from Spain. For the rest of the 19th century, different factions fought over who would rule Mexico. The country lost half its territory to the United States.

The Mexican Revolution began in 1910. This developed to a bloody battle to determine who would rule the country. During this time, a movement began to divide up estates of the wealthy elite and distribute the land to landless peasantry. The Mexican government seized control of all natural resources. The political party that emerged from that conflict, the Institutional Revolutionary Party (PRI), remained dominant in Mexican politics until the elections of 1997. Mexico is sometimes called the "one-party democracy."[1]

Table 7.1 presents selected demographic and economic data for Mexico. The country has a gross domestic product (GDP) of only $3,000, about one-fourth that of the United States. Eleven Latin American and Caribbean nations also have a higher GDP than Mexico. However, the per capita GDP of the three largest Mexican cities (Mexico City, Guadalajara, and Monterrey) is twice the national average. Foreign retailers entering the market can focus on these three large cities and have substantial buying power.

Mexico has .55 retail square feet (0.05 square meters) for every person versus 19 square feet (1.8 square meters) for every person in the United States. Thirty percent of Mexico's population is under the age of 14. This is a sign of great growth potential.

Under NAFTA, Canada and the United States are exempt from quotas in trade with Mexico. This means they can ship unlimited quantities of goods to Mexico and Mexico can ship unlimited quantities back to its two NAFTA partners.

In 1995, Mexico had a nationwide economic crisis and market depression. When the crisis began, merchandise imports were greatly reduced because the peso devaluations nearly doubled the price of those goods. Retailers were forced to change their product mix, shifting from imported products to products produced in Mexico.[2]

DEPARTMENT STORES

Mexico has three major department store chains, El Puerto de Liverpool, Palacio de Hierro, and Sears, Roebuck and Co. J. C. Penney is a newcomer to Mexico, with only two stores. Liverpool and Palacio de Hierro have a long

TABLE 7.1

Mexico: Selected Demographic and Economic Data

	Population (millions) mid-1995	Area (thousands of sq. km)	GNP per capita: Dollars 1995	GNP per capita: Avg. ann. growth (%) 1985–95	PPP estimates of GNP per capita U.S. = 100: 1987	PPP estimates of GNP per capita U.S. = 100: 1995	Life expectancy at birth (years) 1995	Adult illiteracy (%) 1995
Upper-middle-income economies	438.3t	20,514t	4,260w	0.2w			69w	14w
Mexico	91.8	1,958	3,320	0.1	27.8	23.7	72	10

Source: World Bank (1997). PPP = purchasing power parity. t = total. w = weighted average.

history in Mexico. They were both started by French families who moved to Mexico. Liverpool got its name because most of the merchandise the chain sold came from Europe and was shipped through the port of Liverpool, England. When the merchandise arrived in Mexico, the most prominent feature was the shipping stamp, Liverpool. Both Liverpool and Palacio de Hierro have stores throughout Mexico City.

The Zocolo is the central area of a Mexican city. The original stores for Liverpool and Palacio de Hierro in Mexico City are located in the Zocolo, right across the street from each other. When I visited the Liverpool store in 1996, I found it very disappointing, dark and cramped with unmemorable, cheaply made merchandise. Even then the prices were not low. The Palacio de Hierro store across the street had a ceiling reminiscent of Galeries Lafayette in Paris, the dome with the stain glass. The merchandise in this store was not as cramped as that at Liverpool, but again nothing was memorable. Imagine my surprise, then, when I visited the other stores of these two companies and found beautiful modern department stores with first-class merchandise and fixtures. These companies alter their store offerings based on the clientele living in an area. Although U.S. stores appeal to different target markets, they usually change the name of their offerings to maintain their retail image in the minds of consumers.

Liverpool is Mexico's largest department store chain with 18 stores under the name of Liverpool and Fabricas de Francia. Their format is very upscale, which has made it difficult to compete in the rough economic times that have

Photo 7.1
Shoppers flock to a Mexico City department store, the Palacio de Hierro, for a sale that offers a six-month grace period without interest. After the peso devaluation, stores used tactics like this to stimulate sales. Interest rates in Mexico ran as high as 100% in 1995. *Courtesy of AP/Wide World Photos.*

Photo 7.2
Sears was in the Mexico market for nearly 50 years. In 1997, Sears sold the majority of its ownership of Sears Roebuck de Mexico to a Mexican company. *Courtesy of WWD.*

beset Mexico since the mid-1990's. In 1992, Liverpool entered into a joint venture with Kmart. The venture was unsuccessful, and Kmart pulled out of Mexico in 1997.

Sears has operated in Mexico since 1947 under the name Sears Roebuck de Mexico. Sears has greater geographical representation than either Liverpool or Palacio de Hierro. In fact, it is really the only national department store chain, with stores throughout the country. Sears has a true department store image in Mexico, more upscale than its mass merchandiser image in the United States. Even before the bottom fell out of the Mexican economy in 1994, Sears had begun overhauling the chain's image. It trimmed inventory, lowered average price points, modernized advertising, and hired new buyers to enhance the company's image.

The approach taken was to emphasize a "buy Mexican first" strategy to keep costs down. Simply put, the strategy was to offer merchandise of department store quality with the turnover of a mass merchant. This change took place after the company conducted focus group interviews with customers and found that the store was generally overpriced and out of reach for many of the country's middle-class consumers. Since the overhaul, Sear's market share has grown from 15% to 21% in areas where it competes against Liverpool and Palacio de Hierro.[3]

Sears offers the most ample credit plan in Mexico. Sears gained much of its market share in the United States by extending credit to those who typically would not qualify, and 70% of the company's sales come from credit sales.[4] As a country develops a more formalized credit system, this strategy becomes less of a benefit. The company also offers a complete repair service for automobiles and home appliances. Sears was aggressive in developing and operating shopping centers in Mexico[5] and today there are 47 stores in 23 Mexican states.[6] Nearly half of Sears Roebuck de Mexico's square footage is in Mexico City. In 1997, Sears announced that it was selling most of its interests in Sears Roebuck de Mexico to Grupo Carso, which was sold the right to continue using the Sears name and to expand the number of Sears outlets. Sears will retain 15% ownership of the Mexican operations. Grupo Carso also owns the Sanborn retailing chain in Mexico.[7]

J. C. Penney began operating in Mexico in 1994. Its store in Monterrey at the Plaza St. Augustin is one of its most elegant stores. Seventy-five percent of the merchandise consists of imported goods.[8] Until the economic crisis that hit Mexico in the mid-1990s, the major concerns for J. C. Penney were the paperwork and logistics needed to meet Mexico's certificate of origin rules.

SUPERMARKETS AND HYPERMARKETS

Mexico has about 700 stores that offer both groceries and dry goods. Supermarket chains generate only 30% of food sales. The rest of these sales occur through mom and pop stores or street vendors. *Changaros* (tiny independent shops) and *tianguis* (open markets) make up 60% of sales. Because of the predominance of micro-suppliers, the wholesale supply industry is weak. Supermarket managers regard the distribution system as unreliable. The large chains operate their own distribution system with direct links between manufacturers and individual stores.

The supermarket industry is an oligopoly. The three Mexican firms, Cifra, Gigante, and Comercial Mexicana are joining forces with foreign companies to solidify their position and gain market share.

Obtaining state-of-the-art inventory technology is the highest priority for Mexican retailers. Only about one-third of Mexican supermarket products are labeled with bar codes. Some supermarkets put their own scanning codes on merchandise. Investments by foreign retailers have brought technology improvements. The retail industry has received direct foreign investment of $3.1 billion, 12% of total foreign investment in Mexico.[9]

Cifra is the leading retailer in Mexico and the leading investor in technology. The company operates 103 stores, but 80% of these are in the Mexico City area. The company also runs 74 restaurants and 29 apparel and general merchandise stores under the name Suburbia. Eighty percent of Cifra's revenues are from food stores. The company carries no debt and it funds expansion through cash reserves.

Cifra pioneered the idea of membership-based warehouse units. Its first such store, Club Aurrera, is the result of a joint venture with Wal-Mart Stores, Inc., based on that company's Sam's Clubs. Company Focus I.3 (p. 172) provides further information about the Cifra–Wal-Mart joint venture and describes how Cifra has positioned itself to dominate its competitors in the Mexican market.

STREET VENDORS

Street vendors add color to the shopping environment in Mexico. It is difficult to walk a block without being accosted by merchants selling a variety of merchandise. Although we generally think of street vendors as a part of the pre-modern and romantic past in Mexico, they have elevated the practice to a level of great efficiency and productivity. Street vendors take advantage of public space, foregoing the costs of capital investment such as rent. Street vending requires a greater investment of labor relative to inventory, which places a limit on size and necessitates low levels of inventory. These characteristics also contribute to an advantage for street vendors over retail stores: they can be very flexible to market changes.

Because of their location in public space, these mobile retailers respond differently to legal and market situations than do fixed retail sites. In many areas of the world, street vending is either illegal or marginally legal. Governments generally write regulatory systems for retailing with fixed retail operations in mind. Fixed location retailers are easier to monitor and regulate. Mobile retailers have different concerns in conducting business. They must watch inventory more carefully to avoid theft. At the end of the day, the inventory must be packed up and stored somewhere. Inventory control takes on a new meaning, that of protecting the merchandise. Inventory control is labor-intensive and greater trust must be placed in employees. This explains why most street vendors rely only on family members to mind the store. It also limits the growth possibilities of the business.

Street vendors are uniquely suited for sales to pedestrians because they are in public areas.[10] People are less reluctant to stop and inspect a street offering than to step into a store. Vendors are the ultimate purveyors of impulse purchases.

Mexico City has a vibrant street-vending retail sector. There are more than 200,000 vendors in the Federal District alone, which is only half of the entire Mexico City metropolitan area. The number of street vendors has increased since the 1960s. Before that time, the government repressed street vendors, making their operations difficult.

During the 1970s, members of various associations of the blind were given permits to set up metal kiosks at strategic areas within the city. These were perfect sites for taco stands. Permit holders who were blind as well as others who received permits through less than legal circumstances soon began leasing their permits to others. Some of these taco stands were even run as chains of micro-restaurants. Street vendors reemerged in the old areas of the city center in the working-class neighborhoods and in areas behind the National Palace. A retail explosion took place.

Photo 7.3
A temporary market is set up on an overpass in Mexico City. This market is adjacent to a suburban subway stop. Overhead costs are minimal for these retailers, allowing them to sell at very low prices. *Courtesy of the author.*

Photo 7.4
The temporary market is also a gathering place in the community. Fresh fruits and vegetables are sold here. Camera film is one-third the price paid in a regular store. Many vendors sell prepared food that will be taken home and eaten. *Courtesy of the author.*

Vendors began to specialize in a particular type of trade. In one location, vendors specialized in fresh fruits. Another area sold kitchen goods, and another, electrical appliances. The electrical goods area specialized in merchandise that had been smuggled into the country to avoid the high import tariffs then imposed on foreign goods. By 1990, about 20,000 vendors worked in the central areas. Similar magnet markets existed in other areas of the city.

In the **magnet markets,** the key to success was the concentration of similar products in the same area. An entire street would be devoted to leather jackets, or to fancy dresses. Although you might think that this strategy would reduce an individual vendor's profits because of the overly competitive environment, just the opposite is true. As we saw in Chapter 3, geographical location theories explain that creating a central place draws customers. For customers to travel a distance to inspect one leather jacket vendor is not practical. However, if many leather jacket vendors are located together, potential customers are drawn to the area. These vendors emphasize low margins and rapid turnover, providing an attraction for customers throughout the city who want the best selection and price. Promotion is entirely by word of mouth, reducing the cost structure for vendors as compared to fixed-store competitors, who must rely on formal advertising to attract customers.

In residential areas, street vendors followed a different type of marketing strategy. Whereas the magnet markets of the city center tended to be highly specialized, residential street vendors focused on everyday items. Food must be purchased frequently, and transporting food from the city center cost the customers in terms of time and expense. Street vendors of food in residential areas became very popular.

After the period of street-vendor repression ended in the late 1960s, the Mexico City government began to allow *tianguis,* a special type of street vendor. The word *tianguis* comes from the word for market in Aztec. As used in Mexico City, it came to mean a type of rotating market that operated in a circuit, moving to a different neighborhood each day of the week.

The city government allowed these markets in order to reduce the complaints of residents of a particular area who did not want their neighborhoods to be taken over by vendors, but did not mind the inconvenience of having the street hawkers one day a week. Operating in this manner, the *tianguistas* have the advantage of both a fixed market and a mobile market. Instead of having a single market zone, they now had seven zones. The regularity with which they would appear in an area allowed them to build up an established clientele. They began to operate like the downtown magnet markets, focusing on low profit margin and high turnover.

It became important to organize the market zones and to negotiate with officials. This led nearly all street vendors to become members of associations that manage the zones like a corporation. Voting was even coordinated to incorporate vendors into the ruling party.

In the 1960s, when street vending was repressed, doing business was physically dangerous and more expensive. When police found street vendors, they would break up their kiosks and confiscate the merchandise. Even when they were not destroying the street vendors, the police were not inclined to protect them from common criminals. Street vendors became easy targets for thieves who knew they would have their daily earnings on their person. When street vending was legalized, the kiosk owners could afford to invest more money in inventory, and they no longer had to fear the threat of arrest or confiscation.

Street vendors have become a sophisticated retail system in Mexico City. Some *tianguis* may have more than 1,000 vendors that, taken together, equal the same value of goods as a modern supermarket. These neighborhood markets even use layout concepts similar to modern supermarkets. They place key goods, such as meats, dairy products, and other everyday consumer items, at a central location as far away from entrances to the market as possible to draw consumers throughout the market, exposing them to greater amounts of merchandise.

Photo 7.5
Numerous silver shops are found throughout Mexico. Buyers and sellers haggle over the price. *Courtesy of the author.*

The following example highlights the importance of these informal markets within the Mexican retailing environment. Mexico is known for its silver jewelry. On my last trip to Mexico, I was on a quest for the best price for some jewelry for myself and as gifts for others. As I was planning to interview the major department store managers, I began my search in those stores and in jewelry specialty stores. One necklace that caught my eye in a fine jewelry store was nicely polished and displayed in a nice gift box. It cost $500: more than I wanted to spend. During my two weeks in Mexico, I used that necklace as a benchmark for comparison.

In Mexico City, I shopped for silver at the Insurgents' Market, a type of cooperative in which artisans rent spaces in a building and display their merchandise. Walking through the market can be an unnerving experience for U.S. visitors. Hawkers approach customers, draping silver necklaces around their necks without permission. Everyone promises to give the lowest price and provide the finest quality necklaces. Frequently a shop owner will tell you that he made his jewelry himself. This is probably not true. In fact, all sterling silver in Mexico is stamped with a government-required number registering that the silver is solid sterling and identifying the silver shop and the craftsperson who produced the product.

The person from whom I ended up buying several items did, however, have jewelry that looked different from the other merchandise. It was a welcome change to see what appeared to be some creativity after seeing row upon row of identical merchandise: a type of mass production by hand. In Mexico, silver is generally sold by weight, even when it is in the form of finished jewelry. Of course, the price you pay for each gram differs in each store. Several necklace sets at this shop interested me, so I began the negotiation process.

I made an offer. The shop owner made a counter offer. I said I needed to wait until after I had looked in another shop. He counter offered again. Eventually he told me, "Fine, look at other shops, you will not find a better price." He was right; I looked but did not find a better price for the quality of those necklaces. The next day I went back and purchased the merchandise: three silver necklaces with earrings, one set with a bracelet. I purchased all of these items for about the same price as the one necklace in the specialty jewelry store. I did not get a fancy gift box—the items were packaged in fabric bags with drawstring tops—but they are heavyweight, hand-crafted sterling silver jewelry that I doubt anyone I know could tell from the necklace in the specialty jewelry store.

As this example illustrates, the greatest competition for established retailers is from street vendors and informal markets. These forms of informal retailing have very low overhead and greatly reduced tax obligations because of under-reporting of income.

Photo 7.6
A small clothing shop expands into the street to display merchandise. Dozens of shops in Mexico will sell identical lace dresses, tablecloths, and ponchos. Products are so similar because all shops purchase from the same manufacturers. *Courtesy of the author.*

GOVERNMENT REGULATIONS

During the 1980s, the government imposed retail price caps on a wide range of items to control inflation. Mexican workers lost between 30% and 50% of their purchasing power in this period. The 1980s hurt the Mexican retail sector. The country lacked access to foreign capital after the Mexican government defaulted on interest payments to foreign creditors. From 1984 to 1989, the inflation rate was 77%, one of the highest in the world.[11]

Carlos Salinas de Gortari was elected president of Mexico in July 1988. One of his major accomplishments was to make the business environment in Mexico more accommodating. Inflation was reduced from 125% in 1988 to 30% in 1990. Laws related to foreign ownership were relaxed, giving foreign retailers the opportunity to buy out their Mexican partners.

President Salinas pursued deregulatory policies that allowed producers and retailers freedom in labeling and packaging. The Salinas administration also negotiated NAFTA with the United States and Canada. In the first few years of NAFTA, the country's economy was booming and many U.S. retailers began aggressive expansion into Mexico. Then, in late 1994, a currency crisis occurred. The result was a massive devaluation of the peso, which effectively cut consumers' purchasing power in half. Interest rates skyrocketed.

Before the currency devaluation, Mexican shoppers had strong preferences for imported merchandise. Tariffs were 20% on foreign goods, but consumers believed imported merchandise was worth the 20% premium. Imported products made up a large portion of the entire product mix for most retailers. Mexican retailers had good relationships with U.S. suppliers. Accounts payable terms were 30 to 60 days for Mexican suppliers, compared with the 90 to 120 days offered by U.S. suppliers. Purchasing U.S. goods gave the Mexican retailers better working capital efficiencies.[12]

After the devaluation, retailers who purchased merchandise produced in Mexico were hurt, but not nearly as much as retailers who purchased imported merchandise. Sears and Wal-Mart, which had always carried nearly 100% Mexican-produced merchandise, were among those who were not hurt significantly. Retailers who had purchased imported merchandise and then went to pay for it after the currency devaluation found the merchandise cost nearly twice what they had anticipated. Quickly retailers scrambled to find domestic suppliers for merchandise.

FOREIGN RETAILERS

Government policies regulate many aspects of retailing in Mexico. Before 1988, such policies regulated foreign ownership of Mexican companies. However, in the retail sector, these regulations were mainly ignored under the Salinas administration. International firms only need to follow local content and hiring regulations. Getting a permit to open and operate retail stores is difficult. Pizza Hut had to apply for 17 different permits before opening its first franchise in Mexico. In the United States, the company required only two permits. Regulations required that all imported products be labeled in Spanish. This is done either at the point of manufacture or on a customs label affixed at the point of distribution. U.S. firms have complained about this labeling regulation. However, a similar regulation in the United States stipulates that retailers cannot sell merchandise that is not labeled in English.

The major problem for foreign retailers is the lack of retail space or undeveloped land. Mexico City has developed rapidly in the past 10 years. Land became very expensive in the 1990s, and local companies had difficulty accessing capital to purchase retail sites. Mexican retail executives estimate that the minimum efficient size for a discount chain is 20 stores. Without this number, the chain does not have sufficient leverage with suppliers.

Finding local retail managers is also a problem. There are few good buyers and even fewer well-trained store managers. To meet this need, Cifra has begun recruiting senior managers outside the country, pulling from Hispanic populations in the United States and elsewhere.

The planning director of a large Mexican retailer (Grupo Gigante), Juan Carlos Mateos, was quoted in the January 19, 1993, issue of *Financial Times*, "[Foreign firms] supply the know-how and we have the know-who."[13] Four strategic alliances began in the early 1990s: Wal-Mart partnered with Cifra, Fleming joined with Grupo Gigante, Price Club formed an alliance with Comercial Mexicana, and Kmart joined with El Puerto de Liverpool. As I mentioned earlier, Kmart has since withdrawn from Mexico.

The entry of foreign retailers is changing the Mexican retail environment. Many foreign retailers entering the Mexican market have large financial resources. This means that they can pressure gross margin downward to gain market share. As competition increases, marginal players will probably disappear. The competitive environment will grow as joint ventures such as Cifra/Wal-Mart and CCM/Price Club, and foreign retailers such as Carrefour and Auchan do battle either through aggressive expansion or price wars. Table 7.2 summarizes the foreign competitors who have entered the Mexican market since 1990. Of the companies listed, only J. C. Penney has entered the market alone. This is likely a major mistake.

CANADA

COUNTRY BACKGROUND

If Canada and the United States are so similar, why have their retail formats been so different? The answer lies in history, location, and legislation. Before the U.S. Civil War, both Canada and the United States had few large population centers. In the early part of the 19th century, only 12 U.S. cities had a population of more than 5,000. There was little intracity transportation

TABLE 7.2

Foreign Competitors Entering Mexico in the 1990s

Foreign Retailer				
Year	**Country**	**Status**	**Format**	**Units**
1991	Price/Costco (U.S.)	Joint venture with Comerci Clubs	Membership	13
1991	Wal-Mart (U.S.)	Joint venture with Cifra	Supercenters	14
			Sam's Club	28
			Other Cifra	132
1992	Kmart (U.S.)	Joint venture with Liverpool (withdrew in 1997)	Supercenters	4
1992	Radio Shack (U.S.)	Joint venture with Gigante Electronics	Specialty	48
1992	Fleming (U.S.)	Joint venture with Gigante	Supermarket	4
1994	Office Depot (U.S.)	Joint venture with Gigante Office Supplies	Specialty	2
1994	Casino (France)	Joint venture with Central Detallista	Cash-and-carry	3
1994	Carrefour (France)	Joint venture with Gigante	Hypermarket	11
1994	J.C. Penney (U.S.)	No partner	Department	2
1995	Auchan (France)	Joint venture with Comercial Mexicana	Hypermarket	1
1995	Amoco (U.S.)	Joint venture with Femsa Stores	Convenience	1

Source: Compiled by the author.

and low discretionary income. These activities restricted the development of the retail industry.

The Civil War created a need for military supplies that actually pushed the United States into the Industrial Revolution. The industrialization process required concentrations of people in cities and the development of transportation systems between cities to bring workers to and from the newly formed factories. These same intracity transportation systems would also later transport customers to large retailers.[14] Industrialization also increased disposable incomes. Wars are generally good for retailing, and the Civil War was particularly good for the development of the retail industry in the United States.

Canada, in contrast, industrialized late and unevenly. The country's demographics hindered its entry into the industrial age. The Canadian population was small and geographically diverse. By the end of the 19th century, only three provinces—British Columbia, Quebec, and Ontario—were industrialized. Table 7.3 presents selected demographic and economic data for Canada.

Seventy-two percent of the Canadian population live within 100 miles of the U.S. border, located between Windsor and Montreal, a strip of 608

TABLE 7.3

Canada: Selected Demographic and Economic Data

	Population (millions) mid-1995	Area (thousands of sq. km)	GNP per capita		PPP estimates of GNP per capita U.S. = 100		Life expectancy at birth (years) 1995	Adult illiteracy (%) 1995
			Dollars 1995	Avg. ann. growth (%) 1985–95	1987	1995		
High-income economies	902.2t	32,039t	24,930w	1.9w			77w	
Canada	29.6	9,976	19,380	0.4	84.6	78.3	78	a

Source: World Bank (1997). a = less than 5%. PPP = purchasing power parity. t = total. w = weighted average.

miles. This makes cross-border shopping a great concern for Canadian retailers. Retail sales in Canada were up slightly during 1996 and 1997, as the weak Canadian dollar reduced cross-border shopping.[15] In addition, Canada has limited market opportunity. There are only eight major population centers in Canada; these centers have 85% of the retail market. All of these areas have been over-stored and are plateauing. Retailers from the United States have been able to exploit economies of scale in their Canadian operations. One U.S. retailer, Gap, has covered the eight major retail areas with 80 stores.[16]

DEPARTMENT STORES

The department store sector in Canada is in financial trouble. New retail formats such as category killers, superstores, and membership clubs have entered the Canadian markets. The strategic response of the Canadian department stores to the new retailing formats is to focus on soft goods, increasing the floor space for clothing and fashion while decreasing the hardware square footage. Eaton's, a 127-year-old Canadian department store chain, has expanded specific departments while reducing others to become more dominant in selected merchandise lines. Department stores are also emphasizing their own brand names in a strategy of offering higher quality at lower prices. Some department stores have modified this strategy to focus on fewer items with greater depth and breadth. In 1997, Eaton's of Canada came under protection from its creditors and began seeking the possibility of merger or sale to another company. Eaton's, which operates 85 department stores, intends to sell 31 of its existing stores.[17]

The department store share of the retail market has been declining over the past two decades. In 1981, department stores had 9.9% of the market;

this decreased to 7% in 1992. This market share has been lost to discount stores such as Zellers (Canadian), and Wal-Mart (United States). Specialty stores, warehouse clubs, and category killers continue to erode department stores' market share.

The largest department store group in Canada, the Hudson's Bay Company, has been having a difficult time. The group operates 101 department stores trading as The Bay, and 296 as Zellers.[18]

The two major department store groups, The Bay and Eaton's, are trying to reposition to be more upscale. They are focusing on cosmetics, fashion apparel, and home furnishings, while eliminating less profitable hard goods, an area where discounters have eroded the market.[19]

One department store is trying something different. This store, Ogilvy, opened in 1919 on the Rue Sainte-Catherine in Montreal. The store occupies 10,000 square meters (108,000 square feet) and has become a retail landmark in Montreal. About one-fifth of the store's 1.5 million visitors every year are from abroad. Ogilvy has always sold upscale brands in a traditional environment. A kilted bagpiper moves through the store every day at noon. The fifth floor has Tudor Hall, a center for musical performances and other big events. Since 1985, this store has been using a unique retail format. Shop-in-shop tenants occupy more than 90% of the floor space. The tenants must follow strict common standards. Customer services are centralized, sales periods and theme promotions are standardized, and all tenants participate in advertising.[20] This is the same system used successfully in Japanese department stores.

SUPERMARKETS AND HYPERMARKETS

The supermarket industry in Canada is led by Loblaws, Provigo, and the Oshawa Group. The industry is highly competitive, a situation that has led to the use of private label brands. Retailers are trying to gain greater profit margins and increase market share.

Membership warehouse clubs such as Price Club and Costco have increased the competitive pressure. Traditional food stores have cut prices, promoted private labels, added bulk goods, and tested new store formats. Food and drug combination stores are doing well in this experiment to regain market share.[21]

NEW RETAIL FORMATS—FOREIGN RETAILERS

For many years, restrictive legislature, which was similar to that found in Europe, prevented the opening of large format retail stores in Canada. In a series of court decisions since 1988, these zoning regulations have been relaxed. As a result, U.S. retailers have begun expanding aggressively into Canada. Since 1990, new retail format space has doubled in the Greater

Photo 7.7
The Ogilvy store in Montreal opened in 1919 to sell upscale merchandise. This traditional retailer began experiments with shop-in-shop tenants, which increased sales and profits and reduced the store's inventory costs. *Courtesy of Ogilvy.*

Toronto area. Over half this increase has been in the category-killer format. Canadian-owned retailers barely have a majority of the new format square footage. U.S. and European owned companies make up the other 45%.[22]

Category killers offer very narrow but deep merchandise lines. They are not discounters, but instead have the entire category (e.g., books, toys, electronics) covered with a competitive price and vast selection. They get the name category killer because when they enter a market area, other retailers cannot compete with them. A grouping of category killers is referred to as a **power center.** A summary of the new format retailers is provided in Table 7.4.

Wal-Mart acquired 120 Woolco stores (U.S.-based variety stores) in 1994. This acquisition has sent Canadian competitors scrambling. Zellers, a discount department store founded in 1931, and a part of the Hudson's Bay Company since 1978, is the major Canadian competition for Wal-Mart. Zellers had introduced a program called Club Z in 1986 through which club-card-carrying customers could receive points redeemable for gifts from the Club Z catalog. Zellers maintains that one in every five Canadians has

TABLE 7.4

New Format Retailers in the Canadian Market

Store Name	Category
Toys "R" Us	Category killer
IKEA	Category killer
Sporting Life	Category killer
Aikenheads	Category killer
Business Depot	Category killer
White Rose Nurseries	Category killer
Future Shop	Category killer
Winners	Category killer
Alive and Well	Category killer
Idomo	Category killer
Public Optical	Category killer
B. B. Bargoons	Category killer
Hakim Optical	Category killer
Canadian Tire	Category killer
Lenscrafters	Category killer
The Office Place	Category killer
Lewiscraft	Category killer
Loomis and Toles	Category killer
Michaels	Category killer
Value Village	Category killer
Grand and Toy	Category killer
Loblaws	Superstore
Knob Hill Farms	Superstore
A&P	Superstore
Miracle Ultra Mart	Superstore
Price Club	Membership club
Costco	Membership club
Club Biz	Membership club
Club Ultima	Membership club

Source: Jones, K., W. Evans, and C. Smith. (1994). *New Formats in the Canadian Retail Economy, Center for the Study of Commercial Activity.* Toronto, Canada: Ryerson Polytechnic University, p. 168.

received a gift through Club Z. In response to the Wal-Mart acquisition, 62 of the 295 Zellers stores were remodeled and 18 new stores were opened during 1995.[23]

Competition from new format retailers is changing consumers' buying patterns. Consumers are demanding a wider assortment of merchandise, at lower prices, with improved service. As a result, traditional retailers are also being forced to change the way they do business. Canadian Tire is adopting a warehouse format in some of its stores to offer a wider selection and lower prices. Major fashion retailers such as Fairweather, Tip Top Tailors, and Thrifty's are also following this practice.

The new retail formats have polarized shopping. Shopping centers are now perceived as soft goods-oriented. Power centers are viewed as food and hard goods-oriented. The shock of this intense increase in competition has forced traditional retailers to move to larger store formats, raise service levels, and institute more cost-effective management and inventory systems. For instance, Canadian retailing is now embracing electronic data interchange (EDI) for controlling stock and accuracy.[24]

NAFTA has made it easier for U.S. firms to move into Canada; however, the allure of low-cost laborers, available in Mexico, is not an advantage in Canada. Wages in Canada are equal to those in the United States. Canada's greatest attraction for U.S. retailers is its geographic proximity to U.S. retail markets. A warehouse close to the border can service both U.S. and Canadian stores.

Photo 7.8
The Canadian retailer Roots has more than 100 stores in Canada as well as six in the United States and 12 in the Pacific Rim. It specializes in high-quality leather goods, sportswear, and outerwear for children and adults. *Courtesy of Roots.*

SUMMARY

Mexico's retail industry is characterized by a strong informal retail sector that coexists with modern retail formats. Mobile markets move from one residential area to another. These mobile markets create a sense of place.

Mexico's retailers have not expanded nationally. Even large companies have a local or regional presence. Most major Mexican retailers have joined forces with foreign retailers. These joint ventures provide Mexican retailers with needed technological advancements. They provide foreign retailers with knowledge about Mexican culture.

Canada's retailers have not developed into national chains. This has made them vulnerable to competition from new format U.S. retailers. Major U.S. chains are represented in nearly every major Canadian city. However, Canadian retailers have been unsuccessful in their attempts to expand into the United States. The learning that occurs when companies nationalize makes such companies very difficult to compete with, especially on their home field. This factor has played a major role in the failure of Canadian retailers to enter the U.S. market.

KEY TERMS

category killer
magnet market
power center

DISCUSSION QUESTIONS

1. Why are U.S. retailers so eager to move into Mexico and Canada? What factors from Dunning's theory of the eclectic firm (see Chapter 1) would explain this movement?
2. How are retailers affected by the peso devaluation? What strategic changes can a retailer take to reduce the negative effects?
3. The first retailers to move into Mexico and Canada were hypermarkets such as Wal-Mart and Kmart. What makes these operating formats so attractive for these markets? Kmart has withdrawn from Mexico. Can you suggest why they were unsuccessful?
4. Comparatively speaking, there are more U.S. retailers moving into Canada than into Mexico. Using Dunning's theory of the eclectic firm, explain why this is happening.
5. Why is the informal retail sector in Mexico so successful? Will this sector continue to thrive as modern retail formats such as hypermarkets and supermarkets gain momentum?

ENDNOTES

1. "Mexico." (1996). *Craighead's International Business.* Detroit: Gale Research, Inc.
2. Fraschetto, W. (1997). "Mexico." *International Trends in Marketing,* Vol. 14, No. 1, pp. 103–105.
3. "Sears in Mexico: Policing Its Prices." (1995). *Women's Wear Daily,* August 2, p. 16.
4. La Follette, C. (1993). "Retail in Mexico, 1993." Harvard Business School Case 0-793-144, September 28.
5. "Sears Roebuck de Mexico—Company Report." (May 10, 1996). In *InvesText.* Lehman Brothers, Inc. [Database on CD-ROM] Foster City, Calif.: Information Access.
6. Coopers & Lybrand. (1996). *Global Powers of Retailing.* Chain Store Age—Special Report.
7. *Retail News Letter.* (1997). No. 446, May, p. 11.
8. Ramey, J. (1995). "Penney's Long Haul in Mexico." *Women's Wear Daily,* July 12, p. 14.
9. Fraschetto (1997).
10. Cross, J. "Retailing in a Neighborhood Street Market: A Tianguista Family in Mexico." @ http://auc~acs.eun.eg/www/cross/retail2.html.
11. La Follette. (1993).
12. La Follette. (1993).
13. *Financial Times.* (1993), January 19.
14. Burns, D., and D. Rayman. (1996). "Retailing in Canada and the United States: Historical Comparisons." In G. Akehurst and N. Alexander, eds., *The Internationalisation of Retailing.* London: Frank Cass.
15. Anderson, F. (1997). "Canada." *International Trends in Marketing,* Vol. 14, No. 1, p. 78.
16. Coopers & Lybrand (1996).
17. *Retail News Letter.* (1997). No. 446, May, p. 3.
18. "Canada—Hudson's Bay Company." (1997). *Retail News Letter,* No. 449, August/September, p. 3.
19. Coopers & Lybrand (1996).
20. "Canada—Ogilvy Shop-in-Shop Department Store in Montreal." *Retail News Letter,* No. 436, June, p. 3.
21. Coopers & Lybrand (1996).
22. Jones, K., W. Evans, and C. Smith. (1994). *New Formats in the Canadian Retail Economy.* Toronto, Canada: Center for the Study of Commercial Activity, Ryerson Polytechnic University.
23. "Canada—Zellers Continues Building Customer Loyalty." (1996). *Retail News Letter.* No. 432, February, p. 3.
24. Jones, Evans, and Smith (1994).

COMPANY FOCUS II.1

TOYS "R" US

Keirsten Sorensen, Courtney Rising, Cathy Brown

History

Toys "R" Us was started in 1948 by Charles P. Lazarus.[1] Originally, it was a baby furniture store until customers began to request toys.[2] Today, Toys "R" Us has become the world's leading children's retailer, dominating the U.S. toy market.[3] In 1984, Toys "R" Us opened its first international stores, four in Canada and one in Singapore.[4] As of June 16, 1995, Toys "R" Us had opened 300 international toy stores in 20 foreign countries and 618 stores in the United States.[5] In 1997, Toys "R" Us had a total of 1,380 stores, 398 of which were outside the United States.[6]

Toys "R" Us stores are organized like supermarkets. They offer a large selection of toys and brands displayed in warehouse-like buildings.[7] The Toys "R" Us stores, whether international or in the United States, are similarly located in freestanding buildings near shopping centers. All stores are centered on low-priced, brand name goods and self-service.[8]

Strategy

Toys "R" Us decided to expand globally because the company had already dominated the U.S. market. It currently relies on international business as a major means of growth.[9] International efforts focus on opening new stores, unlike U.S. efforts, which rely on getting more business from each store.[10] Internationalizing was favorable for Toys "R" Us because the toy markets around the world are fragmented. This gives Toys "R" Us the opportunity to dominate the market because it offers one-stop shopping.[11]

Toys "R" Us expanded globally with some adaptations to the different markets.[12] The overseas stores were formatted similarly to those in the United States, including an American-style parking lot.[13] The merchandise selection contains about 80% of that sold in the United States, with 20% chosen for local interests.[14] For example, the Japanese market prefers porcelain dolls whereas Germans prefer wooden toys. In Hong Kong, Toys "R" Us carries different versions of the board game Monopoly, and France has a miniature version of the French TGV train.[15] Also in France, there is little interest in baseball compared to the United States.

Toys "R" Us has a goal of opening five stores per year in each country where it does business. All purchasing, marketing, and merchandising are centralized.[16] Toys "R" Us has experimented with franchising in the Middle East. This has allowed the company to enter countries it never thought possible.[17] Toys "R" Us plans to continue these franchises in the future.[18] The company is doing everything it can to continue its reputation as a category killer, but this time internationally.[19]

Internationalization

At present, the best international performance by Toys "R" Us has been in France, Spain, and Japan, with weaker business growth in Canada, the United Kingdom, and Germany.[20] There is tremendous opportunity for expansion in Europe, which provides a well-developed, large market with more than 350 million people who are starving for American products.[21] The newest Toys "R" Us stores were opened in Denmark, Sweden, and Luxembourg.[22] The company's international sales are 24% of total sales. Toys "R" Us attributes its success to the universal attraction children have to toys.[23]

The company puts fear into the hearts of many foreign toy retailers, who do not have the selection or low prices of Toys "R" Us.[24] The latest technology is used to monitor the sales and inventory of the company's overseas stores. Toys "R" Us has created good relationships with its manufacturers by allowing them to grow along with Toys "R" Us. These manufacturers are also able to publicize their names internationally.[25] Toys "R" Us has a standard procedure of borrowing money in each country where it opens new stores. This allows the company to receive tax breaks and decreases the risk of doing business in international markets.[26]

Canada

Toys "R" Us first expanded internationally into Canada, where it opened four stores in 1984.[27,28] Canada was chosen primarily because there was no language barrier and the market was under-retailed.[29,30] The first international stores provided a model as to how other international stores would be marketed and managed, as well as how distribution systems, technology, and the company's low-price strategy would play a part. Toys "R" Us was the first category killer of its kind in Canada, capturing 50% of the Canadian toy market.[31]

Japan

Toys "R" Us entered the Japanese market via a joint venture with McDonald's, in which Toys "R" Us owns 80%.[32,33] The agreement provided that fast-food chains open at the toy stores.[34] The first Toys "R" Us opened in Ami Town, Japan, late in 1991.[35] Serious difficulties caused a delay in entering the Japanese market.[36] Many Japanese toy companies were afraid to supply Toys "R" Us for fear of offending local toy wholesalers.[37] Landlords were reluctant to lease prime space to Toys "R" Us because local retailers were upset. Also, local toy businesses complained that Toys "R" Us would put them out of business.[38] Many toy retailers are now giving in because Toys "R" Us is becoming too successful to ignore.[39]

The company has 24 superstores in Japan and planned for 35 at the end of 1996. Each Japanese Toys "R" Us store generates $5 to $10 million more in sales than a typical U.S. store.[40] Toys "R" Us deals directly with Asian manufacturers and sells products at a larger discount than other Japanese stores.[41] For this reason, the company's entry into the Japanese market caused an extreme fall in the prices of children's' goods.[42] Japanese consumers have apparently changed their habits in response to the new format. There is now a greater emphasis on bargains, variety, and low prices. Consumers feel the service at Toys "R" Us has made shopping a leisure activity for many families in Japan.[43] Toys "R" Us is the first consumer-oriented company to enter the Japanese market, fulfilling the consumer's high expectations.[44]

Middle East

The high risk of entering the Middle Eastern market made franchising an essential route for the company's expansion there.[45] Toys "R" Us opened its first franchise in Dubai. Wishing to move further into this market, Toys "R" Us is seeking to expand in India, Pakistan, and Bangladesh. The company also has plans for stores in Qatar, Bahrain, Oman, and Kuwait.[46] In 1995, Toys "R" Us planned to open franchises in the United Arab Emirates, Saudi Arabia, and Israel.

United Kingdom

In 1985, Toys "R" Us opened five stores in the United Kingdom. It captured 9% of the U.K. toy market in three years.[47] As in the United States, Toys "R" Us is exploring use of the Internet in the United Kingdom. By December 1994, however, increased competition had slowed the company's growth.[48,49]

China

Much of the world's toy manufacturing is located in China with the market developing fastest in the southern region. Although China currently benefits from its most favored nation status with the United States, if this status were taken away, problems would arise for Toys "R" Us. As an example, prices would increase and the company's supply of toys would decrease.[50] This would result in losses for Toys "R" Us of 200,000 or more jobs. In addition to its manufacturing links in China, it has been beneficial for Toys "R" Us to enter the Chinese market because consumers in this market are in need of many products.[51]

Germany

Germany was targeted by Toys "R" Us as an area of fast growth.[52] The company chose to enter the market in 1986 even though labor costs at that time were high.[53,54] In the future, Toys "R" Us plans to open a distribution center in Germany. The company experienced one problem in its entry into the German market. Two prestigious German toy manufacturers chose not to do business with Toys "R" Us out of loyalty to the smaller German retailers.[55] Despite this, in 1990, Toys "R" Us captured 6% of the German toy market.[56] As in the United Kingdom, however, growth slowed down by late 1994 due to competition.[57,58]

Problems and Challenges

Toys "R" Us has faced many challenges during its international expansion. Foreign governments as well as retailers were unsure of the company's effect on their markets. High costs of prime real estate made it difficult to locate retail sites. Differences in zoning and construction practices overseas caused problems when building its stores. Local manufacturers sometimes refused to supply to Toys "R" Us out of loyalty to their smaller local businesses. Other problems included regulated hours of operation, differences in wages and work rules, and cultural barriers. Some of the biggest problems arose due to the company's lack of research into foreign markets. For example, misjudgments were made on promotional strategies, products, and locations. Although Toys "R" Us found international business practices complex, the company is learning from mistakes and successfully moving ahead with its international expansion.[59] The recent bright spots for the company are the United Kingdom and Japan. Profitability in Canada has been restrained by a price war among toy discounters. Sluggish economies in Germany and France, combined with the restrictive shopping hours there, have negatively affected Toys "R" Us sales and profits.[60]

Future Projections

Toys "R" Us is striving to be in every market of the world by 1997–1998. It wants its overseas market share to equal or surpass its current 20% to 25% domestic market share.[61] In 1995, the company opened 50 new stores internationally and only 40 domestically. That was the third straight year in which new international stores totalled more than new domestic stores. In the mid-1990s, Toys "R" Us hoped to open 70 to 80 stores per year overseas by the year 2000, which would have nearly doubled the company's U.S. expansion rate.[62] Its biggest growth was expected to come in the former eastern bloc countries.[63] By 1995, however, its international expansion had slowed. The company planned to open 40 new stores outside the United States that year, most of them in Japan.[64]

DISCUSSION QUESTIONS

1. Toys "R" Us is expanding aggressively in foreign markets. Is this expansion predictable? What elements make international expansion attractive for this company?
2. Would you categorize Toys "R" Us as a global or a multinational company? What characteristics of the company lead you to this conclusion?
3. What country characteristics should a company like Toys "R" Us investigate before entering a foreign market?

ENDNOTES

1. Salmon, W., and A. Tordjman, (1990). "Internationalization of Retailing." *International Journal of Retailing,* Vol. 4. No. 2, pp. 3–16.
2. Katz, M., R. Levering, and M. Mowkowitz. (1990). "The Almighty Consumers: Retailers." *Everybody's Business.* New York: Bantam Doubleday Publishing, pp. 218–219.
3. "Toys 'R' Us—Company Report." (June 16, 1995). Smith Barney in *Investex* [Database on CD-ROM]. Foster City, Calif.: Information Access.
4. Mohnke, M.S. (1992). "Retail & Wholesale: Toys 'R' Us Inc." In A. Hast, ed., *International Directory of Company Histories,* Vol. 5. Detroit: St. James Press.
5. "Toys 'R' Us—Company Report." (June 16, 1995).
6. *Retail News Letter.* (1997). No. 446, p. 14.
7. Katz, Levering, and Moskowitz (1990).
8. Salmon and Tordjman (1990).
9. Salmon and Tordjman (1990).
10. Palmer, J. (1993). "Toys 'R' Us." *Barrons,* No. 12.
11. "Toys 'R' Us—Company Report" (June 16, 1995).
12. Salmon and Tordjman (1990).
13. Mohnke (1992).
14. Mohnke (1992).
15. Reda, S. (1995). "1995 NRF Gold Medal Award Winner Toys 'R' Us." *Stores,* pp. 131–144.
16. Salmon and Tordjman (1990).

17. "Toys 'R' Us to Buy Back 8.8% of Its Shares and Expand Globally." (1994). *Corporate Growth Report,* No. 7056.
18. "Toys 'R' Us to Add Learning Centers, PC Software, Baby Registry in '95." (1995). *Discount Store News,* p. 6.
19. Evans, M. (1995). "From Toronto to Taiwan, TRU Broadens Reach." *Discount Store News,* pp. 28–30.
20. Evans (1995).
21. "Building Around the World." (1995). *Chain Store Age Executive,* pp. 88–92.
22. Liebeck, L. (1995). "Toys 'R' Us Plans U.S. Refinement, International Expansion." *Discount Store News,* pp. 23, 24, 32.
23. Evans (1995).
24. "Toys 'R' Us to Add Learning Centers" (1995).
25. Evans (1995).
26. "Toys 'R' Us to Buy Back 8.8% of Its Shares" (1994).
27. Mohnke (1992).
28. Palmer (1993).
29. Palmer (1993).
30. "Building Around the World" (1995).
31. Evans (1995).
32. Katz, Levering, and Moskowitz (1990).
33. Johnson, J.L. (1994). "Going Global: An Evolving Saga." *Discount Merchandiser,* pp. 46–58.
34. Katz, Levering, and Moskowitz (1990).
35. Mohnke (1992).
36. Palmer (1993).
37. Eisenstodt, G. (1994). "Bull in the Japan Shop." *Forbes,* pp. 41–42.
38. Evans (1995).
39. Eisenstod (1994).
40. Evans (1995).
41. "Japanese Slowdown Leads to Change in Selling, Buying." (1993). *Journal of Commerce,* p. 4B.
42. Johnson (1994).
43. Eisenstod (1994).
44. Johnson (1994).
45. Liebeck (1995).
46. "Toys 'R' Us to Buy Back 8.8% of Its Shares" (1994).
47. Mohnke (1992)
48. Fitzgerald, K. (1995). "Competitors Swarm Powerful Toys 'R' Us." *Advertising Age,* p. 4.
49. Evans (1995)
50. Bouts, L.D. (1994). "Toys 'R' Us Faces International Challenge." *Discount Store News,* pp. 86–88.
51. Johnson (1994).
52. "Toys 'R' Us to Buy Back 8.8% of Its Shares" (1994).
53. Salmon and Tordjman (1990).
54. Palmer (1993).
55. Mohnke (1992)
56. Salmon and Tordjman. (1990).
57. Fitzgerald (1995)
58. Evans (1995)
59. "Toys 'R' Us to Buy Back 8.8% of Its Shares" (1994).
60. "Toys 'R' Us—Company Report." (November 7, 1996). Morgan Stanley & Co., Inc., in *Investext* [Database on CD-ROM]. Foster City, Calif.: Information Access.
61. Palmer (1993).
62. Caminiti, S. (1994). "After You Win the Fun Begins." *Fortune,* p. 76.
63. "Building Around the World" (1995).
64. *Retail News Letter* (1997).

COMPANY FOCUS II.2

LEVI STRAUSS

Wen-Yu Michelle Chen

Levi Strauss & Co. designs, manufactures, and markets brand name apparel, especially its famous blue jeans, as the symbol of American spirit. The company consists of Levi Strauss North America (LSNA) and Levi Strauss International (LSI).

LSNA coordinates the company's strategies in the United States, Canada, and Mexico, whereas LSI markets apparel outside North America. The company operates divisions in North and South America, Europe, Asia, and Australia, and sells its products around the world.

History

Founded in 1850, Levi Strauss began a journey that would eventually make it the world's largest apparel manufacturer and distributor. Blue jeans, which began as the standard uniform of miners in the days of the San Francisco gold rush, became a teenage staple during the 1950s and 1960s. After 100 years of successfully marketing men's pants, a clothing division was established in 1968 to make and sell clothing for women[1] In 1971, Levi Strauss & Co.'s heavily centralized structure became inadequate, and operations were broken into four divisions: jeans, Levi's for women, boy's wear, and men's sportswear.

By 1977, Levi Strauss & Co. had become the largest clothing maker in the world. In addition to its original products, the company had grown through acquisitions and also licensed its name to be used on other products, such as shoes and socks. Sales doubled in just 4 years, hitting $2 billion in 1979. Purchases of Koracorp Industries Inc., a large maker of men's and women's sportswear, in 1979, and Santone Industries Inc., a menswear manufacturer, in 1981, prepared the ground for further growth.

In 1985, as Levi Strauss & Co. continued to restructure and cut back, the company was taken private in a massive leveraged buyout by the Hass family, descendants of its founders. One year later, the company introduced a successful upscale men's pants line, Dockers. As a result of increasing demand around the world for U.S. jeans and the company's introduction of innovative finishes, such as bleaching or stone washing, Levi's sales soared.

Scope of Operation

Retail Formats in the United States

As part of its strategy to create a consistent brand image, Levi Strauss plans to own and operate retail and outlet stores in the United States. These stores would include Original Levi's Stores, Dockers shops, and separate outlet stores, in all cases selling only Levi's or Dockers brand products.

By opening flagship (premier) stores only in key markets and locations, the company may achieve its primary focus of maintaining a high brand image. The locations it seeks are downtown urban sites and selected high visibility regional malls. Levi Strauss is also planning to operate outlet stores in areas other than major markets in key outlet malls. Those company-owned and -operated stores will not be part of the existing retail system Levi Strauss has with Designs Inc.

Designs Inc. Joint Venture

In 1977, Levi Strauss entered into a joint venture with Designs Inc., which operates 119 stores that sell exclusively Levi's brand products. Designs Inc. markets a broad selection of Levi Strauss products in the eastern part of the United States through three formats. Levi's and Dockers clothing and accessories are sold in mall stores called "Designs" and outlet stores called "Levi's Outlet by Designs." The Designs Inc. joint venture also operates "Original Levi's Stores" and "Levi's Outlet" stores.

Other Retail Outlets

In addition to the joint venture, Levi Strauss will continue to maintain its old accounts. Its principal distribution channels are still department stores, specialty stores, and national chains, such as J. C. Penney, Sears Roebuck & Co., and Mervyn's Inc.

At Sears, there are a growing number of stand-alone Levi shops, and retail prices on the company's 501 jeans have risen 40% since 1991. These long-time accounts have helped Levi Strauss reposition 501s as a prestige product. The company believes that its industry leadership and brand strength of its core products are maintained through the use of traditional distribution channels.

Levi Strauss's U.S. sales to its top five retail customers represented 39% of total 1994 U.S. dollar sales. The company's top 25 customers accounted for approximately 66% of these sales. Currently the company's only long-term contract or commitment with any of its customers is the retail joint venture partnership with Designs Inc.

Original Levi's Stores

As part of its efforts to ensure a consistent image for its customers around the world, Levi Strauss distributes products through dedicated retail channels such as Original Levi's Stores. These company stores allow Levi Strauss to showcase the full range of its products. In a fragmented retail economy, the allure of a dedicated distribution channel has great appeal.

These high energy stores not only enhance the company's brand image but also attract a customer who might otherwise not have been exposed to the merchandise. Rather than being in competition with department store chains, retail outlets such as Original Levi's Stores open up another avenue for the business. Ultimately, such brand name stores will help expand retailing in general.[2]

International Retailing Efforts

Levi Strauss International markets jeans and related apparel outside North America and is a major source of operating income for the company. Levi Strauss International is organized along geographical lines consisting of European, Latin American, and Asia Pacific divisions. Europe is the largest LSI division in terms of sales and profits, with the company's affiliates in Germany and Italy being the two largest contributors. Asia Pacific is the second largest LSI division, principally due to the size of its Japanese operations.[3]

Strategy

In some countries, the company's primary retail customers are large "chain" retailers with centralized buying power. In other countries, the retail industry is comprised of numerous smaller, less centralized shops. Some non-U.S. customers are stores that sell only the company's products and are independent of the company.

The company distributes to approximately 1,100 stores outside the United States that sell only Levi's brand products. These stores are strategically positioned in prime locations around the world and offer a broad selection of premium Levi's products using special retail fixtures and visual merchandising.

Considering the increasingly competitive international retail environment, the company further enhanced the Levi's brand image by opening one owned-and-operated "flagship" store in London during 1994, with two more stores planned for Milan and Madrid in 1995.[4]

Pricing

As a status symbol among upwardly mobile young European and Asian consumers, Levi's jeans retail at more than $80 overseas. The same item can be purchased in the United States at Sears or J. C. Penny for $29.99. These price differentials are the key to the company's future.

In the early 1990s, the company's average wholesale price for its 501 jeans in Europe and Japan was $2 more than the retail price in the United States. Sales outside the United States represented 38% of Levi Strauss's revenues, but 53% of its profits.[5]

Distribution

Levi Strauss explores and evaluates new markets on an ongoing basis. In 1994, the company expanded its foreign operations by opening stores in India. It also began looking at a variety of new markets such as Russia, South Africa, China, and Southeast Asia. Countries in which the company recently started doing business include: Hungary, Poland, Korea, Taiwan, and Turkey.

Within the European division, each country's operations are generally responsible for certain marketing activities, sales, distribution, finance, and information systems. The European headquarters coordinates production, advertising, and merchandising activities for core products and also manages certain information systems development activities.

Merchandising and sourcing activities for non-core products are decentralized and located in various countries. Canada, Mexico (both included in the LSNA organization), and the countries of the Latin America and Asia Pacific divisions are primarily staffed with their own merchandising, sourcing, sales, and finance personnel.

For non-U.S. marketing divisions, manufacturing and distribution are independent of the company's U.S. operations. In 1994, however, non-U.S. operations purchased $124 million of products from the company's U.S. divisions. This amount was expected to remain stable in 1995.

Competition

Domestic U.S. Market

Levi Strauss and its largest competitor in the U.S. jeans market, VF Corporation, account for approximately one-half of the units sold in that market. The combined brand share of Levi Strauss's Levi's and Brittania products in the U.S. jeans market is second only to that of VF Corporation's four principle brands: Wrangler, Lee, Rustler, and Lee Riders.

The casual apparel market for men and women is characterized by intense competition among manufacturers and retailers, and ease of entry for new producers. Import competition is more prevalent in the casual apparel market than in the jeans market. Apparel imports have generally lower labor costs and may exert downward pressure on the prices of casual wear products. The situation is limited by U.S. trade policies that restrict apparel imports through quotas and tariffs.

Non-U.S. Markets

There are numerous local competitors of varying strength in most of Levi Strauss's principle markets outside United States, but there is no single competitor with a comparable global market presence. However, VF Corporation is threatening Levi Strauss's leadership because of VF's increasing activity in markets outside the United States.

Environmental Analysis

Economic Factors

Levi Strauss markets products in over 40 countries. As in the United States, demand for jeans in different countries is affected by a variety of factors, including socioeconomic and political conditions such as consumer spending rates, unemployment, fiscal policies, and inflation.

In many countries, jeans are generally perceived as a fashion item rather than a basic, functional product, and, like most apparel items, are higher priced relative to the United States. The non-U.S. jeans markets are more sensitive to fashion trends than the U.S. market.

Sales of Levi's jeans have been flat in the United States. Part of the reason is that the Levi's name has more glamour abroad than it does at home—hence the high selling prices abroad. By selling Levi's chiefly as trendy jeans in Europe and Asia, the company has reinforced a status image for which consumers expect to pay more. In the domestic market, the jeans are more of a commodity item, sold in great heaps at J. C. Penney and Sears.[6]

Policies

Through use of quotas and high tariffs, the textile trade policy of developed countries has increased the cost of importing apparel products produced in countries with lower labor costs. However, this protection of apparel manufacturers in developed countries, particularly the United States, Canada, Australia, and the European Union (EU), is gradually being reduced.

The North American Free Trade Agreement (NAFTA) went into effect on January 1, 1994. Under the agreement, quotas and tariffs are phased out on specific goods of North American origin over a six- to seven-year period. The effect of NAFTA on the sourcing of goods to and from Mexico will have the most immediate impact on Levi Strauss. Once NAFTA is fully phased in, the impact on the company will be an approximately 5% to 18% reduction of tariffs on apparel imports from Mexico, and a 20% reduction in tariffs on apparel imports from the United States to Mexico.

Seasonality

The apparel industry in the United States generally has four selling seasons—Spring, Summer, Fall, and Holiday. New styles, fabrics, and colors are introduced on a regular basis in anticipation of consumer preferences, and are timed to coincide with these retail selling seasons. Historically, seasonal selling schedules to retailers have preceded the related retail season by two to eight months. Outside the United States, the apparel industry typically has two seasons—Spring and Fall. Levi Strauss's business is impacted by the general seasonal trends that are characteristic of the apparel industry.

Advantages of Expansion into Retailing

Whatever the strategy, manufacturers benefit in a number of ways from opening retail stores. For Levi Strauss, the opportunity to operate stores provides a means of controlling its image, creating and enhancing brand identity, and merchandising full product lines.

Levi Strauss has long-established strong global brand equity, which may accelerate its international operations in various nations and shorten the time needed to integrate cultural differences in brand perceptions. Global brand equity is ownership of a brand name recognized throughout the world.

Apparel manufacturing in less developed countries continues to affect global apparel markets, including the U.S. market. By utilizing the lower labor costs and less expensive fabrics of less developed countries, Levi Strauss may reduce its cost structure. The company's U.S.-owned and -operated manufacturing base is trying to stay competitive in jeans production by achieving shorter lead times and greater production flexibility.

Risks of Expansion

Cost Structure

In many foreign countries, so-called accumulators buy products in the United States, which are then shipped to other countries for sale at a higher price, but lower than the retail prices charged by authorized retailers in those countries. Similarly, so-called diverters procure products in the United States at wholesale costs and ship them to other countries for sale at a profit. These diversion tactics reduce the availability of these products for U.S. consumers and also negatively affect both the producers' and retailers' results outside the United States. Both tactics have the potential to negatively impact Levi Strauss's growth outside the United States.

Pricing Strategy

Higher average unit selling prices in the United States for certain products have narrowed the pricing gap between certain U.S. and non-U.S. jeans products, thus discouraging diversion. However, the risks of increasing prices in the United States for certain products include retailer and consumer resistance to pricing that exceeds their perception of the value of Levi's jeans.[7]

International Factors

Levi Strauss's non-U.S. operations, including its use of non-U.S. manufacturing sources, are subject to the usual risks of doing business outside the United States. These risks include adverse fluctuations in currency exchange rates, changes in import duties or quotas, disruption or delays in shipments and transportation, labor disputes, and socioeconomic and political instability. The occurrence of any of these events or circumstances could adversely affect the company's operations and results. For instance, it is not possible to accurately predict the effect that changing political and economic conditions in Russia and eastern Europe will have on the company's ability to expand those operations. Levi Strauss continually evaluates the risk of non-U.S. operations when considering capital and reinvestment alternatives. The company also uses various currency-hedging strategies to mitigate the effects of currency fluctuations.

Conclusion

The global apparel market is shaped by constant change and diversity: demographic fluctuations in consumer population, frequent shifts in prevailing fashions and styles, international trade and economic developments, and retailer practices.

Levi Strauss's success is based on its ability to quickly and effectively initiate or respond to changes in market trends and other consumer preferences, especially now that consumers worldwide are becoming more price- and value-conscious and many competitors are offering lower-priced and innovative products.

Facing the challenges inside and out, Levi Strauss will need to keep its products relevant by shortening the design cycle; restructuring its manufacturing and distribution cycle to keep shelves stocked and replenished in a competitive time frame; continuing to freshen the Dockers brand to appeal to a younger target audience; and capitalizing on the businesswear trend.

The company' business is also dependent on the quality of service it provides to its customers. Retailers are striving to maintain lower inventory positions and to place orders closer in time to requested delivery dates. In response, Levi Strauss will need to improve its product support and delivery performance to fend off the pressure from worldwide retailers.

As it entered the 1990s, Levi Strauss brought its greatest asset, its name and the reputation for quality, into a changing and risky worldwide apparel market. It was unclear whether the company would experience another period of growth, as in the 1960s and 1970s. Nonetheless, the company can count on its already formidable size and strength, which it built up over more than a century, to develop an international retailing network that positions Levi Strauss as the custodian of the original blue jeans, the symbol of the American way of life.

DISCUSSION QUESTIONS

1. Levi Strauss has established its reputation as an apparel manufacturer. What is the term for its expansion into retailing? What are some problems and some advantages associated with this type of expansion?
2. Levi Strauss sells its merchandise at department stores and major specialty stores. Recently, the company began opening stores in factory outlet malls. What do you predict will be the outcome of this strategy?
3. International operations have quite a degree of freedom. Is this type of freedom consistent with the company's objective of protecting and enhancing the Levi's name?
4. What type of ownership advantages does Levi Strauss have? Does its expansion strategy reflect this advantage?

ENDNOTES

1. Levi Strauss & Co. (1995). *Ward's Private Company Profiles*, Vol. 1. Detroit: Gale Research, pp. 460–467.
2. Wilson, M. (1994). "Brand Name, High-Profile Stores Create a Splash." *Chain Store Age Executive*, Vol. 70, No. 2, pp. 22–28.
3. United States Securities and Exchange Commission. (1995). *Levi Strauss Associations Inc. Annual Report.*
4. *Levi Strauss Annual Report* (1995).
5. Munk, N. (1994). "The Levi Straddle." *Forbes*, Vol. 153, No. 2, pp. 44–45.
6. Munk (1994).
7. *Levi Strauss Annual Report* (1995).

COMPANY FOCUS II.3

CIFRA

Tamara Stow

History

Cifra began as a hypermarket and has grown into a company with well over 300 stores and restaurants located throughout Mexico.[1] It was founded by Jeronimo Arango, who was inspired by a New York discount department store. Arango, with his two brothers and $250,000 borrowed from their father, opened the first store, Aurrera Bolivar, in downtown Mexico City in 1958.

Today, Cifra is Mexico's largest retailer and the country's third largest public company. The company's strongest concentration of stores is in Mexico City. For fiscal 1995 and 1996, Cifra's total sales were U.S. $2,551.8 and $2,941.1 million.[2]

One of the main reasons for Cifra's success is its ability to have first mover advantage, that is, the ability of a retailer to capture prime retail locations in developing markets. Cifra was also the first company to offer generic brands and combine clothing, food, and hardware all in the same location. Cifra's penetration of Mexico City is responsible for 90% of the company's overall sales.[3] Not only has Cifra taken a large portion of the city's retail market, but it has greatly diversified its retailing concepts to include supermarkets, discount warehouses, membership clubs, hypermarkets, department stores, and restaurants that cater to various income levels.

Store Concepts

Superama is Cifra's supermarket chain located in Mexico City. It carries a limited number of shop keeping units (SKUs) at higher prices to provide convenience to its customers. The stores average about 15,000 square feet (1,400 square meters) and serve middle to upper-middle income consumers.[4] Along with food, these stores also carry general merchandise and soft goods. Currently there are 37 units in operation with 41 million consumers.[5]

Almancenes Aurrera is a combination supermarket and discount store. This was the original Cifra concept that started in 1958 and had grown to 38 units by February 1994. The stores average 70,000 square feet (6,500 square meters), target middle-class consumers, and serve 72 million people.[6] Since entering into a joint venture with Wal-Mart in 1992, Cifra has been upgrading the image of its Aurrera stores to create a contemporary look and feel. The new image improves the overall organization and gives the stores a more modern feel. Red, being the corporate color, marks customer service areas and draws consumers to new merchandise and sale items. The exterior was redesigned to create smooth traffic flow and sheltered areas were provided for customer comfort. According to Luis Minvielle, Vice President of Aurrera in Mexico City, "The new prototype has changed our business and enabled us to make a giant leap in a short amount of time."[7]

The Bodega Aurrera, like Aurrera, is a combination supermarket and discount store positioned in low-income neighborhoods. This format was developed in 1970, and by 1993, 29 units were in operation.[8] These stores average 46,000 square feet (4,300 square meters) and sell clothing, general merchandise, and groceries to 64 million consumers.

Suburbia is Cifra's department store, which carries clothing, cosmetics, and shoes targeted at lower-middle income families.[9] Twenty-nine Suburbia stores average 55,000 square feet (5,100 square meters) and serve 12 million customers.

Vips is the corporation's family-style restaurant, which is currently owned by Cifra. The plan is to franchise a large number of the restaurants to tion it for new markets. As of the end of 1993, 106 Vips restaurants were in operation[10] serving 44 million people.[11]

Club Aurrera (Sam's Club) is the initial result of a joint venture between Cifra and Wal-Mart of the United States, which was implemented in 1991. The format is similar to Sam's Club, which is owned and operated by Wal-Mart in the United States. The average square footage of Club Aurrera is 98,000 square feet (9,100 square meters), and warehouse clubs serve a consumer base consisting of 70% of small businesses. By 1993, seven clubs were in operation. Aggressive expansion has been planned for the future. Membership clubs are new to Mexico and have become very popular.[12]

Gran Bazar is a test concept for Cifra that sells clothing, food, and general merchandise in a hypermarket format. As of 1993, only two units averaging 180,000 square feet (16,700 square meters)[13] were in operation. Together, Gran Bazar and Almancenes Aurrera make up 35% of Cifra's total sales.[14]

The Supercenter concept combines general merchandise with a supermarket. There are currently two Supercenters in operation, one located in Mexico City and the other in Monterrey. The stores average 160,000 square feet (15,000 square meters) and accelerated expansion is expected in the near future.[15]

Joint Ventures

Beginning in 1991, Cifra entered into its first joint venture with Wal-Mart, the largest retailer in the United States.[16] The joint venture includes all of Cifra's concepts, the Club Aurrera, and the Supercenters, the latter two being joint ventures from their initial opening. This venture has helped Wal-Mart expand into new markets. Strategically, this is also an important move for Cifra, which had up to this point focused on the Mexico City region. Joining with Wal-Mart will give Cifra the financial ability to look outside Mexico City and expand into growing areas, especially along the northern border where the *maquiladoras* are creating a stable economic environment.[17] *Maquiladoras* are factories in Mexico using Mexican workers to produce merchandise for sale outside Mexico. Many United States companies have operations on both sides of the border. They do the labor-intensive processes in Mexico with low-cost labor. Cifra is also expanding into Guadalajara and Monterrey, the second and third largest cities in Mexico.[18]

Initially, the Cifra–Wal-Mart joint venture included only Aurrera Clubs and Supercenters, but today it includes every Cifra concept in Mexico. Not only will Cifra be able to split finances with Wal-Mart, but it will also benefit from the advanced distribution system that Wal-Mart is known for in the United States. From its expansion in the north, the joint venture operations will be able to take advantage of a Wal-Mart distribution center in Texas as well as one that is planned for Arizona. Wal-Mart also brings more advanced technology and a larger supply network that will enable Cifra to focus on expansion more than finances. The two companies share a similar management style, which allows growth and expansion goals to be attained in an efficient manner.[19]

Wal-Mart, Cifra, and Dillards Department Stores, Inc., are participating in a joint venture to open department stores in Mexico. By the end of 1997, however, none of these stores had been built. Dillards will provide the management expertise. Dillards is a family-operated retailer based in Little Rock, Arkansas, with over 200 stores located in the South, Southwest, and Midwest.[20] Wal-Mart and Cifra will each own 25% of the stores operated under this joint venture. Dillards will be the main investor with a 50% share.[21] Dillards targets middle- to upper-middle-class consumers, placing emphasis on fashion and home furnishings.

Cifra, as evidenced by its retailing diversity and joint venture selections, has strategically positioned itself to become the largest retail operation in Mexico, although financially it already beats the competition with one of the best operating efficiency ratios and a debt-free balance sheet.[22] To keep its competitive edge, however, Cifra must be aware of the competition in every segment of its diverse retail concepts.

Competition

Gigante is the second largest Mexican retailer after Cifra. Its main advantage is that it is more geographically diverse with only one-quarter of its operations located in Mexico City. Gigante competes on all economic levels with its retailing concepts, which makes it a competitor to be watched closely. Like Cifra, Gigante entered into a joint venture with a U.S. retailer; in this case, Fleming Companies Inc. in 1992, with a focus on developing hypermarkets.[23] Gigante operates the following retail concepts: The Gigante, The Bodegas Gigante, Hiper G, The Supermarket, Radio Shack de Mexico (a joint venture with Tandy Corporation), and Toks, a family restaurant.[24]

Controladora Comercial Mexicana (CCM) is Mexico's third largest retailer in terms of total sales and, like Gigante, competes with Cifra on all economic levels with different retailing concepts. Also, like Cifra and Gigante, CCM entered into a joint venture with a U.S. retailer in 1991. The venture, with Price/Costco Inc., will develop Price Clubs throughout Mexico. The following operational units are owned by CCM: Commercial Mexicana, Bodega Comercial Mexicana, Sumesa, Price Club de Mexico, the Mega Mercado, and California, the company's restaurant chain.[25]

Although Cifra competes directly on all levels with the above-mentioned retailers, neither Gigante nor CCM have included their supercenter concepts (Hiper G for Gigante and Mega Mercado for CCM) in their joint ventures with U.S. retailers as Cifra has done with Wal-Mart. Therefore, Club Aurrera is expected to grow faster than its competition, which has to bear the financial burden alone.[26]

Soriana is the fourth largest supermarket and discount store in Mexico. It currently runs a chain of 26 hypermarkets. However, unlike Gigante and CCM, this company has only one store format, which is generally about 92,000 square feet (8,500 square meters) with 70,000+ SKUs encompassing a wide variety of merchandise from apparel and food to other general merchandise categories. Also, unlike the other mentioned retailers, Soriana has formed a joint venture with the fifth largest supermarket and discounter in Mexico, Sorimex. Before 1986, the two companies were already operating as a joint venture, but split the relationship when internal family matters conflicted with business. Soriana has expanded its base to include stores in Monterrey as well as the northern border region.[27]

In the area of department stores, Cifra with its department store joint venture partner, Dillards, is competing with El Puerto de Liverpool, the largest department store in Mexico in terms of sales, and Sears Roebuck de Mexico, the second largest department store in Mexico. El Puerto de Liverpool's average store size is about 160,000 square feet (15,000 square meters) and it carries the standard department store merchandise such as clothing, cosmetics, home furnishings, appliances, and furniture. In 1992, Liverpool established a joint venture with Kmart of the United States to expand the Kmart hypermarket in Mexico.[28] However, in 1997, Kmart pulled out of Mexico.

Another Cifra competitor, Smart and Final (SFI), is a cash-and-carry store aimed at the individual consumer rather than small businesses, for whom many of the warehouse clubs are positioned. Food is the dominant merchandise assortment with locations in northern Mexico. Unlike many of the previously mentioned retailers, SFI has chosen to enter a 50/50 joint venture with Casino, a French retailer.[29]

Future Projections

Mexico provides a market that differs from that of the United States and Canada. As of 1993, 20 million people resided in the greater Mexico City area, which is also the wealthiest region in the country with a per capita gross domestic product (GDP) roughly twice the national average. It is also important to note that the population density in Mexico City is approximately 2,100 persons per square mile. As mentioned previously, competitors have an advantage when it comes to geographical disbursement of stores; however, by penetrating and saturating Mexico City, Cifra has been able to capture 22% of Mexico's population and keep distribution costs to a minimum.[30]

Another asset that Mexico brings to the expanding retailer is that of a growing, young consumer population. Thirty percent of Mexico's population is between the ages of 16 and 30, and 12 million Mexicans will enter the work force by the year 2000.[31] At this time, the prime spenders (ages 20 to 49) are expected to make up 40% of the population.[32]

According to the Mexican National Retail Association (ANTAD), there is still plenty of room for self-service expansion within the Mexican borders. Comparatively speaking, only about 600 square feet (56 square meters) of retail space per 1,000 inhabitants is being fully utilized as compared to 19,000 square feet (1,800 square meters) per resident in the United States. This low penetration of retail floor space has made Mexico very attractive to foreign retailers who are interested in expanding their borders. It also gives Cifra an advantage over foreign competitors whose markets are already saturated with retail establishments. It is estimated that floor space in Mexico will increase 8% to 10% in the long run.[33]

The self-service industry has a bright outlook in Mexico and is expected to grow rapidly. Currently, only about 2.1% of the total food and grocery market is serviced by the modern self-service retailers. Both foreign investment and the ability to expand rapidly due to low penetration of floor space give Cifra a true advantage. However, it is still a fact that Mexicans shop predominately at mom-and-pop stores along with outdoor markets, which together share about 60% of the retail market in Mexico. This figure is steadily diminishing as large retailers with more purchasing power consistently offer wider selections, more convenience, and better prices.[34]

Another factor that will contribute to Cifra's growth is the recent government intervention to drive out more than half a million illegal street vendors who smuggle goods across the border, earning an estimated U.S. $35 to $40 billion per year. This is approximately 10% of Mexico's GDP.[35]

The Mexican government also enacted "El Pacto" in 1987 and "PECE" in 1988 with the objective of controlling inflation, restoring confidence in the peso, and renegotiating foreign debt. Within 12 months of their enactments, consumer inflation declined from 160% to 51.7% without a recession, and by 1992, the rate had fallen to 12%.[36]

Cifra's future is bright as it prepares to enter the 21st century with its joint venture partner, Wal-Mart. Wal-Mart and Cifra will invest $200 million to open eight 160,000 square feet (15,000 square meter) Superstores in 1997. They already operate 18 Supercenters and 28 Sam's Club outlets.[37] These two retailers have formed an alliance that dominates competitors in the world's largest free trading zone of over 360 million consumers. In 1997, Wal-Mart acquired a larger stake in Cifra, bringing the two companies even closer. Cifra already has the best technology, greatest efficiency, and lowest-cost structure of any retailer in Mexico. This, combined with the retailing expertise of the largest U.S. retailer, will create an alliance that will form a retailing superpower and leave the competition behind.

DISCUSSION QUESTIONS

1. Is the Cifra–Wal-Mart liaison a strategic alliance?
2. Why are only 2.1% of food products sold at modern supermarkets in Mexico? What advantages do mom-and-pop stores have in this environment?
3. Ninety percent of Cifra's sales are in Mexico City, yet it is Mexico's third largest company. What does this tell you about retail saturation and population distributions in Mexico?

ENDNOTES

1. Lehman Brothers (1996).
2. Fraschetto, W. (1997). "Mexico." *International Trends in Retailing,* Vol. 14, No. 1, pp. 103–106.
3. La Folette, C. M. (1993). "Retail in Mexico, 1993." President and Fellows of Harvard College.
4. "Wal-Mart Encyclopedia, Volume II—Company Report." (August 1,1997). Salomon Brothers, Inc., in *Investext* [Database on CD-ROM]. Foster City, Calif.: Information Access.
5. *Hoover's Handbook of World Business.* (1995–96). Austin, Tex.: Hoover's Incorporated.
6. *Hoover's,* 1995–96.
7. Wilson, M. (1994). "Upgraded Image for Aurrera." *Chain Store Age Executive,* February, pp. 58–59.
8. La Folette (1993).
9. La Folette (1993).
10. "Wal-Mart Encyclopedia" (August 1, 1994).
11. *Hoover's,* 1995–96.
12. "Wal-Mart Encyclopedia" (August 1, 1994).
13. Pardo-Maurer, P., and J. Rodriquez. (1992–93). *Access Mexico.* Virginia: Cambridge Data and Development, Ltd.
14. *Hoover's,* 1995–96.
15. "Wal-Mart Encyclopedia" (August 1, 1994).
16. "Gigante Results and Future Plans." (1994). *Retail News Letter,* November, pp. 6–17.
17. Winsor, A. (1994). *A Complete Guide to Doing Business in Mexico.* New York: American Management Association.
18. Pardo-Maurer and Rodriguez (1992–93).
19. Lehman Brothers (1996).
20. "Dillard Department Stores, Inc." (1992). In A. Hart, ed., *International Directory of Company Histories,* Vol. 5, Detroit: St. James Press.
21. "Gigante Results" (1994).
22. "Prospects for Mexican Consumption—Industry Report." (March 28, 1995). S. G. Warburg and Co., Inc. in *Investext* [Database on CD-ROM]. Foster City; Calif.: Information Access.
23. Pardo-Maurer and Rodriguez (1992–93).
24. "Wal-Mart Encyclopedia" (August 1, 1994).
25. "Wal-Mart Encyclopedia" (August 1, 1994).
26. "Cifra S.A. De C.V. Company Report." (June 28, 1995). Merrill Lynch Markets in *Investext* [Database on CD-ROM]. Foster City; Calif.: Information Access.
27. "Wal-Mart Encyclopedia" (August 1, 1994).
28. "Wal-Mart Encyclopedia" (August 1, 1994).
29. "Kmart in Joint Venture." (1993). *Retail News Letter,* January, p. 14.
30. "Wal-Mart Encyclopedia" (August 1, 1994).
31. Winsor (1994).
32. "Cifra S. A. De C. V." (June 28, 1995).
33. "Cifra S.A. De C.V. Company Report." (January 20, 1994) Merrill Lynch Markets in *Investext* [Database on CD-ROM]. Foster City; Calif.: Information Access.
34. "Cifra S. A. De C. V." (January 20, 1994).
35. "Cifra S. A. De C. V." (January 20, 1994).
36. Winsor (1994).
37. *Retail News Letter* (1997). No. 446, p. 12.

Part III Retailing in Europe

European retailing has been going through a transition in recent years. Retailers are experiencing the same type of consolidation that has already transformed other industries in Europe. The food retailing industry, except in the United Kingdom, is fragmented. Some of the biggest companies are privately held. Takeovers and mergers are occurring in Europe, resulting in greater market concentration held by fewer retailers.

Several characteristics of the retail industry within a country influence the adoption of new logistical technology. These characteristics are (1) scale, (2) concentration of ownership, (3) forms of business, (4) regulation, and (5) profitability. These characteristics provide a useful framework for gaining an initial picture of the retail industry in Europe.

The scale of retailing refers to the size of a country's population in relation to its retail sales. Germany and France are two of the most populated countries in Europe; they also have the most concentrated retail industries. Italy, however, one of the Big Four countries in Europe (along with Germany, France, and the United Kingdom), has a very unconcentrated retail industry. The Big Four account for over 80% of the retail sales within the European Union (EU).

Concentration of ownership in retailing is the size of the retailer in relation to sales. Large retailers use efficient logistics systems to capitalize on their economies of scale. These companies are also good candidates for technical innovation. The opposite is true if ownership is highly fragmented. Six of the top 25 retailers in the world are German (Metro, Tenglemann, Aldi, Karstadt, Otto Versand, and Kaufhof).[1] There are no Italian companies on this list.

Approximately two-thirds of the U.K. stores are independently owned; yet nearly all Italian stores are independents. The United Kingdom averages 165 people per store; Italy, however, averages only 55 people for each store.[2]

Forms of retail business refers to retail organization. In Europe, retail organizations that are owned and operated as a group are called multiples. Multiples are synonymous with the idea of chain stores in the United States. Different European countries have various ideas about what constitutes a multiple. In the United Kingdom, 10 outlets are required to consider a group a multiple. In some other countries, five outlets are considered a multiple. Multiples generally focus on a particular type of merchandise, such as food or electronics. They usually have their own distribution centers where they are likely to introduce innovative logistics systems.

Regulation of retailing refers to government restrictions of retail business activities. Most governments restrict retail activities. The French government has long restricted growth of large-scale retail stores. For example, on November 27, 1995, France renewed a three-year freeze on hypermarkets. This freeze is designed to protect small entrepreneurs. However, there is some evidence that larger companies merge with smaller rivals in response, creating an even narrower group of retailers. The British retailer Tesco's recent acquisition of Wm. Low, the major Scottish food retailer, is evidence of this trend. Auchan, the French hypermarket chain, also recently acquired Docks de France, following this pattern.[3]

Three types of regulations affect retailers. The first type of regulation is related to planning laws, which are commercial zoning restrictions. In the United Kingdom, it may be difficult to obtain sites in the areas around London, as areas called "greenbelts" have been designated around the city in an attempt to control urban sprawl. Many major cities in Europe have these types of planning laws. Belgium has a higher population density, making land scarce. As a result, expansion for large retailers is very restricted.

A second type of regulation restricts the entry of new commercial ventures into an area. The Italian government passed Law 426 in the 1970s. This law froze the development of the Italian retail market, keeping the system fragmented, the domain of independent retailers. The effects of this law will be discussed in Chapter 10. Denmark recently repealed a law that restricted the number of retail outlets that could be owned by one retailer. This law had officially made multiples illegal.

A third type of government restriction controls opening hours. In France, there are no restrictions on the hours of opening. Germany, in contrast, has very strict laws. Most shops are closed from Saturday noon until Monday morning because of these regulations. A few years ago, the German government relaxed the law to allow retailers to stay open one night a week. The government is continuing to relax these regulations.

Profitability of retailers needs to be sufficient to finance innovations and development. Food retailing margins in the United Kingdom have traditionally been higher than those in other parts of Europe. These higher profit margins have been used to develop innovative logistics and technology systems.

The final step toward achieving European unification will be the adoption of a single currency system. This means that instead of having German marks, French francs, and British pounds, all purchases would occur in Euros. Achieving a single currency is not as simple as just making the decision to begin printing Euros instead of marks. The economic environment within each country must be very stable before successful monetary unification can occur. Monetary unification is the process of using one currency throughout the EU countries.

Countries tinker with their domestic currency to achieve economic objectives. The EU has postponed the deadline for achieving a common currency until 1999. Even then, it is projected that only half of the member states will meet the criteria. The five economic criteria were established by the Maastricht Treaty in 1992. The requirements are:

1. *Annual inflation* must not exceed that of the three best performing nations by more than 1.5%.
2. *Public-sector budget deficit* must not exceed 3% of gross domestic product (GDP).
3. *Public sector debt* must not exceed 80% of GDP.
4. *Long-term interest rates* must not exceed those of the three nations with the best inflation performance by more than two percentage points.
5. *The exchange rate* has to be kept within normal bands of Europe's Exchange Rate Mechanism for the previous two years.[4]

These economic performance criteria are difficult to achieve. Perhaps you have been to a circus that included a horseback riding act. Two horses canter side by side around the ring while a rider moves from one horse to another, hangs upside down between them, and generally performs amazing feats. For this act to be performed successfully, the two horses must have the same rhythm in their stride, their legs must extend in unison, and their strides must be equal. This is the type of harmonizing that is required for a country to move from a national currency to a common currency.

Like much of the world, some areas of Europe are experiencing a recession. Most parts of Europe entered the recession later than the United States, and they will probably exit the recession much later. The next four chapters focus on retailing in Europe. Chapter 8 starts with the countries of northern Europe: Great Britain, the Netherlands, and Belgium. Germany and France are featured in Chapter 9. The southern European countries of Spain, Italy, Greece, and Portugal are discussed in Chapter 10. In Chapter 11, the central and eastern European countries are discussed. Finally, several company focuses are included to provide information about retail companies operating in this area.

ENDNOTES

1. Coopers & Lybrand. (1996). *Global Powers of Retailing.* Chain Store Age—Special Report.
2. Cooper, J., M. Browne, and M. Peters. (1991). *European Logistics.* Oxford, UK: Blackwell Publishers.
3. O'Dell, J. (1996). "European Supermarket Chains Feed Merger Pressures, Trends from Poland to Portugal." *Orange County Edition, Los Angeles Times,* August 16, p. D-6.
4. Kamm, T. (1995). "Monetary Chaos Precedes Europe's Single Market." *Wall Street Journal.* July 28, p. A6.

SCOTLAND
NORTHERN
IRELAND
Belfast
Edinburgh
Newcastle
Manchester
ENGLAND
London
Amsterdam
The Hague
Rotterdam
Brussels
NETHERLANDS
BELGIUM

8

Retailing in the United Kingdom, the Netherlands, and Belgium

After reading this chapter, you will understand:

- How government regulations affect retail expansion.
- Why food retailing margins are greater in the United Kingdom than in other European countries.
- The strategy used by retailers with private label food products in the United Kingdom, and how this positioning can be used successfully in other countries.
- Why retailers in the United Kingdom, the Netherlands, and Belgium have expanded internationally.
- The role retail cooperatives have played in these three countries.
- The unique agency system used in mail-order sales in the United Kingdom, and why this system is declining in importance.

THE THREE COUNTRIES included in this chapter share a similar cultural background. The English channel is all that separates the United Kingdom from Belgium and the Netherlands. Although the three countries do not share a common language, most residents of Belgium and the Netherlands speak a second language, and it is often English. Belgium and the Netherlands are very small countries. They have become world traders to survive. Their major retailers have also expanded internationally, because their home markets became saturated. Belgium and the Netherlands have used restrictive legislation to protect small retailers. In Belgium, this restrictive legislation makes domestic expansion nearly impossible.

I will start the discussion with the United Kingdom. The retail industry there is large, mature, and stable. The United Kingdom is also of interest because the study of retailing occurs at a variety of British universities. Some of the best international retailing research has come from professors at these universities. With so much information about retailing available, it can be difficult to select information that distinguishes the industry. I have chosen to focus on the retail characteristics of non-food retailers and food retailers. The next sections of the chapter discuss retailing in The Netherlands and in Belgium.

The discussion of each country includes a set of comparable retail statistics. I have used the statistics published by Corporate Intelligence on Retailing here and throughout Part III. The retail statistics summarize the major domestic and foreign retailers within each country, including sales and number of outlets. Each country discussion also includes a section discussing the government regulation of retailing.

UNITED KINGDOM

COUNTRY BACKGROUND

The United Kingdom (U.K.) is separated geographically and psychologically from the rest of Europe. The Celts arrived on the island about 1000 B.C. Julius Caesar led the Romans to the area in 50 B.C., beginning a period of Roman rule that lasted about 500 years, until the Germanic Angles and Saxons raided the island and forced the Romans to withdraw. In the centuries that followed, the Danish Vikings attacked the Anglo-Saxon settlements periodically. Then, in 1066, French-speaking followers of William the Conqueror defeated the Anglo-Saxons at the Battle of Hastings. Modern Britain carries remembrances from each of these invading groups. Finally, in the 15th century, the people we know today as the English gained control and established the English crown.

The English were great explorers, claiming the world's most extensive overseas empire. They fought the Spanish, the French, and finally the colonies that became known as the United States. At about the time of the

TABLE 8.1

United Kingdom: Selected Demographic and Economic Data

	Population (millions) mid-1995	Area (thousands of sq. km)	GNP per capita: Dollars 1995	GNP per capita: Avg. ann. growth (%) 1985–95	PPP estimates of GNP per capita U.S. = 100: 1987	PPP estimates of GNP per capita U.S. = 100: 1995	Life expectancy at birth (years) 1995	Adult illiteracy (%) 1995
High-income economies	902.2t	32,039t	24,930w	1.9w			77w	
United Kingdom	58.5	245	18,700	1.4	72.0	71.4	77	a

Source: World Bank (1997). a = less than 5%. PPP = purchasing power parity. t = total. w = weighted average.

American Revolution, Britain was experiencing the first phases of the Industrial Revolution.

The 1900s became the "British Century." Britain became the world's leading manufacturing and trading country. In addition, the British were the dominant world power, creating an empire that at its height encompassed a quarter of the world's land area. By the end of the World War II, nearly all of the nations that had flown the British flag became independent nations. However, most have remained members of the British Commonwealth.[1]

The United Kingdom includes England, Scotland, Wales, and Northern Ireland. London is the capital and business center. The major retail centers are Birmingham, in the middle part of the country; Manchester, in the northwest; and Newcastle, in the northeast. Glasgow is the major retail center in Scotland, and Belfast is the center of retailing in Northern Ireland. Because the southeastern portion of the United Kingdom has greater population density and wealth, most retailers have the bulk of their stores there.[2] Table 8.1 presents selected demographic and economic data for the United Kingdom.

The major domestic and foreign retailers in the United Kingdom are summarized in Table 8.2. John Lewis Partnership is the largest department store group. Marks & Spencer is the leading mixed goods retailer. The major mail-order retailer is Great Universal Stores. The four largest retailers are the food multiples: Tesco, J. Sainsbury, Safeway, and ASDA. Table 8.3 summarizes the retail concentration for different types of products.

TABLE 8.2

Major U.K. and Foreign Retailers in the Domestic Market, 1995–1996

Retailer	Operations	Sales (£ millions)	Outlets (no.)
Tesco	Grocery	11,560	545
J. Sainsbury	Grocery/DIY*/hypermarkets	11,146	685
Safeway Group (ex-Argyll)	Grocery	6,069	479
ASDA Group	Grocery	6,010	206
Marks & Spencer	Mixed goods/grocer	5,858	285
The Boots Company	Mixed goods/chemists/DIY/optical	4,191	2,455
Kingfisher	Mixed goods/DIY/electricals/auto	4,072	2,012
Somerfield Holdings	Grocery	3,161	609
John Lewis Partnership	Department stores/grocery	2,541	135
Kwik Save Group	Discount grocery	2,254	979
Sears	Clothing/footwear/sports goods	2,130	1,832
Wm. Morrison	Grocery	2,099	81
Burton Group	Clothing/department stores	2,007	1,900
Dixons Group	Electricals	1,901	802
Littlewoods	Mixed goods/mail-order	1,666	273
Great Universal Stores (GUS)	Mail-order/clothing	1,650	70
CWS Retail	Cooperative grocery/non-food	1,553	797
WH Smith Group	Mixed goods/books/news/music	1,540	964
Co-op Retail Services	Cooperative grocery/non-food	1,490	565
Argos	Mixed goods/catalog showrooms	1,436	370
Spar	Voluntary food group	1,400	2,400
Iceland Frozen Foods	Frozen foods/grocery	1,375	752
Storehouse	Clothing/mixed goods	1,005	435
C&A Brenninkmeyer (Germany)	Clothing	786	188
House of Fraser	Department stores	749	50
Whitbread	Off-licenses*	708	1,601
MFI Furniture	Furniture	706	184
Next	Clothing/mail-order	692	304
Allied Domecq	Off-licenses	670	1,548
Lloyds Chemists	Chemists/drugstores/health food	657	1,491
Costcutter	Food buying group	560	620
Aldi Stores (Germany)	Discount grocery	548	142
Londis	Voluntary food group	500	1,420
United Norwest Co-op Society	Cooperative grocery/non-food	478	300
Harrods Holdings	Department stores/footwear	468	104

TABLE 8.2

Major U.K. and Foreign Retailers in the Domestic Market, 1995–1996

Retailer	Operations	Sales (£ millions)	Outlets (no.)
Midlands Co-op Society	Cooperative grocery/non-food	465	150
Associated British Foods	Grocery/clothing	457	84
Thorn	TV rental	452	652
T & S Stores	CTNs*/convenience stores	445	714
Grattan (Otto Versand Germany)	Mail-order	444	2
John Menzies	Mixed goods/books/news	437	443
Granada Group	TV rental	435	635
Mace	Voluntary food group	420	1,000
EMI	Music/video goods/books	410	191
Wickes	DIY	399	111
Martin Retail (Tog Ltd)	CTNs	393	776
Forbuoys	CTNs	340	685
Signet Group	Jewelry/clothing	337	600
IKEA Habitat (Sweden)	Furniture/household goods	328	46
C & J Clark	Footwear	320	685
Allders	Department stores	310	22
Budgens (Rewe Germany 29.4%)	Grocery	303	103
ALPHA Airports Group	Airport retailing	299	80
Toys "R" Us (USA)	Toys/children's goods	291	51
Netto (Dansk Supermarket Denmark)	Discount grocery	276	85
Wilkinson Hardware Stores	Hardware	275	115
Fitzwilton/Wellworth (Ireland)	Grocery	274	37
River Island (Lewis Trust)	Clothing	267	300
Yorkshire Co-op Society	Cooperative grocery/non-food	248	115
Watson & Philip	Convenience stores	244	461
Empire Stores (La Redoute France)	Mail-order	240	0
Scottish Power	Electrical appliances	240	158
Great Mills (RMC Group)	DIY	234	93
Allied Carpets	Carpets/furnishings	230	207
N. Brown Group	Mail-order	224	0
Greggs	Bakers	220	967
Norweb	Electricals	215	135
Moss Chemists (Unichem)	Chemists	208	446
British Gas	Gas appliances	205	251
Dunnes Stores (Ireland)	Mixed goods/grocery	203	35

Continued

TABLE 8.2

Major U.K. and Foreign Retailers in the Domestic Market, 1995–1996

Retailer	Operations	Sales (£ millions)	Outlets (no.)
Etam	Clothing	202	226
Anglia Regional Co-op Society	Cooperative grocery/non-food	193	95
DFS	Furniture	185	38
Magnet (Berisford)	Furniture	185	200
Carpetright	Carpets/furnishings	185	246
Fenwick	Department stores	184	8
AAH (Gehe Germany)	Chemists	183	309
Asprey	Jewelry	168	43
Matalan	Clothing	163	57
Stylo	Footwear	162	694
The Body Shop International	Beauty and personal products	160	252
Poundstretcher (Brown & Jackson)	Discount mixed goods	160	215
Portsea Island Co-op Society	Cooperative grocery/non-food	160	65
Plymouth & South Devon Co-op Society	Cooperative grocery/non-food	159	75
Greenalls Group	Off-licenses	152	467
Ipswich Co-op Society	Cooperative grocery/non-food	149	75
Laura Ashley Holdings	Household textiles/clothing	148	173
Olympus Sports (Mayfind)	Sports goods/footwear	146	198
Farmfoods	Frozen foods/grocery	144	195
Colchester & E. Essex Co-op Society	Cooperative grocery/non-food	137	60
Oxford, Swindon & Gloucester Co-op Society	Cooperative grocery/non-food	135	90
Vision-Plus/Specsavers	Optical goods	135	300
Owen Owen	Department stores	134	13
Limelight	Furniture/furnishings	133	555
Coats Viyella	Clothing	132	417
MacKays	Clothing	126	270
Oddbins (Seagram)	Off-licenses	125	200
Courts	Furniture	123	85
Dolland & Aitchinson	Optical goods	123	445
New Look	Clothing	120	270
Blockbuster Group (USA)	Video/entertainment goods	119	681
Clinton Cards	Greetings cards	110	486
Edinburgh Woollen Mill	Clothing	108	217

TABLE 8.2

Major U.K. and Foreign Retailers in the Domestic Market, 1995–1996

Retailer	Operations	Sales (£ millions)	Outlets (no.)
Alexon	Clothing	104	603
InterTAN Tandy (USA)	Electricals/computers	103	499
National Co-op Chemists	Cooperative chemists	102	236
Benetton (Italy)	Clothing	100	380

Source: *The European Retail Handbook, 1997 Edition.* (1996). London: Corporate Intelligence on Retailing, pp. 324–325.

£ = British pounds; 1£ = U.S. $1.63. *CTNs = confectioners, news agents, and tobacconists; DIY = do-it-yourself; off-licenses = alcohol shops.

NON-FOOD RETAILERS

Non-food retailing is dominated by multiples, many of these companies such as Marks & Spencer, Kingfisher, Virgin, and The Body Shop have successfully expanded throughout Europe. Likewise, the United Kingdom has attracted foreign retailers. IKEA, the Scandinavian furniture retailer, has 46 stores in the United Kingdom. Toys "R" Us has over 50 outlets and is by far the dominant toy retailer. Tandy has nearly 500 stores and Benetton has 380 outlets.

DEPARTMENT STORES The United Kingdom has one of the oldest and most well-established department store industries in the world. Department stores in the United Kingdom account for 5% of total retail sales. Most department stores are in high street locations. **High street** is the name given to the central business district, an area rather than a single street. This is similar to the American main street. British cities, even those as large as London and Liverpool, have healthy central business district shopping areas.

The department store industry is concentrated. House of Fraser has about 25% of the department store business, but the company has been struggling. Department stores throughout Europe have been losing market share to specialty store chains. The four leading department store groups in United Kingdom control more than 65% of the department store trade.

Mergers and acquisitions have left the major firms with a greater market share. Each group has several different trading names, so people are not generally aware that different department stores are part of the House of Fraser or Burton Group. This is similar to the situation with Federated Department Stores in the United States. Average shoppers in the United States would not know which retailers are a part of Federated and which are part of Macy's group. In fact, few retailing students—or even their professors—can recite the list.

TABLE 8.3

Retail Concentration in the United Kingdom

Share (%) of Retail Sales by Top Five Multiple-store-retailers by Subsector	
Food sector	
Grocers	66.0
Butchers	6.5
Greengrocers	4.5
Bakers	21.5
CTNs*	15.0
Off-licenses*	53.0
Mixed goods and mail-order	
Mixed goods	61.0
Mail-order	95.0
Non-food sector	
Clothing	33.0
Footwear	39.0
Furniture and carpets	14.5
Electrical goods	36.5
DIY*	63.5
Hardware and china	16.0
Booksellers	20.0
Jewelers	43.5
Toys and sports goods	38.0
Chemists[a]	58.0

[a]Chemists exclude The Boots Company.

Note: The United Kingdom has higher-than-average retail concentration in almost all subsectors and the 10 largest retailers combine to have 37% to 38% of all retail sales (1994). Grocery, alcoholic drinks, DIY, mixed goods, chemists, and mail-order all have retail concentrations in which the top five players enjoy more than 50% of sector sales.

Source: ONS (reported 1996), and *The European Retail Handbook, 1997 Edition.* (1996). London: Corporate Intelligence on Retailing, p. 313.

*CTNs = confectioners, news agents, and tobacconists; DIY = do-it-yourself; off-licenses = alcohol shops.

People who only know the name of one retailer from the United Kingdom, probably know of Harrods Department Store. Its semiannual sales are well-known. A visitor to Harrods may imagine bumping into Queen Elizabeth or Prince Charles there. On my first visit, I was surprised by the ambience inside the store. It was more like a museum than a department store.

Photo 8.1
The food hall at Harrods Department Store looks like a museum. This section is located on the London department store's main floor, next to the accessories and perfumes. *Courtesy of Harrods.*

Americans are sometimes surprised that this famous department store sells foods. There are other surprises. Midway through my visit to Harrods, a group of bagpipe performers marched through the store, playing as they went. A stop at the ladies room brought an unpleasant surprise. If you could not show a sales receipt they charged you a pound (U.S. $1.63) to use the facilities. That price did, in fact, include toilet paper.

Concessions are areas within department stores that are leased to suppliers. The suppliers decide what merchandise is presented in that location. Concession areas are used at many department stores in the United Kingdom. At House of Fraser, 32% of sales are from concessions.[3] Profit from these concessions is greater than profit from the company's own merchandise. However, over the long run, the retailer becomes dependent on the relationship. Retailers that allow manufacturers to choose merchandise for their stores are giving up their most important retail function, merchandise selection. A retailer that gives up this function is losing one of its most important strategic options.

Concession sales are similar to the **consignment system.** With a consignment system, a manufacturer puts merchandise in a store and the retailer only pays for the merchandise that is actually sold. The retailer becomes a manufacturer's showroom, providing the physical space for manufacturers. The important thing to remember is that a retailer's primary function is to be an **assembler of lines of goods,** filtering various merchandise offerings and selecting a subset for its customers. Retailers are gatekeepers for products. When retailers allow manufacturers to decide the merchandise that will be in the store, they have given away their most important function. Channel members receive profits based on the value added that they provide to consumers. When suppliers become the assemblers of the merchandise, they obtain a greater portion of the margin. They are also, however, assuming much more risk. This is a very dangerous situation for a retailer.

The major mixed goods retailer in the United Kingdom, Marks & Spencer, takes the opposite approach. The company sells only private label merchandise. Rather than allowing manufacturers to determine what merchandise will be sold through concessions or consignment, Marks & Spencer determines what manufacturers will produce for them. This is the ultimate position of strength within the distribution system. Marks & Spencer is the undisputed channel captain.

MIXED GOODS RETAILERS One of the most famous British stores, Marks & Spencer is unique among British retailers because it sells 100% private label products under the label St. Michael. Marks & Spencer depends on a dedicated core group of United Kingdom-based suppliers. The company encourages supplier consolidation because size allows it to invest in people and machinery as required. The top five general merchandise suppliers for Marks & Spencer account for 45% of the company's total sales. The top 20 suppliers have an 80% share. General merchandise departments depend on 260 suppliers; the food group, on 400 to 450 suppliers.[4] The company maintains a rigorous testing facility to ensure that products live up to the quality of its St. Michael label.

Marks & Spencer provides products in two broad categories, food and general merchandise. Food accounts for 40% of its sales, the rest is made up of womenswear, menswear, childrenswear, toiletries and cosmetics, and home furnishings.

The procurement system used for food and general merchandise is centralized in the company's Baker Street headquarters. Three organizational levels are used in Marks & Spencer's procurement process. Merchandisers handle the day-to-day financial planning and operational responsibilities for

Photo 8.2
Marks & Spencer, the major mixed goods retailer in the United Kingdom, sells 100% private label products. The company sells soft goods, housewares, and food. *Courtesy of SN.*

the buying departments. This includes managing the price structure, margins, and markdowns. Merchandisers also manage the supply base, plan production and commitments, and negotiate price with suppliers. They manage store stocks, the catalog, and the communication of layout and display priorities. The buying department has worldwide responsibility for Marks & Spencer, including international operations. Selectors operate with the guidance of the merchandisers. Selectors are responsible for product development and for each season's range. Selectors work with technology and design experts to create new products. Marks & Spencer's team uses cutting-edge textile and agribusiness technology from around the world. Many commercial innovations have come from technical developments originated or exploited by Marks & Spencer's technology. In one instance, fabric printing technology has been adapted to buttering bread for sandwiches.

Marks & Spencer makes substantial commitments to its suppliers; however, the company is always looking for ways to enhance flexibility. For instance, in some areas Marks & Spencer has made the garments "in the greige," that is, fabric that has not been dyed yet. This allows the company to use information technology to track color preferences and customize these preferences during the selling season.

A close relationship exists between Marks & Spencer and its suppliers. Suppliers may adapt an organizational structure that parallels the Marks & Spencer buying structure. Executive board members of Marks & Spencer and its large suppliers have joint strategy meetings.

Currently, Marks & Spencer is gathering sizing information from its customers. This move is designed to provide better fit and reduce returns.

Measurements are taken in an electronic scanning booth. The booth takes measurements from 46 parts of the body. The last time Marks & Spencer conducted a sizing survey was in 1989.[5] Few retailers have the volume business to undertake such a mass measurement action. Marks & Spencer, however, has a large part of the U.K. market in several categories. The company holds a 35% market share in women's underwear, and a 16% market share in total clothing sales.

At the end of Part I, Company Focus I.1 (p. 159) discussed Marks & Spencer's international expansion. Seventeen percent of the company's sales are generated outside the United Kingdom. The company has made a decision that from Germany westward, all operations will be company-owned; all markets to the east will be franchised.[6] This is an important company decision and fits very much with the theory of international franchising presented in Chapter 4. As you can see from the list of franchised stores and company-owned stores that follows, the company's operations do not currently fit this profile. In the mid-1990s, franchised stores were located in: Austria (3), Bahamas (5), Bermuda (1), Canary Islands (3), Channel Islands (4), Cyprus (8), Gibraltar (1), Greece (9), Hungary (3), Indonesia (5), Israel (6), Malaysia (3), Malta (3), Norway (1), Philippines (7), Portugal (4), Singapore (7), Thailand (4), and Turkey (1). Company-owned stores were located in: Ireland (3), France (17), Spain (5), Netherlands (2), Belgium (3), Hong Kong (8), Canada (50).[7] By 1997, the company had 86 franchises in 24 countries. It is planning 120 franchises in 32 countries by 2001.[8] Including Germany, Poland, South Korea, Taiwan, and Australia.

The company has eight stores in Hong Kong, which continue to experience sales growth. In response to their profitability, the company is considering expansion into mainland China and Japan. However, after visiting the Hong Kong stores, I believe their success is due to the large number of expatriate British citizens living in Hong Kong. Such a large expatriate population in a concentrated area is not likely to exist in even the major cities of China or Japan.

SPECIALTY STORE CHAINS United Kingdom specialty stores have gained reputations worldwide for their aggressive international expansion programs. The Body Shop and Tie Rack, for instance, are so much a part of the American retailing scene that most Americans are surprised to find out they are British companies. At the end of Part III, Company Focus III.2 discusses The Body Shop's use of environmental awareness and corporate ethics to promote its stores. Virgin Records is another company that has expanded aggressively, in this case, both independently and with a variety of partners. Company Focus III.3 details the history and operations of the Virgin Group. Richard Branson, the thrill seeker who founded Virgin, has taken the company through a rapid international expansion cycle.

Specialty stores in the United Kingdom have the largest market share of any retail format in non-food items. They focus on a very specific customer target market. These retailers usually use a global expansion strategy, replicating their successful retail format wherever they go.

MAIL-ORDER Mail-order sales in the United Kingdom are a growth area. Traditional mail-order in the United Kingdom refers to the big book catalogs, often having 1,200 pages. Ninety percent of the sales using these big books are through agents, who receive a 10% commission. The **agent system** uses informal salespersons to take orders from customers. This system is somewhat like the system used by Avon or Mary Kay in the United States. Agents receive the catalog with the understanding that they will show the catalog to customers who will then place orders with them. There are 4.25 million agents in the United Kingdom, and they average 1.9 customers each. This means that most of the agents are simply buying merchandise for their immediate family. The catalogs show the product and the price of the product. Consumers believe that they are getting free credit and delivery; however, the price of the product includes the commission, delivery charge, and a charge for credit.

The other 10% of big book sales are directly to individuals. The catalogs are essentially the same as those used in the agent system; however, prices are lower because of the "unbundling" of the offering. The price in the catalog does not include shipping and commission. Shoppers are charged shipping costs, but since they are ordering themselves, there is no commission charge.

Consumers pay for merchandise over six to twelve months. Both types of big book offerings attract lower-income consumers, who are buying from the catalog to obtain credit. The effective interest rate works out to 50%, or more.[9] On the other hand, the system does make credit available to a segment of consumers who would not be eligible for credit from formal sources such as Visa and MasterCard.

The return rate for merchandise in this system is very high, averaging 35%. Costs for delivery and return of the merchandise, if necessary, are included in the price of the product. With such a high return rate, the cost of distribution becomes a major issue in a company's profitability. Great Universal Stores (GUS) is the largest mail-order operator in the United Kingdom. The company distributes catalogs under four names: Great Universal, Family Album, Marshall Ward, and Choice. After several major postal strikes, GUS decided to operate its own distribution service called White Arrow. This service is now the largest parcel delivery business in the United Kingdom.

Like other mail-order companies, GUS is constantly trying to keep prices stable. The company works on a long lead time, and because the price in the catalog is fixed during the life of the catalog, it must ensure that inflation and increases in production costs do not eliminate profits.[10]

The trend is toward direct-to-customer business, replacing the traditional agency business. In 1997, U.K. catalog sales were split 50/50 between agency and direct sales.[11] The successful direct catalogs are more focused than the big book catalogs. They generally have less than 500 pages. One of the most

Photo 8.3
Great Universal is the major mail-order retailer in the United Kingdom. The thick spine of this catalog cover suggests the breadth of its stock. The company has relied on sales agents, but is moving into greater direct-to-customer sales. *Courtesy of Great Universal.*

successful catalogs in this classification, Racing Green, has only 90 pages. The customers are upmarket of traditional mail-order. They are interested in the product and convenience, not the credit, offered by the mail-order company.

The threat to mail-order is from high street retailers selling branded merchandise, or strong private label merchandise. Mail-order companies have been slow to develop private label merchandise, and selling brand name merchandise that can be used for comparative pricing does not put the mail-order catalogs at an advantage.

In 1996, Marks & Spencer entered the catalog business with a housewares catalog. Sales through the company's Homechoice catalog grew 70% during that year. The catalog offering is an ideal medium for Marks & Spencer. Customers trust the company name, and Marks & Spencer has its own credit system in place. The merchandise is 100% private label, eliminating any direct price comparison. The catalogs also allow Marks &

Spencer to present its full product line. Catalogs also provide an alternative when retail developments are curtailed by restrictive planning. In the United Kingdom, there are only four Marks & Spencer stores with the size to present the total product line. Marks & Spencer is now expanding its mail-order services to clothing.[12]

Mail-order companies from other parts of Europe have begun viewing the U.K. market with interest. Otto Versand and La Redoute have a great deal of experience in direct mail sales and have sophisticated logistics systems. The mail-order industry, like the food industry, has a higher margin in the United Kingdom than on the Continent.

COOPERATIVES United Kingdom retail cooperative societies face a dismal future. Increasingly, co-ops are viewed as the refuge of the old or the disadvantaged consumer. They have not been successful in finding a market position that will allow them to survive alongside the major chain stores.

Retail cooperatives have 3.8% of retail sales in the United Kingdom.[13] The two largest cooperatives are CWS and Co-op Retail Services (CRS), which together account for over 50% of the cooperative societies' sales.[14] The large multiples have gained market share from independents and cooperatives. Cooperatives are the most successful in service sectors such as travel, pharmacy, optical, and funeral furnishings.[15] Most retail cooperatives restrict their business to a single region; however, CWS and CRS are national. Although CWS and CRS are the largest groups of retail societies, they are not the best performing ones.

Cooperatives are more popular with older consumers who have trusted the cradle-to-grave services provided by these groups. The entrance of competitive retail formats such as warehouse clubs and category killers, however, makes the survival of cooperatives even more tenuous.

FOOD RETAILERS

Food retailing in the United Kingdom is distinctive because of the high degree of concentration, the importance of store brands, and higher profit margins than other areas of Europe. The largest food retailers in the United Kingdom are Tesco, Sainsbury, Safeway (Argyll), and ASDA. These retailers create an oligopoly market situation. They are highly competitive, but the focus is on non-price competition. The food industry in the United Kingdom was the last industry to move into the recession, and it has been the last to move out.

Tesco began as two small shops in northeastern London in October 1931. In recent years, the company has been diversifying internationally. In 1993, it acquired Catteau, a French food retailer with 167 stores. In 1994, it acquired Global, a 15-store food retail chain in Hungary. That same year, the company acquired Wm. Low, a Scottish food retailing chain with 57 stores. Tesco now has stores in Poland, the Czech Republic, Slovakia, France, and

Hungary, along with 545 outlets in the United Kingdom. In 1996, the company purchased the MAJ chain of stores that Kmart had previously acquired in the Czech Republic and Slovakia.

Tesco recently overtook Sainsbury as the leading U.K. retailer. Sainsbury had a decline in profits for 1995, the first in its 22 years as a public company. In contrast, Tesco's sales have been buoyant, dramatically increasing its market share. In fact, Tesco's U.K. market share increased from 10.6% to 12.6% in 1995.[16] This was the biggest increase ever for the company. The strategy that brought this upturn is based on changes in the mainstream product mix, improved focus on non-food items, sharper pricing, and the introduction of a company "Clubcard." These elements are helping the company withstand exposure to discount pricing.

When Tesco introduced its Clubcard, a loyalty card used to promote dedicated shopping by consumers, competitors such as Sainsbury dismissed it as just another scheme along the lines of electronic "Green Stamps." However, the strategy has turned out to be highly successful. More than 70% of Tesco's customer base now use the card. Those who bashed the card did not realize its real significance. Rather than being just a high-technology discount scheme, it is used for precise targeting and accumulation of a customer database. The maximum price discount with the card is 1%. Clubcard costs about .5% of turnover but produces a sales increase of 1.5%. By

Photo 8.4
Tesco is the largest food retailer in the United Kingdom. In addition to its traditional supermarket format, the company is experimenting with some new store formats, such as Tesco Metros, the size of convenience stores but selling fresh produce, meats, and freshly prepared foods. The stores are located in high traffic, commercial areas. *Courtesy of Tesco.*

tracking the Clubcard purchase pattern, Tesco can keep track of purchase patterns down to the product group level but not to the detail of individual bar codes. The company is improving the information system, however, and soon it will record every item bought by a consumer.

The database generated by the Clubcard is a powerful marketing tool that will help Tesco make decisions across most business areas. The card can help remove the guesswork from new store location and design decisions.[17] Clubcard information will be very useful in micro-marketing and product extension such as expansion into banking. Company Focus III.1 provides additional details about the company's operations.

A comparison of Tesco's versus Sainsbury's retail strategies is presented in Table 8.4. Sainsbury is diversifying into the United States with its purchase of the Shaws and Giant Foods supermarket chains. The company is also moving into other retail areas by diversifying into do-it-yourself (DIY) with Texas Homecare.

The third largest retailer, ASDA, is hopelessly behind these two leaders. However, its excessive debt burden has forced it to retrench instead of diversifying. The company recently introduced 1,100 ASDA unique products, including baby supplies, coffee, ice cream, and gifts. As a consequence, brand sales grew by 24% and private label penetration rose to more than 33%. The company's market position is one of low prices, large stores, outstanding in-store produced fresh food, and wider range. The ASDA Group is looking for new large superstores and hypermarket sites. The company opened six new stores in 1995. [18]

TABLE 8.4

Retail Strategies Used by Tesco and Sainsbury

	When Introduced	
Retail Strategy	**Tesco**	**Sainsbury**
Value lines	August 1993	
Economy range		September 1995
Loyalty cards	February 1995 (National)	May 1995
One in front	October 1994	October 1994—then withdrawn
Computer for schools	March 1992	
Carrier bag promotion		September 1995

Note: Loyalty cards are cards distributed to entice cusotmers to become dedicated purchasers by giving the cardholder certain benefits. "One in front" refers to speed at checkout: If there are more than two people in line, another checkout counter is opened, so customers never have more than one person in front of them in line.

Safeway (Argyll) is the youngest of the major U.K. food retailers. The company was assembled by acquisition. The Safeway chain was purchased by Argyll in 1987, adding focus rather than breadth. The group has moved out of discounting by selling LoCost, a discount food chain. Eventually, Argyll changed its company name to Safeway, the name of its main supermarket chain.

RETAILER-SUPPLIER RELATIONS In general, retailer-supplier relationships in the United Kingdom are stable and long term. A survey of major U.K. food retailer buyers showed that 50% of the suppliers of retail brands (private label) and 39% of suppliers of manufacturer brands had supplied the retailer for six years or longer. As long as a supplier remains competitive, a retailer will remain a loyal customer because of the cost and time required to develop appropriate products and efficient supply arrangements.[19] Leading-edge retailers are interested in partnership sourcing as a logistics strategy. Cost is important; however, other considerations such as quality, service, and timely delivery are also important sourcing decisions.[20]

By the end of the 1980s, retailer brands accounted for over 30% of U.K. packaged grocery store sales. Retailer brands have pushed weaker secondary and tertiary brands off the shelf. It is common for product ranges to include only three choices; the leading manufacturer brand, the retailer brand, and an alternative manufacturer brand.[21] In interviews I conducted with U.K. food retailers in 1997, I found that the major multiples intend to replace a second-level national brand with a second-level store private label.

There is great variation in retailer brand penetration based on product group. Retailer brand penetration is lowest in snack products (under 10%) and greatest in product lines where there are no dominant manufacturers or in areas where there the products are basically commodity markets. In commodity-type products such as packaged cheese, retailers have an 80% brand share. Retailer brand shares are low in markets with strong manufacturer brands such as canned soups, coffee, and detergents. However, there are other product markets where strong manufacturer brands exist, yet retailer brands have developed a strong market share. Examples of this are baked beans (35% retailer brand share) and toilet tissue (40% retailer brand share).[22]

Retailer brands seem to be most successful in product markets with certain characteristics. Large volume markets not affected by changes in fashion, markets with simple technology, and markets with high profit margins generate high margin for retailer brands.[23] The three major food retailers have taken different approaches to retailer brands. Tesco has the highest level of retailer brands for its packaged grocery product sales (53%). Safeway has the least (29.5%) and Sainsbury is in between (34.9%). These retailers have taken a proactive role in the product development process. The retailer buyer is searching for a manufacturer who will meet the retailers predetermined quality and positioning requirements instead of selecting products from an already existing manufacturer's line.[24] Retailers in the United Kingdom have upgraded their range of retailer brands, from traditional low price/low quality positioning to high quality/value-for-money retailer brands.

These brands are slightly less expensive than the leading manufacturer brand. This repositioning has resulted in the retailer brand being viewed as a brand in its own right. Retailers have also made major investments in new product ranges, packaging, and labeling innovations. The positioning has changed consumer perception of the retailer brand from that of an alternative product option to that of a brand choice option.[25]

United Kingdom food retailers have profit margins that are higher than those in other areas in Europe. Food retailers from the continent view the United Kingdom as a potentially lucrative market for expansion, wanting some of those large margins for themselves, Burt and Sparks term this "margin envy."[26] The average operating margin for the French companies is 2.01% compared with the U.K. average of 6.12%. Using this measure of profitability, the U.K. companies' profits are three times that of the French companies. However, when you examine return on capital employed (ROCE), the profitability average of French retailers (18.72%) is not much lower than the average for U.K. retailers (20.62%).

Accounting methods are quite different in the two countries, making balance sheet comparisons very difficult. The most important difference is in the way land and buildings are depreciated. **Depreciation** means that the value of an asset (e.g., land or buildings) is reduced in value over its lifetime.

Photo 8.5
Private label products are important to all the major food retailers in the United Kingdom. When Sainsbury introduced this Classic Cola product in a distinctive red can, the Coca-Cola Co. protested, claiming that the product was a clear imitation of Classic Coca-Cola. *Courtesy of SN.*

Photo 8.6
Private label products once simply imitated the leading national brands. The new generation of private label products seeks to create a lead product, not a copy of others' success.
Courtesy of SN.

This is a bookkeeping practice and does not necessarily reflect the true value of the property. In France, land and buildings are depreciated over a 20-year period. But until recently, U.K. retailers did not depreciate land and buildings. The belief of U.K. companies was that assets such as land and buildings would continue to increase in value, and therefore should not be depreciated. The collapse of the property market in the early 1990s led U.K. accountants to question the practice of not depreciating land and buildings. In 1994, the major U.K. supermarket chains began to depreciate their land and buildings. This one act brought much of the high profit margins for U.K. retailers in line with those of other continental retailers.

Although U.K. retailers still have higher profit margins, cost differences between the two countries can explain much of the margin imbalance. Another reason for these higher margins is found in the type of competition in the industry. As previously noted, the food retailing industry is an oligopoly with four firms controlling the majority of sales. In an oligopoly, price competition leads to price wars. Companies tend to compete on a non-price basis because price wars will hurt all market players.

Labor costs are lower in the United Kingdom than in France. Food retailers in the United Kingdom employ a much higher proportion of part-time labor, which gives them flexibility by allowing them to staff according to store traffic. In France, which has higher social support costs, employees cost the store more. Finally, U.K. food retailers have typically used a management system that is more centralized than that of French food retailers. This centralized system has given them much greater buying power. Being centralized has also allowed them to get the volume necessary to develop their store brands. And store brands, as we have seen, give retailers higher profit margins.

GOVERNMENT REGULATIONS

Government regulations have influenced all types of large-scale retailers in the United Kingdom. Operating hours, zoning restrictions, and employment options influence a retailer's competitive decisions.

SUNDAY TRADING After World War I, England and Wales passed legislation restricting retail operations on Sunday. Scotland never introduced this type of legislation. Even during the ban, illegal Sunday openings occurred in England and Wales.

The government relaxed the law in 1994. Shops under 280 square meters (3,000 square feet) can open any time they wish on Sundays. Shops larger than this can be open on Sundays, but their opening hours must be restricted to six hours during the day. [27]

Extending hours of operation affects the number of employees needed in the store. Burton's department store has been instrumental in moving employees to part-time positions. It was typical in the past for all retail employees to be full-time. The stores were open about 40 hours per week and all employees worked all hours. Burton's has since moved to flexible working hours. The store hires people according to its busy periods. Instead of calling employees "part-time employees," they are called "key-time employees." Employees who did not want to work the flexible hours were offered severance packages. The remaining employees are paid more than they were before, although their hours are not standard.[28]

ZONING REGULATIONS The U.K. planning process is less prescriptive and gives more power to local authorities than that of many other European countries. In the United Kingdom, the planning process cannot be used for purposes other than to regulate the use of land. Attempts to set social policy, for example, to restrict gambling or use of alcohol, fail. Even environmental policies dealing with energy and waste have been ruled out of order. [29]

The planning process is based on two principles. First, all development, whether a new building or a change in use of any land or building, requires planning permission from the local authorities. Second, there is a system of development plans that sets out policies and arrangements for local areas for a 10- to 15-year period. Development plans are based on a two-tiered approval process. County councils produce broad structure plans, which provide the strategic policy for a county. Local plans are for smaller areas.[30]

Before the 1980s, development plans did not have much effect on retailing. After that, however, the plans included sections on shopping. Since 1996, the planning law PPG6 has been revised. Most of the retail building currently under construction was approved before the 1996 revision. The development plans attempt to ensure that there is not a wasteful "oversupply" of shopping floorspace. Restrictive policies toward superstores (food and non-food) are common. Approval is given only where need can be shown, and where no significant harm will be done to existing shopping centers.[31]

THE NETHERLANDS

The Netherlands has a strong support system for small- and medium-size retailers. The country also has several retail powerhouses, as the following discussion will reveal. Large retailers in the Netherlands have grown because of early and aggressive internationalization efforts.

COUNTRY BACKGROUND

The Netherlands gained its independence from Catholic Spain in 1558. Eighty years of bitter struggle had been necessary to establish the new nation. The period after the country's founding has been called the Dutch "Golden Age." During the next century, this small country played a big role in world history. Access to the sea helped it to become a commercial power. The Dutch competed successfully with England and France for overseas markets and colonies. They became rich on trade with the Far East; for many years they were the only Europeans permitted access to Japan.

The Netherlands was taken over by the French during the Napoleonic Wars, but regained its independence in 1813. From 1815 to 1830, Belgium was included as part of the Kingdom of the United Netherlands. The Dutch were founding members of the European Economic Community and have been one of the strongest supporters of closer economic and political union among the European nations.[32] Table 8.5 presents selected demographic and economic data for the Netherlands.

NON-FOOD RETAILERS

The Netherlands is a major retail market. Per capita, people in the Netherlands purchase 21% more than consumers in the United Kingdom. Dutch companies have successfully internationalized. Dutch retailing, like retailing in France, has many well-established chain stores in the non-food sales area. Table 8.6 lists the major domestic and foreign retailers in the Netherlands.

TABLE 8.5

The Netherlands: Selected Demographic and Economic Data

	Population (millions) mid-1995	Area (thousands of sq. km)	GNP per capita Dollars 1995	GNP per capita Avg. ann. growth (%) 1985–95	PPP estimates of GNP per capita U.S. = 100 1987	PPP estimates of GNP per capita U.S. = 100 1995	Life expectancy at birth (years) 1995	Adult illiteracy (%) 1995
High-income economies	902.2t	32,039t	24,930w	1.9w			77w	
Netherlands	15.5	37	24,000	1.9	70.5	73.9	78	a

Source: World Bank (1997). a = less than 5%. PPP = purchasing power parity. t = total. w = weighted average.

Levi Strauss has 55 outlets. The Body Shop, based in the United Kingdom, has 50 outlets. German mail-order companies such as Quelle, Otto Versand, and Neckermann operate in the Netherlands. Benetton has 59 units, Toys "R" Us, 8 units, and IKEA, 11.

DEPARTMENT STORES Three chains dominate the Dutch department store industry: HEMA, Vendex'Vroom & Dressman, and Bijenkorf. HEMA, which has a 46% market share and sells through 239 HEMA affiliates, has a low-price image. Vendex'Vroom & Dressman (V & D), which has a 38% market share and sells through 63 department stores, has a middle-range image. Bijenkorf, with a 16% market share, sells through six stores positioned in the high-price segment. Bijenkorf and HEMA belong to the Koninklijke Bijenkorf Beheer (KBB) group, meaning that this group controls 63% of the Dutch department store market. The market share of Bijenkorf and HEMA is growing, while V & D has experienced a 3% point decline since 1990.[33]

The KBB Group and V & D are the only two large non-food retailers in the Netherlands. More than 88% of KBB's sales are in the Netherlands. Their stores fall into two sectors, department stores and specialty stores. The department stores account for over half the group's sales. The KBB Group owns FAO Schwartz—this is the only non-European activity of KBB. The KBB Group acquired the stores in 1990 and has suffered losses ever since.

In the process of divestment, V & D is trying to generate the funds necessary to strengthen its core business. As part of this process, the company

TABLE 8.6

Major Dutch and Foreign Retailers in the Domestic Market, 1995–1996

Retailer	Operations	Sales (Guilders billions)	Outlets (no.)
Ahold	Grocery multiple	14.3	1,613
Superunie	Cooperative food group	9.8	1,443
Vendex	Food and non-food	8.0	1,353
KBB	Department stores and non-food	5.6	955
Markant	Wholesale-based food group	3.5	2,085
Schuitema (73% Ahold)	Food voluntary chain	3.1	502
C & A (Germany)	Clothing and textiles	2.9	173
Groenwoudt	Supermarkets/off-licenses/drugstores	2.7	554
Unigro	Food stores	2.5	701
SHV Makro	Cash-and-carries/hypermarkets	2.3	15
Blokker	Household goods and toys	2.3	1,227
Aldi Nederland (Aldi Germany)	Discount food stores	2.0	300
DeBoer	Grocery and drugstores	1.8	489
Intergamma	DIY* and hardware	1.7	185
Spar Nederland	Food voluntary chain	1.2	408
Herman's Groep (Tengelmann Germany)	Grocery and off-licenses	1.1	251
Dirk van den Broek	Grocery and off-licenses	1.1	119
CODIS	Wholesale-based food group	0.9	543
Macintosh	Clothing, auto, and household goods	0.8	223
United Retail Nederland	Electricals buying group	0.8	300
Sperwer	Food voluntary chain	0.8	272
HDB Group	DIY and hardware	0.7	441
Wehkamp (GUS UK)	Mail-order	0.7	0
Zeeman Textiel	Clothing and textiles	0.6	450
P & C Groep	Clothing	0.5	59
Quelle (Germany)	Photo-processing stores and mail-order	0.4	400
Expert (Expert Switzerland)	Electricals buying group	0.3	191
Megapool	Electricals franchised group	0.3	98
It's Electric	Electrical goods	0.3	53
Otto Versand (Germany)	Mail-order	0.3	0
Neckermann Postorders (Karstadt Germany)	Mail-order	0.3	0
Electronic Partner (Germany)	Electricals buying group	0.2	200

TABLE 8.6

Major Dutch and Foreign Retailers in the Domestic Market, 1995–1996

Retailer	Operations	Sales (Guilders billions)	Outlets (no.)
Elektro Vakman	Electricals buying group	0.2	250
Dormael Beheer	Clothing	0.2	241
Intres	Clothing buying group	0.2	593
Free Record Shop	Music and videos	0.2	113
Benetton (Italy)	Clothing	0.1	59
Boerenbord	Agricultural DIY cooperative	0.1	116
Douglas (Germany)	Perfumeries	0.1	63
Hennes & Mauritz (Sweden)	Clothing	0.1	23
Wickes (UK)	DIY superstores	0.1	18
Fleurop	Florists buying group	N/A*	1,750
DA Drogist	Drugstores buying group	N/A	1,300
Moriaan Tabacs	Tobacconists buying group	N/A	1,000
SDO Plus Klus	DIY and hardware	N/A	645
VNR Reformprodukten	Health products buying group	N/A	500
Garant Schuh (Germany)	Footwear buying group	N/A	450
Centrop van Opticiens	Optical goods buying group	N/A	330
Nord-West-Ring (Germany)	Footwear buying group	N/A	300
HomeoPatheek	Homeopathic goods buying group	N/A	235
Schlecker (Germany)	Drugstores	N/A	155
Bata (Canada)	Footwear	N/A	125
Pearle Vision (Cole National USA)	Optical goods	N/A	125
Intersport (Switzerland)	Sports goods buying group	N/A	110
Levi Strauss (USA)	Clothing	N/A	55
The Body Shop (UK)	Personal and beauty products	N/A	50
Sears (UK)	Clothing and sports goods	N/A	50
Carpetland (Taeppaland Denmark)	Carpets and floor coverings	N/A	48
Vobis (Kaufhoff Germany)	Computer goods stores	N/A	25
Boeken en Platen (Bertelsmann Germany)	Books, audio, and video stores	N/A	18
IKEA (Sweden)	Furniture and household goods	N/A	11
Toys "R" Us (USA)	Toy superstores	N/A	8

Source: The European Retail Handbook, 1997 Edition. (1996). London: Corporate Intelligence on Retailing, pp. 200–201.

*1 Dutch Guilder = US $0.48; DIY = do-it-yourself; N/A = not available.

sold its stake in the U.S. department store, Dillards. Other business improvement measures include the introduction of programs to increase productivity, invest in automation and software, upgrade and renovate existing shops, and make changes in logistics.

During the 1960s, V & D used the junior department store as an expansion route. Eventually, the department store industry was saturated in the Netherlands. The company realized that if it wanted to expand in the department store format, it would need to internationalize. In the late 1970s, it acquired 20% of an American department store called The Outlet. The company later sold its share in The Outlet and acquired a 40% holding in Dillards.

COOPERATIVES The Netherlands is home to a strong cooperative movement. About 44,000 small- and medium-size companies belong to business cooperatives. This amounts to 43% of all companies but 61% of sales. The cooperative movement has increased by one-third since 1980.[34] Originally the primary type of cooperative was a buying cooperative. Now franchising is one of the most popular forms of cooperatives. Buyers' cooperatives are based on an association that is nonobligatory. Cooperative members can buy merchandise from the buying organization, or they may buy it elsewhere.

FOOD RETAILERS

Owning a car is very expensive in the Netherlands. Car taxes total about 25% of the price of an automobile, so many people do not own cars. This makes them dependent on bicycles and public transportation to do their food shopping. Dutch consumers shop frequently, and most food sold in the Netherlands is produced there.

Ahold started as a small grocer in 1887 but is now the biggest food retailer in the Netherlands. Ahold ranks 19th on the list of 100 largest retailers in the world. Over 48% of the company's sales are outside the Netherlands. The company operates and franchises more than 612 stores under the name Albert Heijn. Ahold also has major investments in the United States, including BI-LO, Giant Food Stores, Finast, and Stop & Shop. Albert Heijn, the CEO of this company, is credited with developing self-service in the Netherlands. Before opening self-service stores, he needed to update the packaging industry in his country. As noted in earlier chapters, packaging is important to protect merchandise from consumers when self-service is introduced. At the end of Part III, Company Focus III.4 describes Ahold's operations in Europe and abroad.

Ranking 26th on the list of 100 largest retailers in the world is SHV Holdings. The company operates supermarkets under the trading name Makro in 14 countries, generating 85% of its sales through foreign operations.

Retail property development in the Netherlands is tightly regulated, and out-of-town retailing takes second place to city center shopping. As a

Photo 8.7
Albert Heijn is the supermarket format for the Ahold group, the most successful retailer in the Netherlands. The group is also one of the most international of food retailers in the world. The supermarket shown here is in Tilburg. *Courtesy of Ahold.*

result, the Netherlands has half the shopping center development of France or the United Kingdom.

GOVERNMENT REGULATIONS

Local governments restrict expansion of superstores and hypermarkets. Regulations are much stricter than in the United Kingdom. Operating hours are also controlled. Limiting the hours of operation protects smaller stores. The retail environment in the Netherlands is somewhat like the industry in the United Kingdom. The relationship between large- and small-scale retailers is quite good. This may be due to the funding those governments provide for research institutes for small- and medium-size businesses. The research institutes provide small businesses with the type of research information generally available only to larger businesses.

The Netherlands has a well-established social security system for its citizens. This has led to a very equal distribution of income. The top income earners pay 70% of income in taxes. This degree of government support has an impact on the retail industry, by making wages higher. The retail industry is very labor-intensive and employs 13% of the work force. However, the Netherlands is currently experiencing a labor shortage, making it difficult for the retail industry to find employees. The workers in retailing are very young, compared to other employment areas. Forty percent are 22 years of age or younger.[35]

The government in the Netherlands is involved with retail industry in three policy domains:

1. Business establishment policy—measures to guarantee good business practices;
2. Structural policy—measures to support orderly economic trade;
3. Spatial distribution policy—measures to ensure good environmental planning.

The Netherlands is one of the countries that laid the basis for envirnonmental planning. This involvement started with housing laws enacted in 1901. These laws were designed to improve housing conditions, but they also meant that urban development became subject to national legislation. At first, retailing was not included in this planning, but in the 1930s, shops were included for the first time.[36]

During an economic crisis of the 1930s, many of those who became unemployed looked for a solution in the retail trade. Consumer purchasing power declined, yet the number of shops increased significantly. This led to the first government intervention in the retail industry, the Establishment Law of 1937. This law required that retailers obtain a license, which was only given after proof was provided of competence to run a store. The intent of the law was to improve retail trade, but the actual result was to reduce the number of shops.

After World War II, shopping facilities needed to be rebuilt. The government developed a planned-shop hierarchy. The legal framework for the location of shops was formed by a zoning plan. Retail businesses could be established where the zoning plan allowed them. The business location plan of 1954 replaced the old law of 1937. The most significant change in the law was that licenses were tied to specific branches of trade. This kept retailers from responding to changing consumer needs through diversification.

Since 1996, 13 of the largest cities in the Netherlands have been allowed to loosen their restrictive policies related to large-scale (1,500 square meters [16,000 square feet]) retail trade. This was done to encourage greater retail variety, particularly in stores selling bulky merchandise such as large appliances and electronics.[37]

Belgium, the next country discussed, has government restrictions that are more restrictive than those of the United Kingdom or the Netherlands. Retailers from Belgium have expanded internationally, partly to find less restrictive environments, and partly because the country is small, making market saturation a problem.

BELGIUM

COUNTRY BACKGROUND

Two thousand years ago, Belgium sat on the border between the Roman Empire in the south and the area controlled by the Germanic Franks to the north. During the Middle Ages, Belgian cities became the wealthiest and most important trading centers in the world. From the 16th to the 19th centuries, Belgium was controlled by Burgundy, Spain, Austria, France, and finally the Netherlands. The country finally gained its independence in 1830. During the era of European expansion in the late 19th and early 20th centuries, Belgium claimed a vast diamond- and mineral-rich territory in central Africa formerly known as the Belgian Congo. Although the region gained its independence in the 1960s and became the nation of Zaire (renamed the Democratic Republic of the Congo in 1997), close ties remain between the two countries.

The Germans overran Belgium during both world wars. After World War II, Belgium became a founding member of the North Atlantic Treaty Organization (NATO). Brussels, the capital city of Belgium, is now the headquarters of NATO and the European Union (EU).[38] Table 8.7 presents selected demographic and economic data for Belgium.

The major domestic and foreign retailers operating in Belgium are listed in Table 8.8. Thirty of the 49 companies listed are foreign retailers.

TABLE 8.7

Belgium: Selected Demographic and Economic Data

	Population (millions) mid-1995	Area (thousands of sq. km)	GNP per capita Dollars 1995	GNP per capita Avg. ann. growth (%) 1985–95	PPP estimates of GNP per capita U.S. = 100 1987	PPP estimates of GNP per capita U.S. = 100 1995	Life expectancy at birth (years) 1995	Adult illiteracy (%) 1995
High-income economies	902.2t	32,039t	24,930	1.9w			77w	
Belgium	10.1	31	24,710	2.2	76.3	80.3	77	a

Source: World Bank (1997). a = less than 5%. PPP = purchasing power parity. t = total. w = weighted average.

The United Kingdom is particularly well-represented. Wickes has 19 units; Kingfisher, 18; The Body Shop, 18; Thorn, 16; and Virgin, 1.

DEPARTMENT STORES

The largest department store company in Belgium is GIB Group, which is involved with four types of retail activities: food retailing, DIY, department stores, and restaurants. The GIB Group has 20% of the Belgian large-scale food retailing industry. In DIY, GIB ranks 10th worldwide with a presence in five countries. Eighty percent of GIB's total sales are in Belgium, 9% in other European countries, and 11% in the United States. Supermarkets account for 63% of the total, DIY 21%, restaurants 8%, and specialty retailing 8%.[39] The company has entered a strategic agreement with Promodès to enhance buying potential and exchange know-how on logistics, productivity, and computer systems and has sold its Nivelles distribution center to Exel Logistics, a European logistics specialist. The principal reason for taking these actions was to refocus on the company's core activities of retailing and finding specialist partners to improve buying potential and productivity.

In 1992, the company decided to change its operating format and decentralize. This action helped the company see that the group was hindered and needed strategic reorientation, particularly in the food business. The food business accounts for two-thirds of sales but only one-fifth of group operating profit. In restructuring the food business, GIB is using a French model with an accent on price discounting. Gradually, GIB is withdrawing from the department store industry. Separating the group like this could pave the way for a breakup of the company.

The company takes its name—GM-INNO-BM company—from a combination of three department stores, each with a long history. The Grand Bazar d'Anvers was founded in 1885. The Innovation, was founded in 1897, and Bon Marche was founded in 1860. The GIB Group now has only one department store name, INNO, operating 15 department stores. In 1995, a new INNO department store opened in Brussels; it was a rare event. It had been about 25 years since a new department store opened in Belgium. Department stores now account for only 4% of sales in Belgium.

FOOD RETAILERS

The food retailing market in Belgium is highly competitive with low profit margins. Stores have been consolidating, with a 50% reduction between 1970 and 1980. Although, large food retailers sell just slightly over half of the food products sold in the country, many Belgians prefer to shop at traditional food stores. Over half of all Belgians buy their meat directly from a butcher store, and nearly three-quarters buy their bread from a bakery.[40]

TABLE 8.8

Major Belgian and Foreign Retailers in the Domestic Market, 1995–1996

Retailer	Operations	Sales (Bfr billions)	Outlets (no.)
GIB Group	Grocery, DIY, and non-food	178.9	1,047
Delhaize "le Lion"	Supermarkets, discount stores, and drugstores	103.4	450
Colruyt	Discount supermarkets/toys and sports	55.3	137
Louis Delhaize	Grocery and discount food	52.6	202
Aldi (Germany)	Discount food stores	49.0	320
Vente Achat Coop	Wholesale food network	43.0	253
SHV Makro (Netherlands)	Cash-and-carries and electricals	41.4	19
Vendex (Netherlands)	Food and non-food	17.4	278
Unidis (Unigro)	Grocery and cash-and-carries	16.5	990
Trois Suisses (Otto Versand Germany)	Mail-order	10.7	0
Hema/M & S/Press Shop (KBB Netherlands)	Variety stores, clothing, and news	10.0	142
C & A (Germany)	Clothing and textiles	8.7	80
Superconfex/Tonton Tapis (Macintosh Netherlands)	Clothing and household goods	7.2	119
IKEA (Sweden)	Furniture superstores	5.8	7
Gamma (Intergamma Netherlands)	DIY superstores	4.6	37
FNAC Sodal (Pinault Printemps-Redoute France)	Electrical and photo goods	4.4	16
Tera Euro Partner	Electricals buying group	4.1	70
Neckermann (Germany)	Mail-order	4.5	0
Electronic Partner	Electricals buying group	3.6	239
Big Mat/Pointmat	DIY buying group	3.5	25
Wickes (UK)	DIY superstores	3.4	19
Hennes & Mauritz (Sweden)	Womenswear	2.7	17
Bricoman (Leroy-Merlin France)	DIY superstores	2.5	4
Orga	DIY buying group	2.4	43
Krefel (Correxpo)	Electrical goods	2.3	52
Intersport (Switzerland)	Sports goods buying group	2.3	37
La Redoute (Pinault-Printemps-Redoute France)	Mail-order	2.2	0
Minit Corporation	Service and repair stores	1.9	250
Standard Boekhandel	Booksellers	1.9	66

Continued

TABLE 8.8

Major Belgian and Foreign Retailers in the Domestic Market, 1995–1996

Retailer	Operations	Sales (Bfr billions)	Outlets (no.)
Incobe	Furniture buying group	1.9	200
Superbois	DIY* superstores	1.9	22
Home Market (Devresse)	Household goods	1.8	38
Photo Hall (Spector Photo & Distefora Switzerland)	Photo, electrical and computer goods	1.7	40
Hubo	DIY stores	1.7	29
Vanden Borre (Kingfisher UK)	Electrical goods	1.6	18
Expert (Switzerland)	Electricals buying group	1.2	74
Bricosphere (Domaxel France)	DIY superstores	1.2	15
Maxi Toys	Toys stores	1.0	20
Toys "R" Us (USA)	Toys superstores	0.9	3
Go Sport (Rallye France)	Sports superstores	0.6	6
Blokker (Netherlands)	Household goods	N/A*	167
Eram (France)	Footwear	N/A	80
Carpetland (Taeppaland Denmark)	Carpets and floor coverings	N/A	80
Yves Rocher (France)	Perfumery and cosmetics	N/A	60
Ici Paris XL	Perfumery and cosmetics	N/A	50
Free Record Shop	Music and video stores	N/A	28
The Body Shop (UK)	Personal and beauty products	N/A	18
Skala (Thorn UK)	TV and video rental	N/A	16
Virgin (UK)	Media goods superstore	N/A	1

Source: *The European Retail Handbook, 1997 Edition.* (1996). London: Corporate Intelligence on Retailing, pp. 39–40.

Bfr = Belgian Francs; 1 Bfr = US $0.0260; DIY = do it yourself; N/A = not available.

Delhaize le Lion is one of the major food retailers, not just in Belgium, but also in Europe. The company has 394 stores in Belgium. Delhaize has a majority share holding in Food Lion of the United States with 881 supermarkets. Delhaize also operates supermarkets in Prague, operating under the name Delvita. Delhaize acquired controlling interest of Alpha-Beta Vassilopoulos and its 15 supermarkets, in Athens, Greece. Few other foreign retailers have entered the Greek market. The entry of foreign retailers will greatly alter the competitive structure of the industry there.

Food retailing in Belgium is highly concentrated. This is typical of markets in small, highly developed countries. For instance, in the Netherlands, Ahold has 20% of the Dutch market share, and in Switzerland, Migros has 25% of the market share. There is a big division between large- and medium-size retailers and between the hard and soft discount stores. The German company Aldi introduced the discount concept. Interestingly, the Belgian large-scale retail store law (Loi Cadenas) helped the hard discount concept growth. Hard discount stores are smaller than the stores regulated under the law. The Dutch were less receptive to the hard discount concept, largely due to the responsiveness of the Dutch leader Ahold and its supermarket format, Albert Heijn.[41] Ahold has introduced a new store format to respond to the Aldi threat. You can read about this store in the Company Focus III.4.

The segmentation of the Belgian market is similar to the German model of food retailing. The other two models of food retailing in Europe are the French model, dominated by general discounters, and the U.K. model, dominated by quality retailers providing a high level of services. Table 8.9 illustrates the differences between the models. The U.K. model is difficult to export because consumers in other countries have become more price sensitized. This makes the confrontation between the German and French ideas even greater.[42]

TABLE 8.9

Different Types of Food Retailing in Europe

	U.K. Model	French Model	German Model
Concentration	Very high	Rather high	High in discount segment; Average in large-scale food retailing
Type of network	Branch	Mixed (independent and branch)	Branch for hard discounters; mixed for large-scale food retailers
Marketing strategy	Quality	Discount	Discount in hard discounters; choice in large-scale food retailers
Own brands	Widely used	Rather well developed and growing fast	100% in hard discount
Countries involved	United Kingdom Netherlands Switzerland	France Spain Italy	Germany Belgium

Source: Dia-mart—Report in "Les Echos" (1994). Reported in "GIB—Company Report." (February 23, 1996). Credit Lyonnais Laing in *Investext* [Database on CD-ROM]. Foster City, Calif.: Information Access.

Belgium is one of the first battlegrounds for these two ideologies. Colruyt was the first Belgian retailer to find a solution. Colruyt had less market clout than GIB or Delhaize, so its exposure to the hard discounters made it even more vulnerable. Colruyt has successfully shown that it could achieve a viable response to hard discount stores with a soft discount formula based on systematic discounts for brand names.

GOVERNMENT REGULATIONS

Belgium has one of the most restrictive laws regulating large-scale store growth. The law is called the Padlock Law. Originally passed in 1937, the law defined large-scale retailers as those having five or more employees in a town of more than 100,000 population or three people in smaller communities. The law made opening large stores that sold general merchandise very difficult. After World War II, the law was renewed. Retailers could remodel existing stores, but the building of new stores was very difficult.

Department stores waited patiently until the law was overturned in 1961, then jumped at the chance to expand. From 1962 until 1975, there was little restriction on large-scale store growth. The total shopping space increased by 60%. New legislation passed in 1975, the Loi Cadenas, made it nearly impossible to open new large-scale stores in Belgium. Since then, the major department stores and hypermarkets in Belgium have had to saturate their growth needs with international expansion.

SUMMARY

Government involvement influences retailing in the United Kingdom, the Netherlands, and Belgium. The Padlock Law in Belgium is one of the most stringent restrictions on the expansion of large stores. All three countries have had restrictions on Sunday trading, another regulation that favors small-scale retailers.

Retailers in these three countries have looked outside their borders for expansion opportunities. Expansion in the United States, as well as other areas in continental Europe, are attractive options. Lifestyles of people in the United Kingdom, the Netherlands, and Belgium are probably closer to those of the United States than they are to their closer European neighbors.

The United Kingdom has several interesting retail formats that continue to survive alongside the modern retail systems. The agency system used in mail-order is unique. Retail cooperatives have a long and solid history in the United Kingdom, although they are now struggling to survive.

KEY TERMS

agent system
assembler of lines of goods
concessions
consignment system
depreciation
high street

DISCUSSION QUESTIONS

1. Why does a government want to protect small retailers? How does restricting Sunday trading hurt large retailers more than small retailers?
2. There is interest in the U.K. food market because the profit margins reported are higher than margins in other parts of Europe. How can you explain these higher margins? Will retailers from other parts of Europe benefit from these margins?
3. Retailers in the United Kingdom introduced private labels in foods as high-value-added products. Retailers in the United States took just the opposite tactic. They introduced private labels as low-cost alternatives to national brands. What factors contributed to retailers in each country taking each route, and what are the long-term effects of each strategy?
4. Discuss how the agency system affects:
   a. Customers;
   b. The agent;
   c. The retailer;
   d. The retailer's competitors.
5. Using Solomon and Tordjman's theory of global versus multinational retailers discussed in Chapter 1, how would you classify Virgin Records, Marks & Spencer, and The Body Shop?

ENDNOTES

1. "United Kingdom." (1995). *Craighead's International Business, Travel, and Relocation Guide to More than 80 Countries.* Detroit: Gale Research.
2. Coopers & Lybrand. (1996). *Global Powers of Retailing.* Chain Store Age—Special Report.
3. "Great Britain—House of Fraser: What Future After 1995 Results?" (1996). *Retail News Letter,* No. 436, June, p. 10.
4. Bower, J., and J. Matthews. (1994). *Marks & Spencer: Sir Richard Greenbury's Quiet Revolution.* Harvard Business School, Case 9-395-054.
5. "Great Britain—Good Results and New Ideas from Marks & Spencer." (1996). *Retail News Letter,* No. 436, June, p. 9.

6. Hughes, A. (July 9, 1996). "Marks & Spencer—Company Report." UBS Research Limited in *Investext* [Database on CD-ROM]. Foster City, Calif.: Information Access.

7. Hughes (1996).

8. *Retail News Letter.* (1997). No. 445, p. 9.

9. "Great Universal Stores—Company Report." (March 5, 1997). Merrill Lynch Capital Markets in *Investext* [Database on CD-ROM]. Foster City, Calif.: Information Access.

10. Sternquist, B. (1993). Personal interviews.

11. "Great Universal Stores—Company Report." (April 2, 1997). Greig Middleton & Co. Ltd. in *Investext* [Database on CD-ROM]. Foster City, Calif.: Information Access.

12. *Retail News Letter.* (1997). No. 445, p. 9.

13. Sparks, L. (1997). "A Review of Retail Co-Operatives in the UK." *The World of Co-operative Enterprise 1997,* pp.187–192.

14. Sparks (1997).

15. Sternquist, B., and M. Kacker. (1994). *European Retailing's Vanishing Borders.* Westport, Conn.: Quorum Press.

16. "Tesco—Company Report" (October 30, 1995). Williams De Broe in *Investext* [Database on CD-ROM]. Foster City, Calif.: Information Access.

17. "Tesco—Company Report" (October 30, 1995).

18. "Asda Group PLC—Company Report" (March 12, 1996). FT Analysis in *Investext* [Database on CD-ROM]. Foster City, Calif.: Information Access.

19. Shaw, S., J. Dawson, and M. Blair. (1992). "Imported Foods in a British Supermarket Chain: Buyer Decisions in Safeway." *International Review of Retail, Distribution and Consumer Research,* Vol. 2, No. 1, pp. 35–57.

20. Sternquist, B. (1992, 1994). Personal interviews.

21. Burt, S. "Retailer Brands in British Grocery Retailing: A Review." Working Paper 9204, Institute for Retail Studies, University of Stirling: Stirling, UK.

22. Burt.

23. McMaster, D. (1987). "Own Brands and the Cookware Market." *European Journal of Marketing,* Vol. 21, pp. 59–78.

24. Shaw, S., J. A. Dawson, and L. M. A. Blair (1992). "The Sourcing of Retailer Brand Food Products." *Journal of Marketing Management,* Vol. 8, No. 2, pp. 127–146.

25. Sparks, L. (1997). "From Coca-Colonization to Copy-Cotting: The Cott Corporation and Retailer Brand Soft Drinks in the UK and the USA." *Agribusiness,* Vol. 13, No. 2.

26. Burt, W., and L. Sparks. (1997). "Performance in Food Retailing: A Cross-national Consideration and Comparison of Retail Margins." *British Journal of Management,* Vol. 8, pp. 119–136.

27. *Retail News Letter.* (1994). January, p. 8.

28. Thatcher, M. (1993). "Burton Decides to Cut Its Cloth According to Its Changing Business Environment." *Personnel Management,* March, p. 15.

29. Howard, E. (1995), "Retail Planning Policy in the UK. In R. L. Davies, ed., *Retail Planning Policies in Western Europe.* London: Routledge.

30. Howard (1995).

31. Howard (1995).

32. "The Netherlands." (1995). *Craighead's International Business, Travel, and Relocation Guide to More than 80 Countries.* Detroit: Gale Research.

33. "Vendex International—Company Report." (June 1, 1995). Credit Lyonnais Laing in *Investext* [Database on CD-ROM]. Foster City, Calif: Information Access.

34. Nienhuis, J., ed. (1991). *Retailing in the Netherlands.* Netherlands: Center for Retail Research.

35. Nienhuis (1991).

36. Borchert, J. (1995) "Retail Planning Policy in the Netherlands." In R. L. Davies, ed., *Retail Planning Policies in Western Europe.* London: Routledge.

37. *Retail Planning Policies.* (1996). Oxford, UK: Jones Lang Wooton/Oxford Institute of Retail Management.

38. "Belgium." (1995). *Craighead's International Business, Travel, and Relocation Guide to More than 80 Countries.* Detroit: Gale Research.

39. GIB Annual Report (1995).

40. Barents, J., P. Bontinck, and T. E. Hoo. (1988). "Analysis of Retailing in the Benelux Countries." *International Trends in Retailing,* Vol. 5, No. 1, pp. 3–18.

41. "GIB—Company Report." (February 23, 1996). Credit Lyonnais Laing in *Investext* [Database on CD-ROM]. Foster City, Calif: Information Access.

42. "GIB—Company Report." (February 23, 1996).

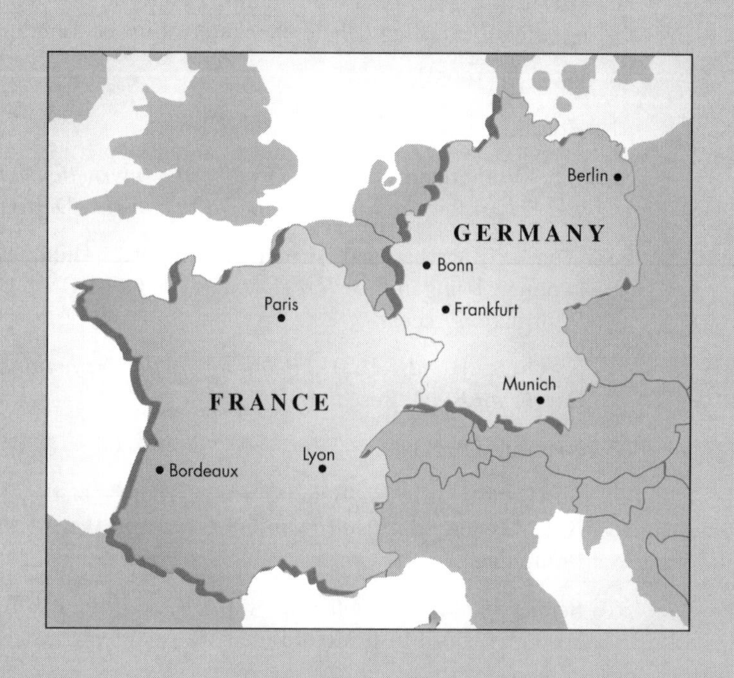
Berlin
GERMANY
Bonn
Paris
Frankfurt
Munich
FRANCE
Lyon
Bordeaux

9

Retailing in Germany and France

After reading this chapter, you will understand:

- How reunification of West and East Germany has affected German retailing.
- Why Germany's concern for the environment and social welfare affects the retail industry and the ability of foreign retailers to enter this market.
- The development of German hard discount food retailers and how this retail format is threatening to take market share from other forms of food retailers throughout the EC.
- How retail competition is altered with a concentrated industry such as Germany's department store sector.
- How French hypermarkets have successfully expanded into Spain and what future expansion can be predicted from this success.

IN THE PREVIOUS CHAPTER, I mentioned ways in which the United Kingdom, the Netherlands, and Belgium are somewhat similar both geographically and culturally. Although Germany and France are considered middle European countries, they do not have a similar cultural perspective. When these two countries are profiled on high context versus low context dimensions, dramatic differences are revealed: Germany is a low context culture, France is high context. By examining these countries using Hofstede's dimensions of difference, you can identify the differences between the Germans and the French.

Despite their cultural differences, I have chosen to discuss these two countries together because they have a similar level of retail development. Both countries have been retail innovators. Both countries have well-developed retail sectors with department stores, food stores, and specialty stores that add value and meaning to consumers. Germany is the largest retail market in Europe. France is the second largest. Retailers in both of these countries are internationally active and threaten the competitive environment when they enter a new market. German retailers have been aggressively moving into the former Soviet-bloc countries of eastern Europe. For some retailers, this means they are reclaiming stores confiscated during the communist takeovers of the early 1950s. French retailers have expanded very successfully into Spain.

GERMANY

COUNTRY BACKGROUND

Germanic tribes defeated the Roman legions in 9 A.D., stopping expansion of the Roman Empire. The German states were again a battlefield during the Napoleonic Wars in the early 1800s. Shortly after this period, the various independent states began the move toward unification. Prussia became the dominant force among these states, leading the emergence of the German Empire. For four decades, Germany dominated the European continent. This was a time of rapid economic and social development for Germans. They surpassed the British and French industrially.

Germans consider the period before 1914 to be a "golden age." However, German leaders became a bit too ambitious, leading to conflict with the other great European powers. The result was World War I. Germany's defeat and the collapse of its empire in 1918 left the country fragile and searching for an identity. Economic problems during the postwar years led to extremism and the rise of Adolf Hitler's Nazi Party in 1933. Germany's militaristic expansion culminated in World War II, when the country was again crushed by Allied Forces led by the United States, Britain, France, and the Soviet Union.

TABLE 9.1

Germany: Selected Demographic and Economic Data

	Population (millions) mid-1995	Area (thousands of sq. km)	GNP per capita Dollars 1995	GNP per capita Avg. ann. growth (%) 1985–95	PPP estimates of GNP per capita U.S. = 100 1987	PPP estimates of GNP per capita U.S. = 100 1995	Life expectancy at birth (years) 1995	Adult illiteracy (%) 1995
High-income economies	902.2t	32,039t	24,930w	1.9w			77w	
Germany	81.9	357	27,510	N/A	N/A	74.4	76	a

Source: World Bank (1997). a = less than 5%. PPP = purchasing power parity. t = total. w = weighted average.
N/A = pre-unification

The defeated country was divided into occupation zones, which were to be treated as single economic and administrative units under the control of the Allies. By 1948, Soviet ambitions in eastern Europe led to the Berlin blockade, and a wall was constructed to divide East from West Germany. On September 20, 1949, the three Western allies merged their zones and turned their powers over to a new German government.

A dramatic currency reform stabilized the German mark and a market economy took off. The Federal Republic of Germany joined NATO in 1955, and in 1957, Germany became a founding member of the European Economic Community.

East Germany did not fare so well. Until 1989, it remained a Soviet bloc country. In May of 1989, eastern Europe's borders began to open, starting with Hungary. Thousands of East Germans escaped to the West through that route. By October of that year, the East Germans who remained were demonstrating in the streets. Soviet President Mikhail Gorbachev decided not to intervene. In November, thousands of partying Germans from both sides tore down the Berlin Wall, signaling the end of East Germany's isolation from the West. A free German election was held in March of 1990, and the West German Chancellor Helmut Kohl won the election on a pledge of speedy reunification. On October 3, 1990 the two Germanies became one again.[1] Table 9.1 presents selected demographic and economic data for Germany.

In discussing retailing in Germany, it is necessary to discuss in some detail the single most important event in recent German history, the unification of East and West Germany.

GERMAN UNIFICATION

I will never forget that Sunday morning in November 1989. The major news event was the fall of the Berlin Wall. Although unexpected, the tearing down of the wall turned out to be prophetic of changes to come in the next few years behind the Iron Curtain. The news coverage that day showed people dancing in the streets and even on top of the Wall. It was a celebration of freedom.

The unification of West and East Germany had a great impact on the retailing industry. Before unification, East Germans could only buy their consumer goods from state-owned stores. These stores were concerned with distributing necessities. Luxuries were considered a waste of resources. Because there were few goods to purchase, the East Germans saved a disproportionate amount of their income. When the wall came down, their pocketbooks came out.

During the first part of 1990, East Germans displayed "consumer tourism," as they traveled across the border to purchase merchandise in West Germany. Sales in West Berlin increased 24% during the first half of 1991, but were down 10% during the second half of 1991.[2] Mail-order houses were early beneficiaries of the unified market, as shoppers placed orders from the newly available catalogs. However, East German consumers did not have to wait until new shopping stores were built to shop closer to home. West German retailers filled trucks with merchandise and then took them to the major East German cities, where they were parked on the streets and operated as "mobile" retail units. This temporary measure lasted only until West German retailers could open stores in the former communist territories. Table 9.2 shows some of these early movers into the East German market.

Photo 9.1
The Berlin Wall divided East and West Germany. In 1989, this wall was torn down, ending official separation of the cities' residents. In 1997, however, there is still a marked difference between East and West Berlin. *Courtesy of AP/Wide World Photos.*

TABLE 9.2

Mechanisms of Expansion For German Retailers

Company	Site Openings	Joint Ventures/ Partnerships	Acquisitions	Logistics
Allkauf	New openings, temporary sites, tents and greenhouses; spending on upgrading	None reported	None reported	None reported
Asko	New openings	Joint venture with consumer cooperatives	None reported	Supply to regional cooperative; development of logistical systems
AWA	New openings, temporary sites, refurbishment	None reported	None reported	Development of logistical systems (wholesale subsidiary supplied East before unification)
Douglas Holdings	New sites	Joint venture with East German druggist and search for new partners	None reported	Warehouse developed in Potsdam
Edeka	New openings	Joint venture with existing East German commercial organizations and independent merchants	None reported	Development of logistical systems
Hertie	New sites, renovation of sites	None reported	Acquisition from Treuhand, acquisition of Centrum department and other ex-state stores	None reported
Horten	New openings	"Loose" joint ventures, partnerships with eastern companies	None reported	None reported
Karstadt	Rented sites, temporary sites, refurbishment	Limited joint ventures with Karstadt acting as wholesale partner	Centrum stores from Treuhand	None reported

Continued

TABLE 9.2

Mechanisms of Expansion For German Retailers

Company	Site Openings	Joint Ventures/ Partnerships	Acquisitions	Logistics
Kaufhof	New sites, new openings (small units)	None reported	Centrum stores and others from Treuhand	None reported
Kaufring	None reported	Cooperative agreements with 101 consumer cooperatives and 18 HO* stores	None reported	Logistical systems and planning
Massa	Temporary sites in prefabs	Joint venture with East German department store	None reported	None reported
Neckermann	None reported	Joint venture in mail-order and travel shops	None reported	None reported
Otto Versand	New sites, stores, and order centers	Joint venture with consumer cooperatives	None reported	Mail-order warehouse systems
Rewe	New sites, temporary sites, tents, refurbishment	Joint ventures in wholesale partnership with HO department stores	Food stores, Treuhand	Logistical systems, warehouse and distribution
Ruefach	None reported	Some joint venture activity	None reported	None reported
Spar	New signing with franchise partners, renovation	Joint venture with HO and other joint ventures with wholesale and retail trade partners	Sites, warehouse and stores from state	Distribution networks
Tengelmann	Department stores, temporary outlets	Joint venture in food retailing with Forum and HO	Wholesale	None reported
F. W. Woolworth	Reopenings of pre-war stores, modernization	None reported	None reported	None reported

*HO = Handelsorganisation, the major retailing organization under the former Communist regime in East Germany.

Source: Clarke-Hill, C., T. M. Robinson, and R. Foot. (1992). "Retailing in Eastern Europe." *International Journal of Retail & Distribution Management*, Vol. 20, No. 6, p. 19.

Photo 9.2
This East German child appears overwhelmed by the product choice available in an East Berlin department store in 1990, after the unification of Germany brought western-style retailing to the East. *Courtesy of AP/Wide World Photos.*

In 1991, East German consumers spent deutsche marks (DM) 145 billion (U.S. $77.8 billion) at retailers. Of this, only 20% was spent with West German retailers. East German retailers commanded 75% of the sales. Over half of all consumer spending was spent with retailers.[3]

Today, Germany has the problem of being "over-stored." This means that there is too much retail space for the population base. This heightened competition means existing players must work much harder to survive. Table 9.3 summarizes the major domestic and foreign retailers in Germany. There has been a strong increase in chain outlets in the inner city areas. More than 45% of all retail outlets in fifteen German cities belong to these chain outlets.

Category killers have also entered the German market. These retailers are locating outside the city centers and creating "destination shopping" in these areas. Economies of scale made it possible for category killers to gain market share based on volume in procurement, logistics, information technology, and national marketing.

Germany has five of the top 100 global retailers listed in Chapter 1 Appendix (p. 44). Metro Holding AG is the second largest retailer in the world. Metro operates a variety of formats in 15 countries. Tengelmann is fifth on the list of top 100 retailers in the world. Tengelmann also operates a variety of formats in 10 countries. Aldi is eighth on the top 100 list. Aldi is a hard discount operator with stores in 10 countries. Karstadt Group ranks 22nd in the world, operating department stores, specialty stores, and mail-order operations in six countries. Otto Versand GmbH ranks 23rd; it operates mail-order systems in 15 countries.[4]

TABLE 9.3

Major German and Foreign Retailers in the Domestic Market, 1995–1996

Retailer	Operations	Sales (DM millions)	Outlets (no.)[a]
Metro Gruppe[b]	Food and non-food	60.6	3,057
Rewe-Gruppe	Grocery and non-food	43.1	9,095
Edeka-Gruppe	Grocery and non-food	41.8	2,733
Edeka	Grocery	31.0	2,004
AVA	Food/DIY°/optical goods	8.6	491
Nanz	Hyper/supermarkets	2.2	238
Aldi	Discount food	32.0	3,125
Karstadt Neckermann	Department stores/mail-order	27.0	740
Tengelmann	Food and non-food	25.1	5,538
Spar Handels	Grocery and non-food	21.2	7,271
Lidl & Schwarz	Discount food and DIY	17.0	1,674
Otto Versand	Mail-order	13.2	26
Quelle Schickedanz	Mail-order and photo stores, etc.	12.1	1,900
C&A	Clothing	7.5	186
Kaufring	Department stores buying group	6.9	1,284
Allkauf	Grocery and non-food	6.4	388
Anton Schlecker	Drugstores and food	5.1	5,340
Dohle Handels	Grocery and non-food	4.8	333
Globus	Hypermarkets and DIY and non-food	4.6	48
VME Möbel	Furniture buying group	4.4	171
Regent Möbel	Furniture buying group	3.8	327
Interfunk	Electricals buying group	3.8	1,600
Atlas	Furniture superstores	3.7	16
Douglas	Drugstores and jewelry, etc.	3.7	1,564
Wertkauf Mann	Hypermarkets and furniture	3.7	36
Norma Lebensmittel	Discount food	3.5	1,005
GfM Möbel	Furniture buying group	3.4	548
Eduscho	Coffee stores/household goods	3.4	1,000
KG Dortmund-Kassel	Grocery	3.3	496
VKG	Furniture buying group	3.2	1,038
Tchibo	Coffee stores and household goods	3.2	850
Musterring	Furniture voluntary chain	3.0	240
Ruefach	Electricals buying group	3.0	2,700
Emil Kriegbaum	Grocery	2.9	104
Bartes-Langness	Grocery	2.8	78
Electronic Partner	Electricals buying group	2.8	2,630
Expert	Electricals buying group	2.8	2,560

TABLE 9.3

Major German and Foreign Retailers in the Domestic Market, 1995–1996

Retailer	Operations	Sales (DM millions)	Outlets (no.)[a]
DMV Deutscher Möbel	Furniture buying group	2.8	474
Intersport	Sports good buying group	2.7	1,200
Woolworth (USA)	Variety stores and footwear	2.7	353
Europa Möbel	Furniture buying group	2.5	248
Bauhaus	DIY	2.4	115
IKEA (Sweden)	Furniture superstores	2.4	22
Robert Klingel (includes Wenz)	Mail-order	2.4	0
Kathreiner	Grocery and DIY	2.3	453
Promohypermarket	Hypermarkets	2.1	36
Der Kreis	Kitchen goods buying group	2.1	771
Co-op Schleswig	Food cooperative	2.1	221
Aral Minimarkt	Petrol station stores	2.1	2,400
Mondial	Carpets and furnishings	2.1	33
Union	Furniture superstores	2.1	9
Musterhaus Kuchen	Kitchen goods buying group	2.1	812
Peek & Cloppenburg (Düsseldorf)	Clothing	2.1	59
hagebau	DIY buying group	2.1	246
Stinnes	DIY	2.0	138
MTG	Furniture	1.8	200
Götzen	DIY/grocery	1.8	158
Bertelsmann	Media goods and mail-order	1.8	300
Tegut Theo Gutberlet	Grocery and discount food	1.8	327
Garant Möbel	Furniture buying group	1.7	1,100
Vedes Spielzeug	Toys buying group	1.7	443
Garant Schuh	Footwear buying group	1.7	1,590
Hornbach	DIY	1.7	50
Ihr Platz	Drugstores/perfumeries	1.7	732
Ratio Handel	Grocery	1.6	27
Ariston Schuh	Footwear buying group	1.6	900
Select	Electricals buying gorup	1.6	832
DM Karlsruhe	Drugstores	1.6	324
Esso Shop & Snack	Petrol station stores	1.6	1,347
Brinkmann	Electrical goods	1.6	25
Shell Shop Select	Petrol station stores	1.6	1,523
Bremke & Hoerster	Grocery	1.5	70

Continued

TABLE 9.3

Major German and Foreign Retailers in the Domestic Market, 1995–1996

Retailer	Operations	Sales (DM millions)	Outlets (no.)[a]
Bunting Handels	Grocery	1.5	68
Deichmann Schuh	Footwear	1.5	800
Telering	Electricals buying group	1.4	1,164
Otto Reichelt	Hypermarkets	1.4	104
Mühller Ulm	Drugstores	1.4	290
Wohngruppe	Furniture	1.3	104
Möbelkraft	Furniture superstores	1.3	2
K + K Klaas & Kock	Grocery	1.3	113
Porta Möbel	Furniture	1.3	49
Interpares Mobau	DIY buying group	1.2	239
Max Bahr	DIY	1.2	72
Pfannkuch	Grocery	1.2	213
Profi Electronic	Electricals buying group	1.2	1,000
dm-drogerie-markt	Drugstores	1.2	340
Dea Shop	Petrol station stores	1.1	1,162
NKD	Clothing	1.1	880
Concorde	Furniture superstores	1.1	23
Nord-West-Ring	Footwear buying group	1.1	1,050
BP Express	Petrol station stores	1.0	1,170
Trend Mobel	Furniture buying group	1.0	170
Aera	Electricals buying group	1.0	300
Markant-Sudwest	Grocery	1.0	96
Hoffer	Discount furniture superstores	1.0	8
Nurnburger Bund	Garden products cooperative	1.0	105
Breuinger	Textiles superstores	1.0	14
Hellweg	DIY	1.0	58
Porst (Distefora/Spector Photo Belgium)	Photographic goods	0.9	2,000
Wirichs	DIY	0.8	57

Source: *The European Retail Handbook, 1997 Edition.* (1996). London: Corporate Intelligence on Retailing, pp. 120–122.

[a]Outlet numbers for the major grocery groups exclude wholesale members.

[b]Metro restructured in 1996 to merge Kaufhof and Asko interests (Asko already having absorbed Massa). Escom went into receivership in 1996.

DM = deutsche marks; 1 DM = US $0.54. °DIY = do-it-yourself.

DEPARTMENT STORES

The past two decades have brought tough times for German retailers. Department stores have been losing market share since their highlight year of 1980. In that year, department stores had 7.2% share of the retail market. In 1994, they had less than 4%. Part of this decline has been due to an increase in the number of large-scale, self-service, and specialty stores in out-of-town greenfield sites. In addition, consumers seem to have become polarized in their expenditures. For everyday products, consumers want to pay the cheapest price, because they regard the products as standard offerings. On the other hand, they shop in high priced specialty stores for products when they perceive a difference of quality or when the product contributes a prestige attraction. For these reasons, two types of retailers are doing well: retailers such as Aldi that offer low prices and self-service, and companies like Douglas that sell a full range of products with high service at higher prices. Department stores, caught in the middle, have lost market share.[5]

The German department store industry is unique in terms of its concentration. For years, the top four German retailers—Karstadt, Kaufhof, Hertie, and Horten—controlled 90% of the department store industry in that country. This is one of the highest concentrations in the world. Besides selling general merchandise, these companies have significant food sales. In the mid-1990s, the two largest companies, Karstadt and Kaufhof, acquired the two smaller companies, Hertie and Horton. Company Focus III.5 profiles the operations of Kaufhof, including its recent efforts to revitalize and expand its operations.

Since Karstadt merged with Hertie, the flagship store of the group is now the famous KaDeWe in Berlin. This store, founded in 1907, became part of the Hertie group in 1927. The original store was demolished in 1943 but rebuilt by 1956. Since 1990, the store has been undergoing a renovation. Twenty percent of KaDeWe's nearly 30 million customers are foreigners.[6] I visited the KaDeWe store in 1997, after the renovation. It is beautiful. The store has a vast range of merchandise. Someone told me it is the largest department store in Europe. The top floor contains the food court, a modern version of Harrod's food court.

Kaufhof, Germany's second largest retailer, is attempting to remedy the problem of declining market share by developing the Galeria concept for its stores. The Galeria concept is to divide sales areas within the store into "shops within a shop." This produces an atmosphere similar to a specialty store with an above-average proportion of higher quality branded name merchandise. Kaufhof obtained the know-how for this concept when it acquired Horten, the concept's original developer, in the mid-1990s. Horten did not start to operate department stores until after World War II. As a result, the company did not get the best retail sites. This forced it to compete in other ways, including the successful Galeria concept.

After unification, companies had the right to lay claims to properties they had owned before the Soviets confiscated them. The major department stores have since been active in rescuing their previous properties. Sometimes the retailers have determined that their previous property is simply too costly to renovate, so they opt to acquire other property.

The former East German government ran 14 Centrum department stores. Three of the four major West German retailers have taken them over. Karstadt took more than six stores, located in Leipzig, Dresden, Magdeburg, Halle, Gorlitz, and Hoyerswerda. Two of these stores, in Gorlitz and Leipzig, belonged originally to the company before their confiscation by the East German State. In addition, Karstadt leases the Magnet department stores in Brandenburg and Wismar. These stores also belonged to the company before their confiscation.[7] Kaufhof took more than five former Centrum stores in Berlin (Alexanderplatz, Chemnitz, Rostock, Suhl, and Neubrandenburg). Hertie took over three stores in Berlin (Hauptbahnhof, Erfurt, and Schweldt).[8]

I visited the Kaufhof store in Alexanderplatz Square, Berlin, in 1997. The store and the merchandise were just a few steps up from offerings you would find at a state-run store. No doubt Kaufhof will remodel the store, eventually bringing it up to the level of the company's other stores. Even seven years after unification, the differences between East and West Berlin are striking. Without getting out of the subway trains, you can tell if the stop was part of what had been East Berlin. Nearly all the East Berlin stops look like underground military barricks: dull, drab, dark, and dirty. The floors are bare concrete, and graffiti covers most walls. The area between what had been East Germany and West Germany is like a wide demilitarized zone. The old buildings have been taken down and the area cleared to bare soil. On my next trip to Berlin, those areas will have bright new architecture. When renovation is complete, the capital will be moved from Bonn to Berlin.

In the past few years, the figures for German department stores have been the worst since the government started keeping records. Often, the key to success in the German retail trade is price leadership through cost leadership. Companies today are spending a great deal on logistics and information technology in an attempt to reduce costs. Analysts predict that traditional department store business will continue to decline. It is estimated that between 30 and 50 of the 380 department stores operated by the two major groups Karstadt/Hertie and Kaufhof/Horten will close by the year 2000.[9]

Germany is in the midst of social upheaval. As Germany's economy has become globalized, high paying German jobs have been exported to other countries. The result has been an erosion of the middle class and an increase of lower paying jobs. When Europe achieves monetary union, a major outcome will be a leveling of European wages. This will result in a further loss of higher paying jobs in Germany. There will be a rising number of low-wage earners and a corresponding above-average increase in the number of low-income groups. This trend will favor discounting formats of retail.

With its acquisition of Horten, Kaufhof gained some prime real estate, and the company is revamping its distribution system. Kaufhof will be replacing its 11 existing warehouses with two large distribution centers in Cologne and Erfurt. These distribution centers, with four regional warehouses for textiles and a warehouse for imported goods, will greatly enhance the company's logistics system. Before this, Horten did not have a logistical planning system; instead, it subcontracted with other companies to handle the function.

German consumers have reached the point where brand name products are considered interchangeable. In a government survey, consumers indicated that 85% of all consumer goods and 65% of all consumer durables received the classification of "good" from consumers. This view of product equality will intensify. Brand names provide added value in very few cases. This makes price a more important parameter, and opens the door for generic products. These generic products have turned into a product group with the greatest value added.[10]

Investment in technical equipment continues to intensify. Retail managers are concerned with integrated inventory control systems and efficient consumer response, automated logistics, data interchange over the entire distribution chain, and scanning equipment. They aim to achieve cost leadership as a basis for price leadership.

MAIL-ORDER

Using 1970 as a base year, the growth of mail-order has increased at a much greater rate than department store sales. German companies are the leaders in mail-order. In the bed linen category, mail-order has 30% of the market. I was surprised to find out that major household appliances such as refrigerators and washing machines are purchased through mail-order. Fifteen percent of the sales in this category are through mail-order. Ten percent of furniture purchases are made through mail-order. Mail-order sales in Germany soared right after unification, increasing nearly 25% in 1990.[11]

Three companies—Quelle, Versand, and Neckermann—control 60% of German mail-order business. Restrictions on opening of new stores and trading hours put mail-order companies in a positive position.

Quelle runs department stores in addition to its mail-order company. Immediately after unification, the company's sales increased almost 25%. Of the 11 million copies of its catalog for that year, Quelle distributed 3.5 million in East Germany. Quelle is opening a huge warehouse facility in Leipzig, using robots that retrieve merchandise from high-level shelving. The choice of Leipzig, in the former East Germany, is an important statement of where the company is pursuing growth.

Quelle expects to grow eastward. The company currently has stores in the Czech Republic, Slovakia, Russia, Slovenia, Poland, and Hungary. Management believes the Leipzig warehouse facility will increase productivity by 25%. Quelle is also starting a 24-hour home teleshopping venture in Germany called HOT (Home Order Television). Quelle is pursuing the

24-hour home shopping system even though German law currently restricts home shopping broadcasting to a limit of one hour per day.[12]

Otto Versand focuses on specialty catalogs within Europe, the United States, and Japan. The company's catalogs include Spiegel and Eddie Bauer.

FOOD RETAILERS

Food retailers have great selling power and great buying power in Germany. This causes a vertical-backward squeeze on food manufacturers. In fact, the food distribution industry is one of the most highly concentrated industries in Germany. In contrast, food manufacturers are very small, having one of the lowest concentration ratios of any industry in Germany. This creates an imbalance in the distribution power. The big food distributors are an oligopoly as sellers and an oligopsony of purchasers.[13] **Oligopsony** means there are few buyers and many suppliers. Food manufacturers have a limited number of companies to whom they can sell. This gives the food retailers a great deal of power. Food retailers are highly integrated, both vertically and horizontally.

Aldi and Tengelmann are two of the giants of food distribution in Germany. Their organizations independently coordinate their purchases without the use of wholesalers. The food divisions of major department stores also operate this way. The companies centrally coordinate volume purchases of inventory that they sell directly to the factory rather than going through wholesale channels.

Photo 9.3
Aldi is a German hard-discount food retailer with a unique format, 100% private label products offered in a small-scale warehouse-type layout. This format enabled the company to expand in countries where hypermarkets and supermarkets were restricted by planning laws. *Courtesy of SN.*

Rewe and Edeka are companies that began as cooperatives but have evolved into corporate entities. Retail cooperatives have a long history in German food distribution. In 1997, Rewe had 11,013 stores.[14]

Markant is the largest voluntary chain in Germany. Members of voluntary chains are joined by contractual arrangements to a group of wholesalers to gain a steady source of suppliers.

The excitement in food retailing today centers on integrated inventory control systems and efficient consumer response, automated logistics, data interchange over the entire system, and scanning. This greater workflow efficiency and productivity will help the retailers achieve cost leadership as a basis for price leadership. Otto Reichelt AG, in Berlin, is trying to encourage customers to scan goods themselves so the store can eliminate the checkout clerks.[15]

Discounters are typically working with a margin of 10% to 15%. Aldi earns a pretax return of 3% to 5%, with a 14% trading margin.

GOVERNMENT REGULATIONS

Germany is one of the "greenest" countries in the world. The Germans introduced an important environmental law in December 1991. This law places the responsibility for reuse or recycling on manufacturers and distributors. The first stage of the law included regulations regarding the disposal of packaging used for transport. The second and third stages were put into effect over the next two years.

Such laws, although good for the environment, make product sales from one European country to another more difficult. Manufacturers must provide special packaging for the German market or make all packaging more environmentally friendly. Another law recently passed in Denmark requires that soft drinks be sold in glass bottles with refundable deposits. Suppliers often decide it is not cost-efficient to make modifications just for the Danish market. The German market, on the other hand, is large enough to make adaptation feasible.

Karstadt, the department store and mail-order giant, has been a leader in being "green." The company won an award in 1992 for its interests and services in environmental protection.

Germany has had very stringent land-use planning ordinances; however these laws are designed at the local, not national, level. This town planning is most noticeable when entering a city or town. There is no urban sprawl. No outdoor billboards welcome new visitors. A single sign is likely to be found with the name of the town. Where the town ends, fields begin. Germany's laws require that stores locate in downtown areas; consequently commercial sites for large retailers are difficult to come by. Since 1968, the land-use plans have required that retail development follow the central place hierarchy discussed in Chapter 3. Demand for essential supplies should be met in neighborhood centers, demand for nonessential specialized goods should be met in medium-size centers, and demand for fashion and luxury goods should be met in city centers.

While I was working on this book, I spent some time in Germany conducting research. After completing a series of meetings in Frankfort, I drove two-lane roads back to Munich. I started Saturday morning. By the time I stopped a little after two in the afternoon to purchase some film, all of the stores were closed. I had to buy my film at a convenience store attached to a gas station because these were the only places open for business. The Ladenschlussgesetz (shop closing hours' law), put into effect in 1956, stipulates that stores will close at 6:30 P.M. on weekdays, except Thursdays when they can stay open until 8:30, and at 2:00 P.M. on Saturdays (with longer opening on the first Saturday of each month). A new agreement allows opening from 6:00 P.M. to 8:00 P.M. on weekdays and from 6:00 A.M. to 4:00 P.M. on Saturdays. The individual Lander, or state in Germany, can adjust closing times by two hours either side of the 4:00 P.M. Saturday closing time.[16]

My scenic tour was even more peaceful than I had expected because the downtown areas were deserted. I imagined that people were at home with their families, and I found this an interesting contrast to life in other parts of the world. Saturday afternoon is one of the busiest days for retailing in the United States and Asia.

This may be changing. As East Germany rebuilds, the German economic machine will speed up.

In 1996, there were 207 shopping centers in Germany. Thirty-five of those were opened in 1995. Before 2000, 41 new centers will open. Of the 41 centers to be built, eight will be in Berlin.[17]

Photo 9.4
German retailers close on Saturday afternoon and remain closed on Sunday. This specialty store is selling Wrangler jeans for DM 89.95, or about U.S. $60. *Courtesy of the author.*

FRANCE

COUNTRY BACKGROUND

France has always been a crossroads of Europe. Julius Caesar conquered the region, which he called Gaul. It was a part of the Roman Empire for 500 years. With the collapse of the Roman Empire, a tribe of people called Franks moved in. In the ninth century A.D., this area was the major component of the Frankish empire created by Charlemagne. The Franks intermarried with the Gallo-Roman population they ruled and became Romanized themselves, giving a Romanized version of their name to the country, France.

France was one of the first European countries to move from feudalism to a nation state. French armies were the most disciplined of any in their day, warring with England and others countries. During the rule of Louis XIV (1643–1715), France was the premier power in Europe.

Louis, however, was overambitious, which led to financial difficulties for France in the 18th century. A bad economy and popular resentment against the rich led to the French Revolution of 1789–1794. Interestingly, the French revolutionaries were inspired by the revolution of the American colonies against England a decade earlier.

France had 26 changes in government between 1946 and 1958. By the time Charles de Gaulle became prime minister in 1958, government instability had led the country to come close to a military coup.[18]

France has one of the oldest and most diverse retail networks.[19] It is the home of both the department store and the hypermarket format. France is Europe's second largest retail market, after Germany. Although France and the United Kingdom have about the same population, French consumers purchase over half as much again as consumers in the U.K. market. The country is also known in retailing for identifying a good idea and transmitting that idea throughout the world. For the French, inspiration begins with the arts and finds practical application in the way they do business. Table 9.4 presents selected demographic and economic data for France.

France can claim nine of the top 100 retailers in the world. The French hypermarket format has spread throughout the world. Two companies, Carrefour and Promodès, receive nearly 40% of their sales outside France. Carrefour is the ninth largest retailer in the world. Operating hypermarkets, discount, convenience, and specialty stores in 14 countries. Promodès ranks 16th, using hypermarkets, supermarkets, cash-and-carry, and convenience store formats in seven countries. Seventeenth in the world is Auchan, operating hypermarkets in four countries. Casino is 28th. It operates hypermarkets, supermarkets, and convenience stores in three countries. Pinault-Printemps-Redoute is 29th. This company uses mail-order, department stores, supermarkets, and specialty stores in 17 countries to obtain its sales volume.[20]

TABLE 9.4

France: Selected Demographic and Economic Data

	Population (millions) mid-1995	Area (thousands of sq. km)	GNP per capita Dollars 1995	GNP per capita Avg. ann. growth (%) 1985–95	PPP estimates of GNP per capita U.S. = 100 1987	PPP estimates of GNP per capita U.S. = 100 1995	Life expectancy at birth (years) 1995	Adult illiteracy (%) 1995
High-income economies	902.2t	32,039t	24,930w	1.9w			77w	
France	58.1	552	24,990	1.5	77.6	78.0	78.0	a

Source: World Bank (1997). a = less than 5%. PPP = purchasing power parity. t = total. w = weighted average.

A summary of the major domestic and foreign retailers in France is included in Table 9.5. Metro, the cash-and-carry store from Germany, is the leading foreign retailer. Metro has 54 outlets and the 14th largest sales of any retailer in France. Kingfisher, from the United Kingdom, has two major chains in France. But International, of which 26% is owned by Kingfisher, is a furniture and electrical appliance retailer. Darty, a part of Kingfisher, operates 145 electrical goods stores. Trois Suisses is a mail-order company operated by Otto Versand of Germany. Toys "R" Us has 40 toy stores in France. The United Kingdom's Marks & Spencer operates 17 stores in France.

NON-FOOD RETAILERS

France is a country with many regions that maintain a strong identity. Originally, retail chains developed in regional areas. These regional chains are now giving way to national chains. Nearly 75% of France's population lives in urban areas, with 9.3 million people in Paris alone. Few French towns and cities do not have a Carrefour, Leclerc, or Promodès hypermarket. The market is considered saturated. Thus, instead of opening new stores at home, the French majors are closing unprofitable stores at home and moving into foreign markets.[21] Construction costs are lower and competition less severe in their selected foreign markets.

There have been some notable failures of French company expansion. Galeries Lafayette opened a store in New York City that did not prove successful and was closed. Carrefour's initial foray into the United States was

TABLE 9.5

Major French and Foreign Retailers in the Domestic Market, 1995–1996

Retailer	Operations	Sales (Ffr billions)	Outlets (no.)
Leclerc	Food and non-food members group	129.3	1,100
ITM Intermarché	Food and non-food members group	128.7	2,716
Auchan	Food and non-food multiple	113.4	1,431
Promodès	Grocery multiple	102.3	2,669
Carrefour	Food and non-food multiple	89.7	741
Casino	Grocery multiple	58.3	2,837
Systême U	Food buying group	45.4	860
Pinault-Printemps-Redoute	Department stores and non-food	41.1	474
Cora Bouriez	Grocery multiple	43.0	240
Galeries Lafayette	Department and variety stores	29.0	254
Comptoirs Modernes (23% Carrefour)	Grocery multiple	27.0	734
Francap Distribution	Food buying group	18.5	856
Castorama	DIY* superstores	13.8	122
Metro (Germany)	Cash-and-carries	13.0	54
Baud Groupe	Grocery multiple	9.5	1,270
Groupe André	Footwear and clothing	8.8	1,775
But International (Kingfisher UK 26%)	Furniture/electricals (includes franchises)	8.7	231
Darty (Kingfisher UK)	Electrical goods	8.7	145
Domaxel	DIY buying group	8.2	530
Trois Suisses (Otto Versand Germany)	Mail-order	7.2	0
Guyenne et Gascogne	Grocery multiple	6.9	139
Eram	Footwear and clothing	5.9	1,400
IKEA/Habitat (IKEA Sweden)	Furniture and household goods	5.2	46
Cedico/Cedimarché (Tesco UK)	Grocery multiple	5.1	109
Groupe CAMIF	Mail-order	4.9	0
Co-op Atlantique	Food cooperative	4.8	355
Toys "R" Us (USA)	Toy superstores	4.7	40
Co-operateurs Normandie Picardie	Food cooperative	4.6	376
ANPF/Mr Bricolage	DIY buying group	4.2	286
Moblier Européen	Furniture/electrical goods	4.2	295
Bigmat	DIY buying group	4.0	252

Continued

TABLE 9.5

Major French and Foreign Retailers in the Domestic Market, 1995–1996

Retailer	Operations	Sales (Ffr billions)	Outlets (no.)
Schiever Distribution	Grocery multiple	4.0	600
Relais H (Matra Hachette)	News kiosks	3.7	900
Catena France	DIY stores/superstores	3.5	290
Lidl (Lidl Germany)	Discount food stores	3.3	445
Dolfus-Mieg	Textiles and haberdashery	3.3	260
Co-operateurs d'Alsace	Food cooperative	3.2	270
France Loisirs (Bertelsmann Germany)	Mail-order	3.2	208
Connexion	Electricals buying group	3.0	165
Hutte (Intersport Switzerland)	Sports goods buying group	3.0	518
C & A (Germany)	Clothing and textiles	2.9	48
Cime-Camiaeu	Clothing	2.8	425
Centrale Pro & Cie	Electricals buying group	2.8	1,500
Gitem	Electricals buying group	2.7	750
Etam	Womenswear and lingerie	2.6	475
Interdiscount (Spector Photo Group Belgium)	Electrical goods	2.5	140
Groupe Tabur	DIY and hardware stores	2.4	270
Yves Rocher	Perfumery and cosmetics	2.4	651
Rallye	Sports goods stores	2.3	171
Spar (65% Casino)	Food voluntary chain	2.3	300
Quelle (Germany)	Mail-order	2.3	0
EOCR Euro-Dif	Clothing	2.2	175
PG (Delhaize "le Lion" Belgium)	Supermarkets	2.0	33
Comepa	Hardware buying group	2.0	130
Guilde des Lunetiers Krys	Optical goods buying group	2.0	771
Tati Textile	Textiles superstores	2.0	14
Phildar (Mulliez family)	Woollen goods	1.9	1,550
Alain Afflelou	Optical goods	1.8	456
Aldi (Germany)	Discount food stores	1.8	281
Zannier	Childrenswear	1.8	281
Tripode Jardiland	Garden products buying group	1.8	97
Damart Serviposte	Mail-order	1.8	0
Sadem Jardin	Garden and seeds buying group	1.7	900
Bricorama/Bricaillerie	DIY and garden centres	1.7	86

TABLE 9.5

Major French and Foreign Retailers in the Domestic Market, 1995–1996

Retailer	Operations	Sales (Ffr billions)	Outlets (no.)
Gel 2000	Frozen food centres	1.6	434
La Samaritaine	Department store	1.6	1
La Foir' Fouille/Splash	Discount household goods	1.6	170
Phox	Photographic/audio buying group	1.6	405
Surcouf	Computer superstores	1.6	2
Hyper Media/Vobis/Reno (Kaufhof Germany)	Electricals, computers, and footwear	1.6	50
Obi (GIB Belgium)	DIY superstores	1.5	52
CDM Mobilier	Furniture	1.5	120
Tecniciens du Sport SED	Sports goods buying group	1.5	420
Marks & Spencer (UK)	Mixed goods and grocery	1.4	17
Bon Marché	Department store	1.3	1
Cuir Centre France	Furniture	1.3	78
Mobilier du France	Furniture buying group	1.2	95
Plein Ciel	Stationery buying group	1.0	320
Maty	Mail-order	1.0	0
Expert (Switzerland)	Electricals buying group	1.0	150
Sephora	Cosmetics and perfumery	1.0	50
Virgin Megastores (UK)	Media goods superstores	1.0	5

Source: *The European Retail Handbook, 1977 Edition.* (1996). London: Corporate Intelligence on Retailing, pp. 99–101.

*DIY = do-it-yourself; Ffr = French francs; 1 Ffr = US $0.16.

not successful, and the company needed to withdraw. French hypermarkets have learned that their export efforts are more successful in central Europe and Latin America, where retail development lags behind other areas.

DEPARTMENT STORES

France has been a leader in most retail innovations. The first department store, Bon Marché, appeared in Paris, and France has remained a leader in the department store sector for 130 years. There are 12 department stores in Paris. The largest is Galeries Lafayette, 48,500 square meters (522,000 square feet); then Samaritaine, 48,000 square meters (517,000 square feet); Printemps, 47,500 square meters, (511,000 square feet); Bon Marché, 32,000 square meters (344,000 square feet); and BHV, 29,000 square meters (312,000 square feet).

Photo 9.5
Galeries Lafayette in Paris on Boulevard Haussmann located next to Au Printemps and across the street from Marks & Spencer. The historic Paris Opera House, setting for the Phantom of the Opera story, is across the street. This is the premier retail location in Paris. *Courtesy of WWD.*

Traditional department stores are having a difficult time today in France. Department stores have been hurt by the rapid development of shopping centers on the outskirts of cities. These centers bring together specialty stores and discount chains. In 1996, these out-of-town centers generated 28% of total retail sales in France. Galeries Lafayette's department store divisions have 63 stores, which generate 35% of total group sales. There are two department store formats, the Galeries Lafayette chain (over 5,000 square meters) with 30 stores that convey a fashion image, and the Nouvelles Galeries that are of smaller size with more traditional offerings in 33 stores.[22]

Department stores have not streamlined their distribution systems like their hypermarket counterparts. Printemps is now leading the way to greater technology use, with an investment of $100 million in point-of-sale equipment. This investment is to help the company cut inventory costs and do a better job of targeting the tastes of its customers. Printemps will also increase its emphasis on midpriced clothes to differentiate its stores from downscale discounters.[23]

The French department stores have been caught in a positioning squeeze. During the economic downturn, they stocked more modestly priced merchandise. Then discounters entered the market providing lower prices for the same merchandise. The higher department store overhead did not allow the department stores to compete with discounters on price. However, by repositioning for a more upscale market, the department stores should be helped in the long run.

SPECIALTY STORE RETAILERS Specialty chains are taking market share away from traditional department stores. Nearly all of the foreign retailers entering France are specialty store chains. Part of the reason for this is that the Loi Royer law (described later) does not cover smaller-size retailers. Specialty stores also seem to address the unique French lifestyle.

Gap is increasing the number of its stores in other parts of France. The first Gap opened as a shop-in-shop in Galeries Lafayette. Gap now operates seven stores in France. Marks & Spencer has five stores in Paris and is planning to open more. These stores carry more food products than Marks & Spencer typically sells in its stores in other parts of France, but less food than is sold in U.K. stores. The company plans to continue to increase the proportion of food sold at its outlets in France.

Photo 9.6
Several European countries, including France, allow markdowns only twice a year. The length of the sale periods is also prescribed by law.
Courtesy of the author.

Photo 9.7
In this Carrefour produce section, merchandise is presented in bulk. Customers come to this central location to have it weighed and priced. Carrefour is the French company credited with developing the hypermarket format.
Courtesy of SN.

FOOD RETAILERS

The five main food retailing groups (the independent companies, Intermarché and Leclerc, and the integrated groups, Carrefour, Promodès and Casino) have 64% of the total selling space of supermarkets and hypermarkets in France. In 1997, the share of total hypermarket sales for major hypermarket groups in France were as follows: Leclerc (24.5%), Carrefour (24.2%), Auchan-Mammouth-Docks (24.2%), Grant-Casino (8.5), Continente-Promodès (8.4%), Cora (6.8%), Intermarché (3.3%), and Hyper U (1.6%). In 1996, Carrefour acquired Cora, giving it an even greater piece of the French hypermarket business.[24]

Carrefour is the leader in terms of sales, but ranks second to Leclerc in sales and total units. Leclerc and Intermarché are primarily giant food retailers, although some general merchandise is included in their offerings. The two firms were food retailing's low price leaders in France during the 1980s. The entrance of hard discounters into France has forced hypermarkets to adopt a less price-oriented strategy. In 1997, a new pricing law makes low cost competition even more difficult. The pricing law is discussed at the end of this chapter. The hypermarkets' focus is now on geographical expansion within France in smaller, scaled-down hypermarket formats. This will allow for greater growth in the presence of government limitations.

Promodès strategy is most like that of Carrefour. The company operates in Germany and Italy and has followed Carrefour to Asia. Promodès already has a strong presence in Spain with its Continente subsidiary. The firm is also increasing holdings in France through acquisition of supermarket franchises. Franchise opportunities have flooded the French market in the past few years. Promodès's heavy involvement in franchising makes it more vulnerable in the French retail environment than Carrefour.

Casino is restructuring due to recent acquisitions. Its major competitive edge will be gained through upgrades and modernization of these newly acquired stores. This is the company's most important type of growth. Casino has already brought its pricing into what it feels is a competitive range and does not intend to enter to price-cutting battles with hard discounters.

Promodès and Carrefour invest primarily outside France, where they can obtain a very rapid return on investment. Auchan has opened stores in Spain, Italy, Poland, and the United States. Docks de France has 76% of its sales in France.

French hypermarkets have extended their product lines and are increasing their services. This reflects their strategy of competing in services, not prices. When deep discounters entered the U.K. food market, retailers were forced to trim their margins. This is also occurring in France. In 1996, deep discounters in France had a 6.5% share of the French food market.[25].

Docks de France uses centralized management to improve its purchasing terms. In the early 1990s, it defined a common product range for all its outlets in the food segment and improved logistics throughout the system. Docks de France is now turning its attention to non-food segments. The company has established a common product range in the brown and white goods. It is also starting a "just in time" delivery system.[26]

Promodès, one of the big French hypermarkets, has been aggressively expanding into foreign markets. Promodès is trying a new retail concept that it plans to position between Champion supermarkets and Continente hypermarkets. It will call this large supermarket Hyper Champion. These stores will average 3,000 to 3,500 square meters (32,000 to 38,000 square feet). Promodès has also been internationalizing the deep discount concept in France. These stores, called Dia, are being opened in Italy, Greece, and Portugal.

Promodès is unique in that it has pursued growth in France and overseas with a variety of store concepts. Most of its competitors focus on a single retail form. Promodès has had a centralized organizational structure longer than its competitors. The company is also unique in that it is heavily involved in wholesaling. The group has five sectors: hypermarkets, supermarkets, hard discount, neighborhood stores, and cash-and-carry. When Promodès enters a country, it expects to be one of the top three in that sector. Supermarkets and neighborhood stores are used only in France; they are carryovers from Promodè's wholesale past.[27] Private label is important, constituting 17% of sales in France, an increase of 4% in less than two years.

Promodès has had problems with its German stores. The weak consumer demand in Germany partially explains this. The legal constraints on store openings also make it hard for retailers to succeed in Germany. In France, stores stay open until 9:00 P.M. each night and are open every Saturday and several Sundays a year. In Germany, shop hours were traditionally more restricted, although the law was recently changed to permit stores to remain open until 8:00 P.M. during the week and 4:00 P.M. on Saturdays, with some variations; but German stores are still never open on Sundays.

Carrefour was one of the first retailers to develop the hypermarket in France. The company opened its first store in 1963. In 1973, it expanded to Spain, and in 1975, to Brazil. Carrefour focuses its expansion efforts on countries where modern retailing is not established. In these countries, hypermarkets are a new concept. They attract customers with their large range of food and non-food product lines and competitive prices.

Carrefour has continued to concentrate on hypermarket sectors while other French hypermarkets have diversified into other retailing types. The company currently ranks among the top four retailers in international operating activities. (The others are Ahold, Delhaize, and Promodès.) Ahold and Delhaize are very dependent on the United States, which makes them less risk-diverse. Carrefour is active in France, Spain, Portugal, Brazil, Argentina, Mexico, Italy, Turkey, Thailand, Malaysia, China, Taiwan, Hong Kong, and South Korea.

Carrefour usually sets up joint ventures, and the company earns 96% of its sales from hypermarkets. In Europe, a hypermarket is defined as any store with a floor space of at least 2,500 square meters (27,000 square feet). In France, the stores are much larger, averaging 6,000 square meters (65,000 square feet), and they top 7,500 square meters (81,000 square feet) in Spain. Carrefour gets 60% to 80% of sales from food products and 20% to 40% from non-food. Company Focus III.6, at the end of Part III, provides more details about Carrefour's international expansion and positioning strategy.

Carrefour has shown a willingness to withdraw from markets in which it is not achieving success. This has happened in Germany, South Africa, and the United States. The required time to reach break-even is three years in France. It is 12 to 16 months in Spain, and less than a year in South America and Taiwan. The hypermarkets Carrefour operates in Taiwan are rented. The company intends to use this strategy in its future Asian expansions, as well.[28]

Carrefour has been held up as the textbook example of a multinational company. A multinational company expands internationally, using a decentralized control system. Since 1994, however, Carrefour has been reversing this strategy, moving to centralize its operations. The major benefits of this reversal are in purchasing. By having a larger common product range, the company can centralize negotiation of purchasing terms to obtain better prices. Logistics are also enhanced with centralized control. More uniform product ranges result in cost savings that can lead to increased use of warehouses and loading platforms. This system is more productive than delivery directly to the stores. Centralization allows the company to use data-processing capabilities. This allows Carrefour to manage supplies and inventory, leading to "just in time" delivery and centralized payment of invoices.

Hard discount stores average about 600 square meters (6,500 square feet) with a very limited selection (600 items, compared with 5,000 SKU's for a typical French supermarket of 1,000 square meters (11,000 square feet)). These stores are under the level for regulation, so they have more freedom to open new stores. Leading hard discount chains in France are Lindl (Lindl of Germany), Erteco (Carrefour), CDM (Intermarché), Aldi (Aldi of Germany), Lemutant (Coop Normandie), and Leader Price (Baud/Beatrice Foods).

Surprisingly, a factory outlet center has opened in a northern suburb of Paris. The center is called Quai des Marques and has 36 outlets in a stripped-down setting. Merchandise is 30% lower than the usual price.[29]

GOVERNMENT REGULATIONS

RETAIL PLANNING France, like most European countries, has laws restricting large-scale retailers' expansion. These laws have made expansion in France difficult. The newest laws make domestic expansion almost impossible for large stores.

France has operated under the Loi Royer law since 1973. The original law covered retail developments of 1,500 square meters (16,146 square feet) or larger in towns with populations over 40,000 population, or 1,000 square meters (10,764 square feet) or larger in smaller cities. Predictably, there was a great deal of retail growth in stores falling just under the 1,000-square-meter size. The hard discount format in particular was growing especially rapidly.

French regulators amended the law in 1996 to lower the size requirement for which a permit is needed. Retailers must now get approval for proposed stores of 300 square meters (3,229 square feet). The new law, called Loi Raffarin, is viewed as an anti-hypermarket measure that appeals to small retail representatives. However, the law will also greatly affect foreign hard discounters and category killers, which pose a competitive threat to hypermarkets. Discounters had been adapting to the 1,000-square-meter limit and were increasing their numbers. The question now is, can they shrink below the 300-square-meter mark? The French hypermarkets may favor this law and view it as a protection from discounters.[30]

Despite the restrictive legislation related to opening hypermarkets and supermarkets in France, large-scale food retailers have grown rapidly during the past 20 years. This growth has been at the expense of traditional stores, such as neighborhood stores, department stores, and general stores. Hypermarkets and supermarkets have 58% of the food retailing business and more than 31% of the specialty retailing trade in France.[31] The restrictive legislation helps the large-scale businesses that are currently operating in France. Hypermarkets in France operate at a very large scale. This means that the start-up costs are very big. It takes between six and eight years for a store to break even when it is this large. This is a barrier to entry for newcomers.

The largest shopping center in Europe opened in France during 1996. The Grand Littoral center has 110,000 square meters (1,200,000 square feet). The center has 180 stores, 20 of them large stores. Continente, the French hypermarket, anchors the shopping center. Claiming 28,000 square meters (300,000 square feet), International retailers include Zara (Spain), Toys "R" Us (U.S.), The Disney Store (U.S.), and C&A (Germany).[32]

SALES AT A LOSS In 1997, I conducted a series of interviews in France. I was interested in retailer-supplier relationships. Several people mentioned that the 1997 French pricing law, called Loi Galland, was creating friction between French retailers and their suppliers. Spain has passed a similar law. Like planning laws that regulate the opening of large-scale retailers, I found that many European countries have laws regulating retail pricing and retail price reduction practices.

In some countries, there are no special regulations covering pricing. Denmark, Germany, Spain, Italy, the United Kingdom, and Sweden have quite liberal pricing laws. However, in other countries, **sales at a loss,** as the practice is called, are strictly prohibited. Sales at a loss does not mean the retailer actually sells the merchandise below cost. Instead, it refers to selling a product at invoice price. The invoice cost may not be the actual price to the retailer, however, because a retailer may receive year-end discounts due to volume or for special promotions that the retailer launches for the supplier. The director of France's major retail trade organization explained it to me using the following example:

Four Different Prices

1. *Base cost* (supplier's charge to retailer, or list price)	100
Discount, depending on purchasing terms (delivery or length of time before retailer must pay for merchandise)	−10
2. *Invoice price* (called net price)	90
Conditional discounts, including yearly volume discount	−5
3. *Net/net price*	85
Commercial cooperation costs (in store promotions, etc.)	−10
4. *Real purchasing costs*	75

The "net price" appears on the invoice sent by the supplier to the retailer. However, it may be that the net/net price including the yearly volume discount is really what retailer will pay for the merchandise. The retailer issues an invoice to charge the supplier with the commercial cooperation costs. Those expenses will be reimbursed. The real costs to the retailer for the products are the net/net price: the price after the retailer has received discounts for volume.[33] Laws such as France's Loi Gallard require that the retailer sell for the invoice price.

Because of this law, at least theoretically, the hypermarkets would need to increase the selling prices on very discounted items. This would reduce the price difference between hypermarkets and supermarkets and would make supermarkets more attractive. On the other hand, it could make margins higher across the board, thus hurting consumers. The measure is politically motivated, in part to protect small retailers and more specifically to reduce the attractiveness of the hard discounter food prices.

This law will also make development of private label products more attractive to retailers. Shortly after the law passed, manufacturers began to realize that the predictable response of retailers would be to go in the direction of private label.[34]

Belgium was the first to make it illegal for a trader to offer products at less than the cost at which the product is invoiced, or will be invoiced in the event of resupply. Certain exceptions are made for special sales such as end-of-season or going-out-of-business sales. Portugal's laws require that sale price of an item cannot be lower than the supplier's purchase price plus the tax on the sale.

Luxembourg's Article 20, another law regulating retail reductions, specifies certain exceptions that enable goods to be sold at lower than invoice price. Promotional prices other than seasonal and clearance sales are authorized when these conditions are met: (1) any advertisement of price reductions must clearly state the promotional nature of the offer, (2) the date from which the reduced price is applicable must continue to be shown throughout the period of the offer, and (3) reference may be made to former prices, provided the prices were applied previously on the same premises to identical products for a continuous period of at least two months immediately preceding the date from which the reduced price is applicable. Seasonal sales can occur only twice a year, at the beginning of the winter and summer seasons, and can only last one month at a maximum. Clearance sales are allowed only if a business is closing, moving, or has had an accident that damaged the merchandise.

Germany has a law similar to that of Luxembourg's. Retailers can only advertise sales twice a year, tied to the end of the selling season.

SUMMARY

Germany is best known as the home of hard discounters and a heavily concentrated department store sector. The most memorable event in the country's past two decades has been reunification. Reunification had a major impact on retailing in Germany. Almost immediately, it brought astronomical increases in sales for West German retailers located close to the former border. These sales were from the East Germans who came to spend money the they had hoarded for years, as they waited for the chance to purchase better quality goods. In the long term, unification has had important consequences for retailing. It opened a new country for West German retailers' expansion activities, just when expansion opportunities in West Germany appeared saturated. As a result, German retailers have not been particularly interested in expanding outside Germany. Once these growth opportunities slow, however, a sleek and efficient retail machine can be expected to move into eastern Europe, led by German retailers, armed with knowledge gained through opening up the former East German trade area.

French retailers also found expansion opportunities blocked within their home market. The answer for hypermarkets was to move south, primarily to Spain, but also to Portugal and Italy. France and the southern Mediterranean countries share a Latin-based culture, and the French view these countries as culturally similar to France.

KEY TERMS

oligopsony **sales at a loss**

DISCUSSION QUESTIONS

1. Discuss how Germany's "green laws" affect retailers. Do these laws make it easier or harder for retailers from other countries to enter the German market?
2. How are the German hard discount food retailers different from other food retailers in Europe? What cultural changes would need to take place to make the German hard discounting format attractive in the United Kingdom?
3. Why would the two largest department store groups in Germany acquire the next two largest retailers? What would you expect from an industry that has such a high degree of concentration?
4. Why do you think French hypermarkets have been so successful in southern parts of Europe, and even Mexico and South America, but not successful in northern parts of Europe or the United States?

ENDNOTES

1. "Germany." (1995). *Craighead's International Business, Travel, and Relocation Guide to More Than 80 Countries.* Detroit: Gale Research.
2. Karstadt Annual Report (1991).
3. Karstadt Annual Report (1991).
4. Coopers & Lybrand. (1996). *Global Powers of Retailing.* Chain Store Age—Special Report.
5. "Kaufhof—Company Report." (October 2, 1995). Oppenheim Finanzanalyse GMBH in *Investext* [Database on CD-ROM]. Foster City, Calif.: Information Access.
6. *Retail News Letter.* (1995). No. 425, June, p. 2.
7. *Retail News Letter.* (1991). No. 386.
8. Robinson, T. M., and C. Clarke-Hill (1990). "Directional Growth by European Retailers." *International Journal of Retail and Distribution Management,* Vol. 18, No. 5, pp. 3–14.
9. "Retailers: Germany—Industry Report." (March 6, 1996). BHF Trust in *Investext* [Database on CD-ROM]. Foster City, Calif.: Information Access.

10. "Retailers: Germany—Industry Report" (March 6, 1996), BHF Trust.
11. *Retail News Letter.* (1991). No. 378.
12. *Retail News Letter.* (1995). No. 425, June, p. 5.
13. Sternquist, B., and M. Kacker. (1994). *European Retailing's Vanishing Borders.* Westport, Conn.: Quorum Press.
14. *Retail News Letter.* (1997). No. 447, p. 7.
15. "Retailers: Germany—Industry Report" (March 6, 1996), BHF Trust.
16. *Retail News Letter.* (1995). No. 430, December, p. 7.
17. *Retail News Letter.* (1997). No. 442, p. 6.
18. "France." (1995). *Craighead's International Business, Travel, and Relocation Guide to More Than 80 Countries.* Detroit: Gale Research.
19. *The European Retail Handbook, 1997 Edition.* (1996). London: Corporate Intelligence on Retailing.
20. Coopers & Lybrand (1996).
21. Coopers & Lybrand (1996).
22. Galeries Lafayette—Company Report. (December 4, 1996). SBC Warburg in *Investext* [Database on CD-ROM]. Foster City, Calif.: Information Access.
23. "Europe: Blood on the Shelves." (1996). *Business Week International Editions: International Business—Europe,* Vol. 3462, February 12, p. 18.
24. "Carrefour—Company Report." (March 13, 1997). UBS Research in *Investext* [Database on CD-ROM]. Foster City, Calif.: Information Access.
25. *The European Retail Handbook, 1997 Edition.* (1996).
26. "Docks de France—Company Report." (April 24, 1995). Hoare Govett Securities in *Investext* [Database on CD-ROM]. Foster City, Calif.: Information Access.
27. "Promodès—Company Report." (March 31, 1995). EIFB in *Investext* [Database on CD-ROM]. Foster City, Calif.: Information Access.
28. "Carrefour—Company Report." (March 29, 1995). UBS Research in *Investext* [Database on CD-ROM]. Foster City, Calif.: Information Access.
29. *Retail News Letter.* (1995). No. 423, April, p. 8.
30. *Retail News Letter.* (1995). No. 432, February, p. 4.
31. Docks de France—Company Report (April 24, 1995). Hoare Govett Securities.
32. Jones Lang Wootten. (1996). *Retailing Planning Policies.* Oxford, England: Oxford Institute of Retail Management.
33. "Carrefour—Company Report" (March 13, 1997), UBS Research.
34. Sternquist, B. (1997), personal interviews, France, July.

PORTUGAL
Lisbon
Madrid
Barcelona
SPAIN
Milan
Rome
ITALY
GREECE
Athens

10

Retailing in Spain, Italy, Greece, and Portugal

After reading this chapter you will understand:

- How traditional retailers remain strong in these countries, and the changes that will need to take place before modern retail chains dominate.
- Why retailers from more developed countries and saturated markets are expanding aggressively into these areas.
- How retailers gain by using negative cash flow for expansion and be able to predict how this practice affects high growth versus low growth retailers.
- How restrictive laws affect retailing and the impact these laws have on consumers, local retailers, and foreign retailers.

SPAIN, ITALY, GREECE, AND PORTUGAL form the new Europe. Birth rates have declined throughout Europe, but the decline in population has been much slower in the south than in the north. This shift in population creates opportunities for retailers. Retailing in the Mediterranean and southern European countries is less developed than retailing in the rest of Europe. Most retailers in this part of Europe are mom and pop stores. Countries such as Spain and Italy have 26 stores per 1,000 inhabitants compared with France or the United Kingdom, with eight or nine per 1,000. Women are less likely to work outside the home in these regions. This has two effects: lack of dual earning capacity keeps household incomes low and women have more time to shop, making technological conveniences less important. Retail competition is just beginning to intensify, led by foreign retailers who are entering this region as their own countries become saturated. French retailers have followed this pattern, expanding aggressively into Spain.

SPAIN

COUNTRY BACKGROUND

Spain's history is one of repeated invasions. Celtic tribes came from the north. Phoenicians and Greeks arrived from the south. Romans incorporated "Hispania" into their empire. They introduced the Roman language, laws, and culture, and later Christianity. When the Roman Empire collapsed in the 5th century A.D., Germanic tribes plundered their way through Spain. Finally, the Moors from North Africa swept up through Spain conquering nearly the entire country. The Moors introduced Islam, and under their rule, a rich civilization arose. Cities were prosperous. The environment attracted brilliant writers and great philosophers. With Jews, Christians, and Moslems contributing, Spain became a center for arts and learning for all three cultures. This was in sharp contrast to the rest of Europe in the Middle Ages.

The Moslems gradually fell back in Spain as the strengthening Christian kingdoms of the north pressed forward. The Christians finally took Granada, at the southern tip of Spain, in 1492. That year also marks the beginning of Spain's expansion into the New World, with the voyage of Christopher Columbus, financed by the Spanish monarchs. The next century was Spain's "Golden Age." Its holdings in America produced great wealth. By the end of the century, however, the nation had exhausted itself with war and emigration of people and resources to the New World. Spanish supremacy had ended.

Spain fought a civil war in 1936 in which the fascists, led by Francisco Franco, defeated the Republican forces. It gave aid to the Axis powers during World War II, but did not declare itself part of the conflict. After several decades under Franco's rule, Spain's political system underwent a major change in the 1970s when the country passed a constitution that was approved by popular referendum and sanctioned by its king.[1]

Today, Spain belongs to the youth. It has the largest percentage of persons under the age of 25 in Europe. Many visitors from around the world visit Spain to experience its unique culture in one of the few remaining environments in Europe that is still affordable. Table 10.1 presents selected demographic and economic data for Spain.

Retailing in Spain follows a different pattern than that of northern Europe. Most stores close between 2:00 and 5:00 P.M. for lunch and the siesta hour. Shops do not open in the morning until 10:00 or 10:30 A.M. They stay open until 8:00 or 10:00 P.M. Nearly 40% of a retailer's sales are generated during the weekend. Sunday is just as important a shopping day as Saturday. The most popular time to shop is after 6:00 P.M. when 50% of sales take place. Restaurants do not open until 8:30 P.M. and do not begin to fill until 10:00 P.M. Prime time TV starts at 10:30 P.M.

Two years ago, my son accompanied me to Spain. He was a typical 15-year-old, always hungry. We ended up eating at a McDonald's-type fast-food outlet several evenings because he simply could not wait for the restaurants to open at 8:30. The few times he could last until the formal dinner hour, we were surprised to see families with young children dining out together, often at midnight.

Spain is one of the least saturated markets in Europe. Because of the potential consumer demand, it is viewed as one of the most attractive retail markets in Europe. Variety and chain stores have not yet developed in Spain, and there are no national chains. Wholesalers play an important role in distribution.

TABLE 10.1

Spain: Selected Demographic and Economic Data

	Population (millions) mid-1995	Area (thousands of sq. km)	GNP per capita: Dollars 1995	GNP per capita: Avg. ann. growth (%) 1985–95	PPP estimates of GNP per capita U.S. = 100: 1987	PPP estimates of GNP per capita U.S. = 100: 1995	Life expectancy at birth (years) 1995	Adult illiteracy (%) 1995
High-income economies	902.2t	32,039t	24,930w	1.9w			77w	
Spain	39.2	505	13,580	2.6	50.5	53.8	77	N/A

Source: World Bank (1997). PPP = purchasing power parity. N/A = not available. t = total. w = weighted average.

Spanish retailing has changed rapidly since the 1970s. The Spanish retail market skipped several predictable development stages to progress from outdated to ultramodern retail forms. This means the family food shop was replaced with the giant hypermarket without passing through the intervening stages of supermarket or variety store. A summary of the major domestic and foreign retailers is presented in Table 10.2

Several U.S. companies, such as Federated, Woolworth, and Sears, attempted to enter the Spanish market. They failed and were forced to leave. The biggest success story to date has been the entry of the French hypermarkets' into Spain. French hypermarkets are found throughout Spanish suburbs. During the 1960s, only one Spaniard in a hundred owned a car; now, about one in three has a car. This has contributed to hypermarket growth. Shoppers coming to the hypermarket purchase a volume of merchandise that cannot be transported without an automobile.

On my first visit to Spain, I took the train from Bordeaux, France, to Barcelona, Spain. As I crossed the border on the rim of the Pyrenees mountains, I was reminded of the barren American Southwest. The buildings, roads, and vegetation seemed to come right out of a Zane Grey novel. However, arrival in Barcelona brings the visitor right back to the present day. Barcelona is as sophisticated as any other great European city. The city hosted the Summer Olympics in 1992, and in preparing for this event cleaned up its shorefront and beautified its parks. Throughout the city, wide boulevards open onto lovely parks. Centrally located in Barcelona and in other major cities in Spain, El Corte Inglés is the country's stately department store chain.

Photo 10.1
El Corte Inglés is Spain's largest retailer. This store is one of several located in Mexico City. The stores are full-scale department stores, offering a complete range of hard and soft lines. *Courtesy of the author.*

TABLE 10.2

Major Spanish and Foreign Retailers in the Domestic Market, 1995–1996

Retailer	Operations	Sales (Ptas* billions)	Outlets (no.)
Euromadi & Vima (merged post-1995)	Food purchasing group	1,501.0	2,800
IFA Española	Food purchasing group	1,200.0	2,552
El Corte Inglés	Department stores and hypermarkets	1,093.0	70
Contisa Continente (Promodès France)	Grocery multiple	685.9	1,717
Pryca (Carrefour France)	Hypermarkets	543.4	50
Alcampo/Sabeco/Pan de Azúcar, etc. (Auchan France and Docks de France)	Grocery multiple	403.5	119
Eroski Grupo	Cooperative group	304.3	697
Mercadona	Large supermarkets	223.7	204
UDA-Acosa	Food purchasing group	159.2	4,259
Unagras	Food purchasing group	104.5	2,167
Zara Inditex	Clothing	102.0	370
Makro (SHV Makro Netherlands)	Cash-and-carries	100.4	14
CMD	Food purchasing group	79.9	474
Autoservicios Caprabo	Grocery multiple	68.0	65
Unigro Grupo (Unigro Netherlands)	Supermarkets and cash-and-carries	64.7	218
Simago (Dairy Farm Hong Kong)	Grocery multiple and discount food	60.0	116
Coaliment & Valvi (merged post-1995)	Grocery multiple and franchises	54.7	639
Fadesa-Expert (Expert Switzerland)	Electricals buying group	52.0	775
Superdiplo	Grocery multiple	52.0	68
Cortefiel	Clothing	51.7	350
Syp Grupo	Grocery multiple and cash and carries	50.0	127
Grupo Galicia	Grocery multiple	44.0	93
Enaco Grupo	Grocery multiple	41.0	116
Aldeasa	Duty-free and museum shops	40.4	60
Gallega de Distribuidores	Grocery multiple	39.1	330
Vegonsa	Supermarkets	38.0	81
Gestesa-Master	Electricals buying group	37.0	1,008
Densa-Tien	Electricals buying group	36.0	756
Segesa-Redder	Electricals buying group	32.0	128
Hilario Osoro	Supermarkets	32.0	110
Dinel Milar	Elecricals buying group	30.0	479
Toys "R" Us (U.S.)	Toy superstores	20.0	26

Continued

TABLE 10.2

Major Spanish and Foreign Retailers in the Domestic Market, 1995–1996

Retailer	Operations	Sales (Ptas billions)	Outlets (no.)
Circulo de Lectores (Bertelsmann Germany)	Mail-order	19.0	0
Distop (Carlo de Benedetti Italy)	Grocery multiple	18.5	115
C & A Modas (C & A Germany)	Clothing	15.1	27
MultiOpticas	Optical goods associated group	15.1	265
Venta Catálogo (Otto Versand Germany)	Mail-order	14.5	0
Benetton (Italy)	Clothing	13.7	300
Cadyssa	Drugstores	12.9	68
Hyper L (Leclerc France)	Hypermarkets	12.2	3
Lidl (Lidl Germany)	Discount food stores	11.0	90
General Optica (Dollond & Aitchison UK)	Optical goods	10.8	91
Marks & Spencer (UK)	Mixed goods and grocery	10.0	8
Intersport (Switzerland)	Sports goods buying group	9.1	140
Aki Bricolage (GIB Group Belgium)	DIY* superstores	7.5	3
Schlecker (Germany)	Drugstores	7.5	153
Décathlon (Auchan France)	Sports goods superstores	7.5	9
Alfaro (Caprabo/Ahold Netherlands)	Grocery multiple	7.4	11
Adolfo Dominguez	Clothing	7.3	80
Disclub	Mail-order	7.2	0
Comercial Atheneum	Booksellers	6.8	60
Estableciementos Miro	Electrical goods	6.7	18
Espasa Calpe	Booksellers	6.6	16
Leroy Merlin (Auchan France)	DIY superstores	6.5	9
Hiperpost Club del Libro	Mail-order	6.4	0
Mango (Isna Group)	Womenswear	6.4	130
Camper (Coflusa Group)	Footwear	6.4	18
Merca Plus (Comptoirs Modernes France)	Grocery multiple	6.3	11
Cristian Lay	Mail-order	6.0	0
Ivarte (International Semi-Tech Canada)	Electrical goods	6.0	88
FNAC (Pinault-Printemps France)	Media goods superstores	6.0	3
Radio Castilla	Electrical goods	5.8	3
Levi's Store (U.S.)	Clothing	5.6	111

TABLE 10.2

Major Spanish and Foreign Retailers in the Domestic Market, 1995–1996

Retailer	Operations	Sales (Ptas billions)	Outlets (no.)
Brico Hogar (Teka)	DIY superstores	5.0	9
Cione	Optical goods associated group	4.8	315
Merkameuble	Furniture and electrical goods	4.6	7
Galerias Tarragona	Furniture	4.6	48
Grupo Acevall	Electrical goods	4.4	1
Eugenio Pereda	Sanitary goods	4.3	5
Cadena	Mail-order	4.3	0
Virgin Megastores (UK)	Audio and video superstores	4.3	6
Visionlab y Ferri	Optical goods	4.2	24
Optica 2000	Optical goods	4.1	40
Cenor	Electrical goods	4.1	35
Foto Sistema	Photo goods	4.0	199
Eldisser	Electrical goods	4.0	6
Discoplay	Mail-order	4.0	0
Herbalife España (Herbalife USA)	Dietetic products	3.8	120
IKEA (Sweden)	Furniture and household goods	3.8	5
Hagalo (Bauhaus Germany)	DIY superstores	3.7	3
Alper	Drugstores	3.6	15
Ulloa Optica	Optical goods	3.5	31
Distribución Quelle (Quelle Germany)	Mail-order	3.2	0
Zannier (France)	Clothing	3.0	35
Vobis (Kaufhof Germany)	Computer goods	3.0	14
Farmashopping	Parapharmaceutical goods	2.8	150
Conrado Martin	Perfumery and cosmetics	2.7	12
Almacenes Sancho	Drugstores	2.6	12
Trigasa	Drugstores	2.6	26
Stefanel (Italy)	Clothing	2.5	50
Interdiscount (Distefora Switzerland)	Electrical goods	2.0	30
Coronel Tapiocca	Travel and leisure goods stores	2.0	45
The Body Shop (UK)	Personal and beauty products	2.0	60
Spaghetti	Clothing	1.9	38
Misco España	Mail-order	1.6	0
Jardiland	Garden centers	1.5	6
Bata (Canada)	Footwear	1.3	42

Continued

TABLE 10.2

Major Spanish and Foreign Retailers in the Domestic Market, 1995–1996

Retailer	Operations	Sales (Ptas billions)	Outlets (no.)
Kiara Bijoux	Jewelers	1.3	65
Nectar Beauty (UK)	Personal and beauty products	1.3	44
Oro Vivo	Jewelers	1.3	24
Hiperjoya	Jewelers	1.2	26
Reader's Digest Selecciones (Reader's Digest U.S.)	Mail-order	1.2	0
Complices (France)	Sportswear	1.1	10
Descamps (France)	Household textiles	1.0	42
ComputerLand (U.S.)	Computer goods stores	1.0	6
Buffetti	Office products	1.0	160
Roche Bobois (France)	Furniture	0.8	37
Mr Bricolage (ANPF France joint venture)	DIY superstore	0.8	1
Jacadi (France)	Clothing	0.7	36
C & J Clark (UK)	Footwear	0.7	6
Imaginarium	Educational toys stores	0.7	17
Phildar (France)	Woolen goods	0.7	212
Rodier (France)	Clothing	0.6	15
Kookaï (André France)	Clothing	0.5	12
Casa Santiveri	Natural cosmetics	N/A*	358
Yves Rocher (France)	Cosmetics and perfumery	N/A	178
Boutique de la Prensa (Hachette France)	News kiosks/bookshops	N/A	160
El Reco	Natural cosmetics	N/A	122
El Rastro del Deporte/Décimas	Sports goods	N/A	111
Prénatal (Chicco Artsana Italy)	Babywear	N/A	101
Fotoprix Barcelona	Photo goods and processing	N/A	91
ITM Iberica (Intermarché France)	Grocery multiple	N/A	30
Blockbuster (U.S.)	Video stores	N/A	21
Storehouse (UK)	General goods and maternitywear	N/A	11
Plus (Tengelmann Germany)	Discount food stores	N/A	10
Penny Market (Rewe Germany)	Discount food stores	N/A	10
JJB Sports (UK)	Sports goods stores	N/A	4
Radio Shack (Tandy U.S.)	Electrical goods	N/A	6
Conforama (Pinault-Printemps France)	Furniture superstores	N/A	2

Source: *The European Retail Handbook*, 1997 Edition. (1996). London: Corporate Intelligence on Retailing, pp. 262–264.
Ptas = pesetas; 1 Pta = U.S. $0.006. *DIY = do-it-yourself; N/A = not available.

NON-FOOD RETAILERS

DEPARTMENT STORES El Corte Inglés is the largest retailer in Spain. The company was founded in 1940 as a small clothing store. It now has 26 department stores and 12 hypermarkets. The company's stores are found in the main population centers. Until 1994, El Corte Inglés had a competitor, Galerias Preciados, with 31 department stores. El Corte Inglés acquired Galerias Preciados in late 1994. The groups had long been rivals. Galerias Preciados was the uncontested market leader until the 1960s, when the company was sold several times, tumbling each time further into decline.

When El Corte Inglés purchased Galerias, the company entered 13 new cities. El Corte Inglés has a hypermarket division, called Hipercore. In Madrid, there are four El Corte Inglés stores, three hypermarkets, and five Galerias. El Corte Inglés is interested in developing specialty formats. It has a toy store strategically positioned to compete with Toys "R" Us. El Corte Inglés is a private group and avoids publicity. The company uses a high degree of vertical integration and is a leader in retailing technology.[2] It also runs the Harris department store company in California.

Company Focus III.6 profiles the operations of El Corte Inglés. Department stores are the conveyers of culture within a country. In this focus section, you will see how El Corte Inglés, as the only remaining department store chain in Spain, engages in a variety of product innovation and extension strategies. The company is selling computers to the government and selling domestic appliances powered by gas to increase gas consumption.

SPECIALTY STORES AND VARIETY STORES There are several successful chains in Spain. Although none of these chains is truly *national*, they have considerable market presence. When I refer to a chain as being national, I mean that it has stores throughout the country, not just in specific regions. Cortefiel is a fashion retail group with 118 men's and women's stores. Cortefiel also has a group of men's leisurewear stores called Springfield. The company is quite aggressive in moving internationally. It has seven stores in Portugal, two in Germany, and plans to open 27 in France. Cortefiel also has a group of 11 stores that sell men's suits, four of which are in France. Cortefiel is the partner of Marks & Spencer in Spain, with stores in Madrid, Seville, and Valencia.[3]

Marks & Spencer gained early experience in the Spanish market by having shop-in-shop arrangements in two of the Galerias Preciados department stores. In a **shop-in-shop** arrangement, merchandise is sold in a type of commissioned sales area. Marks & Spencer would determine what merchandise would be offered for sale, would hire the sales employees, and would pay Galerias Preciados a percentage of the sales. Later, Marks & Spencer opened a 3,000 square meter (32,000 square feet) store in Madrid. The store has five floors of merchandise with a complete range of non-food merchandise and a 600 square meter (6,500 square feet) food department.

HYPERMARKETS The growth of hypermarkets in Spain has been slowing but still continues. Hypermarkets represent 33% of the total food sales in Spain. This is not as concentrated a market as in France, where hypermarkets represent 50% of the market share. Supermarkets have some advantages over hypermarkets in Spain. Only 35% of Spanish customers use their cars to go shopping. Therefore, the proximity of the supermarket over the hypermarket is important.

There are four major hypermarket groups in Spain. Three of the four are associated with French companies: Carrefour has Pryca, Promodès has Continente, and Auchan has Alcampo. The only non-French-based group is Hipercore, owned by El Corte Inglés. Pryca in Spain, like its parent Carrefour in France, has developed a series of private label lines. The Pryca label covers household lines such as food and cleaning supplies. The private label is nearly 10 years old, designed to offer brand name merchandise at lower prices. First-Line is Pryca's household appliances private label line. These products have total guarantees. Some household appliance lines have attained the status of national sales leaders. Pryca also offers a house brand of apparel, Diseno, emphasizing fashion appeal, which is something different for a hypermarket.

FOOD RETAILERS

Spaniards consume 76% of food purchases at home. The major meal in Spain is eaten at midday. Workers go home, have a big lunch and a nap. Most businesses close for two or three hours during the afternoon. However, as cities become more congested, and it takes longer to return to the home, and as women enter the work force, the at-home midday meal is declining. About 25% of the total family income is spent on food and beverage products. The biggest expenditure is for meat (25.6%).[4]

Photo 10.2
French hypermarkets and supermarkets have expanded into Spain. They helped introduce modern food retailing formats. This supermarket offers a variety of fresh and staple food products. *Courtesy of the author.*

Many of the consumers of food in Spain are foreigners. Spain is the world's leader in tourism. Spain has a population of 40 million. In 1995, the country was visited by 64 million tourists.

The food retailing and distribution system in Spain was dominated by traditional grocery stores. However, hypermarkets, supermarkets, and self-service stores have taken over the market. Eighty-four percent of all food products retailed in Spain are sold through these outlets. Food sales are distributed as follows: hypermarkets, 33%; supermarkets and self-services, 35.7%; discounters, 8%; traditional grocery stores, 23.3%; and other categories such as open markets, 12.4%.[5]

Foreign retailers expanded into Spain because there were few legislative restrictions on large-scale retail growth. However, the environment has changed somewhat in recent years, and government regulations are becoming an important consideration.

GOVERNMENT REGULATIONS

The Spanish parliament passed a law in 1996 reinforcing a temporary measure passed in 1993 that restricts the number of opening hours for retailers in Spain. Shops may open for 72 hours per week and can only be open eight Sundays or official holidays per year. The government restricts sales to two months a year. The law will remain in effect until 2001 to allow smaller retailers to modernize. Regions have some autonomy. For instance, in Madrid, large-scale retailers can open 14 Sundays or official holidays per year. In some provinces, stores cannot be open any Sundays or holidays.[6]

The government is also proposing a tax on large-selling units to promote the modernization of small-scale traditional retailing. Part of the plan is to encourage small shopkeepers to take early retirement at 55. They would be paid a stipend if they closed the business, rather than selling it. The money to pay this stipend would come from all retail units of more than 2,500 square meters (2,700 square feet). This proposal will affect about 400,000 jobs. There are 60,000 small independent retailers with 14% of the market. The 300 large units have 30% of the market.[7]

ITALY

COUNTRY BACKGROUND

According to legend, the city of Rome was founded by Romulus in 753 B.C. By the dawn of Christianity, the Roman Empire covered most of the known world, including Europe south of the Rhine and Danube rivers, Great Britain, Romania, the north coast of Africa, and the Middle East. Five centuries later, the empire was in decline. Like Spain, the history of Italy is also one of repeated invasions. Individual city-states flourished, but the Italian provinces did not form a united front until 1861. The relative recentness of the founding of the Italian state may explain why its people usually identify themselves by province first. "I am a Sicilian," or a Sardinian or a Lombard first, an Italian, second. Many people, although they speak Italian outside the home, still speak provincial dialects to family members.

Italy, under Mussolini and the Fascist Party, allied itself with Germany during World War II. The last king of Italy, Umberto II, abdicated in 1946 following a referendum on the question of whether the country should be a monarchy or republic. Despite frequent changes of government, Italy has enjoyed excellent growth in modern times. The country joined the European Community (EC) in 1957.[8] Table 10.3 presents selected demographic and economic data for Italy.

NON-FOOD RETAILERS

Italy has a variety of non-food retailers. Department stores, variety stores, and chains of independent stores have strength in regional locations. Northern Italy is one of the most developed and affluent areas in Europe. Yet it was only after the late 1980s that modern shopping centers and national multiples began to appear. The byzantine structure of Italian distribution has discouraged foreign retailers from entering the market. However, since the 1990s, the largest Italian groups have been seeking foreign participation in developing hypermarkets and superstores. The Italian firms' knowledge of the retail regulations has reduced the risks for these newcomers.[9] A summary of the major domestic and foreign retailers in Italy is presented in Table 10.4.

TABLE 10.3

Italy: Selected Demographic and Economic Data

	Population (millions) mid-1995	Area (thousands of sq. km)	GNP per capita: Dollars 1995	GNP per capita: Avg. ann. growth (%) 1985–95	PPP estimates of GNP per capita U.S. = 100: 1987	PPP estimates of GNP per capita U.S. = 100: 1995	Life expectancy at birth (years) 1995	Adult illiteracy (%) 1995
High-income economies	902.2t	32,039t	24,930w	1.9w			77w	
Italy	57.2	301	19,020	1.8	72.5	73.7	78	a

Source: World Bank (1997). a = less than 5%. PPP = purchasing power parity. t = total. w = weighted average.

TABLE 10.4

Major Italian and Foreign Retailers in the Domestic Market, 1995–1996

Retailer	Operations	Sales (L* billions)	Outlets (no.)
Crai	Wholesale-based buying group	18,000	7,100
Sicom (Conad & Sigma)	Cooperative buying group	12,592	8,029
Co-op Italia	Cooperative regionally based group	12,200	1,194
La Rinascente	Non-food and food stores	6,700	921
Benetton	Young fashion and grocery multiple	5,964	1,140
A & O Selex	Voluntary chain	5,570	1,487
Despar	Voluntary chain	5,060	2,227
VéGé	Voluntary chain	5,000	1,523
Sisa Supermercati	Cooperative buying group	4,500	688
Standa	Variety stores and non-food	4,322	805
C3 Gruppo	Voluntary chain	3,427	694
Sun Supermercati	Grocery multiple	3,409	238
Gruppo Pam	Grocery multiple	3,026	269
Esselunga	Supermarkets	2,826	81
Gea Gruppo	Voluntary chain	2,500	1,420
Finiper	Hypermarkets	2,200	15
Italmec	Voluntary chain	2,157	1,018
Metro (Germany)	Cash-and-carries and discount food	2,143	45
Promodès (France)	Grocery multiple	2,102	228
Unvo	Voluntary chain	2,000	1,208
Gruppo Coin	Department and clothing stores	1,800	213
GET	Electricals buying group	1,160	368
Serta Expert (Expert Switzerland)	Electricals buying group	1,000	300
Lidl (Germany)	Discount food stores	990	140
GRE Idea	Electricals cooperative	700	350
Ecoitalia	Electricals cooperative	600	478
Postalmarket etc (Otto Versand Germany)	Mail-order	552	0
Spar (Austria)	Grocery multiple	550	435
Auchan (France)	Hypermarkets	500	4
Mercatone Uno Service	Furniture and household goods	449	28
ITM Italia (France)	Supermarkets	400	7
Stefanel	Young fashion	325	900
Bernardi	Clothing and textiles	291	137

Continued

TABLE 10.4

Major Italian and Foreign Retailers in the Domestic Market, 1995–1996

Retailer	Operations	Sales (L billions)	Outlets (no.)
Vestro Italia (La Redoute France)	Mail-order	272	0
Vobis (Kaufhof Germany)	Computer goods	230	30
Citta Convenienza	Furniture and household goods	215	8
Compar Bata (Bata Canada)	Footwear	211	180
Intersport Italia (Intersport Switzerland)	Sports goods buying group	201	166
C & A (Germany)	Clothing and textiles	200	20
Oleificio Fratelli	Mail-order	170	0
Max Mara	Womenswear	160	69
Computer Discount	Computer goods	154	64
Comet	Electrical goods	150	11
Superhobby/Mister Brico (Tengelmann Germany)	DIY* superstores	150	24
Media World (Kaufhof Germany)	Audio and video superstores	139	5
Ricordi	Audio and video stores	120	3
CDE Club (Mondadori)	Mail-order	118	0
Butali	Clothing and textiles	115	19

Source: *The European Retail Handbook, 1997 Edition.* (1996). London: *Corporate Intelligence on Retailing,* pp. 171–172.

L = Italian lira; 1 L = U.S. $.0.0005. *DIY = do-it-yourself.

Italy has a declining birth rate and a rising age profile, which reduces the demand for clothing and leisure-related products. As a result, Italian clothing chains such as Benetton and Stefanel have had to expand outside the country. They are also exploring the older age groups.

DEPARTMENT STORES There are only two department store chains in Italy: La Rinascente (13 stores) and Coin (35 stores). Analysts often say that the department store industry is in decline. However, La Rinascente manages to have good operating margins of just under 5%. This is much better than France's Printemps or Galeries Lafayette and Germany's Karstadt and Kaufhof chains. La Rinascente has developed a niche as a quality, value-for-money player.

La Rinascente is Italy's largest and most diversified retail company. Its largest department store is in Piazza Duomo, Milan. This store accounts for 9% of the company's total sales. Forty-three percent of total sales are in food, and 57% are in non-food. When J. C. Penney departed from Italy, the company sold its chain of stores to La Rinascente.

Thirteen percent of sales for La Rinascente are private label. The gross margin on private label is 25%, compared with 15% margin on national brands and 17% on premier brands. Hard discounters entering the market will increase the growth of the premier brand market and may force La Rinascente to follow suit to remain competitive. La Rinascente advertises a low price for national brands. Advertising a price for private label and premier brands is not effective because these labels do not have a universal comparison.[10]

The acquisition strategy used by La Rinascente benefits the company by (1) instantly increasing market share in the more mature supermarket sector without adding to industry capacity, (2) bypassing planning hurdles, (3) completing national coverage, and (4) improving the company's purchasing power.[11] The company generates 90% of its operating profit and 68% of its sales from food.

Italy has five major chain stores: La Rinascente, Standa, Essalunga, Pam, and GS. La Rinascente and Standa sell both food and non-food. La

Photo 10.3
The Galleria is a dome-covered shopping center in Milan, Italy. This center is in the heart of Milan, sharing the square with the major cathedral. *Courtesy of WWD.*

Rinascente also operates department stores, variety stores, supermarkets, hypermarkets, do-it-yourself (DIY), furniture, and appliance stores. Variety stores, supermarkets, and hypermarkets are part of the Standa company. Esselunga, Pam, and GS—the other three chains—are supermarkets.

VARIETY STORES Variety stores throughout Europe have lost market share for the past 15 years. Competition from hypermarkets has been a major hit. Upim, La Rinascente's variety store outlet, reduced its prices in an attempt to compete with hypermarkets. However, it was not successful. Management is now seeking to take advantage of Upim's premier high street locations by repositioning the retailer in a higher market segment. This position will be between hypermarkets and department stores. This strategy will do two things. It will help to protect pricing through a higher quality/value mix, and it will reduce direct confrontation with hypermarkets. The upgrading plans call for Upim to improve presentation and new store layouts, and to increase the share of apparel in the product mix from 50 to 60%.[12]

La Rinascente has centralized all product flow except hanging goods. Under the new system, the company will centrally distribute 60% of Upim's products. This restructuring will not substantially reduce cost, but it will increase purchasing efficiencies and lower stock-holding time.

Upim has franchised outlets, but these outlets will not be required to undergo the same remodeling or merchandising mix changes. Goods for the franchisees will be delivered from the new centralized warehouse, but reordering will not be online. Orders will continue to pass through the La Rinascente head office and be processed by category managers.

NATIONAL CHAINS Benetton is the best-known Italian chain, with operations in more than 100 countries. Its sales are primarily in franchised outlets. The company begins its expansion into a new country by manufacturing in the target country and licensing a local entrepreneur to operate a test outlet. If the results are satisfactory, Benetton will create a 50:50 joint venture with the licensee to increase capacity and establish a production pattern. Benetton's strategy consists of limiting owned fixed assets and maintaining in-house control of the crucial stages of production, such as cutting, dying, and quality control. Benetton's expansion is based on subcontracting. Seventy percent of production is done in Italian cottage industries, where labor costs are lower.

Benetton does not charge a franchisee fee. The company's profits come strictly from sale of the products. The company produces two collections each year, about 1,500 styles in 40 colors. Color is very important to Benetton's success but is very dependent on fashion trends. Benetton has reduced its risk by developing a special dying system. The finished products are dyed, not the fabric. This allows the company to customize colors by country. Benetton has expanded into hypermarkets and supermarkets with the purchase of Euromercato hypermarkets and GS supermarkets.

HYPERMARKETS Italy has one of the most fragmented retail sectors in Europe. This provides unparalleled growth opportunities for retailers who can consolidate existing supermarket capacity and develop the hypermarket and DIY sectors. Hypermarkets have significant growth potential in Italy. In terms of hypermarkets per population, Italy lags behind every major European country. Even if the number of hypermarkets were to double in Italy, the density ratio per million inhabitants would be about the same as that of Spain today. La Rinascente has the greatest market share in hypermarket and home improvement outlets.

Some aspects of the Italian market are much like the Spanish market. La Rinascente's closest competitors are the Spanish hypermarkets Pryca and Continente and their French parents, Carrefour and Promodès. Immature retail markets characterize both the Spanish and Italian markets. Expansion opportunities are available through hypermarkets and commercial centers, extended supplier credit days, and financing by negative working capital.

Over half of La Rinascente's hypermarket sales comes through its Carta Club card. This card gives members a discounted price list on several lines. The supplier pays the price difference. It works similarly to manufacturers' coupons. The card increases repeat retail business and strengthens relationships between La Rinascente and its suppliers. Suppliers can monitor and stimulate the demand for their products. French retailers believe that providing this information could lead to direct supplier marketing of new products to customers. This is misguided. Working with suppliers leads to stronger sales figures and more accurate stock planning.

Non-food in hypermarkets accounts for about 33% of sales. This is expected to increase to 42% by 2005. As a result, hypermarkets should represent 10% of non-food sales by 2005. In France, non-food represents more than 40% of hypermarket sales.

La Rinascente operates 22 hypermarkets under the name of Citta Mercato and more than 120 supermarkets known as Sma. The company is also opening a new format of small hypermarkets trading as Cityper that will open in medium or large towns.[13]

FOOD RETAILERS

The combined shares of the modern hypermarket, supermarket, and hard discount industries account for only 33% of the Italian food retailing market. That means that 67% of all food retailing comes from traditional markets. In perishable food, the small shopkeepers have 78% market share, but only 50% for packaged groceries. Spain and Portugal have similar figures for traditional retail. In food retail, analysts expect that hypermarkets and hard discounters will have the greatest growth. Their respective market shares should grow from 4.7% and 2.4% to 7% and 8% by 2000.[14] Modern retailing in Italy has a 50% market share of packaged groceries, but this is expected to increase to 75% by 2005 as the number of hypermarkets and hard discounters increases. This share is, however, much lower than that of France and the United Kingdom, where 74% and 89% of grocery sales, respectively, are accounted for by modern retail formats.

The largest retail group in Italy is Crai, a cooperative, wholesale-based buying group. This is a very loose buying group, controlling just a small part of the sales of its members' stores. The group does not have much power with respect to suppliers or consumers. Sicom, a cooperative buying group that combines Conad and Sigma, is listed as the second largest retailer in Table 10.4. If sales for Conad and Sigma were listed separately, however, the leading food retailer would be Co-op Italia, a cooperative regionally based group. A & O Selex, Despar, and VéGé are voluntary chains, although most of their members are becoming regional chains.

The food markets in central and southern Italy are not saturated. There are very few hypermarkets, large-scale supermarkets, and discount stores. There are no warehouse club formats in this area.

The type of acquisition activity that is occurring in Italy today is worth noting. Small traditional retailers that cannot afford the trade-off between volume and margin are losing market share and either closing or becoming the target of acquisition. Companies such as Migliarini overextended themselves by making acquisitions. Migliarini, and others like it, have used interest-free debt capital (suppliers' credit) as a source of acquisition funding.[15]

When companies form part of large independent buying groups, such as Végé, they start to realize that buying large volume is not that helpful unless they combine the purchasing function with an electronic data interchange (EDI) system. Until and unless they have both the volume and the electronic data capture, they will be left behind by the modern retailers entering the industry. Likewise, unless the independent stores commit to modern retail formats they will not be competitive. In France, Intermarché and Leclerc found their members increasingly being attracted to the international buying power and tighter supply chains being offered by the multiples. It is likely that the erosion in Italy will be even faster than it was in France, since the store concepts of the Italian independents are more outmoded.

Negative working capital provides operating funds only if a company grows. In Italy, accounts are given 100 days to pay so the use of the negative working capital is very important. Using negative working capital in this way inflates the stock position while absolute levels of borrowed cash owed to suppliers decreases, creating a reversal of the negative working capital advantage. This situation causes smaller, overexpanded retailers to fund part of their acquisition buy-out and their daily working capital commitment through interest-accruing bank finance. The result is a rapid deterioration of earnings and cash flow (Table 10.5).

Large retailers such as Pryca and Continente in Spain are also using negative working capital. However, these companies are rapidly expanding. Their aggressive store opening programs drive sales. These companies also have state-of-the-art information transfer systems that decrease stock-holding times and provide efficient retailer response to nonperforming product lines.[16]

TABLE 10.5

Days Cash Cycle (1993–1994) Among Southern European Retailers

Retailer	Country	Days Cash Cycle
Centros Commerciales Continente	Spain	−96.3
La Rinascente	Italy	−83.5
Hypercor	Spain	−65.6
Alcampo	Spain	−65.2
Pão de Acúcar	Portugal	−62.6
Standa	Italy	−58.8
Meridionale Finanziaria	Italy	−54.5
Prénatal	Italy	−27.1
Simago	Spain	−19.3
Galerias Preciados	Spain	7.7
Centros Commerciales Pryca	Spain	26.7
El Corte Inglés	Spain	81.1
Stefanel	Italy	116.9
Benetton Group	Italy	156.6

Source: "Rinascente—Company Report." (December 11, 1950.) Lehman Brothers Limited in *Investext* [Database on CD-ROM]. Foster City, Calif.: Information Access.

TABLE 10.6

Return on Assets of European Food Retailers

Retailer	1994	1995E*	1996E*
Carrefour	9%	10%	12%
Casino	8%	9%	10%
Colruyt	28%	26%	28%
Continente	45%	33%	49%
Promodès	33%	34%	40%
Pryca	52%	41%	44%
La Rinascente	27%	18%	19%

Source: "Rinascente—Company Report." (December 11, 1995). Lehman Brothers Limited in *Investext* [Database on CD-ROM]. Foster City, Calif.: Information Access.

*E = estimates.

Table 10.6 summarizes the return on assets for several European food retailers. The Spanish and French retailers have proven that an investment in information technology and a tighter logistics chain can enable them to control suppliers and maximize their profits. They do this by trading off the best financial returns to be earned either through cash owed to suppliers (in periods of high interest rates) or through rebates used to bolster gross margin and operating cash flow to the detriment of lower financial returns (in periods of lower interest rates). The Spanish retailers have discovered that putting cash flow gains back into the business provides the best return on capital (operating or negative working capital).

La Rinascente is more cautious and refuses to invest suppliers' cash into expanding the business. The company uses operating cash flows to fund expansion. Using negative capital for aggressive expansion is risky. The La Rinascente group has low yielding assets in the non-food sector. It could use the negative capital to expand its food retailing activities. Food retailing represents 90% of the group's pretax profit compared with 68% of sales.[17]

Although other retailers such as French-based Carrefour are becoming more centralized, La Rinascente is moving to decentralize the power of its head office and impose a less centralized structure. This action will give individual hypermarket managers more autonomy.

Hard discount is the fastest growing retail format in Italy. It is likely that as traditional shopkeepers become caught in price competition, they will view hard discount as an alternative and will reconfigure their existing stores into hard discounters. This strategy is bound to fail, however, because the hard discount success formula is based on volume and economies of scale to compensate for the low margin.

GOVERNMENT REGULATIONS

Italian retail legislation makes the process of opening a new store arduous. The government designed Law 426/71 to protect the interest of small retailers. Under this law, municipalities create a plan for the development of retailing within a community, deciding the amount of sales area needed to serve consumers for each product category. The law does not limit the number of stores in a particular format, for example, department stores or specialty stores. Instead, limitations are imposed based on the product they sell. The products list contains 14 product categories, such as fish stores, book stores, and gift stores. New shops can only be opened if there is a shop space available according to the retail master plan in the area where the store is to be opened. Although changing the master plan is possible, it requires much lobbying.[18]

Retail owners must also learn about running a business and the products they will sell. An owner of a gift shop in Florence explained how the system works. She told me that someone who wants to open a retail store must take a training program and a qualifying certification examination. The examination will have information about business operations and specific details related to the product the retailer will sell. This gift shop owner sells handblown glass, silverware, and crystal. Her qualifying examination would cover these product areas, making sure that she knows product-specific information she can pass on to her customers. She was very surprised that in the United States, you could just decide to open a business, or decide to sell one product one day and another product the next day. Her store had opened in space that had not had a store in it before, so gaining approval was not so difficult. The only other gift store in the area was about five blocks away and was currently closed for several weeks to allow the employees to take their summer vacation. When the gift shop owner's competitors returned from summer vacation, the gift shop owner would close her shop and she and her employees would go on vacation. Time off for vacations is mandated by the government.

Franchise opportunities in Italy generally are limited to sites that currently offer the same product. For instance, a Moto Photo film processing franchise would locate in a space previously operated by an independent film processing store. Most franchisees opening in Italy are opened by experienced business people who view the franchise as an opportunity to gain economies of scale in purchasing and a national advertising campaign.

Franchising has been increasing at a rapid rate. In 1995, Italy had 436 franchisers affiliated with 21,930 franchisees, the largest number in Europe. About 15% of all retail trade in Italy is conducted by franchise trade. Smaller American franchisers have been scrambling to find Italian master licensees. They have not been very successful due to their limited name recognition and inexperience with local business practices. The price they charge for the master license is usually too high, and the assistance they can provide is usually not sufficient for licensees to be interested. Another hindering factor is that in Italy, a separate business license is needed for each outlet. This is difficult to acquire because the franchise will be competing with small independent and local retailers.

In the United States, franchisees pay an up-front fee to the franchiser, and the franchisee pays a continuing franchise fee that is a percentage of the franchisee's sales. Neither of these business practices is commonly used in Italy. The franchiser makes its income from sale of products to the franchisee.[19] This is the system I described earlier for Benetton.

Italians had a chance recently to liberalize the legislation covering retailers. One proposal sought to abolish the licensing system for new store openings. Any new retail opening has to gain approval from the local government. The local government generally follows the advice of established retailers in the area. Hence, licenses are difficult to obtain. The second proposal sought to abolish the regulated opening hours.[20] Sixty percent of the voters voted no to both proposals.

GREECE

COUNTRY BACKGROUND

Greece is the birthplace of Western civilization. The ancient Greeks developed the ideas of justice, liberty, and law that serve as the basis for Western society. Following the collapse of the Roman Empire, Greece continued to play an important role as a center of the Byzantine Empire. When the Turks captured Istanbul in 1453, Greece became a province of the Ottoman Empire. In 1821, Greece began a war of independence, which became a popular cause for the best minds of the Romantic Age of Europe. Independence came in 1827.

Greece sided with the Allies in World War II. The country was invaded by Italy in 1940 and occupied by Germany in 1941. Greece emerged from the war with several possessions given to it by Italy. After the war, pro-Western forces and communists fought a bitter and bloody civil war. It lasted until 1949, when Greece emerged as a democracy.[21] Table 10.7 presents selected demographic and economic data for Greece.

Greece's retail industry is much like that of southern Italy and Portugal. Consumers have low purchasing power, there is an underdeveloped transportation infrastructure, and large-scale retailers are almost nonexistent. Greece has more retail outlets per capita than any other EC country and a greater absolute number than Britain, which has five times the population. Similar to outlets in Italy, the average store employs fewer than two employees. Greece has less than 50 people per square kilometer, compared with the European average of 151. Retail activity is concentrated in major urban

TABLE 10.7

Greece: Selected Demographic and Economic Data

	Population (millions) mid-1995	Area (thousands of sq. km)	GNP per capita: Dollars 1995	GNP per capita: Avg. ann. growth (%) 1985–95	PPP estimates of GNP per capita U.S. = 100: 1987	PPP estimates of GNP per capita U.S. = 100: 1995	Life expectancy at birth (years) 1995	Adult illiteracy (%) 1995
Upper-middle-income economies	438.3t	20,514t	4,260w	0.2w			69w	14w
Greece	10.5	132	8,210	1.3	44.2	43.4	78	

Source: World Bank (1997). PPP = purchasing power parity. t = total. w = weighted average.

centers. The infrastructure needed to support modern retail systems is not present. **Infrastructure** refers to roads, railways, electrical power, and communications equipment.

There are many infrastructure problems, primarily in the transport area. Moving people or merchandise from one area to another is difficult. In Greece, the average travel time needed to reach a major economic center is more than six hours, compared to the European Union (EU) average of four hours. Goods are transported almost exclusively by independent trucking companies.

The major retailers in Greece are listed in Table 10.8.

DEPARTMENT STORES

What department stores Greece has are in Athens. The largest are Minion, Lambropoulous Brothers, Dragonas, and Athenee. Marinopoulos operates a franchisee store of Marks & Spencer. Marinopoulos supplies the capital for the stores, and Marks & Spencer provides the managerial expertise and merchandise.

An impressive shopping center recently opened in Larissa, Thessaly. It is 100,000 square meters (1,080,000 square feet) in size, and includes car parking for 1,200 cars. A Continente hypermarket anchors the center, which has 15 other stores, including Bhs (Storehouse of the United Kingdom in cooperation with Klaoudatos), Marks & Spencer (with Marinopoulos), and Minion, a large department store in downtown Athens. Continente hypermarkets are joint ventures between Marinopoulos and Promodès of France.[22]

FOOD RETAILERS

Fresh products such as vegetables, fruits, fish, and livestock are accumulated in the areas where they are grown by agricultural cooperatives. Some products are consumed locally; the rest are sold to wholesale resellers. The products are transported by road, daily, to the central markets of urban areas. Small and medium transport companies operate the limited number of trucks. The central markets act as major distribution centers for the urban areas and surrounding rural areas. The products are then sold to consumers by local shops.

Supermarket chains buy directly from the central markets and then operate central warehouses to redistribute the products using their own trucking fleet. The central markets do not have modern information systems. Therefore, they cannot monitor inventory accurately. Procurement and distribution are not coordinated, resulting in a great deal of spoilage. Shortages occur unpredictably.

Processed and frozen foods are imported or produced by one of the few modern food companies. These companies generally have central warehousing facilities, which might be fully automated, and operate their own truck

TABLE 10.8

Major Greek and Foreign Retailers in the Domestic Market, 1995–1996

Retailer	Operations	Sales (Dr* billions)	Outlets (no.)
Marinopoulos/Promodès	Grocery and non-food	260.0	135
Elomas	Wholesale food group	132.0	141
Veropoulos Bros	Grocery	130.0	110
Atlantik	Grocery	103.0	45
Sklavenitis	Grocery	100.0	28
Alfa Beta (Delhaize "le Lion")	Grocery	81.6	21
Makro (SHV Makro Netherlands)	Cash-and-carries	75.3	3
Metro	Cash-and-carries and supermarkets	70.0	34
Trofo/ENA	Grocery	67.0	26
Katanalotis Co-op	Grocery cooperative	42.0	135
Massoutis	Grocery	40.0	31
Hellenic Duty Free	Duty-free shops	37.0	28
Pente	Grocery	33.8	42
Tresko	Grocery	25.0	15
Praktiker (Asko Germany)	DIY superstores	23.1	6
Gagoutis	Grocery	12.5	39
Minion	Department stores	11.6	2
Lambropoulos Bros	Department stores	10.0	3
Claoudatos	Department stores and sports goods	5.7	10
Diamantis	Department stores and household goods	5.2	7
Meimarides	Department stores and household goods	5.1	8
Götzen (Germany)	DIY* superstores	4.1	2
Tsitsopoulos	General goods stores	3.3	4
Radio Athinai	Audio and video goods	2.8	7
Hyperemporoki	Department stores	1.3	2
Zazopoulos	Electrical and household goods	1.3	3
Moustakis	Department store	0.9	1
Pappos	Department store	0.9	1
Silber (Electronic Partner Germany)	Electricals buying group	N/A*	80
The Body Shop (UK)	Personal and beauty products	N/A	47
Benetton (Italy)	Clothing	N/A	20
Storehouse (UK)	Clothing, household, and maternity goods	N/A	19
Lidl (Germany)	Discount food stores	N/A	2
Virgin Megastores (UK)	Audio and entertainment goods	N/A	1
Habitat (IKEA Sweden)	Furniture and household goods	N/A	1

Source: *The European Retail Handbook, 1997 Edition.* (1996). London: Corporate Intelligence on Retailing, pp. 133–134.

*Dr = Greek drachmas; 1 Dr = U.S. $0.003. DIY = do-it-yourself; N/A = not available;

fleets. Sometimes, advanced technology, such as on-vehicle terminals for data collection and EDI, is used.[23]

The leading supermarket group in Greece is Veropoulos. It operates 92 stores throughout the country. The company intends to expand the range of private labels. Private labels now represent 7% of group sales. The goal is to increase the private label percentage to 15%.[24]

Alfa Beta Vassilopoulos operates 21 stores in Greece. Profit increased 25% in 1995. Delhaize "le Lion" of Belgium owns 49% of the capital in Alfa-Beta Vassilopoulos.[25]

Portugal is the final country discussed in this chapter. Greece and Portugal share some retail characteristics. They are both very undeveloped, without strong department store competition, few modern retailers, and an infrastructure that restricts the movement of people and goods.

PORTUGAL

COUNTRY BACKGROUND

Celts were the original inhabitants of Portugal, which was subsequently invaded and ruled by Romans, Germanic tribes, and Moors from North Africa. Portugal was liberated from the Moors during the 12th and 13th centuries, becoming a Christian kingdom. It gained independence from Spain in the late 14th century.

The early success of Portugal was tied to the sea. One of the country's explorers, Vasco da Gama, was the first to round the Cape of Good Hope. He became the first European to visit India. Portugal established colonies in the Canary Islands, the Azores, Brazil, and Ceylon. But between 1580 and 1640, Spain retook Portugal, claiming its empire of colonies.[26]

The Portuguese population is concentrated on the coast. The major retail centers are Lisbon, in the south, and Oporto, in the north. The Lisbon region accounts for 21% of Portugal's population. More than 60% of Portuguese are employed in service industries. Lisbon has the highest purchasing power in the country. Metropolitan areas suffer from congestion and rising costs. Oporto is the industrial development area in Portugal. It has 16% of the population and is an area of high purchasing power. The two major cities, Lisbon and Oporto are connected by a new highway. Most of the Portuguese industries and people are between these two cities. Table 10.9 presents selected demographic and economic data for Portugal.

Portugal joined the EC in January 1993. As a requirement for membership in the EC, the country had to eliminate trade barriers with other EC countries. Agricultural imports surged in from other EC countries.

TABLE 10.9

Portugal: Selected Demographic and Economic Data

	Population (millions) mid-1995	Area (thousands of sq. km)	GNP per capita		PPP estimates of GNP per capita U.S. = 100		Life expectancy at birth (years) 1995	Adult illiteracy (%) 1995
			Dollars 1995	Avg. ann. growth (%) 1985–95	1987	1995		
High-income economies	902.2t	32,039t	24,930w	1.9w			77w	14w
Portugal	9.9	92	9,740	3.6	41.6	47.0	75	

Source: World Bank (1997). PPP = purchasing power parity. t = total. w = weighted average.

Subsequently, foreign price competition in fresh fruits and vegetables, from Spain, France, and Holland has led to closure of Portuguese fruit and vegetable producers.

RETAILING IN PORTUGAL

The major retailers in Portugal are listed in Table 10.10. The sales leader is Sonae, the retail group that operates Modelo Continente hypermarkets with Promodès (France) and Sonae fascias (Champion) superstores and cash-and-carries. Sonae also operates Dia, a discount food store.

Jerónimo Martins group, the second largest food retailer, operates Feira Nova hypermarkets with Ahold of the Netherlands, and Pingo Doce, a supermarket chain, also with Ahold. Recheio, a cash and carry operation, is also a part of Jerónimo Martins. The third largest food group is Pão de Acúcar, operated by Auchan of France. This group includes Jumbo, a hypermarket and supermarket group, Minipreco, a discount food retailer, and Extra, a convenience store.

Portuguese retailers generally make purchases from brokers, distributors, cash-and-carry stores, traditional wholesalers, or from retailers' associations and cooperatives. Traditional wholesalers account for nearly 40% of purchases by retailers. Retailers' associations, including cooperatives, account for 11% of retailers' purchases. Retailers' associations are formed by small store owners. The associations help to increase purchasing power. They also provide trade courses and seminars.

TABLE 10.10

Major Portuguese and Foreign Retailers in the Domestic Market, 1995–1996

Retailer	Operations	Sales (Esc billions)	Outlets (no.)
Sonae Group (joint venture with Promodès France)	Grocery multiple and non-food	268.1	147
Jerónimo Martins	Grocery multiple and wholesale	264.3	130
Pão de Acúcar (Auchan France)[a]	Grocery multiple	197.0	150
Uniarme	Food cooperative	146.0	108
Makro (Netherlands)	Cash-and-carries	115.3	6
Ucrepa	Food cooperative	91.4	12,500
Carrefour (France)	Hypermarkets	51.3	2
Grula	Food cooperative	37.0	1,725
Agora Ino	Grocery multiple	27.4	68
Cooperatrres	Food cooperative	12.5	320
Zara Inditex (Spain)	Clothing	12.0	72
A Luta	Food cooperative	6.6	500
AC Santos	Grocery multiple	5.7	19
Carpan	Food cooperative	5.2	600
Pluricoop	Food cooperative	4.9	480
Venda Por Catalogo (Otto Versand Germany)	Mail-order	3.6	0
Toys "R" Us (U.S.)	Toy superstores	3.5	3
Eduardo Martins	Department stores	3.0	4
Aki Bricodis (GIB Group Belgium)	DIY superstores	2.5	3
Bras e Bras	Household goods superstores	2.5	4
Costa e Filhos	Clothing superstores	2.4	4
Americana	Booksellers and stationers	1.9	70
Eschola Directa (Quelle Germany and Sonae joint venture)	Mail-order	1.8	0
Hipermovel	Furniture superstore	1.7	1
Mestre maco	DIY superstores	0.9	3
Benetton (Italy)	Clothing	N/A	50
Feta-Moda	Clothing	N/A	33
Maconde Confeccas	Clothing	N/A	30
Livraria Barateira	Booksellers	N/A	30
Cenoura Lojas	Childrenswear	N/A	30
Lidl (Germany)	Discount food stores	N/A	28

Continued

TABLE 10.10

Major Portuguese and Foreign Retailers in the Domestic Market, 1995–1996

Retailer	Operations	Sales (Esc billions)	Outlets (no.)
Cortefiel (Spain)	Clothing	N/A	27
ITM Intermarché (France)	Supermarkets	N/A	49
El Corte Inglés (Spain)	Clothing and department stores	N/A	10
Tito Cunha	Household goods	N/A	8
Marks & Spencer (UK)	Clothing and mixed goods	N/A	5
Leclerc (France)	Large supermarkets	N/A	5
Habitat (IKEA Sweden)	Furniture and household goods	N/A	3
Mr Bricolage (ANPF France)	DIY superstores	N/A	2
MaxMat (Sonae joint venture with CRH Group of Ireland)	DIY superstore	N/A	1
Conforama (Pinault-Printemps France)	Furniture superstore	N/A	1

[a]Pão de Acúcar was acquired by Auchan (France) in 1996.

Source: *The European Retail Handbook, 1997 Edition.* (1996). London: Corporate Intelligence on Retailing, p. 235.

°Esc = Portuguese escudos; 1 Esc = U.S. $0.005; DIY = do-it-yourself; N/A = not available.

Traditional retail food stores account for more than 40% of Portugal's total retail sales. These retailers are consolidating, and foreign firms are taking market share. By the year 2000, it is estimated that they will have only 20% of sales. On the other hand, hypermarkets and supermarkets, which now account for 35% of all food sold in Portugal, will expand. Discount and cash-and-carry stores are also projected to increase in importance. Most large distribution groups are joint ventures between Portuguese and French companies. These companies have great purchasing power.[27]

GOVERNMENT REGULATIONS

Portugal has passed a law extending store opening hours, allowing stores to open from 6:00 A.M. to midnight on weekdays and Saturdays, and from 8:00 A.M. to 1:00 P.M. on Sundays. Stores at road, air, rail, and ship terminals can be open 24 hours a day. Shopping centers can open from 6:00 A.M. to midnight all days, including Sunday.[28]

Photo 10.4
Private car ownership is important for hypermarket growth. Without cars, consumers purchase only what they can carry home. When cars are available, the average amount spent per customer increases. This hypermarket is Ahold's first venture in Portugal with Jerónimo Martins Retail (JMR). *Courtesy of Ahold.*

SUMMARY

The southern European countries of Spain, Italy, Greece, and Portugal are vastly different from their northern European neighbors. Average income and education level are much lower. Transportation infrastructures are not well-developed. Traditional retailers sell most of the products.

Increasingly, foreign retailers are capturing markets. Their experiences at home have put them in a position to provide competition where little existed before. French hypermarkets have been particularly successful.

Italy represents one of the most regulated retail environments. City planners there control the mix of retail establishments, making it difficult for new entrants. There may not be much impetus to change this heavy regulation.

KEY TERMS

infrastructure **shop-in-shop**

DISCUSSION QUESTIONS

1. In several of these countries there are only one or two department stores. What explains this concentration?
2. What geographical factors have impeded the development of national chains? How has this lack of development positioned local retailers for the onslaught of foreign competition?
3. Retailing in these countries appears to "leap frog" through retail transitions without passing through the normal stages expected as a country develops. What retail groups will suffer because of this?
4. What explanation can you give for the restrictive laws used in Italy? How do these laws affect (a) consumers, (b) local retailers, and (c) foreign retailers?
5. In several of these countries, retailers use negative cash flow. What is this and how does it affect high growth retailers versus low growth retailers?

ENDNOTES

1. "Spain." (1995). *Craighead's International Business, Travel, and Relocation Guide to More than 80 Countries.* Detroit: Gale Research.
2. *Retail News Letter.* (1995). No. 426, July, p. 17.
3. *Retail News Letter.* (1995). No. 427, August/September, p. 15.
4. *Spain Food Market Overview.* (1996). Madrid, Spain: American Embassy.
5. "Carrefour—Company Report," (March 13, 1997). UBS Research in *Investext* [Database on CD-ROM]. Foster City, Calif.: Information Access.
6. *Retail News Letter.* (1996). No. 432, February, p. 16.
7. *Retail News Letter.* (1995). No. 426, July, p. 17.
8. "Italy." (1995). *Craighead's International Business, Travel, and Relocation Guide to More than 80 Countries.* Detroit: Gale Research.
9. *The European Retail Handbook, 1997 Edition.* (1997). London: Corporate Intelligence on Retailing.

10. "La Rinascente—Company Report." (December 11, 1995). Lehman Brothers Limited in *Investext* [Database on CD-ROM]. Foster City, Calif.: Information Access.
11. "La Rinascente—Company Report." (December 11, 1995), Lehman Brothers Limited.
12. "La Rinascente—Company Report." (December 11, 1995), Lehman Brothers Limited.
13. *Retail News Letter.* (1995). No 429, November, p. 11.
14. "La Rinascente—Company Report." (December 11, 1995), Lehman Brothers Limited.
15. "La Rinascente—Company Report." (December 11, 1995), Lehman Brothers Limited.
16. "La Rinascente—Company Report." (December 11, 1995), Lehman Brothers Limited.
17. "La Rinascente—Company Report." (December 11, 1995), Lehman Brothers Limited.
18. Pelligrini, L., and A. Cardani. (1992). *The Italian Distribution System.* Report prepared for the OECD Study on Distribution Systems, University of Bocconi, March.
19. Ishani, M. (1996). *Franchising in Italy. Franchise Update.* Web Services by Los Trancos Systems, LLC [Web site].
20. *Retail News Letter.* (1995). No 426, July, p. 13.
21. "Greece." (1995). *Craighead's International Business, Travel, and Relocation Guide to More than 80 Countries.* Detroit: Gale Research.
22. *Retail News Letter.* (1995). No. 420, January, p. 10.
23. "Distribution of Goods and Services in Greece." ADIGOS—Distribution of Goods and Services. Microsoft Internet Explorer [Web site].
24. *Retail News Letter.* (1995). No. 424, May, p. 13.
25. *Retail News Letter.* (1996). No. 436, June.
26. "Portugal." (1995). *Craighead's International Business, Travel, and Relocation Guide to More than 80 Countries.* Detroit: Gale Research.
27. *Portugal's Food Market.* (1994). Madrid, Spain: Agricultural Affairs Office of the Foreign Agricultural Service/USDA.
28. *Retail News Letter.* (1996). No. 437, July, p. 14.

RUSSIA
St. Petersburg
Moscow
Gdańsk
CZECH
REP
Warsaw
POLAND
Prague
Krakow
Budapest
HUNGARY

11

Retailing in Central and Eastern Europe

After reading this chapter, you will understand:

- The role retailing played in a planned economy and how this limited innovation in the industry.
- How the Marxist philosophy "From each according to his ability, to each according to his needs" is used to plan product distribution in planned economies.
- Why most favored nation (MFN) status is important to retailers in countries with a nonconvertible currency and how this affects retailers' strategic decision-making.
- That even in planned economies, the informal market always operates under a demand economy, whether it is illegal (black market) or legal (free market).
- How consumers who are accustomed to a scarce supply of products view the market differently than consumers who have operated in a system of plenty.

EXECUTIVES WERE SURVEYED about their views of Europe in the year 2000. More than 95% believed that the European market in that year would be double the size of the 1993 market. They were referring to the Pan-European free trade zone, which would encompass the territories including the former Soviet Union and include 800 million people.[1]

Central and eastern Europe offer the type of less-regulated environment western European retailers have had difficulty finding. Many western European countries have regulations that restrict the expansion of large-scale stores, place limits on the hours of operations, and severely restrict the laying off of employees during economic downturns. Although central Europe does not have these restrictions, countries such as Albania, Romania, and Bulgaria are considered 20 to 25 years behind the West economically, and remain unattractive markets for retailers.

There are, however, four countries among the former Soviet bloc nations that are of interest to retailers: Hungary, the Czech Republic, Poland, and Russia. These countries have removed price controls, are making their currencies convertible, and are welcoming foreign investment. The United States government gave these countries **most favored nation** (MFN) status, a designation that provides the most favorable trading conditions with the United States. This means they receive the lowest tariff rates and the most generous quota allotments. The MFN designation generally does not affect retailers within their home country because the designation refers to products shipped to the United States. However, as countries move from planned to free market economies, larger retailers are interested in purchasing imported products to sell in their stores. They need hard currency to buy these products. Retailers may vertically integrate backwards, purchasing a factory to produce export products. Making products for export allows them to generate hard currency. The MFN status is thus important to retailers who want to generate hard currency through export sales.

You cannot understand how much retailing has changed in these countries without understanding what retailing is like under a planned economy. A **planned economy** is one in which the government determines what goods will be produced, where they will be produced, and where they will be sold. Planned economies generally have a blocked or nonconvertible currency. **Blocked or nonconvertible currencies** cannot be bought and sold in the world market. They are kept within the country. The government does this to control how people spend their money. The country gets hard currency by selling products to the outside world and through the currency brought in when foreigners come to the country.

In the first part of this chapter, I will describe how retailing operated in the former Soviet bloc countries under the old planned system. This background section will be followed by a discussion of the four major countries within this group and their retail industries. A cautionary note is in order, however. The retail industries in these countries are small and fragmented and there is little information describing the current situation. Much of the information that is available is speculative.

RETAILING UNDER A PLANNED ECONOMY

Under the Soviet-era planned economic systems, retailing and wholesaling were controlled by the Ministry of Commerce. This government agency determined what products factories would produce, where they would sell them, and their price. Prices were fixed and often stayed the same for decades. Price competition did not exist. If products had different prices in different stores, it was a marking error, not a strategic action.

In such a planned economy, the merchandise price was based on need, not costs of production. A product that was a necessity, such as bread, would have a very low, subsidized price. A luxury product would be priced very high to discourage purchases. In the United States, in contrast, products are priced based on the costs to produce the product, plus expenses and a planned profit. The idea of pricing a product based on production costs seems very strange to people living in planned economies. The basic Marxist philosophy of "From each according to his ability, to each according to his needs" is reflected in the low cost of necessities, and the relatively high cost of luxuries.

I remember reading a newspaper article shortly after Russia removed price controls. The article focused on bakers in Moscow. They had no idea what to charge for their bread. The ingredients used in making the bread came from state-owned factories, and the bakers did not pay for them. A baker's job was simply to mix and bake. After much confusion about what to charge for the bread, they decided they would all charge the same price—the price they had charged before price liberalization.

In this planned economy, both state stores and cooperatives were under the direction of the Ministry of Commerce. Store merchandise came from government sources that were all required to charge government prices. **State-owned stores** were located in the more urban areas and sold a larger proportion of non-food items. **Cooperatives** were most prevalent in rural areas and sold both food and non-food merchandise. In some countries, such as the German Democratic Republic (the former East Germany), Poland, and Hungary, private individuals were allowed to have shops, but the shops had to charge the same prices for products. Private shops had to get their merchandise from the government and had to sell merchandise for government-established prices. These independent stores had little advantage. The government wholesale organization handled the physical distribution of merchandise. Wholesalers were organized by main product groups such as staple foods, fresh fruits and vegetables, furniture, and clothing.[2]

Shopping was not easy under the planned economic system. Shoppers waited in a variety of lines. After entering a store, a shopper would likely wait in one line to request a product or to check the price of a product. If the shopper decided to buy something, for instance, a pork chop, the salesclerk would then give the shopper a bill. The shopper would take the bill to another counter and, after again standing in line, would pay for the pork chop, receiving a receipt that would then need to be taken to a third line, where the shopper would wait to pick

Photo 11.1
Consumers standing in lines are a symbol of a planned market system where there is insufficient supply for the demand. Here, Moscow consumers stand in line to buy oranges. Lines disappear when economies become free rather than planned. *Courtesy of Reuters/ Corbiss-Bettman.*

up the pork chop. This procedure would be repeated for other categories of merchandise. As you can imagine, shopping required a large time commitment. Often shoppers would wait in line only to find out that the store was sold out of the item they wanted. They then had to go to another store and repeat the process.

The government pricing system kept prices artificially low. There was little incentive to increase supply, so consumers competed for the existing, limited supply by standing in line. Some observers estimate that the average Soviet consumer spent two to three hours per day waiting in line. This affected worker productivity. When news of a scarce item became available, workers would simply walk off their jobs to go stand in line, waiting for the chance to purchase the item.

The "waiting in line" phenomenon attracted the interest of several academic studies. One study of Polish consumers found that lines formed for many product and services, including those for which there was no shortage. Lines were more widespread for foods than for non-food products. The longest lines were for meat. Three of the eight meat lines at one department store studied contained more than 100 shoppers.[3]

Products were scarce, in part because the government put highest priority on supporting the military-industrial complex. Consumer products were viewed as frivolous. The situation was compounded by hoarding behavior, as consumers tended to purchase any products they encountered, regardless of their immediate needs. People did this because they were never sure when they would encounter the products again.

Daily shopping was the rule during this era in central and eastern European countries. On each visit to a store, a consumer would buy a few items, generally five to ten. Stores were small and crowded. Crowds were sometimes controlled through shopping basket distribution. Baskets would be issued to everyone who entered the shop, including family members shopping together.

When the limited supply of baskets was exhausted, no more people would be allowed to enter until someone came out.[4]

Customer service was and still is very poor. Salesclerks were rude to customers. Self-service was not available. Most stores used a **responsibility system,** under which the clerks in a shop were collectively responsible for theft. This contributed to a service approach of "guarding" the merchandise from consumers.

Stores were very small and carried a limited amount of merchandise. Customers might enter a food store seeking a particular product and, because of the jumbled merchandising, not find it even if it were there. They would then go to another store, where they might wait in line to gain entry only to find, again, that the store did not have the desired merchandise.

In market economies, advertising plays an important role in communicating product availability to consumers. This type of information source was not available to consumers in the planned economies.

Since economic reforms began, the old systems have been changing, rapidly in some countries and not so rapidly in others. The leaders in this change are Hungary, the Czech Republic, and Poland. Several issues evolve when a country moves from a planned to a free market. People often cannot change as rapidly as markets. The next section will explore these issues.

MOVING FROM A PLANNED TO A FREE MARKET

Privatization is the process of transferring ownership of businesses from the government to individuals. Two main types of privatization have been occurring in central and eastern Europe. In the first type, vouchers are distributed to citizens, giving everyone a share in state-owned companies. Citizens can then sell or trade these vouchers to other citizens. In the second type of privatization, companies are sold directly with domestic investors given priority.

Each country has approached privatization in a different manner. Poland began with sell-offs to company management. However, this proved to be very slow, so the government moved to mass privatization. In mass privatization, companies are given investment funds and the public is able to buy shares in the funds. Hungary has used sell-offs, hoping that this strategy will foster efficient management. It has had limited success. The Czech Republic and Russia have concentrated on the voucher system, which makes the transition faster.[5]

Sell-offs to company management have some advantages and some problems. To begin with, the companies are faced with major repayment schedules. They typically have five or ten years to repay the debt. This leaves little capital for operating expenses, modernization, or product development. These companies typically must look for outside investors. This is an advantage for outside investors, who now do not have to negotiate with the state government. The investment is quicker and easier, and money is not diverted to government coffers. The employees are shareholders so they also gain additional control over the operation of their business.

Another way to gain entry to the central European market is by starting a business from scratch. This is called a **greenfield option.** The meaning of greenfield in this instance is different from the meaning used in the Chapter 8 discussion of retailing in the United Kingdom. In that chapter, I discussed greenfield sites—areas that have not been developed and are being held as green areas in an attempt to prevent or reduce urban sprawl.

Investors who choose to start a new business do not have the problems associated with buying a state-owned business. They can hire the number of employees they think are necessary for the business and not worry about absorbing excess state employees. In the section about the Czech Republic later in this chapter, I will discuss the problems encountered by the Belgian retailer, Delhaize, when it acquired a group of state-owned stores.

Schultz, Belk, and Ger[6] provide a some observations about market privatization and the effect on consumers in countries that are undergoing this change:

1. Changes are occurring at an incredible speed.
2. It is likely that the changes will continue to occur in equally dramatic terms over the next decade or more.
3. There are escalating consumer aspirations and expectations that are as yet unmatched by the available and affordable consumer goods.
4. Differences exist between the small stratum of consumers for new and expensive luxury goods in these countries and the majority who still are barely able to afford essentials.
5. Many consumers in these countries lament the disappearance of their previous economic system. There is clearly dissatisfaction with some aspects of current marketization.
6. There is a powerful influence from images of Western or American consumption and the good life. These global images are primarily obtained from exposure to tourists, travel to neighboring countries, advertising, and mass media.
7. Local conditions continue to exert strong and unique influences in these cultures despite the increasing influence of global images.
8. There is no single adequate theoretical framework that seems to account for the changes taking place. However, there is agreement that the factors of global consumption orientations, information diffusion, and local cultural transformations will be important in any such theoretical framework.
9. There are negative as well as positive consequences of the changes that are occurring. Although the negative consequences are most dramatically illustrated by Croatia and the disintegration of Yugoslavia, the results of marketization were always two-sided, with new consumer desires accompanied by uncertainty, confusion, and frustration in daily consumer life.

The economy of shortage formed consumers' needs and aspirations in the Soviet bloc countries. Satisfying the need for food overcame all other needs in the planned economy. Products that were neither needed nor desired were purchased and hoarded. Consumers could use these hoarded goods to obtain needed goods later, through barter. Luxuries were generally not available. If they were available, it was at an exorbitant price.

In Poland, however, consumers also purchased through the unplanned economy. The unplanned economy depended on theft from state sectors for inputs of materials, labor, time, and machinery.[7] The unplanned economy resolved problems created by the planned economy, such as shortage of necessary goods. The government avoided cracking down on the unplanned economy because it released some consumer discontent created by the economy of shortage. Consumers would obtain products through social networks and would reciprocate with special favors. Vodka, canned ham, and chocolates were favorite commodities used to bribe government officials.

When consumers' consumption aspirations are not met, hostilities can erupt. Armed conflict became a daily event in the former Yugoslavia when Serbian and Croatian forces reinflamed centuries-old ethnic rivalries. The following passage from a book about market development in Yugoslavia and Croatia gives a sense of the disappointment and rage that accompany unmet expectations.

> . . . a genie offers three wishes. For his first wish, the Englishman asks for a cottage overlooking the English channel. The Frenchman requests a vineyard and a chateau with enough rooms to house his mistresses. When the (Slav) is asked, he hesitates for a long time. Finally he points to his neighbor and says. "My neighbor has a goat. I don't have a goat. Kill my neighbor's goat." (And then proceeds to assist the genie in not only killing his neighbor's goat but his neighbor's wife, children, family, friends, and all their relations, so destroying a generation and himself in the process.)[8]

According to **ethnic resource competition theory,**[9] increased rivalry over scarce and valued rewards in the political, economic, and social arenas will exacerbate conflict between groups in society. The more visible the differences between groups, the greater the violence and hostility. Rivalry and hostility will be justified by attributing product acquisition to corruption. Interviews conducted in Croatia confirmed this theory. When citizens pointed out a seaside villa they said, "They stole it from the people. How else could they build a house on their salary."[10] This same kind of justification was used during the Holocaust in Germany.

An **aspiration gap** results when there is a difference between what consumers think they should have and what they have. People suffer disillusionment if their aspired standard of consumption is much less than the actual potential value of their acquisitions. As countries marketize, consumers are exposed to advertising and television programs that intensify their product aspirations.

The four countries included in this chapter are at different levels of marketizing. They can provide an overview of how retail institutions change as a country replaces the planned market with a free market.

HUNGARY

COUNTRY BACKGROUND

Hungary gained independence in 1867 as part of the Austro-Hungarian Empire. After the Allied victory in World War I, the empire was dissolved and Hungary lost two-thirds of its territories. Hungary entered World War

II on the side of Germany. The citizens of Hungry declared a republic in 1946, but the next year the Hungarian communists took power with the help of Russian occupying forces. Soviet forces put down several revolts. In 1968, a sweeping reform of the national economic system replaced central planning and allowed individual enterprises relative autonomy. This economic liberalization and political tolerance made Hungary a maverick among the Soviet bloc countries. By opening its borders with Austria in May 1989, Hungary became a catalyst in the unraveling of communist rule in eastern Europe. Table 11.1 presents selected demographic and economic data for Hungary.

Hungary's approach to the privatization of the retail trade has been different from that used in Poland or the Czech Republic. Those two countries tried to remove the state influence as quickly as possible. The Hungarian authorities had a specific strategic plan. Hungary's approach focused on three objectives: (1) to create a market structure similar to that found in Western economies, (2) to raise revenue that could be used to finance the state budget deficit, and (3) to exert effective governmental control over the privatization process.[11]

RETAILING IN HUNGARY

Hungary is a land of entrepreneurs. In 1989, it was estimated that trade on the black market contributed 30% to 35% of Hungary's gross domestic product (GDP).[12] This strong informal market has a negative effect on retail trade. The country's high **value added tax (VAT)** rates drive consumers to the informal (black) market. A VAT is a tax assessed by each European country, which is like a sales tax. Each country has a different VAT rate. Hungary's rate of 25% is very high.[13] Consumers who buy through the black market, however, do not pay VAT. This is illegal but makes the black market even more profitable.

Hungary's department stores were nationalized in 1948. Until 1966, the government operated the stores as independent units. That year, the government combined the stores into a single company, still under government control. The group was given the name Centrum Aruhaz, but is usually called Centrum. Centrum's major competitor is Skala, a cooperative formed from a department store company and a cooperative wholesaler.

During the early economic reforms, the two groups took different approaches. Skala used concession-type purchasing to offer a wider range of products. This means that Skala allowed manufacturers to display and market merchandise within the store. The manufacturers/ wholesalers carried the product risk. **Product risk** refers to which party absorbs losses for merchandise that does not sell. Having manufacturers to carry the product risk allowed Skala to offer more merchandise and to finance expansion. In contrast, Centrum operated stores as **profit centers.** That is, each store was treated as a self-accounting unit, responsible for achieving a designated profit. In Centrum, responsibility and rewards are highly decentralized.[14]

Skala is moving quickly to modernize stores. Tengelmann, the German retail group, acquired 66% ownership of the company and is providing capi-

TABLE 11.1

Hungary: Selected Demographic and Economic Data

	Population (millions) mid-1995	Area (thousands of sq. km)	GNP per capita Dollars 1995	GNP per capita Avg. ann. growth (%) 1985–95	PPP estimates of GNP per capita U.S. = 100 1987 1995	Life expectancy at birth (years) 1995	Adult illiteracy (%) 1995
Upper-middle-income economies	438.3t	20,514t	4,260w	.2w		69w	14w
Hungary	10.2	93	4,120	−1.0	28.9 23.8	70	

Source: World Bank (1997). PPP = purchasing power parity. t = total. w = weighted average.

tal for financing. The company is investing in new fixtures, layouts, lighting, and computer technology. Its objective is to present an open merchandising approach focused on the upper moderate-income customer.

Non-food retailers are beginning to enter Hungary, but there are also many opportunities for modern chain stores and superstores. Sixty percent of the national economy was in private hands at the end of 1995, and in retailing, this figure will continue to grow. The government continues its privatization efforts, although most of the establishments have been transferred to independent ownership. Often the new owners are people who worked for the store when it was state-owned. Hungary has the highest labor costs in eastern Europe. This gives Hungarian consumers greater spending power than many other eastern Europeans.[15]

New retail developments have increased since a recession lifted in 1994. The Budagyongye shopping center opened in Budapest, and six new centers will be open by 1998. German investors are behind a 24,000 square meter (258,000 square feet) center that opened in Budapest in 1996. All of the center's space was leased out before it opened. Israeli interests are part of a joint venture to build a 42,000 square meter (452,000 square feet) center called Duna Plaza. The largest development of all is the 52,000 square meter (560,000 square feet) Polus center, being constructed on the site of a former Soviet military base outside Budapest. Most of this investment is driven by foreign capital. Foreign retailers are only permitted to own property through a joint venture with a local partner. Table 11.2 summarizes the domestic and foreign retailers in Hungary.

The new shopping centers are open until 8:00 or 10:00 P.M. every day, Monday through Saturday. Sunday opening is uncommon. Smaller shops are open 8:30 A.M. to 5:00 P.M., Monday to Friday and Saturday until early afternoon. Twenty-four hour shops are rare.

The next country I will discuss in this chapter is the Czech Republic. This country is an attractive investment location for foreign retailers. Its retail industry is more developed than most in the region. Because the

TABLE 11.2

Major Hungarian and Foreign Retailers in the Domestic Market, 1995

Retailer[a]	Operations	Sales (HUF[a] billions)	Outlets (no.)
AFESZ Co-op	Regional cooperative organization	150.0	6,000
Plus Discount/Kaiser's/Skala/Obi (Tengelmann Germany)	Discount food, DIY,[a] and general stores	40.0	68
Metro (Germany)	Cash-and-carry	40.0	6
Jééé/Meinl/Nyugat (Julius Meinl Austria)	Supermarkets & food stores	34.3	197
Fotex, which includes:	Non-food multiple	26.0	500
Azur/Dak & Unio	Drugstores and photo goods	N/A[a]	114
Keravill	Electrical and household goods	N/A	78
Ofotèrt/Europtic	Optical and photo goods	N/A	217
Fotex Records	Music and video goods	N/A	4
Domus/Butor/Kristaly	Furniture and glassware	N/A	32
Kontur	Variety stores	N/A	33
Primo/Ruhazati Boltok	Clothing stores	N/A	22
Alfa-Trade (Nash Finch USA)	Cash-and-carries and voluntary chain	25.0	760
Centrum Aruhazak	Department stores (privatized 1994)	18.6	16
Pharmafontana	Pharmacies (privatized 1996)	18.5	197
Profi/duna Füszèrt (Louis Delhaize Belgium)	Supermarkets and food stores	11.0	49
Bakony Füszèrt	Supermarkets and food stores	10.4	N/A
Spar Hungaria (Spar Osterreich Austria)	Food voluntary chain	10.0	37
Mátra Füszèrt	Supermarkets and food stores	8.5	39
Bonbon Hemingway (Austria)	Food stores, confectioners. and sports	8.0	60
Alföld Füszèrt	Supermarkets and food stores	6.0	33
Balaton Füszèrt	Supermarkets and food stores	5.6	26
Global (Tesco UK)	Grocery	4.6	48
Porst (Distefora Switzerland and Spector Photo Belgium)	Electrical goods and photo stores	3.2	250
Eptek Rt	Building products stores	2.9	N/A
Kleider Bauer (Charles Vögele Switzerland)	Clothing stores	2.5	50
Orex	Jewelry stores	2.3	N/A
Komfort	Electrical, photo, and building stores	2.0	59
Quelle (Germany)	Mail-order	1.8	0
Aranypok	Lingerie and accessories stores	1.4	N/A

TABLE 11.2

Major Hungarian and Foreign Retailers in the Domestic Market, 1995

Retailer[a]	Operations	Sales (HUF* billions)	Outlets (no.)
Hernbock	Electrical goods stores	1.2	6
Herbaria	Drugstores	1.0	100
Billa/Penny Markt (Rewe Germany)	Supermarkets and discount stores	1.0	20
Drogeriemarkt (dm drogerie market Germany)	Drugstores	0.5	40
Fonica (50% Salamander Germany)	Footwear stores	N/A	50
Humanic Szivarvany (Leder & Schuh Austria j.v.)	Footwear stores	N/A	40
Aranyok Veres	Clothing stores	N/A	30
Expert International (Switzerland)	Electrical goods buying group	N/A	30
Super Közèrt (Supersol Israel)	Supermarkets	N/A	26
Kolos (Denmark)	Food stores	N/A	25
Levi's Store (USA)	Casual clothing stores	N/A	19
Szegedi Komplett (SPA)	Department stores (privatized 1995)	N/A	12
Reno (Kaufhof Germany)	Footwear stores	N/A	10
Domino	Department stores and mail order	N/A	5
bauMax (Austria)	DIY superstores	N/A	8
Bauwelt (Austria)	DIY superstores	N/A	4
Cotton Bar (Beymen Turkey)	Shirt stores	N/A	4
Cora (France)	Hypermarkets (1996)	N/A	3
Marks & Spencer (UK)	Clothing stores	N/A	2
IKEA (Sweden)	Furniture superstore	N/A	1
Ace Hardware (USA)	DIY and hardware store	N/A	1
Lederland (Vendex Netherlands)	Leather furniture store	N/A	1
Standa (joint venture with CEIC)	General goods store	N/A	1
Otto Katalogusaruhaz (Otto Versand Germany)	Mail-order	N/A	0

[a]Apart from the AFESZ co-op, the major retailers are now mainly those with foreign participation. German groups such as Tengelmann and Metro, together with Julius Meinl of Austria, have overtaken domestic players such as Fotex (undergoing difficulties in 1996) in terms of sales during 1995 and 1996. Bakony Fuszert, one of the remaining state-run food chains, is to be privatized in 1997. Virgin (UK) plans a Megastore for Budapest in 1997.

Source: *The European Retail Handbook, 1997 Edition.* (1996). London. Corporate Intelligence on Retailing, p. 138–139.

*HUF = Hungarian Forints; 1 HUF = US $0.005; DIY = do-it-yourself; N/A = not available.

Czech Republic and Slovakia were one nation when some foreign retailers began entering this market, retailing in Slovakia is also discussed, where relevant.

CZECH REPUBLIC

COUNTRY BACKGROUND

The First Czechoslovak Republic lasted from 1918 to 1938. This was the "Golden Age" of modern Czechoslovakian history. The country enjoyed a prosperous democracy with a lively intellectual and artistic life. However, nationalist tension within Czechoslovakia (conflict between a German minority and the Czech and Slovak majority) made it vulnerable to the international rise of Nazism, which brought down the republic in 1938. After World War II, Czechoslovakia regained its freedom briefly, only to lose it again to the communists, who ruled the country for four decades. The communist party's rule collapsed in late 1989.

Before World War II, Czechoslovakia was considered one of the most developed and sophisticated of European countries. Culture flourished and the retail system was similar to that in France and Germany. After the communists came to power in 1948, they eliminated the private sector, bringing all elements of the economy private sector under government ownership. Predictably, they regarded retailing as an unnecessary function. In planned economies, retailing is believed to serve a negative role of fostering useless competition and unnecessary desires in consumers.

In 1989 and 1990, internal revolutions caused the fall of communism in Czechoslovakia. The transition was so peaceful it was termed the Velvet Revolution. Václav Havel, a prominent playwright, was elected to be the country's first president. In 1993, Czechoslovakia divided into two countries, the Czech Republic and Slovakia. The Czech Republic has a population of 10 million, twice that of Slovakia. Both countries are democracies. They sometimes refer to the 40-year experiment in socialism as "a long, hard and distressing road from capitalism to capitalism."[16] Table 11.3 presents selected demographic and economic data for the Czech Republic.

RETAILING IN THE CZECH REPUBLIC

The retail system, consisting of small, state-owned stores, was called *Potraviny* under the state system. These stores carried a limited selection of locally produced goods. Quality was reasonable, but not on a par with Western standards. People shopped on a daily basis, generally purchasing only three or four essential items. The sale of soft goods and durables was through large, state-owned department stores. The Prior group had a network of stores throughout the former Czechoslovakia. There were other state-owned stores, but all of the state-owned department stores were in major cities.

TABLE 11.3

Czech Republic: Selected Demographic and Economic Data

	Population (millions) mid-1995	Area (thousands of sq. km)	GNP per capita Dollars 1995	GNP per capita Avg. ann. growth (%) 1985–95	PPP estimates of GNP per capita U.S. = 100 1987	PPP estimates of GNP per capita U.S. = 100 1995	Life expectancy at birth (years) 1995	Adult illiteracy (%) 1995
Upper-middle-income economies	438.3t	20,514t	4,260w	0.2w			69w	14w
Czech Republic	10.3	79	3,870	−1.8	44.9	36.2	73	

Source: World Bank (1997). PPP = purchasing power parity. t = total. w = weighted average.

The Czech government is privatizing the *Potravinys*. Those that are not being privatized are making improvements to remain competitive. There are now 286,000 retail stores, of which 284,000 are private. Outside the major cities, *Potravinys* dominate retail trade, and there is no indication this will end.[17] Figure 11.1 shows how the Czech distribution system is organized.

Product procurement in the Czech Republic is modernizing at a rapid rate. Most retailers are increasing their centralized buying functions to maximize buying power. In the past, merchandise would be brought into the country by independent distributors with warehouse capabilities. After it cleared customs, it would be broken into smaller shipments and sent to individual stores. The major distributors have taken over facilities formerly used by the government. However, they are inefficient, opening the door for new third-party suppliers to move in. The market could be even greater, because the central location of the Czech Republic could enable them to become major distribution centers for goods going to other parts of eastern Europe.[18]

Until 1989, there was only one national department store chain, Prior. This chain had 50 stores in the major cities. Stores were poorly organized, showing little expertise in merchandising. Goods were locally produced, and selection was limited. In 1993, Kmart purchased six department stores in the Czech Republic, including the MAJ department store in Prague and five former Prior stores in Plzen, Pardubice, Hradec, Kralove, Brno, and Liberec. Kmart invested $18 million to acquire holdings in the MAJ department store. This acquisition gave Kmart 76% of MAJ holdings and the possibility of purchasing 11 more stores. The MAJ department store in Prague has 8,000 square meters (86,000 square feet). As part of the agreement, Kmart agreed to purchase Czechoslovakian merchandise for its U.S. stores. In 1996, Kmart sold its interest in these companies to Tesco of the United Kingdom. Nearly a year after the sale, several of my colleagues visited the Czech Republic; they were surprised to find that the Kmart signs were still in front of the stores.

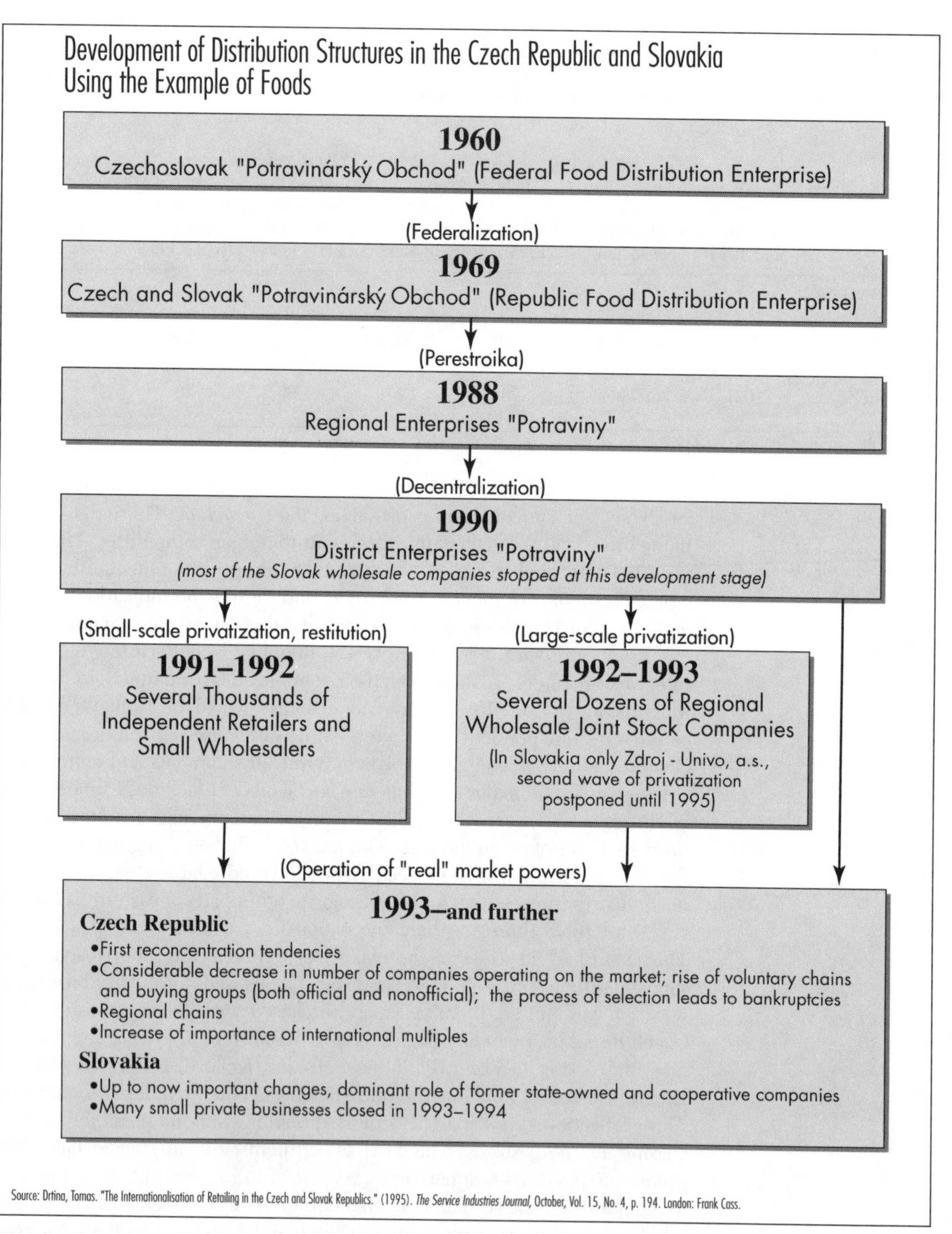

Source: Drtina, Tomas. "The Internationalisation of Retailing in the Czech and Slovak Republics." (1995). *The Service Industries Journal*, October, Vol. 15, No. 4, p. 194. London: Frank Cass.

Figure 11.1
The process of privatizing the food distribution system in the Czech Republic and Slovakia is a lengthy one. Since 1960 they have moved from a centralized distribution system to a decentralized market system.

Kotva, a state-owned store in Prague, has made dramatic improvements and is now the leading department store in Prague. A German investment group is also establishing a department store and supermarket in the center of town, which will operate under the Krone name. Krone was one of the Czech Republic's first foreign retailing investments and has been very successful. Specialty stores such as Benetton, Adidas, Stephanel, Estee Lauder, Marks & Spencer, Kaiser, and Boss are present in the Prague market.[19] Table 11.4 lists the major domestic and foreign retailers in the Czech Republic.

Although all goods supplied to retailers contain bar coding, retailers do not have the scanning capability. The major department stores are investing heavily in information systems but it will be awhile before they meet the standards of the rest of the world.

The introduction of a free market system in the Czech Republic is occurring at a rapid rate. In January 1991, price subsidies were abolished on nearly all products. During the first 10 days, food prices increased by 32%. In response, consumers reduced their purchases and consumption. Retailers reacted by lowering their prices, until a market balance was established. This is often cited as a textbook example of how the market system should work. The price increase in the Czech Republic is the lowest of any of the transitional countries.

In addition to removing price constraints, the Czech Republic also liberalized foreign trade. The new government gave Czech currency convertibility, giving Czech enterprises free access to Western currencies.

Privatization has measured in three stages. First, property nationalized after 1948 was returned to the original owners or heirs. Second, beginning in February 1992, the "small privatization" offered retail outlets for sale at public auctions.

Photo 11.2
By 1997, shops in Prague, the capital of the Czech Republic, offered more merchandise than before large-scale privatization, but customers sometimes still had to wait in more than one line to pay for and pick up their purchases. *Courtesy of Lisa Applebaum.*

TABLE 11.4

Major Czech and Foreign Retailers in the Domestic Market, 1995[a]

Retailer[a]	Operations	Sales (CZK° millions)	Outlets (no.)
Interkontakt[b]	Food and non-food stores	5,400	N/A°
Tesco (UK)	Food and non-food stores	4,100	6
Spar (Spar Handels Germany & Spar Osterreich Austria)	Supermarkets	3,200	202
Ahold (Netherlands) which includes:	Supermarkets and discount food	2,467	180
Euronova	Supermarkets	N/A	96
Mana	Supermarkets	N/A	69
Sesam	Discount food stores	N/A	8
Euronova	Cash-and-carries	N/A	7
Pronto/Paramen Brno (Julius Meinl Austria)	Supermarkets	2,616	50
Delvita (Delhaize "le Lion" Belgium joint venture)	Supermarkets	2,384	27
Kotva (Prague)	Department store	2,000	1
Centex Brno	Clothing	1,500	80
Jednota K Hobby	Food stores	1,100	N/A
Plus Discount (Tengelmann Germany)	Discount food stores	900	24
Magnet (Camif France 51%)	Mail-order	900	0
Billa (Rewe Germany)	Supermarkets and general stores	800	17
Quelle (Germany)	Mail-order/clothing/photo/optical	800	35
Bata (Canada)	Footwear stores	700	30
Krone (Kathreiner Germany joint venture)	Department stores	600	3
Dum Mody (Prague)	Clothing stores	240	2
Boty R Petr (Prague)	Footwear stores	100	40
Porst (Interdiscount Switzerland)	Electrical goods stores	N/A	80
Turex	State-owned cosmetics stores	N/A	32
Rema 1000 (Reitan Norway)	Discount food stores	N/A	20
Expert (Switzerland)	Electricals buying group	N/A	20
NKD (Germany)	Clothing stores	N/A	20
dm-drogerie-markt (Germany)	Drugstores	N/A	20
Mountfield (Czech-owned)	Garden equipment and tools stores	N/A	20
Delta/Diska (Edeka Germany)	Discount food stores	N/A	10
Sklo Bohemia	Glassware stores	N/A	10
Dirk Rossman (Germany)	Drugstores	N/A	10
Benetton (Italy)	Young fashion stores	N/A	8
Netto (Dansk Supermarked Denmark)	Discount fashion stores	N/A	6
baumax (Austria)	DIY superstores	N/A	56

TABLE 11.4

Major Czech and Foreign Retailers in the Domestic Market, 1995[a]

Retailer	Operations	Sales (CZK* millions)	Outlets (no.)
Obi (Tengelmann Germany)	DIY superstores	N/A	4
Levi's Store (U.S.)	Casual clothing stores	N/A	3
Norma (Germany)	Discount food stores	N/A	2
Roller (Austria)	Discount furniture stores	N/A	2
Castel et Freres (France)	Off-licenses	N/A	2
Götzen (Germany)	DIY superstores	N/A	2
Sconto (Mobel Walther Germany)	Furniture stores	N/A	2
Palmers (Austria)	Womenswear and lingerie stores	N/A	2
IKEA (Sweden)	Furniture superstore	N/A	1
Hornbach (Germany)	DIY superstore	N/A	1
Marks & Spencer (UK)	Clothing store (joint venture Ceska Obchodni)	N/A	1
Bauhaus (Germany)	DIY superstore	N/A	1
Globus (Germany)	Hypermarkets/DIY superstores	N/A	1
Bila Labut (Prague)	Department store	N/A	1
Asprey (UK/Brunei)	Jewelers	N/A	1

[a]The above sales and outlet numbers, in most instances, relate to 1994–1995.

[b]The largest domestic retail group is Interkontakt, which has taken over most of the state-owned Pramen and Prior networks. This business is to be floated in 1997. There is no sign of the inflow of foreign retailers slackening, with several German DIY entrants in 1996 and 1997 and Marks & Spencer (UK) opening a store in autumn 1996 in Prague's Myslbek center (three other outlets intended for Plzen, Brno, and Ostrava). Virgin (UK) is reported to be planning its first Megastore in 1997. The Kotva department store in Prague reports that 60% of its customers are foreigners. Tesco (UK) has acquired the Kmart stores, which are in the process of being converted to the Tesco fascia.

Source: *The European Retail Handbook, 1997 Edition.* (1996). London: Corporate Intelligence on Retailing, p. 49–50.

*CZK = Czech korunas; CZK = U.S. $0.029; DIY = do-it-yourself; N/A = not available.

Foreigners were not allowed to participate in the first round of bidding, but they could buy companies from the winning local bidders. Some foreign companies obtained their real estate using this method. The third stage, which is continuing today, is "large-scale privatization." Large, state enterprises are being privatized in various ways. One way is through direct sale to Czech companies or to foreign investors. Other ways are through management buyout, or through transformation into a joint-stock company with shares sold to the public.[20]

Delhaize le Lion, the Belgian-based retailer, owns 75% of Delvita, a supermarket store network in Prague. The Czech government gave the company its choice of a wide range of store sites. Delhaize is converting these stores to make them modern self-service retail centers. Part of the Delhaize contract required them to retain all of the store employees. However, natural attrition has been high because of the demands for efficiency and productivity. In addition, because Czech labor unions do not have the strength of labor unions in western Europe; retail stores are free to lay off employees.[21] Ahold (Netherlands) opened a test discount store in the Czech Republic. It operates the stores under the name of Sesam. These stores average 550 square meters (5,900 square feet) and carry 700 products offered at discount prices. Ahold has 29 other stores in the Czech Republic operating under the Mana food stores name. Most of these stores are supermarkets.[22]

Until 1990, there was no modern retail infrastructure. The surge in tourism has put pressure on the growing retail property market, especially in Prague. New developments such as the Pavillion center and Liberec in Prague are causing rents to rise. The Liberec development of 105,000 square meters (1,130,000 square feet) is funded by Tengelmann (Germany). Retail leases in the Czech Republic are for five to ten years.

Prague's city center, Nove Mesto, was founded in 1348 by Charles IV, but the current city is vibrant and young. Handblown crystal is one of the best buys in Prague. During a recent visit, I decided to purchase some new crystal. There are dozens of crystal shops in each shopping area. I wanted to purchase some handblown glasses with a black tulip base. Many stores sold this particular style, so I decided that it would be worth my time to do a price comparison. The prices did vary.

I wove my way through the city, conducting research for this book and, as an avocation, doing my price study of the crystal. After visiting about a dozen

Photo 11.3
A Slovakian warehouse club has opened in Bratislava. The "Dino" club is functional, not fancy. *Courtesy of SN.*

Photo 11.4
Prague is known for fine crystal. Dozens of small, independent crystal shops line the major shopping streets. *Courtesy of Lisa Applebaum.*

stores that sold crystal, I determined that the lowest price to be found was at one of the major department stores. When I had visited the store, I had noted that it closed at 5:00 P.M. It was now Saturday afternoon. I knew that none of the stores in Prague would be open Sunday, and I was leaving early Monday morning to go back to Germany. This meant that my purchase would need to take place before the store closed at 5:00 P.M. My book research had taken me to the other side of the city. I decided that I had better take the subway to the department store. I arrived there at 4:45 to find the store had closed early. I hurried up a side street I had visited earlier, which I knew had many shops selling the tulip-style glasses. The first store I came to was closed. I went to another; it was also closed. Shops were closing literally moments before I could get to them, and they were all closing before their posted closing time of 5:00 P.M. Finally, I found a shop that was still open. It did carry the glasses, but as I recalled from my earlier, and more leisurely comparison shopping, its prices were the highest I had encountered. By this point, it did not matter. I bought the glasses anyway. I learned two things that day. First, Prague stores no longer use the fixed price system. Second, retailers, even large retailers, open and close at their convenience, not being bound by a responsibility to consumers.

Shopping hours are regulated by local authorities. Only superstores and tourist centers of cities are open on Sunday. Typical hours are from 9:00 A.M. until 5:00 P.M., Monday through Friday, with later closings on Thursday evenings. Shops open on Saturday mornings but usually close at noon or 1:00 P.M. Small shops close for an hour in the middle of the day.[23]

Photo 11.5
Prague streets are full of visitors. Unlike some newly marketizing economies, the Czech Republic has a world class product to sell. This means tourists come to buy goods, not just look at historical buildings.
Courtesy of Lisa Applebaum.

The third country I will discuss in this chapter is Poland. Poland is a large and stable market, with a very undeveloped retail industry. The top five chains have only 6% of retail sales. Poland entered marketization with a fury; the term "shock therapy" is often used to explain how rapidly the country moved from a fixed price system to free market equilibrium.

POLAND

COUNTRY BACKGROUND

Poland is the second largest country in central or eastern Europe, after Russia. The country is named for the Polane, a Slavic tribe that lived in the area more than 1,000 years ago. The name Poland is derived from a Slavic word meaning plain or field, and it aptly describes this country of flat plains and gently rolling hills.

Once, Poles ruled an empire that spanned most of central Europe. But foreign powers conquered Poland, and the land was divided up. Before World War II, Poland was mainly agricultural, with 75% of its people living on farms. In the postwar years, the country became a leading industrial nation. Poland did not become an independent republic until 1918. After

TABLE 11.5

Poland: Selected Demographic and Economic Data

	Population (millions) mid-1995	Area (thousands of sq. km)	GNP per capita		PPP estimates of GNP per capita U.S. = 100		Life expectancy at birth (years) 1995	Adult illiteracy (%) 1995
			Dollars 1995	Avg. ann. growth (%) 1985–95	1987	1995		
Middle-income economies	1,590.9t	60,838t	2,390w	−0.7w			68w	18w
Lower-middle-income economies	1,152.6t	40,323t	1,670w	−1.3w			67w	
Poland	38.6	313	2,790	1.2	21.5	20.0	70	

Source: World Bank (1997). PPP = purchasing power parity. t = total. w = weighted average.

World War II, Poland had a communist government and became part of the Soviet trade bloc, COMECON.

Poland has gone through three phases of planned economy. The first phase, lasting through the mid-1950s involved highly centralized planning. This included the establishment of output objectives for production and strict control over price and margins for the narrow range of goods the government allowed to be produced. The second phase, between the late 1950s and early 1970s, included substantial decentralized planning. Socialist companies could occasionally make their own production and assortment decisions. Price remained centrally controlled. During the third phase, from the mid-1970s through the late 1980s, greater flexibility was permitted to enable socialist enterprises to supply consumers with the goods they wanted, although pricing was still done in a centralized manner.[24]

Poland is now marketizing. The change from socialism to capitalism assumes that the planned economy will increasingly decentralize into private hands, and that the unplanned economy will be absorbed into the overall market economy. Poland has a history of capitalism. Throughout the late 1940s the private sector of Poland was responsible for about 70% of the country's gross domestic product (GDP). From the late 1940s to the early 1960s, however, the government confiscated all businesses. This process is now being reversed, as the large, state enterprises are privatized.[25] Table 11.5 presents selected demographic and economic data for Poland.

RETAILING IN POLAND

Big tents, like circus tents, sometimes house shopping centers in Poland. Grunwaldzki Square, in the city of Wroclaw, is an organized outlet of small merchants that resembles an indoor shopping mall. However, this shopping area is unique. In Poland, each type of retail format has a particular reputation with consumers. Kiosks are viewed as the place to purchase convenience items, such as soft drinks and cigarettes. Department stores have standard quality levels. Open-air markets offer the lowest prices with varying quality levels, but generally lower quality than other retail outlets. Grunwaldzki Square is in a different category because it is an outdoor market brought indoors by a tent. Grunwaldzki Square has 2,700 square meters (29,000 square feet) of shopping space with 148 booths. Table 11.6 lists the types booths found in this square.

The two big ticket items wanted by Polish consumers are an automobile and an apartment. Over half of all Polish families do not own a car. Two-thirds of Polish families have lived in the same apartment for the past 20 years. Only one in four Polish families has a telephone, and every Polish family dreams of having one.[26]

The economic transformation in Poland has been affected by consumers' perceptions of the transition process. There are three cultural-historical antecedents associated with this change. First is the socialist legacy. Consumers have been conditioned to wait for the government to tell them what to do. Under the socialist system, people were trained to await orders and to avoid personal initiative. There was no reward for performance, so the work ethic was weak. A popular saying in Russia about the former government-run business system was, "They pretend to pay us and we pretend to work."

The second cultural-historical antecedent is the aspiration gap. As noted earlier in this chapter, this refers to consumers' perceptions of a discrepancy between the goods and quality of life that they believe they should have and what they can achieve. Often, unrealistic beliefs sharpen the aspiration gap about how others live. In less-developed countries, reruns of *Dallas*, *Dynasty*, and *Santa Barbara*—U.S. TV soap operas about extraordinarily wealthy families—have set the stage for people to think that is how all Americans live.

The third antecedent is the **consumerization process.** The change to a capitalist market must be integrated into other aspects of the economy. The Polish people have little experience as a consumer- or demand-oriented culture. Thus, for the market to function effectively, consumer knowledge needs to increase. Even business people have little understanding of how a market economy functions. In all of Poland, only two universities offer a course in retailing.[27]

Since 1990, the development of modern retailing in Poland has not progressed as rapidly as in the Czech Republic or Hungary. The market is overstored in terms of numbers, although not at all in terms of superstores and shopping centers. Poland tops Europe in the number of stores per capita, with 10 stores per 1,000 people. This is over twice the number of stores in Portugal. The Polish market is dominated by small, family businesses, which are often less than 50 square meters (540 square feet) in size. There are practically no supermarkets outside large cities.

Many consumer goods are beyond the resources of the Polish people. And Polish consumers are more price- than brand-conscious. Physical distribution is hampered by the lack of transportation infrastructure. These problems have discouraged foreign investors in Poland. Since 1994, however, several Western retail chains have been operating in Poland. French and German investors were the first to arrive. French firms included Leclerc, Auchan, Docks de France, Casino, Castorama, and Intermarché. Germany

TABLE 11.6

Vendor Booths in Shopping Pavilion, Grunwaldzki Square (Wroclaw, Poland)

Product Type	Number of Booths
Books	3
Cassette tapes	3
Cigarettes	1
Clothing	52
Casual	(47)
Casual/Formal	(1)
Children's	(3)
Leather	(1)
Food	18
Fresh	(3)
Packaged	(5)
Refrigerated	(3)
Mixed	(6)
Pet food	(1)
Kitchen items	3
Personal care	16
Shoes	9
Casual/Seasonal	(7)
Casual/Formal	(2)
Miscellaneous	18
Don't know/Not open	5
Total occupied	128
Unoccupied	N/A*

Source: Lofman, B. (1994). "Polish Society in Transformation." In *Research in Consumer Behavior: Consumption in Marketizing Economies,* C. Schultz II, R. Belk, and G. Ger, eds., Vol. 7, p.40. Greenwich, Ct.: JAI Press.

N/A = not available.

has Dohle HIT, Komm und Kauf, Plus, and Real. Belgium's Globi, Norway's Rema, Denmark's Netto, and Austria's Billa have also opened in Poland.

The Polish government has introduced programs to help small shopkeepers, who have had difficulty being profitable. Unfortunately for foreign retailers, these programs are modeled along the lines of the French restrictions on the opening of large outlets.[28] Polish retailers feel threatened by the foreign shopping chains, and retailers' demands are supported by right-wing political groups. For instance, the Movement for the Reconstruction of Poland (ROP) has called on citizens to shop in Polish stores, even if these stores offer goods at higher prices.

TABLE 11.7

Major Polish and Foreign Retailers in the Domestic Market, 1995

Retailer	Operations	Sales (ZL* millions)	Outlets (no.)
Ruch (privatized (1996)[a]	State-run kiosk network	2,747	17,000
Polski Handel Spozywczy	State-run retail network	740	950
Elektromis JMB Polska (J. Martins Portugal & Booker UK)	Cash-and-carries	285	54
Pek-Pol	Food stores	1,420	250
Makro (Netherlands)	Cash-and-carries	1,416	6
ABCO	Cash-and-carries	287	8
Vobis (Kaufhof Germany)	Computer stores	79	13
Baltona	Household and electricals stores	65	105
Globi (GIB Belgium)	Supermarkets	45	15
Pewex	Food/non-food stores	38	130
Spolem Gdansk	Regional cooperative	30	25
Mitex Trade	Large general stores	28	8
Savia (Tesco UK)	Grocery	16	36
Krakchemia Krakow	Food/non-food stores	5	1
Cepelia	Arts and crafts stores	N/A*	230
Narvesen (Norway)	Railway kiosks	N/A	200
Ahold (Netherlands) (joint venture with Allkauf Germany) which includes:	Cash-and-carries and food stores	N/A	56
Sesam	Discount food stores	N/A	2
Euronova	Cash-and-carries	N/A	10
Mitex (51%)	Supermarkets	N/A	8
Domy Centrum[a]	Department stores	N/A	36
Novita	Supermarkets	N/A	36
Klub Miedzynarodoweij	Booksellers	N/A	31
Levi's Store (U.S.)	Casual clothing stores	N/A	25
Multi (part German-owned)	Supermarkets	N/A	20
Rema 1000 (Reitan Norway)	Discount food stores	N/A	20
Billa Poland (Rewe Germany)	Supermarkets	N/A	16
Reno/Vobis (Kaufhof Germany)[a]	Footwear and computer stores	N/A	12
Netto (Dansk Supermarked Denmark)	Discount food stores	N/A	10
Yves Rocher (France)	Cosmetics and perfumery stores	N/A	10
Przytula Robert (45% Docks de France/Auchan France)	Supermarkets/hypermarket	N/A	9
Rossman (Germany)	Drugstores	N/A	7
Spar Handels (Germany)	Supermarkets	N/A	6
Aldi (Germany)	Discount food stores	N/A	5

TABLE 11.7

Major Polish and Foreign Retailers in the Domestic Market, 1995

Retailer	Operations	Sales (ZL* millions)	Outlets (no.)
IKEA (Sweden)	Furniture superstores	N/A	4
But Hala (Andre France)	Footwear discount superstores	N/A	4
Hit (Dohle Germany)	Hypermarkets	N/A	3
Elektroland (French-owned)	Electrical goods superstores	N/A	3
Palmers (Austria)	Womenswear and lingerie stores	N/A	3
Leclerc (France)	Hypermarkets	N/A	2
Quelle Polska (Quelle Germany)	Mail-order and computer stores	N/A	2
Auchan (France)	Hypermarket/DIY* superstore	N/A	1
Office Depot (U.S.)	Office goods superstore	N/A	1
Geant (Casino France)	Hypermarket	N/A	1
Kings Cross (Coimpredil Italy)	Hypermarket/cash-and-carries	N/A	1
Castorama (France)	DIY superstore	N/A	1
Domaxel (France)	DIY superstore	N/A	1
Stinnes (Germany)	DIY superstore	N/A	1
Taepper Holdings (Denmark)	Carpet store (at IKEA outlet)	N/A	1
Varner Oglaend (Norway)	Clothing store	N/A	1
Vision Express (UK)[a]	Optical goods store	N/A	1
Bon Prix (Otto Versand Germany)	Mail-order	N/A	0

[a]The Ruch organization, which had central sales of ZL 2.7 in 1995, is being privatized and one possible acquirer is Hachette (France). The Domy Centrum department stores are also being privatized (Jerónimo Martins of Portugal is a contender). Carrefour (France) is involved in a major shopping center development in Krakow. C & A (Germany) has been reported as planning a store in Warsaw. Vision Express (UK) plans up to 30 optical goods outlets. Kaufhof was operating two Reno shoe shops but closed these in 1995. It is undergoing more success with its chain of Vobis computer stores.

Source: *The European Retail Handbook, 1997 Edition.* (1996). London: Corporate Intelligence on Retailing, p. 223.

*ZL = Polish zlotys; 1 ZL = U.S. $0.29; DIY = do-it-yourself; N/A = not available;

The Globe Trade Center in a Warsaw suburb is one of the first purpose-built developments of any size in the country. Carrefour is involved in a major center being built in Krakow. This center will house 100 retailers.[29] Table 11.7 summarizes the major domestic and foreign retailers in Poland.

The Association of Private Retail Trade and Services (ZPHU), a Polish retailers association, estimates that 20% of the food trade in Poland is controlled by foreign retailers. Retailers belonging to ZPHU are calling for a ban on supermarkets doing business on Sundays and holidays. They also would like to limit supermarkets to cities with more than 100,000 residents and even then restrict their building to the outskirts of cities. There are also plans to create local committees, much like what France uses, to determine the locations for new supermarkets and the price for which land can be sold to Western shopping chains. Polish retailers would also like the state to finance the domestic retail trade through a lending program.[30]

RUSSIA

Russia is the final country to be discussed in this chapter. Demographic and economic data comparable to those listed for other countries were not available for Russia.

COUNTRY BACKGROUND

By 1800, the Russian Empire reached from Poland in the west to Alaska in the east. Following the defeat of Napoleon in 1812, Western ideas caught the attention of Russian citizens. The Russian Revolution against the czarist system occurred in 1917. A provisional government assumed power, but it was overthrown in a Communist coup led by Vladimir Lenin. Lenin's death in 1924 precipitated an internal power struggle from which Josef Stalin emerged as the absolute leader. From the 1930s to 1953, the Stalinist regime killed large numbers of people in purge trials, mass executions, and mass deportations to slave labor camps.

In June 1941, Hitler invaded the Soviet Union. After sustaining great losses, the Soviets were able to resist the Germans. After Stalin's death in 1953, Nikita Khrushchev was elected first secretary of the Communist Party. Khrushchev presided over Moscow's cruel suppression of Hungary, and aided the communist revolution in Cuba. In Russia, he was relaxing censorship over literary works and releasing thousands of prisons from the infamous Gulag (labor camp system in Siberia).

In March 1985, Mikhail Gorbachev assumed the leadership of the Soviet Union. He introduced *perestroika* and *glasnost* as the new focus of Soviet economic and foreign policy. This new openness paved the way for an unprecedented reform of the entire Soviet system.

RETAILING IN RUSSIA

It is easy to see why the Russian people might want to return to a planned economy. People are disillusioned. Visitors can see the problems as they approach the central subway stations in Moscow. Long lines of people are selling personal items. This type of selling has gone on for years, although it is illegal. In a letter from Moscow, one observer made this note:

> I was in the passage between Revolution Square and Nikolskaya Street when suddenly the hundred or so women standing along the wall began to flutter and then melt into the crowd in a kind of wave; in an instant, a "market" had disappeared. The reason was the approach of two policemen, whose arrival had been silently sig-

naled down the whole queue. The police strolled into a shop to admire some computer games, the objective of their demarche, and pretended at least to be unaware of the dispersal they had caused. Fifteen seconds had not passed before the hundred sellers and their goods had emerged from the crowd and were back to the wall. There is a Russian saying to the effect that no matter how often one scatters the crows they will just circle and roost again. The roles had been played out.[31]

The black market was the most effective consumer product distribution system in Soviet Russia. A wider variety of products and services were available through black market transactions than through official channels of distribution. In the summer of 1990, 42% of meat, 55% of vegetables, and 75% of potatoes were sold through the black market system.[32]

Today, street kiosks line the roads and cluster near subway and train stations. Although originally the kiosks were temporary structures, more recently they are being replaced with permanent structures. The kiosks are also selling more standard products such as soft drinks and alcohol and fewer artisan-crafted products such as baked goods.

The major department store in Russia is GUM, located in Moscow. GUM originated as an open-air market for bakers, spice merchants, tanners, hatters, and clothmakers. In 1888, the city government and the merchants incorpo-

Photo 11.6 A Russian street scene featuring open vegetable carts and an enclosed kiosk. *Courtesy of Patricia Huddleston.*

Photo 11.7 The major department store in Russia is GUM, which attracts 250,000 shoppers a day, including 20,000 foreign visitors. About 44% of the sales space is used by cooperative agreements with foreign and Russian retailers. GUM directly operates 29% of the space. The remainder is leased by independent retailers. *Courtesy of Patricia Huddleston.*

rated a company, the Great Merchant's Galleries with the shopkeepers as the majority shareholders. A competition was held to find an architect to design the Galleries' home. The architect who was selected, Alexandre Pomerantsev, proposed a three-part shopping gallery with exterior turrets and glass ceilings. After the Russian Revolution took place, the gallery was nationalized and for many years it served as office space. In 1953, the Soviet government decided to create GUM, the Russian acronym for State Universal Store.

The flagship store has a prime location, just opposite the Kremlin in a castle-like structure. This GUM store is twice as large as Bloomingdale's 59th Street flagship store in New York City. It draws 250,000 shoppers a day, including 20,000 foreign visitors.[33] The business part of GUM is privatized. The building is listed as a historical monument owned by the government of the Russian Federation, so the building itself cannot be privatized. GUM leases the premises from the Moscow government. The lease, signed in 1992, expires in 2042.

GUM operates 16,000 square meters (172,000 square feet) directly and leases another 16,000 square meters of shopping space to other retailers. The flagship store is divided into 125 trading sections, each representing an individual boutique or specialty shop. Approximately 44% of the sales space is used in cooperation agreements with foreign and Russian retailers. An additional 29% is occupied by shops directly operated by GUM. The rest are leased by independent retailers.[34]

The amount of space leased by independent retailers increased throughout 1994 and reached a peak in 1995. Management has restructured the operation of the main store since 1994. They are bringing in higher-margin foreign retailers. Instead of subleasing space to retailers, GUM creates joint ventures with them. This allows GUM to share in the upside, with guaranteed minimum profits. Chanel, Escada, and Botany 500 have smaller shops in GUM. Galeries Lafayette has an 800 square meter (8,600 square foot) space in which private label clothing and accessories are sold. These aspects make GUM more like a shopping mall than a department store.

Karstadt operates a 2,100 square meter (23,000 square foot) store in GUM, which provides the salespeople, warehouse space, and currency facilities. Karstadt imports the merchandise and interior displays and trains the sale associates. Karstadt and GUM together set the retail prices.[35]

There is a plan by GUM to refurbish the useable space in the main stores. The plans call for increasing the current area from 16,000 square meters (172,000 square feet) to 45,000 square meters (484,000 square feet). This will not be completed until the year 2002.[36] About 24% of the current selling space is used for direct subleasing. Tenants pay a fixed annual charge. Direct subleasing contributes 25% of the company's gross profits. The Moscow government limits GUM's rights to sublet, and GUM cannot lease more than 25% of trading space at its own discretion. If it exceeds this limit, it must pay the city 50% of the difference between its cost per square meter and the amount paid for the excess leased space.

The joint venture agreements have the following provisions:

- GUM's partner pays for design and refurbishment of the new shop and for installation of sales equipment and displays. In addition, it contributes marketing know-how.
- GUM and its partner sign a supply contract (or a consignment agreement) with 90 days delayed payment after delivery. Merchandise is selected jointly by GUM and its partner.
- GUM provides retail premises, warehousing facilities, and staff, and guarantees security.
- The target gross margin is specified in the agreement. The tenant guarantees that the space will generate enough profit to meet this target. The average target gross margin is around $3,500 per square meter per year.[37]

In these joint venture arrangements, GUM buys merchandise from the partner and serves as a retailer. When products are sold, it makes a margin on the sale. At the end of each quarter, GUM reviews the sales, calculating the gross profit generated by each square meter under each cooperative agreement.

A chain of 14 smaller shops is operated by GUM in Moscow and is expanding into Russia's other regions. The smaller shops do not have the same productivity as the main store. There are plans to remodel all the stores in an effort to bring them up to the main store's level of profit. Currently, the other stores have sales of $3,640 per square meter, compared to the main stores' $8,311 sales per square meter.

The operating profit per square meter for GUM is $919, well ahead of the two other major publicly held Russian retail companies. TsUM made $360 per square meter in 1995 and Petrovsky Passazh made $500. The two best non-Russian comparisons are May Department Stores in the United States making $253 per square meter and Lojas Americanos in Mexico, making $89 per square meter.[38]

Retail space that will go for $3,000 to $5,000 per square meter in Moscow, would cost $1,100 to $1,200 in the United States and $1,200 to $1,500 in Europe. Several new shopping areas are being proposed in Moscow. These areas may present competition and push retail prices down. The major foreign partners in GUM are listed in Table 11.8.

GUM buys goods from various wholesalers or directly from domestic producers. It sells merchandise at an average markup of 20%. GUM's management has improved the choice of goods the store offers. The company entered several long-term agreements with prominent Russian producers for direct supply of goods. In 1995, GUM opened a centralized buying department to optimize sourcing and provide a consistent supply of popular products.[39]

Currently, there is little direct competition for GUM. TsUM is the second largest retailer in Moscow. It has 9,000 square meters (97,000 square feet) of prime space opposite the Bolshoi Theater and the Metropol Hotel. Most of the customers are non-Muscovites with low to average incomes. Target customers for GUM are from the middle to upper middle class, while TsUM has relied on cooperation with domestic and low-profile foreign retailers. It uses a disorganized retail strategy, narrow range of goods, and poor presentation. The same goods are often sold in several locations in the store, for different prices. It is an old Woolworth-type store.[40]

Petrovsky Passazh is an upscale shopping arcade close to TsUM. Its target market is the top-income, newly rich Muscovites. The store is 4,018 square meters (43,249 square feet), divided into 38 boutiques selling luxury goods. Petrovsky Passazh sells Giorgio Armani, Nina Ricci, Bally, Kenzo, Guerlain, and Longines. This company does not deal directly with the suppliers, but instead goes through Russian intermediaries. It pays more for its products because of this purchasing system. Prices at Petrovsky Passazh are high.

Manezhnaya Ploshchad is a massive underground shopping center on Manezh Square near the Kremlin. The complex, run by the government, is expected to become a four-story shopping mall with recreation areas, a parking lot for 700 cars, and 35,000 square meters (375,000 square feet) of shopping space. Gostinny Dvor, another project run by the government, is located in a historical building, just around the corner from GUM. Before the 1917 revolution, it was known as the Middle Trading Stalls, housing small stores of Russian merchants and serving as a hostel (*gostinny dvor* in old Russian means guest house). The retail stores that will be part of this

TABLE 11.8

GUM's Largest Foreign Partners

Company	Sales Area (sq. m.)
Karstadt	2132.0
Galeries Lafayette	801.7
Steilmann	420.0
la Mode	223.0
Samsonite	208.0
Botany 500	177.8
Wella	159.0
Salamander	147.6
Yves Rocher	145.2
Christian Dior	144.6
Reebok	136.0
Estee Lauder	134.0
Hogel	129.0
Tefal	120.0
Escada	111.2
Pfaff Burda	104.0
Soap Berry Shop	97.4
Benetton Sport	92.1
Claude Litz	87.9
Lego	82.9
Clinique (Estee Lauder)	76.0
Others	117.5
TOTAL	5,846.9

Source: "GUM—Company Report." (October 22, 1996). Credit Suisse First Boston, Ltd., in *Investext* [Database on CD-ROM]. Foster City, Calif.: Information Access.

complex could present competition for GUM. The rents here are scheduled to be between $1,500 and $1,700 per square foot.[41]

SUMMARY

Under planned economies, prices of products are low but goods are scarce. Changing from a planned to a demand economy is a difficult process. Until the principles of supply and demand take effect, skyrocketing inflation and product shortages occur. Planned economies comprised of state-owned stores and cooperatives never had to be accountable for product sales. Under the responsibility system, sales employees were accountable for theft but they were not responsible for sales and profits. Learning how to price products and services and how to advertise those services is a trial-and-error process. Company Focuses III.8 and III.9 tell the story of two companies making this transition.

Of the countries discussed in this chapter, Russia has the longest and hardest road ahead as it struggles to make the transition to a free market economy. The other eastern European countries had a recent history of capitalism. Communist rule did not begin in Hungary, the Czech Republic, and Poland until after World War II. Thus, one can find citizens who remember what life was like before the centrally planned economy. In Russia, which became a communist nation in 1917, people do not remember what it was like to have a free market.

The planned market experiment in Russia and the Soviet bloc failed. Hungary was the first eastern European country to open the door to market reform, and other eastern European countries followed. Much work will be needed in these countries to rebuild their economies.

This chapter concludes Part III on retailers in Europe. Our attention now turns to Asia. There are some obvious similarities between eastern European countries and the People's Republic of China (PRC). The PRC is also in the process of moving from a planned to a free market system. The country's state-owned stores are being turned over to private owners. This move to a market economy is made easier by the involvement of retailers from Japan, Hong Kong, and Taiwan. Retailers from those Asian countries are moving the PRC forward, similar to French and German retailers in eastern Europe. In the case of the PRC, the move is from east to west. In Europe, the move was from western Europe to eastern Europe.

We are witnessing a natural experiment, the first time countries have changed from planned economies to free markets. Each country is approaching the transition in a different way. In the end, they may be able to tell us whether an approach such as a Poland's "shock therapy" or China's "putting a toe in the water" makes the transition easier.

KEY TERMS

aspiration gap
blocked or nonconvertible currency
cooperatives
consumerization process
ethnic resources competition theory
greenfield option
most favored nation
planned economy
privatization
product risk
profit centers
responsibility system
state stores
value added tax (VAT)

DISCUSSION QUESTIONS

1. Under a planned economy, retailing is considered to be a nonproductive activity. Why would market planners have this attitude?

2. Use ethnic resource competition theory to explain why consumers would try to disguise consumption.
3. How could U.S. TV shows like *Dallas* and *Dynasty* affect consumers in these marketizing economies? If your explanation did not include the concept of aspiration gap, look back over the discussion of that concept and reframe your discussion.
4. Why is most favored nation status important to retailers in planned economies?
5. Why do we say that the informal economy is the market system that operates under a demand economy. When the informal market system is illegal (black market) how are prices for goods in that market affected?

ENDNOTES

1. Hall, L. (1992). *Latecomer's Guide to the New Europe: Doing Business in Central Europe.* New York: American Marketing Association.
2. Seitz, H. (1992). "Retailing in Eastern Europe: An Overview." *International Journal of Retail and Distribution Management,* Vol. 20, No. 6, pp. 4–10.
3. Turban, J. (1977). "Some Observations on Retail Distribution in Poland." *Soviet Studies,* Vol. 29, pp. 128–136.
4. Davies, B., and R. Schmidt. (1991). "Going Shopping in Poland: The Changing Scene of Polish Retailing." *International Journal of Retail and Distribution Management,* Vol. 19, No. 4, pp. 20–27.
5. KPMG—International (May 1996). Central Europe. *Microsoft Internet Explorer*. [Web site]
6. Schultz, C., R. Belk, and G. Ger, eds. (1994). *Research in Consumer Behavior: Consumption in Marketizing Economies,* Vol. 7. Greenwich, Conn.: JAI Press.
7. Sampson, S. (1991). "May You Live Only by Your Salary! The Unplanned Economy in Eastern Europe," *Social Justice,* Vol. 15, No. 3/4, pp. 135–159.
8. Goldman, M. (1991). *What Went Wrong with Perestroika.* New York: W.W. Norton and Company, p. 116.
9. Samarasinghe, S.W.R. de A., and R. Coughlan. (1991). *Economic Dimensions of Ethnic Conflict.* New York: St. Martin's Press.
10. Pecotich, A., N. Renko, and C. Shultz. (1994). "Yugoslav Disintegration, War, and Consumption in Croatia." In C. Schultz, R. Belk, and G. Ger, eds., *Consumption in Marketizing Economies,* Vol. 7. Greenwich, Conn.: JAI Press, pp. 1–27.
11. Earle, J., R. Fryman, A. Rapaczynski, and J. Turkewitz. (1994). *Small Privatization: The Transformation of Retail Trade and Consumer Services in the Czech Republic, Hungary and Poland.* Budapest: Central European University Press.
12. "Hungary: From Reds to Riches." (1989). *Euromoney,* May, pp. 28–35.

13. Coopers & Lybrand. (1996). *Global Retailing: Assignment Eastern Europe.*
14. James, P. (1992). "Retailing in Hungary: Centrum Department Stores." *International Journal of Retail and Distribution Management,* Vol. 20, No. 6, pp. 24–29.
15. *The European Retail Handbook, 1997 Edition.* (1996). London: Corporate Intelligence on Retailing.
16. Drasny, T. (1992). "Retailing in Czechoslovakia, Retailing in Eastern Europe." *International Journal of Retail and Distribution Management,* Vol. 20, No. 6, pp. 30–33.
17. Pellet, J. (1995). "Retailing in Eastern Europe." *Discount Merchandiser,* Vol. 35, July 1, p. 72.
18. Pellet (1995).
19. Pellet (1995).
20. Drtina, T. (1996). "The Internationalization of Retailing in the Czech and Slovak Republics." In G. Akehurst and N. Alexander, eds., *The Internationalization of Retailing.* London: Frank Cass & Co., pp. 191–203.
21. Sternquist, B., personal interviews.
22. *Retail News Letter.* (1995). No. 421, February, p. 4.
23. *The European Retail Handbook, 1997 Edition.* (1996).
24. Lofman, B. (1994). "Polish Society in Transformation." In C. Schultz, R. Belk, and G. Ger, eds., *Research in Consumer Behavior: Consumption in Marketizing Economies,* Vol. 7. Greenwich, Conn.: JAI Press, p. 30.
25. Lofman (1994)
26. Styezek, D. (1992). "Family Living Standards: Uncertain Futures." *Warsaw Voice,* October 18, pp. 12–13.
27. Lofman (1994).
28. *The European Retail Handbook, 1997 Edition.* (1996).
29. *The European Retail Handbook, 1997 Edition.* (1996).
30. "Supermarkets: Super Targets." (1996). *Warsaw Voice,* November 24, p. 10.
31. Fenster, E. (1995). "Letter from Moscow." *Small World,* Vol. 1, No. 6, November/December, p. 10.
32. Peck, M. J., & T. J. Richardson. (1991). *What Is to Be Done? Proposals for the Soviet Transition to the Market.* New Haven, Conn.: Yale University Press.
33. Raper, S. (1992). "Moscow's GUM Gearing for Growth." *Women's Wear Daily,* September 9, p. 24.
34. "GUM—Company Report." (October 22, 1996). Credit Suisse First Boston in *Investext* [Database on CD-ROM]. Foster City, Calif.: Information Access.
35. Raper (1992).
36. "GUM—Company Report" (October 22, 1996), Credit Suisse First Boston.
37. "GUM—Company Report" (October 22, 1996).
38. "GUM—Company Report" (October 22, 1996).
39. "GUM—Company Report" (October 22, 1996).
40. "GUM—Company Report" (October 22, 1996).
41. "GUM—Company Report" (October 22, 1996).

COMPANY FOCUS III.1

TESCO

Andrea Rehm, Cynita Thomas, Ramsey Watkins, Rosalyn Williams

History

Tesco, one of the leading food retailers in Great Britain, was started in 1919 on the east side of London, when John Edward Cohen opened of his first grocery store. Who could have known that something so small would grow into a chain with over 545 stores in England, Scotland, and Wales? Today, the company is the largest U.K. food retailer.

After Cohen became a successful market trader, he officially founded Tesco in 1931. He derived the company's name by combining his own initials with those of a particular tea that he carried in the store. Cohen visited the United States, where he became a student of the American food retailing system. This trip gave Cohen the concept of the supermarket and provided the basis for his first self-service store. During this time, Tesco made shares available to the public, which allowed for increased expansion over the next two decades.

The growth that followed was almost solely provided by the acquisition of smaller grocery chains: Burnard's in 1955, Williamsons Ltd. in 1959, Charles Phillips & Company in 1964, and the Adsega chain in 1965.[1] In the midst of these acquisitions, the first Tesco supermarket was introduced in 1956. This introduction was followed by the development a higher margin, non-food merchandise department located in the bigger stores. The next step was the establishment of the first "superstore," taking up 49,000 square feet (4,550 square meters).[2]

During the 1970s, Cohen used the knowledge gained from his stay in the United States to make Tesco known for its "pile it high, sell it cheap" image. However, this approach quickly backfired in a decade when quality reigned over quantity and market changes were abundant. Inflation and recession also prevailed throughout this decade. Tesco's slump was exacerbated by an insufficient variety of merchandise, and a lack of customer service. In these circumstances, an unfortunate price war was started with the company's leading competitor, Sainsbury. To turn Tesco around, drastic measures were necessary, and a large-scale modernization program was undertaken. This process included closing unprofitable stores, implementing a computerized distribution system, offering higher quality goods, and pursuing the supermarket concept more strongly. Tesco also developed its own line of private label products to help beat the slump.[3]

Although the recessionary slump continued into the early 1980s, Tesco managed to establish a chain of discount stores known as Victor Value, which were later sold to H. Williams Company. By 1985, Tesco (now Tesco PLC) had opened its 100th superstore after a zoning controversy at the location in Brent Park, Neaspen. Once Tesco won the battle to build there, it became London's largest food retailer.[4] In 1985, the company also expanded its stores and warehouses, and completed the takeover of the 40-store chain, Hillards PLC. Tesco was successful with this strategy and overtook Sainsbury as the U.K. supermarket leader in 1996.

Strategy

Tesco's basic strategy has continued to benefit the company by doing one thing, *putting the customers' needs first.* This is accomplished by developing the product, price, and promotion around the customer. Tesco represents *value,* and it creates *loyalty* for those who shop there. For example, the Clubcard used by the company to earn greater sales and provide customer value has become quite successful. Through the Clubcard, Tesco can gather information about who purchases what and how much they spend. This provides the company with enough information to indulge consumers in savings on their favorite brands as well as maintaining a personal relationship with them. During the Clubcard introduction, competitors such as Sainsbury stated: "We estimate that an electronic Green Shield stamp promotion would cost at least £10 million [U.S. $16.3 million] just to administer. That's wasted money which brings no benefits at all to the customers. We have no plans to go that route. We will continue to focus our efforts on delivering good food for less."[5] This response proved to be shortsighted.

Within months, the Clubcard had built up a membership of over 5 million users and created a 17% spontaneous awareness rating along with 15% usage. The company's advertisements summed it up: "Tesco's Clubcard: The most popular loyalty scheme in the UK. . . ."[6]

In addition to strong efforts such as the Clubcard, Tesco also formed a joint venture with Virgin Cola in 1994. This gave Tesco the exclusive right to carry the cola for a certain period of time in order to keep up with the competition and increase sales.[7]

Advertising plays a key role in the company's strategy. By using a "no quibble moneyback guarantee," Tesco has gained some popularity. The strong new character developed for the company's television ads delivers humor and creates a consumer liking. "In its new ads Tesco promotes the theme that the customer comes first."[8] By caring about the customers' wants and needs, Tesco has developed a most important concept: value for the consumer as well as a profit for itself. The company conducted a survey of its customers' preferences and then designed prototype stores based on these concepts. In 1997, some of these new prototype stores opened. The aisles are two or three times the width of those in regular supermarkets. Fresh produce is offered at the front of the store, and the stores do not have any doors. Panels are retracted when the store is open and a specially designed air system keeps temperature-controlled air in the store.

Stores and Location

The format of Tesco stores has changed steadily over the years. The company still has superstores containing grocery items, and 15% of non-food items, including such goods as clothing, toys, garden tools, and car repair accessories. At present, Tesco also has 80 superstores, which now include home entertainment departments. A planned increase to 110 stores is in progress. Clothing has also been a successful addition, and an increase from the 116 stores already carrying apparel to 147 stores is also being implemented.

Along with the superstores, Tesco has three new store formats: Metro, Express, and Compact. The Compact store is similar to a superstore, but on a smaller scale. It is easier to find sites for these smaller stores and they are less expensive. Their locations include such spots as markets and towns, the edges of high street, and also around already operating superstores. Compact stores provide convenience to the consumer with quality goods at a nearby location. Fourteen stores were scheduled to open in 1995, and the company planned to open more if they continued to be successful.

Tesco currently has 15 Metros, five of which are old and have been converted. Plans for Metro include either converting or opening 75 more stores over the next few years. This will contribute a significant profit to the company because of less warehouse space and more retail space due to internal extension in eight of the stores. Metro stores are located in city centers where their target market consists of workers, as well as local residents. The stores are the size of convenience stores but they carry nearly a full range of products including high quality fresh produce.

The last of Tesco's new store formats is the Express. This is a petroleum station as well as a convenience store. Because the petroleum is bought and sold by Tesco directly, it cuts down a great deal on cost. The convenience store mixes Tesco's own private label products in with the other products it carries. In 1995, three sites were open with 10 more planned over the course of that year. Plans called for increasing the speed by opening over 100 stores in the near future, including 15 to 20 opening in 1995–1996.

Compact, Metro, and Express are strong additions to Tesco's company profile, generating 8.6% of Tesco's 12.9% total sales increase. With the expansion of all three of these stores, Tesco stands to become even more successful and profitable.

Logistics System

Tesco's distribution system has moved through several phases over the past three decades. Initially, distribution centered on the delivery of products directly from the manufacturer: an approach known as Operation Checkout. Although 80% of all supplies came from the manufacturers, resources were becoming scarce. Soon, Tesco faced problems in handling the increased volume, and in peak weeks, the stockrooms would be stored with excess goods. Another problem faced by the company was irregular delivery times. Delays would often last up to six hours, causing customers to wait while empty shelves were refilled.

Due to the unpredictability of Tesco's distribution system in the 1970s, a move toward centralization was unavoidable. Under this strategy, Tesco gained control of the system as well as reducing lead time. Instead of not knowing exactly when a shipment would be delivered, centralization provided a maximum 48-hour lead time. Tesco has identified seven key benefits to this strategy:[9]

1. A change to fixed distribution facilities.
2. Improved lead times.

3. Common handling systems used at distribution centers and stores.
4. Adoption of multishift working.
5. Computer software modeled company decisions.
6. Dedicated distributors met high levels of performance.
7. Technology to control inventory.

Tesco now has a network of distribution centers that are linked by computer to all if its stores.

After studying its logistics system, Tesco developed composite distribution. This allows the company to both store and deliver a wide variety of products that require special attention, such as those that must be kept within a certain temperature range. Both warehouses and vehicles have temperature-controlled departments that enable any combination of goods to be transported to stores. Frozen foods can be kept frozen, fresh foods kept cool, and hot foods kept hot. These goods are stored in one of eight distribution centers located throughout the United Kingdom. Of these eight, only two are actually operated by Tesco. The remaining six are operated by contracted distribution centers, third-party distribution providers. Supermarket chains in the United Kingdom are leaders in the use of this system. Each auto center is responsible for its appointed 50 stores located in various regions of the country. Composite distribution has reduced stock levels held at stores, improved product quality, and reduced waste. The centralization of this distribution system also played a key role in the modernization of Tesco as a whole.

Competition

Tesco faces many small forms of competition, but its main competition comes from Sainsbury, Safeway, and ASDA. These four powerhouses control over one-third of the United Kingdom's grocery market.[10] Originally, Tesco's quality did not compare to that of its competition. Although both Sainsbury and Safeway led the way with their innovations, Tesco improved the innovations. As a result, Tesco now holds the top spot in retail food.[11]

The changes employed by Tesco include "Tesco Value," quality goods for a low price, and better advertising. Tesco also beat out the competition with the innovation of the Clubcard, which both Sainsbury and Safeway now incorporate into their strategy.

The fierce competition between these companies (especially Sainsbury and Tesco) makes attaining and holding the number one market position difficult. Sainsbury has had to severely cut down on the prices of its private label products in retaliation to Tesco's efforts.[12] Although this may be a wise move on the part of Sainsbury, Tesco is sure to retaliate, not only to keep its sales, but to prevent a price gap from developing.

On another level, Sainsbury and Tesco also fought head to head for the acquisition of Wm. Low, a grocery store that operated 57 stores in Scotland and northern England. Sainsbury started a bidding war after learning of Tesco's interest. However, Tesco counteracted with a higher bid and obtained the company. This acquisition posed a large problem for Sainsbury, as both companies had no stronghold on the Scotland market before Tesco's takeover.[13]

Conclusion

Since Tesco overtook Sainsbury as market leader among the U.K. food retailers, it has been a constant struggle to stay on top. Tesco must continue to implement new ideas and innovations if it wants to retain the top spot.

DISCUSSION QUESTIONS

1. What kinds of strategies could Tesco implement to produce a more efficient distribution system without using centralization?
2. Tesco operates in an oligopoly situation. The four major food multiples in the United Kingdom control over 60% of the market share. What effect does price cutting have in a market like this? What are some other methods of competing?
3. A major part of Tesco's sales are private label/private brand merchandise. What particular benefits does this have in an oligopoly market?

ENDNOTES

1. *International Directory of Company Histories*, Vol. 2. (1990).
2. *International Directory of Company Histories*, Vol. 2. (1990).
3. *International Directory of Company Histories*, Vol. 2. (1990).
4. *International Directory of Company Histories*, Vol. 2. (1990).
5. "From High Street to Quality Street." (1995). *Financial Times*, April 21, p. 24.
6. Snowdon, R. (1995). "Tesco Ups the Ante with Humorous Ads." *Marketing*, June.
7. *Financial Times*, October 13, 1994.
8. Lee, J. (1995). "Tesco Express Gets Green Light." *Marketing*, April 13, p. 1.
9. Smith, D. L. G., and L. Sparks. (1993). *The Transformation of Physical Distribution in Retailing: The Example of Tesco PLC.*
10. *The Economist*, December 4, 1993.
11. "From High Street to Quality Street" (1995).
12. "Store Wars." (1993). *The Economist*, Vol. 329, p. 3.
13. *Retail News Letter.* (1994). No. 416, August.

COMPANY FOCUS III.2

THE BODY SHOP

Amy Ruis, Rana Bardos, Sara Veliquette

History

The Body Shop is an international retailer, based in the United Kingdom, that sells skin and hair care products. The company began in 1976, in Brighton, England because the founder Anita Roddick was looking for a way to earn extra money for her family. One of the concepts that makes this company so unique is its commitment to the environment. The Body Shop products are sold in refillable plastic bottles, which decreases waste. At first, the use of refillable bottles was simply a money-saving strategy. However, this developed into a fantastic marketing strategy.

On her opening day, Roddick offered 15 products in the plastic bottles with handwritten labels. Her first day's sales totaled $208.00.[1] Now, 21 years later, The Body Shop has more than $1 billion dollars in sales and 1,500 stores in 47 countries. The Body Shop employs 2,500 people. Approximately 80% of all managerial positions are held by women.

The Body Shop has achieved its growth through franchising. Much of The Body Shop's profit remains in the United Kingdom and Ireland. However, stores outside these countries have shown remarkable growth. The Body Shop is one of the most successful international retailers in the world today.

Product Development and Marketing

Innovative products produced with natural ingredients are the key to The Body Shop's growth. The Body Shop creates, produces, and sells skin and hair care products along with other related items that are naturally based,[2] such as Brazil Nut conditioner, Blue Corn scrub mask, Honey Stick Lip balm, and Avocado Body Butter.[3] The Body Shops' core product range consists of about 450 lines in a variety of bottle sizes. However, the company is constantly updating and developing new products. Each shop carries a comprehensive list of all ingredients,[4] along with an outline of the company's views on animal testing and the purchasing of supplies from the Third World.[5] The buying of supplies from indigenous populations is called The Body Shop Community Trade program. Originally called "Trade Not Aid," this program was launched in 1987 and includes such strategies as buying blue corn from the Pueblo Indians in New Mexico.[6] The Body Shop strives to help communities in need through purchases and trade, which enables these communities to boost their economies.

Customers are also offered pamphlets on recycling and education about acquired immunodeficiency syndrome (AIDS). The Body Shop has a goal of educating the world on these and other topics. The Body Shop conveys the message, "If you think education is expensive, try ignorance."[7]

The Body Shop's marketing techniques started in 1976 when the first store opened. That store was painted green to cover the cracks on the damp walls, not to represent plant life as some people have thought. Roddick found her now award-winning bottles from the urine sample department at the local hospital. The bottles were inexpensive and fit into her budget at that time. The Body Shop promotes recycling with its customers by encouraging them to return used bottles for refills. At first, this was done because there was not enough money to purchase new containers. The bottles were labeled with handwritten round stickers, which are sometimes thought to symbolize the earth. In fact, the labels were selected because they were cheap. The labels also provide product ingredients. This helped customers understand why the products were sometimes lumpy and came in strange colors.

The Body Shop's prices may be higher than those of some other retailers. The management philosophy is that their products are of a higher quality and the cheaper products are inferior.[8] The Body Shop invests little money in advertising. Instead, the company and its founder, Anita Roddick, rely on media attention. It is a promotional strategy in itself.[9] Roddick first learned about the power of the press when her first store was threatened with a lawsuit. The store had opened right next to two funeral parlors. The funeral parlors did not want a store name, "The Body Shop," so close to their corpses. When this story was covered by the local paper, store business took off;[10] Roddick has used this type of publicity to her advantage ever since.

A television report criticized The Body Shop for using products tested on animals. Prior to 1996, The Body Shop's policy was not to use any products or ingredients tested on animals within the last five years. The television program pointed out that since it takes that long for the products to gain approval, The Body Shop really was not as concerned with animal testing as it implied by its policy statements. The report made it look as if The Body Shop's position was purely a marketing strategy. This attack on The Body Shop's image led to a six-week legal battle in British courts. The Body Shop won the case by proving to the court that its stores carry pamphlets explaining its "Against Animal Testing" policy. The court agreed with The Body Shop, and its image remained intact. The publicity from this lawsuit showcased The Body Shop's image, ideals, and commitment to the environment. This is just another example of how The Body Shop uses promotion without advertising. Management believes it is a waste of time and money to extensively advertise its products. They believe advertising is an unnecessary cost that would have to be passed on to consumers.[11,12]

Competition

The Body Shop's sales in the United States have not been satisfactory. A variety of copycat retailers in every mall have taken The Body Shop's concept and done it better. In 1996, The Body Shop hired a new U.S. CEO, a former executive from IKEA, to help turn the company around.[13]

Other cosmetic companies have tried to copy The Body Shop's success. In the United States, they have been successful. Estee Lauder has launched a "natural" ingredients line called Origins. The Limited's Bath and Body Works is very similar to The Body Shop.[14] Other brand competitors include H2O plus, Garden Botanika, Goodbodies, and Naturistics. Although these products are marketed with a similar theme (natural products in recyclable bottles), none can boast the environmental activism of The Body Shop. According to Roddick, this is a crucial advantage her company has over her competitors. "Customers don't enter my store just for the products but [because they support] the company. They come in for the conversation, the link with the community."[15]

Corporate Responsibility

Roddick's believes that businesses should create positive social change. This business idealism movement is growing rapidly. It now extends into the United States, Europe, and Mexico. She has developed good networking strategies through shared areas of interest. The Body Shop is exchanging best practices and creating new markets with customers who are informed and morally aware. They are succeeding and flourishing as businesses and as didactic forces. Through this, they create the impression that they are here to stay.

Through her company, The Body Shop, Roddick advocates replacing the idea of free trade with that of fair trade or sustainable trade. Fair trade acts as a crutch to communities and families, along with demonstrating respect for them. It also protects the environment and teaches others to respect human rights. To back this strategy of fair trade, Roddick defines corporate responsibility in the following way: "We have to rethink our approach to these issues. And then we have to act, in ways big and small, to bring sustainable and healthy growth across the globe. Our political postures must change—we have to stop endlessly whining for easier rules, lower costs, and fewer restrictions. And our business practices must change. We have to take longer term views, invest in communities, and build long lasting markets."[16]

Millions of bars of soap are sold at The Body Shop every year. Originally, the company purchased the soap from a supplier whose cheap prices were due to the use of immigrant labor. This went against The Body Shop's corporate ethics, so the company built its own soap factory in an area of high unemployment. This is an example of a moral business decision by The Body Shop. These decisions are successful because customers understand that their purchases are moral choices as well. The Body Shop feels that businesses should be held environmentally and socially accountable.

Roddick has come up with ideas to reduce transitional difficulties and create more economic gain, which she uses in her business strategy. One project entails the Nanhu cacti. This project first started in 1992 with the Nanhu Indians, who live north of Mexico City. They use techniques perfected by the Aztecs to help them make body scrubs from the fibers of the cacti. Many of the men have left to seek work in the United States and Mexico City. The women have banded together to keep their communities intact. Thanks to the effort put forth by The Body Shop and nongovernmental organizations, the women are making a living. The Body Shop is working with them to find new products that use the cacti, thus diversifying their economic base. This is another example of The Body Shop's Community Trade program.

Another Body Shop project deals with General Paper Industries, producers of hand-made paper in Nepal. A community fund was established from the profits derived from this factory. This fund is used for a variety of purposes that help the community. For instance, there is a medical fund; a scholarship for girls; and a revolving loan of sorts that helps women to start their own small businesses, as Roddick did. These projects help to expand opportunities, uphold communities, and increase income.[17]

Roddick has requested that the International Chamber of Commerce (ICC) pass two propositions related to ethical international business practices. The first proposition seeks to define native intellectual property rights. For example, corporate botanists rely on the knowledge and ideas of local farmers and herbalists. These native experts direct the researchers to valuable plants and potential applications that have been created over the centuries. There are no regulations requiring the researchers to compensate these natives in any way. This is one of the reasons why change is needed regarding fair trade and respect for native people.

The second proposition requests the ICC to make an aggressive move to develop a Corporate Code of Conduct. This code would be based on principles that are formal and well-voiced. If this code were followed, it would end the excuse that competition makes ethical actions impossible. Everyone could accept the idea of competing in nondestructive ways that are harmless to the community and environment.

Environmental Awareness

When Roddick founded the company, she outlined a set of specific principles to follow. For instance, she felt that there was no need to test her products on animals and she wanted naturally based ingredients. Other principles entailed using minimal packaging and avoiding product advertising. The company has been involved in strong environmental and political issues, such as ozone depletion, the burning of the rain forest, and human rights. It has been standing behind these principles and issues since 1976. Making a difference in the community has also been an issue for The Body Shop. Each shop encourages its employees to participate in community service projects and allows them up to four paid hours per month to do so. This helps to show the strong dedication put forth by The Body Shop.

In the United States, The Body Shop's core issues are HIV/AIDS awareness and education, and stopping violence against women. In 1993, the company launched its eye-catching HIV/AIDS campaign, called "Protect and Respect," featuring photographs of infected individuals by noted photographer Annie Leibovitz. In 1995,

The Body Shop launched its ground-breaking campaign to "Blow the Whistle on Violence Against Women."[18]

Finally, The Body Shop has shown its commitment to environmental issues by moving ahead without European Community (EC) guidelines. It did not wait for the EC to ratify environmental auditing. The company measures its waste and energy use, and has built a wind farm to put the energy back into the national grid.

Franchising

The Body Shop's growth is financed through franchising. This has enabled the company to expand into foreign markets quickly. The Body Shop maintains tight control of its global franchising to uphold its good image as perceived by customers. Several features must be approved by The Body Shop's Franchise Department. These include setting, design, and layout. The franchiser must also sign an agreement stating that it will upgrade the store, if needed, to the specifications required by the Franchise Department.[19]

When starting to expand into a foreign market, The Body Shop has a policy of appointing a head franchisee for a given country or area; then The Body Shop supplies merchandise to that person. The franchisee is obligated to provide a warehouse from which to distribute The Body Shop's products. By using this method, The Body Shop has worked through and overcome many difficulties, such as cultural differences and opinions about institutions through its mass global market. Having a head franchisee with local knowledge and expertise has enabled The Body Shop to become a successful international retailer.

The United Kingdom's market is almost saturated, pushing the importance of global expansion. The Body Shop has been able to finance its mass expansions in other countries because of increased sales and future sales estimates. These estimates appear favorable due to the increasing acceptance of the brand in foreign markets.

Conclusions

The Body Shop is one of the most successful global retailers today. What makes this company unique is its tireless commitment to the environment as well as the people living within it. The company demonstrates strong character with well-rounded moral beliefs, thereby generating a valuable customer base. The Body Shop believes that if other companies followed in its footsteps and focused on developing accurate and broad standards for everyone, instead of for the interests of business, a stronger and more wholesome world could prevail.

DISCUSSION QUESTIONS

1. Like The Body Shop, IKEA has been successful in using environmental, community, and moral issues as company image enhancers. Some organizations are beginning to use this strategy, but considering the success of The Body Shop and IKEA, why aren't more following suit?
2. Discuss the possible disadvantages (if any) when a firm takes an "activist-like" position and integrates it into the corporate mission. Can you think of an example where this approach has backfired?
3. The Body Shop used the master franchise method of expansion. What are some of the advantages and disadvantages of using this approach over direct (individual) franchising?

ENDNOTES

1. Ryan, T. (1993). "Not Just the Bottom Line: The Body Shop Puts Social Responsibility at the Top of It's List." *Honolulu Star Bulletin,* June 25.
2. "Body Shop—Company Report." (October 15, 1993). Panmure Gorden and Co. in *Investext* [Database in CD-ROM]. Foster City, Calif.: Information Access.
3. Conlin, J. (1994). "Survival of the Fittest." *Working Women,* February, pp. 29–31, 68–73.
4. "Body Shop—Company Report" (1993).
5. Conlin (1994).
6. Conlin (1994).
7. Northen, S. (1993). "Marmalade Scrub and Smellies." *Times Educational Supplement,* February 5, p. G4.
8. "Body Shop—Company Report" (1993).
9. Nichols, M. (1994). "Does New Age Business Have a Message for Managers." *Harvard Business Review,* March-April, pp. 52–60.
10. Conlin (1994).
11. Conlin (1994).
12. "Body Shop—Company Report" (1993).
13. Parker-Pope, T. (1996). "Body Shop Prepares U.S. Image Makeover." *Wall Street Journal,* November 12, p. B5.
14. Chatzky, J. (1992). "Changing the World." *Forbes,* July 15, pp. 83–84.
15. Conlin (1994).
16. Roddick (1993), "Corporate Responsibility: Good Works not Good Words." *Vital Speeches of the Day,* October 21, p. 198.
17. Roddick (1993), pp. 196–199.
18. Dubroff, H. (1993). "Body Shop Adds Condoms in New AIDS Campaign." *Denver Post,* August 18, p. 1.
19. "Body Shop—Company Report" (1993).
20. Conlin (1994).
21. "Body Shop—Company Report" (1993).

COMPANY FOCUS III.3

VIRGIN

Yueh-ling Zoe Lai

History

Virgin Group PLC is a privately owned holding company primarily involved with airline, music, video, publishing, and retail ventures. Based in Great Britain, Virgin has operations located in more than 20 countries, including the United States. Virgin Group was the creation of British entrepreneur Richard Branson, who dropped out of boarding school at the age of 17 to start his own magazine called *Student.* Branson was able to convince personalities such as John Le Carre, James Baldwin, and Vanessa Redgrave to contribute articles or be interviewed for his publication. *Student* was short-lived, largely because the young proprietor spotted, in the number of ads for mail-order records, a demand among young British music lovers for cut-rate discs. Mail-order led to the Virgin name (they were young and inexperienced) and a small store, which led to the Virgin record label, which led to more than 100 companies with 11,000 employees in 17 countries. Along the way, Branson would attain cult status in his home country—the result of his business exploits, quests for adventure, and unique personal style.

Scope of Operation

London-based Virgin Group, founded by Branson, operates Virgin Atlantic Airways (VA), Virgin Retail Group, and Virgin Travel Group. It also holds a 10% stake in computer game maker Virgin Interactive Entertainment (VIE).

Virgin Vision was formed in 1983 to distribute film and video products. Virgin Group sales reached 50 million that year. In 1984, Branson launched Virgin Atlantic Airways with only one plane and a London–New York route. VA offered two classes: upper class and an economy class. Virgin Holidays, a tour operator, was formed in 1985, to complement the company's airline operations. The same year, VA won a license to fly to Miami.

The next year, Branson took the company public, selling about 35% of its stock. In 1987, Virgin leased another airplane and set up Virgin Records America. A subsidiary was also established in Japan. The company bought W.H. Allen, a publishing house, and 45% of Mastertronics Group, which then owned the U.K. distribution rights for Sega video games.

In 1988, Virgin opened three megastores outside England and established Virgin Broadcasting and Olympic Recording Studios. Virgin Air became the United Kingdom's number two long-haul airline, after British Air. It began flying to Los Angeles and Tokyo, having acquired its third and fourth planes. Virgin Communications also purchased a stake in Europe's Super Channel.

Branson bought back his company in 1988, then embarked on a selling spree, disposing of Virgin Vision, 25% of its Music Group, and 10% of Virgin Travel Holdings in 1989. In 1990, the company sold 20% of Virgin Retail Europe, and in 1991, Mastertronics.

In 1990, Virgin launched its second record company, in New York, and began collaborating with Marui to establish megastores in Japan. Virgin Publishing was formed In 1991. The same year, VA expanded its service to Japan, and Virgin entered into a joint venture with Sega to develop video games.

Thorn EMI bought Virgin Music (formerly called Virgin Records) for almost $1 billion in 1992. According to the contract, Branson was named president for life. That year, Virgin Retail and Blockbuster Entertainment announced a joint venture to establish Virgin Megastores (retail entertainment and music stores) in Australia, Europe, and the United States. In 1994, Blockbuster announced it would open 50 new Virgin Megastores in the United States by 1997.

In 1996 and 1997, Virgin's expansion continued along the transportation system lines. Virgin acquired Euro Belgium Airlines, which it renamed Virgin Express. This carrier offers short-haul services, low cost, no frills service in Europe. In 1996, Virgin became a major shareholder in Channel Tunnel Rail Link that operates Eurostar (a high-speed train using the Channel), which links London, Brussels, and Paris.

Virgin's division and major companies are as follows:

- Virgin Retail: Virgin Megastores, Virgin Trading Company
- Virgin Travel: Virgin Atlantic Airways
- Virgin Entertainment: Virgin Publishing, Virgin TV
- Virgin Hotels: Necker Island, La Residencia
- Virgin Direct: Personal financial services
- Virgin Cinemas: British cinema chain
- Virgin Investments: Storm Model Management, Eurostar
- Virgin Radio: National and local stations in Britain
- Virgin European Airways: Virgin Express

Virgin Retail Group

Virgin Retail Group has two divisions: Virgin Megastores and Virgin Trading Company. Virgin Megastores are entertainment retail stores in Australia, Europe, Japan, and the United States. Virgin Trading Company sells consumer products, including mineral water, cola, computers, and vodka.

Virgin Megastores

The first Virgin Megastore opened in London in 1979 and immediately offered shoppers the widest selection of music in Great Britain. Today, there are over 60 Virgin Megastores around the world, including Dublin, Glasgow, Liverpool, Tokyo, Frankfurt, Vienna, Marseilles, Barcelona, Brussels, Milan, Amsterdam, Paris, and Athens.

Between 1992 and April 1996, Virgin Megastores opened in Los Angeles, Sacramento, San Francisco, Burbank, and Costa Mesa, California, and in Times Square, New York City. Virgin Megastores carry a broad, eclectic selection of music that is available on compact disc (CD) and cassette, movies on video and laserdisc, multimedia software, and in some stores, graphic novels and books.

Plans called for Virgin Retail to open new Megastores in Las Vegas, Seattle, Denver, Boston, Orlando, and at least one more store in the New York City area. A new store was also planned for Vancouver, Canada.

Competitors

Top international music retailers such as Musicland, Tower Records, HMV, and Virgin Megastores target new areas for expansion in the region as part of their global strategies. Tower Records, HMV, and Virgin Megastores share a common approach to retailing: They are superstores that place an emphasis on providing consumers with the largest variety of music possible. All three retail giants have established the headquarters of their Asian operations in Tokyo in a bid to gain control of the world's second largest music market. Tower has been the leader in moving into Asian markets. Musicland is just beginning to enter the multimedia superstore fray.

Competitive Advantages/Weaknesses

Joint Venture with Blockbuster

Blockbuster, "America's Family Video Store," is collaborating with Virgin's music retailing arm to open a string of megastores. Blockbuster does not offer any pornographic or excessively violent videos, and subjects its employees to drug testing. Virgin, on the other hand, operates a no-censorship policy in its music stores. Virgin received tens of millions of dollars and a swift entry, via Blockbuster's local knowledge, to the lucrative U.S. market. It also has sole operational and management control of the stores. Blockbuster, one of the fastest-growing retailers in the United States, received a 75% equity stake and added further momentum to its diversification into music retailing. It is beneficial for Virgin to enter the U.S. market via the joint venture with Blockbuster.

Impact of Selling of Virgin Records

Branson sold Virgin Records to Thorn EMI for almost $1 billion in 1992, when he desperately needed to buy back his company after a frustrating year as a public corporation. As Virgin Megastores opened around the world, Branson longed to return to the record industry. Yet, EMI had made him sign a "non-compete" clause to keep him out of the industry.

Introduction of New Formats

The market should be stimulated by the introduction of new formats such as digital cassettes and mini-discs. Historically, the introduction of a new format has always been beneficial to the recorded music industry by adding further impetus to sales growth. For instance, cassettes grew at twice the market rate when they were introduced in the 1970s, and CDs grew at ten times the rate during the 1980s. There is no reason to believe that the current new formats should be anything but positive. This is illustrated by the major changes that occurred with the introduction of the CD. Music is recorded onto a CD in a digital format. The digital format offers a significant increase in quality and performance over the analog formats (vinyl and cassettes). Although digital cassettes and mini-discs should stimulate this market, they are not expected to have the same dramatic impact as the introduction of the CD.

Virgin Trading Company

Virgin Trading Company sells cola, spring water, vodka, and computers. When Canadian soft drink producer Cott approached Branson with a proposal to put the Virgin name on its new cola formula in 1994, Branson examined the cola market and became excited about the prospects for the business. First, it was an industry where the Virgin brand image was naturally at home: young, fun, slightly hip, slightly irreverent, but where quality mattered. A cola drinker wants the same product whether bought in a pub, a cinema, or out of a machine. Second, it was the sort of fat, highly profitable industry Branson relishes attacking.

In the United Kingdom, getting giant food retailer Tesco to stock the product was the first phase of the Virgin Cola strategy. Phase two involved winning distribution through garage forecourts, wholesalers, and smaller groceries such as Iceland (which dropped Pepsi in favor of Virgin Cola). Phase three was an "unreal" television advertising campaign, in which Branson's own input and personality were clearly visible (it mocked Coca-Cola, supermodels, businessmen in ties, and advertising generally—and was done on the cheap). Simultaneously, Virgin unleashed a wave of additional soft drink products. Following its launch in November 1994, Virgin Cola took 10% of the take-home cola market and showed a profit in its first year, a result the other cola companies would have described as impossible before 1994. Virgin Cola is now sold in retailers other than Tesco. The service of Virgin Cola occurs often on the back of other Virgin operations.

Competitors

Virgin Cola's plans include taking on American icons Coca-Cola and Pepsi-Cola on their home turf. London-based Cadbury Schweppes, the world's number three soft drink vendor, is a third major competitor for Virgin Cola.

Coca-Cola

The Coca-Cola Company is not resting on its laurels. The world's largest soft drink company with the world's most recognizable brand (its products are sold in over

195 countries) has kept up with consumer tastes of the 1990s. Sassy advertising, new-age products, and increased visibility are moving Coke into new markets at home and abroad. Coca-Cola still dominates the global soft drink market. Coke has 41% of the U.S. soft drink market and 50% of the rest of the world.

Coca-Cola is a phenomenally profitable company. The company earns an even higher return in its European business than it does in the United States. In dozens of national markets, there are powerful distributors desperate for a good product to use in their fight against Coke, typically with price as their most potent weapon. However, the company has been in business for more than 100 years, and competition is nothing new to it.

PepsiCo

Long-time number two player in the cola wars, PepsiCo is widening the playing field. Recently the company has invested more than $2 billion in its worldwide bottling operations. Although dominated by Coca-Cola (Coke brands have 42% of the market to Pepsi's 32%), international markets are less saturated and offer PepsiCo a huge potential for growth.

In 1994, Pepsi-Cola International (PCI) formed a joint venture with Brazil's BAESA to market products in South America. The following year, PCI launched Atlantis bottled water in Asia and Mexico. Other recent investments include plants in China and India. Pepsi Max, which contains an artificial sweetener not available in the United States, is marketed in over 50 countries.

Pepsi is also diversifying its product line. In a joint venture with Lipton, it has won over 30% of the ready-to-drink tea market, a part of the so-called "new-age" beverage segment. The company also has a pact with Ocean Spray to market fruit juices. In 1995, Pepsi began testing Mazagran, a coffee-based drink codeveloped with Starbucks.

Cadbury Schweppes

"If you can't fight 'em, join 'em" seems to be the philosophy of Cadbury Schweppes. The world's number three soft drink vendor after Coca-Cola and PepsiCo, Cadbury has only 4% of the market. But a joint venture with Coca-Cola produces Cadbury's soft drinks in the United Kingdom, while PepsiCo distributes Cadbury products in eastern Europe.

In an effort to increase its market share, especially in the United States, Cadbury bid $1.3 billion in early 1995 for the 74% of U.S. soft drink maker Dr. Pepper/7Up Cos. it did not already own. This acquisition made it the third largest U.S. soft drink company and follows a number of other recent purchases, including A&W, the U.S. soft drink company, and French chocolatier Banque D'Or.

Cadbury's next move is the conquest of China, with chocolate. Its joint venture plant near Beijing began production in 1995.

Competitive Advantages/Weaknesses

Extended Distribution Channels

Virgin Cola is to be sold in 10,000 U.K. pharmacies. Unichem, the leading pharmacy wholesaler to the independent chemist sector, will handle Virgin Cola's sales. Unichem, which owns the 350-strong Moss chemists chain, will be able to supply Virgin Cola to all of its 5,000 member outlets. In addition, there is an opportunity to sell Virgin Cola to the remaining 5,000 independent chemists in United Kingdom. This would help Virgin Cola boost its market share and sales volume.

Virgin Spirit

Branson absolutely believes in the power of brands, much the way that Procter & Gamble or Coca-Cola does. This belief is at the core of his business empire. Virgin, with its youthful, dynamic image could create a good brand name in the cola market.

Blocked Supermarket Channels

Virgin was unable to get shelf space in half the British supermarkets—no small problem when four grocery chains control more than 60% of the market. The reason: Coke and Pepsi locked up the shelves with exclusive agreements and got down-and-dirty on price.

Conclusions

For both Virgin Megastores and Virgin Cola, embedding the Virgin brand name into the target consumers' minds via advertisement, public relations events, or publicity is the most effective way of retailing. The prime locations of Virgin Megastores, in big cities where many people pass by every day, could be one of the strengths for Virgin Megastores. The other strength, the Virgin spirit, is compatible with the targeted young customers, the spacious interior, the over 100,000 titles, and wide range of selections. Virgin Megastores satisfies the increasingly sophisticated needs of today's youth. Virgin Cola, facing Coca-Cola and PepsiCo, should certainly employ the resources of the Virgin Group PLC. Through the networking of the VIE, Megastores, VA, Virgin Travel, and Virgin Radio, Virgin Cola could boost the sales volume and market share in the world.

DISCUSSION QUESTIONS

1. Has Virgin overextended itself by diversifying into too many industries (e.g., Virgin Radio, Virgin Travel, and Virgin Cola)? Is this diversification a smart method of entering foreign markets?
2. Discuss the possible drawbacks to Virgin's entrance into the U.S. music retail market.
3. Some authors maintain that upper-income youth are virtually indistinguishable in the triad area: the United States, Japan, and Europe. Is Virgin selling its products or the youth lifestyle?

ENDNOTES

Angelo, B. (1996). "Many Times a Virgin." *Time,* June 24, pp. 51–54.

Dwyer, P., M. Lowry, S. Toy, and P. Oster. (1993). "Shop till you Drop Hits Europe." *Business Week,* November 29, pp. 58–59.

Ferry, J. (1995). "Favourite Fizz-Kid." *Director,* July, pp. 33–38.

Grant, T. (1995). *International Directory of Company Histories,* Vol. 12. Detroit: St. James Press.

Laushway, E. (1993). "Row Over Virgin's Sunday Sale." *Europe,* Vol. 330, October, pp. 40–42.

Schultz, R. (1991). "Megastores May Mean Megabucks for the Virgin Group in Japan." *Tokyo Business Today,* February, p. 39.

Snowdon, R. (1995). "Virgin Assault on Soft Drinks." *Marketing,* May 4, p. 2.

Snowdon, R. (1995). "Virgin Lines up Spirit Launches." *Marketing,* February 23, p. 4.

Spain, P. J., and J. R. Talbot. (1996). "Hoover's Handbook of World Business." *The Reference Press.*

Sparks, L. (1997). "From Coca-Colonization to Copy-Cotting: The Cott Corporation and Retailer Brand Soft Drinks in the UK and US." *Agribusiness,* Vol. 13, No. 2, pp. 153–167.

"Thorn EMI—Company Report." (April 16, 1993). Panumure Gordon and Co. in *Investext* [Database on CD-ROM]. Foster City, Calif.: Information Access.

"Virgin's Chaste Union." (1993). Management Today, January, p. 11.

Web site: virgin.com/history.html.

COMPANY FOCUS III.4

AHOLD

Wen-Yu Michelle Chen

Koninklijke Ahold NV is one of the top international retailing organizations, with 3,000 retail sites on four continents.[1] The formats include supermarkets, specialty stores, hypermarkets, discount stores, and cash-and-carry outlets in the United States, Europe, Asia, and Latin America. The company is primarily focused on distributing and selling food products.

History

Ahold's history is traced back to 1887, when the first small neighborhood Albert Heijn grocery store was opened. Now with 665 stores throughout Holland, the Albert Heijn chain remains the company's flagship, even as Ahold's interests in the last 20 years have expanded well beyond Holland.

With its Albert Heijn supermarket chain, Ahold is the market leader in the Netherlands and holds a 73% interest in wholesaler Schuitema. In Portugal, Ahold co-owns (49%) one of the leading supermarket and hypermarket chains. In the Czech Republic, Ahold owns several store chains, including the Mana supermarket chain.

International Expansion

United States

In the United States, Ahold operates six supermarket chains (see Table 1)—BI-LO, Giant Food Stores, Finast, Edwards, Mayfair, and Tops—totaling over 650 stores. With its acquisition of Stop & Shop in 1996, Ahold became one of the top five U.S. supermarket organizations.[2]

Ahold's six U.S. chains share certain facilities: The American Sales Company, a distribution center in Lancaster, N.Y., which supplies all of the store chains; and Ahold Information Services, an information processing center based at BI-LO's headquarters, which handles administrative processing for all of the companies.[3]

Tops

The Tops Market chain was acquired by Ahold in 1991. It is the dominant food retailer in Buffalo, New York, serving a population of some three million people in western and central New York and northwest Pennsylvania.The stores that comprise Tops Market retail operations include five categories: Tops International Super Centers, Tops Super Centers, Tops Food Markets,

TABLE 1

Ahold's U.S. Acquisitions

	Chain	Location	Number of Stores	Sales ($)
1977	BI-LO	Mauldin, S.C.	203	1.9 billion
1981	Giant	Carlisle, Penn.	61	1.3 billion
1988	Finast	Maple Heights, Ohio	43	900 million
1991	Tops	Buffalo, N.Y.	168	1.6 billion
1995	Mayfair	N.J., N.Y.	28	250 million
1996	Stop & Shop	Mass., Conn., R.I.	176	4.1 billion

Vix Deep Discount, and Wilson Farms Neighborhood convenience stores.

Finast

Finast's store network was part of First National Supermarkets, which was acquired by Ahold in 1988. At the time, Finast in Ohio operated as the Ohio division of First National, while the eastern division operated Edwards and Finast stores. Years later, the two divisions were split into separate operating companies under the Ahold USA banner.

The chain serves customers in the greater Cleveland and northeast Ohio markets. A well-targeted, low-price, low-cost strategy made Finast the area's major food retailer.

Edwards

Edwards Super Food Stores evolved from First National in 1993. The stores are located in New Jersey and serve an affluent, densely populated market in the Northeast. In 1996, the 28 Mayfair stores were integrated into the chain.

Giant

Giant, which was acquired by Ahold in 1981, operates about 70 supermarkets in Pennsylvania, Maryland, Virginia, and West Virginia. The store chain ranks as one of the top-performing supermarkets and its sales are among the highest in its markets. The company is also in a major expansion phase.

BI-LO

BI-LO, built on a commitment to low prices, high quality, and excellent service, is a market leader in the southeastern United States. By mid-1995, BI-LO operated over 266 supermarkets and was continuing to upgrade and remodel stores. Integration of Red Food supermarkets into BI-LO's store chain took longer than planned because of the need to restructure computer systems and rebuilding consumer loyalty.

Stop & Shop

Stop & Shop has long been a market leader in the New England states. It joined the Ahold family in 1996. Edwards was merged into Giant and Stop & Shop took over 28 Edwards stores in New England and New York. The other 16 former Mel's units on Long Island were transferred to the Edwards/Giant organization.[4] At the end of the reorganization, Stop & Shop had 185 supermarkets in the Northeast.

The Netherlands

Ahold operates six store chains with a total of some 1,600 outlets: Albert Heijn (supermarkets), Gall & Gall (liquor stores), Etos (health and beauty care stores), Jamin (confectionery stores), De Tuinen (nature products), and Ter Huurne (stores on the Dutch-German border). In addition, Ahold holds a 73% interest in Schuitema, a wholesale supplier of independent grocers. An institutional food supply company (GVA) and the production companies Marvelo, Meester, and Nistria also are part of the Dutch operations. The total number of outlets in The Netherlands (excluding Schuitema) is 1,572, including 477 franchise stores. Total sales area is 7,664,000 square feet (712,000 square meters).

The "Today for Tomorrow" distribution system, in which store orders are filled within 18 hours, is now operative throughout the Netherlands. Heightened efficiency led to elimination of some positions, but an extensive retraining and outplacement effort made it possible to avoid involuntary layoffs.

Albert Heijn introduced a new store prototype in Haarlem. The store is laid out like a village. The outer area is the bargain aisle, designed to keep customers away from hard discounters like Aldi.[5] Toward the center of the store, products are arranged by consumption time, that is, breakfast, lunch, and dinner.[6]

Mini-stores and a large supermarket in Beek further expanded the range of store formats within the Albert Heijn family. In early 1996, Albert Heijn and Shell began a joint trial, offering a special assortment of products in several Shell station shops.

By the end of 1995, Ahold Specialty Stores operated 933 outlets, including 308 franchise stores. The Gall & Gall liquor store chain increases its market share significantly from 21.6% to 23.4% in a shrinking market. The Gall & Gall chain had 444 stores by the end of 1996.[7] The strong performance was due to improvements in marketing, assortment, and store organization.

De Tuinen natural products and Etos health/beauty care stores also showed exceptional sales growth and improved assortment, increasing 16% in 1996.[8]

Europe

Through its Jerónimo Martins Retail (JMR) joint venture in Portugal, Ahold is co-owner of the country's leading supermarket chain, Pingo Doce (110 stores in 1997), and the Feira Nova hypermarket chain (12 stores in 1997). In the Czech Republic, Ahold owns the Mana supermarket chain, the Sesam discount chain, and Euronova cash-and-carry centers. Through a joint venture in Poland with Allkauf of Germany, Ahold has 30 stores and four cash-and-carries, two Sesam discount stores, and a share in eight supermarkets. In Belgium, Ahold owns a food production company, and in Spain, the company has a joint venture with Caprabo, a Barcelona-based food retailer. By the end of 1996, the company had acquired 11 supermarkets in Madrid.

Associated Marketing Services (AMS), the synergy marketing alliance linking 12 leading European food retailers, including Ahold, achieved combined benefits through extensive programs with suppliers. One of the most important results was introduction of the Euroshopper product line.

Cooperation among members of the European Retail Alliance (ERA), consisting of Ahold, the British food retailer Argyll, and the French food retailer Casino, was, for the most part, confined to information exchanges in 1995. In February 1996, the partners ended their cross shareholdings in each other.

The Far East—Asia

Ahold began its development in Southeast Asia by signing a cooperative agreement in Indonesia and opening an Ahold Asia Pacific office in Singapore. In March 1996, joint venture contracts were signed in Malaysia and Singapore.

Ahold opened two Tops Supermarkets and 16 BI-LO discount stores in Malaysia. The company acquired 31 existing supermarkets in Thailand in a joint venture with Central Robinson Group. Most of these stores are located in department stores and operate under the Central and Robinson names. They will be remodeled under the Asian Tops format during 1997. Free-standing Tops stores will follow.[9]

Tops supermarkets are also being opened in Indonesia, Singapore, and the People's Republic of China (PRC). Ahold's China partner is Zhong hui Supermarket Company, a subsidiary of China Venture tech Investment Corporation (CIVIC). The Ahold joint venture in the PRC includes 15 existing food stores in Shanghai. In January 1997, the first of these stores was remodeled into a Tops Supermarket.[10]

With existing purchases from supermarkets running at a fraction of those in the Western world (penetration is only 2% to 3%, against 65% to 80% in Western countries), the growth possibilities in the Far East are promising. Ahold believes it is possible that within by the year 2005, some 10% of its total sales will derive from the Far East.

Competition

Ahold's competitors in the United States are five food retailing groups that are of comparable size or operate in the regions where Ahold is also active, and three European food retailers, which are large internationally active companies. In addition, other local companies relative to the Dutch market will be discussed in this section.

United States

Competition is on the rise, particularly in BI-LO's and Tops' operating areas. To protect and increase their market positions, the Ahold chains redoubled their emphasis on value-added products and services, efficiency measures, and better utilization of scale through intramarket cooperation.

The major U.S. competitors are:

- Kroger, number one in the United States and operating in 24 midwestern and southern states.
- Safeway, operating in 18 Pacific, southwestern, and mid-Atlantic states in addition to western Canada.
- Winn-Dixie, operating in 13 southern and central states.
- Food Lion, operating in 14 southeastern states.
- Hannaford Bros., operating in seven New England and southeastern states.

However, with the acquisition of Stop & Shop, Ahold is now the market leader in the eastern United States and is among the top five nationwide retailers, after Kroger, American stores, Safeway, and Wal-Mart.

Europe

The French company Carrefour is Ahold's major competitor due to its exceptional growth opportunities in emerging markets such as Asia and eastern Europe. Carrefour operates in France, southern Europe, the United States, Latin America, and Asia. Carrefour is expected to make a substantial contribution, more than Ahold at the present time. Other European competitors are:

- J. Sainsbury, the U.K. company, operating in the United Kingdom and the United States.
- Delhaize "le Lion," the Belgian group, operating in Belgium, the United States, Greece, and eastern Europe

Increasingly, supermarkets are being customized on a store-by-store basis to respond to market needs and to take advantage of market opportunities. There is much experimentation with local store formats, which, when proven successful, are then tested at other locations. Concentration within the retail sector through mergers and acquisitions is continuing apace, implying that retailers will become even larger than their suppliers. Because it aims to be among these market leaders, Ahold will be forced to undertake acquisitions or mergers during the next 10 years.

In the meantime, Ahold has proven to have the confidence and ability to operate different store formats in every segment of retail sector. At present, the company operates a range of food retailing formats, from small discount stores to hypermarkets, and it has not ruled out expansion into non-food retailing, either by expanding its existing activities, or through acquisition or merger.

Conclusions

Ahold is taking an innovative approach to its international development, particularly in areas such as Asia, where it is not yet established but which offer major opportunities based on the company's existing strengths and skills.

The challenge that confronts Ahold is to maintain the regional identities of its divisions while developing operation synergies on an international retailing base. With a highly decentralized organization, the company permits itself to concentrate on activities that meet the needs of the local consumer.

DISCUSSION QUESTIONS

1. Discuss the implications of entering a foreign market though the acquisition of other firms. What problems are involved in this type of expansion that you would not expect when opening new stores?
2. How did Ahold benefit from its affiliation with the European Retail Alliance (ERA)? (This buying alliance is discussed in Chapter 4.)
3. Ahold has expanded in the United States, Portugal, the Czech Republic, and Poland. This pattern does not seem to fit a pattern predicted by Dunning's theory of the eclectic firm. Can you offer an explanation for expansion in the countries chosen?

ENDNOTES

1. *Ahold Annual Report* (1996).
2. *Ahold Annual Report* (1996).
3. Garry, M. (1996). "Walk on the Wild Side." *Progressive Grocer,* Vol. 75, No. 3, pp. 38–44.
4. *Ahold Annual Report* (1996).
5. Sternquist, B. (1997). Personal interview.
6. *Ahold Annual Report* (1996).
7. *Ahold Annual Report* (1996).
8. *Ahold Annual Report* (1996).
9. *Ahold Annual Report* (1996).
10. *Ahold Annual Report* (1996).

COMPANY FOCUS III.5

KAUFHOF

Elizabeth Deboer, Karen Engelhardt, Monika M. Lederer, Melissa Smith, Deborah Trabin

Kaufhof is Germany's second largest retailer. Its original activity was department store retailing in large inner city locations. Kaufhof has expanded its format considerably in Germany and throughout Europe. The group operates through 175 subsidiaries, 105 of which are located in Germany and 70 throughout Europe. Kaufhof's principle subsidiaries include specialty stores, wholesale services, travel services, and mail-order.[1]

Management Strategies

Kaufhof's most important management strategy is to pursue diversification into specialty store retailing.[2] Department store sales for Kaufhof, which made up approximately three-fourths of profits, declined to about half of the profit total, while sales from specialty stores have continued to rise rapidly despite economic recession.[3] Based on the success of these specialty stores, management is trying to reduce the proportion of sales in department stores to 30% and to increase the proportion of specialty stores to 30% by the year 2000. Management has identified the growth areas in which to expand its specialty stores. These are the areas of consumer electronics and tourism.[4]

Kaufhof has also engaged in revitalizing some of its stores by altering formats. The company acquired the Kerber chain of stores (consisting of four stores) and the Loh chain (consisting of eight stores). These stores are less than half the size of an average Kaufhof Warenhauser department store. Accordingly, this acquisition has permitted Kaufhof to gain greater expertise in managing small stores and alternating the format of existing stores. Sales per employee at the Kerber outlets are about 15% higher than sales per employee at the larger Kaufhof Warenhauser stores. This success prompted the transfer of several Warenhauser stores to the Kerber format.[5]

In the past few years, Germany has been expanding limited access zones in the inner cities in hopes of discouraging the use of cars. This has forced larger department stores in these areas to reformat their product lines due to the stores' inaccessibility by car. Large items, such as furniture and white goods, could not be sold because of the lack of available parking. Kaufhof decided to turn its inner city stores into luxury shops that will appeal to a buyer who is out enjoying the shopping experience rather than out buying staple provisions. Merchandise such as delicatessen foods and cosmetics are featured in these luxury stores.[6]

In another area of advancement, Kaufhof recently developed a customized desktop computer program. This system is based largely on key technical trends, including downsizing to client/server systems, using Intel Corp. Windows-based graphical user interfaces and local high-speed networks.[7] The system works through a series of three-dimensional icon screens. Clicking onto these icons launches various applications, including word processing and e-mail. Plans for future expansion of the system focus on the use of multimedia. Computer analysts are expanding the option of using videos for distributing information such as interoffice memos. In addition, a Windows-based telephone will soon be brought online. The idea is that users can click on telephone icons to place calls instead of trying to reach clients and customers through the use the existing phone system.

The main challenge faced by Kaufhof in implementing the new computer system is motivating users to take advantage of all the information available to them.[8]

Logistics

Kaufhouf's logistics system is currently under revision. The company decided that its decentralized distribution system with 16 warehouses has increased overhead costs as well as limited stock flexibility.[9] In response, it has decided to reduce the number of its warehouses to three; one will be located in southeastern Germany, one in southern Germany, and one in western Germany.[10] In addition to the warehouse reductions, Kaufhof implemented a point-of-sale system for inventory control.

Competition

Kaufhof's largest competitor is the current number one German retailer, Karstadt.[11] Karstadt, like Kaufhof, has holdings in the areas of department stores, tourism, and the specialty store market.[12] Karstadt is reported to have higher undisclosed reserves, a superior financial structure, a more modern materials management system, and greater earnings power than Kaufhof. However, Kaufhof has expanded substantially in the area of specialty stores, which is a particularly profitable area. Much of this expansion is in the consumer electronics field, which in past years has seen high turnover rates. Kaufhof has also sold property to management companies to raise capital as well as to utilize tax benefits. Additionally, Kaufhof carried its start-up costs in eastern Germany as an asset, allowing for a more favorable outlook.[13]

Further competitive opportunities exist for Kaufhof. The specialty store market in areas of building materials and furniture has been relatively untouched. These areas are expected to have significant growth potential. Kaufhof already has experience in these areas and by increasing its investment, the company could gain a competitive advantage over Karstadt.[14]

Expansion

Currently, strategic mergers are used as the method of choice for expansion in Germany. Karstadt acquired the number three retailer, Hertie. In what may be viewed as a defensive move, Kaufhof recently began increasing its ownership position of Horten from 12% to 58%.[15]

Personnel

Kaufhof employs approximately 59,000 people, including permanent staff, part-time staff, and trainees. The average period of service of an employee is ten and a half years.[16] Seventy-two percent of employees are women. To better help staff members balance an occupation and home life, Kaufhof offers flexible work schedules and many part-time positions.

Personnel development measures are designed to meet the specific needs of Kaufhof's departments. Seminar courses provide training in management techniques and strategic thinking. In addition, creativity and managerial conduct are also emphasized. Special seminars are given at the work place in areas of customer service, product knowledge, and business organizations methods as well.[17]

Labor Relations and Working Conditions

The German labor force as a whole is highly skilled and very qualified. Compared to the standards of other countries, Kaufhof's level of training, discipline, and efficiency is very advanced. Government policy tries to protect the rights of employees and chooses as an objective to spread work over as many full-time employees as possible in attempt to reduce the level of unemployment. These provisions guard against pressure from employers and also provide for legal minimum holidays and limitations on working hours.

In relation to working conditions, the average monthly income of male German industry employees is deutsche marks (DM) 4,400 (U.S. $2,358). General managers of foreign subsidiaries receive anywhere from DM 10,000 (U.S. $5,360) to DM 12,000 (U.S. $6,432). Before unification, workers in former German Democratic Republic (East Germany) earned 40% of what those in West Germany did. Agreements between employers and unions try to raise earnings and strive for equal wage levels in the east and west. Employers legally must pay full salaries to employees when sick, up to the first six weeks. In addition to the sick pay, Kaufhof offers benefits that include annual bonuses, allowances for staff meals, and personnel discounts. Payroll costs are frequently the single most important component in the cost of doing business.

In general terms, the hourly work week in Germany by law is 38 to 40 hours. Currently, a typical work week is 36 to 37 hours per week, but the trade union's goal is to establish a 35-hour work week. The rates for overtime range between 175% and 150% of base salary, and could double if employees work on bank holidays or Sundays. It used to be that larger companies required overtime work, but that is no longer true. Employees are legally entitled to 15 paid vacation days per year. Trade unions often improve these conditions to 25 to 30 days as a holiday entitlement. Thirty to 32 days is generally the norm for upper-level management.[18]

Advertising

Germany has been operating on a fundamental "craftsman" tradition that has, in turn, developed into a production orientation and a controlled, but, competitive environment. Advertising is highly regulated and price competition is not the basis for advertising. Products are developed on the basis of niche marketing and personal selling is viewed as more effective than mass media approaches. The German focus on product orientations has led to a corresponding focus on product quality and customer-oriented service policies. Advertising in Germany relies primarily on print versus television media with a heavy information orientation. The German approach to advertising appeals is direct and factual.[19]

Certain members of the European Parliament have expressed a desire for a unification of national laws and the establishment of an independent media council. A guiding principle of this idea is that all broadcasts should follow the lines of the law within the country in which they originate. To comply with this proposal, Kaufhof will follow the lines of the law within Germany, since a substantial amount of its broadcasts originate there.

To ensure circulation of broadcasting in the EC, the "TV without Frontiers" directive makes minimum requirements for broadcasting advertisements. It provides for a separation between broadcasting and advertising. It also sets general standards in regard to the breakdown of programming for advertisements.[20]

This new directive prohibits surreptitious advertising and any advertising containing subliminals. Also banned under the stipulations of the directive is any advertising that discriminates on the basis of race, sex, nationality, or religious or political grounds. The "TV without Frontiers" also prohibits broadcasting of programs that may seriously impair the physical, mental, or moral developments of children and young people. This includes pornography and violence.[21] Kaufhof must adhere to these regulations when planning its advertisements.

"TV without Frontiers" sets basic rules in the targeting of advertising. Advertising must not exploit persons in order to get them to buy a product (e.g., appeals toward the inexperience of children as consumers). Member states retain the responsibility of regulating their own advertising in the broadcast laws. The directive laws define more restrictive conditions for member states that want to ban advertising coming from another member state that they feel violates their own advertising regulation. In this sense, Kaufhof could advertise in other nations as long as its advertisements do not violate any of the stipulations in Germany's law dealing with foreign advertisement.[22]

DISCUSSION QUESTIONS

1. Through mergers and acquisitions, the department store industry in Germany has become an industry with 2/90 concentration. That is, the two major department store groups, Karstadt and Kaufhof have 90% of the sales. What other structural characteristics would you expect in this industry? Will there be price competition?
2. Germany does not allow comparative advertising. For example, you cannot compare your product to a rival product. Price is also not an advertising feature. What is left? How can a department store wage a successful positioning campaign with these promotional restrictions?
3. In Chapter 9, I spent quite a bit of time discussing the effects that unification had on retailing in Germany. Did the unification of East and West Germany have any special effects on department stores as compared to specialty stores?

ENDNOTES

1. "Kaufhof Holding Company Report." (January 1, 1994). Barclays De Zoete Wedd Securities in *Investext* [Database on CD-ROM]. Foster City, Calif.: Information Access.
2. Hoare Govett Securities Ltd. (August 5, 1993). In *Investext* [Database on CD-ROM]. Foster City, Calif.: Information Access.
3. Hoare Govett Securities Ltd. (August 5, 1993).
4. Schroeder Securities Ltd. (May 13, 1993). In *Investext* [Database on CD-ROM]. Foster City, Calif.: Information Access.
5. Hoare Govett Securities Ltd. (August 5, 1993).
6. Schroeder Securities Ltd. (May 13, 1993).
7. Heichler, E. (1993) "Windows LANs Meet Up." *ComputerWorld,* April 19, p. 50.
8. Heichler (1993).
9. Schroeder Securities Ltd. (May 13, 1993).
10. Vereins-Und Westbank Ag. (June 23, 1993). In *Investext* [Database on CD-ROM]. Foster City, Calif: Information Access.
11. Shearlock, P. "Not the Dream Ticket." (1994). *The Banker,* April, pp. 47–48.

12. "Karstadt/Kaufhof—Company Report." (January 25, 1994). Westlb Capital Management GmbH in *Investext* [Database on CD-ROM]. Foster City, Calif.: Information Access.
13. "Karstadt/Kaufhof—Company Report." (January 25, 1994).
14. "Karstadt/Kaufhof—Company Report." (January 25, 1994).
15. "Germany—Kaufhof Acquires a Majority Control of the Horten Department stores." *Retail News Letter,* July, 1994, pp. 8–10.
16. Kaufhof Annual Report. (1991). pp. 16–17, 27–37.
17. Kaufhof Annual Report (1991).
18. The preceding paragraphs were compiled from Price Waterhouse and Co., *Doing Business in Germany,* (1991).
19. Graham, J. L., M. A. Kamins, and D. S. Oetomo. (1993). "Content Analysis of German and Japanese Advertising in Print Media from Indonesia, Spain, and the United States." *Journal of Advertising,* Vol. 22, pp. 7–8.
20. "Audiovisual Communications—Europe 1994 Industry Report." (April 28, 1994). Coopers & Lybrand Europe in *Investext* [Database on CD-ROM]. Foster City, CA: Information Access.
21. "Audiovisual Communications—Europe 1994 Industry Report" (April 28, 1994).
22. "Audiovisual Communications—Europe 1994 Industry Report" (April 28, 1994).

COMPANY FOCUS III.6

CARREFOUR

Linda S. Niehm

History

Postwar France was a hotbed of opportunity for entrepreneurs. Food retailing was destined for growth because of the French preference for fine cuisine. Two French businessmen, Marcel Fournier and Louis Deforrey, entered the market in the 1950s. Stores were evolving from small, family-run operations to supermarkets. The pair had experience in department store retailing and wanted to expand their business interests by starting a supermarket. Fournier and Defforey had reason to think big in regard to French food retailing. Department stores were thriving. Large assortments of merchandise in one location appealed to consumers. Free service (self-service shopping with carts or baskets) had been widely accepted. Department store goods were pricey, however, and store locations in the city center were not convenient for food shopping. There had to be a better solution for food shopping in France.[1]

Fournier and Defforey saw an opportunity to incorporate multiple food shopping preferences under one roof. A new concept in retailing was launched in 1960 from the basement of Fournier's department store in Annecy, France. Their new venture, named Carrefour, was an expanded supermarket featuring a wide assortment of merchandise, fast service, and low prices. This store within a store was an instant success, selling out of all merchandise in four days. Success with this format prompted the owners to open their first free-standing store in 1963. It offered a wide assortment of food and non-food merchandise and on-site parking. This large-scale facility ushered in the era of the hypermarket.

Carrefour's business continued to increase throughout the 1960s and 1970s, as management added more conveniences to their hypermarket offerings, such as an on-site gasoline and service center. Their strategy of low prices, decentralized power, reduced overhead, and rapid stock rotation proved to be highly successful. Hypermarkets boomed throughout the 1960s and 1970s in France, with Carrefour leading the way. Competitors, such as Auchan, Casino, and Euromarché soon entered the market. Today, hypermarkets represent the most dominant retail format in France.[2]

Small business, long supported and nurtured by the French government, began to experience extreme competition from hypermarkets during the late 1970s and 1980s. The French government imposed expansion limitations on hypermarkets as a protectionary measure for small businesses. Limited growth opportunities resulted and fierce competition erupted among food retailers. Carrefour and other large French retailers were forced to seek other avenues of territorial expansion. French retailing became fragmented, and Carrefour's stock went public for the first time.[3] These combined push factors signaled a new direction for Carrefour and the internationalization of French food retailing.[4]

Carrefour was successful in its early internationalization efforts. Brazil, Argentina, and Spain were easy and profitable points of entry. Acquisitions and joint ventures dominated the firm's international retailing activity. French hypermarkets, led by Carrefour, comprised over 75% of all foreign joint ventures in food retailing during the period between 1970 and 1990.[5]

Hypermarkets matured in France during the 1980s. Carrefour strategically reduced the size of some stores and formed retail partnerships to diversify product offerings. Private label products were introduced in 1976 as a low-priced alternative. Carrefour's name and brand image quickly ranked it as France's private label leader.[6] Carrefour was France's leading hypermarket retailer in 1988 with 65 domestic stores. Internationally, Carrefour's reach extended to 10 countries. International efforts continued to thrive with 115 locations in Europe and South America.[7]

Success in multiple foreign markets encouraged Carrefour to introduce its hypermarket format to the United States. In 1988, a new 330,000 square foot (31,000 square meters) store was opened in suburban Philadelphia. Sixty checkout lanes, wide aisles, and roller skating clerks were featured in this super-sized marketplace. Carrefour failed to do its homework, however, using a low-key French advertising approach to introduce the store. The response was lackluster. Labor union disputes added to management's frustration during the first two years of operation. A second store opened in a nearby New Jersey suburb in 1991. It produced an equally dismal showing. Carrefour learned a costly lesson in its U.S. venture: What works in France does not necessarily translate well to other countries.[8] The American consumer was already well served by a variety of food retailing formats.[9] The hypermarket's size did not lend itself to efficient shopping and consumers were not receptive to Carrefour's merchandise assortments.[10] In 1993, Carrefour closed both of its U.S. stores, realizing this pilot effort did not warrant further expansion.[11,12]

Carrefour's founding families stepped down from active directorship in the early 1990s, although they continue to participate in an advisory capacity. A decision was made by corporate management for Carrefour to own and manage stores of only 2,500 square meters (27,000 square feet) or more in size. Carrefour sold some of its smaller stores and bought larger ones in this consolidation process. Daniel Bernard, previously of the Metro Group, was named CEO in 1992. He is credited with revolutionizing Carrefour by spearheading store consolidation and centralized management.[13–15]

French hypermarkets had nearly reached saturation in the early 1990s. Government restrictions on growth continued to tighten. Carrefour grew domestically through acquisition of existing supermarkets and hypermarkets, diversification of formats, and store concentration. Euromarché and Montlaur were purchased and Carrefour's hard discount division, Erteco, was launched. Frozen food specialty retailer, Picard Surgelés, was purchased in 1994 as part of consolidation efforts.[16]

Growth in domestic market activity has complimented Carrefour's rapid international expansion. Carrefour was active in 18 countries in 1997. Growth will continue to come from expanded foreign operations and European discounting efforts. In 1997, 30 to 40 new Carrefour store openings were planned abroad.[17,18]

Strategy

Financial strength, management know-how, and longevity give Carrefour a decided advantage in global retailing. Many firms are internationalizing, but key strategic differences position Carrefour for sustained growth in the global arena. The main points of Carrefour's strategy are:[19–21]

1. *Multiple formats.* Diversification of formats will continue to strengthen the firm's position in established markets (e.g., France). This will be achieved through acceleration of discount operations, supermarkets, and scaled-down versions of the hypermarket. Smaller stores meet French regulations for store size and allow flexibility in competitive European markets.
2. *Sustained international growth.* Carrefour will continue international expansion due to saturation of its home market. Growth will be targeted for either developed countries with low inflation rates

or undeveloped retail markets. Carrefour's hypermarket format is ideally suited for low income, high population countries. This practice allows the company to divide its risk among countries where currencies evolve at different rates.

3. *Shared risk.* Entry into new markets will be facilitated by opening small pilot stores that can later be expanded. Renting versus buying store space and forming strategic partnerships are other risk-reducing strategies. Cross ownership is preferred over joint venture partnerships. The firm's policy is to not increase the number of stores in any country unless several have proven to be successful. Its closure of unprofitable stores in the United States and Italy reflects this policy.
4. *Cultural adaptation.* Carrefour exports its basic concepts as it expands internationally. Key concepts include: low prices, large selection, a convenient location, and usually a flat-store format. Carrefour adapts merchandise to the local environment and consumers' needs. The firm assimilates into the culture and economy where it is installed and essentially becomes part of that country. Merchandise supply sources are then obtained on a regional level. Carrefour strives to expand credit repayment terms while developing regional networks.
5. *Improved efficiencies.* Optimization of sourcing and distribution synergies between global region is a current strategic emphasis. Carrefour cultivates relationships with local suppliers by region in an effort to reduce dependency on imports. This provides economic benefits to Carrefour and reduces the time it takes to break even in a new country.[22] To obtain better operating efficiencies and economies of scale, Carrefour is shifting from its traditional decentralized management to a centralized process in France. Centralization will eventually be implemented in all of Carrefour's global regions.
6. *Strength in food, non-food, private label.* A current directive is to strengthen non-food merchandise lines (e.g., computers, software, services) while maintaining strength in food retail operations. Flexibility is exhibited in the ratio of food to non-food offerings varying with consumer needs and the economy. Rapid expansion is taking place in food retailing on a global scale. Carrefour is moving toward global branding of merchandise to efficiently supply its vast market in both food and non-food lines. As mentioned in Chapter 9, Carrefour began centralizing its operations in 1994. The company is moving toward central purchasing and price negotiation with vendors. By 1997, 30% to 40% of dry goods and about 20% of fresh foods were being bought internationally through Carrefour's central purchasing offices.[23] Its private label is already strong in Europe and South America.

Scope of Operations

Carrefour is one of the world's most international retailers. Only Ahold, Delhaize, and Promodès are as international as Carrefour.[24] The firm ranks ninth among the world's top 100 retailers with turnover totaling U.S. $24.577 billion. International sales contribute 37.1% of total earnings,[25] and Carrefour possesses great potential for continued long-term growth and international expansion.

Acquisitions of smaller hypermarkets, such as Euromarché and Montlaur have allowed Carrefour to concentrate and dominate the hypermarket sector in France, and consolidation was further achieved by the 1994 purchase of Picard Surgelés. Carrefour's discount division, Erteco is still active in France but has pulled out of business in Spain, the United Kingdom, and Italy. Less successful ventures were those in retail dense markets in the United States and Germany.[26,27]

In December 1996, Carrefour bought 41% of Grands Magasins B, which controls 100% of Cora. Cora is a French hypermarket with nearly 7% market share. Cora's acquisition gives Carrefour an attractive piece of the French hypermarket business. This is particularly important since the tightened Loi Raffarin legislation, discussed in Chapter 9, makes opening new large stores very difficult.

A review of Carrefour's global market activity demonstrates integration of these strategic directives. The four primary countries in which Carrefour operates are France, Spain, Brazil, and Argentina. Recent joint ventures and acquisitions have expanded Carrefour's hypermarket locations to Taiwan, Italy, Turkey, Malaysia, Mexico, Thailand, Portugal, China, South Korea, and Hong Kong. Taiwan represents the strongest showing of the Asian operations. The remaining countries are composed of new entries or slow performers, such as Italy. For the first time in its history, the firm has greater corporate involvement outside of France than domestically. The company continues to demonstrate growth through discounting and acquisitions in Europe.[28–32]

France

Hypermarkets and hard discount food formats are the cornerstones of Carrefour's retailing efforts in France and Europe. Approximately 96% of Carrefour's sales come from hypermarkets. These vast stores average 8,000 to 9,000 square meters (86,000 to 97,000 square feet). Approximately 60% to 80% of sales come from food products. Stores feature wide aisles, massive merchandise displays, some specialized stores within a store, and selected services. Hypermarkets dominate store formats in France and are still gaining market share.[33] Because of government ceilings on hypermarket growth, it is doubtful that more than one new store will be added in France per year. The long-term plan is to progressively reduce Carrefour's dependence on the French market.[34–37]

Carrefour leads the integrated hypermarket group in France. It owns 13 of the 25 largest French hypermarkets and ranks third in domestic food retailing behind Leclerc and Intermarché. Carrefour had 117 hypermarkets in France in 1995, accounting for 57% of total group sales. A 2% increase in sales growth was recorded during the year and Carrefour's hypermarkets continued to gain market share.[38] The contemporary hypermarket has adapted its original concept to accommodate changing consumer lifestyles and the competitive retail environment. Today's stores focus more on wide merchandise assortments (food and non-food, including jewelry, phones, and computers) and improved customer services.[39]

Carrefour would like to maintain a high discount image. For example, it reimburses customers if they offer proof of a competitor's lower price and will refund their money within 30 days if they are not satisfied with their purchase.[40] Carrefour still finds price a difficult obstacle to overcome in the presence of deep discounters such as Aldi and Lidl. To counter this competitive threat, Carrefour narrowed the European playing field through acquisitions (Euromarché and Montlaur) and expansion of its Erteco discount division. These moves have allowed for aggressive expansion of floor space.[41,42]

Acquisition of existing supermarkets and involvement in hard discounting are avenues of growth for Carrefour and large European retailers. Hard discount stores have been exceptionally well received in Europe. Each store is fairly small, approximately 600 square meters (6,500 square feet), and carries a limited selection of about 600 competitively priced items.[43–46]

Carrefour France reorganized into five regional divisions in 1994 to improve logistics and operating efficiencies. A centralized approach is new for Carrefour. Traditionally, department managers were permitted autonomy in merchandising and sourcing decisions.[47] The move has been positive in terms of margin enhancement, better merchandising, and replenishment efficiency for French stores. Carrefour is encouraging similar restructuring in its other global regions.

Euromarché is Carrefour's largest acquisition to date. Transformation of these stores has taken time and resulted in some short-term profit reduction for the company. Despite this factor and a downturn in French consumer purchasing, Carrefour continues to record significant growth earnings. Projected sales and profit earnings for 1996 were expected to exceed the 20% mark. Main competitors in the French food retail group are: Intermarché, Leclerc, Promodès, and Casino. Together with Carrefour, they represent 64% of the total supermarket and hypermarket floorspace in France.[48–50]

Erteco

Erteco, Carrefour's discount division, holds a very competitive market position among hard discounters in France. Hard discounters account for about 4% of the food retail market share. Erteco ranks number two behind Lidl in an increasingly dense field of competitors. The division is managed independently of Carrefour's hypermarkets and includes the subsidiaries of Europa Discount and Ed. There were 569 Carrefour discount stores throughout Europe in 1995, with 179 in France. By 1997, however, Carrefour had pulled its hard discount format out of Spain, Italy, and the United Kingdom.

Picard Surgelés

In 1994, Carrefour acquired a majority share (79%) in Picard Surgelés, a frozen food specialty store with 240 outlets. The number of stores increased to around 250 by the end of 1995, with major expansion beyond the traditional Paris market. Picard enjoys a 25% market share in the Paris region, but only 5% nationwide. The new acquisition accounted for only 1% of Carrefour's overall sales in 1995. It was viewed as a defensive versus a strategic move in Carrefour's effort to consolidate French food retailing. Picard's contributions to Carrefour are mainly indirect, centering on its strong private label and innovation in frozen foods. Some Picard products will also be sold in Carrefour stores internationally. Carrefour will probably not see additional expansion into specialty retailing.[51]

Spain and Portugal

Pryca, Carrefour's Spanish hypermarket division, holds the bulk of the firm's operations outside France. The Spanish retail market has not yet reached maturity, so Pryca could see substantial growth beyond its current 50 units. Pryca operates one-quarter of all hypermarkets in Spain, but this number could easily double in the next several years.[52] Pryca leads the five major Spanish hypermarkets in market share (35.3%) and is the low price leader.

Continente poses the greatest competitive threat, with 40 stores. It is followed by Eroski, Alcampo, and Hypercor. Pryca and its competitors are all very strong players in the Spanish market. This fact raises some questions about the long-term expansion possibilities for hypermarkets in Spain. Pryca should logically begin to investigate options in emerging world markets. This would be in conflict, however, with Carrefour's strategy and will pose the biggest limitation for the Pryca division. A more plausible scenario is for Pryca to merge with French food retailer Comptoirs Moderns and become a stronger force in the Spanish supermarket sector. This strategy would also benefit the parent company, Carrefour, as it is a shareholder in Comptoirs Moderns.[53,54]

Pryca opened five stores in Spain in 1995. To achieve greater growth and productivity in this market, it must increase its logistics and computerization systems. For example, product bar codes were only added in 1994. The firm is totally decentralized and optimal efficiency has yet to be reached. Carrefour is attempting to remedy Pryca's inefficiencies by implementing centralized buying and management practices as in France. The low cost of personnel in Spain will be a continuing benefit for Pryca.[55]

Closely related to Pryca Spain are the two Portuguese stores, which were part of Carrefour's purchase of Euromarché in 1992. Accounting for only 1% of Carrefour's total 1994 group sales, the Portuguese stores are just now approaching profitability level. They will continue to follow a course similar to Pryca's Spanish stores.[56]

Other European Markets

Turkey

Turkey is a test market for Carrefour. Its attractions include a lack of chain store development, the presence of a young population with purchasing power, and consumers' preference for westernized products. Carrefour's initial store got off to a great start in 1993 but was slowed by a downturn of the economy in 1994. Management still saw promise in Turkey, however, and planned to open another store in 1996. It will be joined by Metro/Makro, the Dutch discounter, and the United Kingdom's Marks & Spencer, which also see potential in the Turkish market.[57]

Italy

Carrefour is returning to Italy following a poor showing in the late 1970s. In 1993, Carrefour opened a new hypermarket near Venice. It then acquired a majority share in Societa Sviluppo Commerciale (SSC), owner of the Gran Sole hypermarket chain. A total of six stores were acquired, and results have been mixed. The Italian market is fragmented and suffers from conflict between retail newcomers and independent Italian retailers. Further expansion in Italy will be difficult in the hypermarket format. No new store openings were planned in 1995, and management does not look for much contribution to group earnings in the near future. Carrefour has attempted to counter the hypermarket problem by diversifying its Italian formats. Six stores were opened in Italy under Carrefour's subsidiary, Europa Discount.[58–60]

Eastern Europe

No plans are currently in play for expansion in other regions of Europe. Present market conditions do not meet Carrefour's criteria for entry. Carrefour will continue to monitor the political and economic environment in eastern Europe, but changes are likely to be slow. Poland seems to be the best fit for Carrefour's initial entry.[61]

Latin and South America

Brazil

Carrefour's Brazilian stores are typically located in the city center. They are not as technologically modern as French stores. Brazilian stores do not presently use conveyors or scanning devices. Food comprises 80% of sales, and they function as a mass merchandiser. Price is not yet a competitive feature in Brazil as low price leaders do not exist. This is changing, however, with the entry of Wal-Mart and other discount retailers to the region.[62]

Carrefour's 38 Brazilian hypermarkets recorded a sales increase of 33% in 1994, making this one of the firm's strongest international divisions. However, high inflationary conditions in Brazil negated any appreciable increases in profitability. The division accounted for 11% of total 1994 group sales and planned to expand in 1995–1996 by five stores. Carrefour's experience in foreign markets allows the company to monitor effectively economic conditions and adjust its course of action accordingly. Profitability was projected to increase by approximately 15% in 1995–1996.[63]

Much of Brazil is underserved in general merchandise retailing. Combined with the projected economic upswing, this paints a bright picture for Carrefour's opportunities in the region. Competition will intensify with Wal-Mart and its joint venture partner Brazilian retailer Lojas Americanas. Like Carrefour, the partnership is aiming to exploit regional opportunities. Two supercenters and three wholesale clubs were planned for 1995–1996. Their presence along with Paõ de Acucar, a major Brazilian retailer, pose a new competitive threat to Carrefour. The effect will be moderated by minimal penetration of modern retailing in the Brazilian market.[64,65]

Argentina

Profitability is unstable for Carrefour's 12 Argentinean stores. Newly implemented government taxation and increases in the value added tax (VAT) have fostered recessionary conditions. Total growth was projected to be 10% to 12% annually for 1995–1996 and three new stores were planned. More floor space will be devoted to food lines as Carrefour adapts to local economic conditions. Food currently represents about 80% of consumer purchases. Carrefour will also wage battle with Wal-Mart in the region where six new stores are targeted.[66,67]

Mexico

Carrefour saw success in Brazil and Argentina as an invitation to expand into Mexico. Mexico has a large consumer population accustomed to being served by modern retailing operations. Wal-Mart and Price-Costco have already taken advantage of the Mexican consumer base and the country's proximity to the United States. Numerous supercenters and warehouse clubs are already in place there under these two names. Wal-Mart's joint venture with Mexican retail giant Cifra has further strengthened its presence south of the border.[68]

Carrefour's strategy of adaptation allowed it to overcome a relatively late entry into the Mexican market. Sourcing goods from area suppliers made it resilient during the 1994 Mexican economic crisis. Most U.S.-based competitors were forced to alter their expansion plans and experienced losses by sourcing primarily U.S. goods. Carrefour also exploited its supplier network, developed over years of doing business in South America. It had the added benefit of established suppliers who are familiar with the Hispanic culture. Carrefour's experience in operating in diverse economic climates provided added insight during the economic downturn. Similar to its pattern in Argentina, the firm reduced floorspace devoted to non-food items, adapting to consumption patterns in the local economy.[69,70]

Demonstrating its preference for joint ventures, Carrefour forged a partnership with Mexican retailer Gigante in 1994. Two hypermarkets were jointly opened, finding immediate success in the Mexican retail climate. Later that year, Carrefour broke from its usual one- to two-year "wait and see" expansion strategy. Seeing Mexico as particularly advantageous, the firm expanded at a fairly rapid pace. It totaled seven Mexican hypermarkets at the end of 1995. Floor space of Carrefour's Mexican hypermarkets totals 78,661 square meters (846,697 square feet). The Mexican stores were expected to make significant contributions to group sales in 1996.[71]

Other Countries

New entries in Asia and Europe account for only 2% of Carrefour's total group sales. However, opportunities created by political and economic restructuring make Asian countries especially attractive for retailers. Carrefour recognizes the potential purchasing power of large Asian populations. It is fast establishing itself as a major player by installing pilot stores in targeted regions of Asia. These stores will serve as a proving ground for further expansion in the region.[72–76]

Taiwan

Carrefour entered Taiwan in 1989, leasing space through a joint "sales shop" agreement. Land costs, availability of retail space, and government-imposed limitations precluded a joint venture arrangement. The original space was an existing vertical store format. Despite the structural layout, the pilot store was successful. Sales growth of nearly 30% was recorded the first year. Carrefour has since bought land and built ground-level stores with attached parking. In 1995, eight stores were operating in Taiwan. Carrefour's plans call for opening two to three stores annually with market capacity for an estimated 25 stores. Sales are projected to grow at the rate of about 27% annually. Taiwanese stores are a highlight of Carrefour's early Asian efforts. They have managed to make a positive contribution to earnings in three years versus the estimated five for new openings. In 1994, Taiwanese stores accounted for 2% of overall group sales.[77,78]

Malaysia

Carrefour's second point of Asian entry was Malaysia. The Malaysian store opened in September 1994 with selling space of 6,500 square meters (70,000 square feet). Still in its pilot stage, it is difficult to project Carrefour's long-term performance in this setting.[79]

Thailand

A joint venture with Thailand's leading retailer, Central Group, paved the entry to a market of 58 million consumers. Carrefour's potential in this market appears great. The economy is growing and supports a fairly high standard of living. Carrefour holds a 40% share in the joint venture and should encounter little initial competition in the sparse retail sector.[80,81]

China

Following years of operation as a closed economy, the Chinese government opened the door to foreign investors in 1992, though foreigners could enter only as minority partners in joint ventures. Chinese citizens are eager to satisfy years of delayed consumption. Finding the economic climate strategically advantageous, Carrefour sought to form a joint venture with Chinese retailer Lin Hua. Lengthy negotiations ensued between the two groups. A joint subsidiary was formed and two stores opened in Shanghai and Beijing late in 1995. An agreement was recently signed with a second Chinese group for another store in Beijing. Details are sketchy on this venture.[82,83] In Chapter 14, on retailing in the People's Republic of China, you will find out why Carrefour stores are no longer allowed to use the Carrefour name in Beijing.

Lack of supplier networks, insufficient infrastructures, and logistical dilemmas will likely plague the early years of Carrefour's Chinese operation. Hypermarkets are a totally new concept for China. Educating the consumer and training staff will pose additional challenges. Carrefour's initial stores are smaller than average (4,000 square meters [43,000 square feet]) with the capacity to enlarge. Despite some negatives, many other foreign firms are testing China's retail waters. Wal-Mart, Japanese retailer Yaohan, and Marks & Spencer are the most active firms to date. Carrefour will continue to monitor market viability, but the potential in China appears significant.[84,85]

South Korea

South Korea offers a population 44 million strong. Other assets include a high standard of living, well-developed transportation systems, and a strong economy. Relaxation of foreign investment limitations permitted Carrefour to buy land for a store site, but at a very high price. Leasing of store space is not possible in South Korea, so Carrefour had to deviate from its usual strategy to enter the burgeoning market. The first South Korean store was set to open in 1996. Carrefour is in the process of identifying key markets and setting up pilot stores throughout Asia. Exceptions will be Japan, Hong Kong, and Singapore, which do not meet Carrefour's criteria for hypermarket suitability.[86]

Competitors

Europe

European retailers approaching Carrefour's degree of internationalization are the Dutch firm Ahold, Delhaize of Belgium, and Promodès of France. All have substantial operations outside their home markets of northern Europe. Promodès appears to be the strongest competitive force for Carrefour if it can sustain its presence in Asia. The firm is Carrefour's major competitor in Spain. However, its expansion into already saturated German and Italian markets casts some question on its ability to go head to head with Carrefour in emerging markets.[87]

Ahold and Delhaize are likewise dependent on the mature U.S. market. Ahold may be impeded in its competitive efforts due to financial commitments. It has typically used acquisition versus joint ventures as an entry mode. The firm has numerous facilities to upgrade and is undergoing costly restructuring. Carrefour, on the other hand, has a very healthy debt-equity ratio and high cash flow. It is compared in financial strength to European retailers J. Sainsbury and Tesco.[88]

Latin America

Retailers in the United States have enjoyed significant presence in Mexico and South America for several years. Wal-Mart is Carrefour's most significant competitor in food and general merchandise retailing in the region. Several formats are represented by Wal-Mart: the Wal-Mart superstore and Sam's Clubs (with joint partner Club Aurrera) in the warehouse sector, supermarkets, and discount stores. Wal-Mart and Carrefour entered the region for similar reasons: it is a less developed retail sector, with less competition, cheap land costs, and fewer government restrictions and regulations.[89–91]

Wal-Mart's strategy is to open enough stores in a geographical area to gain competitive advantages with suppliers on pricing. Wal-Mart established solid bases in Mexico in 1991, Puerto Rico in 1993, and opened pilot stores in Brazil and Argentina in 1995. At the end of 1995, a total of 14 superstores were in place in Mexico, two in Brazil, and one in Argentina. Modes of entry include direct ownership, acquisition, and joint ventures. Perhaps Wal-Mart's most significant association is its joint venture with Cifra, Mexico's largest retailer. By the end of 1995, the two firms were to be jointly operating 100 units. Wal-Mart plans to continue this rapid penetration in its quest to become the major international retailer of the 21st century. Chile will be the next likely target. Kmart will provide marginal competition for Wal-Mart and Carrefour in Mexico.[92,93]

Hard discounters will also provide heavy competition in Central and South America in the form of food warehouses. Dutch cash-and-carry retailer Makro has been in Brazil since 1972 and currently operates 24 warehouses there. It will be competitive with Carrefour's hypermarkets and Wal-Mart divisions such as Sam's Clubs. Makro is more food oriented than Sam's Clubs, requires no membership fees, offers both bulk and consumer sizes of products, and maintains discount pricing (slightly higher than Sam's Clubs). Sam's Clubs feature high inventory turn, more general merchandise, and a required membership fee. Prices are on the average 8% lower than Makro. Both firms, along with Kmart, will provide substantial competition for Carrefour in both food and non-food categories.[94,95]

Asia

Taiwan and China will be competitive focal points for Carrefour in the new Asian markets. Taiwan is a thriving market for Carrefour. It is joined there by Promodès and Ahold in the hypermarket format. Makro also has discount warehouse stores in place. Growth and cost restrictions may make it difficult to see rapid growth for all foreign retailers. Makro closed two of its seven Taiwanese stores due to government regulations and zoning restrictions. Hypermarkets in Taiwan are beginning to go the route of membership clubs to avoid similar regulatory conflicts. This list includes Carrefour, Societe, and Ka Hong Group, Taiwan's largest hypermarket.[96]

All entries into China are very new. Potential in this market is significant, providing the Chinese government gives its support and cooperation to these ventures. Activity of competitors (Ahold, Promodès, Makro, and perhaps Wal-Mart) should be carefully monitored.

Conclusions

By 1999, 75% of the European food and non-food market will be served by 8 to 12 multinational retailers.[97] The hypermarket will continue to be the firm's main focus, but new formats are possible. Carrefour is testing new formats such as Erteco and Picard Surgelés. Carrefour, presently the world's ninth largest retailer, will undoubtedly be one of the multinational giants in a variety of ways. Twenty plus years of experience place Carrefour in a prime competitive position in the future of international retailing.[98]

DISCUSSION QUESTIONS

1. Carrefour has enjoyed continual global growth and expansion during the past two decades. Will its current strategy be sufficient for continued success in the changing global retailing environment? What potential threats and opportunities will confront Carrefour in this changing environment? Are any strategic modifications suggested in light of these threats and opportunities?
2. Carrefour has a history of being a "first mover" in international markets. This is usually accomplished in a step-by-step pilot store process. The rapidly expanding global retailing picture does not always make this time-consuming process plausible. Compare and contrast the pilot store process with the options of joint ventures and acquisitions. Which would be the most advantageous for Carrefour under specified market and environmental conditions?
3. What market and environmental characteristics make a global region best suited to Carrefour's interpretation of the hypermarket and discount store formats? What new global regions might be potential targets for expansion of these two formats and why?

ENDNOTES

1. Kepos, P., ed. (1995). *International Directory of Company Histories,* Vol. 10. Detroit: St. James Press.
2. Spain, P. J., and J. R. Talbot, eds. (1995). *Hoover's Handbook of World Business 1995–1996.* Austin, Tex.: The Reference Press, Inc.
3. Kepos (1995).
4. Spain and Talbot (1995).
5. Burt, S. (1991). "Trends in the Internationalization of Grocery Retailing: The European Experience." *International Review of Retail Distribution and Consumer Research,* Vol. 1, No. 4, pp. 487–515.
6. Kepos (1995).
7. Spain and Talbot (1995).
8. Fong, D. (1989). "Cherchez la Store." *Forbes,* January 9, pp. 311, 314.
9. "Is US Hypermarket Ready? Carrefour Is Not So Sure." (1989). *Chain Store Age Executive,* January, No. 1, Vol. 65, pp. 49–50.
10. Johnson, J. L. (1990). "Carrefour Revisited." *DM,* August, pp. 24–30.
11. Kepos (1995).
12. Spain and Talbot (1995).
13. "Carrefour—Company Report." (July 21, 1995). Morgan Stanley & Co., Inc. in *Investext* [Database on CD-ROM]. Foster City, Calif.: Information Access.
14. *Euromonitor 1995: World Retail Directory and Sourcebook.* (1995). London: Euromonitor PLC.
15. Spain and Talbot (1995).
16. *Euromonitor* (1995).
17. "Carrefour—Company Report." (March 13, 1997). UBS Research Limited in *Investext* [Database on CD-ROM]. Foster City, Calif.: Information Access.
18. "Carrefour—Company Report." (March 13, 1997), UBS Research Limited.
19. "Carrefour—Company Report" (July 21, 1995). Morgan Stanley & Co., Inc..
20. "Wal-Mart—Company Report." (October 11, 1995). Salomon Brothers, Inc. in *Investext* [Database on CD-ROM]. Foster City, Calif.: Information Access.
21. "Carrefour—Company Report." (March 29, 1995). UBS Research Limited in *Investext* [Database on CD-ROM]. Foster City, Calif.: Information Access.
22. "Carrefour Hipermercados." (1996). *Gigante Home Page.* Address: http://www.gigante.co. (Alta Vista).
23. "Carrefour—Company Report." (March 13, 1997), UBS Research Limited.
24. "Carrefour—Company Report" (March 29, 1995), UBS Research Limited.
25. "F & S Index US." (1996). *Points de Vente,* February 26, p. 15.
26. "Carrefour—Company Report." (September 19, 1995). UBS Research Limited in *Investext* [Database on CD-ROM]. Foster City, Calif.: Information Access.
27. *Euromonitor* (1995).
28. "Carrefour—Company Report" (July 21, 1995), Morgan Stanley & Co., Inc..
29. "French Retailing: Sector Analysis." (October 11, 1995). Salomon Brothers, Inc. in *Investext* [Database on CD-ROM]. Foster City, Calif: Information Access.
30. "Carrefour—Company Report" (March 29, 1995), UBS Research Limited.
31. "Carrefour—Company Report" (September 19, 1995), UBS Research Limited.
32. "F & S Index International." (1995). *Tribune,* April 21, p. 3.
33. "Carrefour—Company Report" (March 29, 1995), UBS Research Limited.
34. "Carrefour—Company Report" (July 21, 1995), Morgan Stanley & Co., Inc.
35. "French Retailing: Sector Analysis" (October 11, 1995), Salomon Brothers, Inc.
36. "Carrefour Hipermercados" (1996).
37. Spain and Talbot (1995).

38. "Carrefour—Company Report" (September 19, 1995), UBS Research Limited.
39. "F & S Index International." (1994). *Tribune,* September 9, p. 3.
40. "Carrefour Hipermacados" (1996).
41. "Carrefour—Company Report" (March 29, 1995), UBS Research Limited.
42. "Carrefour—Company Report" (September 19, 1995), UBS Research Limited.
43. "Carrefour—Company Report" (March 29, 1995), UBS Research Limited.
44. *Euromonitor* (1995).
45. Kepos (1995).
46. "F & S Index International" (1994).
47. Johnson (1990).
48. "Carrefour—Company Report" (March 29, 1995), UBS Research Limited.
49. "France—Large food retailers in 1994." (1995). *Retail News Letter,* No. 422, March, p. 5.
50. "France—Increased sales in 1995 for Carrefour." (1996). *Retail News Letter,* No. 432, February, p. 5.
51. "Carrefour—Company Report" (July 21, 1995).
52. "Carrefour—Company Report" (March 29, 1995).
53. "Carrefour—Company Report." (March 28, 1995). Credit Lyonnais Laing in *Investext* [Database on CD-ROM]. Foster City, Calif.: Information Access.
54. "Carrefour—Company Report" (July 21, 1995), Morgan Stanley & Co., Inc.
55. "Carrefour—Company Report." (May 1, 1995). Massonaud-Fontenay in *Investext* [Database on CD-ROM]. Foster City, CA: Information Access.
56. "Carrefour—Company Report" (July 21, 1995), Morgan Stanley & Co., Inc.
57. "F & S Index International." (1996). *Grocer,* February 17, p. 26.
58. "Carrefour—Company Report" (March 29, 1995), UBS Research Limited.
59. "F & S Index International." (1994). *Sole,* January 4, p. 21.
60. "F & S Index International." (1994). *Sole,* March 1, p. 10.
61. "Carrefour—Company Report" (May 1, 1995), Massonaud-Fontenay.
62. "F & S Index International." (1994). *LSA,* No. 1395, April 28, p. 9.
63. "Carrefour—Company Report" (May 1, 1995), Massonaud-Fontenay.
64. "Carrefour—Company Report" (May 1, 1995), Massonaud-Fontenay.
65. "F & S Index International." (*LSA*, 1994).
66. "Carrefour—Company Report" (May 1, 1995), Massonaud-Fontenay.
67. "Carrefour—Company Report" (July 21, 1995), Morgan Stanley & Co., Inc.
68. "Carrefour—Company Report" (May 1, 1995), Massonaud-Fontenay.
69. "Carrefour—Company Report" (May 1, 1995), Massonaud-Fontenay.
70. "F & S Index International." (1994). *Tribune,* March 16, p. 14.
71. "Carrefour—Company Report" (May 1, 1995), Massonaud-Fontenay.
72. "Carrefour—Company Report" (May 1, 1995), Massonaud-Fontenay.
73. "Carrefour—Company Report" (July 21, 1995), Morgan Stanley & Co.
74. "Carrefour—Company Report" (March 29, 1995), UBS Research Limited.
75. "Carrefour—Company Report" (September 19, 1995), UBS Research Limited.
76. *Euromonitor* (1995).
77. "Carrefour—Company Report" (May 1, 1995), Massonaud-Fontenay.
78. "Carrefour—Company Report" (July 21, 1995), Morgan Stanley & co., Inc.
79. "Carrefour—Company Report" (May 1, 1995), Massonaud-Fontenay.
80. "Cárrefour—Company Report" (May 1, 1995), Massonaud-Fontenay.
81. "F & S Index International." (1994). *Tribune,* March 21, p. 31.
82. "Carrefour—Company Report" (May 1, 1995), Massonaud-Fontenay.
83. "F & S Index International." (1994). *Tribune,* August 24, p. 7.
84. "Carrefour—Company Report" (May 1, 1995), Massonaud-Fontenay.
85. "F & S Index International." (*Tribune,* 1994)..
86. "Carrefour—Company Report" (May 1, 1995), Massonaud-Fontenay.

87. "Carrefour—Company Report" (March 29, 1995), UBS Research Limited.
88. "Carrefour—Company Report" (March 29, 1995), UBS Research Limited.
89. "Wal-Mart—Company Report" (October 11, 1995), Salomon Brothers, Inc..
90. "Carrefour—Company Report" (March 29, 1995), UBS Research Limited.
91. "Wal-Mart to Open in Brazil, Argentinia." (1994). *Discount Store News,* September 5, p. 16.
92. "Wal-Mart—Company Report" (October 11, 1995), Salomon Brothers, Inc..
93. "Wal-Mart to Open in Brazil, Argentina." (1994).
94. "Wal-Mart—Company Report" (October 11, 1995), Salomon Brothers, Inc..
95. "F & S Index International." (*Tribune*, 1994).
96. "F & S Index International." (1995). *LSA*, April 13, pp. 22–23.
97. "F & S Index International." (1994). *LSA*, No. 1401, June 9, p. 3.
98. "Carrefour—Company Report" (July 21, 1995), Morgan Stanley & Co., Inc.

COMPANY FOCUS III.7

EL CORTE INGLÉS

Kelly Rae Pizzuti, Lori Garijo, Patricia Johnson, Alisa Gish

History

El Corte Inglés Group, a private company, was founded in 1940 by Ramon Areces Rodriguez. Areces Rodriguez had first worked with his uncle Cesar, and cousin Fernandez at the department store El Encanto in Cuba. In the early 1920s, he and his uncle left Cuba for a year and a half and worked for a U.S. firm, to develop a better grasp of retail management techniques.[1]

In 1928, Areces Rodriguez moved to Spain and bought out a tailor's shop. The store was immediately successful, and 12 years later, El Corte Inglés moved into what would become the company's first shopping center site. In an odd twist, Ramon's cousin Fernandez bought the original store, which would soon become El Corte Inglés's arch rival, Galerias Preciados.[2]

By 1960, El Corte Inglés had fallen on hard times. Its main competitor, Galerias Preciados, outperformed it, with a turnover 20 times greater than that of El Corte Inglés. In response, Areces Rodriguez developed a new strategy, positioning his store in such a way that Galerias Preciados would no longer be a direct competitor.[3]

Strategy

During the Spanish Civil War, the clothing industry in Spain faced many problems due to shortages of raw materials and the availability of capital to buy machinery. To prevent the possibility of such shortages hindering the future success of El Corte Inglés, an independent company, Induyco (Industrias y Confecciones, S.A.), was formed in 1949 exclusively to manufacture clothing for El Corte Inglés. Induyco later began to trade its products with other businesses.[4] Although Induyco was incorporated as El Corte Inglés, S.L. in 1952, it is not a part of the El Corte Inglés Group. This strategy appears beneficial to both parties. El Corte Inglés benefits by having a clothing manufacturer, and by also trading with other businesses outside the El Corte Inglés Group; Induyco benefits by ensuring its continued success as a "separate" entity.

Another example of the group's vertical integration strategy is illustrated in the formation of the fully owned subsidiary, Construccion, Promociones e Instalaciones, S.A. This subsidiary primarily deals with the construction needs of the firms within the El Corte Inglés Group.[5] This also illustrates the paternalistic management style of El Corte Inglés's founder, Ramon Areces Rodriguez. By forming new companies and subsidiaries whose focuses differ from that of the parent company, El Corte Inglés benefits from a family-like structure. The companies and subsidiaries take care of each other, without needing assistance from firms outside the group.

Before 1960, El Corte Inglés's chief competitor, Galerias Preciados was the leading Spanish department store.[6] To compete with Galerias Preciados, El Corte Inglés changed its strategy. Galerias Preciados was selling wide assortments of products at low prices. El Corte Inglés countered this strategy by focusing on personalized service and offering specialized products.[7] El Corte Inglés gave consumers a choice in the type of department store they wanted to patronize based on differences in product assortment, available services, and price.

El Corte Inglés excels in an important retailing area, the placement of its stores in prime locations. In the United States, many department stores are located in suburban shopping mall sites. In direct contrast, European department stores are usually located in urban areas.[8] Not only are the El Corte Inglés department stores located in urban areas, but the firm has managed to locate its stores in ten of the twelve major cities of Spain, including four stores in the capital city, Madrid.[9,10] El Corte Inglés has recently opened a store in the city of Valladolid, making it the second El Corte Inglés store in that area.[11] This placement of stores in almost all of the major cities in Spain ensures El Corte Inglés's firm grip on the department store market in that country.

El Corte Inglés's expansion skills can be seen in the formation of the group's largest subsidiary, Hypercor, S.A. Consumers in Europe embraced the concept of the hypermarket format very quickly, and Hypercor was founded with the intention of being El Corte Inglés's representative in the hypermarket sector. Hypercor operates as a traditional hypermarket with some of the characteristics of a department store.[12] By expanding in this area of retailing, El Corte Inglés ensures that the group's interests are not concentrated in just one area, which is beneficial to the group in the event of a sharp decline in the department store sector. The shares of hypermarket retailers in the Spanish clothing trade have increased from 5% in 1986 to 12% in 1994,[13] and the popularity of the hypermarket sector has been beneficial to the El Corte Inglés Group. In recent years, Hypercor has enjoyed an increase in net profits and there are plans for self-financed expansion for the profitable subsidiary.[14,15]

Examples of El Corte Inglés's expansion through joint ventures and the formation of other subsidiaries include:

- A 1993 joint venture with the Walt Disney Company to commercialize Disney products to be sold in the El Corte Inglés stores.[16]
- An agreement with the Spanish insurance company Generali, to introduce a comprehensive insurance policy exclusively to the customers of El Corte Inglés.[17]
- Formation of the publishing company Editorial Centro de Estudios Ramon Areces, S.A., which publishes texts for universities.[18]
- The creation of Bricor, a new subsidiary dedicated to developing a chain of "do-it-yourself" (DIY) units.[19]

In addition to expanding in its home country, Spain, El Corte Inglés has been expanding internationally.

Subsidiaries, Joint Ventures, and Franchises

El Corte Inglés recognizes the opportunities available through joint ventures and subsidiaries. Through a strategy of vertical expansion and integration, and its development of diversified services and activities, El Corte Inglés has grown to include the following principle subsidiaries. Hypercor, S.A.; Viajes El Corte Inglés, S.A.; Informatica El Corte Inglés, S.A.; Construccion Promociones e Instalaciones, S.A.; Centro de Estudios Ramon Areces, S.A., and the Harris Company (U.S.A.).[20] Along with these principle subsidiaries, the company has also entered into various agreements and collaborations with other firms.

One of El Corte Inglés's fully owned subsidiaries, Hypercor S.A., was founded in 1979. This subsidiary combines the low prices of a traditional hypermarket with the range of products and level of customer care typical of a large department store. Combining grocery stores, non-food retailing, and service businesses, Hypercor grew tremendously during the 1980s, making it El Corte Inglés's largest subsidiary.[21] Perhaps trying to establish a specialty aspect to El Corte Inglés, the company has recently created a subsidiary, Bricor, to hone in on other DIY markets.[22]

El Corte Inglés signed an agreement with Zenith Data Systems in 1993, the first distribution agreement the company had dealing with personal computers (PCs) in six years, under which it planned to supply the Spanish government with Zenith computers.[23] In 1988, El Corte Inglés had formed its own subsidiary in the information technology market. This subsidiary, Informatica El Corte Inglés, opened a plant in Madrid, the largest city and the capital of Spain, to produce 60,000

PCs a year.[24] In late 1993 and early 1994, Informatica El Corte Inglés reached an agreement of its own with a computer services company, Investronica. The two companies are combining both their services and their products in hopes of improving the efficiency of their existing commercial agreement. Informatica El Corte Inglés is contributing its service aspect, which is aimed at large companies and institutions.[25] In 1995, Informatica El Corte Inglés reached another agreement dealing with its Inves brand computers, the third largest company in the Spanish PC market. The agreement with U.S. software giant Microsoft's Spanish subsidiary gave Inves immediate access to Microsoft's new Windows 95 operating system, launched in 1995.[26]

A $12 million computer program has been launched by the Spanish government. The program is funded by contributions from companies such as IBM. Villena, a sleepy Spanish town with 31,000 people, is the guinea pig in the experiment. Nearly all the homes have been supplied with computers and high-speed ISDN digital lines. In fact, the town has one-fifth of all the ISDN digital lines in Spain. Residents are using chat rooms, making ticket reservations, and shopping online.[27] El Corte Inglés as the dominant retailer in Spain is making the change to computer systems a high priority.

In its collaboration with the insurance company Generali, El Corte Inglés agreed to sell a new home insurance product developed by Generali. Habitat 2000 is an insurance policy that contains exclusions and provides that consumers receive 100% of replacement value of covered items. This is an advantage for El Corte Inglés because the product is offered through it, exclusively.[28]

In another effort to attract customers, El Corte Inglés reached an agreement with the Spanish gas company, Gas Natural, under which the department store is selling domestic appliances powered by gas in an effort to increase gas consumption in Spain. As a result of this agreement, these appliances will be produced locally, instead of being imported from Italy and the United Kingdom.[29]

In early 1994, El Corte Inglés formed two agreements for use in a special promotion focusing on products from the Mediterranean. The first agreement was actually with 123 separate Israeli manufacturers from which the company purchased a variety of products, ranging from beachwear to fashion accessories to 10,000 bottles of wine from the Golan Heights Winery. This as not the first time El Corte Inglés had purchased Israeli products, having done so since 1979 through export companies such as The Export Institute. This particular company arranged for 75 exporters to display their goods for El Corte Inglés buyers, resulting in 31 Israeli companies making their first-ever exports.[30] El Corte Inglés also signed an agreement with J. Malki Industries, a manufacturer located in Beit Dagan, for a shipment of goods such as cosmetics and soaps based on minerals from the Dead Sea, to be displayed as part of the "Mediterranean Week" promotion.[31]

It is evident that El Corte Inglés, in addition to being extremely successful in the hypermarket and department store division, believes in the power of expansion to other markets. By creating subsidiaries, joint ventures, and franchises, El Corte Inglés is effectively capturing a part of the specialty market that cannot be achieved through the superstores. Through these other ventures, the company is targeting the market that prefers to shop in smaller stores that specialize in the merchandise they are looking for. It is targeting those consumers who do not wish to deal with the immensity of a superstore.

Conclusions

Through expansion and continuous strategic planning, El Corte Inglés has become one of the largest and best retailers in Spain. El Corte Inglés is successful at identifying opportunities open for expansion and moving quickly to fill particular niches in the market. From its beginning as a tailor shop through its emergence as a superstore, its ownership of a hypermarket, and its entry into the do-it-yourself market, the hotel industry, and the computer industry, El Corte Inglés has demonstrated its ability to identify and respond to the needs of its customers.

DISCUSSION QUESTIONS

1. One of the strategies used by El Corte Inglés since the late 1940s is vertical integration. Discuss the characteristics of vertical integration and determine whether or not El Corte Inglés should continue to use this strategy.
2. Could the takeover of Galerias Preciados by El Corte Inglés hurt or diminish the success of this firm? If yes, explain your reasoning.

ENDNOTES

1. Hast, A. (1992). *International Directory of Company Histories,* Vol. 5. Detroit: St. James Press.
2. Hast (1992).
3. Hast (1992).
4. Hast (1992).
5. Hast (1992).
6. *Retail News Letter.* (1995). No. 426.
7. Hast (1992).
8. Sternquist, B. HED 45 Lecture, September 25, 1995.
9. *Department Stores in Europe 1992.* (1992). Europe: Management Horizons.
10. Estell, 1992.
11. *Retail News Letter.* (1995). No. 421.
12. Hast (1992).
13. *Retail News Letter.* (1994). No. 419.
14. *Retail News Letter.* (1994). No. 419.
15. *Retail News Letter,* (1994). No. 410.
16. *Retail News Letter,* (1993). No. 398.
17. *Cinco Dias.* (1994). June 16.
18. Hast (1992).
19. *Retail News Letter.* (1994). No. 409.
20. Hast (1992).
21. Hast (1992).
22. *Retail News Letter.* (1994). No. 409.
23. *Cinco Dias* (1994).
24. *Retail News Letter.* (1995). No. 421.
25. *Cinco Dias* (1994).
26. *Expansion,* June 16, 1995.
27. Vitzthum, C. (1997). "Ancient Spanish Town Becomes Infoville." *Wall Street Journal,* August 4, p. B38.
28. *Cinco Dias* (1994).
29. *Expansion,* June 16, 1994.
30. "J Malki Soaps up Spain." (October 29, 1993). *Israel Business Today,* in *Investext* [Database on CD-ROM]. Sagit Publishing International Ltd.
31. "J Malki Soaps up Spain" (October 29, 1993).

COMPANY FOCUS III.8

NOVOARBATSKY GASTRONOM

Patricia Huddleston and Linda K. Good

If "location, location, location" is the hallmark of retail success, then Novoarbatsky Gastronom (New Arbat Supermarket) has it made. Situated in the heart of Moscow, Russia, on New Arbat Street, next to the Irish House and the Valdai shopping center, it would be difficult to find a more advantageous location. The Irish House, one of the first successful foreign retail joint ventures in Moscow, sells imported food, electronics, and apparel such as Levi's. It was one of the first places in Moscow where Russians and tourists alike could purchase a large assortment of imported goods, and it has attracted hordes of customers from the day it opened. The Valdai center, built in 1993, is a magnet for the affluent "New Russians" and tourists, featuring joint venture designer boutiques and other shops with luxury goods. Arbat Street's open market was historically a mecca for foreign tourists seeking Russian souvenirs and handicrafts. Although the open market has disappeared, nearby Old Arbat Street remains a major shopping destination for tourists. Strategically located several hundred meters away from Novoarbatsky Gastronom is a metro stop, so traffic in this area is always heavy.

By Russian standards, even under the planned economy, Novoarbatsky Gastronom was a unique food market. Unlike the majority of food stores in central Moscow before 1991, it was usually well-stocked with products and even offered some imports. This was made possible because even during the planned economy, there was the opportunity to purchase about 25% of the assortment at "free (market) prices." With such initial advantages, success in the market economy would seem to be guaranteed.

Organizational Structure

Formerly a state-owned firm, Novoarbatsky Gastronom became a joint stock company in 1992, which means that employees and outside investors were able to invest in it. The board of directors, which consists of five people, is voted in by employees and meets once a month. Seven department managers are hired by and report to the board of directors, a situation that is not common in the United States. The store director has been with the firm since 1973.

Novoarbatsky Gastronom has seven departments, including bread, wine, meat (specialty and fresh meats), fruits, vegetables, and dairy products, and each department has its own "chief" or manager. The firm employs about 1,000 full-time workers, including those who operate the bread bakery and shop. Typically, employees work 15-hour shifts every other day, with two one-hour breaks each shift.

Since 1991, the store has undergone some extensive remodeling, made possible by Finnish and Italian investors. A sausage shop, which sells precut and prepackaged meat, was built because it is more profitable than purchasing from suppliers. In addition, a "fast-food" restaurant was opened that sells pizza, hamburgers, and some Russian dishes, such as borscht. A Baskin-Robbins outlet inside the shop attracts many customers, especially ice-cream loving Russians.

Originally a one-unit firm, Novoarbatsky Gastronom has expanded in recent years. In 1993, the firm opened a new bakery and bread shop, which is open 24 hours a day, and the aroma of freshly baked bread permeates the area surrounding the store. In 1996, Novoarbatsky owned four shops on nearby Old Arbat Street, a pedestrian street. All four shops are small, and three of the four sell meats, sausages, and some produce. One of these is a special shop where military veterans can buy goods more cheaply; this is a vestige of the old system of doing business in which there were special shops for select groups of Soviets. Management estimates that these four remodeled shops have increased sales volume by 20%.[1]

Challenges and New Business Practices

According to the store director, the unstable economic conditions and lack of legal structure are two of the biggest challenges to doing business.[2] Another challenge that surfaced in 1995–1996 was the appearance of wholesale markets where consumers can buy large quantities of goods more cheaply than in the traditional shops. Novoarbatsky management is fearful of losing some of its customers to these markets because the firm cannot offer the same low prices. One strategy management plans to use to compete with the wholesale markets is to lease space and start a wholesale business in nonperishable goods. However, Novoarbatsky has not currently targeted any particular type of customer for this wholesale business. According to the director, "Life dictates what we must do today."[3] So if retail competition is great, the firm will need to diversify into other lines of business.

In the past two years, new supermarkets have opened in residential districts surrounding Moscow, and management is concerned that people will not want to travel to the city center to do their food shopping. To combat these new competitors, Novoarbatsky sells products its competition does not, for example, semi-cooked meat and fish products. The firm has established a reputation for the freshness of its prepared foods, an advantage it feels the competition cannot match.

Although management expresses concern over the increased level of competition, advertising is limited to in-store announcements, and sampling is the most frequent form of promotion used. Management does not see a need for media advertising because Novoarbatsky is well known and has an excellent reputation. In addition, its suppliers (e.g., Coca-Cola and Pepsi) advertise heavily, and customers are drawn into the store as a result of their advertising. Novoarbatsky supports this with in-store efforts such as sampling.

According to the store director, these challenges are what make doing business in the "New Russia" more interesting.[4] She and the other managers like the new decentralized decision-making, freedom to choose suppliers, and greater reliability of goods supply. The Ministry of Trade used to make product assortment decisions and there was usually an unspecified delivery period for goods. The store never knew which supplier would supply what, what the quality would be, or even what products they would receive. Now, the quality and supply of food products is much more consistent.

Between 1991 and 1993, Novoarbatsky Gastronom was dependent on imported products to provide a complete assortment. In 1993, about 50% of products were imported. In 1996, this dropped to about 40% because Russian producers began to offer higher quality products on a more consistent basis.[5] Some locally produced products, such as vodka and confections (candy), are in higher demand than imports, so Novoarbatsky stocks them. The store director observed that it is difficult to convince foreign suppliers to provide Russian labels for products so that consumers know how to use them. The suppliers are reluctant to do so unless a large volume is ordered. Now that staple products are readily available from Russian producers, imported products will be unique, high quality goods unavailable from Russian suppliers; for example, frozen cakes from Vienna with an 18-month shelf life.[6]

How have priorities changed for Novoarbatsky Gastronom during the transition to a market economy? In 1991, the highest priority of the store director was to find goods to stock the shelves, because a wide assortment of products was not yet available and the most important task was simply to stock the shelves. Now that the supplies of food products have increased, the first priority of the store director is to buy products demanded by customers. For example, a survey of customers found that they wanted cheaper milk products; the store has worked with suppliers to find them. After supplying what customers want, the next priority is to increase the range and quality of goods.

More demanding customers are having an influence on priorities because the next stated priority of the store director is to increase the service level to customers. Increased competition has made Novoarbatsky more customer-oriented. Employees are hired from schools that specialize in trade. Salesclerks participate in sales training seminars to learn how to treat customers more politely.

DISCUSSION QUESTIONS

1. Are these the right strategies for Novoarbatsky Gastronom to prosper in the increasingly competitive Moscow business climate?
2. What should Novoarbatsky Gastronom do to maintain market share as supermarkets open in residential districts in Moscow?

ENDNOTES

1. Huddleston, P., and L. K. Good (1993–1996), personal interviews.
2. Huddleston and Good.
3. Huddleston and Good.
4. Huddleston and Good.
5. Huddleston and Good.
6. Huddleston and Good.

COMPANY FOCUS III.9

PUSHKIN MINI-LAUNDRY

Patricia Huddleston

Every businessperson's dream is to "corner the market" in a product or service that everyone needs. Such has been the case of the Pushkin Mini-Laundry-Business Development Center. Opened in February 1996, it was the only commercial laundry in Pushkin at that time.

Pushkin, located approximately 12 kilometers (7.5 miles) outside of St. Petersburg, Russia, has a population of about 150,000 people. When the former government-owned commercial laundries and dry cleaners closed several years ago, no new ones emerged immediately to replace them. Although a 1989 study of Russian consumers revealed that 66.4% of respondents owned a washing machine, many Russians are accustomed to washing their clothes by hand, in the bathtub. Few Russians own a dryer, so clothing is usually dried on a clothesline outside the flat during the warmer months and inside during the winter. Russian washing machines are considerably smaller than those found in the United States, and wash cycles can take up to two hours to finish, which makes doing laundry a time-consuming and cumbersome process. The chance to finish a week's worth of laundry in a two- to three-hour time span makes a commercial laundromat a convenient alternative to time-starved Russian women.

History

Pushkin Mini-Laundry was developed with the assistance of the Business Development Center (BDC) of St. Petersburg and the Employment Committee of the mayor's office of St. Petersburg. This center was funded through the United States Agency for International Development (USAID) and was one of the most expensive USAID projects in Russia, with support totaling over $100,000.

In February 1995, a seminar was held in St. Petersburg for unemployed people and businesspeople interested in starting their own businesses. A mini-laundry project had been successfully initiated in Moscow, and the owners of this mini-laundry (Blue Krystal) spoke to the participants. As a result of this meeting, enough interest was expressed to conduct market research. The participants in the seminar decided to found a noncommercial organization to support the development of a service-oriented business. This organization, the BDC, was registered in May 1995. During the summer of 1995, market research conducted in the St. Petersburg region to assess the demand for laundry cleaning services confirmed that such a demand existed.

A funding request was submitted to USAID via the BDC to develop a mini-laundry and training center. The purpose of the training center was to prepare entrepreneurs to own and operate their own mini-laundries through hands-on training at an operational laundry facility. Local strategic partners in this venture were the Pushkin Chamber of Commerce and city administration of Pushkin. They worked with the BDC to locate a site for the training center. A small house on one of the major streets in Pushkin, easily accessed by several bus lines, was selected. Once the site was located, renovation of the building began in September 1995. The Pushkin Chamber of Commerce negotiated with its members and other local firms to give discounts on materials and labor for construction of the laundry. An engineer, employed by the Pushkin Chamber of Commerce, worked with construction firms for six months to ensure that the work was completed properly and on time. The director of the Chamber of Commerce estimated that the cost of the renovation would have been two to three times higher without the Chamber's assistance. The manager and staff of the mini-laundry provided some "sweat equity" in the venture. For example, instead of spending 8 million rubles (about $1,400) on landscaping, they did it themselves.

While construction of the laundry was taking place, training materials for the entrepreneurs were developed by personnel at the BDC, and training of the first group of students took place in November 1995. Some of the topics included in the training were how to write a business plan, arranging financing, designing security systems, and providing services of a Western-style laundry. Participants were required to complete 60 hours of practical training in which they learned to operate the equipment, make minor repairs, and work with customers (e.g., how to use machines and detergents properly).

Decorated with red, white, and blue banners symbolizing the support of the U.S. government, a press conference was held to herald the official opening of the Pushkin Mini-Laundry-Business Development Center. Officials from USAID, the city of Pushkin, and the Pushkin Chamber of Commerce were present. Although the official opening was February 27, 1996, the laundry was not actually open for business until about a month later, disappointing customers who stopped by hoping to use the facilities. The facility is brightly lit and spotless; it is equipped with 20 Maytag washing machines and dryers, provided at a substantial discount by the Maytag Company. For customer convenience, detergents can be purchased on site. Ironing boards, irons, and a lounge area are also available.

Promotional Strategies

The mission of the Pushkin Mini-Laundry-Business Development Center is twofold: first, to provide excellent, state-of-the-art laundry services to the citizens of Pushkin, and second, to train students to open their own mini-laundries. Currently, the mini-laundry employs a manager (deputy director), one attendant, and a director of the BDC. The director is responsible for the recruitment and training of students. The manager is responsible for the operation of the laundry, training of the attendants, and customer service.

So, have customers flocked to the mini-laundry? Is it turning away business? Are there long queues to use the machines? Well, not yet. Six months into this venture, the mini-laundry was serving approximately 30 to 40 customers a day. This was an increase from three to four per day when it first opened. The goal is to attract 50 to 60 customers per day; however, the laundry could handle 100 per day.

What strategies are being used to attract customers? Initial market research revealed that younger people were most likely to use the self-service laundries, whereas older people will continue to wash clothing the old-fashioned way, by hand. With this information in mind, a variety of promotional strategies were used to attract potential customers. Flyers were distributed at the railway station and in the mailboxes of large apartment buildings in Pushkin. These flyers offered a free wash or a 50%-off coupon. Results showed more people responded to the 50%-off coupon. English versions of the flyers have also been distributed to attract foreign customers already familiar with commercial laundromats.

Media advertising has included a local cable television commercial which showed people washing clothes in the laundromat. To reduce advertising expenses, the management was able to barter laundry services with the local television station in exchange for air time. Other promotional strategies include transit advertising signs at bus stops that advertise express wash and self-service, and the manager plans to develop outdoor advertisements. Of the strategies used thus far, the most effective has been the flyers. They cost about one cent per flyer, and approximately 5,000 are distributed per month.

Initially, this was the only commercial laundry in central Pushkin, but in 1996, a competitor entered this market. Located approximately eight blocks from the mini-laundry, it is a smaller operation and current customers of the Pushkin Mini-Laundry who visited this facility ultimately returned because they said the machines were smaller and the atmosphere was not as nice.

How is the training aspect of the business progressing? There are difficulties here, as well, and this aspect is not profitable at the present time. Although the BDC has been able to recruit five to seven clients per month, the director acknowledges that people interested in the laundry business constitute a narrow segment that is difficult to reach. Thus far, no monetary resources have been committed to recruit students. However, The BDC has been able to generate some publicity through interviews with journalists. Articles have appeared in *St. Petersburg Press, Business Man* (a Russian publication), and a local Pushkin paper.

This venture appears to be facing other problems as well. One of its strategic partners, the Pushkin Chamber of Commerce, has expressed concern that the BDC wants to sever its relationship with the Chamber even though its financial situation is precarious. For the past year, the Pushkin Chamber of Commerce has provided both advisory and financial assistance to the laundry-BDC, and it was instrumental in getting this venture on its feet. The Chamber of Commerce holds the lease on the building in which the laundry-BDC is located and the rent of $300 per month is paid through the Chamber account. The Chamber negotiated with the City of Pushkin for lower rent for this venture. For several months, when the laundry did not generate sufficient cash flow to pay overhead expenses, the Chamber loaned it the money to cover the rent. The Chamber of Commerce also paid the utilities up front, and it took the mini-laundry several months to repay them. The director of the BDC wants to be an independent venture without the involvement of its strategic partner. However, the Chamber of Commerce has spent considerable financial and personnel resources to get this venture up and running and believes that its reputation is at stake, especially if this venture fails. One stipulation of the initial agreement was that the Pushkin Chamber of Commerce would share the profits, which would then be reinvested in assisting other local businesses. Although not yet profitable, Pushkin Mini-Laundry-Business Development Center wants to operate independently of the Pushkin Chamber of Commerce and retain its profits.

DISCUSSION QUESTIONS

1. What strategies should be used to attract potential entrepreneurs as students to the BDC?
2. Should Pushkin Mini-Laundry-Business Development Center sever its ties with the Pushkin Chamber of Commerce?
3. What strategies can be used to attract a larger customer base to maximize use of these facilities?

ENDNOTES

Afanasenko, V.I., Director, Pushkin Chamber of Commerce. (1996). Personal interview.

History of the Program to Support the Development of Private Mini-Laundries in St. Petersburg. (1996). St. Petersburg: Internal Document Business Development Center.

"Laundromat Opens in Pushkin." (1996). *St. Petersburg Press,* February 27–March 4, p. 14.

Understanding the Soviet Consumer. (1991). Ithaca, N.Y.: W-Two Publications, Ltd.

Part IV Retailing in Asia

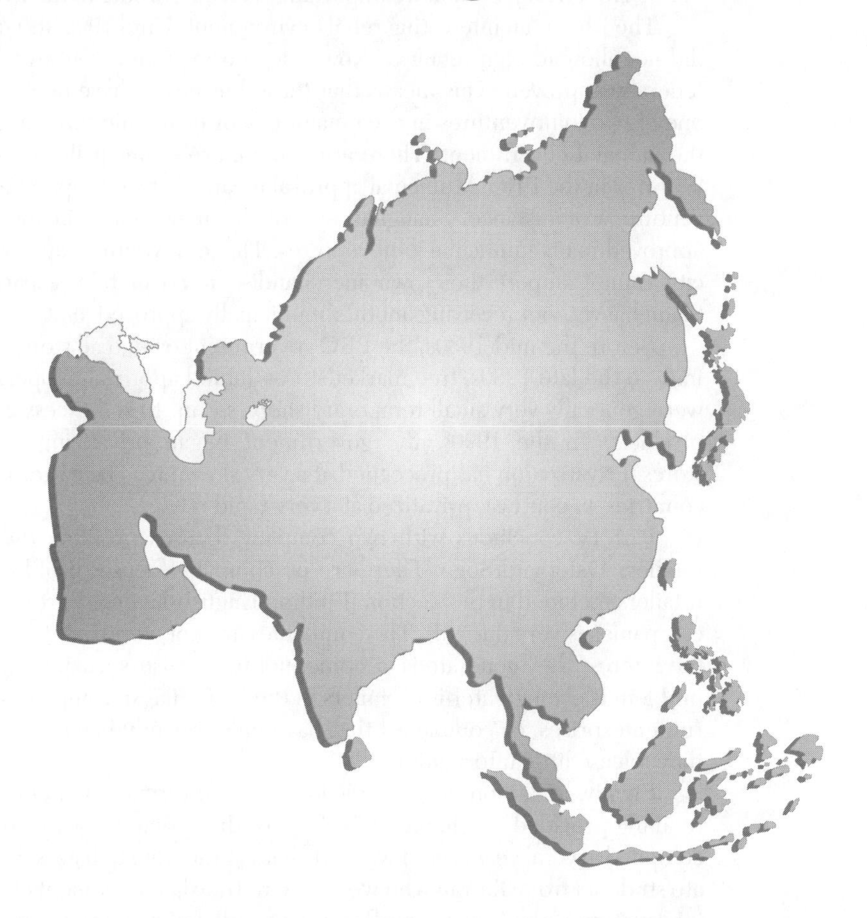

The countries discussed thus far in this book share a broad European heritage. In Part IV, our focus shifts to Asia: specifically, Japan, Hong Kong, Taiwan, and the People's Republic of China (PRC). The first chapter in this section considers Japan's distribution system, which is nearly opposite to that of the United States. Differences between developed and less developed countries are to be expected. However, it is surprising to see so many differences between two highly developed countries. These differences are explored in Chapter 12.

There are several areas populated by Chinese. In Chapter 13, I discuss similarities among the three groups of Chinese in the PRC, Hong Kong (since 1997 a special administrative region of the PRC), and Taiwan. Hong Kong and Taiwan are populated with immigrants from the PRC. The retail industries in Hong Kong and Taiwan display some characteristics of Japanese distribution and some American types of distribution. In July 1997, Great Britain's lease on Hong Kong expired. Hong Kong reverted to the PRC. This makes Hong Kong even more important as an entry route to the PRC.

The PRC is an interesting retail environment. Until 1992, its government did not allow foreign retailers. Now, a few foreign joint ventures have been federally approved. This means that these businesses have been selected as one of two joint ventures in each major city or economic zone sanctioned by the national government. There are many more municipally approved joint ventures in the PRC. Municipal approval means that a city approves the joint venture. For instance, Shanghai, one of the major cities in the PRC, has approved many municipal joint ventures. The joint ventures approved by the city cannot import their own merchandise nor can they expand outside Shanghai without receiving another municipally approved joint venture.

Before the mid-1980s, the PRC government owned all stores. From the mid- to the late 1980s, free market stores gained approval to operate. These were generally very small temporary shops set up to sell excess agricultural products. In the 1990s, the government began privatizing state-owned stores. Privatization has proceeded at a very slow rate. The eastern European countries, in contrast, privatized at a very rapid rate.

Part IV concludes with two company focuses profiling the Japanese retailers Daiei and Sogo. There are no company focuses profiling Chinese retailers included in this section. Finding English-language articles on these companies is very difficult. The companies are not world giants, and most of the interest they generate is at home, not in English-speaking regions. The problem is even greater for retailers in the PRC. These companies are state-run enterprises, or companies that have only recently been privatized, and they release little information.

Finally, a caution is given regarding the information about Taiwanese retailing provided in Chapter 13. Much of the research for this section was compiled several years ago. I was fortunate at the time to have several graduate students from Taiwan who were able to translate documents for me. The information is the best I can offer. I have updated some statistics, but other statistics are tied to these original Chinese documents. I had the choice of eliminating them, to keep things current, or providing them with the caution that they are dated. I decided that it was better to provide the information.

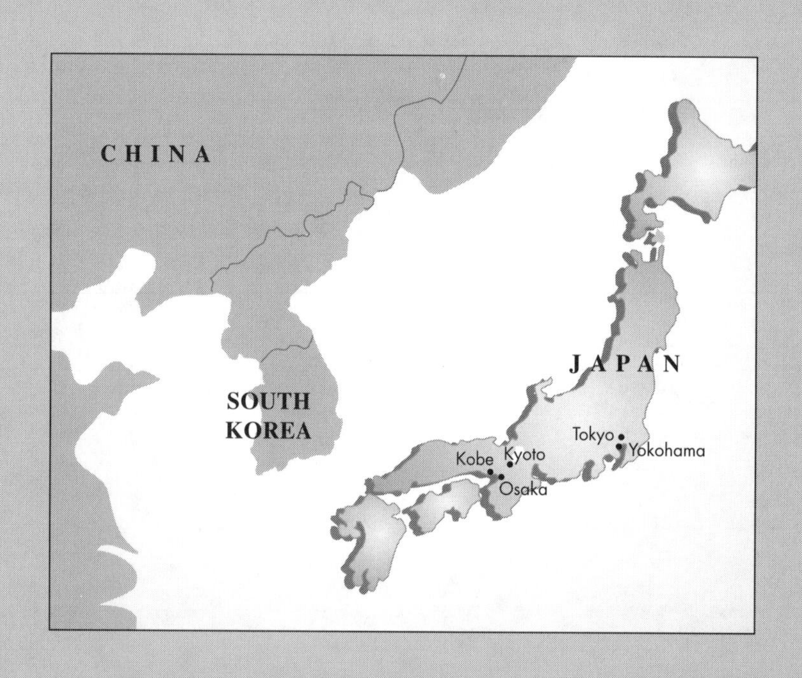
CHINA
SOUTH KOREA
JAPAN
Tokyo
Yokohama
Kyoto
Kobe
Osaka

12

Retailing in Japan

After reading this chapter, you will understand:

- How the Japanese use group affiliation (frame theory) to structure and regulate relationships.
- Why doing well in Japan has been difficult for foreign businesses.
- The details of the Japanese buying system.
- How to use Dunning's theory of the eclectic firm to explain which Japanese retailers will internationalize and where they will go.
- How modern and traditional retail systems coexist in this developed society.

THIS CHAPTER EXPLORES the unique characteristics of the retail system in Japan, particularly the distribution system, which differs from that of many other highly developed countries, including the United States. The chapter begins with a look at theories and concepts that can help us to better understand the Japanese business culture. Next, the major Japanese retail formats are discussed. The Japanese department store industry is among the most developed in the world. However, restrictive legislation has made domestic expansion difficult. This and other factors have prompted Japanese retailers to expand into international markets. This chapter concludes with a discussion of these factors.

COUNTRY BACKGROUND

For much of their history, the Japanese have kept others outside their world. In the 4th century A.D., the title "Emperor of Japan" was given to a major clan leader. Myth-makers added the belief that the emperor was descended from the Sun God, and people soon came to believe in his divinity. This belief continued until Hirohito (the 124th emperor, crowned in 1926) told the Japanese citizens that he was not divine in a proclamation that was part of the surrender agreement after World War II. Today, there are still some Japanese people who believe the emperor is divine.

Many religious and cultural influences came to Japan from China. Traditions that we consider Japanese, such as Zen, the tea ceremony, and bonsai trees, all came from China 1,000 years ago. The Japanese writing system also comes from the Chinese. In 1542, the first Europeans (Portuguese) arrived in Japan. The first Christian missionary, Francis Xavier, came five years later. Will Adam, the first Englishman, came in 1600. He was followed by the Dutch in 1609.

Japan established trade with the Europeans in the mid-16th century. However, Japanese rulers viewed the rapid spread of Christianity by European missionaries as a threat to their power. They eradicated Christianity in 1639 and expelled all foreigners except the Dutch and Chinese. Foreigners were kept out for the next 200 years.

In 1854, Commodore Perry roared into Tokyo Bay with a fleet of boats. He demanded that Japan open its ports to trade. The Japanese, realizing they were outnumbered, opened their doors to trade with the United States, Britain, the Netherlands, and Russia. They then began a mad rush to catch up with the industrialized nations. The Japanese were highly successful. In just 50 years, they defeated China in the war of 1895. Ten years later, the Japanese did the unthinkable. They defeated imperial Russia.

Japanese leaders were convinced of their ability and right to dominate the world. They annexed Taiwan, took over control of Manchuria from Russia, and overpowered Korea. Japan's support of the Allies in World War I gave the country financial rewards and convinced its leaders that they were destined to lead the rest of Asia to prosperity. A depression in the 1930s, lack of natural resources, and overpopulation led to Japan's expansionist zeal.

Japanese air fleets attacked the United States (Pearl Harbor) in 1941. During World War II, the United States destroyed much of Japan's navel power. The war ended in 1945 when the United States dropped atomic bombs on Hiroshima and Nagasaki.

After the surrender, U.S. forces occupied Japan, helping to set up a new constitution. The United States also helped to construct an industrial machine that would transform Japan's military capabilities to peaceful use. The emperor was retained as a figurehead with no governmental authority or power. Emperor Hirohito died in January 1989, and his son, Akihito, inherited the title.

Table 12.1 presents selected demographic and economic data for Japan.

Japan is a high context society. Much meaning is derived through the setting of communication, not just the words. I discuss the meaning of high context in Chapter 3. Several years ago, I taught a class in Japan. One of my students gave me a book by Chie Nakane, a well-known Japanese anthropologist. He said it would help me understand the Japanese I met. Nakane begins her lesson about the Japanese with two concepts, attribute versus frame orientation. [1]

ATTRIBUTE VERSUS FRAME THEORY

Societies that are attribute-oriented separate an object into elements. These elements are the **attributes,** the specific features of a product or person. If all the elements are added together, we get an evaluation of the object or person. For instance, in considering a vacation destination, I would probably evaluate the hotel for price and value, amenities in the area such as beaches or museums, and consider the time and cost expended to reach the destination. In the end, some good attributes, such as low cost, might sway me toward my ultimate choice. However, in an attribute-oriented society, assessment of one object does not directly influence assessment of other objects.

In a frame-oriented society, every object is set in an environment—the frame of reference for the object—and it is the entire frame that the society evaluates. Suppose an American and a Japanese man meet at a dinner party. In response to the question, "what do you do?", the American would likely respond by mentioning his professional area, "I am a lawyer." The Japanese would likely mention his company, "I work for Isetan." The

TABLE 12.1

Japan: Selected Demographic and Economic Data

	Population (millions) mid-1995	Area (thousands of sq. km)	GNP per capita: Dollars 1995	GNP per capita: Avg. ann. growth (%) 1985–95	PPP estimates of GNP per capita U.S. = 100: 1987	PPP estimates of GNP per capita U.S. = 100: 1995	Life expectancy at birth (years) 1995	Adult illiteracy (%) 1995
High-income economies	902.2t	32,039t	24,930w	1.9w			77w	
Japan	125.2	378	39,640	2.9	75.3	82.0	80	a

Source: World Bank (1997). a = less than 5%. PPP = purchasing power parity. t = total. w = weighted average.

Japanese response would be the same, whether the person was a cleaning person or the CEO of an international company. Americans cite an attribute: "I am a lawyer." Japanese cite a **frame,** the setting for attributes: "I work for Isetan."

Figure 12.1 illustrates how two objects—a blind date and a supplier—could be described using an attribute versus a frame perspective. The personal ads in the classified section of most local U.S. newspapers are rampant with attributes.

> Tall, dark, and handsome, SWM, lawyer, seeks sweet but swinging SWF. Must be tall, thin, blond, and tan. . .

Japanese matchmakers would start with an overview of the blind date's family, company employment, and educational affiliation:

> An oldest daughter of a prestigious Tokyo family, an employee of Sony electronics company, and 1993 graduate of Tokyo University. . .

This information presents three frames: her family, her employer, and her educator.

Attribute versus frame orientation explains in large part why U.S. companies have not been successful in the Japanese market. Consider this scenario. An American handbag salesperson calls on a Japanese retail buyer. The American sells the handbags by highlighting all the features—the fine quality leather, the style, and the competitive price. The salesperson is selling the attributes. These attributes are of secondary consideration to the Japanese buyer. While the American seller is trying to sell the handbags, the Japanese buyer is evaluating the company. He is interested in the reputation

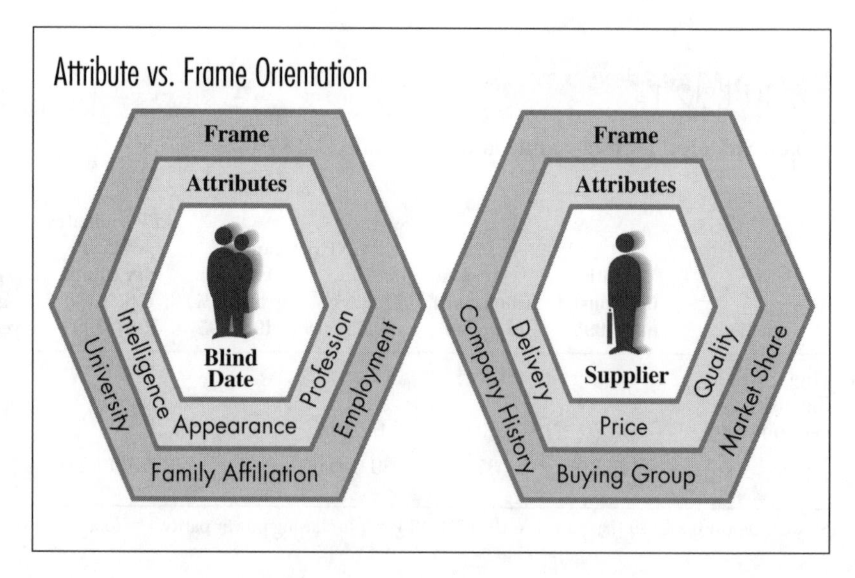

Figure 12.1
While attributes are isolated features, frame orientation requires context. Frame features for a blind date might include such information as university attended, family affiliation, and employer. Frame orientation for selecting a supplier might include company history, buying group affiliation, and market share. Frame is based on association with others; attributes are individual qualities.

of the company in the United States, its market share, and the formal and informal business relationships the company may have with other companies. The American salesperson is selling attributes, but the Japanese buyer is buying the company within its business frame. Product attributes are important, but only after the Japanese buyer has established the acceptability of the company as a supplier.

The relationship of suppliers to retailers shows evidence of this frame orientation. A Japanese retailer would not change suppliers because a competitive supplier offered a lower price. However, this attribute, price, is very important in the United States. If a lower-priced supplier were available, a U.S. business would consider changing suppliers.

THEORY OF JAPANESE BUSINESS RELATIONS

The attribute versus frame orientation is an important introduction to Japanese thinking. Shimaguchi goes further in explaining some important differences in how the Japanese conduct business. Three concepts that can help us understand Japanese business activities are pseudo-harmonism, eclecticism, and exceptionism.[2]

PSEUDO-HARMONISM

The Japanese have a saying: "The nail that sticks up gets hammered down." This adage reflects the concept of pseudo-harmonism. **Pseudo-harmonism** means that you pretend harmony exists, whether it exists or not. A nail that sticks up is not harmonious with the other nails. Similarly, an employee who sticks out, as either superior or inferior to other employees, disrupts the harmony of the work-place. The Japanese want to get along with others, and they suppress things and people that ruffle relationships. So in business relationships, like personal relationships, there is an attempt to maintain peace and harmony.

In my early days of doing research in Japan, I told a Japanese research colleague that I would like to interview an important woman executive. I had read about this woman in several major publications. His response was, "It will be difficult." At the time I thought he was saying, "It will be difficult, but probably can be arranged." As time went on, though, and I never seemed to get any closer to setting up the interview, I realized that when my colleague said, "It will be difficult," what he really meant was, "There is not a chance you will get to talk to this person." Rather than saying no, he just postponed the issue, maintaining harmony.

The same response occurs in business transactions. If a retail supplier is late with a delivery, the Japanese retailer might respond graciously, helping the supplier to give explanations about why the merchandise was delivered late. There is disharmony, the supplier has not lived up to his end of the agreement, but the Japanese retailer will pretend nothing is wrong.

Have you ever fought with a significant person in your life, yet pretended that everything was all right when you went out in public? This is pseudo-harmony. The difference is that in the United States, we save such social protection for our loved ones. In Japan, it extends to business relationships. Japanese business relationships are like intimate family relationships. This designation also applies to the next concept, eclecticism.

ECLECTICISM

Eclecticism means that decisions are made in a circular manner. In Japan, business solutions often are a compromise or midpoint among the different business options. Decisions are made by consensus. Contracts pass through multiple levels of decision-makers, a system known as ***ringi.*** In the *ringi* system, decision-makers affix their seals of approval. These seals are not a signature but a chop. A **chop** is a group of characters on a circular seal, which is used instead of a signature in Japan and China. A person's chop is registered with the authorities, and it becomes the official signing instrument for that person.

I have talked with U.S. businesspeople who were very displeased with the outcome of their negotiations with Japanese companies. They carried out talks with a Japanese team for several weeks, expecting a contract to be signed before they left the bargaining table. In the end, however, the Japanese team said they would need to take the agreement back to Tokyo to have headquarters sign off on it. The U.S. representatives were disappointed, believing they had negotiated in good faith with a Japanese representative who was authorized to make decisions. However, the Japanese action in this instance is very predictable. Among Japanese, all of those involved consider the final agreement, not just the members of the negotiating team.

The next concept is exceptionism. This concept is tied directly to high context cultures, for whom the meaning of the rule is affected by the situation.

EXCEPTIONISM

The working method in Japan is exceptionism, or the ruleless rule. **Exceptionism** means that rules change with the situation. A flexible, freestyle approach characterizes this system. The Japanese rebate system is an example of this absence of rigid rules. Suppliers have discretionary rebates. For instance, a supplier might give a retailer a rebate because the retailer's daughter is getting married. There are a wide variety of discretionary rebates. These practices confuse outsiders.

The Japanese government periodically gives the appearance of trying to reduce exceptionism, making rules that are clear to all the market players. Shimaguchi uses the pharmaceutical industry as an example. During fierce competition in the industry, manufacturers would provide *tempu* (additional products), a type of rebate. Physicians who placed large orders might receive 200% *tempu;* that is, two products given to them for every one bought. When the government discouraged this practice, the industry switched to another system, called *okiwasure* (leave and forget). The manufacturer would simply deliver more goods than ordered and then forget to correct the error.[3]

Japan's distribution system is a curious combination of a traditional system and a modern retail system. The traditional system refers to mom and pop stores. These stores are located close to where consumers live. The modern retail system refers to self-service convenience stores and mass merchandisers using modern distribution technology. Japan has a large number of retail stores per consumer. Its trading partners say Japan's distribution system is closed to outsiders. There is some truth and a lot of fiction in this contention.

CHARACTERISTICS OF THE RETAIL SYSTEM

The frame orientation introduced at the beginning of this chapter can help us to understand characteristics of the Japanese retail system. In Japan, retailers and their suppliers work as partners. Generally, the relationship between a buyer and a supplier is very long term. Adding a new supplier is not an everyday event.

Photo 12.1
The Marui department store in Tokyo offers a wide variety of housewares and apparel. The symbol that looks like "OlOl" is the company logo, representing Marui. *Courtesy of the author.*

SUPPLIER SUPPORT

Suppliers in Japan provide several of the functions handled by retailers in the United States. In Japan, suppliers hold merchandise until the retailer needs it, monitoring the stock within a store and replenishing it as needed. Japanese suppliers may restock convenience stores four times per day. In department stores, suppliers provide salespersons to sell their merchandise. These employees provide the suppliers with important market information. Suppliers provide financial support for remodeling a department store, or for recreating a window display. If a Japanese department store needs a new elevator, the store would likely assess its suppliers to have them pay for part of the elevator.

Japanese manufacturers allow retailers to return unsold merchandise. This is a type of consignment system. With a **consignment** system, manufacturers determine what merchandise will be displayed, hire sales employees to sell the merchandise, and accept return of unsold merchandise. Manufacturers, not retailers, are responsible for the risk of product acceptance. In Japan, retailers became **manufacturers' showrooms;** that is, they function like a real estate leasing agent rather than an assembler of merchandise assortments. Retailers lease their real estate, that is, the display area in the store, to manufacturers. This system gives power to the manufacturers. **Power,** in this context, refers to influence in the distribution channel.

I have been doing Japanese distribution research for thirteen years. Ninety percent of the articles I read mention the high ratio of retailers and wholesalers to consumers. This ratio is about twice the ratio in the United States. Japan's critics often cite this as the primary reason foreign manufacturers have a difficult time entering the Japanese system. They believe that wholesalers and manufacturers have close interlocking relations and disregard foreign products. ***Keiretsu*** refers to a system of formal business relationships linking financial institutions and manufacturing companies. Although *keiretsu* relationships are important in Japan, they do not play a major role in Japanese retailing. Retailers and their suppliers are not so purposely linked but rather are linked through mutual obligation.

If foreigners know one piece of information about Japanese distributions, it is that there are multiple wholesalers. The length of the channel is much longer than in the United States. Three years ago, after conducting hundreds of hours of interviews with department store managers and buyers, I wanted to start talking to their wholesale suppliers. Throughout the interviews, which we always conducted in Japanese, the buyers would refer to their suppliers. My Japanese colleague and I assumed most of the suppliers they were referring to were wholesalers. Weeks before I was to return to Japan for more interviews with wholesalers, my Japanese colleague called and said "There are no wholesalers." I said, "What do you mean, no wholesalers?" He replied, "All the department store buyers we have been interviewing buy direct from the manufacturer."

This is an embarrassing mistake to admit. We had spent years talking to department store managers and buyers and had not discovered they buy

Photo 12.2
This mother and child are selecting a toy from a vending machine. In Japan, vending machines are very sophisticated; chilled fresh beef, fancy cakes, and even ladies' lingerie are sold through them. Small stores use vending machines to extend their hours of operation. A liquor store owner might sell five or six different sizes of cold beer, several types of hard liquor, and several varieties of hot and cold *sake* through a vending machine outside the store. *Courtesy of AP/Wide World Photos.*

direct from the manufacturer. We had not even bothered asking, because we thought we knew the answer. Small retailers do buy from wholesalers, but these retailers only purchase a small amount of imported merchandise. They are not a viable distribution route for foreign products. The myth of multiple wholesalers is so strong, we did not question it. If we had not set out to interview wholesalers, we might not have found out the truth.

An economist, David Flath, made a very important contribution to our knowledge about Japan. He studied channel length (number of wholesalers) used in Japan and other parts of the world. He found that if you control for product perishability, there is no difference between channel length in the United States and Japan.[4] For example, fresh fish passes through a lengthy channel in both the United States and Japan. Japanese people eat a lot of fresh fish, and they value product freshness in a variety of food products. It is this emphasis on perishable products that lengthens the distribution channel, not excessive wholesaler processing.

THE BUYER IS KING

Japan is a hierarchical society. When the Japanese exchange business cards, the purpose is not to learn the other person's name, it is to establish the status of the new acquaintance. Without this information, they do not have the necessary information to talk with strangers, or even to know where they should seat them. In Japan, people are seated around a conference table in the order of their group status.

Relationships have a formal meaning in Japan. They clearly define the role of buyer and seller in Japanese culture. Japanese businesspeople view buyers and sellers vertically. Buyers are superior to sellers. Sellers must conduct themselves in a subservient manner, respecting this difference. U.S. businesspeople view buyers and sellers as equal, having a horizontal relationship. A supplier offers something for sale, if the buyer wants to purchase it, fine; if not, that is fine also.

CONSIGNMENT

After World War II, a shortage of products in Japan meant that anything could be sold. The suppliers, wholesalers, and manufacturers began to have merchandising power. This supplier's market significantly decreased the merchandising power of department stores. During rapid economic growth, department stores tried to enlarge their stores and increase stock. They became careless about product selection. To ensure access to distribution outlets, manufacturers instituted a consignment system under which retailers could return merchandise that did not sell. This movement to the consignment system significantly reduced the retailers' power in the channel system. Manufacturers also began to send their own representatives to the stores. They did this to make sure the retailer presented their products properly and to provide information about sales volume.

Japanese retailers and their suppliers have long-term relationships. One part of this relationship is to provide merchandise on a consignment basis. If the merchandise does not sell, it can be returned to the manufacturer. Consignment sales are used in many different lines of merchandise, such as clothing and footwear. In the United States, consignment is used in cosmetics but not in most other product areas. Using consignment spreads the product risk. If merchandise produced by the manufacturer does not sell successfully in the retail store, then both the retailer and the manufacturer share the cost of this product failure. The retailer loses opportunity costs. **Opportunity costs** are what the retailer would have earned if another, better-selling manufacturer had that shelf space. The manufacturer must absorb the cost of producing the product if it does not sell.

The effect of using the consignment sales method is that merchandise is generally more standard. Manufacturers are less likely to take great product risks because they are responsible for product failure. Effects of the consignment system are presented in Figure 12.2.

Using a consignment system will result in lower retail margin, less product variety, less imported merchandise, as well as higher supplier margins and consumer costs. The retail margin is less because the manufacturer, not the retailer, is taking product risk. Taking greater risk gives greater margin. With consignment, we would expect that the retail margin is reduced but the

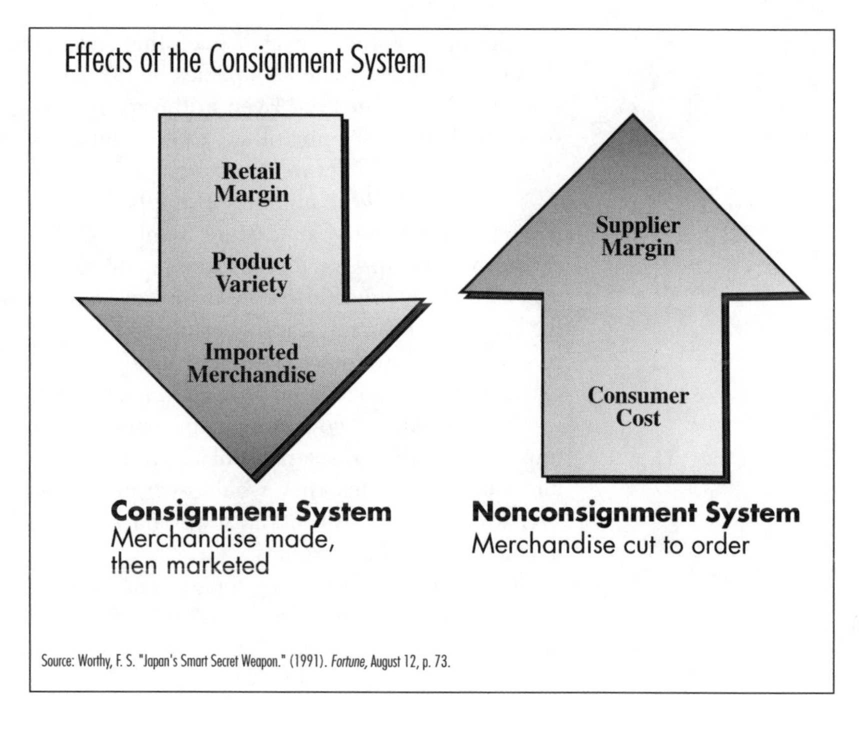

Figure 12.2
Consignment systems prevail in Japan. Under the consignment system, the manufacturer carries the product risk by accepting the return of unsold merchandise. The consignment system lowers retail margins because the retailer assumes less risk. It also lowers product variety because manufacturers assume the cost of failed innovations, and lowers imported merchandise because of the cost of merchandise returns. The consignment system raises manufacturer margins, because the supplier takes the product risk. It also raises consumer prices because merchandise is not rapidly marked down so it will sell.

manufacturer's profit margin is increased. Product variety is reduced because the manufacturer seeks more staple products with more predictable demand. The consignment system discourages imported purchases because of the shipping costs involved in product returns.

ROLE OF RETAIL BUYER

In the United States, retail buyers are considered profit centers. Retailers in the United States evaluate buyers on how they have increased sales and profits on a year-to-date basis. They evaluate buyers on maintained markup, returns, and inventory turnover. If buyers do not purchase merchandise that is saleable, with an adequate maintained margin, the retailer cannot make a profit. Management rewards buyers financially and with promotion for profitable figures. Buyers who do not perform well are demoted or fired.

A different situation exists in Japan. Japanese buyers are rewarded based on seniority. They are not considered profit centers and are not constantly monitored to determine markup, returns, and inventory turnover. Although most large Japanese retailers do have buyers, these buyers work closely with the retail department sales manager and the manufacturer from whom they purchase. Purchases are rarely the decision of one individual.

Because of the prevalence of the consignment system in Japanese department stores, some companies do not have buyers. Department managers serve this function. Even in those companies where there is a highly developed central buying office, there is much greater interaction between the buying and selling function in Japan.

Stores control the number of suppliers that can deal directly with them through the issuing of an account number. Only suppliers that have proven themselves obtain a number. I asked Japanese buyers and merchandise managers about the procedure used to approve a new vendor for the stores' buying list. Their response was quite similar. The final question is, "Can our current suppliers produce this merchandise?" The bias is against buying from any new vendor, not simply from a foreign vendor.

The Japanese government pressures large retailers to buy more imported merchandise, particularly from the United States. Retailers I interviewed said that they would give preference to a U.S. manufacturer over a new Japanese vendor. Stores buyers attend foreign products trade fairs to find suitable products.

Competition among the department stores focuses on non-price competition. Negotiations with suppliers reflect this. Rather than negotiate price, buyers negotiate margin.

BUYING METHODS

Japanese department stores use three types of buying agreements: *kaitori shiire, itaku shiire,* and *uriage (shoka) shiire.*

KAITORI SHIIRE In the *kaitori shiire* system, there is no return unless the product is damaged or faulty. This is like the system used in the United States. The retailer pays for the merchandise in cash, usually one month after delivery. The returns system continues under the euphemism of product exchange. The retailer receives a margin of about 50% on sales.

ITAKU SHIIRE *Itaku shiire* is the equivalent of consignment sale. Here, the risks pass to the department store upon delivery, but payment to the supplier occurs one month following sale to the consumer. Therefore, if the merchandise does not sell, it is returned to the wholesalers. Retailers can set the price if they want, or they can allow the wholesaler to set the price. If retailers want to put the merchandise on sale, they must receive the approval of the manufacturer or wholesaler. Retailers receive a margin of about 30%. In this system, the retailer is responsible for damaged or stolen merchandise.

URIAGE (SHOKA) SHIIRE *Uriage (shoka) shiire* means, literally, digestion purchase. Product and product risk pass to the department store upon delivery, but payment to the supplier occurs the month following the sale to a customer. Perishable foods are purchased using this system. *Uriage shiire* began when department stores expanded from the sales of kimono products to perishable foods. Department stores did not have the product knowledge needed to manage the sale of perishable goods. Under *uriage shiire,* the wholesaler keeps track of sales and pays the retailer about 3% of sales.

LONG-TERM RELATIONSHIPS

As previously noted, Japanese buyers are linked to suppliers through long-term business commitments. Most buyers and suppliers have been business partners for decades. They do not base the relationship strictly on price, but instead on mutually beneficial concerns and decision-making. Like a family, the partners may argue with each other and voice dissatisfaction with the business relationship, but they remain true to each other.

The relationship situation between suppliers and retailers is not part of the *keiretsu* system, mentioned earlier. The *keiretsu* system, used in manufacturing and in the commodities trade, is a formal linking of businesses. The retailer-supplier link is more informal than this. However, major retailers belong to specific buying groups. These groups have a financial link with other business partners which, when all things are considered, are the preferred partners for all types of business relationships.

SALES EMPLOYEES SENT BY MANUFACTURER

Much of the sales staff in a Japanese department store is not hired by the department store, but instead is hired by various manufacturers and sent to the store to sell merchandise. In a department store that has 60% to 80% consignment merchandise, the manufacturer would also send about 60% to 80% of its sales employees. These sales employees are dressed just like other sales employees so custmers in the store do not know whether the department store or a manufacturer paid the person. The sales people do not sell only their manufacturer's products.

An observer might think the department stores are forcing the manufacturers to provide sales employees, but manufacturers would explain that having the sales employees in the store is their most important type of market research. By having their employees talk with customers, the manufacturers receive grassroots information about what customers want. Information is one of the most important competitive factors in marketing. Sales employees provide this important information, which gives their employer access to the information. This offers competitive strength.

HIGHLY COMPETITIVE, BUT NOT ON PRICE

Manufacturers attach a price to products and, because of the consignment system, can convince retailers to keep the price at their suggested level. If markdowns are to be taken, the manufacturer has the major determination of whether, and when, a markdown will take place.

This pricing system is a part of the larger marketing system in Japan, where most merchandise is produced before demand is known. The Japanese manufacturer determines what merchandise will be made available. The manufacturer's representatives work with retail buyers to determine what merchandise and what volume of merchandise will be offered in each store. If the merchandise does not sell, the manufacturer accepts the return of unsold merchandise. When the merchandise is returned to the manufacturer, it is usually destroyed rather than being sold at a reduced price. To reduce the price would erode the price image of the company.

In the United States, in contrast, manufacturers produce merchandise lines that are then shown to retail buyers at markets and trade shows. Buyers review the line and place orders. After the manufacturers review the orders they have obtained from buyers, they decide what merchandise to produce. If manufacturers have just a few orders for a particular model, they will not produce that product. They will tell the retail buyer that an item is not available due to insufficient demand. In Japan, merchandise is made, then sold. In the United States, merchandise orders are taken, and production is based on orders. Figure 12.3 graphically illustrates the difference between how the Japanese and the U.S. product development process is carried out.

Photo 12.3
Fresh strawberries are sold in a gift box as a delicacy. The price is 2,500 yen, about $25 for 12 strawberries. *Courtesy of the author.*

Photo 12.4
A melon, two grapefruits, and three oranges in a gift box sells for nearly $100. Two melons in a gift box commands a price of nearly $120.
Courtesy of the author.

REBATE SYSTEM

The Japanese rebate system is a very good example of eclecticism and exceptionism. A Japanese businessman once told me, when you understand the Japanese rebate system, you will understand Japanese distribution. He was trying to convey to me the complexity of this system. Taga and Uehara[5] classify rebates into six areas: quality rebates, payment debt rebates, target achievement rebates, physical distribution rebates, sales promotion rebates, and special rebates.

Quantity rebates are given to retailers based on order size or total quantity ordered throughout the period. **Payment date rebates** are given to buyers who pay their bill before a certain deadline. **Target achievement rebates** are paid according to how well the buyer has met sellers' agreed-upon targets in areas such as total sales and new customers. **Physical distribution rebates** are given when the buyer helps the seller with the physical distribution of the goods ordered. These rebates might include repackaging rebates when a retailer, at the request of the supplier, makes changes in packaging, putting several items together or dividing items into smaller groups. Inventory burden rebates also fit under this classification for buyers who, at the request of the seller, share the costs of risk and of special inventory. **Sales promotion rebates** are refunds paid to the retailer who shares the work or cost of conducting a special sales promotion (advertising, displays, and so on). **Special rebates** are based on the supplier's overall evaluation of how much the retailer contributed to the supplier's business.

There are some important differences between the United States and Japan in how rebates are used. In the United States, rebates are usually

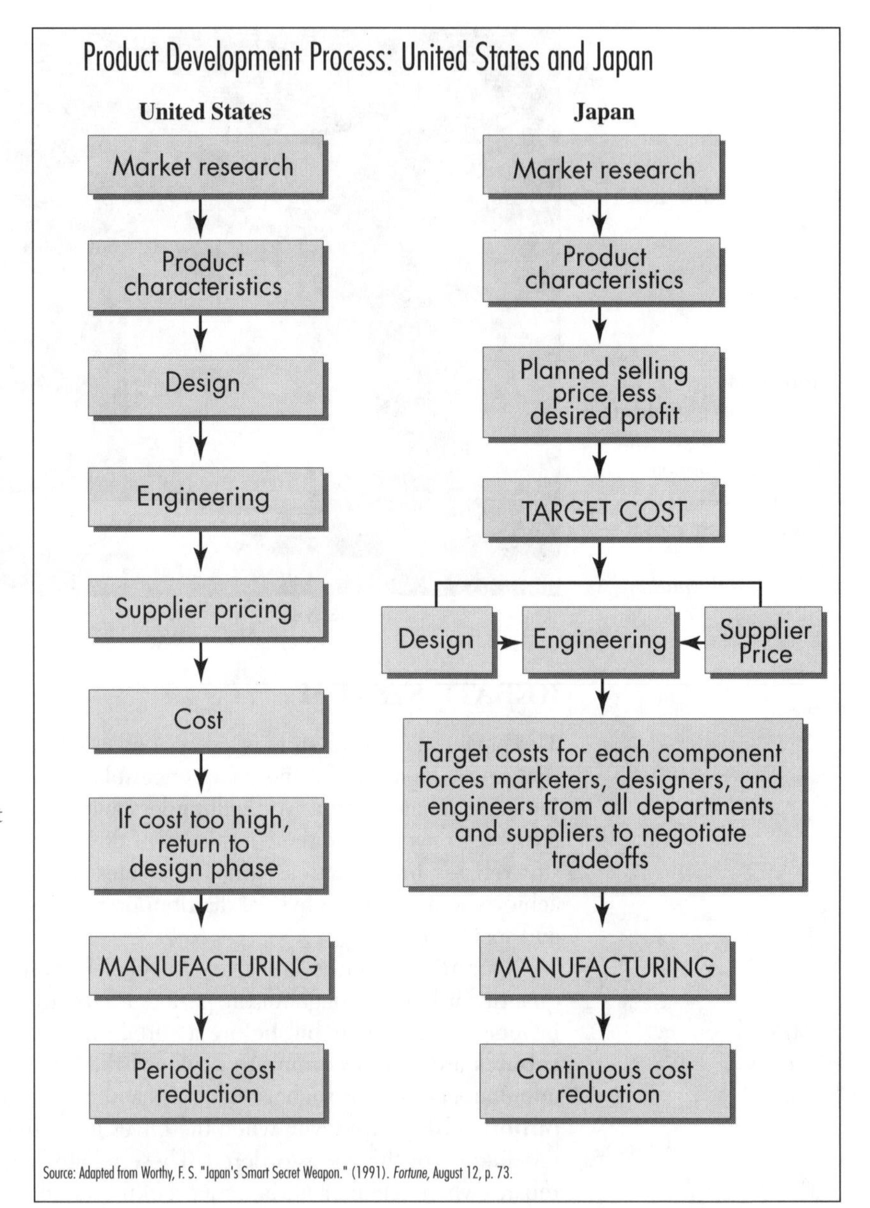

Figure 12.3
The product development process in the United States differs from that in Japan. In Japan, most products are produced and then sold. In the United States, manufacturers produce samples, take orders from retail buyers, and then produce products to fill the orders. Japan uses product engineering for continuous cost reduction.

given as immediate discounts. The manufacturer subtracts a quantity rebate on the invoice the retailer receives as a bill. If retailers pay the bill within a certain time period, they are entitled to subtract a payment date rebate. Retailers take these rebates immediately. In Japan, they pay the rebates at the end of each accounting period, which is normally once a year. In Chapter 9, in which I discussed the "sales at a loss" law, these year-end rebates were an important consideration in the real price of a product.

Manufacturers in the United States generally give sellers 30 days to pay for merchandise. Japanese suppliers generally extend 90 days' trade credit. This longer time in Japan gives the retailer time to sell the merchandise before payment is due, eliminating the need for external inventory financing. This concept was discussed in Chapter 10. Retailers in many countries use this negative capital (unpaid accounts payable) to finance store expansion.

In the next section, I will discuss the retail formats used in Japan. Japan has a well-developed department store sector and strong national specialty store chains. Food stores range from superstores to mom and pop operations. In the 1990s, discount stores began to operate throughout Japan. True brand name discounting occurs only in selected product categories, but it is a growing trend.

RETAIL FORMATS

DEPARTMENT STORES

HISTORY Japanese department stores have a long history. Most department stores have their roots as either kimono shops or railroad terminal stores. **Kimono shops** are stores that originally sold textile merchandise. The featured cloth was custom-made into clothes (kimono) or household items. The oldest Japanese department stores such as Mitsukoshi and Takashimaya began this way. **Terminal stores** began much later as stores selling everyday items to people going through the train station. This broad classification of kimono versus terminal stores is one basic way to determine the type of department store with which you are dealing. Years ago, the department stores that originated as kimono shops carried higher-price/higher-prestige products, and those that originated as terminal stores carried everyday products. This distribution does not remain. Several present-day stores, such as Tokyu and Hankyu, share a similar ending, *kyu*. This tells you that they began as terminal stores; ***kyu*** means the express train line. Another way of classifying stores is as urban versus local.

In the Edo era, from the early 17th century to the late 19th century, Japan experienced a period of scarcity. Manufacturing power increased, which caused the economy to grow. The number of merchants increased, and the kimono merchants were the center of this boom. Matsuzakaya originated as a kimono shop in 1611 in Nagoya. Shirakiya, which is now Tokyu Department Stores, began as a kimono shop in Tokyo in 1662. Mitsukoshi (Echigoya) began in 1673. Daimaru (1717), Sogo (1830), and Takashimaya (1831) were some of the other early retailers. Sogo is profiled in Company Focus IV.2. Six of the 10 largest department stores operating in Japan today originated before 1850.

Echigoya (Mitsukoshi) began some innovative new sales ideas. It was the first company to establish a fixed price, rather than the negotiated prices that had been prevalent earlier. It was also the first company to sell cloth by the piece rather than by the entire roll. A third unique policy was to allow

Photo 12.5
Kimono sales used to occupy a full floor in large department stores. Today kimono are still sold but occupy a smaller area, like a bridal shop. Kimono are worn for traditional occasions, such as weddings, funerals, and New Year celebrations. *Courtesy of the author.*

customers to return merchandise. Echigoya became a corporation in 1893. Other stores followed this course.

Takashimaya, in these early years, developed a four-point policy: (1) sell good products at lower prices to earn profits, (2) set the right price, with no overcharging, (3) tell customers the good and bad points about products, and (4) treat customers equally, not discriminating against the poor, and not cheating customers.

After Japan opened itself to foreign countries in 1867, kimono shops adopted new ideas that suggested a modern society. They started selling Western clothes. They sent employees on overseas buying trips to buy goods for import and to bring back samples that could then be produced in Japan. They also began to send Japanese goods to international expositions. The birth of department stores was largely influenced by an economic boom between 1894 and 1904.

Department stores enjoyed an era of major prosperity around 1923. They expanded to stock products of all types. By 1910, they began door-to-door and mail-order sales. Innovations such as elevators (1911) and escalators (1914) were added. The stores provided ultimate service such as sending cars to pick up customers and providing home delivery service. The department store became the symbol of modern life in the big city.

Then came the great earthquake of 1923 in Tokyo. Department stores began to sell daily goods rather than the luxuries they had been specializing in before the disaster. Before this period, department stores would require that customers remove their shoes before entering the store. After the disaster, department stores no longer asked customers to change into slippers. These two changes popularized the department store, making it seem less exclusive but still high image. After 1925, kimono shops *(gofuku-ya)* changed their names to department stores *(hyakka ten).* During the Showa era (1925), department stores greatly increased in number. Hankyu was the first company to start a railroad terminal store in 1929 in Osaka.

Competition among the departments stores increased. Stores offered discount sales, and they expanded their free delivery areas. They began giving customers free subway tickets and providing private bus pick-up service. These aggressive actions by the department stores created ill will with other retail stores. An anti-department store movement began. In 1932, the Japan Department Store Association announced a self-control declaration. In this self-regulation, the department stores agreed to: (1) stop door-to-door discount sales, (2) stop expansion of branch stores for several years, (3) end loss leader promotions, (4) stop providing cars to pick up customers, (5) reduce the area for free delivery, and (6) have three-day holidays each month.

In 1936, the first Hyakkaten-Ho (Department Store Law) was enacted. During World War II, there was great confusion within the country, and after the war, department stores rapidly recovered support of the consumers because of increased demand. The major period of prosperity for department stores arrived around 1955. Many terminal department stores came into existence around this time. In 1956, the second Hyakkaten-Ho was established. As a result of this second department store law, department stores focused their growth in smaller cities rather than in big urban areas.

The growth rate for department stores before 1962 exceeded the growth rate in personal consumption. After 1962, the growth rate for department stores slowed because of competition from supermarkets and specialty shops. In response to this competition, department stores took one of two routes. They either specialized in becoming the prestigious stores (e.g., Takashimaya and Mitsukoshi) or shifted toward one of two strategies, specialization or mass marketing.

During the 1960s, urban department stores increased the number of stores in suburban areas and local cities. It was also during this time that local department stores became affiliated with urban department stores by organizing into six major buying groups.

The six major buying groups are: Mitsukoshi, Daimaru, ADO (Isetan, Matsuya, and Marui), Japan Department Stores Management Association (Seibu stores and affiliates), and High-Land Group (Takashimaya). Each group includes a variety of affiliates. The Mitsukoshi group has more than 50 members, yet it only operates 14 stores in Japan; the other members are non-Mitsukoshi stores in Japan.

Local stores benefited by receiving financial backing, management training and support, and private label products, and through the establishment of co-buying systems. The importance of the buying groups has declined because the urban department stores did not follow through on their commitment to provide these benefits. Merchandising was weak, and the merchandise often did not match the needs of local consumers. The strong local department stores tried to react to the local needs and establish a base as the

Photo 12.6
A chart on the sales floor shows the array of Seibu Department Store private label products.
Courtesy of the author.

top store in the area. They developed subsidiary supermarket chains, and also became aggressive in obtaining merchandise, focusing on apparel and food.

From 1975 to 1985, department stores had poor performance. They failed to react to the more individualized needs of consumers. After the oil crisis in the early 1970s, consumer demand was depressed; this forced department stores to reexamine their strategy. Department stores streamlined management by reducing the number of employees and motivating employees through a more specialized job system. Department stores also refurbished the physical aspects of the store by remodeling or building new stores.

SERVICE ORIENTATION When I first started doing research in Japan, department stores were doing well. The top 10 department stores occupy huge sections of prime city real estate. Department stores are designed to be cradle-to-grave providers of products and service. The basement level(s) of a store—sometimes there are two of them—sell grocery products. These Japanese stores were the first department stores I had ever visited that sold food. Department stores in the United States do not sell food, other than gourmet products, because food does not generate a high gross profit margin. The ground floor of a Japanese department store is laid out like a U.S. or European department store. Cosmetics, jewelry, and accessories are featured on this floor. The next three to six floors contain men's, women's, and children's apparel. Additional floors are devoted to housewares, appliances, furniture, and stationery. The top floor is likely to contain a restaurant, a pet store, and an outdoor amusement area for children. At one department store in Ginza, I even noted an area where you could select grave markers and commission the appropriate engraving.

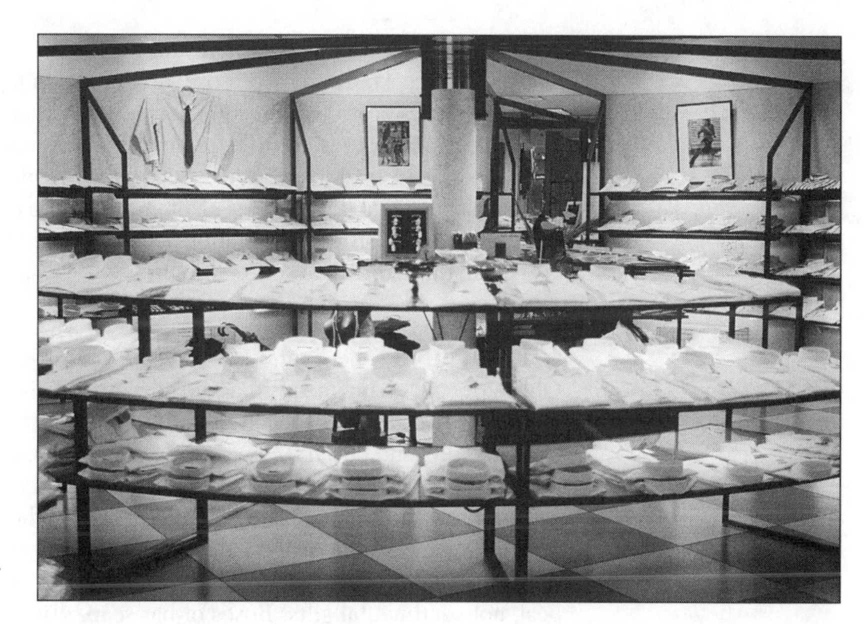

Photo 12.7
A vast display of men's dress shirts in a Japanese department store. Displays are generally sleek and artistically presented. *Courtesy of the author.*

Department stores have an area they call their community college. It is an educational facility where they teach courses. This is not the same type of community college we have in the United States, where students take courses for an associate's degree or take general college requirements and transfer the credits to a four-year institution. The Japanese department store community colleges offer courses in geography, languages, cooking, and flower arrangement. They design the courses to enhance the quality of homemakers' lives and stimulate purchase of supplies from the department store. A few years ago, a popular class was "How to hold a cocktail party." Few Japanese consumers have ever given, or been to, a cocktail party. The department store would arrange for teachers who would inform the homemaker-students about the tangible and intangible aspects of a cocktail party. The tangible aspects would include how much wine, mixer, and liquor is needed; what kinds of glasses are used to serve the drinks; and which drinks require an olive, and which a cherry. One intangible aspect includes how to select people with good communication skills to provide sparkling conversation. Another intangible is how the hostess should move around the party, introducing guests to others they might find interesting.

Of course, after learning the skills required to hold a cocktail party, the homemakers will want to hold an actual party. The department store is prepared to offer assistance. Most Japanese homes are too small to hold a reasonably sized cocktail party. The department store can solve the problem by renting some of its fully furnished modern apartments specifically designed for this purpose. The hostess will also need to rent or purchase glasses, flowers, food, and drink. The department store will arrange all these things. Japanese do not initiate conversations with people to whom they have not been introduced. This can hamper a cocktail party, where the purpose is to engage in conversation. The ultimate cocktail party accessory you can rent in Japan is a friend. For a fee, special agencies provide interesting people you can hire to attend your cocktail party and . . . be your friend. These hired friends mingle with guests and keep the conversation lively. As I said earlier, Japanese department stores want to convey the idea that they provide all of life's needs to their customers.

Department stores' reputations for high quality service and products also make them the ideal source for gifts.

GIFT-GIVING There are two *obligatory* gift-giving seasons in Japan. Obligatory gift giving means that the gifts are not given out of a sense of sentiment, but because it is socially required. During the two seasons, *O-chugen* (June or July) and *O-seibo* (December or January), gifts are given to those to whom you are obligated. This would include your boss, your children's teachers, perhaps the matchmaker that brought together you and your spouse. This gift-giving is not reciprocal. You do not expect your boss or your children's teacher or your yenta to give you a return gift. Obligatory gifts are practical, not sentimental gifts. Boxes of bar soap, dried fish, and washcloths are traditional gifts. A six-pack of beer is a popular contemporary gift. Fresh fruit in a gift box from a prestigious department store is another popular gift. Department stores set up special display sections to sell these obligatory gifts. They also provide consultants to help young wives select the appropriate gift. Individuals and companies purchase gifts during these seasons, which can account for 40% of the department store's total yearly sales. Since the recession in the 1990s, sales during the gift seasons have decreased; however, they are still a major part of department store sales.

RECENT INITIATIVES From 1985 to 1990, department stores continued to lose market share to other retail formats although retail sales in general were healthy. Retailers were riding the crest of the economic bubble. In the early 1990s, department store sales began falling. They continued to fall until September 1996, when department stores experienced their first six-month rise in sales in four and a half years.[6] However, the joy was somewhat short-lived. The Japanese government increased the national consumption tax from 3% to 5% in April 1997. Retail sales for June 1997 showed a drop of 4% over the previous year.

Sales of the top 20 department stores for 1996 are listed in Table 12.2. These figures are for individual store sales. A summary profile of the major department store companies is included in Table 12.3.

Department stores are trying to streamline their operations by reducing the number of employees. Mitsukoshi (42nd among the top 100 global retailers) and Takashimaya (35th among the top 100 global retailers) have opened new store formats that use fewer sales employees and offer more distinctive merchandise. They are hoping that changes such as these will make shopping exciting and fun for younger women. The target for many retailers is the

TABLE 12.2

Leading Japanese Department Stores by Sales, 1996

No.	Company	Business Region	Sales (Yen millions)	% Change 1995–1996
1	Mitsukoshi (Nihonbashi)	Tokyo	320,177	1.3
2	Hankyu	Osaka	274,991	0.3
3	Seibu (Ikebukuro)	Tokyo	268,518	0.0
4	Kintetsu	Osaka	267,937	2.3
5	Isetan	Tokyo	262,567	3.0
6	Takashimaya	Osaka	254,525	8.3
7	Takashimaya (Nihonbashi)	Tokyo	243,286	4.9
8	Daimaru	Osaka	240,594	−0.8
9	Takashimaya (Yokohama)	Kanagawa	195,605	−1.7
10	Tokyu (Shibuya)	Tokyo	167,225	1.8
11	Tobu	Tokyo	163,284	3.7
12	Matsuzakaya	Nagoya	158,916	2.2
13	Odakyu (Shinjuku)	Tokyo	158,613	−0.3
14	Takashimaya	Kyoto	131,640	2.3
15	Hanshin	Osaka	114,358	0.9
16	Keio (Shinjuku)	Tokyo	113,274	3.8
17	Daimaru	Kyoto	106,338	1.5
18	Sogo	Chiba	101,546	7.4
19	Sogo	Hiroshima	94,048	5.6
20	Matsuzakaya (Ueno)	Tokyo	92,480	−0.1

Source: *Nikkei Ryutsu Shimbun,* (1997). February 18.
1 yen = U.S. $0.0084.

under-30, unmarried Japanese woman. These women are employed but still live at home. They have a full paycheck to spend and few expenses. However, such women have been shunning the traditional department stores, which they view as boring. Many are shunning Japan's retailers totally, opting to take shopping vacations in Europe or the United States, instead.[7]

MAIL ORDER In 1993, while I was conducting interviews in Japan, everyone was talking about individual import programs. Department stores would conduct classes, somewhat like the cocktail party class described earlier, to teach Japanese consumers how to shop through foreign catalogs. The department stores would have collections of hundreds of catalogs, such as Lands' End and Eddie Bauer. It struck me as unusual that a department

TABLE 12.3

Leading Japanese Department Store Companies by Sales, 1996

Overall Retail Rank	Company	Description
5	Mitsukoshi	Mitsukoshi, Ltd. was established in 1673 and incorporated in 1904. The company operates 14 department stores in Japan. Overseas subsidiaries operate Mitsukoshi stores in Hong Kong, the United States, the United Kingdom, Germany, Spain, Italy, France, Guam, and the Netherlands. Overseas sales accounted for less than 10% of fiscal 1995 revenues.
8	Takashimaya	Takashimaya Company, Ltd. was established as a clothing retailer in 1831 and initiated department store operations in 1922. Department store business operations accounted for 81% of fiscal 1996 revenues; automobile interior products, 7%; interior construction works, 6%; real estate rental, leasing, and management, 1%; mail-order sales, financial services, and other, 5%. The company has 39 consolidated subsidiaries, 27 in Japan, nine in the United States, and one each in the Cayman Islands, Holland, and Singapore. Overseas sales accounted for less than 10% of fiscal 1996 revenues.
9	Daimaru	Daimaru, Inc. was incorporated in 1920, succeeding traditional kimono shop operations started in 1717. The company operates seven department stores in Osaka, Wakayama, Kyoto, Kobe, and Tokyo, and its seven domestic consolidated subsidiaries operate three department stores in Kochi, Asahiya and Nagasaki; operate supermarkets in Osaka; wholesale merchandise; and rent and lease real estate. The company also operates other Daimaru department stores in Japan, Hong Kong, Singapore, Thailand, Australia, the United States, and France through unconsolidated subsidiaries and affiliates. Department store operations accounted for 73% of fiscal 1996 revenues; supermarket operations, 14%; wholesale of food and sundry goods, 11%; and other, 2%. The company has 15 consolidated subsidiaries, 14 in Japan and one in Hong Kong.
12	Matsuzakaya	Matsuzkaya Co., Ltd. was established in 1910 and is a department store operator. The company is also involved in supermarket operations, wholesale of textile/fiber products, manufacturing of furniture, and other services. Department store operations accounted for 86% of fiscal 1996 revenues; supermarket operations, 9%; wholesale of textile products, 3%; furniture manufacturing, 1%; and other, including precision equipment manufacturing, cleaning service, catering, and insurance agency businesses, 1%. The company has 24 consolidated subsidiaries, 23 in Japan and one in the United States.
13	Isetan	Isetan Co. Ltd. was established in 1930. The company stands today as one of Japan's top-ranking retail conglomerates and operates six department stores in the Tokyo area, as well as two stores in Shizuka and Niigata as consolidated subsidiaries. Department store operations accounted for 90% of fiscal 1996 revenues and real estate operations, supermarket operations, cafes and restaurants, ladies and gents clothing stores, and other, 10%. The company has 14 consolidated subsidiaries, eight in Japan, two in China and one each in the United States, Hong Kong, Malaysia, and Singapore.

Business Region	Sales (Yen millions)	Five-Year Average Growth Rate	Net Income (Yen millions)	Five-Year Average Growth Rate (Net Income)
Tokyo	1,018,134	−1.51	−2,567	N/A*
Tokyo/Osaka	1,226,932	−0.98	19,856	−3.67
Kansai area	795,365	−1.75	6,689	5.9
Nagoya	519,147	−1.25	16	−74.9
Tokyo	568,195	0.66	−31,702	N/A

Continued

TABLE 12.3

Leading Japanese Department Store Companies by Sales, 1996

Overall Retail Rank	Company	Description
16	Tokyu Department Stores	Tokyu Store Chain Co., Ltd. was established in 1956 to operate a chain of supermarkets. The company has 86 stores in operation, mainly in Tokyo and the surrounding Kanto area. Directly operated stores accounted for 70% of fiscal 1996 unconsolidated revenues; franchised stores, 28%; real estate business and other, 2%. Unconsolidated revenues accounted for 94.8% of fiscal 1996 consolidated revenues. Tokyu Corporation is the major shareholder with 21.27% of issued stock.
18	Hankyu Department Stores	Hankyu Department Stores, Inc. was established in 1947 and is a major department store chain comprising five stores in the Kansai area and three in Tokyo. Department store sales accounted for 83% of fiscal 1996 revenues; supermarket/variety stores sales, 13%; manufacture of foodstuffs, 1%; financing and leasing, 1%; and other products and operations including clothing, pharmaceuticals, and transportation services, 2%. The company has 24 consolidated subsidiaries, 22 in Japan and one each in the Netherlands and the United States.
24	Sogo	Sogo Co., Ltd. was established in 1830 and incorporated in 1919 and operates three department stores, one each in Osaka, Kobe, and Tokyo. Department store operations accounted for 75% of fiscal 1996 revenues; wholesaling, importing, and exporting of clothing, sundry goods, household goods, and other, 14%; and other operations including interior decoration works, restaurants/cafes, and insurance agency business, 11%. The company has one consolidated subsidiary in Japan, which is engaged in restaurant operations. The company has an overseas unconsolidated subsidiary, which is engaged in restaurant operations in Taiwan.
28	Odakyu Department Stores	Odakyu Electric Railway Co., Ltd. was established in 1948 and is a leading railway company operating the Shinjuku-Hakone line. Department stores and other sales operations accounted for 57% of fiscal 1996 revenues; railway and other transport operations, 26%; real estate business, 5%; and other operations including hotels, restaurants, and leisure services, 12%. The company has 22 consolidated subsidiaries in Japan.

Source: Compiled from *World Scope* (CD-ROM).

N/A = not available.

1 yen = U.S. $0.0084.

Business Region	Sales (Yen millions)	Five-Year Average Growth Rate	Net Income (Yen millions)	Five-Year Average Growth Rate (Net Income)
Tokyo	289,898	165	1,753	−5.45
Osaka	437,660	1.15	1,286	−27.48
Tokyo/Osaka	168,722	−12.41	5,099	1.49
Tokyo	573,510	7.79	3,375	−11.40

store would be teaching its customers how to import merchandise themselves. However, this illustrates how much importance department stores place on their roles as cultural agents to the community. Initially I thought the individual import phase would pass; however, it is still quite popular. Major department stores also sell merchandise through catalogs. It is very popular to purchase *O-seibo* and *O-chugen* gifts through catalogs.

SUPERSTORES AND SUPERMARKETS (GENERAL MERCHANDISE RETAILERS)

Chains of general merchandise retailers and supermarkets are the biggest retail companies in Japan and have been since the early 1970s.[8] Six of the major Japanese general merchandise stores rank high among the 100 largest global companies. Daiei (6), Ito Yokado (7), Jusco (13), Mycal, formerly known as Nichii, (24), and Seiyu (27). The Japan Chain Store Association requires that members have at least 11 outlets and annual sales exceeding 1,000 million yen. The Japanese census differentiates department stores and large general merchandise stores on the basis of whether they use personal sales or self-service techniques. Self-service general merchandise outlets are called ***sogo supa,*** or general superstores.[9] There are also specialty superstores ***(supa).*** A general supermarket would sell a variety of merchandise and food. A specialty superstore would sell one type of product, such as computers or appliances. Food superstores, apparel superstores, and electronics superstores are prevalent in Japan. Superstores are different from specialty stores in that they must derive only 70% of their sales from one product (e.g., apparel) as compared with the 90% of sales from a single product for specialty stores. Specialty *supas* must have more than 500 square meters (5,382 square feet) of sales space.

In the early 1990s, supermarket sales fell for 21 months in a row. Sales rose during fiscal 1994, however, profits continued to fall. Factors behind the falling unit prices included a stronger yen, cheaper import goods because of deregulation, retailers developing private brands, and advancement in cost-saving technologies for labor and store expenses. A list of the major superstores is included in Table 12.4. Company Focus IV.1 discusses Daiei, a superstore and the largest retailer in Japan.

CONVENIENCE STORES

This category of retailer is very successful in Japan. Convenience stores were introduced during the 1980s. Many convenience stores are part of the largest superstore groups. When large retail groups were blocked from expansion because of the Large Scale Retail Store (LSRS) Law, they opened convenience stores. The convenience store in Japan is a major home office connection, often offering photocopying and facsimile services. Convenience stores provide a merchandise mix based on prepared foods and

TABLE 12.4

Leading Japanese General Merchandise Chains by Sales, 1996

No.	Company	Sales (Yen Millions)	% Change 1995–1996	Store No.	Store No. 1995–1996
1	Daiei	2,432,396	0.2	375	365
2	Ito-Yokado	1,561,348	1.1	158	155
3	Mycal (Nichii)	1,070,843	7.8	142	144
4	Jusco	1,207,984	6.6	239	209
5	Seiyu	951,282	−0.9	204	208
6	Uny	667,101	9.6	136	126
7	Marui	500,326	3.0	34	33
8	Izumiya	382,471	0.4	68	65
9	Kope Kobe	376,235	7.2	171	168
10	Nagasakiya	359,093	−1.3	95	94
11	Maruetsu	310,007	−0.3	188	182
12	Tokyu Store	285,950	6.7	88	86
13	Suya	274,420	3.6	131	122
14	Heiwado	265,205	10.5	80	73
15	Toku Benimaru	261,161	2.7	71	67
16	Life Corporation	249,570	12.9	119	101
17	Inageya	182,189	1.1	119	118
18	Yaohan Japan	162,979	0.1	58	56
19	Kasumi	137,004	6.6	84	78
20	Tokyu Store	117,236	−4.1	55	54

Source: *Nikkei Ryutsu Shimbun.* (1997) February 18.
1 yen = U.S. $0.0084.

simple household goods such as cleaning materials, stationery, toiletries, and leisure products such as books and magazines. Some convenience stores stay open 24 hours a day.

In order to qualify as a convenience store, the store must employ self-service, operate more than 16 hours a day, have a sales floor space of less than 200 square meters (2,153 square feet), take less than 30% of total sales from fresh foods, and have fewer than two closing days per month.[10] A list of the major convenience stores is included in Table 12.5.

TABLE 12.5

Leading Japanese Convenience Stores, 1995

No.	Company Name	Sales (Yen billions)	Year-on-Year % Growth	Outlets
1	Seven-Eleven Japan Co.	1,477	6.1	6,373
2	Daiei Convenience Systems Inc.*	885	7.8	5,683
3	FamilyMart Co.	543	11.7	3,402
4	Sun-Shop Yamazaki Co.	362	2.5	2,724
5	Circle K Japan Co.	293	14.3	1,806
6	Sunkus & Associates Inc.	214	15.4	1,273
7	Ministop Co.	106	13.4	710
8	Kasumi Convenience Networks Co.	94	4.9	832
9	Seicomart Co.	91	9.9	592
10	Kokubu & Co.	90	2.3	617

*Changed its name to Lawson Inc. in June 1996.
Source: *The Nihon Keizai Shimbun,* reprinted from "Convenience-Store Growth Not So Easy." (1997). *Nikkei Weekly,* September 30, p. 9.
1 yen = U.S. $0.0084.

THE LARGE-SCALE RETAIL STORE LAW

Japan has many small retail stores. These small stores are often called mom and pop stores because they are family-owned and operated. Business analysts refer to this as a traditional structure. Historically, Japan consisted of small villages separated geographically by mountains and bodies of water. Consumers had limited incomes, little storage space in their small homes, and a preference for fresh, not processed food. This profile translates into frequent, small, unit purchases. The Japanese government also views retailing as a social welfare system, absorbing surplus labor. Thus, it was in the government's interest to protect the small-scale retailers. When department stores became popular in Japan, legislation was introduced that guaranteed the long-term survival of the mom and pop stores.

Between the First and Second World Wars, Japan experienced a depression. The number of small retailers increased but their profitability declined.[11] During the same period, department stores increased in number and operated more efficiently than the small retailers. Small retailers united in a national movement. They drew public attention and sympathy to the plight of the small retailers. This publicity led to the passage of the first Department Store Law. This law required that large stores get government approval to open a department store, to open a branch store, or to increase floor space in their current

Photo 12.8
Japanese beef is heavily marbled. This means that there is a great deal of fat (white areas) in the meat (red areas). Most Japanese beef is not eaten in thick chunks; instead it is sliced thin and cooked on a flat grill or boiled in water. *Courtesy of AP/Wide World Photos.*

stores. After the Second World War, this law was repealed. Over the years,. conflicts between small retailers and department stores again grew heated. In 1956, the second Department Store Law was put into effect.

Department stores were not the only type of large retailers growing in Japan. Supermarkets and self-service stores grew rapidly in the 1960s. These large stores other than department stores were not covered by the Department Store Law. If retailers divided their business into several different legal entities and each group operated only one or two floors of a large building, it could escape the application of the second Department Store Law. These stores were called "quasi-department stores."

Small stores demanded regulation of all large stores. The strong political lobby was again successful in passing the Large Scale Retail Store (LSRS) Law in 1973. This law regulated stores with retail floor space exceeding 1,500 square meters (16,146 square feet) and eliminated the loophole that allowed "quasi-department stores" to be legal. Eventually the law was extended to cover retail stores with as little as 500 square meters (5,382 square feet).[12]

The LSRS Law required that stores wishing to open or expand must apply to the LSRS directors. The Council for Coordination of Commercial Activities (CCCA), organized under the local Chamber of Commerce and Industry of each community, had a great deal of impact on the decision-making. Small retailers had authority to decide whether they wanted competition from large-scale stores. Approval of a large-scale store application was lengthy, sometimes taking 10 years.

Foreign producers and foreign retailers cited the LSRS Law as an important nontariff barrier to market penetration in Japan. Ultimately, Japan

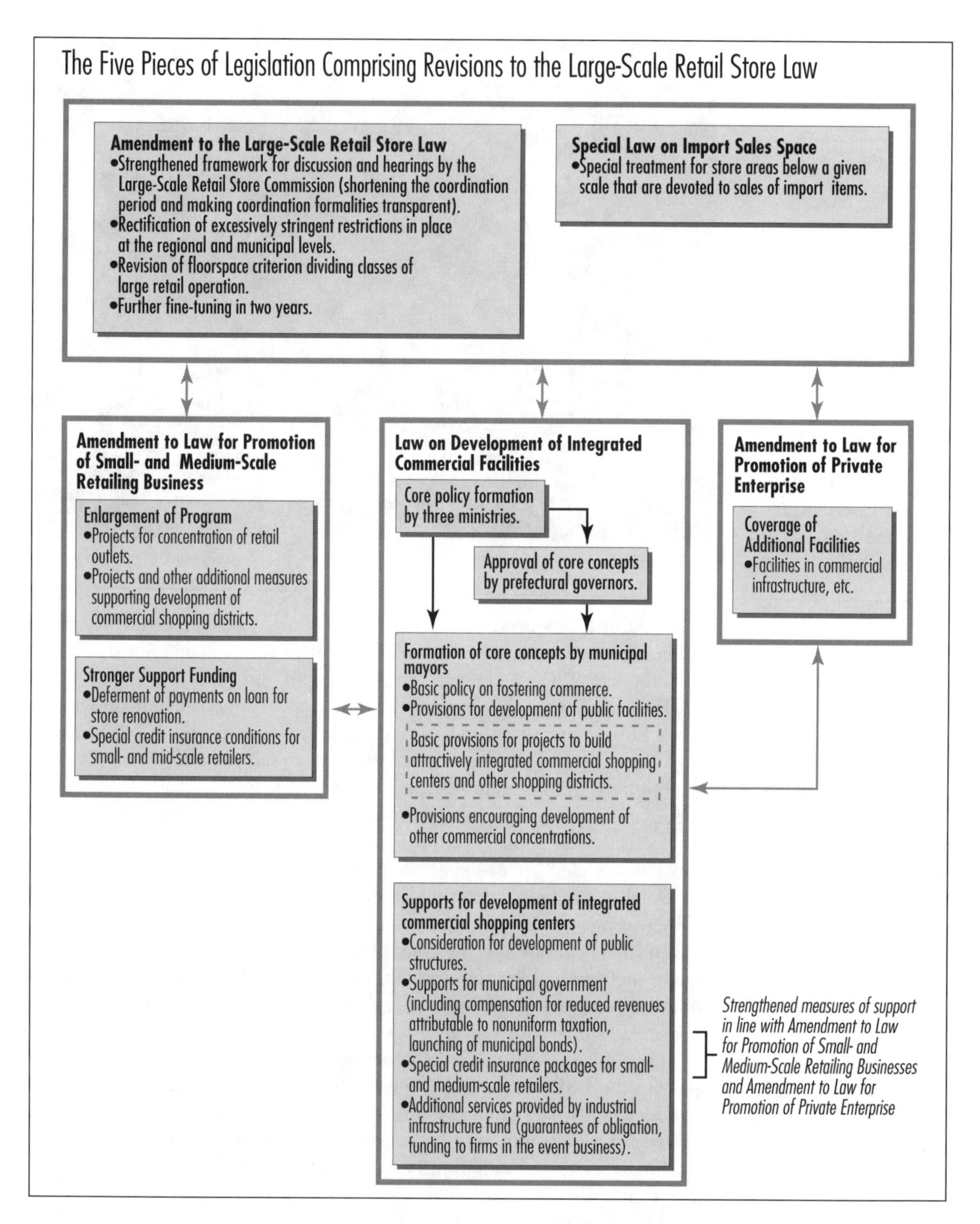

Figure 12.4 The Large-Scale Retail Store Law was a major impediment to large-scale store growth. Small retailers were allowed to approve or disapprove stores that wanted to locate in their area; it could take 10 years to receive approval for a new store. This law has been revised, making it much easier for new stores to open.

promised to deregulate the retail industry and to cut the time required for approval of new stores to 18 months. This amendment to the LSRS was enforced in January 1992. The legislation introduced a modified framework for processing new store applications under which application processing time was limited to one year and the CCCA, the chief body charged with processing applications, was eliminated. The revised law raised the floorspace criterion from 500 square meters (5,382 square feet) to 1,500 square meters (16,146 square feet).[13] Figure 12.4 represents changes in the LSRS Law.

The loosening of the LSRS Law came at a time of great economic recession in Japan. Although the reform was pushed through as a result of pressure from Japan's trading partners, five large foreign retailers have jumped at the chance to enter Japan.

Japanese retailers have been very successful internationally. In several areas such as Hong Kong, Taiwan, and Singapore, they have a majority of the department store market share. Some Japanese retailers are more successful in foreign countries than they are at home. Dunning's theory of the eclectic firm (see Chapter 1), can explain some of this internationalization.

INTERNATIONAL EXPANSION OF JAPANESE RETAILING

There are three primary factors in the Japanese retail environment that make international markets particularly attractive: (1) competition from mass merchandisers and discounters, (2) government restrictions on expansion of large department stores, and (3) the high cost of labor and land in Japan.

COMPETITION FROM MASS MERCHANDISERS AND DISCOUNTERS

Japanese mass merchandisers, also called supermarkets, carry clothing, appliances, and often food. Although they carry the same merchandise mix as department stores, they are not brand name discounters. They carry merchandise with brand names different from those of the traditional department stores. Often the same manufacturer will produce brand name merchandise for department stores and brand name merchandise for supermarkets, but consumers do not associate the two brand names with each other. The difference between the positioning of the two store formats is that department stores carry a luxury image whereas mass merchandisers provide goods for everyday needs.

Since the 1950s, there has been a significant change in the structure of retailing in Japan.[14–16] The first major push for department stores to diversify geographically came from competition with mass merchandisers. During the 1950s, department stores commanded large market share. Mass merchandisers appeared in Japan around 1955, and in just 10 years captured 5.4% of retail sales compared to 9.1% at department stores.[17] By 1982, the percentages had reversed, and mass merchandisers obtained a 19.5% share as compared to 7.8% held by department stores.[18] Although sales for major department stores grew in 1991, pre-tax profits declined by as much as 25%,[19] while mass merchandisers posted gains in both sales and profitability.[20] As their market share eroded domestically, department stores were forced to seek international markets where competition was not as severe.

Japanese retailers are successful in various regions of the Far East. By 1989, the 14 Japanese department stores in Hong Kong held 30% of the department store market.[21] More recently, Japanese stores have moved into Vietnam[22] and the People's Republic of China.[23]

This expansion into overseas markets has met with political obstacles in some countries, particularly Thailand. Daimaru was the first Japanese department store to open in Thailand, closely followed by Sogo and Tokyu. Japanese presence has prompted the 80-member Thai Department Store Association to put pressure on the government to restrict foreign retail operations. They charge that Japanese companies have posted large losses in Thailand to gain market share.

GOVERNMENT RESTRICTIONS ON EXPANSION

Distribution policy in Japan is closely coordinated and imposes further restrictions on department stores' domestic expansion.[24] The goal is to develop a retail industry in harmony with local communities. Policies support the efforts of small- and medium-scale retailers to create a town-like environment.

As discussed earlier, the LSRS Law, protects the interests of small retail stores, and impedes expansion of department stores and mass merchandisers.[25] The effect of this law has been to slow the modernization of older stores. Large chains diversify into retail and service areas previously dominated by convenience stores and fast-food chains.[26] In 1992, and again in 1996, the LSRS Law has been revised, making opening new stores easier. The result has been an increase in retailers expanding in Japan.

HIGH COST OF LAND AND LABOR

Land prices and construction costs in Japan are the highest in the world. There is no early return on investment in a new building project. "It takes ten to twelve years for a new department store to become profitable, and fifteen to twenty years before it breaks even on investment costs."[27] In places like Hong Kong, Singapore, Taipei, and Bangkok, retail footage is expensive, but it is available.

Both low-cost labor and available retail space have made relocation attractive to Japanese retailers. Labor cost to sales is 5% in Singapore versus 10% in Japan. Department stores develop strategies to reduce investment costs overseas. The Sogo department store, for example, has expanded rapidly in the Pacific Rim. As detailed in Company Focus IV.2, in Taipei, Sogo entered a joint venture with Pacific Construction. Pacific Construction provided the land and

51% of the building and start-up costs.[28] Sogo executives estimated that Pacific Rim locations would be profitable in less than four years, and they were, even without investment incentives such as those offered by Pacific Construction.

Hong Kong has offered additional special opportunities. Local Hong Kong retailers became reluctant to expand domestically because of the uncertainty associated with Hong Kong's much-heralded reversion to Chinese rule in 1997. A department store retailer's major investment is in land and the store buildings, assets that are difficult to relocate if the political environment changes. The reluctance of local department stores to expand has enhanced the market attractiveness of Hong Kong for foreign department stores. Joint ventures with foreign-owned companies are considered politically safer than alliances with other Chinese.

SUMMARY

Japanese retailing is influenced by unique Japanese business practices. The concept of frame is evident in the way decisions are made, relationships are maintained, and merchandise is procured. The concepts of pseudo-harmonism, eclecticism, and exceptionism help us to understand the complex environment of Japanese businesses. Much of the antagonism between Japan and its trading partners stems from lack of understanding of these important cultural dimensions. These concepts also help to explain the unique features of the Japanese retail system.

Suppliers in Japan provide extensive support to retailers. They hold merchandise until it is needed at the retail level, a natural just in time procurement system. Suppliers accept unsold merchandise returns, sharing the risk of product failure. Retail buyers work with suppliers to determine what merchandise will be offered for sale in the store. Many of the sales employees in a large store, such as a department store, are hired and paid by the manufacturer, not the retailer. These sales employees provide an important information-gathering service for manufacturers. Interacting with consumers, these manufacturers' sales representatives gain important information about what consumers want. They relay this information to their manufacturing employers. This type of information is power in the distribution system.

Japan has a highly developed retail system with extensive offerings in most of the format categories. The department store industry is one of the most developed in the world. These department stores offer cradle-to-grave service to their customers.

The LSRS Law has made domestic expansion difficult. The law has recently been revised, making it less of an impediment to domestic expansion. This law, as well as other domestic issues, such as intense competition and high cost of land and labor, have influenced Japanese retailers to expand internationally. Japanese retailers have been very successful in expanding throughout Asia. In the next two chapters, we will discuss the impact Japanese retailers have had in the overseas Chinese market and in the People's Republic of China.

KEY TERMS

attributes
chop
consignment
eclecticism
exceptionism
frame
itaku shiire
kaitori shiire
keiretsu
kimono shops
kyu
manufacturers' showrooms
monopsonist
opportunity costs
payment date rebates
physical distribution rebates
power
pseudo-harmonism
quantity rebates
ringi
sales promotion rebates
sogo supa
special rebates
supa
target achievement rebates
terminal shops
uriage (shoka) shiire

DISCUSSION QUESTIONS

1. The relationship between Japanese buyers and sellers is vertical. Buyers are considered superior to sellers and therefore are treated in a deferential manner. How would this distinction put foreign sellers at a disadvantage?
2. Americans believe in being very explicit. We are taught to talk about situations that make us angry. What Japanese concept would this violate?
3. The Japanese government has tried to discourage manufacturers from sending sales employees to work in stores. This is partially due to pressure from the U.S. government. The U.S. government maintains that this practice is a type of nontariff barrier. The Japanese manufacturers continue to send sales employees to the retail stores, calling them volunteers instead of sales employees. This is an example of one of the Japanese business relationship concepts. Which concept is it?
4. How does using consignment affect the types of products sold? If the system is used throughout Japan, would you expect to find more or less product similarity than in other countries not using consignment?
5. Using Dunning's theory of the eclectic firm (Chapter 1), explain how the international expansion issues would affect a company's decision to internationalize. Are these factors related to ownership, internationalization, or locational advantages?

ENDNOTES

1. Nakane, C. (1970). *Japanese Society.* Berkeley: University of California Press.
2. Shimaguchi, M. (1993). "New Development in Channel Strategy in Japan." In M. R. Czinkota and M. Kotabe, eds., *The Japanese Distribution System.* Chicago: Probus Publishing Co., pp. 173–190.
3. Shimaguchi (1993).
4. Flath, D. (1990). "Why Are There So Many Retail Stores in Japan?" *Japan and the World Economy,* Vol. 2, pp. 365–386.
5. Taga, T., and Y. Uehara. (1994). "Some Characteristics of Business Practices in Japan." In T. Kikuchi, ed., *Japanese Distribution Channels.* Binghamton, NY: Haworth Press, pp. 71–87.
6. *Retail News Letter.* (1996). No. 438, p. 10.
7. "Sales, Not Suntans, Lure Women Abroad." (1996). *Nikkei Weekly,* October 7, p. 18.
8. Larke, R. (1994). *Japanese Retailing.* New York: Routledge.
9. Larke (1994).
10. Larke (1994).
11. Suzuki, T. (1993). "Trade Issues in Distribution." In M. R. Czinkota and M. Kotabe, eds., *The Japanese Distribution System.* Chicago: Probus Publishing Co., pp. 219–230.
12. Suzuki (1993).
13. Watanabe, T. (1994). "Changes in Japan's Public Policies Toward Distribution Systems and Marketing." In T. Kikuchi, ed., *Japanese Distribution Channels.* Binghamton, N.Y.: Haworth Press, Inc., pp. 17–32.
14. Murata, S. (1973). "Distribution in Japan." *The Wheel Extended,* Autumn, pp. 4–11.
15. Czinkota, M. (1985). "Distribution of Consumer Products in Japan." *International Marketing Review,* Autumn, pp. 39–50.
16. Tajima, Y. (1971). *How Goods Are Distributed in Japan.* Shibuya, Japan: Walton-Ridgeway and Co.
17. Distribution and Marketing in Japan (Series 3. Retail and Wholesale Distribution). (1985). *Second Workshop on Japan's Distribution Systems and Business Practices.* Tokyo: MIPRO.
18. Distribution and Marketing in Japan (1985).
19. "Department Stores Hit Declines in Pretax Profits." (1991). *Nikkei Weekly,* November 2, p. 14.
20. "Supermarkets Ring Up Solid Gains." (1991). *Nikkei Weekly,* November 2, p. 14.

21. Hock, T. L. (1989). "How the Japanese Are Winning the Retailing War." *Asian Finance,* January 15, pp. 26–27.
22. Yamamuro, A. (1994). "Seiyu Steps Gently into Vietnam." *Nikkei Weekly,* August 8, p. 18.
23. Goll, S. (1995). "China's Big State-Owned Retail Stores Form New Ventures with Foreign Firms." *Wall Street Journal,* March 13, p. B5a.
24. Goldman, A. (1992). "Evaluating the Performance of the Japanese Distribution System." *Journal of Retailing,* Vol. 68, No. 1, pp. 11–39.
25. Dawson, J., and T. Sato. (1983). "Controls Over the Development of Large Stores in Japan." *Service Industries Journal,* Vol. 3, No. 2, pp. 136–145.
26. Goldman, A. (1991). "Japan's Distribution System: Institutional Structure Internal Political Economy and Modernization. *Journal of Retailing,* Vol. 67, No. 2, pp. 154–182.
27. Lein, F. (1987). *Department Stores in Japan.* Tokyo: Sophis University Bulletin, No. 115, p. 10.
28. Goldstein, C. (1988). "The Bargain Hunters." *Far Eastern Economic Review,* May 26, p. 82.

Taipei
TAIWAN
Hong Kong
Kaohsiung

13

Retailing in Overseas China

After reading this chapter you will understand:

- **How Chinese cultural values shape Chinese business activities and consumer behavior.**
- **The relationship between the overseas Chinese and the mainland Chinese.**
- **The role Japanese retailers have played in retailing in Hong Kong and Taiwan.**
- **The difference between Chinese and Japanese methods of retailing.**

MANY CHINESE have left their homeland, mainland China, throughout history. These enclaves of Chinese have started or enhanced new countries with their commercial ingenuity. We credit the Chinese with developing the first system of writing, explosives, and according to some people, even spaghetti. It should come as no surprise that when Chinese immigrants move away from their home country they take with them a large number of commercial skills and abilities that allow them to be successful in other markets. Chinese immigrants helped to develop the commercial activities of Malaysia, Singapore, Thailand, Australia, and the Philippines. Ninety-seven percent of the population of Taiwan and Hong Kong is Chinese.

The Chinese people who are the focus of this chapter are the overseas Chinese, those who live in Hong Kong and Taiwan. Their relationship to the mainland, the People's Republic of China (PRC), is an important factor in understanding the present-day situation in this region. The PRC has always considered Taiwan and Hong Kong as its rightful possessions. On July 1, 1997, Hong Kong was returned to PRC control after a long British lease. Ultimately, the PRC is seeking to reunite Taiwan with the mainland, as well.

CHINESE CULTURAL VALUES

The reason Chinese immigrants have been so successful in so many parts of the world may be partially understood by looking at a group of similar values held by both mainland and overseas Chinese. These values reflect a long-term orientation to the world.[1]

MAN-NATURE ORIENTATION

The Chinese regard human beings as a part of nature, and they believe people should not try to overcome or master nature, but rather, adapt in harmony. In Chapter 2, I told you about *feng shui* and the Regent Hotel. The Chinese man-nature orientation influenced the construction of this building. Originally the building was to have had glass windows looking out on one side only, into the harbor. However, during construction, a Chinese spiritualist was consulted about the building. He predicted the building would have terrible problems if it blocked the exit of spirits from the harbor. According to the spiritualist, the walls of the building would trap the spirits inside. This consultation led the builders to change the structure, making it glass on three sides. In this way, the spirits of the harbor could flow right through the building and not cause trouble.

The Chinese man-nature orientation leads to low expectations toward products. If the performance of a product does not meet expectations, there is less dissatisfaction because this confirms *yuarn,* the belief that predetermined conditions decide what will happen in life. The Chinese attribute success or failure of a product to fate rather than to the expertise of a particular company. They are, therefore, reluctant to complain about products. If a Chinese consumer purchases a product that does not act properly, he or she is likely to attribute it to fate rather than to blame the company. Concepts such as consumer dissatisfaction and complaining behavior thus have less relevance in China than in the United States.

Photo 13.1
Boat ferries patrol Aberdeen harbor in Hong Kong. A group of Hong Kong residents live on boats, such as those in the rear of the picture. Children swim in the murky water between the boats. Dogs race around the boat decks, and chickens squawk from cages. It is not unusual to see children emerging from a residential boat to go to school in immaculate-white starched shirts and sharply pressed gray wool shorts. *Courtesy of the author.*

MAN-TO-HIMSELF ORIENTATION

The concept of man-to-himself orientation refers to how the Chinese view their role in life. Traditional Chinese are raised to believe that they are not worthy. This leads to self-abasement throughout their lives. In Western cultures, for example, a person will say "thank you" in response to a compliment. A Chinese person will deflect a compliment, saying, "I am not worthy of that compliment."

The Chinese are situation-oriented and pragmatic. The extended family raises children; this leads to an attitude that is less dogmatic and more flexible. Chinese children learn that the correct response is based on the situation, not on an abstract ideal. In some ways, this corresponds to the Japanese view of frame orientation. The individual alone is not important. It is the environment, the frame, that gives importance to the nature of the individual.

There is an important distinction between the Chinese and Japanese view of man-to-himself. The ideal for a Chinese person is to be an individual, worthy of respect and reverence. In Chinese culture, entrepreneurs are admired and respected. In Japan, the greatest esteem is given to an individual who is a part of the major group. Working for a large, respected corporation conveys respect in Japan, not being an entrepreneur. These differences are very apparent in the way the Chinese and Japanese have made themselves known in world retail markets. Japanese expansion has been through large-scale stores, department stores, and mass merchandisers; Chinese expansion has primarily been in independent family-owned businesses. The

Chinese preference for family businesses and the link to their clan is further explained by the next concept, relational orientation.

RELATIONAL ORIENTATION

Relational orientation refers to respect for authority. Chinese students respect their teachers and teachers are expected to teach them, not be their friends. Confucius established five cardinal relationships:

- Sovereign and minister
- Father and son
- Husband and wife
- Old and young
- Between friends

Chinese are expected to act according to the norms prescribed for each instance of interpersonal relations. The king must act kingly, the minister ministerly, the husband husbandly, the wife wifely, the old old, the young young, brothers brotherly, and friends friendly. These relationships are fostered with favors and gifts. The Chinese give gifts for different reasons than the Japanese. The gift should match the income of the giver; this gives face to the receiver of the gifts. Friends should return gifts of comparable or even higher value when possible.

Chinese business people exchange favors when supplying goods on credit without signing any legal documents, believing that the signing of any legal document will end the reciprocity of doing favors. Informal channels of communication are very important in product selection by Chinese consumers. Brand loyalty is very strong, based on previous experiences with a brand. For the Chinese, the past plays an important role in what should happen in the present.

PAST TIME AND CONTINUITY ORIENTATION

The past rather than the present or future is the dominant time dimension of the Chinese. Ancestor worship is one part of this dimension, but it is much more complex than this alone. Respect for family is very important. The following proverb illustrates the feeling of most Chinese: "Among the three unfilial duties, to have no heir is the greatest." For a son to leave no heir is a big problem in Chinese cultures, and the concept at the center of the 1993 movie, *The Wedding Banquet.* In this movie, a handsome Chinese man is hassled by his mother to get married and provide an heir. He sets up an extensive list of spousal requirements: the bride must have multiple doctorates, be beautiful, musical, and so on. All this is a guise to cover the fact that he is gay and in love with a wonderful male companion. The story is funny, touching, and illustrative of the importance of producing an heir in Chinese culture.

An identification with the past reflects a certain type of cultural thinking. Sociologists call this type of time orientation **circular thinking.** To such cultures, the future is not predictable; therefore, the past is used as the point of reference. People in Western cultures, in contrast, use **linear thinking.** We believe that what has happened in the past can be used to alter, or change, the future. Linear thinkers believe that one learns from the past to shape the future.

ACTIVITY ORIENTATION

The dimension of activity orientation refers to how people in a particular culture prioritize their actions. For the Chinese, knowing one's place in society is important to group functioning. People's actions convey their knowledge of their position within society. Among Chinese, there is a high degree of moral self-control or self-regulation. The culture has established rules, and people are expected to follow these rules. If a person is rich and powerful, that person should do what is expected of someone who is rich and powerful. Likewise, if a person is poor and humble, he or she should do what is expected of someone who is poor and humble. There are five major themes in Chinese behavior, as follows:

1. *All men are born unequal. To the Chinese, the naturalness, necessity, and inevitability of hierarchy is self-evident. An efficient society requires a broadly accepted ordering of people. The alternative to hierarchy is chaos and anarchy, which together are worse than a harsh authority.*

   This view was challenged in mainland China beginning in the 1950s, when the equalizing views of communism were being spread throughout the country. During the Cultural Revolution, students were encouraged to chastise their teachers, and large public demonstrations were held to put into their places those who had been viewed as superior to others.
2. *The bases of inequality are achievement (usually academic), wealth, and oral example (speaking ability). The last is especially important for commanding political authority.*

   I know a very successful Chinese American who graduated from an Ivy League university and teaches at one of the best universities in the United States. However, in the eyes of his parents, he is not successful because his advanced education has not brought him great wealth. He is a university professor, not a wealthy company executive.
3. *Laws negotiated by human beings are rigid, artificial, and insensitive to the changing circumstances of life. The judgment of wise and compassionate people is a better way to regulate personal, social, and political relationships.*

   This view corresponds to the British system of law called common law, in which laws change based on precedence. The United States also uses common law. The basic idea is that law should reflect changes in society. As people's ideas about right and wrong change with societal change, the law should also change. Chinese law is very contextual. Right and wrong are not determined in an isolated situation, but instead are based on the situational constraints.

4. *People exist in and through relationships with others. The goal of socialization is to train children for lifelong interdependence with others by developing skills and values that promote harmony. The family is a fundamental cradle of sure support across time and requires especial commitment from its members.*

   Before the civil war in China, this philosophy governed most of human interaction. The Confucian relationships identified earlier governed people's interactions. However, the political changes in mainland China disrupted these philosophical ideals. When the communists took control of mainland China in 1949, they required that allegiance to family be eliminated. They did this to foster commitment to the greater, larger group. During the Cultural Revolution, families were separated, with various family members sent off to different regions of China. Many families were separated for 10 years. Communist leaders used this technique to diminish the strong bond of family. According to the party, comrades were to be the basic support groups, not family.

5. *The need to master ideographs, the basic symbols of the Chinese written language, reinforces an academic emphasis on memory, attention to detail, and lengthy homework. It also strengthens a predisposition toward perceiving stimuli as whole rather than as collections of parts, and high spatial intelligence.*

This belief continues. Chinese children, both on the mainland and in the overseas communities, are exposed to great amounts of detailed memorized learning. Whereas Western cultures view school success as largely determined by innate ability, Chinese cultures view school success as work- or application-driven.

These Chinese values refer to deeply held tendencies of all three groups of Chinese enclaves: mainland China, the special administrative region of Hong Kong, and Taiwan. History will help us understand how these groups became scattered.

FLIGHT FROM THE MAINLAND

In 1950, the Chinese city of Shanghai was a booming commercial center. Sections of the city, called concessions, housed enclaves of foreigners. The French Concession, the American Concession, the Russian Concession, and others essentially determined their own governance. Foreign residents lived in mansions. European-style office buildings line the Bund, the major boulevard, paralleling the harbor in Shanghai. The city was called the Paris of Asia. Today, the architecture along the Bund is a mix of European styles, the

Photo 13.2
A street scene in busy Tsim Sha Shui, the Kowloon side of Hong Kong Harbor, sometimes called the tourist ghetto. Most corporate offices and the financial district are located on the Hong Kong side. In Tsim Sha Shui, every area of land is used, and neon lights promote every kind of pleasure and product imaginable. These shops are not selling low-priced trinkets, but expensive watches, jewelry, and designer clothes.
Courtesy of the author.

buildings now housing Shanghai's government offices. At night, as one travels along the Bund, floodlights illuminate the buildings, giving the illusion that things are as they were in 1950.

During Liberation, when the Communist party took power in the early 1950s, two groups of Chinese citizens left the country. The defeated military group left for Taiwan, the commercial group, for Hong Kong. These two communities have grown and prospered.

HONG KONG

COUNTRY BACKGROUND

Captain Charles Elliot secured Hong Kong Island for England after the first Opium War with China in 1841. At the time, Hong Kong was mainly a barren rock, but it was surrounded by a perfect natural harbor. In 20 years, Hong Kong became the center of a thriving opium trade from India. Opium was the major Western export to China. Actually, the second Opium War was fought over the right to sell opium to China. The Chinese rulers did not want to allow the British to sell the drug in China. Britain won the war, and with it, the right to expand its opium trade. The British first annexed Stonecutter's Island (Hong Kong Island) and then Kowloon, the community on the other

TABLE 13.1

Hong Kong: Selected Demographic and Economic Data

	Population (millions) mid-1995	Area (thousands of sq. km)	GNP per capita		PPP estimates of GNP per capita U.S. = 100		Life expectancy at birth (years) 1995	Adult illiteracy (%) 1995
			Dollars 1995	Avg. ann. growth (%) 1985–95	1987	1995		
High-income economies	902.2t	32,039t	24,930w	1.9w			77w	
Hong Kong	6.2	1	22,990g	4.8	70.7	85.1	79	8a

Source: World Bank (1997). a = data refer to GDP. PPP = purchasing power parity. t = total. w = weighted average.

side of Hong Kong Island, in 1860. Today, the two sides are connected by subway, bridges, and the Star Ferry.

In 1898, the Chinese rulers were forced to lease Hong Kong, Kowloon, and the area of the New Territories to the British for 99 years. The British considered the lease a gift; they did not pay any rent. For the Chinese, however, 99 years is a short period in history. In 1997, the Chinese reclaimed their rights to Hong Kong, and it reverted back to mainland Chinese control. The PRC has frequently stated that Hong Kong will continue to function as it has for the past 50 years. Despite these reassurances, many people have their doubts that this will be true.

During World War II, Hong Kong was attacked by the Japanese. The colony surrendered on Christmas Day 1941. The Japanese occupied the area until August 1945. Many Hong Kong families were ruined, and their money converted to yen. After the war, the Japanese debts were discharged by the surrender treaty.

When the communists took over mainland China in 1949, millions of refugees fled to Hong Kong. They came with the desire to get rich, or stay rich. By the 1980s, Hong Kong and the surrounding areas had become one of the world's wealthiest business centers. There are more Rolls Royces per capita in Hong Kong than anywhere else in the world. Table 13.1 presents selected demographic and economic data for Hong Kong.

I have spent more time in Hong Kong than in any other city in the world. The city has an excitement—and a smell—that is unique. What is a Hong Kong smell? Describing it is difficult, but forgetting it is impossible. Part of the smell is the harbor. Hong Kong, the city proper, is on one

Photo 13.3
Wet markets are informal commercial sections that sell fresh fruits and vegetables. Vendors gather together to create a central place. Prices here are lower than in supermarkets or department stores. Products are not refrigerated. *Courtesy of the author.*

side of the harbor; Tsim Tsa Tsui (Kowloon) is on the other side. Both sides of the harbor are considered Hong Kong. The cultural center, the boardwalk, Regent Hotel, Golden Mile, and Peninsula Hotel are all on the Tsim Tsa Tsui side. Mandarin Hotel, Pacific Place, Victoria Peak, and the Hong Kong race track are on the Hong Kong side. Going from one side to the other takes about one minute on the subway, and about five minutes on the Star Ferry.

Shopping is everywhere. Every block is filled with shops, intermixed with fancy hotels and department stores. In small shops, customers bargain for the best prices; in department stores, designer boutiques, and chain stores, the prices are set.

Hong Kong is one of the world's leading business and financial meccas. Many businesses have their Asian headquarters here. Hong Kong is also a major tourist destination. Groups of tourists from Japan, Taiwan, and other parts of Asia come to Hong Kong to shop. The average Hong Kong tourist spends U.S. $219 per day. Japanese tourists spend U.S. $345 per day. Over 50% of this expenditure is on shopping.[2]

The future of Hong Kong is uncertain. Despite assurances by the mainland Chinese government that the free enterprise system will be allowed to continue in Hong Kong for 50 years, there is anxiety about the future. After the June 1989 crackdown on student protesters in Tiananmen Square, many Hong Kong residents had more reason to worry.

That is the background of Hong Kong. This history plays an important role in how retailing has developed in Hong Kong. It will also affect what will happen in the future.

Hong Kong is a dazzling, confusing, and very exciting place to shop. Take one turn off a major street and you are likely to encounter snake skins dangling from a shop's ceiling and live sea creatures looking at you from water tanks. In sharp contrast are the major global retailers who have locations in Hong Kong. Nearly every major designer label has a shop here. Toys "R" Us, IKEA, Footlocker, and Benetton have stores scattered throughout Hong Kong.

INDEPENDENT RETAILERS

Open-air markets exist for a variety of merchandise. These markets can be an eye-opening experience for Western shoppers. On one of my trips, I took my son with me to Hong Kong. I had often heard about the jade market, but had never been there. This seemed like an interesting adventure for my son. We took a taxi to the open-air market. Arriving a little before the jade market had opened, we took a stroll around the area. Surrounding the jade market was an open-air food market. Live chickens squawked in cages, live snakes hissed at us from open-air pits. We were the only Caucasians in the area. No one spoke English, and we did not speak Chinese.

Photo 13.4
Wing On is one of the major department stores in Hong Kong and one of three department store groups (the other two are Sincere and Shui Hing) that was originated and is currently owned by Hong Kong Chinese. The store has remained under Kwok family management since the late 1800s. *Courtesy of the Wing On Corporation.*

Then the doors to the jade market opened. This was an area covered with a roof, but with just a metal cage around the vendors. We approached a vendor just completing his set up. We were the only customers in the market. I picked up a jade necklace and inquired the price. The vendor did not speak English, but we communicated in the universal shopping language. He held up a calculator and offered a price, first in Hong Kong dollars, then in the U.S. equivalent. It was about U.S. $100. I shook my head and walked away. The man pursued me, clicking out another price on the calculator, $75. I shook my head and walked away. He came after me again, this time pounding out a price of $50. I really was not interested in the necklace and tried to indicate that the price was not the issue. I believed this would stop him. My son was becoming quite upset at this point. He was only 10 years old, and did not like this man hassling his mother. The man did not stop; on the next approach, he grabbed my arm and started dragging me back to his stand. He presented the necklace to me again to examine. He then tapped out his price, $20, a steal. Unable to imagine why he had dropped the price so low, I bought the necklace. Later, when talking to a Chinese friend, I found out why the vendor gave me such a great deal. Some Chinese vendors are very superstitious. They believe that their first customer of the day determines how their day's sales will go. To lose a first customer is a bad omen. The vendor offered to sell me the jade necklace at a loss to make sure he got this first sale. Likewise, many vendors believe that their last sale of the day is an omen for the next day's sales. My advice to shoppers is therefore to go early or come late, when shopping in the open-air markets.

These are the more exotic markets. There are also major shopping centers and shopping districts with full-scale department stores. The department stores are either Chinese- or Japanese-owned. They carry designer brands, regular national brands, and private label merchandise, all of which is sold at a fixed price.

DEPARTMENT STORE INDUSTRY

Many retailers, primarily Japanese, have viewed Hong Kong as an accessible laboratory where they can learn how to sell successfully to the Chinese. Their strategy is to start with Hong Kong, where the market is wide open, and move to mainland China, where the greatest opportunities in the world exist. Japanese department stores in Hong Kong control more than 50% of the market. Competition from Japanese department stores has made the industry much more competitive. A breakdown of the department store industry in Hong Kong is presented in Table 13.2. There have been some changes in the past few years. Isetan, a Japanese department store, has pulled out of the Hong Kong market. Seibu, another Japanese department store, opened a spectacular store in Pacific Place, on Hong Kong Island in

TABLE 13.2

Departmental Store Retailing in Hong Kong[a]

Retailer	Ownership	Established	Location	Market Segments
Sincere Co.	Chinese	1900	DesVouex, HK, Argyle St. Kowloon; nine locations	Families
Shui Hing	Chinese; member of International Group of Department Stores (IFDS) with headquarters in Switzerland	1961	Tsim Tsa Tsui (Golden Mile) store is being closed; five locations throughout Hong Kong	Tourists
Wing On	Chinese	1907	15+ locations	Families, middle-income households, local residents
Lane Crawford	Chinese	1850	Queens Rd., (Kowloon); 12+ locations	Upscale
Seibu	Japanese-owned originally, now licensed to Hong Kong retailer Dixon Concepts	1990	Pacific Place	Upscale
Uny Co. (HK Ltd.)	Japanese	1987	Taikoo Shing	Local residents, middle-income households
Jusco	Japanese	1987	5+ locations	Middle-income consumers, value-oriented
Yaohan	Originally Japanese; owner relocated corporate headquarters first to Hong Kong and now to Shanghai	1984	Shatin, New Territories; locations throughout New Territories	Local
Isetan (withdrew from the Hong Kong Market in 1996)	Japanese	1973	Tsim Tsa Tsui	Japanese tourists, younger locals
Matsuzakaya	Japanese	1975	Causeway Bay, UC Kin City	Consumers who prefer medium to high priced goods
Marks & Spencer	British	1988	Ocean Center, Mon Kok, Pacific Palace, Times Square; eight+ locations	Locals and middle- to upper-middle-income expatriates living in Hong Kong, tourists
Daimaru	Japanese	1975	Causeway Bay, reducing space	Middle- to upper-middle-income locals
Sogo	Japanese	1985	Causeway Bay	Middle-class locals
Mitsukoshi	Japanese	1980	Causeway Bay, Tsim Sha Tsui location closed	Japanese tourists
Tokyu	Japanese	1982	Tsim Tsa Tsui	Japanese tourists, younger locals

[a]Retailing changes very quickly in Hong Kong, so it is difficult to give an accurate picture.

Recent Changes
Traditional department store that has adopted new supermarket image. New additions include bath department, cookware corner, coffee shop. New marketing to seek out broader base to include 20–30-year-olds. Sincere has stores in Taipei and Shanghai. Both of these stores opened as much more upscale that the main store in Hong Kong. Store in Shanghai has repositioned downward.
Traditional department store/men's and women's specialty store. Shanghai store opened in 1993.
Bought 40% of Seiyu (Shatin) store. Overseas ventures in PRC.
Overseas ventures in Taiwan, Singapore, and Australia.
High priced and innovative, Seibu Pacific Place was part of Seibu-Saism Group. (Seiyu also bought 40% share of Wing On Department Store.) Wanted to be forerunner of Japanese stores in Hong Kong for the 1980s. Failed.
Seeks to promote gift-giving, an age-old tradition in Japan, to show affection for loved ones.
Plans to invest in 15 retail shops in the territory over the next five years, including locations in Causeway Bay, Tsim Tsa Tsui, and New Territories. Has used New Territories to move into China. Successful operations in Shanghai and Beijing.
Plans on investing heavily in foodstuff market. Opened the largest retail shopping center in China, New Age Department Store with Shanghai Number One Department Store in Pudan, an economic development zone in Shanghai. Outlook is not prosperous for this store and a lot of money is involved. In 1997 Yaohon sold most of its interest to Chinese partner.
Fashion-oriented, European and designer Japanese.
Offers merchandise that is "different" from other stores: 60% to 65% of items in Matsuzakaya are from Europe and the United States, about 30% from Japan.
Opening more specialty stores, such as lingerie in Ocean Center. Several Marks & Spencer shops are located in the same shopping area.
First Japanese department store in Hong Kong. More traditional Japanese products.
Large mass merchandiser. Many Japanese products. Largest department store in Hong Kong. In a favorable position because it owns its own building.
High prestige. Source for high quality gifts.
High prestige.

1990. Although the store still has the Seibu name outside, it is now licensed to Dixon Concepts, a retail group that runs many of the luxury specialty stores in Hong Kong. Dixon Concepts is also the group that is buying Barneys New York after Barneys filed for bankruptcy. Just two years ago, 10 of these stores were Japanese, four were Chinese, and one British. Today, eight of the stores are Japanese, five are Chinese, and one British. More Japanese department stores are set to close by the end of 1997. The primary reason is spiraling rents. Isetan maintains it pulled out of Hong Kong because of a fall in Japanese tourist traffic. Mitsukoshi closed a store in Tsim Tsa Tsui when the landlord wanted to triple the rent. Sogo is the only Japanese department store that owns its own building. Rental contracts are generally for three years, with landlords getting a 2% to 3% increase. A few years ago, there were three Japanese retailers in Tsim Tsa Tsui—Isetan, Mitsukoshi, and Tokyu. Now only Tokyu remains. The rest of the Japanese department stores are on the Hong Kong side.

Several new shopping centers offer wide assortment of designer boutiques and specialty stores. One of these, Times Square, is a large American-style atrium shopping center, similar to Pacific Place. I visited this shopping center in 1997. It was churning with people. Marks & Spencer has a specialty store in this center.

IMPORT ORIENTATION More than 70% of the merchandise sold in Hong Kong's department stores is imported.[3] This is ironic when one considers that Hong Kong is one of the largest exporters in the world. However, most of the merchandise produced in Hong Kong is **made for export,** that is, manufactured in Hong Kong to be sold in the United States or Europe. Hong Kong's manufacturers do not attempt to make their products appropriate for Chinese consumers. For instance, Chinese consumers are smaller and do not fit the standard Western clothing sizes. Furthermore, most Hong Kong department stores are single-store operations. They simply do not have the sales volume that would meet the minimum order requirements of the Hong Kong manufacturers.

Some of the merchandise produced in Hong Kong is also sold in a variety of specialty stores and factory outlets, but these are mainly designed for the tourist trade. Outside the department stores, price haggling is an accepted and expected practice. Shopping is sport in Hong Kong. It is also a popular activity for a date.

ROLE OF BUYERS Chinese department stores such as Wing On and Shui Hing have professional buyers, and they view their buyers as profit centers. Buyers attend markets in Europe and the United States. Both of these retailers belong to cooperative buying groups outside Hong Kong. Japanese department stores carry merchandise from Europe and Japan. Marks & Spencer is the only British retailer in Hong Kong. It carries 100% private label merchandise that is produced primarily in Great Britain.[4]

Photo 13.5
Much of Hong Kong is built on steep hills. This shopping street threads through a busy pedestrian area. Stores extend beyond their structures, capturing part of the busy sidewalk. *Courtesy of the author.*

The Chinese department stores in Hong Kong have a flavor more like those of Europe or the United States than Japan. The opposite is true in Taiwan. Taiwan's Chinese-owned department stores are more oriented to Japanese-style merchandise and layout. In Hong Kong, stores use professional buyers, like the United States. Taiwan's department stores, in contrast, use consignment and either do not have professional buyers or have buyers who are very inexperienced.

TAIWAN[5]

Demographic and economic data comparable to those listed for other countries were not available for Taiwan.

COUNTRY BACKGROUND

Taiwan's earliest inhabitants were non-Chinese aborigines. Taiwan became a protectorate of the Chinese Empire in 1206 A.D., although migration from the mainland only began in the 17th century. The first Chinese immigrants came from Guangdong and Fujian provinces, escaping persecution. Beginning in the 1400s, large numbers of Chinese immigrated from Fujian Province. At that time, Taiwan was a prefecture of Fujian Province.

Europeans arrived in the 1500s. The Portuguese explored the area in 1590, calling it Beautiful Island (Isla Formosa). The Dutch, who came in 1624, set up forts on the island. Then Spaniards arrived in the north. In 1641, the Dutch threw the other foreigners out. They controlled the island for the next 20 years. By this time, the Ming dynasty of mainland China had been conquered by the Qing dynasty, and the defeated Ming fled to Taiwan. The Ming immigrants soon expelled the foreigners and took the island for their own. Their rule was short. The Qing dynasty took control of the island in 1683 and held it until 1895. At that time, the island was given to Japan as a result of China's defeat in the Sino-Japanese war. Japan developed and exploited the island, and locals were forced to serve in its army during World War II. After the war, the island was returned to the mainland Chinese.

By 1949, a civil war was raging on the mainland of China. The war was fought between the Nationalists (Kuomintang), led by Chiang Kai-shek, and the communists, led by Mao Zedong. When the Nationalists were defeated, Chiang and more than 1.5 million of his followers took boats across the Formosa Straits to Taiwan. A fleet of U.S. army boats prevented the communists from pursuing the Nationalists.

The Nationalists, known in Taiwan as the KMT, crushed local organizations, suppressed dissidents, and ruled under martial law until 1986. Chiang was president of the Republic of China until 1975, when he died. He always maintained that he would return to the mainland. His wish was for the two Chinas, the People's Republic of China (mainland) and the Republic of China (Taiwan) to be united. Upon Chiang's death, his son assumed control and began taking greater steps toward a freer country. Martial law was ended in 1987, and a new representative assembly elected at the end of 1991.[6]

DEPARTMENT STORES

When I visited Taiwan in 1987, Sogo department store had just opened in Taipei. Other department stores were scrambling to replicate the modern professional atmosphere created by this Japanese giant. The major department store groups were beginning to seek professional assistance from the only professional retailers they knew, the Japanese.

Small independent shops were everywhere. Streets were jumbled, and moving from one place to another took an immense amount of time. McDonald's was one of the very popular restaurants. The small shops sold expensive, low-quality merchandise. The department stores sold Japanese-style clothes, protectively wrapped so that consumers could not spoil the merchandise. Salespersons in department stores lounged on merchandise, ignoring consumers. I had not yet been to mainland China, but later I was to recall the experience of shopping in Taiwan's department stores as being one step up from the mainland Chinese stores. If I were to make a continuum, it would look like this:

PRC **Taiwan** **Hong Kong**

←——————————————————————→

Taiwan's economic progress has been great since 1987. Taiwan's retail formats include traditional grocery stores, convenience stores, supermarkets, department stores, and superstores. The growth of convenience stores has forced 90% of the traditional grocery stores out of business. Supermarkets have developed a strong customer base, but they have not yet replaced conventional open-air markets. Growth rates from 1994 to 1995 by retail format were: convenience stores (19%), supermarkets (8%), department stores (11%), and superstores (30%).[7]

Hypermarkets focus on the value-oriented consumer who buys in bulk. Taiwan had seven hypermarkets in 1993, eight in 1994, 10 in 1995, and 13 in 1996. It was estimated that by the end of 1997, there would be 16. The average purchase at a Carrefour hypermarket in Taiwan is $33. This is the lowest amount of any of their stores. In Portugal, the average purchase amount was $54, and in Brazil, $49. However, the Taiwan hypermarkets are in heavily populated areas so the number of transactions is great.[8] Far Eastern Department Stores (FEDS) operates two hypermarkets under its subsidiary, Far Eastern Enterprise (FEE). These stores use a format similar to that of Kmart and Sam's Club in the United States. In 1997, Makro had six food stores in Taiwan and Carrefour had 13.

HISTORY The history of Taiwan's department store industry can be traced back to 1958 when Da-Hsin, Taiwan's first contemporary department store, was established in Kao-Hsiung. Because most of Taiwan's department stores were small, with limited cash flow, they have widely adopted consignment sales. Lack of merchandise differentiation, stemming from consignment, resulted in a serious problem with vicious price competition. The Taipei Coordinated Department Store Association (TCDSA) was formed in 1980 as a way to alleviate this devastating price competition among stores. Recently, collaborative agreements have attracted the attention of Taiwan's department stores. These strategic alliances have advanced Taiwan's department store industry, and have offered foreign retailers entry into the Taiwanese market.

The development of Taiwan's department store industry has lagged far behind that of its Western counterparts. The industry has been extensively influenced by the Japanese because of geographical proximity, cultural resemblance, and the colonization of Taiwan by Japan earlier in this century.

In 1958, three independent retail stores had merged into Taiwan's first contemporary department store—Da-Hsin. By offering a variety of merchandise, Da-Hsin distinguished itself from its predecessors and pioneered the development and prosperity of Taiwan's department store industry. Another distinctive practice adopted by Da-Hsin was presetting and maintaining fixed prices. At the time, "bargaining" was the purchasing strategy used by Taiwan's businesses and consumers.[9]

Ti-I department store, which became Today (FIT) department store in 1981, was the next major entrant to the department store industry, in 1965. During the 1960s and 1970s, shopping at department stores was a symbol of elegance and superior social status for Taiwanese. Consumers perceived that merchandise sold by department stores was higher in quality and more costly than that sold through other retail establishments.[10] Stimulated by the success of Da-Hsin and Ti-I department stores, many newcomers, including Far Eastern, Hsin-Hsin, Hsin-Kuang, Lai-Lai, Sesame, and Evergreen, were established to meet increasing market demand.

Following the prosperous affiliation of Taiwan's Evergreen department store with Japan's Tokyu department store in 1977, many local department stores began to initiate coalitions with foreign, particularly Japanese, retailers. However, the collaborative agreements between local department stores and foreign partners were limited to management contracts. The Taiwanese government only opened its doors to foreign investment in 1987. The Pacific-Sogo (Pacific of Taiwan and Sogo of Japan) alliance was the first joint venture in the Taiwan retail market. Before this agreement the relationships between Taiwanese stores and foreign retailers were just collaborative agreements to transfer management knowledge. There are now seven major Taiwanese-foreign retailer joint ventures. Au Printemps is the only European retailer; the rest are all Japanese. Taiwan's foreign investment administration prohibits the control of the major share of local-foreign joint ventures by a foreign party.[11] In the Pacific-Sogo joint venture, for example, the local company owns a 51% share, the Japanese partner, 49%.

The Japanese brought to the Taiwan market better customer service, information management, and accounting control. Department stores offer services such as currency exchange and classes for expectant mothers. The stores have become much larger. Larger size is needed to provide the more extensive customer facilities, like children's play areas, restaurants, and theaters.[12]

Far Eastern Department Stores is the largest department store chain in Taiwan, with 12 stores. The company's market share has declined over the past few years due to competition from Japanese department stores. However, FEDS has strong competitive advantages, which include an extensive store network, volume purchasing, value pricing strategy, superstore expansions, experienced management, and support from a network of companies associated with Far Eastern Group. Far Eastern Department Stores reaches consumers of most income groups. As living standards rise, FEDS's upscale shopping is expected to register solid growth.[13]

Taiwanese department stores are often called "little banks." Their sales are made on a cash basis. Concession sales account for 90% of total sales. Payments to concessionaires, after subtracting fees, are made 45 days later. If concessionaires want to receive payment earlier, they receive a reduced payment. Department stores with average daily sales of New Taiwan (NT) $20 million, have a great deal of cash on hand, providing them with greater liquidity and working capital.[14]

In Taiwan, the department store share of total retail sales is comparatively insignificant: only 5.9% compared to 35.8% in Japan. Taiwan's department stores have historically been criticized for unreasonable profits and unacceptable, exorbitant prices. Today, Taiwanese consumers still believe that department store prices are higher than those of other retailers.[15]

CONSUMERS As shown in Table 13.3, statistics based on actual sales divided by product category indicated that textile/apparel and related products accounted for 67.4% of Taipei department stores' annual sales in 1986.[16] Other product categories included food, hardware, stationery and toys, home appliances, furniture, drugs, and others. Product categories sold by Taiwan's department stores, and percentages of sales, were similar during the period from 1984 through 1986. This indicates that both shopping patterns and merchandise assortments remained quite stable.

TABLE 13.3

Average Sales of Major Product Categories (%) at Taiwan Department Stores

	%		
Product Category	**1984**	**1985**	**1986**
Textile/apparel	65.1	64.0	67.4
Foods	14.2	15.0	14.3
Hardware	6.4	6.4	5.1
Stationery/toys	5.7	5.7	5.4
Home appliances	5.4	5.1	4.9
Furniture	1.0	0.7	0.6
Drugs	0.1	0.1	0.1
Others	2.1	3.0	2.2
Total	100.0	100.0	100.0

Source: Wu, S.- C. (1987). "The Study of Improving Large Scale Department Stores' Productivity." Unpublished thesis, Chinese Culture University, Taiwan, p. 34. (In Chinese).

Ming-Chuan Junior College of Business in Taiwan conducted a study of the shopping patterns of department store consumers (Table 13.4). Respondents were asked to indicate product categories purchased frequently at department stores. Consumer responses indicated that almost 35% of total purchases were for apparel and accessory products.[17] When the sample was further divided into male and female subgroups, it was found that 33% of total purchases for males were apparel and accessory products versus 43%

TABLE 13.4

Product Categories Most Frequently Shopped at Taiwanese Department Stores

	%		
Product Category	**Male**	**Female**	**Total**
Apparel and accessories	32.8	43.2	34.4
Daily necessaries	36.0	26.0	31.3
Foodsf14.4	24.8	19.6	
Home appliances	9.0	2.2	5.7
Furniture	1.7	1.3	1.5
Others	4.5	2.5	3.5

Source: Chang, C.-H. (1988). "The Study of Department Store Consumers' Behaviour." *Chuan-Hsin Magazine,* No. 6. p. 13. (In Chinese).

TABLE 13.5

Perceptions of Department Stores by Taiwanese Consumers

	Reasonable Price (%)	**Superior Quality (%)**	**Store Image (%)**	**Shopping Atmosphere (%)**
Department store	12.7	32.0	78.8	44.8
Designer store	5.6	42.2	4.6	24.5
Exporting goods store	54.6	1.6	1.1	10.8
Specialty store	21.9	20.9	12.7	18.0
Missing data	5.2	3.3	2.9	2.0

Source: Kuo, C.-H. 1989). "The Predication of Department Stores' Present and Future: Based On Consumers' Preferences." *Direct Marketing,* No. 25, pp. 39–51. (In Chinese).

for females. Table 13.4 also shows that daily necessaries accounted for 31% of purchases made at department stores. Other product categories purchased included food products, home appliances, furniture, and others.

Department stores are perceived by Taiwanese consumers as having better store images than the formats of other retail outlets. A survey conducted by Fu-Jen University, Taiwan, found that department stores' high prices were most frequently criticized by shoppers. The general picture of Taiwanese consumers' perceptions of department stores is shown in Table 13.5; only 13% of consumers perceived the department store's prices as reasonable.[18] In this study, most (79%) of the Taiwanese consumers preferred the department stores' image; 45% agreed that department stores offered better shopping atmospheres; and 32% expressed a positive view of the quality of the department store products.[19]

When Taiwanese consumers were asked about their reasons for shopping at department stores, wide variety of merchandise was the most frequently mentioned reason.[20] Other reasons included product quality, shopping comfort, and store image. On the other hand, consumers said that prices and service were unsatisfactory (Table 13.6).[21] A survey conducted in 1986 indicated that 80% of Taiwanese consumers had negative attitudes toward the department stores' prices and discount promotions.[22] In another survey, 50% of consumers claimed dissatisfaction about price when shopping at department stores, while 33% deemed reasonable price to be the most significant criterion for being a "good" department store.

TABLE 13.6

Reasons Cited by Taiwanese Consumers for Shopping at Department Stores

Reason	Percentage
Completeness of assortment	33.6
Quality of product	22.4
Shopping comfort	17.2
Store image	12.0
Price	6.5
Service	4.8
Postal service	3.5
Total	100.0

Source: Chang, C.-H. (1988). "The Study of Department Store Consumers' Behaviour." *Chuan-Hsin Magazine*, No. 6, p. 13. (In Chinese).

CHARACTERISTICS OF THE INDUSTRY Consignment sales, the existence of the Taipei Coordinated Department Store Association, and alliances with Japanese retailers are three distinctive aspects of Taiwan's department store industry.

Two-thirds of department store sales in Taiwan are associated with consignment (Table 13.7). Under this practice, 10% to 30% of sales in department stores come from consignors, who are manufacturers or retailers.[23]

The substantial affiliation of Taiwanese department stores with foreign businesses, particularly Japanese retailers, includes alliances ranging from management contracts to joint ventures. Table 13.8 provides an overview of these store alliances. Evergreen Department Store initiated the first Taiwanese-Japanese alliance with Japanese Tokyu Department Store in 1977. The 1987 Pacific-Sogo joint venture between Taiwan's Pacific Construction and Japan's Sogo was a successful strategic alliance. They built the first joint venture department store in Taipei.

INDUSTRY STRUCTURE: FIVE COMPETITIVE FORCES

Porter[24] provides a framework for analyzing the structure of an industry as a means of detecting how change will occur. Competition focuses around five

TABLE 13.7

Percentages of Consignment Sales and Conventional Sales of Taipei's Leading Department Stores

Department Store	Conventional Sales (%)	Consignment Sales (%)
Ton Ling	15	85
Re Bar	20	80
Lai-Lai	30	70
Sincere	30	70
Sunrise	30	70
Ming Yao	30	70
Evergreen	35	65
Homey	40	60
Pacific-Sogo	45	55
Today	50	50
Far Eastern	60	40
Average	33.7	66.3

Source: Chou, M.-P. (1986). "Department Store Industry: The Perspectives of Past, Present, and Future." *Da-Yeh Financial Investment Magazine.* (In Chinese.)

TABLE 13.8

Taiwanese Department Store Joint Ventures

Est.	Name	Taiwanese Partner	Foreign Department Store	Store Size (sq. meters)	Location
1987	Pacific Sogo	Pacific Construction	Sogo	29,040	Taipei
1991	Shin-Kong Mitsukoshi	Shin Kong	Mitsukoshi	21,780	Taipei
1991	Ta Lee Isetan	Ta Lee	Isetan	33,000	Kaohsiung
1994	Da Yeh Takashimaya	Da Yeh Development	Takashimaya	49,500	Taipei
1995	Han Shin	Han Lei Group	Han Shin	59,400	Kaohsiung
1995	Kuang San Sogo	Kuang San Construction	Sogo	56,100	Taichung
1995	Printemps	Deh Geh Enterprise	Au Printemps	39,600	Taipei

Source: Ren, A. (1996). "Far Eastern Department Stores—Company Report." Bankers Trust Research, June 24, in *Investext* [Database on CD-ROM]. Foster City, CA: Information Acess.

interacting forces: (1) threat of new entrants, (2) threat of substitute products or services, (3) rivalry among existing competition, (4) bargaining power of suppliers, and (5) bargaining power of buyers (Figure 13.1). The pressure of these forces will determine the intensity of competition and ultimately how the industry will be reorganized. The discussion that follows will look at how these five forces affect the Taiwanese market.

BARGAINING POWER OF BUYERS In 1990, Taiwan had the largest cash hoard in the world—U.S. $66 billion in non-gold foreign reserves[25]—making it the world's third greatest economic power.[26] With an annual economic growth rate of nearly 10%, its per capita gross domestic product (GDP) reached U.S. $7,509 in 1989, compared to U.S. $3,993 in 1986, almost doubling within three years.[27]

This consistent economic growth pattern is due to export-oriented industrialization, which has effectively transformed Taiwan from a lesser developed nation to a newly industrialized economy. These and several other factors, such as low unemployment and an increase in per capita income, have helped Taiwan's promising retail environment. With a 40% average savings rate, Taiwanese consumers used to be conservative in their spending,[28] but the increase in disposable income has led them to spend more freely.[29]

Although Taiwan's consumers have gained economic strength, this has not been paralleled by growth of a highly service-oriented retail system. The consumer-retailer relationship in Taiwan still resembles that of a developing country where suppliers dictate market practices. When merchandise is pur-

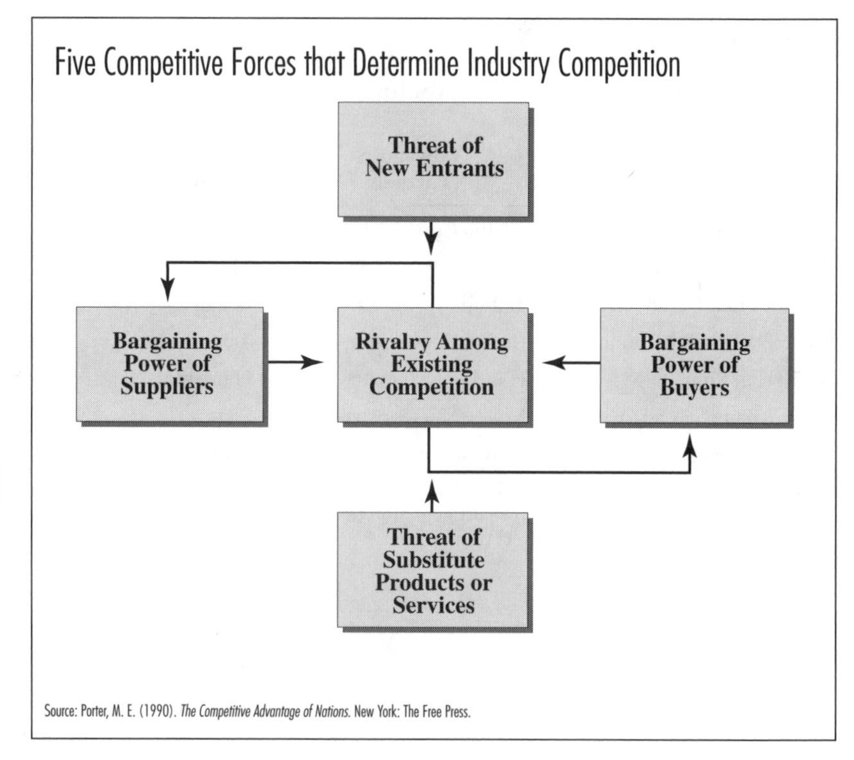

Figure 13.1
Five forces determine industry competition. The bargaining power of suppliers, the bargaining power of buyers, the threat of substitute products or services, and the threat of new competitors increase rivalry among competitors. This rivalry influences the bargaining power of buyers and suppliers. In suppliers' markets where there are few suppliers, suppliers do not need to be very concerned with their role performance; they know that they are the sole source of supply for their captive retailers. In buyers' markets competitive rivalry is high, forcing suppliers to compete for clients.

chased in Taiwan, the sale is final. Generally, no returns are permitted. Entry of foreign retailers will likely shift this balance, giving consumers access to service-oriented businesses.

THREAT OF SUBSTITUTE PRODUCTS OR SERVICES Opportunities for foreign consumer-goods manufacturers and marketers exist because of Taiwanese consumers' preference for foreign products. Chu[30] found that Taiwanese consumers perceive imported merchandise to be better than domestic in product quality and product image. Further, according to a survey conducted by *Tu-Po Magazine* and Harvard Management Consultant Company in 1987, the purchase ratio of imported to domestic products was 3.2:1 for durable goods and 1.6:1 for nondurable goods.

Another study found that the price of imported merchandise was 50% higher than that of domestic goods.[31] However, the appreciation of the New Taiwan dollar has helped to decrease the price of foreign products.[32] An increase in domestic labor costs[33] has also made domestic products more expensive.

With a considerable trade surplus and sizable foreign-exchange reserves, the Taiwanese government initiated the "Buy Imports" campaign to encourage Taiwanese consumers and businesses to purchase foreign products as a means of balancing trade with foreign countries.[34] This is particularly advantageous to U.S. businesses because there is a "Buy American" campaign to encourage the Taiwanese consumption of American-made goods and services, and also a "Don't Buy Japanese" campaign to discourage the buying of Japanese products.[35]

RIVALRY AMONG EXISTING COMPETITORS The intense competition that exists among Taiwan's department stores is largely due to too many department stores competing in a limited marketplace. For instance, in 1989 in Taipei, 20 department stores competed in a marketplace with a population of 3 million as compared to the general ratio 1:300,000 in developed countries.[36] In addition, the consignment system means that there is little merchandise differentiation among department stores. Product similarity makes price competition even greater because retailers lack competitive advantages.[37] Fierce price competition initiated a chaotic era, usually referred to as the "discount war,"[38] in which every department store relied heavily on offering the lowest price. However, the excessive use of this strategy made consumers suspicious and had a detrimental effect on the department store business.[39]

THREAT OF NEW ENTRANTS Taiwan's department stores have been forming alliances with foreign retailers, mostly Japanese department stores. Sincere (Taiwan-Hong Kong) and Printemps (Taiwan-French) are the only department store not invested in by Japanese retailers. In the hypermarket and supermarket industries, there are non-Japanese dominated joint ventures. Because of growing consumption power and increasing market demand for fashionable foreign products, management contracts and joint ventures present promising opportunities for both local and foreign retailers. The first alliance between Taiwanese and Japanese department stores was the management contract of Evergreen (Taiwan) and Tokyu (Japan) in 1977.[40] Ten years later, Pacific-Sogo, the first Taiwanese-Japanese joint venture was established after the deregulation of foreign investment. Pacific-Sogo is now the leading department store in Taiwan, with one-tenth of Taipei's market share. The success of the Pacific-Sogo is further evidence of preferences for foreign products and services.

Due to geographical proximity and cultural similarity, Taiwan's retail industry was influenced by Japan. Taiwanese consumers also exhibit a strong preference for Japanese merchandise. This strong preference is believed to be the reason for Japanese retailers' success in Taiwan. Nevertheless, because of the Taiwanese authorities' "Buy American; Don't Buy Japanese" policy, the robust market demand still presents promising opportunities for U.S. retailers.

BARGAINING POWER OF SUPPLIERS As noted earlier in the chapter, consignment sales account for two-thirds of the department store sales in Taiwan. The majority of Taiwan's department stores generate only limited cash flow and lack a solid financial base.[41] This encourages the practice of consignment sales. Under the consignment system, department stores receive 10% to 30% of sales as a commission from the consignee (depending on the product category).[42] For example, the commission for apparel is 30%, whereas that percentage for cosmetics is 15%. Although the percentages are different for each store, consignment sales account for about 66% of Taiwanese department stores' sales, whereas only 34% are direct purchase.[43] Although consignment sales reduce risk and eliminate a retailer's need for substantial cash flow for inventory, they also reduce the store's ability to carry out marketing strategies.

Dissimilar business objectives of department stores and consignees commonly cause conflict within the distribution channel. Indeed, conflicts arise frequently between department stores and consignees.[44] Additionally, human resource management presents a major challenge for administration because most salespersons are employed by the manufacturer or supplier who has a consignment contract with the store. Human resources statistics for Taipei's major department stores, including employees who were hired by consignees and those who were directly employed by department stores, are given in Table 13.9.

The consignment system gives channel power to the manufacturers. As the percentage of consignment merchandise increases, the market sophistication of the retailer decreases. New entries into the Taiwan retail market will likely gain a competitive edge by handling their own product risks. Also, because of transportation logistics, imported merchandise is rarely ever returned to the vendor; therefore, a parallel should occur between an increase in direct purchasing and retailer dominance.

Currently, merchandise sold in Taiwan department stores is very similar, leading to merchandising monotony. Foreign market entrants can play on this product redundancy as a competitive strategy. In addition,

TABLE 13.9

Employment Statistics of Taiwan's Department Stores

Department Store	Store-hired Employees	Consignee-hired Employees
Far Eastern (J.A.)	180	180
Far Eastern (P.C.)	300	300
Lai-Lai	210	310/350
Today (O.M.)	220	210
Today (N.K.)	328	432
Re Bar	189	300
Sincere	150	100
Homey	80	480

Source: Lin, I.-C., and W.-C. Ling. (1988). "An Overview of Human Resources for Department Store Industry." *Chung Hsin Magazine*, No. 6, p. 33.

because most department stores in Taiwan are single-store operations, their ability to use some of the market strategies used by U.S. retailers, such as private label merchandise, is significantly reduced. As Taiwan moves from a supplier's market to a buyer's market, a significant shift in channel power is expected from manufacturers to retailers. Traditionally, department stores in Taiwan have been weak channel members. It is predicted that these retailers will gain channel strength, however, bolstered largely by foreign investment. This environment is a rich opportunity for foreign investment.

FUTURE OF THE OVERSEAS CHINESE

Hong Kong and Taiwan will have a major impact on retail operations in mainland China. In each community, foreign retailers, primarily the Japanese, have been testing their retail formats, adjusting their business strategies to bring them in line with what is needed in the larger market, the PRC. Over the years, I have talked with retailers in Hong Kong about their relationship with the PRC. In the early 1980s, most business people indicated that they did not anticipate much change occurring when Hong Kong reverted to Chinese rule in 1997. After Tiananmen Square in 1989, the view was very different. Many major retailers changed their country of domicile from Hong Kong to other countries, such as Bermuda. Others changed their Hong Kong passports to foreign passports if they had the opportunity.

In the years since Tiananmen Square, the views have softened. Some major retailers, who vowed never to enter the mainland market after their stores were confiscated in the 1950s, have been courted by the PRC government. The opportunity presented by the vast population of the PRC, combined with the relatively weak competition has made expansion there very attractive for major Hong Kong retailers.

I visited Hong Kong just four months before the July 1, 1997, turnover to China. I stayed for a week before going on to Shanghai and Beijing. Although I wonder how different Hong Kong will be the next time I return, I expect more change to occur in Shanghai and Beijing than in Hong Kong over the next few years.

SUMMARY

Both Hong Kong and Taiwan have been greatly influenced by Japanese retailers. Their modern retail formats have been adapted from small family-owned businesses to major retail concerns. Competition from foreign firms has marked their retail development.

Retailers and consumers in Hong Kong and Taiwan share may cultural attributes with their neighbors in mainland China. Categories of shared cultural values include man-nature orientation, man-to-himself orientation, relational orientation, time orientation, and activity orientation. Although their economies diverged after mainland China become communist in 1951 and Hong Kong and Taiwan did not, important cultural connections remain.

The overseas Chinese in Hong Kong and Taiwan are an important link to mainland China. When Hong Kong reverted to mainland China on July 1, 1997, I watched the ceremony from a Paris hotel room. There was much nostalgia about an era that had passed. Chinese businesspeople from Hong Kong that I talked with were not happy with the change of ownership, but they accepted it. Earlier, there had been great concern about what the change would bring. When the actual change occurred, there was little alarm. Business continued as usual. The Chinese military was benevolent to people in Hong Kong during the transition. Perhaps this event is the beginning of something even bigger; it may be a prelude to the eventual unification of all the overseas Chinese.

In the last days of October 1997, the Hong Kong stock market suffered monumental declines. Wall Street reacted with a similar drop. Then all the financial worlds seemed to pick themselves up. It is another statement about how interconnected Asia and the United States have become. In November 1997, the leader of the PRC completed a visit to the United States, the first visit of any mainland Chinese leader since the 1989 incident. Crowds protested the PRC's human rights agenda. Nevertheless, in the end, the importance of trade and a global economy were the dominant theme of this occasion.

KEY TERMS

circular thinking
linear thinking
made for export

DISCUSSION QUESTIONS

1. Japanese department stores have been very successful in the Hong Kong and Taiwanese markets. Are they successful because they are Japanese? If not, how can you explain this success? Recently, the Japanese department stores have begun leaving Hong Kong. Would you expect a similar departure from Taiwan? Why?
2. How do Chinese cultural values help to explain the differences between retailing in overseas Chinese enclaves and Japan?
3. In many parts of Hong Kong and Taiwan, prices are not fixed; buyers and sellers negotiate prices. This does not happen in Japan. Recall the discussion of retailing in developing countries, in Chapter 3. When do markets become more formal?

ENDNOTES

1. Yau, O. H. M. (1988). "Chinese Cultural Values: Their Dimensions and Marketing Implications." *European Journal of Marketing*, Vol. 22, No. 5, pp. 44–57.
2. *Statistical Review of Tourism* (1988). Hong Kong: Hong Kong Tourist Association, p. 41.
3. Sternquist, B. (1994). "Gatekeepers of Consumer Choice: A Four-Country Comparison of Retail Buyers." *International Review of Retail, Distribution and Consumer Research*, Vol. 4, No. 2, pp. 159–176.
4. Phillips, L. A., B. Sternquist, and S. Mui (1992). "Hong Kong Department Stores: Retailing in the 1990s." *International Journal of Retail & Distribution Management*, Vol. 20, No. 1, pp. 16–24.
5. Adapted and reprinted by permission from Chang, L. D., and B. Sternquist (1993). "Taiwanese Department Stores Industry." *International Journal of Retail & Distribution Management*, Vol. 21, No. 1, pp. 26–34.
6. *Craighead's International Business*. (1996). Detroit: Gale Research.
7. Ren, A. (June 24, 1996). "Far Eastern Department Stores—Company Report." Bankers Trust Research in *Investext* [Database on CD-ROM]. Foster City, Calif.: Information Access.
8. "Carrefour—Company Report." (March 13, 1997). UBS Research Limited in *Investext* [Database on CD-ROM]. Foster City, Calif.: Information Access.
9. Chang, C.-H. (1988), "The Development of Consignment Sales." *Chuan-Hsin Magazine* (Taiwan), Vol. 6, pp. 116–118.
10. Chiu, C.-S. (1990). "The Study of Introductory Development of Contemporary Retail Organization." Unpublished thesis, National Politics University (Taiwan).
11. Price Waterhouse (1979).
12. Ren (June 24, 1996).
13. Ren (June 24, 1996).
14. Ren (June 24, 1996).
15. Chiu (1990).
16. Wu, S.-C. (1987). "The Study of Improving Large Scale Department Stores' Productivity." Unpublished thesis, Chinese Culture University (Taiwan).
17. Chang, H.-M., S.-L. Yeh, and J.-C. Li (1988b), "The Study of Department Store Consumers' Behavior." *Chuan-Hsin Magazine* (Taiwan), Vol. 6, pp. 13–15.
18. Kuo, C.-H. (1989). "The Prediction of Department Store's Present and Future: Based on Consumers' Preferences." *Direct Marketing* (Taiwan), Vol. 25, pp. 39–51.
19. Kuo (1989).
20. Chang, Yeh, and Li (1988).
21. Chang, Yeh, and Li (1988).

22. Lin, I.-C., and W.-C. Ling. (1988). "An Overview of Human Resources for Department Store Industry." *Chuan-Hsin Magazine,* Vol. 6, pp. 92–96.
23. Kuo (1989).
24. Porter, M. E. (1990). *The Competitive Advantage of Nations.* New York: The Free Press.
25. Lee, D. (1991). "Rebuilding a Tiger: Who'll Get the Lion's Share." *Business Week,* March 25, pp. 46–47.
26. Montagu-Pollock, M. (1991). "All the Right Connections: Chinese Management Has Amazing Advantages Over 'Modern' Methods." *Asian Business* (Hong Kong), Vol. 27, No. 1, pp. 20–24.
27. Scogna, L. (1990). "Taiwan: Growth and Reduced Barriers Increase U.S. Opportunities." *Business America,* Vol. 111, No. 8, pp. 33–34.
28. Droker, L., and R. J. Sander. (1989). "Market Taiwan: Recent Changes Create New Opportunities." *Business America,* June 19, pp. 2–9.
29. Worthy, F. S. (1988). "Tightwad Taiwan Starts to Spend." *Fortune,* Vol. 118, No. 13, pp. 177–182.
30. Chu (1987).
31. Caplen, B. (1989). "Selling Quality in Cloneland." *Asian Business,* Vol. 25, No. 5, pp. 62–63.
32. Scogna (1990).
33. Lam, D. K.-K. (1989). "The Neglected Market: Opportunities in Taiwan." *Canadian Business Review,* Vol. 16, No. 3, pp. 45–48.
34. Lee (1991).
35. Worthy (1988).
36. Kuo (1989).
37. Chou, M.-P. (1986). "Department Store Industry: The Perspectives of Past, Present, and Future." *Da-Yeh Financial Investment Magazine* (Taiwan).
38. Shen, I-H. (1988). "An Overview of Taipei Coordinated Department Store Association." *Chuan-Hsin Magazine,* Vol. 6, pp. 112–115.
39. Lin and Ling (1988).
40. Lin and Ling (1988).
41. Chiu (1990).
42. Kuo (1989).
43. Chiu (1990)
44. Chang, Yeh, and Li (1988).

Beijing
PEOPLE'S REPUBLIC
of CHINA
Nanjing
Wuhan
Shanghai
Guangzhou
Shenzen
Hong
Kong

14

Retailing in the People's Republic of China

After reading this chapter, you will understand:

- How a planned economy handles the distribution of products.
- How the retailing system in the People's Republic of China (PRC) is similar to distribution in the central and eastern European countries before marketization.
- The role of state-owned stores in the PRC and how the distribution process has changed since market reforms.
- The rules regulating foreign joint ventures in the PRC and how this affects foreign retailers operating in China.

THIS IS AN EXCITING TIME to be studying retailing in the PRC. Sales in China during the first six months of 1993 were up 24% from the same period of 1992. China's retail market is expected to triple by the year 2000.[1] In this chapter, I will outline how retailing was conducted in China before market liberalization, followed by a discussion of the current retail system. Although foreign retailers are interested in entering this huge market, most are worried about the control still exercised by the central government. Indeed, there is good cause for concern. In the last section of this chapter, I will focus on the PRC's joint venture laws, and their implications for foreign retailers.

Table 14.1 presents selected demographic and economic data for the PRC.

COUNTRY BACKGROUND

It is easy to forget that communism in the People's Republic of China (PRC) is a relatively recent phenomenon, in the span of Chinese history. China has a vibrant commercial past. Since the days of Marco Polo, China was sought as a trading partner by Western nations. Endowed with tremendous riches in natural resources and artistic expression, it was and is a country with tremendous market appeal.

Around the middle of the Ming dynasty (1368–1644) China's economy, consisting of agriculture and the handicraft industry, operated under a capitalist system. The silk and cotton industries were prosperous in southeastern China. Thousands of textile and cotton workshops emerged, utilizing low-cost labor, and the beginning of a class system emerged. The succeeding Qing dynasty (1644–1911), rather than encouraging these capitalistic enterprises as had its Ming predecessors, instead placed limits on the size of factories and imposed high taxes on merchants. The Qing dynasty also pursued a closed-door policy to foreign trade, discouraging Chinese merchants from seeking foreign markets. This desire for isolation was reflective of a historical desire for self-sufficiency. The only port the Qing dynasty kept open was Guangzhou, where tea, silk, medicine, and porcelain were traded for woolens, cotton textiles, and spices.

Trade was unbalanced, favoring the Chinese exports. British colonialists demanded that China purchase additional British products, or more specifically one prize product of the British, opium. When China refused to cooperate by refusing to legalize the opium trade, the British threatened military force. The Treaty of Nanjing (1842) concluded the first Opium War with Great Britain. China agreed to open the port of Shanghai and four other ports to Western trade. American and western European businesses set up shop in Shanghai. The architecture of the Bund district in Shanghai reflects this European influence.

By 1860, following the second Opium War and a second round of treaties, China had deteriorated into a colonial society. The government was powerless to stop foreign land-grabbing and to protect the rights of its citizens. In 1868, a sign posted over the entrance to a new municipal park in Shanghai was a testimony to China's deterioration; the sign read, "No admittance for dogs and Chinese." Thousands of gambling houses, opium dens, and brothels had emerged in the city. It was a mecca for American and European investors. Prosperity was not limited to foreigners. A ruling merchant class of Chinese also emerged.

TABLE 14.1

People's Republic of China: Selected Demographic and Economic Data

	Population (millions) mid-1995	Area (thousands of sq. km)	GNP per capita: Dollars 1995	GNP per capita: Avg. ann. growth (%) 1985–95	PPP estimates of GNP per capita U.S. = 100: 1987	PPP estimates of GNP per capita U.S. = 100: 1995	Life expectancy at birth (years) 1995	Adult illiteracy (%) 1995
Low-income economies	3,179.9t	40,606t	430w	3.8w			63w	34w
China	1,200.2	9,561	620	8.3	6.3	10.8	69	19

Source: World Bank (1997). PPP = purchasing power parity. t = total. w = weighted average.

In the late 19th and early 20th centuries, most foreign goods gained acceptance through constant advertising in the modern media. About 200 foreign-owned newspapers and magazines were published in China throughout the 19th century. The Chinese publishing giant Commercial Press launched 16 magazines between 1903 and 1937. Radio broadcasting in China dates to 1922. In 1927, the Sun Sun Company, a Shanghai department store, established a station that broadcasted market news, current events, and Chinese music. By 1936, Shanghai had 36 Chinese-run stations. Massive department stores with names such as Sincere, Wing On, and Shui Hing sprouted up on Nanjing Road, the major shopping boulevard.[2] These luxury stores were parallel to Macy's and Gimbels in the United States and Harrods in London.

The division between the moneyed entrepreneurs and the working class broadened. Starvation, prostitution, and opium addiction were prevalent. The Bund, the beautiful boulevard in Shanghai that surrounds the harbor, was strewn each morning with corpses. China was troubled with civil strife from 1921, leading to civil war. During the first civil war, the two major political groups, the Nationalists and the communists, agreed on a policy of strikes and boycotts that ultimately led to the dispossession of the propertied class and foreigners. During World War II, the two parties put aside their differences and cooperated in the fight against Japanese expansionism. But the end of the war brought renewed hostilities. Eventually, the Nationalists found themselves overpowered and left the mainland to form their own government, the Republic of China, which we know as Taiwan, on the island of Formosa.

Photo 14.1
The Shanghai Wing On department store as it appeared in the early 19th century. The owners were Chinese immigrants who went to Australia and then returned to China to open a retail store. In the 1950s, when all commercial property was being converted to state ownership, the store was taken over by the government. *Courtesy of the Wing On Corporation.*

On October 1, 1949, communist leaders and 300,000 citizens gathered in Tiananmen Square, Beijing, to attend the ceremony that marked the formal beginning of the People's Republic of China. The government set a deadline of January 1956 for the transformation of private businesses to "whole people enterprises." Over the next five years, the state expropriated all of the major industries. The luxurious department stores such as Sincere, Wing On, and Shui Hing were taken over by the communist government and their names changed to less descriptive terms, such as Number One Department Store and Number Two Department Store. The door between China and the West closed.

During the Cultural Revolution, from 1966 until 1976, people in positions of authority—government officials, teachers, and managers—were persecuted. Eerie sameness, adopted by many as a survival tactic, settled in: everyone dressed alike, thought alike, and shunned anything intellectual. The overthrow of the counter-revolutionary group in late 1976 signaled the beginning of a new historical period in China. The Cultural Revolution was over and socialist modernization became the new focus. The policy line became "emancipating the mind, using the brain, seeking truth from facts, and unity to look forward." This is the paradigm of modern China.

Except for a brief retrenchment following the 1989 Tiananmen Square incident in which Chinese army troops confronted student demonstrators, killing an unknown number of protestors, China has continued to modernize at a very rapid rate. Foreign investment in China increased steadily throughout the late 1980s and early 1990s and this trend is expected to continue.

Photo 14.2
The Shanghai Wing On became the Shanghai Number One Department Store and is the best-known store in China. This is a picture of it today. Recent renovations call for a doubling of the current space. *Courtesy of the Number One Department Store.*

BEFORE MARKET REFORMS

China is a large and diverse country. Retail market reforms have occurred first in the major special economic zones and cities, before slowly spreading out to other areas. I will discuss the retail industry before market reforms in some detail because in most parts of China, that is still the system today. Only in the most economically developed areas has rapid retail modernization occurred.

Beginning in the 1950s, retail sales in China were controlled by the Ministry of Commerce, now known as the Ministry of Domestic Trade. In the pre-reform system, modeled after the Soviet distribution system, products were categorized into three types. Category 1 included items vital to the national economy and people's livelihood. Products such as rice, cotton, coal, and fuel were included in this list. The distribution of these products was monopolized by designated state-run units.[3] Category 2 included products such as bicycles, watches, sewing machines, and radios. Industrial ministries controlled the distribution of these products. Category 3 included merchandise considered nonessential; these products were controlled by provincial and municipal governments.

Under this system, known as the *fenpei* system, distribution operated strictly as a case of allocation. The State Planning Commission would decide on general production goals for the factories in China. The factories would then be allocated raw materials and told to produce the necessary products. After production, the goods would be shipped to the Ministry of Commerce Central Distribution Centers. In addition to the product orientation, China's distribution system used a three-tier wholesale structure. Three major distribution centers in Tianjin, Shanghai, and Guangzhou served many second- and third-tier distribution centers at the local level. Wholesalers and retailers were owned by the government and served within this allocation function not as market players, but as storage facilities for merchandise.

This planning system could be justified when the PRC had an undersupply of merchandise, but it made less sense when merchandise shortages did not exist. During the 1980s, foreign manufacturing firms were allowed to set up joint ventures in China. These joint ventures provided upgraded production technology and product design. The undersupply situation was eliminated. Competition over product quality and efficient distribution prompted changes in the wholesale and retail distribution system.

Governments at the municipal level were given the right to set up and run wholesale activities. Large department stores were also permitted to purchase directly from manufacturers. The control of product pricing was deregulated. Prices could now be negotiated based on quantity ordered and various other considerations.

By the late 1980s, China's distribution system contained a variety of wholesale and retail owners. By 1992, state-owned units accounted for just 41.3% of total retail sales. Collectives in addition to private and individual enterprises made up 27.9% and 20% respectively.[4] By the end of 1995, the distribution was state-owned stores, 30%; collective-owned, 19%; and individual, 30%. Joint venture sales in 1995 still did not make up even 1% of sales.[5]

RETAIL OWNERSHIP

The Chinese government, like other centrally planned economies, viewed distribution as a nonproductive business activity. Rather than putting money into selling merchandise, it was believed that people should put their efforts into producing the products. As a result, the distribution system in the PRC is still inefficient, but it is rapidly being modernized in major cities.

A striking contrast can be seen in how the former Soviet Union and China have approached developing a market economy. In the Soviet Union, the political system was changed first. The removal of the communist party from power set the stage for transformation of the economic system. The result has been tremendous hardship, including consumer shortages and tremendous inflation. In contrast, the PRC has altered the economic system first, moving toward a free market before leaving the political security of a communist/socialist system. Unlike the former Soviet Union, the PRC has had an abundant supply of merchandise and comparatively low inflation.

GOVERNMENT-OWNED STORES

State-owned stores and cooperatives were the only type of retailers allowed in China until the late 1980s. **State-owned stores** include department stores, food stores, and specialty stores owned by the government. **Cooperatives** are quite similar to state-owned stores except the business is owned by a group. A list of the top 10 Chinese retailers is presented in Table 14.2. A more detailed list of large retailers is included in Table 14.3; this is a list of the 50 largest retail stores in terms of sales, square footage, and profitability. The list is for 1991 data, so use the information cautiously. However, it is the only place in which I have found this type of detailed information. Also, because many of these companies are being privatized, this type of information may not be available in the future.

To encourage market reforms the government has allowed **shareholding,** transferring ownership to private individuals. Seven of the top 10 department stores in the PRC are now shareholding companies. These companies include Shanghai Number One Department Store, Tianjin Leader International, Beijing Xidan, Beijing Wangfujing Department Store, Wuhan Shopping Arcade, Guangzhou Nanfang Building, and Shanghai Yuyuan Shopping Center.

TABLE 14.2

Top 10 Chinese Retailers

1994 Sales Ranking (1993)	Name of Store	1994 Sales RMB* (billions)	Increase 1993–1994 (%)
1 (1)	Shanghai Number One Department Store	2.76	41%
2 (5)	Beijing Wangfujing Department Store	1.68	53%
3 (7)	Wuhan Shopping Arcade	1.51	16%
4 (6)	Zhongxing-Shenyang Commerical	1.40	35%
5 (–)	Beijing Urban Rural Trading Centre	1.31	50%
6 (9)	Guangzhou Nanfang Department Store	1.30	24%
7 (4)	Shanghai Hualian Commercial	1.23	0%
8 (8)	Nanjing Xinjiekou Department Store	1.20	26%
9 (–)	Wuhan Zhongnan Commercial Building	1.16	49%
10 (–)	Dalian Shopping Arcade	1.11	37%

*RMB = renminbi; 1 renminbi = U.S. $0.12.

Source: Hong Kong Trade Development Council/Asian Strategies Ltd, reported in *Setting Up Shop: Retailing in China.* (1996). China: FT Pitman Publishing, Pearson Professional Asia Pacific, p. 94.

TABLE 14.3

China's 50 Leading State-Owned Retail Stores (Ranked by 1991 Gross Sales)

Rank	Store Name	Gross Sales RMB* (1000)	Cost and Expenses RMB (1000)	Net Income RMB (1000)
1	Shanghai Number One Department Store	95,993.78	3,780.65	8,688.38
2	Shanghai Hualian Commercial Building	70,084.79	2,308.79	6,926.99
3	Beijing Xidan Market	68,849.89	2,881.31	6,044.64
4	Beijing Department Store	65,132.62	2,832.84	6,554.74
5	Zhongxing-Shenyang Commercial Building	57,842.00	3,559.00	4,018.00
6	Tianjin Hualian Commercial Building	51,678.45	2,053.00	3,795.11
7	Nanjing Xinjiekou Department Store	48,382.00	1,767.10	3,941.43
8	Wuhan market	47,119.62	2,072.66	3,525.64
9	Harbin Number One Department Store	45,845.00	2,656.00	4,745.00
10	Dalian Market	44,951.02	2,861.20	2,979.41
11	Beijing Longfu Store	42,149.03	2,616.13	3,285.17
12	Guangzhou Nanfang Store	41,605.00	4,412.00	1,617.94
13	Harbin Qiulin Company	40,899.00	1,906.30	4,467.00
14	Nanjing People's Market	36,412.81	1,599.11	2,501.59
15	Tianjin Quanyechang	35,121.49	1,595.33	2,764.48
16	Tianjin Department Store	34,773.96	1,781.11	2,316.39
17	Beijing Dong'an Market	32,725.06	1,077.54	3,386.66
18	Shenyan Joint Operation Company	31,376.58	1,772.91	2,305.19
19	Wuhan Zhongnan Commercial Building	31,100.87	1,423.85	2,140.64
20	Hangzhou Jiefang Road Department Store	30,263.23	1,064.00	2,749.58
21	Beijing Friendship Commercial Group	29,200.00	2,585.00	6,075.00
22	Chongqing Department Store	27,009.89	1,583.54	2,211.82
23	Znongxing-Dalian Commercial Tower	26,562.20	2,284.40	1,456.20
24	Changchun Department Store	25,004.69	1,344.60	2,215.10
25	Zhengzhou Commercial Tower	25,003.00	1,874.00	1,277.00
26	Hangzhou Department Store	24,512.32	1,162.27	1,905.44

Annual Average Employees (Persons)	Annual Average Current Funds RMB (1000)	Business Areas sq. m.	Original Fixed Assets RMB (1000)	Profit	Net Income per Employee RMB	Net Income per sq. m. RMB
3,200	8,994.28	21,540.00	3,067.07	5.11%	2,715.1188	403.3603
2,415	5,738.90	13,500.00	1,365.96	6.59%	2,868.3188	513.1104
2,789	5,737.62	13,000.00	3,765.40	4.59%	2,167.3144	464.9723
3,194	5,512.77	18,000.00	4,870.17	5.71%	2,052.2041	364.1522
3,652	6,953.00	24,000.00	1,829.00	0.79%	1,100.2191	167.4167
1,803	3,631.00	14,000.00	5,061.00	3.37%	2,104.8863	271.0793
2,265	4,902.38	12,000.00	1,470.00	4.49%	1,740.1457	328.4525
2,618	5,843.50	16,557.00	4,048.29	3.08%	1,346.6921	212.9395
3,015	4,101.00	20,000.00	5,336.00	4.56%	1,573.7977	237.2500
3,101	5,038.50	36,000.00	6,173.29	0.26%	960.7901	82.7614
2,586	5,066.00	22,472.00	5,555.56	1.59%	1,270.3674	146.1895
4,267	8,030.00	19,400.00	3,259.00	−6.72%	379.1751	83.3990
1,986	4,014.70	19,200.00	2,429.80	6.26%	2,249.2447	232.6563
2,463	3,721.52	12,000.00	1,552.52	2.48%	1,015.6679	208.4658
2,120	3,052.49	10,639.00	2,542.68	3.33%	1,304.0000	259.8440
2,150	3,187.38	12,674.00	2,232.46	1.54%	1,077.3907	182.7671
1,435	2,469.04	6,000.00	147.01	7.06%	2,360.0418	564.4433
1,962	5,473.99	16,500.00	4,171.90	1.70%	1,174.9185	139.7085
1,923	2,863.28	19,000.00	2,821.39	2.30%	1,113.1773	112.6653
1,310	2,456.07	11,000.00	1,877.53	5.57%	2,098.9160	249.9618
1,756	11,372.00	13,605.00	5,282.00	11.95%	3,459.5672	446.5270
1,330	2,637.22	11,556.00	1,210.94	2.33%	1,663.0226	191.4001
1,869	3,305.20	28,700.00	38.60	−3.12%	779.1332	50.7387
1,650	2,969.20	20,000.00	3,587.00	3.48%	1,342.4848	110.7550
2,147	5,829.00	17,885.00	2,762.00	−2.39%	594.7834	71.4006
1,157	2,383.49	13,000.00	4,717.24	3.03%	1,646.8799	146.5723

Continued

TABLE 14.3

China's 50 Leading State-owned Retail Stores (Ranked by 1991 Gross Sales)

Rank	Store Name	Gross Sales RMB* (1000)	Cost and Expenses RMB (1000)	Net Income RMB (1000)
27	Cjangsha Zhongshan Commercial Tower	24,356.70	1,521.45	1,650.82
28	Wuxi Commercial Tower	24,235.50	1,043.70	1,910.86
29	Guangzhou Xindaxin Company	23,892.50	2,057.20	1,745.70
30	Beijing Chang'an Market	23,700.00	1,647.00	1,549.00
31	Chengdu People's Department Store	23,536.85	1,761.72	1,730.06
32	Taiyuan Tianlong Commerce Trade Corporation	23,515.37	1,517.63	1,668.43
33	Nanjing Market	22,523.10	1,267.40	1,441.29
34	Guagzhou Department Store	22,026.71	2,661.13	1,066.36
35	Dalian Department Store	21,022.00	1,169.00	1,578.70
36	Kunming Department Store	20,980.05	1,399.44	1,458.74
37	Xi'an Minsheng Department Store	20,608.49	1,282.02	1,002.07
38	Shijiazhuang People's Market	20,577.00	1,388.40	1,593.40
39	Tangshan Department Store	20,234.27	1,325.43	1,510.05
40	Jinan People's Market	20,218.00	1,257.60	1,481.90
41	Wuhan Zhongxin Department Store	20,211.49	1,093.19	1,162.75
42	Wuhan Hanyang Department Market	20,090.00	1,216.00	1,033.00
43	Tianjin Market	20,042.99	1,212.13	1,179.36
44	Taiyuan Wuyi Department Store	19,003.55	1,187.14	1,515.66
45	Xuzhou Department Store	18,694.68	1,298.17	1,108.11
46	Wuhan Liuduqiao Department Company	18,453.70	911.00	986.50
47	Mudanjiang Commercial Tower	18,254.00	1,384.00	1,237.00
48	Urumqi Friendship Market	18,003.07	1,331.60	1,446.28
49	Chengdu Department Store	17,656.00	1,305.00	1,178.00
50	Fuzhou Dongjiekou Department Store	17,301.51	1,196.97	1,281.33

**RMB = renminbi; 1 renminbi = U.S. $0.12.*

Source: *Chinese Statistical Yearbook.* (1993). Beijing: China Statistical Publishing House, pp. 262–265.

Annual Average Employees (Persons)	Annual Average Current Funds RMB (1000)	Business Areas sq. m.	Original Fixed Assets RMB (1000)	Profit	Net Income per Employee (RMB)	Net Income per sq. m. (RMB)
1,804	4,345.51	16,500.00	4,091.10	0.53%	915.0887	100.0497
1,474	2,513.98	21,585.60	4,363.22	3.58%	1,296.3772	88.5248
1,900	3,820.40	7,244.00	3,027.00	−1.30%	918.7895	240.9856
1,625	1,610.60	8,800.00	8,742.50	−0.41%	953.2308	176.0227
2,914	4,377.58	21,200.00	400.51	−0.13%	593.7062	81.6066
1,602	3,231.95	30,000.00	4,457.66	0.64%	1,041.4669	55.6143
1,628	2,089.00	11,000.00	3,260.00	0.77%	885.3133	131.0264
2,105	2,245.00	15,000.00	6,602.00	−7.24%	506.5843	71.0907
1,481	1,806.40	13,000.00	1,443.70	1.95%	1,065.9689	121.4385
1,567	3,512.58	10,159.00	1,346.16	0.28%	930.9126	143.5909
1,576	3,438.69	12,823.50	459.95	−1.36%	635.8312	78.1433
1,423	1,786.00	10,300.00	1,865.50	1.00%	1,119.7470	154.6990
1,732	1,745.00	2,000.00	2,856.70	0.91%	871.8533	755.0250
1,795	2,396.00	13,000.00	2,135.00	1.11%	825.5710	113.9923
1,372	2,581.32	8,000.00	904.00	0.34%	847.4854	145.3438
1,348	2,443.00	10,439.00	2,217.00	−0.91%	766.3205	98.9558
1,181	2,842.60	14,270.00	296.75	−0.16%	998.6113	82.6461
1,382	1,646.93	10,200.00	2,208.45	1.73%	1,096.7149	148.5941
1,398	2,093.96	12,500.00	2,525.94	−1.02%	792.6395	88.6488
1,032	2,151.00	4,200.00	321.00	0.41%	955.9109	234.8810
1,652	3,568.00	25,200.00	1,327.00	−0.81%	748.7893	49.0873
1,259	2,573.67	15,000.00	2,260.04	0.64%	1,148.7530	96.4187
1,293	2,917.00	11,000.00	2,812.00	−0.72%	911.0596	107.0909
1,083	1,509.61	8,368.00	438.54	0.49%	1,183.1302	153.1226

Throughout China, many state-owned department stores, specialty stores, and food stores can be found in each of the major cities. The setup of stores is similar. Merchandise is displayed behind counters. In a department store, you may find a counter of sweaters. Sweaters samples are hung up behind the counter, with the actual inventory under the counter. In a specialty store selling light fixtures, samples of fixtures are displayed in a glass display case. Once a consumer makes a selection, the salesperson brings a light fixture out from the storage area. In a food store, cans of peaches are stacked up and displayed behind the counter. If a person is interested in buying a can of peaches, he or she asks the salesclerk for one. These state-owned enterprises have similar customer service, product offerings, and price.

CUSTOMER SERVICE Consumers who want to see a product must request that product from the salesperson; however, crowded stores make it difficult to receive attention from salesclerks. Salesclerks are not compensated according to sales volume, so they have little motivation to serve customers efficiently. As one Chinese consumer told me, "You enter a Chinese store and immediately beg for someone to sell you merchandise; salesclerks do not seem to want to be bothered, they waste time, your time and my time, because they have nothing better to do." In fact, salesclerks were so predictably rude that the state government created a list of phrases that salesclerks are banned from using. A list of these statements is presented in Box 14.1.

Photo 14.3
State department stores used to sell all merchandise behind counters. Much of the merchandise is still sold in this manner. Customers must ask to see a product. Sales employees were held responsible for product losses so they "guarded" merchandise to protect it from customers. *Courtesy of the author.*

BOX 14.1

Service With Some Bile

By Seth Faison

Shanghai—It may be hard for many Americans to imagine under what circumstances a salesclerk might actually say to a customer, "Stop shouting, can't you see I'm eating?" But in China, it is common for clerks to abandon their post without notice, and to ignore —or even insult—customers who happen to come along.

One of the legacies of Communist rule has been atrocious service. For years such workers could justify their laziness by decrying attentive service as bourgeois. They could rest assured they would not be fired for performing badly. Managers, too, had few incentives to motivate their staff to do better.

Now market economics are taking over, and with competition emerging, things are changing, even service. But improving service one step up from bad still leaves the customer with pretty bad.

There is a surplus of pretty bad service in any number of Chinese stores, airports and hotels. But a year ago, as part of a nationwide politeness campaign, the Chinese Government began enforcing a strict policy aimed at reining in the hostility common at the counter. Just a few months ago, it published a list of 50 phrases that are banned from use at any service counter.

"Didn't you hear me, what do you have ears for?" is one such forbidden phrase. "Are you finished talking?" is another. Both hint at the animosity that often erupts at the counter.

If one measure of China's progress toward a functioning economy is a program in which store managers actually demand that their staff be courteous, another is how hard it is to change an old system when the authorities rely mostly on a campaign in the newspapers.

Still, the publication of a list of 50 officially banned phrase offers a clue to understanding how bad service is, rather than a reflection of any genuine effort to improve it.

"Buy it if you can afford it, otherwise get out of here," speaks to the impatience that salesclerks are loathe to hide. "What can I do? I didn't break it," echoes the reluctance to take responsibility for a store's faulty products.

Wang Dao, deputy office director at Shanghai's Number One Department Store, one of the stores chosen to lead the campaign, said: "These phrases were chosen because they are so common. Otherwise why would we pick them?"

A ban on such phrases is unlikely to work in any comprehensive way, since the authorities who are so good at policing dissidents are not yet as strict in the service industry. The Chinese have become inured to political campaigns, too, knowing they must heed them in the short term but that enthusiasm will wane after a while.

So far now, many salesclerks are at least pretending to treat the politeness campaign earnestly.

"It's very serious," said Lin Gan, a 45-year-old salesclerk at the electronics counter in the Number One Department Store. "We're not allowed to stand around in groups of more than two. We're not allowed to fold our arms. And, of course, we have to watch what we say."

One floor down, however, in the men's garment section, six salesclerks were huddled, all arms folded, chatting away while two customers tried to get help.

"Okay, okay, what do you want?" one salesclerk, Ye Ping, said finally, skating close to one of the banned phrases.

"I've been in this store 38 years," said Ms. Ye after the customer left without buying anything. Queried about her attitude, she replied, "I've worked hard all these years. I don't see why we are always asked to do better."

Mr. Wang said his store was serious about the campaign and enforcing it with fines and dismissals.

How many of his 2,000 clerks have been fired since the store began its strict policy a year ago?

"No one yet," Mr. Wang said.

How many have been fined?

"It's hard to give an exact number," he said.

Mr. Wang added hopefully: "Change is not going to come overnight. It's going to take some time."

Continued

Service with Some Bile
continued

Hey, Rude Clerks: No. 49!

In China, store clerks were so predictably rude that the government banned 50 of their choicest phrases:

1. Hey!
2. Old man.
3. Hey, soldier!
4. Country bumpkin.
5. Darkie (refers to dark-skinned Chinese).
6. What does it have to do with you?
7. Who told you not to look where you're going?
8. If you don't like it, go somewhere else.
9. Ask someone else.
10. Didn't you hear me? What do you have ears for?
11. Take a taxi if you don't like the bus.
12. Get out the way, or you'll get killed!
13. That's just the way things are!
14. I don't care whom you complain to.
15. Are you finished talking?
16. If you're not buying, what are you looking at?
17. Buy it if you can afford it otherwise get out of here.
18. Are you buying or not? Have you made up your mind?
19. What are you yelling about? Wait a while.
20. Don't you see I'm busy? What's the hurry?
21. Hurry up and pay.
22. I can't solve this. Go complain to whomever you want.
23. I don't know.
24. I just told you. Why are you asking again?
25. Don't stand in the way.
26. I have no change. Wait here.
27. Why didn't you choose well when you bought it?
28. Go ask the person who sold it to you.
29. If you don't like it, talk to the manager.
30. Time is up, be quick.
31. The price is posted. Can't you see it for yourself?
32. No exchanges, that's the rule.
33. If you're not buying, don't ask.
34. You're asking me. Whom should I ask?
35. Stop shouting. Can't you see I'm eating?
36. It's not my fault.
37. We haven't opened yet. Wait a while.
38. What are you doing? Be quick.
39. I'm not in charge. Don't ask me so many questions.
40. Didn't I tell you? How come you don't get it?
41. I have no change. Go get some yourself.
42. Don't push me.
43. If you want it, speak up; if you don't, get out of the way. Next!
44. Don't talk so much. Say it quickly.
45. Now you tell me. What have you been doing all this time?
46. The busier I am, the more you bother me. How annoying!
47. Why don't you have the money ready?
48. What can I do? I didn't break it.
49. Don't play the fool with me.
50. Get at the end of the line!

Source: Originally published in the *New York Times*, October 11, 1996. Reprinted with permission from the *New York Times*.

In department stores, inventory is held on the selling floor; thus, if a size is not behind the counter it is not available. Most state-owned department stores do not have dressing rooms, so customers are not able to try on merchandise other than outerwear such as coats and gloves. In addition, merchandise is generally not returnable. However, the non-returns policy is flexible. Chinese consumers I talked with said that if the salesperson knows you or if you are a frequent customer and you purchase a defective or unsuitable product they may allow you to return the item. To be competitive, state stores are also beginning to add dressing rooms. In many stores, you will notice a wooden box with a door, often on wheels. This box is a portable dressing room.

Department stores are beginning to offer their own store credit cards, and some stores offer delivery and alterations, but customer service is not a high priority for the state-owned department stores. China, like Taiwan, may require the market entry of Japanese department stores to significantly alter the perception of what constitutes customer service.

PRODUCT Just a few years ago, state-owned stores had to buy products from designated state wholesalers. After the economic reforms, department stores were allowed to buy directly from domestic manufacturers; however, they still cannot purchase imported merchandise directly. State-owned stores are still required to buy products from domestic manufacturers or from government-controlled import/export agencies. Although these import/export agencies are primarily in the business of exporting Chinese products, they may receive a request by a state store to purchase merchandise for the store during their overseas trips. For instance, a few years ago a manager told me that if Number One Department Store decided that it needed some personal computers to sell, it would request that the Light Industries Division of the Import/Export Commission buy some computers for it the next time the division was on a selling trip to the United States. Often these exporters have little product knowledge and resort to purchasing whatever seems like a good buy, rather than the products consumers want to buy. This is particularly true if the state store does not specify brand names and product specifications. A few selected retailers, about four in each of the major cities, are now being given permission to import merchandise directly. Number One Department Store is one of the stores that has been given permission to import on its own.

Compared to the United States or western Europe, the products produced in China's domestic factories are of low quality and unimaginative style. But when the products of joint venture manufacturers are added to this product line, many high priced and high quality products, as well as and low priced and low quality products, are available.

SECURING MERCHANDISE Department stores in the United States and most developed countries employ individuals whose primary responsibility is to procure merchandise for the retail store to sell. These retail buyers are experts in the product area. The retail buyer is considered a profit center for U.S. companies. In most Chinese department stores, there are no individuals whose sole responsibility is to procure merchandise.

In a Chinese department store, merchandise is arranged around hundreds of display counters. At each counter, there is a counter manager and from six to 12 salesclerks. The counter manager selects merchandise for sale at his or her counter. In larger stores, manufacturers' representatives come to the retail store. The store may designate an area for product display. This is like a mini-showroom, where the counter manager examines the samples of merchandise and places orders. In other department stores, the counter manager travels to the manufacturer's facility to select merchandise. In all of the stores where I have conducted interviews, the counter manager's primary responsibility was to sell merchandise and coordinate the activities of the salesclerks; buying merchandise was a secondary responsibility.

It is even more accurate to say that the large stores do not select merchandise, they select vendors. When department store management signs up a new clothing supplier, they set certain sales targets for the prescribed launch period. In premier shopping areas of Beijing, the rent can be as high as U.S. $7 per square meter per day. If sales are good, the excess amount of sales is subject to a commission rate of about 30%. If sales are less than expected, the supplier will be asked to replace products or withdraw from the store. Stores usually do not make an advance payment for merchandise, but agree to pay for the portion of merchandise sold, generally at the end of 30 days. The payment process is actually much slower; three to six months is the average payment period for major state-run department stores. State-run department stores also have strict documentary requirements for garment suppliers. One Hong Kong retailer with operations in China said that the invoices are printed by the government with tracking numbers that work like a U.S. social security number for the IRS.[6] Suppliers need to produce the following documents: business registration, trademark registration, tax registration, and quality control certificate.[7] In a Chinese store, the merchandise is displayed with a yellow and red chart that includes the price and detailed information about where the product was produced. The source of origin is not just for foreign-produced products, but also for products produced in the PRC. The invoice also tells the region in China where the merchandise was produced.

The consignment system, which is quite prevalent in Japan and Taiwan, is also used in the PRC. The purpose for using the system in the PRC is very different from that in Japan, however. In Japan, the system is used so manufacturers can protect the image of their brand. Merchandise is not marked down, which would lessen the prestige of the product. In the PRC, consignment is not used to protect the manufacturer's image, it is just considered a safe method for retailers. In both the PRC and Japan, manufacturers, not retailers, are assemblers of lines of merchandise. When manufacturers determine what merchandise should be offered for sale in a department store, they glean market information.

Currently, the responsibility for determining what merchandise to display in a space falls on the manufacturer. Chinese retailers, like many Japanese retailers, thus serve as manufacturers' showrooms.

As retailers in the PRC become assemblers of merchandise, they will gain market power and become channel captains. Some companies such as Beijing Wangfujing Department Store are working to reduce their dependence on consignment, realizing that taking product risk is the primary way to increase margin. Beijing Wangfujing Department Store does business with 2,000 industrial factories. This merchandise comes from all over China, but primarily from the Beijing area. The store serves both as a retailer and as a wholesaler to smaller companies. Its plans are to have 15 stores throughout the country by the year 2003.[8] In one year, Beijing Wanfujing moved from the fifth-ranking Chinese retailer to become the second; a 53% increase. This was the best performance of any of the top 10 Chinese

Photo 14.4
Typical interior of a PRC state department store. The interiors are dark, and merchandise is displayed behind counters or on metal racks. Stores are being rapidly remodeled; however, even in major cities they still look like this. *Courtesy of the author.*

retailers. I talked with the president of this store in 1997. She is a very impressive businesswoman who is approaching her company's growth very strategically. One of her goals is to train professional buyers for the store and reduce their use of the consignment system.

Because the major department stores all obtain their merchandise from the same suppliers, there is a general feeling of sameness in product offerings. Large retailers in all product areas also serve as wholesalers for products to smaller retailers, further contributing to the problem of similar merchandise.

Merchandise produced in state-owned, or previously state-owned, factories is very reasonably priced. Imported merchandise or merchandise produced in foreign joint venture factories is expensive. Imported merchandise carries high tariffs, even after a series of tariff reduction actions. Imports from Hong Kong fall under the preferential tariff rate, the rates for apparel products range from 60% to 100%. For imports from countries such as the United States, the rates are 90% to 150% for apparel products.[9]

Foreign joint venture manufacturers are allowed to sell some of their production domestically. The amount they can sell depends on their location, but generally they can sell 30% of their output.

PRICING Before market reform, Western observers might have assumed that prices will vary according to store location or store prestige. However, the prices at state stores were nearly identical. Price differences were more of a market aberration—a mistake—than a competitive tool. After the market reforms, state stores began using price as a market tool. State stores have an advantage over joint venture retailers because the state stores pay very low rents, yet have prime locations. Products sold in state stores used to be subject to strict price controls, but as the economic reforms continue, these price controls have largely been eliminated.

Previously, the PRC used a two-tiered monetary system. This type of system was very common in planned economies before market liberalization. In the years before 1995, whenever I went to China, I would trade my U.S. dollars for Foreign Exchange Certificates (FEC). These notes were printed in currency equivalent to the Chinese People's currency, or renminbi (RMB). There were some places such as foreign hotels, fancy taxi cabs, and Friendship stores, where only FEC could be used. Some state-owned department stores had luxury floors, or sections of floors, where products could only be purchased with FEC. You could use FEC anywhere; it was the preferred method of payment. If I took an inexpensive taxi, or purchased merchandise in a regular state-owned store, I could pay in FEC, but I would receive my change in RMB. I could use this RMB to purchase other merchandise in state-owned stores or ride in inexpensive taxis, but I could not use RMB in foreign hotels, or Friendship stores, or to pay for FEC taxis. Also, when I got ready to leave China, I could get U.S. dollars in exchange for my FEC money, but I could not redeem my RMB for anything. This led to several mad spending sprees in the airport shops prior to departure. Just before my trip in 1995, the dual monetary system was eliminated. Now, everything is priced in RMB, there are no foreign-currency-only stores, and all taxis accept RMB.

Price controls are determined on a municipal basis. For instance, Beijing and Shanghai might have different pricing systems based on their local economies and product abundance. This caused me some problems when I first started doing research in the PRC. I would do interviews in Shanghai, finding out about the regulated gross margin requirements, and then go to Beijing, where I would be told something completely different.

Originally, there were 146 products under government price control. In addition, 69 products had a regulated gross margin; that is, the rate was stipulated by the government. Now, except for times of product scarcity, there are no regulated prices or regulated gross margins.

FREE MARKET STORES

The first free market outlets were run by farmers selling their excess production. Originally, farmers had to turn all their production over to the state. Then the government began allowing them to sell any excess production. The term **free market** means that the seller, not the government, is free to set the price.

Gradually, entrepreneurs started to sell other kinds of merchandise such as clothes, footwear, and accessories. The Chinese students I interviewed told me there were only limited types of products they would buy at these early free market stores. They would buy products such as food, clothing, or accessories—items whose quality they could evaluate on the spot. However, they would not buy items such as electronic appliances because if something was wrong with the product, the free market retailer would not stand behind it. This is similar to the risks in buying from street vendors in New York or any major city in the United States. You would probably only buy products whose quality you felt you could evaluate.

At first, free market stores were all mobile units located in various parts of the city. In a few years, however, these stores were allowed in permanent buildings. The government licenses these free market stores and collects taxes on their transactions. To prevent under-reporting of earnings, government "snitches" patrol the area. These people observe sales transactions and use these observations to estimate the actual sales for the shop.

The mobile free market shops are very small. Many are constructed from polypropylene wrap, which is draped over metal pipes. Each evening, merchandise is packed back into cardboard boxes and taken home. A typical shop may sell only men's shirts, in five or six colors, all the same style. The goal of the mobile shop owners is to save enough money to rent a space in an actual building.

The first free market stores purchased their merchandise from special economic zones where joint venture manufacturers produce products for export. The free market retailers I talked to in Shanghai bought their merchandise from Shenzen, an area close to Hong Kong. They would travel to that area by train and bring back as much merchandise as they could carry. All purchases were made in cash, and there were no special allowances or trade credit.

Just a few years ago, free market shops were only allowed in a designated free market street so consumers would not be confused by finding state stores and free market stores side by side. Now, free market stores are everywhere. Before free market stores became so prevalent, they were known for carrying higher quality, more stylish, but higher priced merchandise than that in state stores. Now that most of the PRC retail market is a free market, the caution about buying in a free market does not exist.

SUPERMARKETS

The number of supermarkets in China has risen remarkably in only a few years. In 1993, nothing I encountered in Guangdong, Shanghai, or Beijing deserved that label. In each of these areas, a half-dozen local chains have now upgraded their stores and companies such as Hong Kong's Park 'n Shop, the Netherland's Makro hyperstores, the United States's Sam's Club, and Japan's Jusco have opened operations in China. Carrefour has invested in stores in Shanghai and Beijing.

In 1991, I visited my first state-owned supermarket. It had a casket-type freezer, containing frozen meat. I asked the store manager if many consumers had freezers. He said no, consumers purchased the frozen meat, took it home, and thawed it. Today, supermarkets have frozen food sections, selling ice cream, meats, fish, vegetables, and prepared local foods. In 1997, I noticed a flood of large shops and small shops selling Wall's frozen ice cream bars. These ice cream freezers would be left outside the store, due to a lack of space. On nearly any commercial block, you would encounter one or more of these Wall's ice cream freezers. Later, I found out from a consulting company that the Wall's company gave the retailers the freezers to promote their products. The company has been successful; the product is everywhere.

Exporters from the United States say it is not easy to sell imported merchandise in the PRC. Import duties that are often above 50%, quarantine restrictions that are long and arbitrary, and restrictive import licensing serve as import barriers. Some consumer-ready products find their way into the PRC market through so-called **converters,** individuals or groups who use false invoicing to avoid high duties, bans, and quarantine restrictions.[10]

Starting December 1, 1996, Chinese law began requiring that all food products, both local and imported, have Chinese labels clearly stating the type of food, brand name, trademark, manufacturer name and address, country of origin, ingredients, date of production, and "sell by" date. Foreign languages can also appear on the label, but the Chinese language requirements must be met.

Most Chinese consumers prefer to buy fresh food products. They purchase meat, poultry, seafood, and produce in traditional open-air wet markets. However, all other grocery products and even some of these wet market items are appearing in supermarkets.

In Shanghai, as in other parts of China, the most popular grocery outlets are still the wet markets. Consumers shop daily in the wet market, which is usually about a 10-minute walk from their homes. Prices in the wet markets are

Photo 14.5
Produce section in a traditional Chinese food store. There is no self-service; customers tell salesclerks what they want, and the salesclerks handle the produce.
Courtesy of the author.

lower than those in supermarkets. The first supermarket opened in Shanghai in 1990; by 1995, there were 704, belonging to 20 different supermarket companies. Joint venture retailers such as Carrefour, Yaohan, Park 'n Shop, and Metro are adding sophistication to the entire distribution chain.

Shanghai has a five-year city plan to phase out wet markets and provide incentives to supermarkets to become the primary food retailing points in the city. The city government requires new stores to have produce and meat sections, as well as refrigeration and freezer space. A survey of Shanghai consumers found that 11% shop regularly for groceries in supermarkets. The group that does shop in supermarkets is a higher-income group. Ninety percent of consumers over age 55 said they preferred wet markets. Younger and higher-income consumers said they will shop in Western-style supermarkets to meet their food needs.[11] Chinese households spend 41% of their incomes on food.

A 1995 national survey found that 96% of Chinese living in major cities had refrigerators; only 25% of those living in rural areas had refrigeration. Less than 2 out of 100 people surveyed had a freezer. Microwaves are rare in China, except in major cities. In Guangzhou, 7% of the population owned microwave ovens. However, it is estimated that this will climb to 40% to 50% in the next few years.[12]

Shanghai has one of the most developed series of chain food retailers. Hualian has over 100 stores. Hualian was a state-owned department store that has become a shareholding company. The group has expanded its department store offerings and has moved aggressively into supermarkets. Hualian's major competitor is Lian Hua, another company that is aggressively expanding into supermarkets throughout the city.

FOREIGN RETAILERS IN CHINA[13]

The PRC opened its doors to foreign joint ventures in manufacturing many years ago. But, as I have mentioned before, retailing is considered a nonproductive activity in planned economies. Thus, until 1991, foreign retail joint ventures were not allowed. Initially, the government announced that it would approve a limited opening of its retail sector for foreign investors on an experimental basis. Six cities (Shanghai, Beijing, Guangzhou, Tianjin, Qingdao, and Dalian) and five special economic zones (Shenzen, Zhuhai, Shantou, Xiamen, and Hainan) were designated as areas open to foreign retailers. Only two foreign joint ventures would be approved in each of the 11 areas, for a total of 22 foreign joint ventures with state (Beijing-level) approval.

The initial joint venture regulations included several other stipulations. First, the joint ventures could not be majority or wholly foreign-owned operations. Second, they could not wholesalers. Third, although these state-approved joint ventures could import goods, these goods could not exceed 30% of their total sales. The joint ventures would also be

Photo 14.6
A butcher in a traditional Chinese food store cuts meat directly for the customer. Big slabs of meat hang from hooks, and the butcher carves off what the customer requests. *Courtesy of the author.*

required to pay any quotas and licenses if they imported merchandise. At that time, the two-tiered system of foreign exchange, which I described earlier, was still in effect. As a result, the joint ventures had to generate hard currency to pay for any imports. In effect, retailers would first have to produce merchandise, then export and sell it, to obtain currency needed to pay for imports.

These first 22 state-approved joint ventures were equity joint ventures. In an equity joint venture, the partners share the risk. In Beijing, the Lufthansa Shopping Center and Dong'an Shopping Center are the two state council-approved foreign joint ventures. The Dong'an Shopping Center is still under construction, just across from Wangfujing Department Store. In Shanghai, there are four state council-approved joint ventures because Shanghai encompasses both the city and the Pudan special economic zone. These four ventures are the Orient Shopping Center, Next Age Department Store (Yaohan and Number One Department Store), Shenhua Department Store (Jusco-Japan), and Friendship Store Run Hua (China Resources of Hong Kong). Table 14.4 lists the state-approved joint ventures as of March 1997.

A second type of joint venture is a locally (municipal level) approved joint venture. These ventures, approved by cities such as Beijing, Shanghai, and Guangzhou, have not received approval from the state council. In such cooperative joint ventures, the foreign firm provides all the money and management; the Chinese partner provides the location and local business knowledge. Foreign-capitalized department stores in

TABLE 14.4

China's State Council-Approved Joint Venture Retail Projects, March 1997

	Location	Foreign Party	Chinese Party
Beijing Lufthansa Center	Beijing	Singapore Group	Beijing Friendship Commercial Services Corp.
Dong'an Shopping Center	Beijing	Sun Hung Kai Properties (Hong Kong)	Beijing Dong'an Group
Next Age Department Store	Shanghai	Yaohan International (Japan)	Shanghai Number One Department Store
Orient Shopping Center	Shanghai	Shanghai Industrial Investments (Hong Kong)	Jin Jiang Group
Shenhua Department Store	Shanghai	Jusco (Japan)	N/A
Friendship Store	Shanghai	Run Hua China Resources (Hong Kong)	Hua Lian Department Store
Hualian	Tianjin	Shun Tak (Hong Kong)	Tianjin Hualian Commercial Building; Heping District Construction & Development Co.
Chia Tai International	Tianjin	Chia tai (Thailand)	Tianjin Leader Group
Qingdao Number One Parkson Department Store	Qing Dao	Malayasia Group	Qingdao Number One Department Store Corp.
Dalian International Commercial Center	Dalian	Mycal (Nichii)	Dalian Department Store Co., Ltd.
Hualian	Guangzhou	Hong Kong Broadway Group	Guangdong Commercial Enterprise Group
Longhu Shopping Center	Shantou	Thailand	Tianjin Huddlestonualian Commercial Building; Shantou China Travel Service Co.
Zheng Jia	Guangzhou	Hong Kong	Guangzhou Zheng Jia Enterprise and Trade Development Co.
Qingdao Jusco	Qingdao	Jusco	Qingdao Municipal Logistics Corp.
Wal-Mart	Shenzhen	Wal-Mart (U.S.)	Shenzhen International Trust and Investment Corp.
Wuhan Weilai Central Department Store	Wuhan	Taiwan	Wuhan Central Department Store (Group) Co., Ltd.
Makro	Beijing	Makro (Netherlands)	China Native Products Import and Export (General) Co.
Ito Yokado	Beijing	Ito Yokado (Japan)	China Candy and Spirits (Group) Corp.

Source: Sternquist, personal interviews, March 1997.

Shanghai include Sincere, Shui Hing, Printemps, Wings of Hong Kong, Isetan and Yaohan of Japan, and Sunrise of Taiwan. These businesses do not have approval to import goods and legally must go through a Chinese partner or trading company. However, the state council has ordered the State Administration of Industry and Commerce to withhold business licenses to such joint ventures and to deny their imports entry into the country. In response, local officials have been battling with the state council. These officials want to be able to attract retail foreign joint ventures to their localities.

Of even more importance, the central government has been sending signals that the municipally approved joint ventures are not legal entities, because they were not approved by the central government. Remember, only two joint ventures within each city can have central government approval to date. Shanghai has approved 50 retail joint ventures, which the central government might now consider illegal. Among these ventures, in addition to those previously mentioned, Printemps and Yaohan's Megamart, and Carrefour's cooperative joint venture with Lin Hua. One of Wal-Mart's stores in China is a centrally approved venture; the other is not. The state government conducted a study of these municipally approved joint ventures, the results of which are not yet available. However, it is not likely that the state council will close these businesses down. Although they received only a type of backdoor approval, they have been allowed to operate.

The state council has approved two foreign companies, Makro and Ito Yokado, to develop retail chains. However, the process is still unclear, as the companies will still need to receive individual municipal approval.

The Orient Shopping Center was the first foreign joint venture to open in Shanghai. The store opened at the termination point of an as yet-to-be-constructed subway line. The first time I visited the store, the merchandise was positioned at a very high price point. I saw few customers buying; they came mainly to look. Since then, consumers in Shanghai have benefited from greater disposable income. It also seems to me that the store has positioned itself a bit more downscale, and it now seems to be doing quite well. The Oriental Shopping Center is unique among Chinese department stores. It has buyers for each department. It is not a manufacturer's showroom. There are no leased departments. The merchandise mix is one-third imports from abroad, one-third products produced in foreign joint venture manufacturing facilities in the PRC, and one-third products produced in domestic factories. Like all Chinese department stores, its employees are all full time; however, the store does not generally accept employees sent from the manufacturer. When a new product is introduced, the manufacturer may send employees to provide information, but these comprise only a small part of the store's total sales staff. The store's top floor sells imported luxury goods. All of the sales employees there have college degrees. During my 1997 visit, the training manager took me to that floor and asked the salespeople to explain to me, in English, the fine

Photo 14.7
Large video display panels are found in the center of some major PRC shopping centers. This video display is in the Next Age Department Store, the Yaohan–Number One Department Store joint venture. Yaohan, a Japanese firm, has experienced financial difficulty and, in 1997, sold most of its holdings to the Chinese partner. *Courtesy of the author.*

points of the products they were selling. Although when I had visited the floor the day before, no one had spoken to me in English, but with the training director's encouragement, the salespeople readily demonstrated unexpected talents.

The Number One Department Store–Yoahan joint venture in Shanghai (Pudan area) called the Next Age Department Store, is about as large as Macy's in New York's Herald Square. Actually, the store consists of a variety of stores holding areas leased from Next Age. A major Korean department store, Shinsagae, leases one floor. Another Korean company operates a supermarket, which is located on the top floor. Next Age put the food market on the top floor because the store management thought it would generate the most traffic. People would go to the top floor and would be exposed to the merchandise on the other floors along the way. I think this store has a difficult battle ahead. It is located in a new area, with few wealthy residents. The area will change, but it may be years before Next Age's customer base can support it. In August 1997, reports were beginning to surface that Yoahan would sell all but a very small percentage of its ownership in Next Age Department Store.

The PRC is still formulating the laws regulating foreign retail joint ventures. However, many retailers are eager to enter China's vast market—(so eager they are willing to invest in a country in which such laws have not been clearly determined. Table 14.5 contains a list of some of the foreign retailers now operating in China.

TABLE 14.5

Selected Foreign Retailers in China

Department Stores	Supermarkets	Fast-Food	Other
Seibu	Yaohan	McDonald's	A. S. Watson
Lane Crawford	Wellcome	KFC	Giordano
Jusco	Park 'n Shop	Cafe de Coral	Benetton
Wing On	Daiei	Fairwood	Crocodile
Pacific Concord	Carrefour	Vie de France	Nike
New World	Nichii	Pizza Hut	Theme
Sincere	NTUC Fairprice	Pizzeria Uno	Lacoste
Printemps	Jusco	Yoshinoya	Bossini
Emporium	Makro	Dairy Queen	Walt Disney
Yaohan	Metro	Baskin Robbins	
	Ito Yokado		
	Wal-Mart		

Source: Adapted from *Setting Up Shop: Retailing in China.* (1996). China: FT Pitman Publishing, Pearson Professional Asia Pacific, p. 17.

CONSUMER BEHAVIOR IN THE PRC

Virtually every Chinese person under 25 years of age is a single child, accustomed to having been indulged by his or her family. China's one-child policy has been highly successful in controlling its population. Although women can have more than one child, they pay a high fine and face social ostracism from co-workers. Thus, most second pregnancies result in abortion and eventual sterilization. However, a trend among the newly rich Chinese is to have a second or third child to demonstrate wealth. The penalty for having a second child is different in each municipality. In Shanghai, the fine is three times the annual salary of the mother and father.[14]

The PRC's State Statistical Bureau estimates that monthly household income is about U.S. $1,500 per year. Bear in mind that rent, transportation, utilities, health care, and staple foods are subsidized. In addition, Chinese workers save nearly 40% of their income, more than any other nation except Singapore. Thus, the purchasing power of Chinese consumers is actually two to three times the $1,500, equaling that of consumers in Malaysia or Thailand.[15]

Shopping has become an important social occasion in the major cities of the PRC. Major streets such as Nanjing Road in Shanghai resemble Hong Kong's Golden Mile at night. Families and dating couples stroll the streets window-shopping and responding to street vendors. According to Shanghai

Photo 14.8
This pedestrian bridge is located at the most important four corners of shopping in Shanghai. The street directly below is Nanjing Road. No. 1 Department Store and the new addition to No. 1 Department Store are located here. Several state stores in the area have been privatized and remodeled. *Courtesy of the author.*

Number One Department Store manager Wu Zheng Lin, "People already own washing machines, they are putting their money into buying clothes."[16]

Good packaging materials are not currently available in China. Therefore, commodities are easily damaged. Often the damage rate exceeds 10%.[17] Just a few years ago, I saw clerks in food stores attaching labels to canned goods as they set them on the shelves. Chinese consumers complained about opening a can that says applesauce only to find green beans instead.[18] As a precondition for successful distribution of self-service consumer products, the state of the packaging industry needs to be improved. Consumers need the reassurance provided by high quality packaging. They need to know that the package has protected the product and kept it fresh for their use.

Credit is just beginning to be offered by major retailers, but the credit is offered on a formal, not an informal, basis. Stores are issuing their own credit cards. Joint venture stores typically accept credit cards such as MasterCard and VISA, but state-owned stores deal in cash only. The push to accept credit cards came not because retailers saw it as an opportunity to sell a greater volume of merchandise, but because they viewed the credit cards as a way to capture hard currency. Consumers will benefit from the increased use of credit. As I discussed in Chapter 3, credit allows consumers in less developed countries to purchase the best product for their needs, not simply the products they can afford today.

Photo 14.9
Bicycles are still a major mode of transportation in the PRC. Bicycles are used to transport merchandise from warehouses to the retail stores. *Courtesy of the author.*

CHINA'S RETAIL EVOLUTION

Chapter 3 discussed Saimee's propositions regarding economic development and retail changes.[19] These six propositions were developed to explain the changes in retailing as a country moves from developing to developed (Table 14.6). The PRC is a developing country and, as such, shares many of the characteristics proposed by Samiee. However, the change from a planned to a free market economy alters the situation somewhat. Table 14.6 illustrates how Saimee's propositions can be applied to the PRC today.

Until the 1980s, all merchandise sold in the PRC was distributed through government wholesalers. Even today, nearly all of the imported merchandise comes through government import/export agencies. Until recently, prices were set by the government for all merchandise. Now, price controls remain only for essential products, and the controls are administered by the municipality rather than by the federal government.

Consumers in the PRC have a pent-up demand for consumer products, particularly imported products. This sudden release of purchasing power is not something one would expect to find in a typical developing country. It is

TABLE 14.6

Evaluation of Samiee's (1993) Research Propositions, as Applied to the PRC

Channel/ Retailing Element	Proposition	Application to PRC
Environment	The level of economic development significantly influences the structure of the distribution channels in less developed countries such that:	
	▮ Channels are longer and less efficient	▮ Yes, government wholesaler
	▮ Channels are a major source of employment	▮ No
	▮ Major segments of the population are self-sufficient (e.g., food and apparel)	▮ No, but because of government control
	▮ There is a seller's market in many product categories	▮ Yes, but not because of supply
	Government regulations and controls influence the distribution channels through:	
	▮ Frequent or ongoing price controls, subsidized products, and rationing leading to the presence of black markets	▮ Yes
	▮ Consumers practice forward-buying in hyper-inflationary environments	▮ No hyper-inflation
	▮ Government-supported or -owned distributors and cooperatives	▮ Yes
	Buyers and sellers in the channel know each other well and channel operations are influenced by high-context cultures that impact various aspects of business communications and negotiations.	Yes, there is collusion between producer and retailer
Consumer Characteristics	Consumer characteristics in less developed countries lead to retailers' need for smaller but more frequent purchases from their suppliers, which, in turn, may lead to product and package modification by manufacturers. Typically, the following are expected:	
	▮ Smaller packages of products	▮ No
	▮ Smaller cases containing a larger variety of products	▮ No
	▮ Product modifications to ensure longer shelf life	▮ Just beginning
	▮ Package modifications to ensure safe delivery	▮ Mainly in joint venture stores

Continued

TABLE 14.6

Evaluation of Samiee's (1993) Research Propositions, as Applied to the PRC

Channel/ Retailing Element	Proposition	Application to PRC
	▮ Retailers offer credit to their regular clientele on an informal basis	▮ No
	▮ Shopping is a more important form of social interaction as compared with developed nations	▮ Yes
Channel Characteristics	Channel structures are fragmented and the networks are uncoordinated. The channel is further characterized by:	
	▮ Relatively small institutions	▮ No, large government stores, large joint venture stores
	▮ Channel members are generalists and their functions become more specialized (i.e., separated) with economic development	▮ Yes
	▮ Retail establishments vary in form and functions performed and may cater to a different class of customers as compared with developed nations	▮ Not for state stores
	▮ Limited financial and managerial resources	▮ Yes, for free market stores
	▮ Adoption and popularity of self-service retailing are dependent on the availability of packaged goods and shortage of labor	▮ Packaging, yes; shortage of labor, no
	▮ Limited presence of vertical marketing systems	▮ Yes
Retail and Wholesaling Practice	As compared with developed nations, less developed countries' retailing practices are characterized by:	
	▮ Limited working capital of channel members, particularly retailers	▮ Yes
	▮ Intermediaries typically obtain financing for purchases with no or low interest or carrying charges from suppliers	▮ No
	▮ Dominance of family-owned and -operated firms	▮ No
	▮ Sporadic or routine importing by various channel members	▮ No, except black market from Hong Kong
	▮ Limited vendor loyalty	▮ No, consignment system
	▮ More emphasis on carrying and dispensing bulk or staple products	▮ Yes

TABLE 14.6

Evaluation of Samiee's (1993) Research Propositions, as Applied to the PRC

Channel/ Retailing Element	Proposition	Application to PRC
Channel Communication	Channel communication is characterized by the limited availability and use of print media and various forms of intra-channel promotion;	▮ No
	Numerous brokers and agents are instrumental in the communications process as they expedite transactions, such that:	
	▮ They assist in providing total market coverage	▮ No
	▮ They are specialized by customer/channel member, region, or product	▮ No
Market Research	The following patterns are generally expected:	
	▮ Very little use of formal market information is made by less developed countries' channel members	▮ Yes
	▮ The use of market research increases with greater economic development and the size of the channel member	▮ Still to come
	▮ Less developed countries' retailers typically do not have marketing research departments and seldom use outside suppliers	▮ Yes
	▮ Informal and underground distribution channels play major roles in less developed countries, and this activity is not reflected in official statistics	▮ Yes
Channel Performance	Retail performance is lower than in the developed markets and characterized by:	
	▮ Flexible, but generally low, channel mark-ups	▮ Not flexible for government stores
	▮ The practice of one-price policy increases with greater foreign participation in the distribution sector	▮ No, one price existed before, now more price variability
	▮ Prices, terms of sales, and payment arrangement are negotiable	▮ No
	▮ Low net profit margins	▮ Yes

Source: Adapted from Samiee, S. (1993). "Retailing and Channel Considerations in Developing Countries: A Review and Research Propositions." *Journal of Business Research*, Vol. 27, pp. 103–130.

the result of government relaxation of import restrictions. A seller's market originally existed for imported products, not because of supply but because of government restrictions. Now that nearly every type of product can be imported, prices reflecting tariffs keep demand in line. Those retailers selling imported goods operate on relatively high margins.

In most developing countries, there are few large-scale retailers; however, in the PRC there are many large department stores. Many of these department stores, which are now owned by the state or are in the process of being privatized, originated as foreign retailers confiscated during communist takeover in the 1950s. As Samiee points out in his propositions, in most developing countries there is a dominance of family-owned businesses. This is not so in a planned economy, where the state owns all companies. Likewise, the pricing situation is different. In planned economies, price is set by the state, with little variation. This is in contrast to the flexible pricing system used in developing countries. The state no longer controls price in the PRC. However, the former state stores enjoy lower rent or mortgage costs than do foreign joint ventures.

As Samiee posited, the packaging industry is an important market complementary to self-service. In the PRC, the packaging industry is undeveloped. Much product loss occurs because sufficient packaging is not available. Merchandise is protected from consumers through physical barriers such as counters or salespersons. Joint venture stores are leading the way in packaging innovation.

SUMMARY

The PRC is in the process of liberalizing its retail trade. Until 1991, foreign joint ventures were not allowed in the country. Today, the government is playing a major role in determining how much foreign retail investment it can tolerate. The federal government has approved the establishment of only two joint ventures in each of 11 major urban areas. Municipalities such as Shanghai are also approving retail joint ventures with limited commercial rights. All types of joint ventures face burdens that will make their operations difficult.

A striking contrast can be seen in the ways in which the former Soviet Union and the PRC have approached the challenge of developing a market economy. In the Soviet Union, the political system was changed first, then the economic system. The result has been tremendous hardship, including consumer shortages and inflation. In contrast, the PRC has altered the economic system first, moving toward a free market before leaving the political security of a communist/socialist system. Unlike the former Soviet Union, the PRC has had an abundant supply of merchandise and comparatively low inflation.

An important trade issue currently being debated in the United States is whether to retain most favored nation (MFN) status for the PRC. Most favored nation status is the designation given to the United States's best trading partners. This designation is used largely as a political tool. If the United States uses this tool against China, Hong Kong will suffer. This is because over two-thirds of Hong Kong's exports are re-exports from the PRC. There are so many countries eager to do business with the PRC that the country would likely feel little effect from the removal of MFN status.

It is a unique experience to witness the change of a country from a planned to a free market economy. The PRC has gone full circle: from capitalism to communism in the 1950s; from market planning to the beginnings of a free market in the 1990s; free market to planned and back to free market in only 50 years.

KEY TERMS

cooperatives
converters
free market
shareholding
state-owned stores

DISCUSSION QUESTIONS

1. Why would a government consider retailing a nonproductive activity?
2. The change from guarded merchandise to self-service is an important change in retailing. We think of self-service as a way to reduce expenses; customers help themselves, therefore, a store needs fewer sales employees. However, in the PRC, the change to self-service is not implemented to save money. What advantages do consumers have in a self-service environment?
3. Why would foreign retailers enter a country that has not established joint venture laws?
4. Using Dunning's theory of the eclectic firm described in Chapter 1, can you explain why Japanese retailers have been attracted to the PRC? Why would Japanese retailers be more likely to enter this market than U.S. or European retailers?

ENDNOTES

1. Ho, D., and N. Leigh. (1994). "A Retail Revolution." *The China Business Review*, January-February, pp. 22–27.
2. Xu, B. (1990). *Marketing to China.* Lincolnwood, Ill.: NTC Publishing Co.
3. Hong Kong Trade Development Council Research Department. (1994). *Retail and Wholesale Distribution of Consumer Goods in China.* Hong Kong: Hong Kong Trade Development Council.
4. Hong Kong Trade Development Council Research Department (1994).
5. *China Statistical Yearbook.* (1996). Beijing: China Statistical Publishing House.

6. Interview conducted by B. Sternquist in Hong Kong (March 1997).
7. Hong Kong Trade Development Council Research Department (1994).
8. Interview conducted by B. Sternquist (March 1997).
9. Hong Kong Trade Development Council Research Department. (1995). *Market Report on Wholesale and Retail Distribution of Garments in China.* Hong Kong: Hong Kong Trade Development Council.
10. Rutledge, R., and J. Patmon. (1996). "South China Food Market Overview." FAS Online, AGR No. CH6610. (July 9).
11. *China Food Market Overview.* (1997). Report Code CH9662V, AGR No. CH6810. (March).
12. Rutledge and Patmon (1996).
13. Adapted and reprinted with permission from Sternquist, B., Z. X Qiao, and Y. Chengmin. (1995). "China: The Planned to Free Market Paradigm." *International Journal of Retail and Distribution Management,* Vol. 23, No. 12, pp. 21–28.
14. Faison, B. (1997). "Chinese Happily Break the 'One Child' Rule." *The New York Times,* August 17, p. A1.
15. Goll, S. (1995). "China's Big State-Owned Retail Stores Form New Ventures with Foreign Firms." *Wall Street Journal,* March 13, p. B5A.
16. Goll (1995).
17. Lo, T., O. Yau, and Y. Li. (1986). "International Transfer of Service Technology: An Exploratory Study of the Case of Supermarkets in China." *Management International Review,* Vol. 26, No. 2, pp. 71–76.
18. Interviews conducted by B. Sternquist in the PRC (1992, 1995).
19. Saimee, S. (1993). "Retailing and Channel Considerations in Developing Countries: A Review and Research Propositions." *Journal of Business Research,* Vol. 27, pp. 103–130.

COMPANY FOCUS IV.1

DAIEI

Yung-Fang Chen

History

Daiei, Inc., is the largest retailer in Japan. Its first store opened in front of Senbayashi Station in Osaka in 1957 as a small retail shop selling foodstuffs, sundries, and drugs.[1] In the 1960s, it added perishable foods, clothing, and consumer electronic appliances to its retail line, and began to aim at becoming a general *supa* (superstore). The Kobe-based company quickly expanded the store and became a national chain based on a nontraditional high-volume, low-price strategy.[2] Daiei's style of offering cheap prices, which is based on a narrow margin but quick inventory turnover strategy, has won the support of consumers, thus enabling the company to build 225 general merchandise stores throughout Japan since 1957.[3]

Isao Nakauchi, the founder and chief executive of Daiei Inc., is a living legend in Japanese retail annals. The drugstore that Nakauchi opened in 1957 was modeled after one he had seen in a James Cagney movie.[4] After visiting Sears, Roebuck & Co., he was so impressed by their competitive pricing he decided to treat Japan to American-style discounting. Consequently, he deserves much credit for bringing chain stores with low-cost and good quality merchandise to Japan.[5] Nakauchi is often considered the consumer's champion because he dismisses the argument that Japanese consumers are happy to pay high prices for high quality. He believes that people want to buy daily necessities cheaply, so he offers consumers the best deal possible.[6] Although Nakauchi's fortunes are estimated to be at least $680 million,[7] he has never let up; Nakauchi will not be content until he makes Daiei the most powerful retailer in all Japan.[8]

Strategy

Home Expansion Orientation

One thing that differentiates Daiei from other chain stores in Japan is its home expansion orientation. While many of Daiei's chain competitors are preoccupied with international expansion, especially to the Asian markets such as Malaysia, Hong Kong, and Singapore, Daiei's main focus is at home. The company keeps busy figuring out how to build sales at home and finding ways to expand in Japan.[9] Daiei aims to have 1,200 supermarket chain stores in Japan, or about one Daiei's store for every 100,000 people. Nakauchi also wants Daiei to operate a chain of neighborhood shopping centers. A typical shopping center is featured as a one-story supermarket combined with drug, variety, and other stores. The top management at Daiei opened over 50 outlets of this type for places with a population of between 30,000 and 50,000.[10] Trade press refer to Daiei as "Wal-Marting" Japan.

In 1996, Daiei began plans to open up to 1,000 small supermarkets and convenience stores in the PRC. The stores will be concentrated in Shanghai, Beijing, and Tianjin.

Best Price Strategy

Daiei is challenging retail price maintenance used in Japan. In addition, after a series of mergers, the company has developed far more influence over its suppliers. To provide the best deals to its customers, Daiei has made great headway in taking control of its pricing. A number of price-side moves are designed to position its chain stores as the nation's low price sellers. For example, in a strategic move intended to get ahead of the consumer-driven loop, Daiei has become the first Japanese chain to make a major commitment to Every-Day-Low-Price (EDLP) selling.[11] This price cutting strategy has been successful in cutting into the profits of Daiei's competitors, however, it also cut into Daiei's profits. For the fiscal year ending August 31, 1996, profits for the company fell 82% over the previous year.[12] In another price-side move, Daiei makes use of several private labels in its stores.[13]

Search for Efficiency

Daiei's search for efficiency can be illustrated in two aspects. One is associated with its operation. The other is on the distribution side. Recognizing that more than 50,000 manufacturers in Japan have registered their product codes and marked an approximately 3 million items, Daiei has adopted the same Japan Article Number (JAN) code for all of its merchandise, including clothing.[14] Point of sale technology such as side scanners and automatic checkout devices are used to speed up front-end efficiency. This decreases inventory by tracking what customers really want and improves turnover of products.[15] The improved efficiency in sales and distribution has also contributed to Daiei's declining recruitment. Because of this, Daiei has not increased its hiring of high school graduates.[16] To train its executives in managing the multiunit retail company, Daiei is continuing to recruit newly graduated university students, although at a slightly lower level.[17]

Daiei is an unusual Japanese retailer. The company takes the product risk by bypassing the wholesalers and refusing to accept the manufacturer's suggested prices. Instead, Daiei imports a growing share of its merchandise directly from foreign makers to cut prices. It also opened Japan's first wholesale club.[18] In doing this, however, Daiei is obstructed in many ways. For example, because of government regulations that protect the interests of small shopkeepers, Daiei has found it difficult to swamp small operators by means of fast-turn, low profit selling strategies.[19] The price reform that has taken place at the initiative of Daiei is also hindered by the *tatane* system developed by the Economic Stabilization Board.[20] Matsushita Electric Industrial Co., the powerful consumer electronics maker, refuses to supply Daiei with its electronics products under labels like National and Panasonic because Daiei sold its refrigerators, rice cookers, and color TVs at half price.[21]

Centralized Procurement and Internationalization

With an emphasis on high-volume merchandising, Daiei uses centralized procurement and creates a large-scale, vertically integrated network from producers to its retail stores. To provide shoppers with the best goods at the most affordable prices, the company cultivates suppliers and develops merchandise throughout Japan and around the world. For instance, Daiei told more than 300 of its food-processing suppliers that it expected them to reduce their prices by approximately 1%.[22]

The company has liaison branches in Singapore, London, and New York.[23] Daiei also operates procurement offices in several overseas locations, including Hong Kong, Korea, Taiwan, China, the Philippines, Thailand, Indonesia, Australia, the United Kingdom, and the United States, so that it can ensure supplies of merchandise with good prices and variety.[24] In 1996, Daiei extended its interest to mainland China. Through joint ventures, Daiei plans to invest 13 billion yen (U.S. $110 million) to build a shopping center in the center of Beijing in collaboration with a Chinese partner.[25] Other than this project, there is no indication of any strategic intent for Daiei to open up stores and start selling abroad.

Environmental Consciousness

Approximately 40% of Japan's total plastics output ends up as waste, of which 12% is recycled, 23% is buried, and 65% is incinerated.[26] In response to the increasing customer concern about the environment, Daiei focuses on recycling and offers stamps to be redeemed for discounts to those not requiring shopping bags.[27] To reduce the number of plastic shopping bags, this bag reuse project started in 1991.[28] Daiei's customers can receive 100 yen (U.S. $0.84) shopping coupons by reusing the same bag 20 times or refusing a new bag 20 times. The company has also introduced plastic bags that degrade in sunlight. The evidence indicates that the number of customers using the bag-reduction plan keeps increasing, yet time is still needed to assess its effectiveness.[29]

Strategic Relationships

Daiei and Marubeni

Daiei's close relationships with several manufacturers and big trading houses help the company to lower the costs of product development and distribution. One example includes the major alliance forged between Daiei and Marubeni. Through a strategic cooperation with the trading firm Marubeni, clothing, food, interior accessories, sporting goods, and wrapping material at the Daiei stores will be co-developed by the two companies and procured by Marubeni. With respect to the food business, Daiei uses a Marubeni poultry factory in China to develop products and produce shrimp. Reliance on Marubeni's coffee plant in Brazil, fish-processing plant in Alaska, and stock-raising farm in Australia are also being considered to help streamline distribution costs. In the field of clothing, Marubeni will develop low priced business outfits in China for the new pact with Daiei. In turn, Marubeni will be able to utilize its plants abroad and benefit from Daiei's retail know-how.[30]

Daiei and Excel

In April 1990, Japan's beef import regulations were liberalized. Daiei imports over 14,000 tons of beef annually. To cut costs, the company entered into a joint venture with Excel Corp., the third-largest beef processor in the United States. Through its collaboration with Excel, Daiei is able to jointly raise and process cattle in Kansas. Using Excel's feed-lot operation technology, Daiei secures a supply of low-cost U.S. beef and can produce beef at lower costs than in Japan. This agreement enabled Daiei to import enough cattle to supply beef for all Daiei's outlets through Japan.[31]

Daiei opened a meat specialty store called Kansas City that is intended to dominate the market segment partial to Western meats.[32] It will offer a wide selection of American-style beef and other Western meats at competitively lower prices. The typical price for the popular cuts sold at this store is 20% lower than that of other supermarkets. Kansas City occupies 7,500 square feet (700 square meters) in the basement of a large Daiei retail complex in Kobe. The meat store is decorated with a Western atmosphere using figurines of cattle, lots of woods, and female employees dressed as cowgirls. The store's logo features the image of a bull, the Kansas state flag, and other flags to remind consumers that many of the products are imported.[33] At this store, beef dominates sales; 40% of the beef is from the United States and of that, 70% actually comes from Kansas. Another 40% is imported from Australia, and the remaining 20% is sourced domestically. In addition to meat, Kansas City also offers wine, spices, and other accompaniments.[34]

Marketing

Pricing Strategy—EDLP

The pricing strategy in terms of EDLP differentiates Daiei from the other competitors. Daiei's competitively low price is realized through the company's centralized procurement systems, international sourcing, and direct purchase from makers. At some Daiei stores, Roman letters claiming EDLP were hung to remind customers of Daiei's low prices. Nakauchi believes that Daiei must have low prices in order to meet consumers' demands, and that Daiei's use of EDLP can gradually change the Japanese distribution system to an American-style distribution system.[35]

As the domestic demand for imported products has increased, Daiei has decided to import more products into Japan. Following the relaxation of rules governing large stores by Japan's Ministry of International Trade and Industry, Daiei put more U.S. products, ranging from Kansas beef to Coleman outdoor goods, on its shelves.[36] Daiei also opened special departments of 100 square yards (9.3 square meters) within its supermarket stores in Chiba, primarily to sell imported European goods.

Daiei is a pioneer in selling private label products at cut-rate prices. A large amount of its floor space is devoted to display these items.[37] Again, Daiei's aim in creating store brands is to boost demand by lowering prices. Currently, the exclusive private labels at the Daiei stores include Kroger, under licensing agreement with the U.S. retailer.

Store Formats

Daiei became a big discounter in Japan by directly managing its sales floors and by buying products made in China.[38] Daiei introduced men's suits priced in the range of 20,000 to 30,000 yen (U.S. $170 to U.S. $250) at the end of 1993. In addition, its discount food retailing is usually under the Hyper Mart and Topos banners (food and general merchandise units) and Big-A box stores.[39] A box store is a no-frills retailer selling merchandise in boxes on pallets. Daiei started Big-A as an experiment without providing full lines of merchandise. As a chain of 50 box stores in Tokyo, Big-A offers food sectors at provocatively low prices for the consumers. The success of Big-A demonstrates the Japanese consumer's desire for discounting retailing.

Department Stores, Convenience Stores, and Restaurant Chains

Daiei pays a franchising fee and a royalty based on store turnover to the French department store chain Printemps. Three Au Printemps department stores have opened to date, and Daiei uses its French partner's expertise in store layout, merchandise display, and management. Daiei's convenience store operations include 4,100 units under the Lawson banner and a few under the Sun-Chain banner. Restaurant chains are also operated by the Daiei group through franchising with Wendy's and Big Boy of the United States.[40]

Wholesale Membership Club

Daiei opened the first wholesale membership club store in Japan in Kobe in October 1992.[41] The choice of the store's name, Kuo's, was inspired by Wal-Mart

Stores' use of the Sam's Club name, which derives from the name of its founder, Sam Walton. Likewise, Kuo is an alternative pronunciation of the written character Isao, Nakauchi's first name in the Japanese language. Kuo's is a full-scale membership club in Japan and an extremely new business format to both its operator and the Japanese consumers. The focus of product selection in the club is on branded merchandise, and the store format closely follows American-style membership clubs.

About 146,000 people joined the membership in its first year.[42] A qualified member pays a $28 annual fee plus a one-time sign-up charge of about $4 to cover the costs of card insurance.[43] The biggest draw of the club store is the prices charged on its products. The club offers up to 80% discounts on everything from Coach bags to refrigerators to salad oil.[44] Because the wholesale club concept is virtually unknown to the public, Daiei intended to limit the club rollout to approximately 10 stores and see what the outcome would be after a year and a half or 18 months.[45] Meanwhile, the company planned to promote the club membership to its Orange Membership Card holders. The Orange Member Card is Daiei's in-house credit card, which can be used at all of the 219 retail outlets operated by Daiei under its own banner in Japan.[46]

Conclusions

Daiei is in the midst of a major restructuring program designed to separate its retail and non-retail operations. The objectives of this five-year plan are (1) to revamp the company's financial structure, (2) to establish new management systems, and (3) to efficiently administer subsidiaries and group companies.[47] In other words, this plan enables the top executives to pick strategically critical problems and examine almost every existing store in the group. The Daiei group is considering its centralized management style, and horizontally decentralized management is being suggested as Daiei continues to stretch into businesses other than retailing operations such as real estate and finance.

Daiei will need to broaden its appeal beyond price. Uniqueness and quality of merchandise, personalized services, convenience and/or appearance, and presentation of products are also important elements to consumers of each niche market. For example, in emphasizing low price offering at its supermarkets, Daiei should use more supportive advertisement to educate and reinforce consumers about its marketing uniqueness such as EDLP and distinctively imported products. Finally, differentiation and upgrading of the tone and content of the company's advertising and appropriate use of media should be carefully selected if different market segments are targeted.

DISCUSSION QUESTIONS

1. Daiei's alliance with Marubeni lowered product development and distribution costs. Considering the various locations of Marubeni's plants, discuss how the lowered costs are possible.
2. Daiei has aggressively introduced private label products into its stores. The company hopes to have an even larger percentage of product sales come from private label goods. Suggest some brand image management strategies that could help Daiei achieve this goal.
3. What are the advantages and disadvantages of centralized management versus a horizontally decentralized management system for the Daiei company?

ENDNOTES

1. Yamagiwa, K. (1993). "Middling Through; Distribution Reform Is Stuck Halfway." *Japan Update*, December, pp. 10–11.
2. Johansson, J. K. (1990). "Japanese Service Industries and Their Overseas Potential." *Service Industries Journal*, Vol. 10, No. 1, pp. 85–119.
3. Daiei Company Report (1993).
4. Smith L. (1985). "Japan's Autocratic Managers." *Fortune*, January 7, Vol. 111, No. 1, p. 59.
5. Holden, T. (1991). "A Retail Rebel Has the Establishment Quaking." *Business Week*, April 1, (3206), pp. 39–40.

6. Wagstyl, S. (1989). "Japan's Master of Retailing." *World Press Review,* January, No. 1, p. 52.
7. Wagstyl (1989).
8. Holden (1991).
9. Merrefield, D. (1992a). "Japan's First Full-Scale Club Planned." *Supermarket News,* August 10, p. 6.
10. Aizawa, Y. (1993). "Daiei Founder Recasts Expansion to Secure Future of Retail Giant." *Nikkei Weekly,* October 18, p. 1.
11. Merrefield (1992a).
12. "Daiei Finds New Price Slashing Cuts Both Ways." (1996). *Nikkei Weekly,* October 21, p. 9.
13. Merrefield (1992a).
14. "JAN Source Marking Becomes the Vogue in Apparel Industry." (1991). *Office Equipment and Products,* April, p. 34.
15. Merrefield (1992).
16. "Supermarkets, Stores Halve Recruitment for '94." (1993). *Nikkei Weekly,* November 15, p. 12.
17. "Tight Job Market For '94 Grads." (1993). *Nikkei Weekly,* October 11, p. 3.
18. "Japan Shops the Wal-Mart Way." (1993). *The Economist,* February 6, Vol. 326, No. 7797, pp. 67–68.
19. Merrefield (1992a).
20. Yamagiwa (1993).
21. Sterngold, J. (1994). "An Untraditional Retailer in Japan Is on a Roll and Gains Influence." *New York Times,* March 14, p. D4.
22. "Daiei Demands Price Reductions From Suppliers Before Merger." (1993). *Nikkei Weekly,* December 6, p. 10.
23. Johansson (1990).
24. Daiei Company Report (1993)
25. "Japans Einzelhandel has China im Visier." (1992). *Narchrichten fur Aussenhandel,* August 10, p. 5.
26. "Plastic Waste Seen Being Applied to Power Generation." (1991). *Japan Chemical Week,* January 24, p. 5.
27. "Wrapped in Environmentalism." (1991). *Washington Post,* April 23, p. D1.
28. Ishihara, Y. (1991). "Stores Eye Recycling, Reuse of Bags to Help Conservation." *Japan Times Weekly International Edition,* March 25–31, Issue 12, p. 15.
29. Ishihara (1991).
30. Matsuzaka, T. (1994). "Daiei, Marubeni Forge Major Alliance." *Nikkei Weekly,* February 21, p. 10.
31. "Daiei, US Firm Will Join to Raise Cattle in Kansas." (1990) *Asian Wall Street Journal Weekly,* August 27, p. 6.
32. Dowdell, S. (1992). "Corralling Japan's Meat Market." *Supermarket News,* October 5, p. 43.
33. Dowdell (1992).
34. Dowdell (1992).
35. Merrefield (1992a).
36. Holden (1991).
37. Bivins, J. (1988). "Japan: Land of Contradictions." *Chain Store Age Executive,* March, Vol. 64, No. 3, pp. 14–18.
38. "Daiei to Sell Low-Priced Men's Suits." (1993). *Nikkei Weekly,* April 5, p. 10.
39. Merrefield (1992a).
40. Merrefield, D. (1992b). "Japan's Pricing Pioneer, Daiei: Chain Is Taking Everyday-Low-Price Approach." *Supermarket News,* October 5, p. 1.
41. "Daiei Opens Kuo's, Japan' 1st Club." (1992). *Discount Store News,* October 5, p. 1.
42. Thornton, E. (1994). "Revolution in Japanese Retailing." *Fortune,* February 7, pp. 143–146.
43. Merrefield (1992b).
44. Thornton (1994).
45. Merrefield (1992b).
46. Merrefield (1992b).
47. Aizawa (1993).

COMPANY FOCUS IV.2

SOGO

Yung-Fang Chen

Sogo was established in 1830 and incorporated in 1919. Department store operations are the core business of this Japanese company, accounting for 75% of revenues. Wholesale business, wholesaling of clothing, sundry goods, household goods, and so on, account for 14% and other operations, the remaining 11%.[1] The company had a $37 million loss in 1995 but regained profitability in 1996.

Organizational Structure and Philosophy

Sogo uses a centralized management style for all of its stores. Its largest shareholder, Hiroo Mizushima, a former International Bank of Japan executive and legal scholar, accounts for 5% of equity and essentially controls the company.[2] President Hiroo Mizushima's most important management strategy is to "build a retail behemoth"[3] and to "aim to reign supreme in all districts that it enters."[4]

Such a strategy perhaps originated during Sogo's early years, when as a young department store, it was pitted against traditional giants such as Mitsukoshi and Isetan. President Mizushima believes that every new Sogo store must have the largest floor space in the area it is serving in order to overwhelm its rivals. This strategy makes Sogo "more like a shopping mall than a traditional department store,"[5] and explains why all of its outlets are major-scale department stores of over 10,000 square meters (108,000 square feet) and why the average floor space of all Sogo stores (including those in the planning stage) is around 18,000 square meters (194,000 square feet).[6]

The company expands overseas as quickly as possible targeting the international retail markets that are not covered by the established companies. Sogo's expansion pace during the 1980s was extremely rapid. It opened up 25 stores in the United States, Europe, and Southeast Asia in this period. The company has since slowed its pace and even closed several international locations.

Merchandising Mix and Sales Breakdown

A breakdown of the merchandise sales for Sogo's major three stores located in Japan reveals that Sogo's apparel sales account for 41%, food comprises about 20%, followed by variety goods (including cosmetics, sporting goods, jewelry, and timepieces) at 15%, personal effects products at 11%, household utensils (including furniture, carpets, and curtains) at 10%, restaurant and tea shops at 2%, and others at 1%.[7] Because Sogo considers women's apparel, food, and home furnishings as its major profit generators, the company plans to devote more retail space to these items in the stores. In particular, it plans to merchandise women's apparel on more floors to give it additional emphasis.

Compensation and Employees

Unlike such rivals as Seibu, Takashimaya, or Mitsukoshi, Sogo is short of so-called asset-based advantages associated with innovative, unique products or a prestigious store image that can be used to obtain market power. Nor is it strong in its transaction-based advantages with respect to information systems or volume buying that can help it enjoy economies of scale. Nevertheless, Sogo demonstrates a superior performance in its low level of selling, and general and administrative expenses, which, in turn, are reflected in its low level of wages and salaries. As an example, in fiscal 1989, Sogo's payroll was equal to 7.5% of sales, which was far lower than the average of 9.6% for the seven other major department stores including Seibu, Mitsukoshi, Takashimaya, Daimaru, Marui, Matsuzakaya, and Isetan. In addition, the wages Sogo paid to its regular employees were 3% lower than the simple average for the other seven department stores. If part-timers are included, its average payroll was 15% lower than those of its rivals.[8] Three major factors have contributed to Sogo's lower payroll burden. One is associated with a higher dependence on sales personnel sent from its suppliers. It is even said that Sogo has been able to open up to three stores a year because it relies on suppliers for inventory and sales personnel to a much greater extent than any other Japanese department store group.[9] Another factor is directly tied to its gradual shift to part-timers, which has a tremendous impact on payroll burden. The third factor is related to the swift pace of new store openings. This is because more regular employees are sent to the new associate stores in the group than is the case with its rivals.[10] As a result, it is not surprising to find that Sogo's sales productivity per employee is higher and more efficient than its rivals. This efficient manpower management seems to work well to help offset the company's relatively low gross profit levels.[11]

Reasons for Overseas Expansion to Southeast Asia

In addition to President Mizushima's personal ambition, Sogo's enthusiasm for overseas expansion can be attributed in part to the limitations placed on the opening of new stores in Japan under the controls of the Large-Scale Retail Store Law. The fierce competition from the other major department stores, increasing challenges from specialty shops, and a possibly saturated home market are also impetuses that are pushing Sogo to expand internationally. International expansion provides a less restrictive market for the company's growth. Another benefit of overseas expansion derives from the much lower initial costs involved in running the overseas stores as compared to those in Japan.[12] In addition, because it lacks significant ownership advantages, Sogo will be in a more advantageous position if it expands to less developed countries where it can have locational advantages in terms of cultural and geographical proximity, first-mover advantages, lower costs of land and labor, unmet consumer demands, and site availability in those countries.[13] Meanwhile, in response to Asia's growing ranks of middle-class consumers, Sogo, along with many other Japanese retailers, has rushed to enter this area.

Current Operations in Southeast Asia

Hong Kong's geographical location as a major trading and financial center, coupled with a favorable taxation system, attracted Sogo to expand there in 1985. The Sogo Department Store in Hong Kong is highly popular and is considered likely to demonstrate an appeal to a broader market. Sogo makes extensive use of concessions at its stores in order to boost its image and fashion. Consumers in Hong Kong can therefore can find concessions by Chanel, Gucci, Dunhill, and Pierre Cardin on Sogo's ground floor.[14]

Sogo opened its first store in Singapore in 1986, in the center of the city. In July 1993, the company opened another small department store, Tampines Sogo, with 5,400 square meters (58,000 square feet) of floor space in the Singapore suburb of Tampines. This is the core outlet in the DBS Tampines Buildings, an eight-story structure.[15] Sogo is improving and remodeling this store in an attempt to upgrade the store's image and merchandise. The remodeling will change Sogo from a general retailer to a specialty store.[16] Along with vigorous inventory and cost controls, in Singapore Sogo adopts centralized management by developing strategies associated with a unified merchandise selection, pricing policy, interior design, and advertising to appeal to the target audience.[17]

Through a joint venture, Sogo established strong ties with its Taipei partner, Pacific Construction, and made its debut in the Taiwanese market in November 1987.[18] Because Pacific Construction provided the land and 51% of the building and start-up costs,[19] the initial operating costs involved in opening the Pacific Sogo Department Store in Taipei were very low. In Taipei, Sogo developed a unified merchandise style and amiable shopping environment to appeal to young, affluent consumers. In addition, rather than a hodge-podge merchandising mix, only 20% of floor space was handed over to specialty boutiques and cosmetic counters, according to Roy Wang, vice-general manager of Pacific Sogo.[20] After the gleaming 12-story, 300,000-square-foot (28,000 square meters) Pacific Sogo opened on Taipei's newly fashionable Chung Hsiao East Road, consumer response outpaced the company's most optimistic projection—a target that had been projected to take three years but turned out to break even before the end of its first year.[21]

Sogo's success has shocked not only many of the domestic department store sectors, especially those in Taipei, but has also forced locals to relearn their business.[22] For example, taking defensive strategies, many local companies have signed management contracts or joint ventures with other Japanese retail groups such as Tokyu, Mitsukoshi, and Isetan to help them modernize their displays, businesses, and operations in the Japanese way.[23] Furthermore, reacting to intense competition from Sogo, the Far Eastern Department Store, Taiwan's biggest department store, has begun revamping its outlets, changing its merchandising mix, repositioning itself, and pursuing a major expansion program. Not only has Far Eastern refurbished its existing stores, but it also has extended its business through new store openings in cities other than Taipei, and through completion of Far Eastern Plaza, which contains a department store, office tower, hotel, and luxury apartments.[24]

Lured by the growing affluence of the Southeast Asia region, Sogo recently announced a venture valued at 1 billion ringgits (U.S. $379 million) with the Malaysian Government. A part of this project was expected to be a giant department store.[25] In Thailand, where real incomes are lower, the Sogo Department Store adjusted its sights downward from the middle- and higher-income market segment that it would normally target. However, because of the rapid development of suburban areas in the northern and northeastern sections of Bangkok, large number of middle-class residents are moving away to the suburban locations. This is bad news for Sogo, with its city center location. Another obstacle troubling the Sogo store is Thailand's prohibitive tariff rates. These high tariffs have forced Sogo to develop entirely new supply networks. Often, however, the locally manufactured consumer products are not of the same quality as the Japanese products usually sold at its stores.[26]

In Indonesia, under the foreign investment laws, Sogo's participation is limited to a technical-assistance agreement with a local company, Sogo Lestari Indonesia, through which it licenses its name and concept to that company and provides only technical advice. Currently, in Jakarta, the verb "to sogo" is equivalent to "to be overcharged."[27] On the other hand, the Indonesian retailers have opposed the entry of Sogo because they believe it is likely that Sogo will buy back the local store if the Indonesian market is deregulated.[28]

Current Marketing Strategies

Facing a financial trauma, Sogo is slowing down its pace of expansion "as a result of changed economic circumstances," according to Terumori Ashida, a Sogo executive director. Sogo is attempting to cut back on capital expenditures by reducing the number of planned new store openings and forgoing renovation of existing properties.[29] However, the goal of being "Japan's number one department store" remains.

To achieve this goal, the company is continuing to double the capacity at its Causeway Bay store in Hong Kong with the goal of making it the biggest department store in that area. Two new Asian openings, one in Kuala Lumpur and another at Tampines, a new town in Singapore, are also planned, although Sogo has halted its planned entry into mainland China. To boost margins, the company will be enhancing the private label brands sold in the Sogo stores while simultaneously cutting back on rented floor space to a level more in line with its overseas stores, where Sogo now controls 70% of the floor space.

One approach that is especially different from many of its competitors is Sogo's decision not to slim down the numbers or types of products it offers at its stores. Sogo's Ashida explains the reason, "We need to remain one-stop shops. When a department stores loses that special characteristic, it will be all downhill from there."[30]

Sogo launched its own brand, Sogo original products, in 1995.[31] Sogo original has a low price line and another line for stylish products. Over 3,000 types of Sogo originals were launched. This was a big departure for a retailer that had relied nearly exclusively on consignment sales. Sogo had a devastating year in 1995, although it is unclear whether this was related to the introduction of the company's private label.

DISCUSSION QUESTIONS

1. List and discuss the "push" and/or "pull" factors that preceded the expansion of Sogo into international markets.
2. Has Sogo's expansion followed what we would predict using Dunning's theory of the eclectic firm (Chapter 1)?
3. In Chapter 12, I discussed the Japanese practice of having manufacturers send sales employees to work in retail stores. Sogo uses this system quite a lot. In this company focus, you learned one of the positive effects of this system—reduced overhead costs for the retailer. What are some of the negative features? Are these negatives of greater or lesser importance in a foreign country?

ENDNOTES

1. *Japan Company Handbook.* (1996). Tokyo: Keizai, Inc.
2. "FF Analysis: Sogo Company Report." (December 15, 1989). Merrill Lynch Markets in *Investext* [Database on CD-ROM]. Foster City, Calif.: Information Access.
3. Friedland, J. (1993). "Sogo's Woes: Japanese Retailers Pay Price of Rapid Expansion." *Far Eastern Economic Review,* April 15, Vol. 156, No.15, p. 64.
4. Maruki, T. (1991). "Overseas Expansion by Japanese Retailer Picks up Momentum." *Tokyo Business Today,* May, p. 42.
5. Friedland (1993).
6. Maruki (1991).
7. *Japan Company Handbook* (1993).
8. "FF Analysis: Sogo Company Report" (1989).
9. Maruki (1991).
10. "FF Analysis: Sogo Company Report" (1989).
11. "FF Analysis: Sogo Company Report" (1989).
12. Sternquist, B., and T. Ogawa. (1993). *Internationalization of Japanese Department Stores.* East Lansing: Michigan State University.
13. Sternquist, B. (1997). "Internationalization of Japanese Department Stores." *International Journal of Commerce and Management,* Vol. 7, No. 1, pp. 57–73.
14. McGoldrick, P. J., and S. S. L. Ho. (1992). "International Positioning: Japanese Department Stores in Hong Kong." *European Journal of Marketing,* Vol. 26, No. 8/9, pp. 61–73.
15. "Sogo to Open Second Singapore Outlet." (1993). *Nikkei Weekly,* July 19, p. 10.
16. "Sogo Upgrading Its Singapore Stores." (1996). *Business Times* (Singapore), August 22, p. 5.
17. Goldstein, C. (1988a). "The Bargain Hunters." *Far Eastern Economic Review,* May 26 , Vol. 140, No. 21, pp. 82–84.
18. Tanzer, A. (1990). "Selling the Japanese Way of Life," *Forbes,* September 3, pp. 58–60.
19. Goldstein (1988a).
20. Goldstein, C. (1988b). "Local Under Pressure to Upgrade Outlets." *Far Eastern Economic Review,* May 26, Vol. 140, No. 21, pp. 84–86.
21. Goldstein (1988a).
22. Goldstein (1988b).
23. Goldstein (1988b).
24. Einhorn, B. (1992). "Far Eastern Department Store: Taking on the Japanese." *Asian Business,* June 28, No. 6, p. 8.
25. "Japan's Retailers Look to Southeast Asia, Lured by Growing Affluence of Region." (1991). *Wall Street Journal,* May 20, p. A12C.
26. Goldstein, C. (1988c)."Free-Spending Japanese Boast Superstore Sales," *Far Eastern Economic Review,* May 26, Vol. 140, No. 21, pp. 84–85.
27. Friedland, J. (1992). "Sogo, So Good: Invisible Hand." *Far Eastern Economic Review,* February 20, Vol. 155, No. 7, p. 50.
28. Davies, K. (1993). "The International Activities of Japanese Retailers." In *Proceedings of the 7th International Conference on Research in the Distributive Trades.* Stirling, Scotland: University of Stirling Institute for Retail Studies, pp. 574–583.
29. Friedland (1993).
30. Friedland (1993).
31. "Sogo Heading to Low Price Products." (1995). *Commercial Times,* March 22, p. 35.

Part V Regionalization and Internationalization of Retailing

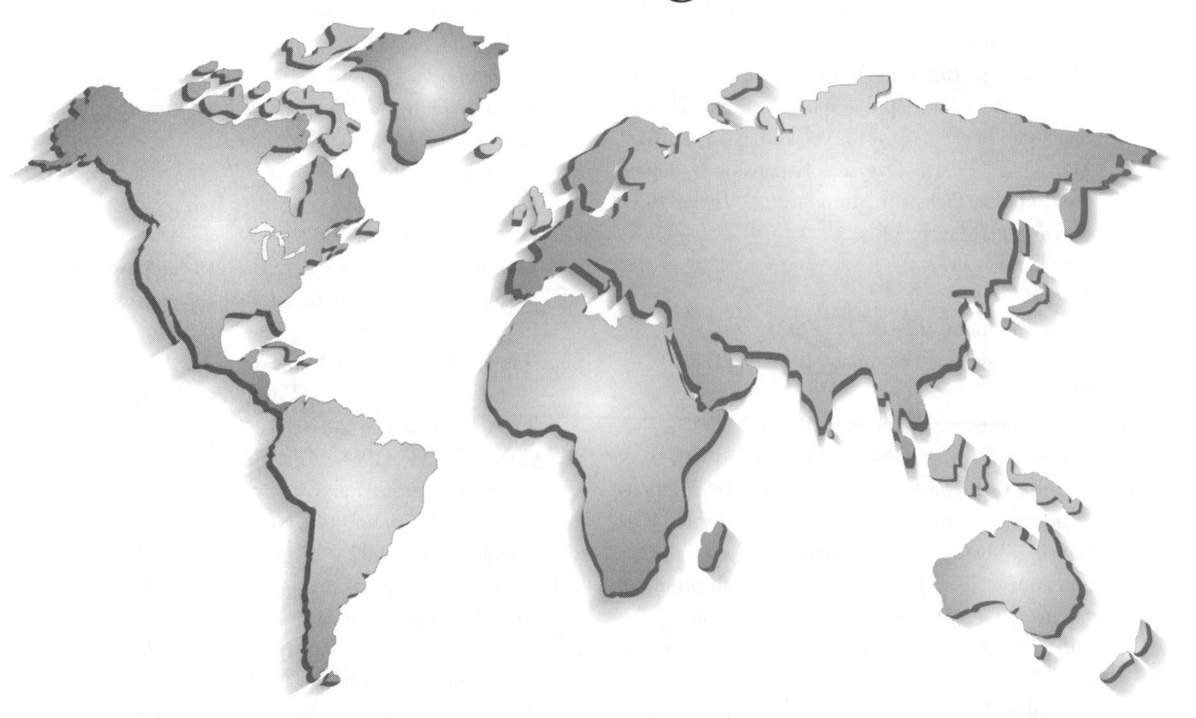

This section consists of a single chapter, entitled "Prognosis for the Future," along with two final company focuses. The concepts presented in this final chapter are not new. The first five chapters of this book presented concepts and theories that are used here to construct a framework for predicting (1) those retailers that will internationalize, (2) where they will internationalize, and (3) how the pattern of internationalization might vary based on the experience of the retailer.

The macro-marketing environment introduced in Chapter 1 forms the basis for Dunning's locational advantages. Dunning's ownership advantages represent the basic reasons why companies pursue international expansion. International culture and human behavior, the topic of Chapter 2, also influences whether a company can adapt to a variety of locations. Multinational companies, one of the two expansion types described initially in Chapter 1, choose to adapt to cultural differences, unlike the second expansion type, global companies, which expand using their standard format.

Risk is a concept introduced in Chapter 4, on licensing and strategic alliances. When handled directly by a company, international expansion provides great learning. A portfolio of methods for handling situations emerges, giving the retailer tools for further adaptation and expansion. Direct exposure provides the greatest learning, but also presents the greatest financial risk.

Chapter 15 presents the strategic international retail expansion (SIRE) model to join these theories. In using this model, an important first step is to watch and observe whether predicted types of actions occur. It is important to take a medium- to long-term view, as the expected short-term results of some types of expansion will look very positive, but after the initial depletion of resources, the effects may not be as positive.

At the end of Chapter 15, I identify five countries for which I predict an interesting retail future. I consider these five to be countries to watch. In each country, a macro-environmental change is altering the retailing environment, opening up opportunities for future internationalization.

Two final company focuses are presented at the end of Part V. The first focus is a profile of Coles-Myer, the leading retailer in Australia, and the dominant company in a variety of retail formats there. It is an excellent example of a company that, by staying in the home market, has dominated its home turf. Coles-Myer's expansion to New Zealand, described in this focus, is a predictable step, according to the SIRE model. The second focus describes IKEA, the international furniture retailer. IKEA is often used as a textbook example of a global company. It has been very strategic in its expansion, carefully evaluating and researching markets before entry.

PEPSI
CỬA HÀNG
BÁNH KẸO ĐỒ HỘP RƯỢU BIA
NƯỚC GIẢI KHÁT. MỸ PHẨM
177 NG VĂN TRỖI Q.PN
PEPSI
SÁP ĐEN 1BC
PEPSI
PEPSI
177
Heineken
333
Heineken
333
Tiger
Heineken
Tiger
Schweppes
333

15

Prognosis for the Future

After reading this chapter, you will understand:

- How to apply Dunning's theory of the eclectic firm, stages theory, and risk theory to predict retailers' methods of international expansion.
- Why franchising and licensing arrangements, although methods for rapid growth, dissipate retailers' ownership advantages.
- Why retailers would select a global versus multinational method for internationalization.
- Where the attractive new markets for international expansion are located, and what market characteristics make these areas attractive to international retailers.

THIS CONCLUDING CHAPTER pulls together many of the concepts and theories introduced earlier in this book to provide a model for analyzing and predicting patterns of internationalization by retailers. Some of the content presented in the first part of this chapter reiterates or expands on content included in Part I of the book, particularly Chapter 1. This restatement of key concepts and theories is necessary to build the framework for the analysis presented here. The final part of the chapter identifies five countries that I believe will be key markets for future international expansion efforts, as well as specific retailers who are already taking the first steps to enter these markets. The model of strategic international retail expansion (SIRE) presented in this chapter should help you develop your own prognosis for the future of international retailing.

INTERNATIONALIZATION OF RETAILING[1]

Several trade and academic journals have devoted special issues to the topic of the internationalization of retailing. These issues often begin with a discussion of what constitutes retail internationalization. Does retail internationalization exist when a retailer agrees to allow a foreign retailer to operate under its name in a licensing agreement? Does it exist when a retailer begins to source from international vendors? An important distinction in the discussion was made by Pelligrini,[2] when he developed a scheme to explain paths for growth. Pelligrini identified the search for growth to be related to (1) an attempt to extend the application of a firm's proprietary know-how to extract the implied rents, and for (2) an attempt to optimize the scale of operations (economies of scale) or the mix of operations (economies of scope) to reduce costs and increase efficiency. He makes the point that while these actions can be proactive, they can also be reactive.

In this chapter, I will consider only the strategic internationalization of retailing. By this I mean that a retailer purposely considers internationalization options as a part of its overall market expansion strategy. By this definition, international sourcing would not be a part of the strategic internationalization of retailing. However, the retailer who allows a foreign retailer to license its company name would be making a strategic internationalization of retailing decision. This retailer would be choosing a low risk alternative to extend the application of the firm's proprietary knowledge to extract the implied rents.

The model of strategic international retail expansion (SIRE) that is the basis for this chapter is presented in Figure 15.1. This model is meant to be normative, not descriptive. **Normative** means it explains how things *should* be done. A descriptive model could be used to summarize or describe how retailers are actually internationalizing. However, many retailers are making mistakes and failing in their internationalization efforts. A failure is far more valuable to a retailer than a success, because one can analyze a failure and learn from it. Carrefour, the French hypermarket chain, is an excellent example of a company that enters and then withdraws from markets in which it is not succeed-

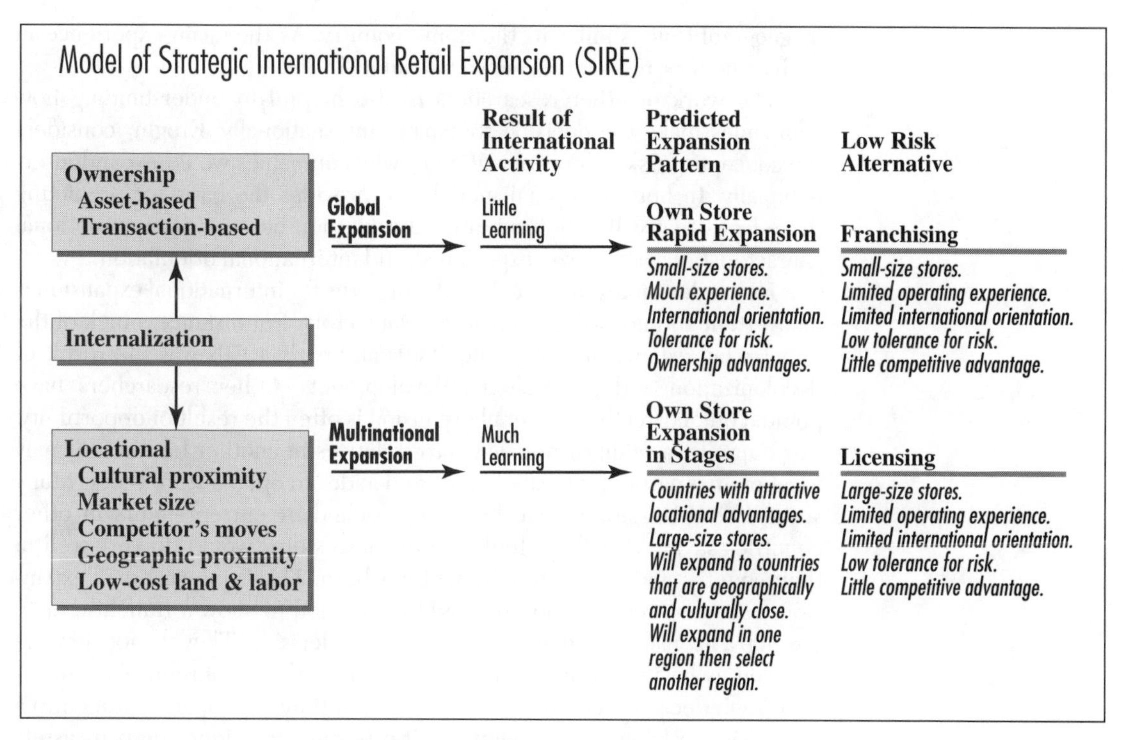

Figure 15.1
The SIRE model provides a way of mapping how ownership factors, the need to internalize company information, and locational factors influence international activity. Companies that have extensive ownership advantages are likely to use a global mode of expansion, expand in their standard format at a rapid rate, and learn little through their international expansion because most decision-making is centralized. Franchising is the low risk alternative available for global companies. Companies that focus on locational advantages will use a multinational mode of expansion. These companies are decentralized, changing their offerings with each country they enter. Because they are constantly making these changes, they learn much from international expansion, eventually assembling a portfolio of knowledge about how to operate internationally. Licensing is the low risk alternative available to a multinational retailer.

ing. As a result, the company has compiled a vast portfolio of information about how to do business in other countries. Normative models are not used to describe, but to prescribe. The accuracy of this model can only be assessed after a long period of time, when the final results of retailers' actions are known.

This model contains elements of theories described earlier in the book. Dunning's theory of the eclectic firm, hereafter referred to as "eclectic theory," focuses on ownership, locational, and internalization factors that influence a company to seek international expansion.[3] The focus of Salmon and Tordjman's[4] theory is on global versus multinational retailers, a distinction based on a centralized versus a decentralized dichotomy. Several researchers have explored the stages theory of international expansion. According to this theory, retailers will begin their international expansion in countries that are culturally or geographically similar to the home country. As they gain experience in each country or region, they move into another area.

The work of other researchers is also helpful in understanding how companies make the decision to expand internationally. Eroglu[5] considers the concept of risk as an explanation of why companies would expand internationally. In her conceptual model, she provides the basis for predicting those firms that will seek international expansion because of organizational characteristics such as size, experience, and international orientation.

Hollander[6] notes that much of the impetus for international expansion is inadvertent and not based on commercial factors. For instance, much of the initial retail expansion during the 1960s and early 1970s was the result of decolonization and post-colonial developments. Other researchers have pointed out, correctly, that retail expansion is often the result of opportunity. For example, a retail owner may have relatives in another location, or may vacation in a particular location, and so decides to open a store there. Many successful chain stores have been approached by entrepreneurs in other countries saying that they think one of these stores would do very well in their country, and therefore a franchise is born. This is international expansion, but many retailers do not view the decision to allow a franchise or to develop a licensing arrangement as a strategic decision. They do not view the decision as having an impact on their other market expansion plans; however, such decisions do have an impact. Each time a company enters into a franchising or licensing arrangement, it is renting its unique company assets to others. In doing this, the company needs to consider what it is losing in opportunity costs for internal market expansion.

The remainder of this chapter will explore factors related to the strategic international expansion of retailers, their reasons for expanding internationally, and predictions for where they will go next.

ECLECTIC THEORY

Dunning's eclectic approach[7] is recognized as a conceptual framework for explaining foreign direct investment. The model, described in Chapter 1, includes three types of advantages, which influence foreign direct investment. These advantages are ownership advantages (O), locational advantages (L), and internalization advantages (I). Pellegrini[8] applies the OLI model to retailing and provides some insightful expansion of the locational factor.

OWNERSHIP ADVANTAGES As discussed in Chapter 1, ownership advantages include innovative or unique products or processes a company can use to obtain market power. Included in this grouping are asset-based advantages and transaction-based advantages. Remember that asset-based advantages refer to an organizational innovation or unique products. A private label line is an example of asset-based advantages. In 1997, as I was conducting interviews for a research project on food retailers, people kept mentioning Aldi, the German hard food discounter that is rapidly internationalizing. Aldi sells 100% private label food. Everyone I talked with raved about Aldi's outstanding private label merchandise, and people from the United Kingdom to France told me about Aldi's superb private label champagne priced at only $14.

Transaction-based advantages come about because of the way things are done. Volume buying or economies because of centralized management are examples of transaction-based advantages in retailing. Carrefour is an example of a company that has always been very decentralized; however, the company is now centralizing its buying and product procurement. Carrefour is doing this to gain economies of scale in this area. Suppliers, such as Carrefour's, that deal with a strong international retailer will thus need to have a **global pricing structure.** This does not necessarily mean that the price is the same anywhere in the world, but rather that price differences are (1) explainable across countries and continents, (2) simple, (3) fully published, and (4) repeatable yet adaptable to local marketing needs. Suppliers will no longer be able to have, for example, a U.K. price list and a German price list.[9]

LOCATIONAL ADVANTAGES Locational advantages relate to how suitable the host country is with respect to a firm's strategies. Pellegrini's 1991 work identifies locational issues relevant to retailing. Several of these issues were introduced initially in Chapter 1. While presenting in full here, I have expanded Pellegrini's list, adding my own observations of countries that illustrate these issues.

1. *Cultural proximity.* People in some countries share similar patterns of life. Australians and New Zealanders have very similar lifestyles. As you will see in Company Focus V.1 on Coles-Meyer, this Australian company's first international extension was to New Zealand. Lifestyle is more important than language in determining cultural proximity. However, cultural proximity is more important for mass retailers and becomes less significant when retail concepts involve narrowly defined consumer markets that are similar in various countries.
2. *Market size.* Market saturation in the home country is an impetus for foreign direct investment by retailers. Ample space for expansion must be available, particularly if the firm needs to reach a certain size to exploit economies of scale. Legal restrictions governing growth in the home country can be considered a motive for companies to move to foreign locations. Examples of this effect have been presented throughout this book. French hypermarkets dominate the Spanish market. Delhaize "le Lion" owns the leading supermarket chain in the Czech Republic. German department stores have expanded rapidly into the former East Germany. Japanese department stores have expanded into Hong Kong, Singapore, and the People's Republic of China (PRC). France, Spain, and Portugal have just tightened requirements that limit large-scale

retailers' growth, pushing retailers in these countries to expand outside national borders. This also gives existing retailers certain benefits because market entry has been blocked for competitors. These restrictions encourage companies to acquire other companies because they cannot build their own new stores. In 1997, for instance, Auchan acquired Docks de France; both companies are major French hypermarkets. Carrefour later acquired Cora, another hypermarket. As a result, concentration in this industry is greatly increased, mainly because new stores cannot be opened.

3. *Competitors' moves.* A first-mover advantage is very important to retailers. Within any major city, there are only so many prime retail sites. Competitors who secure prime retail locations may block out other firms. The larger the retailer considering international expansion, the more crucial it is to be an early mover. Smaller retail spaces are generally not a problem. Nevertheless, like a strategic game of chess, the early moves of a large retailer set the stage for a long-term competitive advantage. Makro and Carrefour both had an early presence in China, Malaysia, South Korea, Taiwan, and Thailand. In Mexico, Argentina, and Brazil, the pattern of Carrefour and Wal-Mart reflects each other. Sam's Clubs opened in Mexico in 1991; by 1996, the company had 57 stores. Carrefour opened in Mexico in 1994; by 1996, it had 13 stores. In Argentina, Carrefour opened nine stores in 1994; by 1996, it had 15 stores. Wal-Mart opened in Argentina in 1995 and by 1996, had six Sam's Club's. Carrefour opened in Brazil in 1994; by 1996, the company had 44 stores. Wal-Mart opened in Brazil in 1995 and by 1996, had five stores. These retailers have executed a well-planned strategic game of expansion.[10]
4. *Geographical proximity.* Expanding closer to home reduces transfer costs related to transportation and corporate communication. Geographical proximity is more important for retailers selling private labels that they produce in a central location. It is less important for decentralized companies, because they are allowed to operate as independent units, generally sourcing from within the country. For instance, even before the devaluation of the peso, Sears Mexico and Wal-Mart Mexico purchased 80% to 90% of their products from Mexican sources.[11]
5. *Low-cost land and labor.* Land and labor are important expenses for large-scale retailers. In rapidly developing countries, retail rents can sky rocket. Japanese department stores opening in Hong Kong were provided with subsidized land and reduced taxes to make their investments more attractive. Sogo purchased its property in Hong Kong when it first entered the market. According to a 1995 survey, Causeway Bay in Hong Kong had taken over the top position from Pedder Street, also in Hong Kong, as having the most expensive commercial rents in the world, up to $10,000 per square meter (U.S. $930 per

square foot).[12] Japanese retailers who did not own their own property in Hong Kong faced rents that were two or three times this amount. The second stage of the retail leap frog is now occurring. Isetan opened stores in Hong Kong during the previous decade. These stores are now closed. Instead, Isetan is opening stores in the PRC. This movement is not strictly due to low-cost land, because the rental cost is very high for good locations in major PRC cities. However, Isetan is likely gambling that prices will soar as others join the retail pioneers in the PRC. When Jusco, a Japanese general merchandise store, entered Hong Kong, it located its stores in suburban areas where rents are not so expensive. Jusco has also reduced its labor costs by employing part-time employees, primarily housewives. The company would not have such easy access to this employment pool in the central business district of Hong Kong.

INTERNALIZATION ADVANTAGES Internalization advantages have to do with keeping company secrets. All companies have secrets—information that helps to make them unique or successful, or both. Internalization refers to the process of keeping this information within the company. The greater a company's ownership assets, the more important it is to protect these assets by guarding company secrets. For many years, the methods McDonald's uses to keep its french fries crisp were a closely guarded secret. The company found that soaking the potatoes in cold water before freezing them would keep them crisp. With this method, they could use potatoes that had been bought in bulk throughout the year. Before learning this technique, McDonald's had used one type of potato during one part of the year and a different type of potato for the rest of the year.

In retail franchising, a company sells or leases assets to other firms. Therefore, franchising is a particularly dangerous idea for retailers with strong asset- or transaction-based ownership advantages. Retailing innovations are difficult to defend from imitators. Competitors can freely copy them because there are no patents on retail know-how. Therefore, to maintain a competitive advantage, a retail company needs to internalize its innovations. The only way for a retail company to keep its operating secrets is to open wholly owned subsidiaries in various countries. This is too expensive for many companies, which are forced to franchise their retail innovations to expand rapidly. However, over time, these companies may come to regret this decision because they have lost the market opportunity of that area.

Joint ventures offer less protection of secrets than wholly owned subsidiaries, but are often necessary when entering a different cultural environment or because of government regulations. Many developing countries, such as Taiwan, Thailand, and the PRC, require that the controlling interest of multinational companies rest with domestic ownership.

THEORY OF GLOBAL VERSUS MULTINATIONAL EXPANSION

INVESTMENT A company's motivation for expanding internationally through investment usually falls under one or more of the following three choices. In general, companies investing in foreign retailers are looking for (1) a higher-than-domestic return on investment, (2) a safe foreign international investment, or (3) access to retail know-how. Most companies identify investment choices by looking for lucrative areas in which to expend excess assets.

Although investment is considered a strategic internationalization option, it does not lead to other strategic options. When a company uses investment strategy, it learns little about international expansion. Ahold is the seventh largest food retailer in the United States. Few people realize that this Dutch company owns BI-LO, Giant Food Stores, Tops Markets, and Stop & Shop. Ahold purchased these chains but retained their management and operating systems. The company sought an investment that would largely run itself. No doubt Ahold has learned about retailing in the United States after this investment, but it is not the same kind of direct, sink-or-swim learning that would be obtained if the company operated its own stores.

The two major strategic alternatives available for international retail expansion are global and multinational. The characteristics of global versus multinational strategies are presented in Table 15.1.

GLOBAL RETAILERS Global retailers, as we saw in Chapter 1, reproduce a standard product in each country they enter. These retailers generally have great asset-based ownership advantages, such as a globally recognizable company name (e.g., Levi's), or a successful private label (e.g., Gap). Other global retailers have strong transaction-based ownership advantages; for example, McDonald's fast-food system. Generally, reproducing a standard product requires centralized management decision-making. Many global retailers begin with decentralized management and then, to gain greater control of their rapidly expanding company, move to a more centralized management system. Global retailers expand internationally using a standard retail format. Each store looks similar. The products are much the same. Fixtures look like they belong to the same family. In its early years, The Body Shop allowed its stores to select one of three color schemes. The stores were also free to sell merchandise other than The Body Shop line. However, these freedoms were later eliminated to provide a more unified store image. In Company Focus V.1, following this chapter, the Scandinavian retailer IKEA is profiled; it is one of the classic examples of a global company.

Generally, global retailers are vertically integrated backward, producing their own private label lines. It is often difficult to determine to what degree the success of a global retailer can be attributed to its retail format and to what degree it is due to the product itself. Because these retailers produce their own private labels, the lead time for product development is longer

TABLE 15.1

Characteristics of Global versus Multinational Strategies

Global	Multinational
Centralized management	Decentralized management
Standard format	Adapted format
Rapid expansion	Expansion in stages
Private label	National brands and private label

than for a traditional retailer. This means that their product lines are more stable and less fashion sensitive.

Some retailers that do not sell private label merchandise can still be considered global retailers. However, these retailers operate in industry segments in which the merchandise is either mainly consignment merchandise (e.g., Toys "R" Us) or brand merchandise but with special "makeups" for the retailer (e.g., Foot Locker).

Some global retailers take steps to reduce lead time. Benetton, as I have noted before, dyes its garments after production, in the country where they will be sold. By doing this, the company can capitalize on changes in color preferences. The company has two shows, producing over 7,500 styles per year.[13] It operates 14 factories in eight countries, and has 16 licensing agreements in 28 countries for the Benetton trademark in the production of clothing. During Benetton's initial international expansion, the company concentrated on securing prime locations in which to operate its own stores, so it would get to know the market. Today, the company has 80 offices worldwide, each responsible for a specific geographical area. Over 7,000 independent stores now sell the Benetton product. Store owners do not pay Benetton a royalty; the company's profits come from product sales.

Benetton's distribution system looks like a franchise system, but the company maintains it is not a franchise because it does not charge royalties or dictate the operating format of individual stores. The company does not want to be directly involved in the selling phase. Initially, financing was 50-50, with Benetton providing 50% of the costs and the store owner the other 50%. Later, the company found that potential store owners were willing to underwrite all the costs of opening a Benetton store.

MULTINATIONAL RETAILERS In contrast to global retailers, multinational retailers are decentralized, and they alter their offerings based on cultural differences. Multinational retailers generally have transaction-based ownership advantages. These transaction-type assets generally depend on an industry infrastructure such as a refrigeration system and packaging industry to do business. The location factors in Dunning's theory are more important to multinational retailers than to global retailers. Companies such as France's

Carrefour and Germany's Tengelmann are multinational companies. Expansion of multinational retailers is generally more sporadic than that of global retailers. Table 15.2 details Carrefour's international expansion efforts, listing entries and, more important, exits over the years.[14] Generally, multinational retailers concentrate their expansion within a geographical area, filling that area before moving to a new country or region.

These retailers change their retail offering based on customer and cultural differences. This strategy requires a great deal of learning. Each country mastered gives the retail firm a broad knowledge base. However, because these companies are decentralized, this knowledge base often remains within each country. Carrefour, after operating as a very decentralized company, began to centralize the development of private label lines in Europe. To accomplish this, the company had buyers from each of the major countries

TABLE 15.2

Carrefour's Record of Overseas Expansion in the Hypermarket Format, 1978–1997

Year of Entry	Country	Status
1969	Belgium	Out in 1978
1969	United Kingdom	Out in 1983
1972	Italy	Out in 1984
1973	Spain	54 stores in 1997[a]
1974	Brazil	45 stores in 1997
1976	Austria	Out in 1979
1977	Germany	Out in 1979
1982	Argentina	17 stores in 1997
1988	United States	Out in 1994
1989	Taiwan	16 stores in 1997
1990	Portugal	3 stores in 1997
1993	Italy	7 stores in 1997[b]
1994	Mexico	16 stores in 1997
1994	Malaysia	2 stores in 1997
1996	Thailand	5 stores in 1997
1996	China	3 stores in 1997
1996	South Korea	3 stores in 1997
1996	Hong Kong	1 store in 1997
1997	Monaco	1 store in 1997
1997	Turkey	1 store in 1997

[a] Under "Pryca" name. [b] One store under "Al Gran Sole" name.

Source: Carrefour—Company Report. (March 13, 1997). UBS Research Limited in *Investext* [Database on CD-ROM]. Foster City, Calif.: Information Access; and http://www.carrefour.fr/monde.html

Photo 15.1
Yaohan has opened stores throughout the world. In fact, the company is probably better known in China than it is at home in Japan. This store is located in Chicago. The large head is a doll believed to provide good fortune. Owners color in one eye, make a wish, and then color in the other eye when the wish comes true.
Courtesy of SN.

bring samples of their private label products for certain lines, such as dairy. As a European team, these buyers decided which country would produce the private label ice cream, which would produce the private label orange juice, and so on. The basic question the buyers were asked to address was, "Are country differences significant enough to justify all of these different products?"[15]

STAGES THEORY

Learning sets the stage for future investment. For example, U.S. chain stores have learned as a result of their investment throughout this country. This learning may allow them to predict, for instance, that moving into Ontario, Canada will be like moving into Seattle. The ability to make these analogies serves to distinguish those who are able to compete from those who are not.

International expansion can involve different levels of learning. Global companies expand rapidly, using the same standard retail format. They do not learn much about their market environment. Multinational companies change as they move to other countries. Each movement prepares them to move to another location. They arm themselves with an arsenal of stereotypes about doing business in diverse conditions. Retailers who franchise or license their format for other retailers obtain little information that will help them in additional markets. For these retailers, the short-term benefits of franchising and licensing fees are what drives their investment.

Multinational retailers expand into locations that they perceive to have greater locational advantages. Wal-Mart, Sears, and Kmart expanded into

Mexico because of geographical proximity. In addition, because these companies had many customers from border towns in Mexico, they had a chance to get to understand the Mexican culture before making this move.

French hypermarkets expanded very successfully into Spain. The cultural similarities between France and Spain are viewed as much greater than those between France and other European countries.[16] Today, the French hypermarkets' private label products have become the leading national brands in Spain.[17]

RISK THEORY

The reward for risk is margin or profit. Some companies are inherently greater risk-takers than others. Eroglu, in her 1992 article,[18] identified some organizational characteristics that help to explain the risk-taking behavior of companies. She believes that a set of organizational and environmental characteristics influences perceived risk and perceived benefits, two ideas that directly affect the intention to internationalize. The characteristics she places under environment are domestic competitive pressures, external change agent influences, and perceived favorability of the external environment. These characteristics are part of the SIRE model under locational advantages.

The organizational characteristics are firm size, operating experience, top management's international orientation, top management's tolerance for risk, and top management's perception of the firm's competitive advantage. These characteristics will determine whether a retailer selects internalizing or externalizing as its method of international expansion as follows:

- If the company is using a *global* strategic international expansion strategy and it *internalizes* its international expansion, it will open its *own stores* with *rapid expansion* throughout the world.
- If the company is using a *global* strategic international expansion strategy and it *externalizes* its international expansion, it will *franchise* its operations with *rapid expansion* throughout the world.
- If the company is using a *multinational* strategic international expansion strategy and it *internalizes* its international expansion, it will open its *own stores,* expanding in *stages,* beginning with countries with the greatest *locational advantages.*
- If the company is using a *multinational* strategic international expansion strategy and it *externalizes* its international expansion, it will *license* its operations, expanding in stages, beginning with countries with the greatest *locational advantages.*

I believe that several countries will become important targets for retailer internationalization in the next decades. In many cases, locational advantages make these countries attractive; however, a locational advantage for a retailer from Japan will not be a locational advantage for a retailer from the United States. Often countries become attractive market targets because of some macro-environmental change. The end of apartheid is prompting retailers to look at South Africa as an attractive market. South Korea has opened its retail markets to foreign joint ventures in the year 1996; this action makes the country attractive. Vietnam is of interest to many retailers because the U.S. government recently removed a long-standing ban on trading with this country. The five countries I think will be of greatest interest to retailers are summarized in this section.

TARGETS FOR FUTURE RETAIL INTERNATIONALIZATION EFFORTS

SOUTH KOREA

South Korea has the second greatest urban buying power in Asia after Japan. Despite this, its retail sector is less developed than other areas in Asia. This lack of development is due to government restrictions on foreign retailers' participation in the market. Distribution is currently dominated by licensed dealerships. There are many foreign retail names in the market, but they are owned and controlled by Koreans. Small independent retailers dominate the South Korean retailing environment. There are three large retail companies, Lotte, Midopa, and Shinsegae.[19]

Lotte has a management contract with Takashimaya (Japan). This store is in the most prestigious shopping location and has the largest selection of imported merchandise. Shinsegae is owned by the manufacturing giant, Samsung. In 1993, Shinsegae opened E-Mart, the country's first discount supermarket, modeled after the U.S. retailer, Kmart. In 1995, Shinsegae and Price/Costco formed a licensing agreement to open the country's first warehouse club.

Shinsegae leases one of the primary floors of the Next Age Department Store in Shanghai. Shinsegae has also opened up an E-Mart store in Shanghai. Several South Korean specialty stores have also opened in major Chinese cities. One of my university student translators told me it is the Korean retailers, not the Japanese, that are really "hot" in China.

South Korea liberalized its highly regulated retail industry in 1996. This will greatly increase foreigners' access to South Korean consumers.[20] In 1997, however, a currency and liquidity crisis forced the South Korean government to seek a multibillion-dollar bailout from the International Monetary Fund.

SOUTH AFRICA

The retail market in South Africa that has traditionally targeted the white population is mature, with limited growth potential. On the other hand, the majority target market, black South Africans, has great growth potential. An important part of this growth will be in credit sales. This growth happens in all countries with increasing economic development. It is particularly important in the short-run. For instance, Woolworth's sales increased 43% in the first six months after it introduced a credit policy. Long-term benefits to retailers may be less than satisfactory, however, when one considers the risks of (1) inflation rising and causing an increase in interest rates, (2) credit lines reaching their limit and driving up the debtor rate, and (3) political delays to economic recovery, causing lenders to tighten credit policies.[21]

South Africa has a population of 41 million. Three-quarters are native African, 5 million are of European decent, and the remaining 6 million are of Asian and mixed origins. The age distribution of the black population is skewed in favor of youth, with half the population under the age of 25 years. Less than one-third of the population over 16 years of age is economically active. As incomes predictably increase, the potential for low-cost retail operations will be expansive. More of the population is moving to urban areas, and rural growth is half that of urban areas.[22]

The informal economy accounts for 20% of South Africa's gross domestic product (GDP) and employs 4 million people, almost all within the black community. The distribution system is characterized by 20,000 spaza shops inside the townships, in addition to 200,000 door-to-door hawker salesmen. **Spazas** are shops that purchase products from wholesalers and sell them at lower prices than established stores. These shops are mobile or semi-permanent units. **Hawker** salesmen take their books of products to consumers in their homes. Commercial retailers who can tap the target market of this informal economy stand to gain the most in the South African market. A South African company, Pick 'n Pay, is trying to break into this market by acting as a wholesaler to township franchisees.

VIETNAM

Four years ago, I attended an international business symposium in Los Angeles. The entire symposium focused on Asia. There were sessions on Japan, China, Thailand, and Hong Kong. But by far the greatest interest was generated by the seminar on Vietnam. Before going to that seminar, it had never occurred to me that Vietnam was a country of any economic importance. I have since changed my mind.

When Seiyu, a Japanese supermarket, first decided to enter Vietnam, there were very few cash registers in the country. Most of those to be found were in fancy hotels and probably were not operable. There are 70 million people in Vietnam, and even more important, there are a growing number of foreigners and affluent Vietnamese who have prospered from foreign trade.

The new Seiyu store will target the 6,000+ foreign businesspeople. Most of the 3,000 items the store sells will come from Hong Kong, so prices will be high. However, eventually the retailer will substitute local products and suppliers for these foreign imports.[23] Vietnam may become the next Hong Kong or Singapore.

BRAZIL

Brazil is almost the size of the United States. It has more than 160 million people and a growth rate that will increase this number to nearly 200 million by the year 2025. Three-quarters of these people live in urban areas. Brazil

Photo 15.2
Even this small store in Vietnam sells Pepsi.
Courtesy of SN.

is a multicultural, multiracial country with a youthful population. Thirty-five percent of the population is under 15, only 5% over 65.[24]

Department stores have an amazing market share in Brazil: 13%. Recently, however, profitability has been down, as a recession has reduced overall consumer spending. Outlet centers, hypermarkets, and discount stores are gaining market share.

Until recently, technology improvements were restricted due to an import ban. This has been removed and retailers are beginning to improve operational efficiencies. Wal-Mart and Lojas Americanas are the leading joint venture partners. Carrefour currently operates 38 hypermarkets and has further expansion plans.[25]

The greatest opportunities exist outside the major urban areas. São Paulo has 28% of Brazil's supermarkets and accounts for about 47% of supermarket sales. There are 10 other cities in Brazil that have populations greater than 1 million. In addition to geographical opportunities, there are also product category opportunities. Demand is strong for electronics, primarily televisions and computers. Private label accounts for only 2% of sales in Brazil, compared with 17% in the United States, 23% in Germany, and 38% in the United Kingdom.[26]

AUSTRALIA

Most analysts dismiss Australia as a low growth country with limited retail expansion opportunities. There are two major retailers, Coles-Myer and Woolworths. Coles-Myer is the 34th largest retailer in the world. It operates a variety of formats in Australia, including supermarkets, department stores, discount stores, and specialty stores. The company operates only in Australia and New Zealand. Company Focus V.2, at the end of Part V, profiles Coles-Myer. The company has used a high-degree of diversification to achieve its market share in Australia. Woolworths, which is number 51 on the list of 100 largest retailers, operates supermarkets, department stores, and specialty stores in Australia.

The lack of domestic competition makes these retailers vulnerable to foreign competition. Category killers, discount operations, and warehouse clubs have growth potential, as well as well defined specialty store niches.

Australia, geographically, is almost as large as the United States, but has a population of only 18 million. Seventy percent of this population is located in five major cities. This makes market entry less daunting. Australia, like much of the rest of the world, is passing through a recession. As the country's economy pulls out of the recession, retail opportunities should take off.[27]

SUMMARY

The model presented in this chapter is based on four theories that help to predict strategic retail internationalization. The model is not meant to be descriptive, but instead is presented as a normative model based on the four interconnected theories. A descriptive model summarizes what has happened; a normative model predicts what should happen over time. No doubt you can think of global retailers who use franchising and are very successful. However, a long-term evaluation of the success of this strategy is needed. For instance, although a company may look very successful initially, this success is predictable; franchising allows the retailer to expand at a rapid rate without massive corporate investment. In effect, franchising is a short-term solution, providing rapid growth and income.

You will not find many Japanese companies that offer their company expertise to a franchising or licensing arrangement. Their orientation is long-term. Investors are prepared to accept long-term corporate growth rather than short-term profits. Retailers from the United States have been eager to engage in franchising and licensing arrangements. Will they regret this strategy in the coming decades?

Recently I conducted interviews with management at several U.S. national chain stores. These chains are eager to engage in international franchising opportunities and potential licensing arrangements. When I asked them if they would be eager to engage in franchising or licensing in their home market, they indicated that they do not want to sacrifice control of their retail image and identity, and so are not interested in franchising or licensing at home. There will come a time when their view of the world is like their view of the national market. Yet, by then, they may have sold their share of these foreign markets to strangers.

Most U.S. manufacturers sacrificed long-term market presence in Japan by entering licensing arrangements with Japanese companies. The names of these U.S. manufacturers were always represented in Japanese stores; however, Japanese companies produced their products under licensing agreements. Years later, when the U.S. companies wanted to have a larger presence in the Japanese market, the Japanese companies blocked them because of the earlier licensing arrangements.

In some instances, retailers have used licensing to protect their company interests. For example, Price Club entered Beijing through a licensing arrangement with an equity option. This is the only method of entry into the PRC market that does not require the foreign retailer to contribute a large amount of money. I talked with the Price Club's U.S. manager in Beijing. He had also worked on the Price Club's South Korean licensing arrangement. His job was to set up the company, train local managers and move on to the next international assignment. Local companies participating in such joint ventures in the PRC were very disgruntled if the company had to absorb high expatriate manager salaries. **Expatriate** managers are managers from foreign countries. The benefit packages these managers receive for foreign assignments can turn a $70,000 middle manager's salary into a $350,000 expense for the company. The benefits package generally includes a housing allowance, education reimbursement for children, and usually hardship pay. In contrast, the senior managers in the PRC might be paid $6,000.

Five countries—South Korea, South Africa, Vietnam, Brazil, and Australia—offer attractive targets for future retail internationalization efforts. All five countries share some important characteristics. Countries such as South Korea and Vietnam are just now liberalizing their laws regulating foreign ownership of retailing. As I have mentioned before, market reforms in retailing typically come years after market reforms in manufacturing. Furthermore, retailing is viewed as a negative force in many socialist or developing countries. Retailing changes material culture, creating desires that would not occur among a population ignorant of the various products available to consumers elsewhere in the world. It is likely that Japanese retailers will become important players in South Korea and Vietnam. South Korea has a tradition of large-scale stores; Vietnam does not. In Vietnam, shops are very small. Rather than department stores, it is likely that hypermarkets will be the strongest players in Vietnam. Carrefour is a likely early candidate because the company has learned about many foreign markets through its worldwide expansion.

Brazil is attractive to retailers because of its recent economic growth and the probability that it will join a trading alliance like that created by the North American Free Trade Agreement (NAFTA). Brazil is currently the focus of international retailers from the United States and France. It is predictable that retailers who are gaining experience in Mexico will make Brazil their next stage of expansion.

The end of apartheid has made South Africa an attractive market. Although this country has had major department stores and exclusive specialty stores, these stores typically served white customers only. This history of exclusion will not position them well for the upwardly mobile group of black South Africans. New retailers will gain this market.

Australia offers benefits similar to those found in the United States. Although the country is sparsely populated, automobile ownership is high and cars are a major source of transportation. Hypermarkets are favored to expand to this area. Category killers and specialty stores from the United States have entered this market with success.

Retailers have crawled in their international expansion activities. Those retailers who have gained a portfolio of strategies for international expansion are poised to make the leap into future markets. Those who have not conducted their own international expansion, but rather, have given their proprietary knowledge to others, will likely begin to contract their expansion into new markets. The learners in international expansion will be the long-term earners.

KEY TERMS

expatriate
global pricing structure
hawker
normative
spaza

DISCUSSION QUESTIONS

1. Which of Dunning's advantages are more important for global retailers? Which are more important for multinational expansion?
2. When is it worthwhile for a retailer to use an investment strategy for internationalization?
3. How does franchising or licensing hurt a retailer?
4. When does franchising or licensing help a retailer?
5. Evaluate the countries highlighted in this chapter according to their locational advantages. Predict in each case whether you feel U.S., European, or Japanese firms will be the most successful in these markets. What types of retailers do you anticipate being most successful?

ENDNOTES

1. Parts of this chapter are published from Sternquist, B. (1997). "International Expansion of U.S. Retailers." *International Journal of Retail and Distribution Management.* Vol. 25, No. 8, pp. 262–268.
2. Pellegrini, L. (1994). "Alternatives for Growth and Internationalization in Retailing." *International Review of Retail, Distribution and Consumer Research,* Vol. 4, No. 2, pp. 121–48.

3. Dunning, J. H., and M. McQueen. (1982). "The Eclectic Theory of the Multinational Enterprise." In A. M. Rugman, ed., *New Theories of the Multinational Enterprise.* Beckenham, Kent: Croom Helm, pp. 79–106.
4. Salmon, W. J., and A. Tordjman. (1989). "The Internationalization of Retailing." *International Journal of Retailing,* Vol. 4, No. 2, pp. 3–16.
5. Eroglu, S. (1992) "The Internationalisation Process of Franchise Systems: A Conceptual Model." *International Marketing Review,* Vol. 9, No. 5, pp.11–39.
6. Hollander, S. C. (1970). *Multinational Retailing.* East Lansing: Michigan State University.
7. Dunning, J. H. (1981). *International Production and the Multinational Enterprise.* London: Allen & Unwin.
8. Pellegrini, L. (1991). "The Internationalization of Retailing and 1992 Europe." *Journal of Marketing Channels,* Vol. 1, No. 2, pp. 3–27.
9. O'Connor, D. (1997). "Retail Concentration and Multinational Expansion: Two Important Retail Bonds." *Discount Merchandiser,* Vol. 37, No. 5, p. 64.
10. "Carrefour—Company Report." (March 13, 1997). UBS Research Limited in *Investext* [Database on CD-ROM]. Foster City, Calif.: Information Access.
11. Sternquist, B. Personal interviews. (1996).
12. "International—World Rents and Other News." (1995). *Retail News Letter,* No. 429, p. 1.
13. Benetton, L. "Franchising: How Brand Power Works." In P. Stobart, ed., *Brand Power.* New York: New York University Press.
14. Compiled from company reports, source unknown.
15. Sternquist, B., personal interviews (1994).
16. Sternquist, B., personal interviews (1994, 1996).
17. Sternquist, B., and M. Kacker. *European Retailing's Vanishing Borders.* Westport, Conn: Greenwood Publishing.
18. Eroglu (1992).
19. Coopers & Lybrand. (1995). "Global Retailing: Assignment Asia." *Chain Store Age Executive,* January.
20. Coopers & Lybrand (1995).
21. "Pepkor/Edgars/Pick 'n Pay/Wooltru—Company Report." (September 6, 1995). Lehman Brothers Limited in *Investext* [Database on CD-ROM]. Foster City, Calif.: Information Access.
22. "Pepkor/Edgars/Pick 'n Pay/Wooltru—Company Report" (September 6, 1995).
23. Yamamuro, A. (1994). "Seiyu Steps Gently into Vietnam." *Nikkei Weekly,* August 8, p. 18.
24. Coopers & Lybrand (1996). "Global Retailing: Assignment Asia." *Chain Store Age,* April, Section 2.
25. Coopers & Lybrand (1996).
26. Coopers & Lybrand (1996).

COMPANY FOCUS V.1

COLES-MYER

Heather L. Schwark, Regina Cummings, Sunita Surajan

Coles-Myer is the largest retailer in Australia and the 34th largest retailer in the world. In 1995, the company accounted for 16% of total retail sales in Australia and boasted the highest per capita sales of anywhere in the world.[1] Its retail operations span the Australian continent, and it is a leading owner of Australian retail properties. Coles-Myer's extensive real estate portfolio includes prime real estate in regional shopping centers as well as sites in the central business districts of both Melbourne and Sydney.

Coles-Myer is the largest employer in Australia's private sector.[2] The company's diverse business holdings include supermarkets, department stores, discount department stores, clothing stores, liquor stores and wine cellars, restaurants (take-away and sit down), and auto service centers. Coles-Myer now has over 1,700 store locations, and well over 3.6 million square meters (39 million square feet) of selling area alone.[3]

History

On April 9, 1914, George James Coles founded the first Coles variety store in a small working-class suburb in the state of Victoria, Australia. George Coles had for years studied the methods of variety (discount) store retailing in both the United Kingdom and the United States. In 1919, Coles opened a larger variety store in the same city. Two years later, in 1921, Coles's company was incorporated as G. J. Coles & Coy Pty. Ltd. In 1924, another Coles variety store opened in Bourke Street, Melbourne. This was the first Coles store to open in a major city. By 1927, G. J. Coles & Coy Pty. Ltd. had grown to eight stores and become an Australian public company trading on the Melbourne Stock Exchange. In 1928, the first Coles store outside of the state of Victoria opened. That store was located on Pitt Street in Sydney.

In 1930, G. J. Coles & Coy began its first decade of major expansion. In just three years, Coles variety stores were developed in every Australian state. The company enjoyed success and continued to expand even during the Great Depression, despite its customers' tough financial times. Its success was due to the strong commitment Coles had to offering affordable goods to all sectors of the community. The managing director, A. W. Coles, wrote at this time, "A store has no right to success just because it is open for business and has a bright display. The goods must reflect the wishes of the community in which the store is located."[4] The company promise of "Satisfaction Guaranteed or Money Cheerfully Refunded" was introduced in 1938, amidst high inflation and the tail end of the Depression. That Coles promise still stands today.

In 1939, the war prompted nearly all (95%) of Coles's male employees to enlist in the armed forces.[5] Wartime production caused a major shortage of goods, and Managing Director A. W. Coles made a progressive move. He promoted to management positions many women who filled the vacancies left by the male soldiers serving in the war. A. W. Coles retired in 1944 and handed the position over to his brother, E. B. Coles, who led the company through a second major wave of expansion during the 1950s. During this time, Coles acquired major retailers such as Selfridges Ltd. (Australia) in New South Wales (1950); F&G Stores Ltd. in Victoria (1951), and Queensland Penney's Ltd. (1956). It is no wonder that E. B. Coles was nicknamed "The Takeover King."

After finding success in the variety store format, Coles ventured into food retailing. In 1958, the company took over 54 John Connell Dickins Pty. Ltd. grocery stores. In 1959, Coles acquired Beilby's Supermarkets of southern Australia, and one year later, purchased 265 supermarkets from Matthews Thompson in New South Wales. In 1962, customers were treated to a "New World of Shopping" with the opening of the first Coles New World Supermarket in Frankston, Victoria. This was a new concept in food retailing for Australia—selling groceries, fresh meat, fruit and vegetables, dairy goods, produce, and frozen foods all within one store.[6] It gave customers the opportunity to complete all of their food shopping in just one stop, save money, enjoy a wider selection, and experience a higher standard of quality. Coles enjoyed a 30.7% net profit increase that year[7] and carved a lasting impression in the world of food retailing—one that remains to this day.

The next area of exploration for the company was the discount department store. In 1967, Coles's first major discount department store opened in South Australia under the name of Colmart. One year later, Coles began a joint venture with S. S. Kresge Company (now Kmart) of the United States. This joint venture gave Coles a 49% stake and an agreement to open discount stores in Australia under the Kmart name. The first Australian Kmart opened in Coles's homeland of Victoria, in 1969, and exposed Australia to the American discount department store. A great many established Australian retailers fell short of the sales performance achieved by these new Kmart stores, and Kmart (and Coles) blasted to the forefront of Australian retailing. That same year, Coles New World Supermarkets opened its 100th store in Western Australia. Once again, Coles had covered the Australian continent with one of its successful retail formats. George James Coles, the company's founder, lived to see all of these achievements, dying in 1977 at the age of 92.

Continuing its long tradition of positive employee relations, Coles introduced equal benefits for male and female staff in the company's medical scheme and staff superannuation fund.[8] The benefit of these positive employee relations was evident, as over 1,000 of Coles-Myer's employees at the time had been with the company for over 25 years.[9] In December 1978, Coles purchased the remaining 51% stake in Australian Kmart, thus making it a wholly owned subsidiary of Coles Australia.[10]

The 1980s began the third wave of major expansion for G. J. Coles & Coy Pty. Ltd. Claude Fay Cellars, Liquorland, and Mac the Slasher liquor store chains were bought in the late summer of 1981. In 1982, Coles gained the right to operate all of its liquor stores under the name Liquorland. Coles also bought Ezywalkin and Edward Fay Pty. Ltd. in 1981, entering into the footwear market. However, the company rid itself of these ventures in 1988 due to poor profit performance.

The first hypermarket opened in Australia under the name of Super Kmart in 1982. This store was a combination of the Coles New World Supermarket and the Kmart discount department store formats. Many of the Kmarts that opened included automotive sections under the name K Auto, which had first been established in 1961. They sold an extensive range of automotive accessories and parts and offered full servicing and maintenance to fleet and private vehicle operators.[11]

Coles entered the women's clothing business in November 1984 when it purchased 117 Katies Fashion Pty. Ltd. (Australia) stores. These Katies stores provided quality womenswear at reasonable prices, and had a good reputation with the Australian public. Australian customers liked the fact that Katies made a point to stock a major portion of each store with Australian-made merchandise. Later that same year, the 100th Kmart store opened for business in New South Wales, and net profits were over Australian dollars (AD) $100 million (U.S. $74 million).

In 1985, Coles merged with Myer Emporium Ltd., which since 1983, had held the Myer-Grace Bros. chain of traditional department stores. Myer Emporium, Ltd., like Coles, had been in operation since the beginning of the century. The merger with Myer cost Coles just under AD $1 billion (U.S. $740 million), but it brought to the company 56 department stores, 68 Target discount stores, 122 Fosseys discount variety stores, the Country Road chain of 45 stores (which was subsequently sold for a profit of AD $33.27 million [U.S. $24.6 million]), and the Red Rooster chain of fast-food chicken outlets.[12]

The name of G. J. Coles & Coy Pty. Ltd. was changed to Coles-Myer Ltd. and a new corporate symbol adopted in January 1986. Coles-Myer then divided the huge corporation into its first organizational structure, combining each of its formats into five divisions.

The present-day Coles-Myer organization is in three divisions: The Supermarkets Group (which contains both supermarkets and discount stores), the Department Stores Group, and the Specialty Stores Group.

New Zealand Operations

Coles-Myer made its first move overseas with the acquisition of the supermarket chain Progressive Enterprises Ltd. in 1988. This expansion effort came at a time when Coles-Myer was seeking to expand outside of Australia, but the 38% share in Progressive was subsequently sold in 1993.[13] Coles-Myer now focuses its efforts on its Kmart and Katies chains, which have been successful in New Zealand.

Retail Atmosphere in Australia

The Australian retail sector performed at a real growth rate of about 2.4% compared to sales in 1993. By June 1994, Australian retailing was worth AD $101 billion (U.S. $740 million)![14] Even at this rate, the retail sector was performing at somewhat of a lag, as compared to the Australian economy as a whole.

Some of the characteristics of retailing in Australia are the high degree of concentration in a few major retailers, the emphasis on large retail shopping centers, and relatively intense price competition.[15]

Highly Concentrated

Retailing in Australia is very highly concentrated, especially in the food sector. A market is said to be concentrated when four of the top firms control 50% or more of the market share. This is certainly the case in Australia, where exactly half the total annual food sales are generated by the three supermarket giants—Coles-Myer, Franklins, and Woolworths.

Growth of Regional Centers

Large, regional shopping centers (over 46,000 square meters [500,000 square feet] in space) are extremely popular in Australia. These regional centers are responsible for about 18% of the retail sales in Australia.[16] This may not seem like much compared to the estimated 50% of sales generated from regional centers in the United States, but the Australian percentage is much higher than the averages in the United Kingdom and the remainder of Europe.[17]

Intense Price Competition

Intense price competition is also a major factor in the Australian retail environment. When there is a situation of oligopoly, as in the Australian retail sector, competition is not based solely on price. However, if a price war were to ensue, the dominant firm in the industry or the market share leader would be victorious. In an oligopoly, prices are higher than they are in perfect competition, as there are few products, but many consumers.

In perfect competition, the lowest price possible is charged. This is because there are many homogenous products to choose from, and many consumers in the arena. A competitive oligopoly can sometimes produce more intense pricing and margin pressure than is seen in more fragmented markets.[18] This statement sums up what has been occurring in Australia, where in every industry, margins are very low compared to world standards.

Current Retail Formats

The Supermarkets Group

The Supermarkets Group is the largest division in the Coles-Myer organization. Coles Supermarkets and BI-LO are the two food retailing formats that fall under this division. However, the discount stores Target, Kmart, and Fosseys are also in this organizational structure.

Food Retailers

BI-LO is a discount food retailer, and Coles Supermarkets are full-service food retailers. The combination of BI-LO and Coles makes the Supermarkets Group the second-largest food retailer in Australia, with over 500 stores and a 24.6% share of food sales.[19] Woolworths is the leading food retailer, coming in at just above 30% share of sales.[20]

Competition

Coles Supermarkets' major competitor is Woolworths. Coles has had some difficulty keeping up with Woolworths exceptional sales and turnover levels per square meter. Woolworths' main advantage over Coles has been an advertising campaign touting Woolworths as "the Fresh Food People." With the Australian public's recent demand for freshness, this campaign has been extremely successful, enabling Woolworths to gain market share over Coles.

Future Direction

Top managers in the Coles Supermarkets Group are focusing on a four-step program to help improve their performance and regain market position. These steps are:

1. Instituting a major store expansion program, with emphasis on prime locations, as well as opening 25 new BI-LO discount food retail stores by 1998.
2. Making an increased commitment to fresh foods and produce within their Coles full-service supermarkets.
3. Remodeling at least half of their existing store locations.
4. Improving logistical systems, thus lowering costs and, in turn, passing those savings to the customer.

Non-food Retailers: Discount Stores

Coles-Myer owns two of Australia's three leading discount store formats: Kmart and Target. Target and Kmart together account for 75% of the discount store retail sales in Australia.[21] In addition to those market leaders, Coles-Myer also owns Fossey's discount variety stores. Combined, the Discount Stores Group has over 400 locations throughout Australia and New Zealand.[22]

Target is the golden egg in Coles-Myer's discount store basket. It continues to achieve remarkable sales and maintained high profit margins throughout the recent recession and recovery, with 8.8% profit margins in both 1993 and 1994.[23]

Kmart, the first major discount store operation in Australia, reached its peak sales during the 1980s. During the recession, sales plummeted, but since 1993 have begun to rise again. A lack of efficiency in inventory management when major stock reductions had to take place contributed to Kmart's poor performance, drastically reducing profit margin.

Fosseys is a discount variety store with 158 stores throughout Australia.[24] These stores are found primarily in small towns, and a great many Fosseys stores have been closed in recent years due to poor performance. Sales have been on the decline, although in 1994, Fosseys saw its first profit in years.

Competition

The recent entry of category killers as well as specialty furniture, hardware, and appliance retailers pose a threat to discount department stores. Cannibalization in Coles-Myer retail formats is certain; for example, the World 4 Kids toy superstore has taken away toy sales from Kmart.

Future Direction

Target's successes are largely due to its private label apparel line, which is regarded by customers as being extremely high in quality and workmanship, as well as reasonably priced.[25] Target hopes to open another 36 stores by 1998, which is still far below the point of market saturation.[26] Projected sales growth is between 7% and 11% per year. This growth will be due to both store expansion and improved logistics, which will produce economies of scale, thus decreasing costs.[27]

A 6% growth in sales is predicted for Kmart, due, in part, to the opening of 14 new Kmarts by 1998.[28] Regional shopping centers housing Kmarts will also contribute to this growth, with the growing customer attraction to these regional shopping centers. Thirteen of the 14 Kmarts to be opened will be in New Zealand, adding to Coles-Myer's expansion overseas.[29] Improved logistics and cost-cutting measures are a major focus of Kmart's operating plan. Kmart is also introducing a private label line called "Australia's Choice," and these food and beverage products will likely contribute to higher profit margins for the discount store.

Store expansion plans are also being made for Fosseys, although on a different level. The expansion and remodeling efforts are not being done with the hopes of increasing sales and generating higher profit margin, but as an attempt to reposition Fosseys in the minds of the customer (much like Sears did a few years ago in the United States) as a clothing and soft goods retailer.

The Department Stores Group

The Myer-Grace Bros. chain, with over 70 locations, is the largest department store chain in Australia. However, Myer-Grace has seemingly had its heyday. The Myer-Grace Bros. chain of traditional department stores is often mentioned in the same context as dinosaurs, being large, unwieldy, and outdated. Once the flagship of Coles-Myer, contributing 25% of group earnings before interest and taxes (EBIT) in 1990, the chain has had a dreadful performance, now providing just 14% of EBIT.[30]

Competition

The major competitive threats come, once again, from specialty stores and category killers. The loss of market share resulting from these competitors, coupled with poor management, has weakened the foundation on which these department stores once stood. Sales have increased only about 1% per year since 1990, and major stock markdowns have reduced profitability.[31]

Future Direction

Closure of smaller and unprofitable stores is certain, although there are plans in the making for five new stores, all of which will be double the size of most existing Myer-Grace Bros. locations.[32] These new, state-of-the-art department stores will be positioned to attack the specialty stores. Sales growth and improving profit margin will be predicted, thanks to the closing of unprofitable stores, and a decreasing need for stock markdowns.

The Specialty Stores Group

The Specialty Stores Group consists of over 750 locations, with a range of formats.[33] These formats include Katie's womens clothing stores, Liquorland Wine Cellars and liquor stores, Red Rooster take-away restaurants, Chili's Texas Bar & Grill, and two category killers, World 4 Kids and Officeworks. World 4 Kids is a toy superstore that carries a wide range of toys, baby products, and nursery goods.[34] Officeworks carries items ranging from pens and paper to computers, fax machines, and office furniture.[35] In addition, Officeworks has in-store print shops to meet home and business needs. This area of Coles-Myer's operating structure is performing extremely well, achieving tremendous profit margins, despite the category killers' developmental phase expenses.

Future Direction

There is still room for expansion in all of these market areas, and plans are underway for 50 new Katie's (women's clothing) stores and 87 new Liquorland stores and Wine Cellars.[36] The category killers also have expansion plans: at least 10 World 4 Kids stores and over

40 Officeworks stores.[37] However, expansion for the fried chicken (Red Rooster) restaurants is still being considered, as Australians are becoming more health conscious, and the trend toward home-delivered food is increasing. Specialty group sales growth predictions are high. In 1995, a 23% growth rate was projected.[38] Developmental expenses of the newer store formats are beginning to fade, and this should help profit margins.

Strategic Directions

Store Renovation and Expansion

Store renovation and expansion plans are expected to increase both sales revenues and market share. Coles-Myer was expected to spend about AD $4 billion (U.S. $3 billion) between the years 1993 and 1998. This would involve 421 new stores and 1,136 refurbishments, out of a total store base of 1,725 stores.[39] Coles-Myer also plans to gradually close down its unprofitable stores, which will offset its expansion and avoid contributing to over-storing. It is estimated that this will result in a 16% to 17% percent increase in store selling space.[40]

Category Killers

The expansion into the category killer format with World 4 Kids and Officeworks has successfully met consumers' expectations and has forced quite a few independent toy and bicycle stores out of business.[41] This has enabled Coles-Myer to gain market share and has benefited consumers, as well, by driving retail prices down through economies of scale.

Private Label Programs

Coles-Myer has begun a new program aimed at building up its private labels. The company has relaunched and heavily promoted an old supermarket private label, Farmland, with a new range of products that are clearly distinguished from generic lines by high quality products and packaging.[42] Coles-Myer has also developed a private label in its Kmart stores under the name of "Australia's Choice."

Repositioning Efforts

Coles-Myer is also trying to reposition its stores and product offerings to reduce the cannibalization that has been impeding the company's overall progress. In the 1980s, the boom years for discount stores such as Kmart and Target, earnings from these stores were offset by the fact that the customers spending money in Kmart were *not* spending that money in Myer-Grace Bros. department stores. Coles-Myer's new repositioning attempts will likely be geared at exploiting its stores' respective consumer and product profiles.

Cost Reduction

Lastly, Coles-Myer is subjecting all of its retail formats to a major cost reduction and operating efficiency effort. This includes better inventory management to avoid the major stock clearances and writedowns such as the loss of AD $22 million (U.S. $16 million) in 1995, taken on a Myer-Grace Bros. stock clearance of AD $75 million (U.S. $55 million).[43]

DISCUSSION QUESTIONS

1. Coles-Myer is one of the few examples of a retailer that dominates its home market. What elements of the Australian retail market make this possible? Where do you see market opportunities for foreign firms such as Carrefour and Makro entering this market?
2. Do you see opportunities for Coles-Myer to expand outside of Australia? What elements of competition experienced by the company at home will help it in a foreign market?

ENDNOTES

1. "Coles-Myer Company Report." (April 1, 1995). McIntosh & Company Limited in *Investext* [Database on CD-ROM] Foster City, Calif.: Information Access.
2. Roberts, J. (1992). *International Directory of Company Histories,* Vol. 5. Detroit: St. James Press.
3. "Coles-Myer Sells Its Share in Progressive Enterprises." (1993). *Retail News Letter,* July.
4. Roberts (1992).
5. Roberts (1992).
6. Roberts (1992).
7. Roberts (1992).
8. Roberts (1992).
9. Roberts (1992).
10. Roberts (1992).
11. Roberts (1992).
12. Roberts (1992).
13. "Coles-Myer Sells Its Share in Progressive Enterprises" (1993).
14. "Coles-Myer Company Report" (April 1, 1995).
15. "Coles-Myer Company Report" (April 1, 1995).
16. "Coles-Myer Company Report." (September 22, 1993). Merrill Lynch Capital Markets in *Investext* [Database on CD-ROM]. Foster City, Calif.: Information Access.
17. "Coles-Myer Company Report." (June 5, 1992). McIntosh & Company Limited in *Investext* [Database on CD-ROM]. Foster City, Calif.: Information Access.
18. "Coles-Myer Company Report." (May 23, 1994). McIntosh & Company Limited in *Investext* [Database on CD-ROM]. Foster City, Calif.: Information Access.
19. "Coles-Myer Company Report." (October 10, 1994). Morgan Stanley & Co. Inc. in *Investext* [Database on CD-ROM]. Foster City, Calif.: Information Access.
20. "Coles-Myer Company Report" (May 23, 1994).
21. "Coles-Myer Company Report." (March 30, 1994). Merrill Lynch Capital Markets in *Investext* [Database on CD-ROM]. Foster City, Calif.: Information Access.
22. "Coles-Myer Company Report" (April 1, 1995).
23. "Coles-Myer Company Report" (April 1, 1995).
24. "Coles-Myer Company Report" (April 1, 1995).
25. "Coles-Myer Company Report" (September 22, 1993).
26. "Coles-Myer Company Report" (October 10, 1994).
27. "Coles-Myer Company Report" (April 1, 1995).
28. "Coles-Myer Company Report" (April 1, 1995).
29. "Coles-Myer Company Report" (April 1, 1995).
30. "Coles-Myer Company Report" (April 1, 1995).
31. "Coles-Myer Company Report" (March 30, 1994).
32. "Coles-Myer Company Report" (April 1, 1995).
33. "Coles-Myer Company Report" (April 1, 1995).
34. "Coles-Myer Ltd. World 4 Kids Targets Chain." (1993). *Retail News Letter,* October.
35. "Mixed Results for Coles-Myer." (1994). *Retail News Letter,* October.
36. "Australia's Coles-Myer to Spend AD $2.83 billion in Expansion Program." (1993). *Wall Street Journal 3 Star,* Eastern (Princeton, NJ) Edition, August 13, p. B5B.
37. "Coles-Myer Company Report" (April 1, 1995).
38. "Coles-Myer Company Report" (April 1, 1995).
39. "Coles-Myer Company Report" (May 23, 1994).
40. "Coles-Myer Company Report" (May 23, 1994).
41. "Coles-Myer Company Report" (April 1, 1995).
42. "Coles-Myer Company Report" (April 1, 1995).
43. "Coles-Myer Company Report" (April 1, 1995).

COMPANY FOCUS V.2

IKEA

Lori Garijo

To succeed as a global retailer, a company must possess several characteristics that ensure longevity and success. The most important of these characteristics is an understanding of the consumers in the market being entered. Cultural differences, government policies, and economic climates are just a few of the variables that need to be examined in gaining that understanding. Two other characteristics of importance are production location and distribution methods. These factors are especially crucial in determining whether it is feasible for a firm to enter the international market. Conversely, if these factors are not wisely managed, they can also determine how quickly a firm will exit the international market.

IKEA is a company that understands what it takes to become a global retailer. IKEA has more than 50 years of experience as a retailer, with over 30 years as an international retailer. IKEA is looked upon as a model for successful entry into international markets, with good reason. In 1997, IKEA has 136 stores in 17 countries.[1]

History

IKEA is a privately owned firm that was founded by Ingvar Kamprad in 1943, in Sweden. The name IKEA is an acronym for the founder's name and the area where he lived. When Kamprad began his business, furniture was not an item that he sold. Vegetable seeds, fish, and magazines were the extent of his merchandising mix.[2] In 1947, IKEA issued a mail-order catalog, and by 1950 included furniture in its offerings. The opening of IKEA's home furnishing showroom in 1953 was followed by a 13,000 square meter (140,000 square feet) store in 1958. Growth continued, and in 1963, IKEA opened a store in Norway, its first outside of Sweden.[3] Although IKEA is still privately owned, the IKEA Group belongs to a Dutch charitable foundation. However, Kamprad continues to oversee many of the company's operations.

Consumers, Environment, and Employees

> The IKEA vision is to contribute to a better everyday life for the majority of people. We do this by offering a wide range of home furnishing items of good design, and function, at prices so low that the majority of people can afford to buy them.
>
> —*IKEA's corporate philosophy*[4]

IKEA is more than a firm that produces and sells furniture to the public, it is a company that cares. IKEA cares about the public it sells to, the workers it employs, and the environment that surrounds us all. IKEA strives to give its customers convenience, assistance, and an all-around pleasant shopping experience. This is accomplished through the use of unique services and unusual store promotions.

Shortly before the opening of its Long Island, New York store, IKEA sent out a mass-mailing of its catalog, to familiarize consumers in the region of its offering. Television ads were also used to stir up excitement. A few weeks before the store opened, IKEA announced that it was giving away all of the furniture pictured on the cover of its catalog, (a living room suite), to the first person to enter the store on opening day. On the day of the grand opening, consumers found more than a promotional gimmick. They found child care services, low-cost truck and car rack rentals (for customers to take their purchases home), instant credit services, decoration services, and a dining facility serving low-cost Swedish specialties. This is one example of how IKEA creates a total shopping experience for its consumers. These types of services are available at most IKEA stores worldwide. Another example of IKEA's fun and unusual promotions occurred in Canada. On February 26, 1996, IKEA invited customers to visit one of its Canadian stores wearing pajamas. The first 100 people to enter the store in their pajamas would get a free pillow and a coupon to use toward the purchase of bed linens and bedroom furniture. This promotion was designed to celebrate leap year.[5]

IKEA also provides convenience for its customers. Realizing that customers would have to travel long distances to shop, after the closing of its Quebec City store, IKEA provided those customers with a home shopping phone order service.[6]

Commitment to the communities it enters is another IKEA hallmark. IKEA has been using Polish suppliers since 1965 and opened its first Polish store in 1990. Another IKEA outlet was opened in the town of Janki, near Warsaw in 1993. The opening of this store was part of an investment that IKEA made to that community. The Janki store was the first stage of achieving a goal; the creation of an "American-style" shopping center in Poland. The goal was realized on September 7, 1995, with the opening of the Regional Shopping Center in Janki. The Janki shopping center is the largest IKEA store in central Europe, and "has become a magnet for weekend family shopping trips."[7]

Consistent with IKEA's vision to create a "better everyday life" is its focus on environmental concerns. In 1993, IKEA began printing its catalog on nonchlorine-bleached paper. The company brochure is also printed on recycled paper, and to save the cost of printing yearly brochures, the brochure is expected to remain current for at least three years.[8]

Recycling is a growing movement in the United States, and it is a cause that IKEA is happy to champion. In many of its stores, the IKEA catalog may be brought back to the store for recycling.[9] After the Christmas season, IKEA offers free mulching to customers who return their trees to the store.

Another example of IKEA's ongoing concern for the environment is its constant search for methods and products that will not cause harm to the environment during the production of furniture. In March 1996, IKEA began testing products from AMT, a California-based company that produces a line of water-based wood coatings.[10] These water-based coatings eliminate the potential environmental hazards that arise from using solvent-based coatings. If the products are approved by IKEA, the company will recommend that its suppliers use the AMT products.[11]

Ingvar Kamprad formed the IKEA Foundation in 1982. The IKEA Foundation presents monetary awards and grants to individuals, companies, and institutions whose contributions in the areas of design, environment, production, and architecture have had a positive effect on the "majority of the people."[12] These awards are presented every three years.

IKEA is also known for its consideration of its employees. When the company closed its Quebec City store, it was concerned with the fate of its employees. IKEA offered workers leaving the company severance pay based on "one month's salary for every year of service plus outplacement support."[13] IKEA also promised to investigate relocation opportunities for its workers.[14]

In France, legislation allows employees to take a six- to 11-month unpaid break for the birth of a child, to create a business, or for a sabbatical leave of absence. To offset the possibilities of financial hardship to its employees, IKEA France has created an unusual agreement with its workers. The agreement is called CET or Compte Epargne Temps (time-saving account), which allows employees to save unused leave, and apply it towards the leave of absence. The employees benefit from a paid leave of absence, and IKEA benefits from the ability to plan employee absences and coordinate replacement workers.[15]

In New York City, the IKEA outpost store is unique because it remains closed during its frequent theme changes. IKEA compensates its employees by keeping workers on the payroll during the downtime. IKEA allows staff to log their hours by doing volunteer work for a charity that they (employees) select.[16]

Suppliers, Distribution, and Information Systems

Using a global sourcing network allows IKEA to minimize costs. This system lowers costs by decreasing the distance needed to ship goods to IKEA's numerous worldwide locations. It is more economical to ship goods manufactured in North America to stores located in North America, than it is to ship them from another country. Suppliers contracted by IKEA are closely monitored and often benefit from IKEA's close supervision. This is a necessity because many of the company's furniture parts come from different manufacturers. For example, the legs of a chair may come from one supplier, the seat from another, and the back from a third; IKEA's strict quality control system ensures that these pieces fit together when the consumer is ready to assemble them.[17] To facilitate the acquisition of suppliers, IKEA has invested in or become a joint owner of furniture industries in many different countries. IKEA suppliers receive training, technical advice, leased equipment, and long-term contracts. In return, IKEA receives an exclusive contract and suppliers who will work closely with its designers to lower costs.[18,19]

IKEA's furniture is boxed in flat packages. This packaging system has three benefits. IKEA benefits by saving money (flat packages save space during transport) and by reducing damage to goods during transportation. Consumers also benefit because most of the packages can easily fit into an average car. Central warehouses are used as a furniture "pit-stop" before it is delivered to the stores. IKEA is trying to develop a more efficient system to reduce the intermediate storage time at the warehouses. Direct delivery to stores and consumers is limited but increasing.[20]

IKEA carries a wide variety of products; more than 12,000 SKUs. To assist in pricing and inventory control, IKEA has enlisted the services of the Oracle Corporation. Oracle is a leading supplier of information management software. IKEA had developed a pricing information system using Oracle's software. The new system allows the individual IKEA stores to set prices and print price tags.[21] Before the development of this system, price tags and product information labels were generated in Sweden and took up to six weeks to reach the stores. The new system also enables the individual stores to quickly adjust prices in their local areas, and update their product information labeling without the time lag from Sweden.[22]

International Furniture Industry

In the international furniture industry, importing to the United States is indicative of success. The United States is the world's largest single furniture market, as well as the largest single manufacturing country, with an annual production of approximately $22 billion. The European market is a close second with an annual production of $19 billion.[23]

Because of the wide variety of designs available to European consumers from European manufacturers, importing to the United States is crucial for a global furniture company. For the same reason, there is little demand for imports from Asia or the United States, and the volume of imports from these two countries to Europe is very small.[24] Two European companies that are considered to be international companies due to their success in importing to the United States are IKEA and Natuzzi of Italy.[25] Another factor contributing to the success of these two companies is their sophisticated channels of distribution, a characteristic not usually attributed to European furniture manufacturers.[26]

The third largest furniture manufacturing market is Asia. The largest Asian importers (labeled the "Asian Tigers" in the furniture industry) are Taiwan, Indonesia, China, Thailand, Malaysia, and the Philippines. Individually, these Asian manufacturers are small when compared to European manufacturers. The exceptions are the Taiwanese companies who are the leading importers of furniture in both the United States and Japan.[27]

The home furniture industry appears to be reasonably free from barriers to importing and exporting products. Growth in this industry can be expected, but factors such as local and worldwide economies could have a slowing effect.[28]

International Entry—United States

When IKEA entered the U.S. market by opening a 169,000 square foot (15,700 square meter) store outside Philadelphia, in 1985, it did not follow the basic rules of international retailing. The company did not appear to research the U.S. market extensively, and although it is often held up as an example of successful international entry, it suffered a few setbacks initially.

IKEA did not anticipate any major problems in its U.S. expansion, but by 1989, several of its stores had yet to show a profit. This concerned the company, because in each new European country it had entered, a profit was realized within the first two or three years of entry.[29] IKEA assumed that the same approach that had worked for it in other countries would work in the United States as well.

One of the problems that IKEA encountered was American indifference to some of its product offerings. American consumers prefer matching bedroom suites—IKEA did not offer any. Americans prefer wide beds—IKEA offered only narrow beds with sheets measured in centimeters. The kitchen cabinets that IKEA stocked in its U.S. stores were too small to accommodate the large dinner plates that Americans normally use. When IKEA's staff noticed that customers were not buying its drinking glasses, but their vases were selling very quickly, management began to speak to customers in an effort to understand the odd buying patterns. It was soon discovered that the U.S. shoppers were purchasing the vases to use as drinking glasses. The glasses IKEA offered were too small for Americans, who prefer ice with their beverages.[30]

Other cultural obstacles that plagued IKEA were an American fondness for liberal return policies, and

American dislike for waiting in long lines.[31] IKEA quickly made the appropriate changes, and the situation improved. Although IKEA was forced to make these changes in order to suit U.S. tastes, the company's core concept remains the same, and its ability to adapt to different international markets is the key to the company's success.[32]

Another primary concern of IKEA when entering a new market is maintaining low costs. High corporate costs lead to higher prices for consumers. Although IKEA has an international reputation for cost trimming, the company did not have a clear strategy on how to cheaply supply the American market. This lack of a clear strategy led to high costs resulting from shipping products to the United States from Europe, as well as availability problems for certain items. To combat these problems, IKEA arranged for a high percentage of the furniture to be produced locally.[33]

IKEA responded quickly and adequately to the problems encountered in the U.S. market. IKEA entered the U.S. market in 1985 and did not realize a profit until 1993; yet the company remained committed to its U.S. expansion. Currently, IKEA has 15 stores in the United States, including a "marketing outpost" store located in New York City.

Innovations: The IKEA Marketing Outpost Store

IKEA's "marketing outpost" store—a concept store in New York City—is located at the busy intersection of 57th Street and Lexington Avenue. The 7,500 square foot (700 square meter) store changes its concept every 8 to 12 weeks and totally shuts down its operations during these changes.[34] The outpost opened in the fall of 1995 with the theme of IKEA COOKS. For the duration of this theme, the outpost featured kitchen furnishings as well as cookware; the sales staff dressed in chef uniforms.[35] By Thanksgiving of the same year, the outpost reopened with the theme IKEA PLAYS. All traces of IKEA COOKS were removed and replaced, including exterior signs, and shopping bags.[36] It was decided that opening a full-scale IKEA store in Manhattan would defeat the low-cost policy of the company. The overhead from operating in an area as expensive as downtown Manhattan would raise prices chain-wide.[37] Sales are not the primary goal of the concept store; instead, the store is used as a marketing vehicle to promote interest in IKEA's nearby stores.[38]

The outpost store features a shuttle bus program called "Passport to Sweden." Customers participating in this program receive a "passport," and if they are intrigued by what they see at the outpost store, they may use their "passport" to take a shuttle bus trip to full-scale IKEA stores on Long Island or in Elizabeth, New Jersey. After several trips, customers may turn in their "passport" (every bus trip entitles riders to a stamp in their passport) for merchandise credit.[39,40] Frequent bus riders are entered into a lottery for a free flight to Sweden. This concept store has proven beneficial to IKEA. According to Martin Dooley, the outpost director of events, the sales of the Elizabeth, New Jersey store have increased significantly.[41]

Future Expansion

IKEA continues to expand globally, and seems intent on opening stores in every country on the planet. The company's planned expansion into Israel created a controversy when, in 1994, Ingvar Kamprad publicly admitted to having affiliations with Nazi extremist groups from 1945 into the 1950s.[42] This admission led to a series of discussions with the Simon Wiesenthal Center, which is committed to focusing attention on people or companies with past Nazi affiliations. After these discussions, the Center, along with other Jewish groups, accepted Kamprad's apology for his past, and announced that they would not attempt to block IKEA from opening a store in Israel.[43,44] In 1995, IKEA announced its plans to open a store in that country.[45]

Currently, IKEA is undertaking expansion plans in the People's Republic of China (PRC). Beijing and Shanghai are the two locations of interest to the company.[46] The PRC is an untapped market for most retailers and is sure to be a profitable one for businesses throughout the next decade. IKEA is wise to get an early start in this emerging market, and it will be interesting to watch the company's future development there.

Conclusions

IKEA has consistently proven itself as a major player in the international business community. IKEA's strong corporate philosophy, cost-saving measures, and commitment to providing convenience and quality furniture for its consumers ensures its high ranking. It is not surprising that IKEA is often held up as a model to businesses attempting to enter international markets.

DISCUSSION QUESTIONS

1. IKEA is often given as an example of a global company. What characteristics of a global company have been highlighted in this case? Do you see any elements of this company's strategy that do not reflect a global strategy?
2. Most global companies are smaller-scaled specialty stores. IKEA enters the market in a larger-store format. Is there something unique about the company's product line that allows it to do this?
3. What do you think are two of IKEA's most significant ownership advantages?

ENDNOTES

1. *Retail News Letter.* (1997). No. 446, p. 14.
2. Jefferys, J. B. (1992). "The IKEA Group." in A. Hast, ed., *International Directory of Company Histories,* Vol. 5. Detroit: St. James Press, pp. 85–87.
3. Jefferys (1992).
4. *IKEA Company Brochure* (1993).
5. "The Best Thing About a Leap Year... Is the Extra Night of Sleep." (February 26, 1996). http://www.newswire.ca/releases/February 1996/26/c3812.html.
6. "IKEA Quebec City." (July 5, 1996) http://www.newswire.ca/releases/July 1996/05/c0637.html.
7. Sosnowska-Smogorzewska, L. (1995). "Pride in Suburban Sprawl." *The Warsaw Voice,* September 17. http://www.contact.waw.pl/voice/v360/ bus01.s html.
8. *IKEA Company Brochure* (1993).
9. Roach, L. (1994). "IKEA: Furnishing the World." *Discount Merchandiser,* October, pp. 46–48.
10. "AMT Environment Products AMV 11/8 VSE." (March 1996). *AMT Environmental Products.* http://www.westergaard.com:8080/ENV/amv3. html.
11. "AMT Environmental Products (1996).
12. "An IKEA Award to Maurice Strong, Canada." (October 6, 1995). http://www.newswire.ca/releases/ October 1995/06/c0851.html.
13. "IKEA to Close Store in Quebec City." (March 8, 1996). http://www.newswire.ca/releases/March 1996/08/c1239.html.
14. "IKEA to Close Store in Quebec City" (1996).
15. *Retail News Letter.* (1996). No. 431.
16. McCarthy, C. (1996). "IKEA's Manhattan Outpost." *Visual Merchandising and Store Design,* May, pp. 36–41.
17. *IKEA Company Brochure* (1993).
18. *IKEA Company Brochure* (1993).
19. "Furnishing the World." (1994). *The Economist,* November 19, pp. 79–80.
20. *IKEA Company Brochure* (1993).
21. "IKEA Corp. Modernizes Operations with Oracle 7." (January 23, 1996), *Oracle Corporation.* http://www.oracle.com/corporate/press/html/ikea.html.
22. "IKEA Corp. Modernizes Operations" (1996).
23. Johnson, C. (1996). "Furniture, Household." In D. M. Sawinski and W. H. Mason, eds., *Encyclopedia of Global Industries.* Detroit: Gale Research, pp. 576-582.
24. Johnson (1996).
25. Johnson (1996).
26. Johnson (1996).
27. Johnson (1996).
28. Johnson (1996).
29. "Furnishing the World." (1994). *The Economist,* November 19, pp. 79–80.
30. "Furnishing the World" (1994).

31. "Furnishing the World" (1994).
32. Begg, D. (1995). "What Does It Take to Be a Global Retailer?" *Discount Merchandiser,* September, p. 48.
33. "Furnishing the World" (1994).
34. Roach (1994).
35. Roach (1994).
36. McCarthy (1996).
37. McCarthy (1996).
38. Roach (1995).
39. Roach (1995).
40. McCarthy (1996).
41. McCarthy (1996).
42. White, G. (1994). "IKEA Founder Issues Apology for Long-Ago Ties to Nazi Groups; Home Edition." *Los Angeles Times,* November 9, p. D-1.
43. White (1994).
44. "IKEA to Establish Franchise in Israel." (1995). *Simon Wiesenthal Center News Release,* November 24. http://www.wiesenthal.com.
45. Torres, V. (1995). "Briefly Retailing; Home Edition." *Los Angeles Times,* November 28, p. D-2.
46. Bergmann, J. (1995). "China Reassessed." *Discount Merchandiser,* May, pp. 94–105.

BIBLIOGRAPHY

Alawi, H. (1986). "Saudi Arabia: Making Sense of Self-Service." *International Marketing Review*, Spring, pp. 21–38.

"Asda Group PLC—Company Report" (March 12, 1996). FT Analysis in *Investext* [Database on CD-ROM]. Foster City, Calif.: Information Access.

Aydin, N., and M. Kacker. (1990). "International Outlook of U.S. Based Franchisers." *International Marketing Review*, Vol. 7, No. 2, pp. 43–53.

Barents, J., P. Bontinck, and T. E. Hoo, (1988). "Analysis of Retailing in the Benelux Countries." *International Trends in Retailing*, Vol. 5, No. 1, pp. 3–18.

Benetton, L. "Franchising: How Brand Power Works." In P. Stobart, ed., *Brand Power.* New York: New York University Press.

Berner, R. (1997). "How Gap's Own Design Shop Keeps Its Imitators Hustling." *Wall Street Journal*, March 13, p. B1.

———. (1997). "Now the Hot Designers on Seventh Avenue Work for Macy's, Sears." *Wall Street Journal*, March 13, p. B1.

Berry, B. (1963). *Commercial Structure and Commercial Blight; Retail Patterns and Processes in the City of Chicago.* Research Paper No. 85. Chicago University of Chicago, Department of Geography.

———. (1967). *Geography of Market Centres and Retail Distribution.* Englewood Cliffs, N.J.: Prentice-Hall.

Borchert, J. (1995) "Retail Planning Policy in the Netherlands." In R. L. Davies, ed., *Retail Planning Policies in Western Europe.* London: Routledge.

Bower, J., and J. Matthews. (1994). *Marks & Spencer: Sir Richard Greenbury's Quiet Revolution.* Harvard Business School, Case 9-395-054.

Bowersox, D., and M. B. Cooper (1992). *Strategic Marketing: Channel Management.* New York: McGraw-Hill, p. 157.

Brown, S. (1995). "Christaller Knew My Father: Recycling Central Place Theory." *Journal of Macro Marketing*, Spring, pp. 60–73.

Bucklin, L. (1966). *A Theory of Distribution Structure.* Berkeley, Calif.: IBER Special Publications.

Burns, D., and D. Rayman. (1996). "Retailing in Canada and the United States: Historical Comparisons." In G. Akehurst and N. Alexander, eds., *The Internationalisation of Retailing.* London: Frank Cass.

Burt, S. "Retailer Brands in British Grocery Retailing: A Review." Working Paper 9204 Institute for Retail Studies, University of Stirling, Stirling, UK.

Burt, W., and L. Sparks, (1997). "Performance in Food Retailing: A Cross-national Consideration and Comparison of Retail Margins." *British Journal of Management*, Vol. 8, pp. 119–136.

Caplen, B. (1989). "Selling Quality in Cloneland." *Asian Business*, Vol. 25, No. 5, pp. 62–63.

"Carrefour—Company Report." (March 29, 1995). UBS Research in *Investext* [Database on CD-ROM]. Foster City, Calif.: Information Access.

Cateora, P. R. (1996). *International Marketing.* 9th ed. Chicago: Irwin, p. 316.

Chang, C.-H. (1988)., "The Development of Consignment Sales." *Chuan-Hsin Magazine* (Taiwan), Vol. 6, pp. 116–118.

Chang, H.-M., S.-L. Yeh, and J.-C. Li (1988b), "The Study of Department Store Consumers' Behavior." Chuan-Hsin Magazine (Taiwan), Vol. 6, pp. 13–15.

Chang, L., and B. Sternquist. (1993), "Taiwanese Department Store Industry: An Overview." *International*

Journal of Retail and Distribution Management, Vol. 21, No. 1, pp. 26–34.

China Food Market Overview. (1997). Report Code CH9662V, AGR No. CH6810. (March).

China Statistical Yearbook. (1996). Beijing: China Statistical Publishing House.

Chiu, C.-S. (1990). "The Study of Introductory Development of Contemporary Retail Organization." Unpublished thesis, National Politics University (Taiwan).

Chou, M.-P. (1986). "Department Store Industry: The Perspectives of Past, Present, and Future." *Da-Yeh Financial Investment Magazine* (Taiwan).

Christaller, W. (1963). *Central Places in Southern Germany.* (C. Baskin, trans.). Englewood Cliffs, N.J.: Prentice-Hall.

Coopers & Lybrand. (1995). *Global Powers of Retailing.* Chain Store Age Special Report.

———. (1995). "Global Retailing: Assignment Asia." *Chain Store Age Executive,* January.

———. (1996). "Global Retailing: Assignment Asia." *Chain Store Age,* April, Section 2.

———. (1996). *Global Retailing: Assignment Eastern Europe.*

———. (1996). *Global Retailing: Assignment Latin America.*

Cross, J. "Retailing in a Neighborhood Street Market: A Tianguista Family in Mexico." @http://aucăcs.eun.eg/www/cross/retail2.html

Czinkota, M. (1985). "Distribution of Consumer Products in Japan." *International Marketing Review,* Autumn, pp. 39–50.

Davies, B., and R. Schmidt. (1991). "Going Shopping in Poland: The Changing Scene of Polish Retailing." *International Journal of Retail and Distribution Management,* Vol. 19, No. 4, pp. 20–27.

Dawson, J., and T. Sato. (1983). "Controls Over the Development of Large Stores in Japan." *Service Industries Journal,* Vol. 3, No. 2, pp. 136–145.

Delnevo, R. (1990). "Tie Rack, plc. Case Study." In M. Abell, ed., *The International Franchise Option.* London: Waterlow Publishers, pp. 339–347.

Distribution and Marketing in Japan (Series 3. Retail and Wholesale Distribution). (1985).

"Distribution of Goods and Services in Greece." ADIGOS—Distribution of Goods and Services. Microsoft Internet Explorer. [Web site]

"Docks de France—Company Report." (April 24, 1995). Hoare Govett Securities in *Investext* [Database on CD-ROM]. Foster City, Calif.: Information Access.

Drasny, T. (1992). "Retailing in Czechoslovakia, Retailing in Eastern Europe." *International Journal of Retail and Distribution Management,* Vol. 20, No. 6, pp. 30–33.

Drtina, T. (1996). "The Internationalization of Retailing in the Czech and Slovak Republics." In G. Akehurst and N. Alexander, eds., *The Internationalisation of Retailing.* London: Frank Cass, pp. 191–203.

Dunning, J. H. (1981). *International Production and the Multinational Enterprise.* London: Allen & Unwin.

Dunning, J. H., and M. McQueen. (1982). "The Eclectic Theory of the Multinational Enterprise and the International Hotel Industry." In A. M. Rugman, ed., *New Theories of the Multinational Enterprise.* Beckenham, Kent: Croom Helm, pp. 79–106.

Earle, J., R. Fryman, A. Rapaczynski, and J. Turkewitz. (1994). *Small Privatization: The Transformation of Retail Trade and Consumer Services in the Czech Republic, Hungary and Poland.* Budapest: Central European University Press.

Entrepreneur. (1996). Seventeenth Annual Franchise 500. January, pp. 211–311.

Eroglu, S. (1992). "The Internationalisation Process of Franchise Systems: A Conceptual Model." *International Marketing Review,* Vol. 9, No. 5, pp.11–39.

"Europe: Blood on the Shelves." (1996). *Business Week International Editions: International Business—Europe,* Vol. 3462, February 12, p. 18.

The European Retail Handbook, 1997 Edition. (1997). London: Corporate Intelligence on Retailing.

Evans, W., H. Lane, and S. Grady. (1992). *Border Crossings: Doing Business in the US.* Scarborough, Ontario, Canada: Prentice-Hall.

Fenster, E. (1995). "Letter from Moscow." *Small World,* Vol. 1, No. 6, November/December, p. 10.

Fladmoe-Lindquist, K. (1996). "International Franchising: Capabilities and Development." *Journal of Business Venturing,* Vol. 11, pp. 419–438.

Flath, D. (1990). "Why Are There So Many Retail Stores in Japan?" *Japan and the World Economy,* Vol. 2, pp. 365–386.

Fraschetto, W. (1997). "Mexico." *International Trends in Marketing,* Vol. 14, No. 1, pp. 103–105.

Galeries Lafayette—Company Report. (December 4, 1996). SBC Warburg in *Investext* [Database on CD-ROM]. Foster City, Calif.: Information Access.

"GIB—Company Report." (February 23, 1996). Credit Lyonnais Laing in *Investext* [Database on CD-ROM]. Foster City, Calif.: Information Access.

Goldman, A. (1991). "Japan's Distribution System: Institutional Structure Internal Political Economy and Modernization. *Journal of Retailing,* Vol. 67, No. 2, pp. 154–182.

———. (1992). "Evaluating the Performance of the Japanese Distribution System." *Journal of Retailing,* Vol. 68, No. 1, pp. 11–39.

Goldman, M. (1991). *What Went Wrong with Perestroika.* New York: W.W. Norton and Company, p. 116.

Goldstein, C. (1988). "The Bargain Hunters." *Far Eastern Economic Review,* May 26, p. 82.

Goll, S. (1995). "China's Big State-Owned Retail Stores Form New Ventures with Foreign Firms." *Wall Street Journal,* March 13, p. B5A.

"Great Universal Stores—Company Report." (April 2, 1997). Greig Middleton & Co. Ltd. in *Investext* [Database on CD-ROM]. Foster City, Calif.: Information Access.

"Great Universal Stores—Company Report." (March 5, 1997). Merrill Lynch Capital Markets in *Investext* [Database on CD-ROM]. Foster City, Calif.: Information Access.

"GUM—Company Report." (October 22, 1996). Credit Suisse First Boston in *Investext* [Database on CD-ROM]. Foster City, Calif.: Information Access.

Hall, E. (1983). *The Dance of Life.* New York: Anchor Books-Doubleday.

Hall, L. (1992). *Latecomer's Guide to the New Europe: Doing Business in Central Europe.* New York: American Marketing Association.

Hall, M. (1951). *Distributive Trading.* London: Hutchinson's University Library.

Ho, D., and N. Leigh. (1994). "A Retail Revolution." *The China Business Review,* January–February, pp. 22–27.

Hoare Govett Securities, LTD, April 24, 1995, Docks de France—Company Report in *Investext.*

Hock, T. L. (1989). "How the Japanese Are Winning the Retailing War." *Asian Finance,* January 15, pp. 26–27.

Hofstede, G. (1980). *Culture's Consequences: International Differences in Work-Related Values.* Beverly Hills, Calif.: Sage Publications.

———. (1992). "Motivation, Leadership, and Organization: Do American Theories Apply Abroad?" In H. Lane and J. DiStefano, eds., *International Management Behavior,* 2nd ed. Boston: PWS-Kent, pp. 98–122.

Hollander, S. C. (1970). *Multinational Retailing.* East Lansing, Mich.: Michigan State University.

Hong Kong Trade Development Council Research Department. (1994). *Retail and Wholesale Distribution of Consumer Goods in China.* Hong Kong: Hong Kong Trade Development Council.

———. (1995). *Market Report on Wholesale and Retail Distribution of Garments in China.* Hong Kong: Hong Kong Trade Development Council.

Howard, E. (1995), "Retail Planning Policy in the UK. In R. L. Davies, ed., *Retail Planning Policies in Western Europe.* London: Routledge.

Hughes, A. (July 9, 1996). "Marks & Spencer—Company Report." UBS Research Limited in Investext [Database on CD-ROM]. Foster City, Calif.: Information Access.

Huszagh, S. M., F. W., Huszagh, and F. McIntyre. (1992). "International Franchising in the Context of Competitive Strategy and the Theory of the Firm." *International Marketing Review,* Vol. 9, No. 5, pp. 5–18.

International Franchising Association (IFA). (1992). *Franchising in the Economy: 1989–1992.* Washington, D.C.: IFA Educational Foundation.

Ishani, M. (1996). *Franchising in Italy. Franchise Update.* Web Services by Los Trancos Systems, LLC. [Web site]

James, P. (1992). "Retailing in Hungary: Centrum Department Stores." *International Journal of Retail and Distribution Management,* Vol. 20, No. 6, pp. 24–29.

Johansson, J. (1997). *Global Marketing: Foreign Entry, Local Marketing and Global Management.* Chicago, Ill.: Irwin.

Jones Lang Wootten. (1996). *Retailing Planning Policies.* Oxford, England: Oxford Institute of Retail Management.

Jones, K., W. Evans, and C. Smith. (1994). *New Formats in the Canadian Retail Economy,* Center for the Study of Commercial Activity. Toronto, Canada: Ryerson Polytechnic University.

Jordon, M. (1996). "Marketing Gurus Say: In India, Think Cheap, Lose the Cold Cereal." *Wall Street Journal,* October 11, p. A9.

"Kaufhof—Company Report." (October 2, 1995). Oppenheim Finanzanalyse GMBH in *Investext* [Database on CD-ROM]. Foster City, Calif.: Information Access.

KPMG—International (May 1996). Central Europe. Microsoft Internet Explorer. [Web site]

Kuo, C.-H. (1989). "The Prediction of Department Store's Present and Future: Based on Consumers' Preferences." *Direct Marketing (Taiwan),* Vol. 25, pp. 39–51.

La Follette, C. (1993). "Retail in Mexico, 1993." Harvard Business School Case 0-793-144, September 28.

"La Rinascente—Company Report." (December 11, 1995). Lehman Brothers Limited in *Investext* [Database on CD-ROM]. Foster City, Calif.: Information Access.

Lam, D. K.-K. (1989). "The Neglected Market: Opportunities in Taiwan." *Canadian Business Review,* Vol. 16, No. 3, pp. 45–48.

Larke, R. (1994). *Japanese Retailing.* New York: Routledge.

Lee, D. (1991). "Rebuilding a Tiger: Who'll Get the Lion's Share." *Business Week,* March 25, pp. 46–47.

Lein, F. (1987). *Department Stores in Japan.* Tokyo: Sophis University Bulletin, No. 115, p. 10.

Lin, I-C., and W.-C. Ling. (1988). "An Overview of Human Resources for Department Store Industry." *Chuan-Hsin Magazine,* Vol. 6, pp. 92–96.

Lo, T., O. Yau, and Y. Li. (1986). "International Transfer of Service Technology: An Exploratory Study of the Case of Supermarkets in China." *Management International Review,* Vol. 26, No. 2, pp. 71–76.

Lofman, B. (1994). "Polish Society in Transformation." In C. Schultz, R. Belk, and G. Ger, eds., *Research in Consumer Behavior: Consumption in Marketizing Economies,* Vol. 7. Greenwich, Conn.: JAI Press, p. 30.

Love, J. (1995). *McDonald's: Behind the Arches.* New York: Bantam Books.

Martin, R. E. (1988). "Franchising and Risk Management." *American Economic Review,* Vol. 78, No. 5, pp. 954–968.

McCracken, G. (1988). *Culture and Consumption.* Bloomington, Ind.: Indiana University Press.

McMaster, D. (1987). "Own Brands and the Cookware Market." *European Journal of Marketing,* Vol. 21, pp. 59–78.

Montagu-Pollock, M. (1991). "All the Right Connections: Chinese Management Has Amazing Advantages Over 'Modern' Methods." *Asian Business* (Hong Kong), Vol. 27, No. 1, pp. 20–24.

Murata, S. (1973). "Distribution in Japan." *The Wheel Extended,* Autumn, pp. 4–11.

Nakane, C. (1970). *Japanese Society.* Berkeley, Calif.: University of California Press.

Nienhuis, J., ed. (1991). *Retailing in the Netherlands.* Netherlands: Center for Retail Research.

O'Connor, D. (1997). "Retail Concentration and Multinational Expansion: Two Important Retail Bonds." *Discount Merchandiser,* Vol. 37, No. 5, p. 64.

Peck, M. J., & T. J. Richardson. (1991). *What Is to Be Done? Proposals for the Soviet Transition to the Market.* New Haven, Conn.: Yale University Press.

Pecotich, A., N. Renko, and C. Shultz (1994). "Yugoslav Disintegration, War, and Consumption in Croatia." In C. Schultz, R. Belk, and G. Ger, eds., *Consumption in Marketizing Economies,* Vol. 7. Greenwich, Conn.: JAI Press, pp. 1–27.

Pellegrini, L. (1991) "The Internationalization of Retailing and 1992 Europe." *Journal of Marketing Channels,* Vol. 1, No. 2, pp. 3–27.

———. (1994). "Alternatives for Growth and Internationalization in Retailing." *International Review of Retail, Distribution and Consumer Research,* Vol. 4, No. 2, pp. 121–148.

Pellegrini, L., and A. Cardani. (1992). *The Italian Distribution System.* Report prepared for the OECD Study on Distribution Systems, University of Bocconi, March.

Pellet, J. (1995). "Retailing in Eastern Europe." *Discount Merchandiser,* Vol 35, July 1, p. 72.

"Pepkor/Edgars/Pick 'n Pay/Wooltru — Company Report." (September 6, 1995). Lehman Brothers Limited in *Investext* [Database on CD-ROM]. Foster City, Calif.: Information Access.

Phillips, L. A., B. Sternquist, and S. Mui (1992). "Hong Kong Department Stores: Retailing in the 1990s." *International Journal of Retail & Distribution Management,* Vol. 20, No. 1, pp. 16–24.

Porter, M. E. (1990). *The Competitive Advantage of Nations.* New York: The Free Press.

Portugal's Food Market. (1994). Madrid, Spain: Agricultural Affairs Office of the Foreign Agricultural Service/USDA.

"Promodès—Company Report." (March 31, 1995). EIFB in *Investext* [Database on CD-ROM]. Foster City, Calif.: Information Access.

Ren, A. (June 24, 1996). "Far Eastern Department Stores-Company Report." Bankers Trust Research in *Investex* [Database on CD-ROM]. Foster City, Calif.: *Information Access.*

Retail Planning Policies. (1996). Oxford, UK: Jones Lang Wooton/Oxford Institute of Retail Management.

"Retailers: Germany—Industry Report." (March 6, 1996). BHF Trust in Investext [Database on CD-ROM]. Foster City, Calif.: Information Access.

Robinson, T. M., and C. Clarke-Hill (1990). "Directional Growth by European Retailers." *International Journal of Retail and Distribution Management,* Vol. 18, No. 5, pp. 3–14.

———. (1994). "Competitive Advantage Through Strategic Retail Alliances: A European Perspective," presented at Recent Advances in Retailing and Service Science Conference, University of Alberta, Canada, May 1994.

———. (1995). "International Alliances in European Retailing." In P. McGoldrick and G. Davies, eds., *International Retailing Trends and Strategies.* London: Pitman Publishing, pp. 133–150.

Rostow, W. W. (1960). The Stages of Economic Growth. London: Cambridge University Press.

Rutledge, R., and J. Patmon. (1996). "South China Food Market Overview." FAS Online, AGR No. CH6610. (July 9).

Saimee, S. (1993). "Retailing and Channel Considerations in Developing Countries: A Review and Research Propositions." *Journal of Business Research,* Vol. 27, pp. 103–130.

Salmon, W. J., and A. Tordjman. (1989). "The Internationalization of Retailing." *International Journal of Retailing,* Vol. 4, No. 2, pp. 3–16.

Samarasinghe, S.W.R. de A., and R. Coughlan. (1991). *Economic Dimensions of Ethnic Conflict.* New York: St. Martin's Press.

Sampson, S. (1991). "May You Live Only by Your Salary! The Unplanned Economy in Eastern Europe." *Social Justice,* Vol. 15, No. 3/4, pp. 135–159.

Schultz, C., R. Belk, and G. Ger, eds. (1994). *Research in Consumer Behavior: Consumption in Marketizing Economies,* Vol. 7. Greenwich, Conn.: JAI Press.

"Sears Roebuck de Mexico—Company Report." (May 10, 1996). Lehman Brothers, Inc. In *Investext.* [Database on CD-ROM] Foster city, Calif.: Information Access.

Second Workshop on Japan's Distribution Systems and Business Practices. Tokyo: MIPRO.

Seitz, H. (1992). "Retailing in Eastern Europe: An Overview." *International Journal of Retail and Distribution Management* Vol. 20, No. 6, pp. 4–10.

Shaw, S., J. Dawson, and M. Blair (1992). "The Sourcing of Retailer Brand Food Products." *Journal of Marketing Management,* Vol. 8, No. 2, pp. 127–146.

———. (1992). "Imported Foods in a British Supermarket Chain: Buyer Decisions in Safeway." *International Review of Retail, Distribution and Consumer Research,* Vol. 2, No. 1, pp. 35–57.

Shen, I-H. (1988)., "An Overview of Taipei Coordinated Department Store Association." *Chuan-Hsin Magazine,* Vol. 6, pp. 112–115.

Shimaguchi, M. (1993). "New Development in Channel Strategy in Japan." M. R. Czinkota and M. Kotabe, eds., *The Japanese Distribution System.* Chicago: Probus Publishing Co., pp. 173–190.

Shook, C. and R. Shook. (1993). *Franchising: The Business Strategy That Changed the World.* Englewood Cliffs, N.J.: Prentice-Hall.

Spain Food Market Overview. (1996). Madrid, Spain: American Embassy.

Sparks, L. (1997). "A Review of Retail Co-Operatives in the UK." *The World of Co-operative Enterprise 1997.* pp.187–192.

Sparks, L. (1997). "From Coca-Colonization to Copy-Cotting: The Cott Corporation and Retailer Brand Soft Drinks in the UK and the USA." *Agribusiness,* Vol. 13, No. 2.

Statistical Review of Tourism (1988). Hong Kong: Hong Kong Tourist Association, p. 41.

Sternquist, B. (1994). "Gatekeepers of Consumer Choice: A Four-Country Comparison of Retail Buyers." *International Review of Retail, Distribution and Consumer Research,* Vol. 4, No. 2, pp. 159–176.

———. (1997). "International Expansion of US Retailers." *International Journal of Retail & Distribution Management,* Vol. 25, No. 8, pp. 262–268.

———. (1997). "Internationalization of Japanese Department Stores." *International Journal of Commerce and Management,* Special Issue on Global Retailing, Vol. 7, No. 1, pp. 57–73.

Sternquist, B., and M. Kacker. (1994). *European Retailing's Vanishing Borders.* Westport, Conn.: Quorum Press.

Sternquist, B., X. Q. Zhou, and Y. Chengmin. (1995). "China: The Planned to Free Market Paradigm." *International Journal of Retail and Distribution Management,* Vol. 23, No. 12, pp. 21–28.

Styezek, D. (1992). "Family Living Standards: Uncertain Futures." Warsaw Voice, October 18, pp. 12–13.

Suzuki, T. (1993). "Trade Issues in Distribution." In M. R. Czinkota and M. Kotabe, eds., *The Japanese Distribution System.* Chicago: Probus Publishing Co., pp. 219–230.

Taga, T., and Y. Uehara. (1994). "Some Characteristics of Business Practices in Japan." In T. Kikuchi, ed., *Japanese Distribution Channels.* Binghamton, NY: Haworth Press, pp. 71–87.

Tajima, Y. (1971). *How Goods Are Distributed in Japan.* Shibuya, Japan: Walton-Ridgeway and Co.

Terpstra, V., and K. David. (1985). *The Cultural Environment of International Business.* Cincinnati, Ohio: South-Western Publishing Company.

"Tesco—Company Report" (October 30, 1995). Williams De Broe in *Investext.* [Database on CD-ROM]. Foster City, Calif.: Information Access.

Thatcher, M. (1993). "Burton Decides to Cut Its Cloth According to Its Changing Business Environment." *Personnel Management,* March, p. 15.

Turban, J. (1977). "Some Observations on Retail Distribution in Poland." *Soviet Studies,* Vol. 29, pp. 128–136.

U.S. Department of Commerce, 1988.

"United Kingdom." (1995). *Craighead's International Business, Travel, and Relocation Guide to More than 80 Countries.* Detroit: Gale Research.

"Vendex International—Company Report." (June 1, 1995). Credit Lyonnais Laing in *Investext* [Database on CD-ROM]. Foster City, Calif.: Information Access.

Watanabe, T. (1994). "Changes in Japan's Public Policies Toward Distribution Systems and Marketing." In Kikuchi, ed., *Japanese Distribution Channels.* Binghamton, N.Y.: Haworth Press, Inc., pp. 17–32.

Wolfe, A. (1991). "Single European Market: National or Euro-Brands." *International Journal of Advertising,* pp. 49–58.

Worthy, F. S. (1988). "Tightwad Taiwan Starts to Spend." *Fortune,* Vol. 118, No. 13, pp. 177–182.

Wu, S.-C. (1987). "The Study of Improving Large Scale Department Stores' Productivity." Unpublished thesis, Chinese Culture University (Taiwan).

Xu, B. (1990). *Marketing to China.* Lincolnwood, Ill.: NTC Publishing Co.

Yamamuro, A. (1994). "Seiyu Steps Gently into Vietnam." *Nikkei Weekly,* August 8, p. 18.

Yau, O. H. M. (1988). "Chinese Cultural Values: Their Dimensions and Marketing Implications." *European Journal of Marketing,* Vol. 22, No. 5, pp. 44–57.

INDEX

Key terms and the pages on which their definitions appear are indicated by **boldfaced** type.

Regional cooperative group, 152, 157